S0-CBV-609

Pragmatism and Social Theory

Hans Joas

Pragmatism and Social Theory

The University of Chicago Press
Chicago and London

Hans Joas is professor of sociology at the Free University of Berlin.

The University of Chicago Press, Chicago 60637
The University of Chicago Press, Ltd., London

Printed in the United States of America

02 01 00 99 98 97 96 95 94 93 5 4 3 2 1

ISBN (cloth): 0–226–40041–7 ISBN (paper): 0–226–40042–5

Library of Congress Cataloging-in-Publication Data

Joas, Hans, 1948–
Pragmatism and social theory / Hans Joas.
p. cm.
Includes bibliographical references and index.
1. Sociology. 2. Pragmatism. I. Title.
HM26.J63 1993
301—dc20 92-19533
CIP

♾ The paper used in this publication meets the minimum requirements of the American National Standard for Information Sciences—Permanence of Paper for Printed Library Materials, ANSI Z39.48-1984.

Contents

Acknowledgments

I would like to extend my sincere gratitude to Jeremy Gaines, Raymond Meyer, and the late Steven Minner for their translations of the various essays included in this work. Jeremy Gaines translated the Introduction, chapters 2, 3, 4, and parts of chapter 5. Raymond Meyer translated chapters 1, 6, 7, and 8, as well as parts of chapter 5 and the Conclusion. Steven Minner translated the major part of chapter 9.

Further acknowledgments are given as footnotes to chapters.

Introduction: Steps toward a Pragmatist Theory of Action

This volume includes a number of my studies on American pragmatism, on the history of its reception, which has been far from free of misunderstandings, and on its possible significance for contemporary social theory. These studies, which were written over the course of the last few years and several of which have already appeared in this or that volume in Germany and elsewhere, document a learning process, one full of twists and turns, the aim of which has meanwhile come more sharply into focus. The current clearer view of the goal, however, does not diminish the value of the terrain that has been covered up to this point. Consequently, the present collection does not involve one continuous text running from beginning to end, but rather a series of studies, each of which is complete in itself. The resulting mosaic-like structure nevertheless clearly reveals a recognizable, distinct pattern.

All these studies start from the premise that American pragmatism possesses an incredible modernity. Admittedly, there are sharp differences between the works of Charles Sanders Peirce, William James, John Dewey, and George Herbert Mead, and each respective oeuvre is in some way tied to the period in which its author lived and to certain peculiarities of American culture. Nevertheless, from the end of metaphysical certainties these thinkers have drawn conclusions whose radicalism has to date not been sufficiently acknowledged. Indeed, they avoided replacing metaphysical assumptions with new certainties based on some philosophy of history, or theory of Reason, and did not regard the end of these certainties as a cause for desperation. Rather, their endeavor under these conditions was geared to inquiring after the possibilities of science and of democracy and to finding a meaningful life for the individual. As they saw it, neither science nor democracy had ceased to have validity simply because it no longer seemed possible to provide any final justifications for them.

I feel confirmed in fundamentally sensing that pragmatism is extremely modern by the fact that a great many of the major representatives of contemporary American philosophy expressly situate themselves in the pragmatist tradition or are situated there by others. The list of names such as Richard Rorty and Richard Bernstein, Stephen Toulmin and

Thomas Kuhn, Willard Van Orman Quine and Donald Davidson, Hilary Putnam and Nelson Goodman shows at the very best the degree to which pragmatism has remained a medium of discourse at American universities, despite its having been severely constrained there for decades. We are speaking, admittedly, of a medium of discourse and not of some clearly delineated school or fixed position, for it goes without saying that to call any one of the intellectuals mentioned here a pure pragmatist is a questionable undertaking, and to assign all of them to pragmatism is impossible if the concept "pragmatism" is to retain any measure of selectivity. At this juncture it is merely important to emphasize that pragmatism is the focus of debate in the United States with regard to arriving at a precise definition of a postscientistic philosophy, of a philosophy "beyond realism and anti-realism," as Richard Rorty has called it. Disregarding the obviously spectacular exceptions—Karl-Otto Apel and Jürgen Habermas (as well as a few other specialists there)—in Germany, by contrast, pragmatism is even today having a very rough time of it. In the German discussion, the casual prose of William James and the sober, commonsense style of John Dewey have difficulties making themselves felt against the shrill voice of Friedrich Nietzsche and the visionary tone of Martin Heidegger. Yet, Germans as well as Americans have every reason not to treat democracy and the social sciences as part of the obsolete nineteenth-century faith in progress, as Nietzsche and many of his disciples did. American pragmatism was not some naive form of scientism and it did not hinge on some blindly optimistic faith in the spread of democracy. It only appears as such to those who rule out there being postmetaphysical justifications for democracy and science.

The renaissance of pragmatism in American philosophy has admittedly been restricted to traditional core areas of philosophy. In the philosophy of science and in epistemology, in aesthetics and ethics, one can discern contributions that are "neopragmatist" in nature. By contrast, only rarely are links established to political philosophy and social philosophy. And, aside from Richard Bernstein, there is an even greater distance from discussions of sociological theory. A book such as Richard Rorty's *Contingency, Irony and Solidarity*[1] moves with the greatest of elegance between the philosophical and literary discourses; however, a discourse in the social sciences is so conspicuously absent that one could be forgiven thinking that it does not exist at all.

One cannot contend that this indifference on the part of philosophers corresponds to a disinterest in issues of contemporary philosophy on the part of sociological theorists. Quite the opposite is the case. Within sociology, as Jeffrey Alexander has correctly diagnosed,[2] a "new theoretical movement" has emerged. By this he means that the times are gone when sociology—following the disintegration of the "orthodox consensus" of the Parsonian variety which had prevailed in the nineteen-fifties and nineteen-sixties—could content itself with the mere peaceful coexistence of the widest variety of paradigms. The mere coexistence of approaches which either took the form of established, respectively distinct traditions or had to be eclectically linked by individual sociologists was increasingly felt to be unfruitful. This should not be read to say that a uniform theory has taken the place of this pluralism or even that hopes have arisen of such a theory becoming established in the near future. Nor does it mean that there no longer exists within the social sciences that form of empiricist self-understanding which has virtually ceased to be advocated within philosophy today. It does mean, however, that the philosophical demand for the justification of every single theoretical proposal has grown enormously. Alexander himself prefaced his ambitious attempt to revive the Parsonian synthesis with a complete volume dealing with the results of postempiricist or postpositivistic philosophy of science. Even the model of rational action, which is in many respects the least theoretically sophisticated of all social scientific approaches, is justified in such subtle terms by its current proponents—such as Jon Elster—that it no longer looks like a Cinderella from the social sciences in the court of the philosopher king. Taking motifs from sociological systems theory, Niklas Luhmann has erected a theoretical edifice of intimidating proportions; the key to this intricate building does not lie in the traditional sociological discussion about "action" and "system," but rather in the philosophical dimensions of the definitions he gives of the concepts "meaning," "communication," and "self-referentiality." In the case of Jürgen Habermas's *The Theory of Communicative Action*, there is no need to prove that we have to do here with a sociological theory with strong philosophical foundations. Anthony Giddens does his utmost to avoid being drawn into providing a philosophical justification for the valuative implications of his theory of structuration, yet it is plain to see that his innovations would be impossible if they were not linked back to modern philosophy. In the case of Alain Touraine, the underlying philosophical dimension only remains concealed because he essentially adopts it from the political philosophy of Cornelius Castoriadis. Indeed, even the large number of sociologists who strive for a comprehensive sociological theory by taking up Max Weber's oeuvre can be divided into two camps: those who tend to be neo-Kantian and the rather more Nietzschean variants.

To date, the increased need to provide philosophical justifications and the "new theoretical movement" have not, however, led to the discussion of sociological theory being linked to the renaissance of pragmatism in philosophy. The most important motive behind the studies presented here is to help forge such a link. This book is not a book about pragmatism as such, but on pragmatism, as it is mirrored in different classical and contemporary versions of social theory, and on the potential of pragmatism for the solution of crucial problems in social theory. It is my contention that American pragmatism is characterized by its understanding of human action as a *creative* action. The understanding of creativity contained in pragmatism is specific in the sense that pragmatism focuses on the fact that creativity is always embedded in a *situation,* i.e. on the human being's "situated freedom." It is precisely this emphasis on the interconnection of creativity and situation that has given rise to the repeated charge that pragmatists merely possess a theory that is a philosophy of *adaptation* to given circumstances. This accusation fails to perceive the antideterministic thrust of the pragmatists. In their view the actors confront problems whether they want to or not; the solution to these problems, however, is not clearly prescribed beforehand by reality, but calls for creativity and brings something objectively new into the world. Even the assertion that actors confront problems, which indeed force themselves to be tackled, is frequently misunderstood to mean that pragmatism disregards the subjective components involved in defining a situation as a problem situation and thus takes an objectivistic concept of the problem as the point of departure. Contrary to this, the pragmatists quite readily accept the subjective constitution of a given worldview, but nevertheless regard the emergence of the problems within reality, as subjective as it is, as removed from arbitrary subjective reach.

At this juncture, it is perhaps best to trace the importance of the idea of situated creativity for pragmatism in the works of all four major representatives of pragmatism, without, however, attempting a broader description of the basic ideas of pragmatism.[3] The decisive innovation in Charles Peirce's logic of science—namely, the idea of abduction—is aimed precisely at generating new hypotheses and pinpointing their role in scientific progress. Peirce's speculative philosophy of nature is built around the question of under which conditions the New can arise in nature. His philosophy also endeavors to find a niche for artistic creativity in an age characterized by both the dominance of science and Darwinism, a way of thinking that brought the Romantic philosophy of nature to an end.[4] Of William James it can be concluded from his biography that for him the conflict between a belief in free will with religious justifications and naturalistic determinism was not simply an intellectual problem, but rather one that actually paralyzed all his mental powers. Accordingly, his attempt to find a way out of this dilemma by regarding the ability to choose as itself a function crucial to the survival of the human organism in its environment not only signaled the beginning of functionalist psychology, but was also a step which unleashed his lifelong productivity. John Dewey's work was crowned by his theory of art, or, rather, his theory on the aesthetic dimension of all human experience. Far from being geared exclusively to solving problems of instrumental action, the unifying element running through Dewey's work, with the numerous areas it covers, takes the shape of an inquiry into the meaningfulness to be experienced in action itself. As for George Herbert Mead, his famous theory of the emergence of the self is primarily directed against the assumption of some substantive self; his concept of the human individual and the individual's actions is radically "constructivistic." In all four cases the pragmatists' ideas are not devoted to the creative generation of innovation as such, but to the creative solution of problems. Despite all the pathos associated with creativity, the pragmatists nevertheless endeavored to link it to the dimension of everyday experience and everyday action.

This linkage can be viewed as characteristic of American intellectual history. As early as the German debate on pragmatism prior to the First World War, when the stereotypes about the land of the dollar helped to prevent any serious discussion of pragmatism in Germany,[5] one of the few German philosophers who had tackled the new theory emphasized this connection. Günther Jacoby concurred with the opinion that pragmatism was a uniquely American philosophy:

> not as a philosophy of the dollar, however, but as a philosophy of life, of human creation, of possibilities. For the American pragmatists, cognition is thus not a process of acquisition in the narrower sense, but rather a process of life in the broader sense. . . . For the joy in creating things oneself and the belief in the greatest creative possibilities of the human being: that is indeed American. In America itself pragmatism is a doctrine of cognition as a creative life process, and at the same time it is the belief that every insight contains the greatest variety of possibilities in itself, just as every piece of factual insight itself has become "real" among countless other possible insights.[6]

In American thought ideas of creativity are connected with the idea of democracy to an extent far greater than was ever possible in Germany. Although one would not wish to paint things too baldly in black and white, it can be said that in Germany theories about creativity have always been dominated by an aestheticist ideology of genius.[7] In the United States, by contrast, even Emerson, for all his undoubted elitism, had associated Romantic motifs with the active shaping of nature. Especially in the Progressive Era, the instinct of workmanship, as Thorstein Veblen put it, represents a value-laden concept for defining everyday creativity. It is not the artist but the engineer and the inventor[8] who are the incarnations of creativity, without this, however, becoming transformed into a technocratic ideology. When conservative cultural critics, from Daniel Bell to Niklas Luhmann and Allan Bloom, pour scorn on the concept of creativity as the democratization of the ideology of genius, as "democratically deformed geniality" (Luhmann),[9] they inadvertently become the targets of their own criticism. It is precisely American intellectual history which is capable of showing us that the myth of the genius should rather more be described as "undemocratically deformed creativity."

It is surely one of the major tasks of research on pragmatism to place that body of thought as a theory of situated creativity in the more profound context of its original, American environment. For a long time, another major deficit was the lack of adequate attention paid to the link between pragmatism and similar currents of thought in the German, French, and Anglo-Saxon intellectual worlds. This lack has been remedied in a brilliant manner by a young American historian, James Kloppenberg.[10] Although his assertion that a "transatlantic community of discourse" existed between 1870 and 1920 would appear exaggerated in view of the degree to which national discourses increasingly sealed themselves off from the international community during this period, Kloppenberg nevertheless demonstrates quite convincingly that there was a convergence of discourses which were originally very different in approach. This convergence occurs, on the one hand, at the level of philosophy; here Kloppenberg elaborates the features American pragmatists, British neo-Hegelians, German hermeneuticians, and French neorationalists have in common, while remaining sensitive to the differences between them. This confluence also took place at another level, for there was a convergence between the philosophical innovations of this period and the political search for a path that transcended dogmatic liberalism and revolutionary socialism. Kloppenberg's account considers democratic socialists such as Eduard Bernstein, Jean Jaurès, and the Webbs along with the major figures of American progressivism of that period, and he goes on to claim that an affinity existed between pragmatist philosophy and the theoretical basis of a radical-reformist form of social democracy. He argues vehemently that the welfare states which exist today cannot rightfully refer to themselves as the fully fledged realization of this theoretical foundation. Irrespective of the precise shape these historico-political interconnections may take, for the purposes of a social theory with pragmatist foundations the crucial component of this line of argumentation is that here the pathos of creativity does not engender visions of a permanent revolution or of a macro-subject that can shape society by totalitarian means, but instead is related to the program of a democratic welfare state. "Steady, incremental change through the democratic process, with all its confusions and imperfections, is the political expression of this philosophical creed. These ideas, moderate, meliorist, democratic, and sensitive to the possibility that no perfect reconciliation of liberty and equality can be attained, are the consequences of pragmatism for politics."[11]

The essays collected together in this volume deserve varying degrees of retrospective commentary. The first chapter of the book centers on reconstructing the influence which the philosophy of pragmatism has had on American sociology. After a characterization of the basic features of pragmatism, the presentation then focuses on the sociological research done by the Chicago School between 1895 and 1940 and the fragmentary continuation of this tradition at a later date in the writings of the symbolic interactionists. The image which emerges is that of an important, if clearly deficient, transformation of pragmatism into a theory of the social sciences and empirical social research. Since the completion of this essay, and in addition to a further helpful overview of the Chicago School, by Dennis Smith, which foregrounds its "liberal" critique of capitalism,[12] various works have appeared which not only contextualize the Chicago School in terms of a history of science—as I do here—but also within a history of civilization. The attempt to trace the School's relationship to the history of American journalism, especially to urban documentary reporting, has yielded results as interesting as those which have come to light in the course of initial efforts to establish a closer link between the history of sociology and Chicago's literary history.[13] (In this regard, the connection between pragmatist thought and modern architecture in Chicago has only been dealt with in passing to date.) All these contributions generate highly tangible evidence for the claim that pragmatist theories are intimately bound up with modernity.

The following chapters of this book deal with reactions to American pragmatism. First of all, a comparison with pragmatism is given of the theories of Emile Durkheim, the classical figure of French sociology. This study initially draws on the little-known lectures which Durkheim held on pragmatism in 1913–14, after completing his last major work, namely the study of the elementary forms of religious life.[14] However, I am concerned not only with correcting Durkheim's misconception of pragmatism, which he understood to be "logical utilitarianism," but, more importantly, with establishing the similarities and the differences between pragmatism and Durkheim's program of a sociology of knowledge, i.e. of a theory of the social constitution of the fundamental categories of knowledge. Such a comparison reveals flaws on both sides and points up the opportunities for reciprocal rectification. (Whereas the essay in question concentrates exclusively on Durkheim's late work, I have meanwhile tried elsewhere to identify the role played by the problems of creativity in Durkheim's entire oeuvre and thus to trace a line of continuity there with regard to the issue of how a new morality and/or new institutions could arise.)[15] The study on the attitudes of the "Frankfurt School," which emigrated to the United States, toward pragmatism, the American social sciences, and American society as a whole is intended to show how strongly the representatives of Critical Theory adhered to a Marxist functionalism and the degree to which their efforts to reinstate a concept of "objective reason" fell far short of drawing on the decisive innovations of pragmatism. This resulted in deficits in a whole series of thematic areas. Up to now, a euphemistically positive view of the accomplishments of Critical Theory has helped impede the further continuation of the pragmatist intellectual heritage. This essay on the Frankfurt School is followed by a study on the history of the German misunderstandings of pragmatism. It is a sad story, which ranges from the reduction of pragmatism to a utilitarian theory of truth in the debates prior to the First World War, via the hidden pragmatism of Max Scheler and Martin Heidegger, all the way to the appropriation of pragmatism for the purposes of a fascist philosophy of the deed. Most of the German émigrés, and not only those of the Frankfurt School, remained prisoners of this history of misconceptions, and it was not until the nineteen-sixties that Karl-Otto Apel and Jürgen Habermas, in particular, were able to pave the way for a new approach.

The following part of the book contains outlines on contemporary attempts to devise grand sociological theory; I have attempted to point out critically those problems inherent in the works themselves for which, in my opinion, elements of pragmatist theory would appear to offer promising solutions. The most important of these studies deal with the works of Jürgen Habermas, Cornelius Castoriadis, Anthony Giddens, and Jeffrey Alexander. Since each of these four authors has been remarkably productive, the conclusions I come to can, of course, not be regarded as valid for all time. A few relativizing remarks are therefore in order in all four cases.

What prompted my taking issue with Jürgen Habermas's *Theory of*

Communicative Action was my surprise at how little this author had adopted from pragmatism for his theory as a whole. After all, Habermas had repeatedly documented his orientation toward the pragmatists Peirce and Mead and had, in the above work as well, justified the fundamental paradigm shift "from purposive action to communicative action" by citing Mead and (albeit problematically) Durkheim. For me it was a matter of describing the relative poverty of Habermas's theory of action in relation to the phenomenal variety of action and to pinpoint that Habermas's problematical understanding of the logical status of the theory of action inherently compels him to receive functionalism in a specific manner. To the present day, the "theory of communicative action" appears to me to rely on an inconsistent link between hermeneutic and functionalist components. In his replies to his critics and in a series of more recent works Habermas has sought to clarify his position, and in the process he has eliminated most of the reasons for my criticisms of the dualism of system and life-world in the area of political sociology.[16] This, however, does not apply to the issue of what constitutes action in terms of the theoretical basics involved. In a direct reply to my criticisms[17] he rejects the entire question of an anthropological theory of action and contends that he was only concerned to provide an explanation of social action. But if such a narrow definition is taken, then not only play and art, but in fact the whole area of "labor" would fall outside the domain of social theory. This surely cannot seriously be his intention. If Habermas replies to my criticism by contending that with regard to his social-theoretic aims "the juxtaposition of communicative and strategic action (has) the advantage . . . of stressing consensus and influence—those two mechanisms of action coordination which, from the rationality-theoretic viewpoint of whether the rational potential of speech has been exhausted or not, form completely alternative options," then this reply still confirms two of the criticisms raised. First, it shows that the question as to a theory of action is obscured beneath that of a theory of action coordination; and secondly that the latter, furthermore, was from the outset discussed from the vantage point of a theory of rationality. Both are legitimate approaches, of course, but they are by no means plausible decisions from the standpoint of pragmatism. Surprisingly, Habermas subsumes every attempt to create a nonfunctionalist sociological theory that has action-theoretic foundations under a concept of praxis philosophy which he has obviously derived from a study of Georg Lukács. Habermas's dictum is simply not true both in that in such approaches collective actors are hypostatized and in that they are necessarily bound up with a "form of society based on labor." Just as a praxis philosophy in a Lukácsian guise can hardly be helped by grafting spare parts from symbolic interactionism on to it—as Habermas chidingly notes[18]—by the same token spare parts from Luhmann's systems theory will hardly resolve the dilemmas of Critical Theory. Indeed, Habermas's own confrontation with the debate on postmodernism in his lectures on "the philosophical discourse of modernity"[19] may in fact enable us to realize that the problems he so brilliantly demonstrates call for a more profound relativization of "rationality" than the concept of communicative rationality permits. I believe that the concept of creativity does more justice to the provocative issues raised in the postmodernism debate.[20]

Cornelius Castoriadis's work is most certainly situated in the tradition of the praxis-philosophical interpretation of Marxism. It is, however, so strongly permeated with the experience of totalitarianism and is so original in its link on the one hand to Aristotle and, on the other, to the social phenomenology of Maurice Merleau-Ponty that any reduction of Castoriadis's thought to the tried-and-true arguments against praxis philosophy would also be illegitimate. Rather, Castoriadis's theory is currently the most original attempt at a political philosophy derived from the idea of creativity. In the study presented here, the focus will be on the basic features of Castoriadis's theory of the institution and his understanding of society as the result of a process of institutionalization which is engendered by the ability to project meaning, to draw on the "imaginary." Nevertheless, I contend, Castoriadis has not managed to develop an adequate theory of modern democracy on this basis. The final statement in my essay asserts that Castoriadis sidesteps the central problem involved in applying his praxis philosophy to social theory, namely "how to uphold the project of autonomy when the myth of revolution is dead." I do not believe that the events of autumn 1989 in Eastern and Central Europe—including those in the city in which I am penning these lines—have disproved this statement. If we do not wish to speak in terms of a collapse of the post-Stalinist regime, but rather to speak of a revolution, then surely it was a revolution without an innovative program. For the problems of democracy were not solved, but instead placed on the agenda there. However, it is not only in the realm of politics that there are clear differences between Castoriadis's theory and a contemporary form of pragmatism. Various critics have remarked that in the second, constructive section of his major work to date Castoriadis tends to lose sight of the dimension of action. His theory of creativity runs the risk of not being a theory of creative *action.* Whether or not Castoriadis will be able to avert this danger is something which will be shown by his next, eagerly anticipated major work.[21]

I myself have referred to the theory of Anthony Giddens as a sociological transformation of praxis philosophy, for I think that this description best characterizes the degree to which his theory both parallels and is distinct from a sociological transformation of pragmatism. An exceptionally broad international discussion has ensued in recent years with regard to Giddens's work and it is impossible to assess what the outcome of the debate will be.[22] Shortly after publishing his major theoretical work, *The Constitution of Society,* Giddens himself presented a substantial work on the history and sociology of the nation-state and violence in which he—and here he resembles both Michael Mann and John Hall in Great Britain, but also Randall Collins and Theda Skocpol in the United States—sets out to eliminate one of the most disturbing weaknesses in the formation of sociological theory.[23] However, the way in which these problems are linked to basic theoretical questions can only be elaborated in a different context.[24]

Jeffrey Alexander's work comes from a tradition that is completely unlike that of pragmatism or Western Marxism. It approaches the Parsonian heritage in a highly critical and creative manner in the endeavor to develop an adequate sociological theory by reshaping that body of thought. In the study presented here I have attempted a careful examination of Alexander's metatheoretical considerations and of his interpretation of the classic sociological figures—Marx, Durkheim, Weber, and Parsons. My intention is to prove thereby that the scheme of "utilitarianism versus normativity," which Alexander culls from Parsons, does not suffice either as an adequate description of the problem which the sociological classics had posed themselves or as the basis on which to develop a satisfactory theory of action. Again, I appeal to a third position, namely that of the theory of creativity. Alexander has recently undertaken relatively major revisions of his theory.[25] He accuses Parsons in increasingly radical terms of failing to recognize the contingency of human action both in microsociological as well as macrosociological contexts. This allows him to draw constructively on the works of the symbolic interactionists and on a historically sensitive functionalism, such as that put forward by Shmuel Eisenstadt. In the way in which it perceives the problems, neofunctionalism is increasingly centering on the key issues which are also being tackled by current major sociological theories in Europe. The hubris of this school so noticeable at the outset appears to have waned significantly.

The chapter "Role Theories and Socialization Research" deals with empirical research on the concept of role-taking in research on socialization. The goal of this study is to provide an example which demonstrates the empirical fruitfulness of a key concept of the pragmatist idea of human action.

The volume concludes with a text which I wrote as a retrospective on the book I wrote ten years ago on the American pragmatist George Herbert Mead. This study deals with the normative implications of pragmatist theory and—of all of the works collected here—provides the clearest indication of what the pragmatist theory of action from which I expect so much in terms of social theory would look like.[26]

Notes

1. Richard Rorty, *Contingency, Irony and Solidarity* (Cambridge, 1989).

2. Jeffrey Alexander, "A New Theoretical Movement," in Neil Smelser (ed.), *Handbook of Sociology* (London, 1988), pp. 77–101.

3. See the section on "Pragmatism as the Philosophical Source of the Chicago School" in the following essay, "Pragmatism in American Sociology."

4. See Douglas R. Anderson, *Creativity and the Philosophy of C. S. Peirce* (Dordrecht, Netherlands, 1987).

5. Cf. the study "American Pragmatism and German Thought: A History of Misunderstandings" (in this volume).

6. Günther Jacoby, "Der amerikanische Pragmatismus und die Philosophie des Als Ob," in *Zeitschrift für Philosophie und philosophische Kritik* 147 (1912), pp. 172–84. See especially p. 173.

7. Jochen Schmidt, *Die Geschichte des Genie-Gedankens in der deutschen Literatur, Philosophie und Politik 1750–1945,* 2 vols. (Darmstadt, 1985).

8. On Emerson cf. Eduard Baumgarten's interpretation, *Der Pragmatismus: Die geistigen Grundlagen des amerikanischen Gemeinwesens,* vol. 2 (Frankfurt, 1938), p. 3–96. Thorstein Veblen, *The Instinct of Workmanship* (New York, 1914). Sherwood Anderson's novel *Poor White* left a deep impression on me as a literary treatment of creativity among inventors.

9. Daniel Bell, *The Cultural Contradictions of Capitalism* (London, 1979); Niklas Luhmann, "Vom Zufall verwöhnt: Eine Rede über Kreativität," in *Frankfurter Allgemeine Zeitung,* June 10, 1987; Allan Bloom, *The Closing of the American Mind* (New York, 1987), pp. 180 ff.

10. James T. Kloppenberg, *Uncertain Victory: Social Democracy and Progressivism in European and American Thought, 1870–1920* (New York, 1986).

11. Ibid., p. 194.

12. Dennis Smith, *The Chicago School: A Liberal Critique of Capitalism* (New York, 1988).

13. Rolf Lindner, *Die Entdeckung der Stadtkultur: Soziologie aus der Erfahrung der Reportage* (Frankfurt, 1990); Eugene Rochberg-Halton, "Life, Literature and Sociology in Turn-of-the-Century Chicago," in Simon Bronner (ed.), *Consuming Visions: Accumulation and Display of Goods in America, 1880–1920* (New York, 1989), pp. 311–38. Cf. also the book by this author entitled *Meaning and Modernity: Social Theory in the Pragmatic Attitude* (Chicago, 1986). Also Heinz Ickstadt, "Concepts of Society and the Practice of Fiction—Symbolic Responses to the Experience of Change in Late Nineteenth Century America," in Marc Chénetier and Rob Kroes (eds.), *Impressions of a Gilded Age: The American Fin de Siècle* (Amsterdam, 1983), pp. 77–95.

14. Emile Durkheim, *Pragmatism and Sociology* (Cambridge, 1983).

15. Hans Joas, "Emile Durkheim's Intellectual Development," in a forthcoming anthology of essays edited by Stephen Turner on Durkheim. The essay on Alexander in this volume contains hints for these interpretations.

16. Jürgen Habermas, "A Reply," in Axel Honneth and Hans Joas (eds.), *Communicative Action,* tr. J. Gaines and D. Jones (Cambridge, 1991), pp. 214–64; "Volkssouveränität als Verfahren: Ein normativer Begriff von Öffentlichkeit," in *Merkur* 43 (1989), pp. 465–77; preface to the new, 1990 edition of *Strukturwandel der Öffentlichkeit* (Frankfurt, 1990), pp. 11–50.

17. *Communicative Action,* p. 249f.

18. Ibid., p. 250.

19. Jürgen Habermas, *The Philosophical Discourse of Modernity,* tr. F. Lawrence (Cambridge, 1987).

20. For the time being, see my lecture on "Participation—Yuppification— Violence: On Creativity Today," in: Wolfgang Zapf (ed.), *Die Modernisierung moderner Gesellschaften.* Verhandlungen des 25. Deutschen Soziologentages (Frankfurt/M., 1991), pp. 205–11.

21. A new collection of essays by Castoriadis has appeared only recently; this is not the book referred to here. Cf. Cornelius Castoriadis, *Le monde morcelé* (Paris, 1990). Indispensable for the discussion of Castoriadis's work is Giovanni Busino (ed.), "Pour une philosophie militante de la démocratie: Autonomie et autotransformation de la société," in *Revue européenne des sciences sociales* 27(86) (1989). Cf. in this connection especially the contributions by Bernhard Waldenfels, "Der Primat der Einbildungskraft," in Busino, "Pour une philosophie," pp. 141–60, and Johann Arnason, "The Imaginary Institution of Modernity," in Busino, "Pour une philosophie," pp. 269–92. The works of the former Budapest School (Agnes Heller, among others) are to be situated in the context of this discussion on a new version of praxis philosophy, as well as those of Roberto Mangabeira Unger (*Politics: A Work in Constructive Social Theory,* 3 vols. [Cambridge, 1987]) and Johann Arnason (*Praxis und Interpretation* [Frankfurt, 1988]); cf. also my critique in *Soziologische Revue* 12 (1989), pp. 263–65.

22. This can be seen from the publication of a large monograph on Giddens's work and three collections on the discussion about it: Ira Cohen, *Structuration Theory: Anthony Giddens and the Constitution of Social Life* (New York, 1989), as well as the collections edited by Jon Clark, David Held and John Thompson, and Christopher Bryant.

23. Anthony Giddens, *The Nation-State and Violence* (Cambridge, 1985).

24. On this point, see my works on a sociological theory of war and peace. An overview is provided in my essay "Between Power Politics and Pacifist Utopia: War and Peace in Sociological Theory," in: *Current Sociology* (1991), pp. 47–66.

25. Jeffrey Alexander, *Action and Its Environments: Toward a New Synthesis* (New York, 1988). Cf. also by Alexander, *Structure and Meaning. Relinking Classical Sociology* (New York, 1989). A German parallel to American neofunctionalism can be found in the works of Richard Münch.

26. My essay "The Democratization of Differentiation: On the Creativity of Collective Action," in Jeffrey Alexander and Piotr Sztompka (eds.), *Rethinking Progress* (Boston, 1990), pp. 182–201, gives an initial overview of such consequences in social theory. My book *The Creativity of Action* (published in German, Frankfurt, 1992) develops this theory in a systematic way.

1 Pragmatism in American Sociology[1]

When American sociology set out on its triumphal march around the world after the end of the Second World War, it had passed its own historical turning point only a short time before. The combination of Lazarsfeld and Merton, as the sociological approach after that turning point was described (Shils 1970, p. 794), linked together a quantitatively oriented and sophisticated empirical social research with a structural-functional theory stripped of its philosophical and historical context and origins and trimmed down to a "middle range" of application. This combination offered itself as the summing up of all that was valuable from the legacy of the classical European sociologists and as the way of conveying this legacy into the basic store of theory and method of a professionally safeguarded and cumulative acquisition of knowledge. To be sure, the stability of the discipline's identity was bought at the high price of the suppression of traditions that could be integrated into sociology's new image only with great difficulty. In this regard it is most striking that, although Parsons grappled with the interpretation of Durkheim, Weber, and Pareto for hundreds of pages in his first great work, *The Structure of Social Action* (1968a), in that discussion he not only presented a completely inadequate picture of German idealism and Marxism, but even considered the American traditions of social theory as hardly worth mentioning. He literally did not devote a single word to the accomplishments of John Dewey's and George Herbert Mead's pragmatist social philosophy, or to the pioneering methodological achievements of the Chicago School of sociology and the theoretical implications of their large-scale empirical investigations. American ideas and research that were not deemed worthy of attention even in their country of origin could hardly expect to find better treatment outside the United States, given the general leftist or Eurocentric scepticism about American thought.

This does not mean that this tradition has died out completely. In numerous subfields of sociology, ranging from research on socialization to

Published in English as "Symbolic Interactionism," in *Social Theory Today*, edited by A. Giddens and J. Turner (Cambridge, Eng./Stanford, Calif.: Blackwell Press [Polity Press]/Stanford University Press, 1987), pp. 82–115.

criminal and urban sociology and including occupational sociology, works of the Chicago tradition play an important role and have contributed to the fruitfulness of investigations carried out in these areas. Scattered fragments of this tradition, such as Mead's conceptions of the self and of role-taking, the "Thomas theorem" on the effective character of all components of a situation that are regarded as real, and the fundamental notion of the biographical method all belong to the standard stock of sociological knowledge. Certainly, many representatives of this tradition found themselves in relative isolation or had to assume the role of a more or less "loyal opposition" to the mainstream of sociology. In the sixties, the tradition, especially in the form given it by Herbert Blumer (1969), became the object of an almost fashionable interest. It became so, though, in a theoretically muddled combination with phenomenological and other approaches that yielded the so-called interpretative approach (Wilson 1970). In the very recent past, there have been an increasing number of attempts to overcome this tradition's temporary concentration on microsociological phenomena and to achieve an understanding of its premises and principles through an examination of its history.

These attempts have taken two sharply distinct forms. On the one hand, the movement toward the neopositivist theory of science and behaviorist psychology holds out the promise of overcoming the "astructural bias" of the symbolic-interactionist tradition.[2] From the standpoint of the history of sociological theory, this line of thought seeks to insure its validity by attempting to make a metatheoretical conflict between nominalist and realist views the guiding thread for distinguishing the strand of the tradition originating with Peirce and Mead from the one that leads from James, via Dewey, to Blumer.[3] On the other hand, there are the efforts to uncover and extract the macrotheoretical assumptions that had always been implicit in the concrete research carried out within this tradition, and to join them together to make a coherent whole, a theory of "negotiated order." In the most recent writings of symbolic interactionists one can also find signs that they are concerning themselves with the ideas of structuralism and poststructuralism (Perinbanayagam 1985).

No matter how one assesses these different tendencies, they are all indicative of the intent actively to introduce into the general theoretical discussion the legacy of the sociological tradition that has its roots in the Chicago School. This is by no means typical for this school. For many decades, the Chicago tradition was continued less through the elaboration of a systematic theory and the tradition's theoretical self-grounding than by means of exemplary research and oral transmission. This fact could itself become a point of reference in the self-understanding of symbolic interactionists, as well as for an account of the history of this school of thought (Rock 1979). Parsons's silence was, so to speak, repaid in the same currency. It is difficult to say whether this theoretical self-isolation was due to a justified mistrust of analytical construction of theory, in contrast to the symbolic interactionists' own program of formulating an empirically grounded theory (Glaser and Strauss 1967), or simply to the Chicago theorists' inability to oppose to the comprehensive, theoretically and historically broadly inclusive approaches such as those of Parsons (or of Marxism and Critical Theory) something even approximately equivalent in scope.

It is from this position that the difficulties of reviewing symbolic interactionism arise. In the following account, one certainly has to define symbolic interactionism as it is generally understood. The name of this line of sociological and sociopsychological research was coined in 1938 by Herbert Blumer (1938). Its focus is processes of interaction—social action that is characterized by an immediately reciprocal orientation—and the investigations of these processes are based on a particular concept of interaction which stresses the symbolic character of social action. The prototypical case is of social relations in which action does not take the form of mere translation of fixed prescriptions into deeds, but in which definitions of the relations are, rather, jointly and reciprocally proposed and established. Social relations are seen, then, not as stabilized once and for all but as open and tied to ongoing common acknowledgment.

Now, it would be entirely inadequate to confine a delineation of symbolic interactionism to this central insight and to the theoretical and methodological preferences arising out of it. The widespread criticism of symbolic interactionism is alone sufficient to make it necessary to go beyond this first level of presentation. Such criticism is directed chiefly against the limitation of symbolic interactionism to phenomena of interpersonal immediacy. However, it also accuses symbolic interactionism of ignoring questions of power and domination. There is imputed to it a view of the complex of macrosocial relations as merely the horizon of life-worldly sociality as well as a complete unawareness of the societal mastery of nature or the fact that societal conditions may become autonomous in relation to the actions and orientations of the participants in social actions. Although many of these criticisms do in fact apply, at least partially, to Herbert Blumer's program and to the sociologists who follow that program, their justification is nevertheless doubtful when one considers the breadth of the theoretical and empirical work produced by this line of research.

For the true significance of symbolic interactionism and its potential theoretical fecundity can only be understood when it is viewed against the background of the old Chicago School, which it continues while omitting some aspects of that school's thought. Such a consideration of symbolic interactionism, therefore, constitutes another strand of the following account of that tradition. Symbolic interactionism is regarded as the continuation of certain parts of the thought and work of the loose-knit interdisciplinary network of theoreticians, social researchers, and social reformers at the University of Chicago which exercised a determining influence on American sociology between 1890 and 1940, during the discipline's proper phase of institutionalization. To be sure, this school had no unequivocally key theoretician or clearly outlined program of research; rather, the Chicago School consisted of a complex nexus of important and less important thinkers and researchers who influenced one another in ways that can now hardly be reconstructed.

An account of this school that wants to include a description of its theoretical system must, then, undertake to reveal and extract the underlying structure of the shared assumptions of the members of this school, and do so without creating a false impression of the school's absolute homogeneity or temporal stability. Yet this is not the principal difficulty. That difficulty lies, rather, in the fact that the Chicago School, which could be described as a combination of pragmatist philosophy, of a politically reformist orientation to the possibilities of democracy under conditions of rapid industrialization and urbanization, and of efforts to make sociology into an empirical science while attaching great importance to prescientific sources of experiential knowledge, was itself only a partial realization—from the theoretical standpoint—of the possibilities inherent in the social philosophy of pragmatism.

Hence, the third strand of the present study: the reconstruction of pragmatism as the philosophical source of the Chicago School and of symbolic interactionism. This, of course, does not mean that greater importance or more enduring validity is to be ascribed to the elaboration of philosophical notions as such. What is meant, rather, is that in the philosophy of pragmatism can be found fundamental ideas about the theories of action and social order which have the greatest relevance for the theoretical labors of present-day sociology. These foundations of a theory of action and social order have not been adequately integrated into sociology. The Chicago School and the vital tradition of symbolic interactionism owe a large part of their importance to the transformation of these fundamental ideas into concrete social scientific theory and empirical research. It can be shown, however, that this took place only fragmentarily, and that some of the unsolved problems of this tradition can be solved by means of a reconsideration of its starting point. The following account thus begins with an analysis of pragmatism's significance for social theory. This is followed by an examination of the most important stages of the development of pragmatism in its sociological form as represented by the work of W. I. Thomas, Robert Park, Herbert Blumer, and Everett Hughes, and of the situation at the present time. An assessment of the theoretical yield from this tradition for contemporary construction of theory concludes this examination of the pragmatist school of sociology.

I Pragmatism as the Philosophical Source of the Chicago School

Pragmatism is a philosophy of action. However, it did not develop its model of action as did Parsons and, at least according to the latter's interpretation of them, the classical sociological thinkers, by posing and answering the question: What dimensions must be added to the utilitarian notion of the solitary actor rationally pursuing his ends, if the undeniable but—within the framework of utilitarianism—inexplicable fact of the existence of social order is to be theoretically grasped? Pragmatism is, certainly, no less critical of utilitarianism than were the classical theorists of sociology. It does not, however, attack utilitarianism over the problem of action and social order, but over the problem of action and consciousness. Pragmatism developed the concept of action in order to overcome the Cartesian dualisms. Out of this enterprise there emerged an understanding of intentionality and sociality that differed radically from that of utilitarianism. The concept of rationality and the normative ideal of this mode of thought are theoretically grasped in the idea of self-regulated action. Pragmatism's theory of social order, then, is guided by a conception of social control in the sense of collective self-regulation and problem-solving. This conception of social order is informed by ideas about democracy and the structure of communication within communities of scientists. The actual importance of this type of social order in modern societies poses one of the main problems of pragmatism's political philosophy and of the sociology based on that philosophy. Let us now consider these matters in detail.

The emancipation of the individual from the self-evident validity and authority of received institutions and ideas that took place in the early modern period attained its most extreme and uncompromising expression in the thought of René Descartes. He elevated the individual's right to doubt into the establishment of the self-certainty of the thinking and doubting ego as the firm foundation of a philosophy. Of course, the self-evident, taken-for-granted existence of the world over against the individual consciousness, of the body of the thinking ego as a component of this world and of the other thinking subjects in the world was thereby abolished. An epistemologically oriented philosophy was thereby able to substantiate its claim to be foundational vis-à-vis the sciences. At the same time, though, it incurred the difficult—or impossible—tasks of constituting the world, the body, and the "you," the subject encountered by the ego, on the basis of the thinking ego. It was against this entire program that the central idea of pragmatism was directed. The pragmatist places in doubt the meaningfulness of the Cartesian doubt.

> We cannot begin with complete doubt. We must begin with all the prejudices which we actually have when we enter upon the study of philosophy. These prejudices are not to be dispelled by a maxim, for they are things which it does not occur to us *can* be questioned. Hence this initial skepticism will be a mere self-deception, and not real doubt; and no one who follows the Cartesian method will ever be satisfied until he has formally recovered all those beliefs which in form he has taken up. It is, therefore, as useless a preliminary as going to the North Pole would be in order to get to Constantinople by coming down regularly upon a meridian. A person may, it is true, in the course of his studies, find reason to doubt what he began by believing; but in that case he doubts because he has a positive reason for it, and not on account of the Cartesian maxim. Let us not pretend to doubt in philosophy what we do not doubt in our hearts. (Peirce 1934, pp. 156ff.)

This critique of the Cartesian doubt is anything but a defense of unquestionable authorities against the emancipatory claim of the thinking ego; it is, though, a plea in defense of *true* doubt, that is, in defense of the anchoring of cognition to real-problem situations. Cartesianism's guiding notion of the solitarily doubting ego is supplanted by the idea of a cooperative search for truth for the purpose of coping with real problems encountered in the course of action. One could be tempted to attribute to this transformation the same historical significance as that accorded the philosophy of Descartes.

The consequences, at least, of this transformation of the guiding idea of philosophical reflection are extremely far-reaching. Indeed, the entire relationship between cognition and reality is changed. The concept of truth no longer expresses a correct representation of reality in cognition, which can be conceived of using the metaphor of a copy; rather, it expresses an increase of the power to act in relation to an environment. All stages of cognition, from sensory perception through to the logical drawing of conclusions and on to self-reflection, must now be conceived anew. Charles Peirce had begun to carry out this program. William James applied it to a great number of problems, chiefly of a religious or existential nature. Led perhaps by his desire to demonstrate the impossibility of finding solutions to these problems that could be made universally binding, James narrowed, and thereby weakened, pragmatism's basic idea in a decisive fashion. In contrast to Peirce, he formulated the criterion for truth in terms of actually occurring results of action rather than those that could generally be expected to occur. In his psychology, James did not take action as his starting point, but instead the pure stream of conscious experience. He did, however, develop extraordinarily penetrating and impressive analyses showing the selectivity of perception and the apportionment of attention as a function of the subject's purpose. Peirce exercised almost no influence at all on sociologists; James's writings did have influence, but it was very diffuse and manifested itself primarily in a sensitization to the subtleties of subjective experiences. Pragmatism's decisive influence on sociology took place only through John Dewey and George Herbert Mead. These two men, who had initially pursued a program of "naturalized" Hegelianism, i.e. Hegelianism recast in terms of the evolutionary processes of nature, and who, like Feuerbach,[4] had felt themselves thereby elevated above the Cartesian constraints on thought, recognized the crucial importance of a regrounding of pragmatism on the foundation of the biological and social sciences.

This regrounding of pragmatism at first assumed the form of a functionalist psychology. The intent of this psychology was to interpret all psychical operations and processes—and not only the cognitive ones—in terms of their functionality for the solution of problems encountered by subjects in the course of their conduct. This enterprise meant the rejection of traditional epistemological approaches to the interpretation of psychical phenomena as well as a critique of all the psychologies that more or less embody these obsolete philosophical positions. The most famous document of the new approach is John Dewey's trail-blazing article "The Reflex Arc Concept in Psychology," published in 1896 (Dewey 1972); its most thorough elaboration, however, is to be found in George Herbert Mead's lengthy, but still almost unknown study "The Definition of the Psychical" (1903).

Dewey's critique is directed against a psychology that believes it has found its object in the establishment of law-like causal relations between environmental stimuli and the organism's reactions. Dewey denies that we can legitimately conceive of actions as additively composed of phases of external stimulation, internal processing of the stimulus, and external reaction. To this "reflex arc model" he opposes the totality of the action: it is the action that determines which stimuli are relevant within the context defined by the action. The elements of an action that are regarded as discrete according to the reflex arc model are, rather, Dewey asserts, functional distinctions within the action; the unity of an action breaks down, and the functionality of these distinctions becomes clear, whenever the execution of an action is interrupted. The sensation enters into the subject's conscious awareness as an external stimulus when its nature is *unknown;* and we become aware of the necessity of a reaction as such when we do *not* know how we should react. Accordingly, Mead defined the psychical as "that phase of experience within which we are immediately conscious of conflicting impulses which rob the object of its character as object-stimulus, leaving us so far in an attitude of subjectivity; but during which a new object-stimulus appears due to the reconstructive activity which is identified with the subject 'I' as distinct from the object 'me'" (Mead 1903, p. 109).

Admittedly, Dewey's and Mead's critique, insofar as it is presented here, is principally aimed at theories that reduce action to environmentally determined conduct. However, the model of action employed in this critique also shows the modification of the meaning of intentionality in comparison with those theories that regard action as the realization of pre-set ends. In pragmatism, precisely because it considers all psychical operations in the light of their functionality for action, it becomes impossible to hold the position that the setting of an end is an act of consciousness per se that occurs outside of contexts of action. Rather, the setting of an end can only be the result of reflection on resistances met by conduct that is oriented in a number of different ways. Should it prove impossible to follow simultaneously all the various guiding impulses or compulsions to action, a selection of a dominant motive can take place which then, as an end, dominates the other motives or allows them to become effective only in a subordinate manner.

Such a clear orientation to an end is by no means the usual case, however. By its nature, action is teleological only in a diffuse fashion. Even our perception is shaped by our capacities and possibilities for action. Only under constraint by himself or another, though, will the actor narrow down the wealth of his impulses and sensibility to a clear line of action toward a single end. Dewey and Mead were interested in children's play not only because of their desire to bring about educational reform but because such play also served them as a model of action that was subject to little pressure to achieve unequivocal ends. In their analyses of experimentation, they developed a definition of creative intelligence as the overcoming of action problems through the invention of new possibilities of action; this capacity for invention or creativity, however, presupposes the conscious manipulation of the form of action called play, the "playing through" of alternative courses of action. At this point in the development of Dewey's and Mead's thought it is already clear that, in comparison to the utilitarian approach, the pragmatist theory of action both opens up new domains of phenomena and makes it necessary to reconceive the known domains, and does so in a way which is unexemplified in the critique made of utilitarianism by the classical sociological thinkers.

Let us now consider briefly three possible objections to the pragmatists' model of action. The criticism that this model narrows the concept of action in an instrumentalist or activist way should have already lost much of its plausibility through the indication above of the significance for pragmatism of play and creativity. This criticism can be refuted most powerfully by means of Dewey's writings on aesthetics (Dewey 1934) in which it is exactly the subject's passive readiness to experience, and the rounding-off of experience in a present, that are demonstrated. For Dewey, pragmatism was nothing less than a means to criticize those aspects of American life "which make action an end in itself and which conceive ends too narrowly and too 'practically'" (Dewey 1931, p. 16). Thus the choice of action as the starting point of philosophical reflection does not mean that the world is degraded to mere material at the disposal of the actors' intentions; this objection is still based on the Cartesian dichotomy, the overcoming of which is precisely what is at issue. Only in action is the qualitative immediacy of the world and of ourselves revealed to us.

The next conceivable objection finds fault with consciousness being bound to the present moment in the pragmatist model of action. This charge can be rebutted by pointing out the central importance of "habits" in that model. Solutions to action problems are not stored by the actors in their consciousness but employed for new actions, which, being routine in character, run their course outside the actors' consciousness. It is only the new action problem that renders the routines and "habits" ineffectual and requires new learning.

A third problem, and the most difficult for pragmatist social philosophy, is that the model of action described above is so general that it does not even distinguish the actor's relation to objects of his environment from his relation to his fellow subjects. The transformation of the Cartesian ego into the community constituted by collective problem-solving had at first been only asserted. Peirce had been able, certainly, to link his idea of the critical community of scientists with his theoretical model of action immanently, insofar as he declared all cognition to be symbolic. His theory of signs contains, in addition to the object signified and the qualitative peculiarity of the sign-bearer, an interpreting consciousness belonging to a subject who wants to convey his intention to another or to himself.[5]

Peirce was not able, however, to provide a true theory of the subject that communicates with itself and with others. Cooley had been the first to proclaim the necessity of a "social" or "sociological" pragmatism[6] and to develop a theory of the self and its dependence on primary groups. In elaborating this theory, though, he had proceeded in a manner that was still very inconsistent. He did not root consciousness in action with logical rigor, and formulated an emotive rather than a cognitive theory of the self. This problem of arriving at a pragmatist analysis of situations of social interaction and individual self-reflection was the crucial coupling necessary for linking pragmatist philosophy with anti-utilitarian social psychology and sociology. Far more than even Dewey, George Herbert Mead, in his analysis of the origin of human gestural and linguistic communication, was the one who thought through this problem and step by step reached a solution to it. And because he was credited with solving this problem, Mead became the strategically central figure of the Chicago School. This is true regardless of how unimpeachable his solution was and how thoroughly sociologists were acquainted with his thought.

It would be incorrect to understand Mead's contribution[7] as a simple reversal of the relationship between the individual and the collectivity—now to the advantage of the collectivity. The true meaning of his achievement lies, rather, in the fact that he fundamentally changed the way of looking at the problem. Fully in the spirit of pragmatism, he investigated the type of action situation in which a heightened attentiveness to objects of the environment does not suffice to guarantee a successful continuation of the action. What he had in mind was interpersonal action problems. In social situations the actor is himself a source of stimuli for his partner. He must, therefore, be attentive to his own ways of acting, since they elicit reactions from his partner and thereby become conditions for the continuation of his own actions. In this type of situation, not merely consciousness but self-consciousness is functionally required. With this analysis of self-reflectivity, Mead sought to reconstruct pragmatistically the legacy of German idealism.

Mead developed the conditions of the possibility of self-reflectivity out of a theory of the origins of specifically human communication and sociality. In a series of articles written around 1910, he arrives step by step at the fundamentals of the theory of symbolically mediated interaction.

He maintains that the transformation of phases of action into gestural signs makes it possible for an actor to react to his own actions, thereby to represent with his own actions those of others and to cause his own actions to be anticipatorily influenced by the virtual reactions of others. Human behavior becomes oriented to the possible reactions of others: through symbols, patterns of reciprocal expectations of behavior are formed, which, however, always remain embedded in the flow of interaction, of the verification of anticipations.

The conceptual results of this innovation are quite well known—the notions of role-taking, of the self, of the generalized other, etc.—and an explanation of them can be omitted here. More important for the purposes of the present account is the fact that Mead undertook to extend his approach into the domain of cognitive problems. On the basis of this social turn of pragmatism,[8] he gives a new interpretation of the constitution of the physical object, of the body image, and of subjective temporality. Together, these fragments make it possible to understand action as self-controlled behavior, and to see a concept of self-control that is not instrumentalistically restricted as pragmatism's concept of rationality.

In particular, Mead establishes the conditions of symbolic interaction and self-reflection. His analyses are guided by a normatively ideal conception of the structure of social order that is based principally on an ideal of democratic self-government combined with Peircean ideas about free and unrestricted communication within the community of scientists. In the central theoretical parts of his work, however, this notion is not used to elaborate a theory of society that could also be put to sociological use. This development is more commonly found in those writings belonging to his political journalism.

John Dewey's writings go further in this regard, especially the discussion in his book *The Public and Its Problems* (1927).[9] There Dewey argues in defense of a theory that takes the process of collective action as its starting point. This action encounters problems and leads to unintended or unanticipated consequences, which must be reflectively "processed" by the acting collectivity. Within the framework of communal standards, the consequences of action are perceived, interpreted, assessed, and taken into consideration in the preparation of future actions not only by institutions that have specifically been assigned those tasks, but also by all the individuals and collectivities affected by the consequences. In this process of interpreting and assessing the consequences of collective action, communication among all those concerned plays an essential role; everyone affected is motivated to participate in such communication, to manifest that he or she is affected by and concerned with the consequences. Dewey's political philosophy thus does not assume an antagonism between individuals and the state, but instead takes as its starting point the internal problems of group action. In the public that is founded in group action, as the community of communication made up of all those affected by and concerned with the consequences of such action, both the independent state and the autonomous individual are constituted.

In this theoretical model, communication for the purpose of solving problems of collective concern becomes an essential condition of social order. This becomes even clearer when one compares this notion with the competing theories of social order. Thus conceived, social order does not require the "like-mindedness" of society's members; human communication links together individual uniqueness and the shared or universal recognition and use of symbolic systems. Dewey's political philosophy is also directed against the Hobbesian tradition of thought, which can conceive of social integration as effected only through the agency of external authorities.

Lastly, Dewey's program, like the earlier reflections of Cooley, is explicitly opposed to a "naturalization" of the market and to a conception of it as a self-regulating, problem-solving mechanism. It is precisely the consequences of the interconnection of actions having economic ends that require a collective interpretation and assessment. In the specific way that the notion of "social control" was used by this group of thinkers, this notion did not refer to a guarantee of social conformity but, rather, to conscious self-regulation, to the idea of self-government effected through the medium of communication and understood as the solving of collective problems. Thus this concept of "social control" was, in the theory of social order, the equivalent of the concept of "self-control" in the theory of action.[10] Neither concept was intended for use in value-free description. Rather, they both contained immanent criteria for judging the rationality of actions or of social orders. That does not mean that they were merely evaluative concepts. They were to demonstrate their revelatory power precisely in actual analyses of human actions and societies. On the one hand, pragmatism's social philosophy thus provided a complex of fundamental concepts for social scientific research and theory construction. On the other hand, it ascribed to these very social sciences an enormous moral and political importance. For they were supposed to aid human communities in improving their potential for collective action and, in a world that had lost all metaphysical certainty, make a decisive contribution to promoting the solidarity of a universal human community that collectively recognizes, discusses, and solves the problems of humanity.

II The Development of the Chicago School

Those investigating the theoretical content of the thought and work of the old Chicago School must begin by freeing themselves from several widespread misconceptions about that school if they are to appreciate the real accomplishments of this group of researchers and thinkers.[11]

The first of these misconceptions is that the school had an exclusively empirical orientation and that it not only failed to systematize theoretically the results of its researches, but regarded them as emanations of the objects of research. This assessment is accurate insofar as this school, faithful to the spirit of pragmatism, placed great value on empirical research. In the history of social science, it stands in the middle between the speculative evolutionist social philosophy of sociology's early years and modern empirical social science. It is also true that in retrospect the school for the most part produced a mosaic of quasi-ethnographic studies rather than enduring theoretical treatises. But this fact should not be allowed to give the misleading impression that the works of the school's members do not share an at least implicit theoretical framework. Although it is not exactly identical in each study, nevertheless an implicit general theoretical framework of pragmatism—which was however given hardly any explicit metatheoretical grounding—can be uncovered in the individual substantive theorems of the Chicago School.

Just as mistaken as this assessment is the view that the Chicago School was merely interested in bringing about social reform, or the belief that the specific nature of this school consisted of a more or less secularized Protestant social reformism.[12] In this regard too one could speak of an intermediary position in the history of social science, namely a position between the absence of, and the complete, professionalization of the social sciences. All the central figures of the Chicago School were opposed to social research conducted without professional standards, which merely made the public conscious of the existence and extent of social problems. They were, furthermore, clearly aware that although the professionalization of the social sciences had to be based on improved research methods and a universalistic frame of reference—as opposed to mere reformism—it should not consist of the renunciation of all extrascientific mandates. Finally, as far as the Christian character of the Chicago School is concerned, it can certainly not be found in the thought and writings of such important members as Thomas and Mead. Nor is it possible to speak meaningfully of a merely secularized form of Christianity, in view of the extremely anti-Puritanical motives of many of the school's members.

A third misassessment regards the Chicago School as the epigonous result of the study of the writings of European thinkers and the appropriation of their ideas. It is true, certainly, that above all German thought—as it went through the transition from historicism to sociology (represented by Dilthey, Windelband, Rickert, Tönnies and Simmel)—and German ethnology and folk psychology (*Völkerpsychologie*)—which sought to explain the cultural life of nations or peoples—exercised a formative influence on many important figures in the school. Much attention was given to the sociological theories of Durkheim, Tönnies, and Simmel. There were, in particular, affinities between members of the school and Simmel, inasmuch as Simmel was searching for a concept of society that would neither reduce society to a mere aggregation of individuals nor reify it into an entity completely transcending individuals.[13] Yet it is completely misleading to regard the ideas of the Chicago School as deriving from the thought of Simmel, or even to assume a general superiority of European social scientific thinking at this time. If the thesis is correct that the theoretical framework of the Chicago School has its origin in the social philosophy of pragmatism, then it will also have been shown that the school had its starting point in an authentically American school of thought, and not in European philosophy. Even Parsons's later admission that Cooley, Thomas, and above all Mead had developed a sociopsychological theory of internalization that constituted an important advance over the classical European social theorists,[14] does not go far enough, as it isolates this accomplishment from the conditions in which it was made and from the consequences resulting from it. That is, the pragmatist critique of rationalistic individualism was not acknowledged in its full breadth.

This fact is expressed most strikingly in the myth of the dominance of Herbert Spencer's utilitarian individualism over pre-Parsonian American sociology. For the period prior to the Chicago School, and for the speculative sociologists outside this school, it is indeed true that a great deal of work was given over to a theoretical modification of Spencer's assertions. However, the fact is that for all the social theorists from this period whose works are still read today—Peirce, James, Baldwin, Mead, Dewey, Cooley, Veblen, Thomas, and Park—Spencer was "more whipping boy than master."[15] The first important textbook of American sociology, W. I. Thomas's *Source Book for Social Origins* (1909), can be understood, in long stretches, as a polemic against Spencer. Since the end of the American Civil War, many American thinkers had renounced allegiance to atomistic individualism and set out on a search for new theoretical and practical models of the formation of community. Their solutions to the problem of a new basis for community took extremely diverse forms and extended from a return to the communitarian ideals of early Puritanism, through a mysticism of nature, attraction to Catholicism, utopian schemes and experiments, and on to a glorification of America's colonial past or of the former conditions in the Southern states. In most instances, the attempt was made to introduce the moral claims of individualism into these models of community.

The way in which pragmatism was transformed into sociology was, of course, determined in a decisive manner by the conditions of American society, of the University of Chicago, and of political connection of early American sociology to its environing society during the period when it originated, at the beginning of the 1890s and in the years following. In this period, the United States was going through a phase of rapid industrialization and urbanization.[16] The influx of immigrants was enormous; for the most part they came from cultural backgrounds very different from the Protestant tradition. The dissolution of the politically and economically strongly decentralized structure of the United States, together with the simultaneous economic changes per se, provided a foundation for a profound modification of the class structure of American society. A part of this change that must be especially mentioned was the rise of a new "professional" middle class. Politically, these changes were accompanied by many efforts to achieve social reforms, which earned for this epoch the name "the progressive era." Common to these reform efforts was the goal of preserving the democratic ideals of the self-government of local communities under the new conditions of a hegemony in American society of the great corporations and the central federal government; this was to be done by developing the ideals of small local communities into a form appropriate to the new urban communities. Chicago was one of the centers of these reformist enterprises. The intellectuals of the Chicago School were closely associated personally with many of these efforts and remained so in large part even during the conservative period of the twenties. The principal themes of the Chicago School were therefore the problems of the modern city, especially of Chicago itself. The choice of the topics of its sociological studies can almost always be accounted for by this focus of concern.

The institutional conditions of the recently founded University of Chicago favored an orientation toward research and interdisciplinarity.

At this university the emphasis, for the graduate students, was on learning through research, and for the infrastructure, on cooperatively conducted research. The establishment of a professional journal, the *American Journal of Sociology*, in 1895 and the publication of textbooks by Thomas and by Park and Burgess gave support to the undertaking of the sociologists at the University of Chicago. There sociology did not find it necessary to struggle for its existence against the *power* of the older disciplines, especially political economy, but was able, under much more favorable conditions than elsewhere, to give its full attention to them *intellectually*, and to demarcate itself from them.[17] It was closely connected with ethnology, with philosophy and educational theory (in the persons and thought of Dewey and Mead), and with the institutionalist, anti-marginalist economics of Thorstein Veblen.

The founders of sociology at the University of Chicago in the strict sense are, with the exception of Albion Small, today forgotten and rightly considered to be of no significance as theorists. Small can be described as a combination of speculative "systems sociologist" and administrative initiator of empirical sociological research. His own theoretical position, which he apparently did not in any way make a guideline for the empirical sociological research carried out at the University of Chicago, could be called "collective utilitarianism," that is, it was a theory that accounted for social life through the processes engendered by the conflict among interest groups. Against the force of the pragmatist ideas, though, this approach had little chance of prevailing. In the work of William Isaac Thomas, an early graduate of the University of Chicago who then joined its faculty, there occurred the first important linking of pragmatism and sociological research.

Thomas's intellectual roots lay in ethnography and folk psychology.[18] These two fields of research gathered and investigated materials pertaining to the cultural variety of peoples and eras in a holistic and—compared to introspectionist psychology—"objective" fashion. Methodologically, Thomas remained faithful to an ethnographic procedure, but now applied to nonexotic objects; theoretically, in the debates around the elaboration of a social psychology, he was interested in a theoretical model that gave close attention to the influence of culture on individual and collective behavior. In his early writings, he gradually distanced himself from the contemporary notions of a biological determination of racial and sexual differences. The basic features of his own theoretical model, however, are pragmatist. In the introduction to his *Source Book for Social Origins* (1909), a central theoretical position was already given to the "habits" model of action. When confronted with unfamiliar stimuli, habits break down, a state of affairs that constitutes a crisis which can be overcome only by a conscious operation ("attention") on the part of the subject, through which new habits of behavior originate. He also opposes the concept of control to all the other key concepts then in use, such as imitation, conflict, coercion, contract, and "consciousness of kind."

More clearly than the pragmatist philosophers, Thomas emphasized the cultural character of behavioral habits and the embedding in a collectivity of even individual initiatives: "The level of culture of the group limits the power of the mind to meet crisis and readjust" (Thomas 1909, p. 20). Culture, as Thomas understood it, embraced the most diverse material, technical, and cognitive resources of a community. Methodologically, this orientation leads to the search for procedures which make it possible to reconstruct the dynamics of subjective response to, and solution of, action problems. For Thomas, this does not yet mean participant observation or interaction-process analysis, but rather the gathering and interpretation of material about the subjective perspectives of actors. In contrast to Durkheim's maxim in *Rules of Sociological Method,* social facts are not to be explained solely through other social facts. Thus it is not statistical procedures of analysis that are primarily applied; instead individual perceptions and new creations are to be recognized as the mediating link between social facts. Therefore, in sociological studies, materials are to be gathered and examined which approach most closely to the ideal of autobiographical self-presentation and thus to the narrative unity of human existence. Accordingly, for Thomas and the whole Chicago School, a demarcation of their thought and research from psychology did not play an important role, as it did for Durkheim. The theoretical model of a social psychology prevented the identification of psychology with the atomistic individualism they were combating.

Subjective response to, and coping with, the transformation of a "traditional" society into a "modern" one was the research topic with which Thomas advanced his reflections furthest, in a combination of theory and empirical research that was admittedly often loose. Quite early in his career, he became interested in the problems of black Americans, of the Jewish socialists in the United States, and of the immigrants of various nationalities (Bressler 1952). His most extensive study dealt with the Polish immigrants (Thomas and Znaniecki 1926), and became recognized as one of the paradigmatic works of the Chicago School. Thomas followed it with other studies of problems concerning immigrants, as well as of other topics having to do with social adaptation, including one on juvenile prostitutes (Park and Miller 1921;[19] Thomas 1923), without, however, making really significant theoretical advances.

Thomas's theoretical model, as it is presented chiefly in the preliminary methodological remarks to *The Polish Peasant* (1926) and in other parts of that study, expands the pragmatist model of action in two respects: first, the model is made sociologically more concrete and, second, it is expanded to include collective action. It is made concrete inasmuch as the subjective operation of defining a situation is considered with greater exactitude. Received orientations of conduct are seen as the result of definitions of situations that have previously been successful. With the concept of "attitude," these definitions are formulated with reference to action and distinguished from the psychology of consciousness. Attention is paid to the social role of the definer of situations. It is clear that these definitions always contain an element of risk. They do not necessarily have to form a unitary coherent system, or to cover all situations equally well. Situations continually arise for which fixed definitions of situations do not suffice. Thomas asserts that it is possible to divide motives of action into four classes. These are: the desire for new experience; for mastery of a situation; for social recognition; and for certitude of identity.

This sketch of a theory of motivation shows that Thomas had gone beyond the notions of instinct psychology without accepting the explanations proposed by psychoanalysis, which he considered to be monocausal. His theory included motives that lay beyond material self-preservation or egoistical pursuit of individual interests, and resembles most strongly the "humanistic" psychology that was developed later. He made a contribution to the theory of personality with his notion of "life organization," the subjective shaping of the life course. Using this category he distinguished three personality types: the "philistine," with a rigid orientation of his life; the "Bohemian," who has no coherent character structure; and, lastly, with a clearly positive valuation, the creative personality, who is able systematically to guide his own development.

The expansion of the pragmatist model of action to include collective action changes the view of the disintegration of "traditional" orientations or societies. On this new view, disorganization and crisis always present an opportunity for creative reorganization. Thomas was not a cultural pessimist who saw in the modern era only the disintegration of "community." He did not believe in the rigid opposition of strong institutions and anomic loss of orientation; rather, his interest was directed to the collective processes bringing about the formation of new institutions. For him "the stability of group institutions is thus simply a dynamic equilibrium of processes of disorganization and *reorganization*" (Thomas and Znaniecki 1926, p. 1130).

This view of society and history made *dépassé* the dichotomous historical categories that had exercised such great influence at the beginning of sociology. No longer was community opposed to society, mechanical to organic solidarity; these oppositions were replaced by continuous processes of institutional disintegration, of the successful or failed formation of new institutions. It was no longer necessary to deny the importance for modern societies of crucial components of earlier societies, such as the family and membership of ethnic groups. These had, to be sure, been changed, but their importance had not necessarily been diminished. The relationship between individual and collective action, or between individual and collective disorganization and reorganization, was explicitly not regarded functionalistically, that is, the opportunity for individual reorganization also existed under conditions of social disorganization. In his empirical research on Polish immigrants, Thomas undertook to investigate the different phases of the crisis-fraught process of adaptation undergone by these immigrants by using empirical materials corresponding to each of the phases (Madge 1962, pp. 52–87). On the basis of letters, a picture of Polish peasant society was drawn which showed that society from extraordinarily diverse aspects. The disintegration of this society in the spreading industrial capitalism and its first efforts to reorganize itself were documented with articles from Polish newspapers. The personal disorganization of the immigrants was presented with the help of extensive autobiographical material. Information about the social disorganization of the immigrant's culture in the United States was gathered from court and parish records. In this way, despite all the problems of the relationship of theory and empirical research, as well as of the elaborateness of theory and methods of empirical research, an impressive pioneering sociological work was written that today must be accorded the status of a classic.

For some time, William Thomas was the most important sociologist of the Chicago School. When, in 1918, he was actually dismissed by his university owing to a conspiracy directed against his political and moral nonconformity, his position as unofficial head of the school was filled by a man whom Thomas himself had brought to Chicago a few years before, and who, even prior to their acquaintance, had displayed a very strong affinity with Thomas's orientations and the themes of his thought and research: Robert Park. Until the middle of the thirties, Park was the decisively influential figure in the school. His importance is even greater than that of Thomas, inasmuch as he was effective through his many students and through the organization of research projects, and not just through his own studies.

In light of the many twists and turns of his life, which brought him to a professorship only after he had passed the age of fifty, it seems almost as if Park was predestined for the role he played at the University of Chicago.[20] He had, as a student, come under the crucially important influence of John Dewey, had worked for many years as a newspaper reporter, and had obtained a doctoral degree in Germany with a critique, influenced by Simmel, of contemporary crowd psychology, and had published his dissertation in German. Additionally, having been for years a close collaborator of the black reformer Booker T. Washington, he knew the problems of blacks in the United States better than any other white person of that period. Moreover, these different activities were by no means so unrelated as they might at first appear. Park's creative personality, at least, succeeded in integrating them. From Dewey's philosophy Park had taken over, in particular, the emphasis on democracy as a social order and on public communication as the prerequisite for democracy. His work as a journalist gave him an intimate knowledge of public communication and provided material for his sociological reflections.

Park would later define "news" as information that is of interest to all because it concerns them, the interpretation of which, however, is still open (Park 1972). More than Dewey, Park was interested in the empirical reality of the processes by which public opinion is formed, and of the dynamics of the discussion processes which frequently lead to non-consensual results. His passion for giving first-hand reports and his commitment to the blacks in America were both fueled by a deep hunger for experiences lying outside the narrow cultural and moral confines of the parochial Protestant American milieu. While scarcely any awareness of the plight of blacks in the United States can be found among the majority of progressive intellectuals of the period, Park saw that, prior to the question of the integration of new immigrants into the American society, the existence of a black population made it necessary to reflect on the possibility of "social control," of democracy under the conditions of cultural heterogeneity. Finally, in his German dissertation Park had undertaken to employ Dewey's concept of democracy as a formal concept in Simmel's sense of the term. By taking this step, Park achieved two things. From the standpoint of the theory of action, the problem of creatively achieving consensus was recognized as being of central importance, and it was shown, counter to the aims of the European crowd psychologists, that there is indeed a possible rationality of collective decision-making processes. What Park did with Dewey's concept, however, also yielded an alternative to the dichotomous theory of historical transformation with its opposed categories of "community" and "society." This alternative was the transformation of traditional communities either into mass societies or into democratically integrated societies. Park was intensely interested by the creative possibilities both of the masses and of public discussion.

This fact makes it understandable that for him the collective behavior out of which institutions first emerge, and in which they are changed, became the proper object of sociology. In the large introductory textbook written by Park and Burgess (1921)—the "green Bible" of American sociologists between the two world wars—sociology is defined as the science of collective behavior. That does not mean, of course, that individual action is to be ignored or excluded from the domain of sociology, but rather that it is to be understood as collectively constituted in its orientation.

For Park, society does not confront the individual solely as an agency of restraint, of coercion, or of obligation. It is also experienced as a source of inspiration, of an expansion of the self, and of a liberation and enhancement of hidden personal energies. The condition of collective action is the existence of "collective representations," which are constituted in communication. The focus of such an approach must, therefore, be on the different types of constitution of such collective representations: these extend from systems of religious symbols to public opinion, and also include phenomena such as fashion.

This notion does not take us outside the terrain that is thoroughly familiar to pragmatist social philosophy. The language in which Park and Burgess express these ideas in their textbook is obviously influenced by Durkheim.[21] More strongly than the French theorist, though, they stress the modern and everyday forms of the emergence of collective representations. One might easily conclude that this is little more than a mere formulation of well-known fundamental ideas in a Durkheimian manner and in a way that is closer to empirical reality. This impression disappears, though, when it is recognized that for Park only one of two types of social order is captured by this view of society: the type of "moral order," of collective action that is regulated with reference to values and meanings. To this type, however, there is opposed another, which Park designates "biotic" or "ecological" order.[22] The reason for the introduction of this second type of social order was evidently the difficulty of conceiving—on the basis of its characteristic model of social order—of systematic deviations of the results of collective action from what is collectively intended, or systematically occurring results of uncoordinated action. Park found the archetype for this "human ecological" theory in plant ecology, which in turn was partially influenced by models of the market economy. These models seemed to him suitable for the scientific representation of processes of competition for scarce resources, and for the resulting reciprocal adaptations and spatial and temporal distributions.

Park's theory was fruitful to the extent that it took seriously the relationship of social processes to their physical environment. This theory was the origin of many impulses, for example for the investigation of the origin and change of function of neighborhoods and for research on the spatial or regional diffusion of social phenomena. The models used in these studies, however, constantly ran the risk of "naturalizing" social phenomena and of thereby giving a deterministic interpretation of them. Ralph Turner pointed out this crucial weakness.[23] The distinction of the two types of social order has to do not with different social spheres, but with the intentional or unintentional character of the results of social action.

This fact, however, gives rise to the problem of applying these models of social order and, above all, of their integration to produce a single coherent theory of society. Park's lack of theoretical clarity here leads to a mere combination of a democratically oriented macrosociology with underlying assumptions of a competition and a struggle for survival that are considered natural. A theory that would reconcile economy and society is not achieved. The gap between the two parts of Park's theory is bridged with evolutionist assumptions about the gradual transformation of the unplanned, competitive sector of societies into the democratically self-determined sector: "The evolution of society has been the progressive extension of control over nature and the substitution of a moral for the natural order" (Park and Burgess 1921, p. 511). This implicit view also distorts the idea of "natural history" and in particular influences the famous "stage model" of the development of race relations from "competition" through "conflict" to mutual "accommodation," and, finally, "assimilation." As Park and his students typically employed these ideas, it was not a matter of ideal types of processes, but of deterministic schemata of stages. As such, of course, they can easily be criticized, whether by drawing attention to ethnocentric features of the way certain phenomena of urbanization are viewed, or by adducing the experience of entirely different courses of development of race relations than that leading to assimilation.[24] Park, though, used the deterministic character of his models for the purposes of a polemic against the unrest of the American blacks and against reformist intellectuals acting on behalf of others.

Obviously, then, it cannot be claimed that Park and his students succeeded in transforming pragmatism into a satisfactory theory of society. About central questions that such a theory must answer in the twentieth century, such as the development of class relations, bureaucracy, or international relations, this approach has nothing to say. They did, however, succeed in elaborating a flexible, theoretical, and macrosociologically oriented frame of reference for the many empirical studies of phenomena of everyday life in the modern (American) big city. In the course of the twenties and thirties, a plethora of such studies was carried out that is impressive even today. Some of them have remained famous because of their methods and findings, for example, Nels Anderson's study *The Hobo* (1923), Frederick Thrasher's investigation of criminal youth gangs (1927), and Clifford Shaw's biography of a juvenile criminal (1930). The first sociological studies by black sociologists of the problems of American blacks have their origin in Park's school. In each case it is striking how enormous was the distance from a perception—whether moralistic or social reformist—of the social phenomena from the standpoint of the middle classes. What was produced by Park and his students was a mosaic of studies of metropolitan life full of first-hand descriptions that were of almost literary quality; but it was certainly not a social science methodically progressing by means of the testing of hypotheses or theoretical generalization.

Although it is not possible here to discuss in detail the work of other important thinkers of the Chicago School of this period, some of them should at least be mentioned. Chief among them is Park's friend and coauthor Ernest Burgess, who, to be sure, tended to an even stronger determinism in his urban sociology than Park. He unequivocally subsumed the sphere of the economy under the ecological model and was a proponent of the famous theory of concentric circles of urban development, which he had based on the case of Chicago. He made an important contribution to the sociology of the family, in which he introduced the view of the family as a processual unity of interacting personalities, without, however, the methodological instruments corresponding to this program, and under the assumption of the unilinear evolutionary development of the family "from institution to companionship" (Bogue 1974). Ellsworth Faris (1937), in many short articles, and very influentially in his teaching, advocated central ideas of pragmatist social philosophy, and made use of them in an original manner principally to criticize behavioristically reductionist views and the claims of instinct psychology. Louis Wirth,[25] who was influential in the late thirties and the forties, investigated the Jewish ghetto entirely in the manner advocated by Park; on the other hand, though, he proposed a theory of the large city that, completely contrary to the typical approach of Park's school, interpreted life in the large city according to the scheme of the *replacement* of community bonds by societal relations.

It would also be inappropriate to speculate here about the reasons for the much-debated demise of the Chicago School in the thirties.[26] In the context of the present account, it is not the details of the history of sociology that are of interest but the subsequent fortunes of pragmatist theory. How did this theory deal with new problems and with the old, unsolved ones? What became of it after the ebbing of the progressive optimism of the theory's founders about the possibilities of reform? What became of the dualism of moral and biotic orders?

It is customary to see the continuation of this tradition principally in Herbert Blumer's programmatic writings on social psychology. As important as these are, they form too narrow a foundation for examining the tradition's continuation. Thus the eminently inspiring work of Everett Hughes is given equal importance here with that of Blumer. In the writings of these two men, two ways of treating the problems that have been raised can be studied.

Herbert Blumer's work, with its merits and weaknesses, has been of decisive importance for the self-understanding of subsequent generations of proponents of symbolic interactionism. After writing a dissertation in which he reviewed the methods of social psychology, Blumer became well known in the thirties in particular through two works (Blumer 1928, 1939). He examined in an extremely critical manner the relationship between theory and empirical research in Thomas and Znaniecki's study of the Polish peasant; and in an article for a handbook in which he systematized the premises of the tradition of the Chicago School, he invented the name "symbolic interactionism." The relationship of theory and empirical research in the social sciences became a subject of lifelong interest to Blumer. In opposition to the survey research and professionalized data analysis that was attaining dominance in the social sciences, he developed more and more the thesis that an intimate relation of the social scientist to the object of his investigation was required. For all the sociologists who tended to interpretative methods, to the inclusion in sociological research of subjective experiences, to a use of theoretical concepts that made them more sensitive to empirical reality, his methodological protests and programs became an extremely important point of reference. Even more than Mead and the other sociological thinkers from whom he had learned, Blumer raised the processual character of all action to a methodological tenet. Phase models of action could never be more than only approximately correct if the continuous re-adaptation to new or changed environmental conditions was just what was characteristic of action. His systematizations also offered an account of the central premises of pragmatist thought that was at a greater remove from philosophy and easier to use for the purposes of the sociological researcher.

In his substantive studies on ethnic topics and on collective behavior,

Blumer strove to go beyond and even to supplant psychologistic and functionalist explanations; also, in contrast to Park, his writings are not guided by evolutionist ideas. If, however, Blumer's work is measured against the questions faced by the contemporary theory of society, then it becomes obvious that his writings simply provide no answer to many of these. The problem implicit in Park's dualism of "moral" and "biotic" order is not taken up again in any way. In his version of symbolic interactionism, Blumer confines himself to tackling those problems which lie within the conceptual framework of the "moral order." He avoids problems which apparently cannot on principle be located within this framework, or whose assignment to the "moral order" seem intuitively to be possible only with difficulty. Thus it was possible to consolidate a fruitful paradigm without greatly advancing the confrontation with other theories.

This qualification does not hold for Everett Hughes, the Chicago tradition's leading sociologist of occupations and work.[27] In his work, Park's dualism is preserved, but its form is changed. The distinction between a sector of society that is normatively or communicatively integrated and a societal domain regulated through market processes or the unplanned interconnections among the results of actions is transformed in such a way that, although now every organization or institution continues to be analyzed using the model of normative integration, the relations among these institutions or organizations appear as competition among collective actors—very similar to the "collective utilitarianism" that can be found, say, in the theory of Albion Small at the inception of the Chicago School. Hughes regards every institution as a part of an organic system that is not further specified, for which it has certain functions to fulfill but which, as a totality, exhibits no integrative system of values. The concept of collective consciousness is no longer referred to society in its entirety, but applied now only to the individual macroscopic actors. In this position there lies, certainly, an undeniable possibility for fruitful analysis of empirical reality, which was subsequently developed, both within and without the framework of symbolic interactionism, in the theory of reference groups. At the same time, though, this restricted application of the concept of collective consciousness also means the loss of a concept of society as a unitary political and social order.

Like that of Park, Hughes's oeuvre includes a great number of small studies and only a few large ones. His importance lay in his ability to maintain a consistent point of view while remaining close to empirical reality, and to make it operative in the research of his students. Also significant were his efforts to guide others to the investigation of institutions as living wholes, and of competition among ethnic groups. Of greatest importance, however, were his studies on occupational sociology. It is not surprising that occupational sociology attracted the attention of the continuators of the Chicago tradition, who were interested in making fruitful use of their ideas about the structure of social order in empirical research. For occupations are the patterns of activities specialized in accordance with a division of labor, in which the mediation, through different interests, relations of forces, and processes of negotiations, of a structure that only apparently results from objective constraints is manifested with particular clarity.

Hughes directed his attention especially to the professions, the occupations requiring university training, for the greater latitude they allow individuals to shape their own work makes evident the theoretically predicted essential feature of the division of labor, namely that it is neither technologically, nor ecologically, nor normatively determined, but can be understood only by reference to the action of the pertinent individuals or occupational groups. Since for Hughes the question of a macrosocietal, institutionalized commonwealth did not arise, he had no difficulty in making the professions the topic of his reflection and research, without holding any simple belief in their self-justification. He examined critically the ideologies of different kinds of professions as means for achieving freedom from control and attaining to high status. He was interested in the techniques and tactics used to avoid undesirable tasks and to conceal mistakes from subordinates and clients. Thus his concentration on professions in which firm guidelines or prescriptions play a minor part, and in which there exists the necessity for those exercising the professions to "create" their own roles, does not in any way originate in an uncritical attitude toward the ideology of these professions. In the course of Hughes's research studies of industrial workplaces were also conducted. In these investigations, the crucial point was that even under the most restrictive conditions, occupational activity cannot be understood without taking into consideration the workers' own definitions of their situation and their struggle for autonomy.

At the beginning of the fifties, the Chicago School, whose dominance had ceased at the end of the thirties, lost its most important representatives at the University of Chicago itself: Ernest Burgess retired, Louis Wirth died, and Herbert Blumer went to California. The end of the Chicago School in the narrower, definitive sense should be dated at this time. The school's intellectual legacy, which was not equally elaborated in all its aspects, was then passed on and developed further along the most diverse paths. The best-known use of this legacy is the elaboration of a symbolic-interactionist social psychology by Tamotsu Shibutani (1961), Anselm Strauss (1959), and Norman Denzin (1977a),[28] as well as of a role-theory and family sociology by, among others, Ralph Turner (1970). The continuation of Hughes's work can be followed in the outstanding sociological studies of the professions, and especially of medicine, by Eliot Freidson (1970), Howard Becker (Becker et al. 1961) and Anselm Strauss. In addition, Becker in large measure opened up a new field of research with his influential study, undertaken completely in the spirit of the Chicago tradition, on "outsiders" and the genesis of deviant behavior (Becker 1963). Gregory Stone and many others have contributed to the sociological understanding and explanation of many phenomena of everyday life (Stone and Farberman 1970). At the margin of this school stands the brilliant and highly original work of Erving Goffman.[29] If one considers all these topics and researchers together, the picture one sees is certainly that of a vital and viable current of research. However, of these many paths of research only one appears to lead toward an overcoming of the theoretical isolation of this school. This is the one that has developed on the foundation laid chiefly by the studies of Anselm Strauss and that is presented in the writings of younger sociologists as the "negotiated-order approach."

The elaboration of this approach, too, was carried out entirely in the empirical style of the Chicago tradition: on the whole, by means of thematically limited, specific case studies rather than through mere elaboration of concepts. The starting point for the development of this approach can be located where the research on professions conducted by members of the Chicago School, chiefly in the studies of hospitals, led to a distinct perspective regarding the sociology of organizations.[30] It was initially the reaction to a process of change, namely the increase in the number of types of professionals carrying out their professional activities within complex organizations, that brought about a shift of interest away from the "professions" to the "professional organizations." In the analysis of the "hospital" as a typical example of such an organization, the models of organizational sociology of the rationalist-bureaucratic and functionalist types proved to be inadequate. The structures of the division of labor within the hospitals proved to be, from the outset, quite indefinite, the goals nonspecific, and the rules equivocal. Only a continuous process of tacit agreements, unofficial arrangements, and official decisions among the various professional groups concerned, parts of professional groups, and individuals regarding the strategy of the total organization and the way it divides up work makes the functioning of such an organization possible. From this is derived the general principle asserted by this sociology of organizations: that organizations are to be conceptualized as "ongoing systems of negotiation."

According to this theory, organizations are not formations structured by univocal, normative rules; the action performed within them is not determined by a mere application of prescriptions or guidelines free of all intervention by the actor's self. Reflection and dialogue are required not just for the alteration of rules and norms, but also for their maintenance and reproduction. For their existence, organizations are dependent on their continuous reconstitution in action; they reproduce themselves in and through the medium of action. Goals and strategies of organizations are a matter of controversy; agreement can assume many different forms, including those of intentional or knowingly tolerated intermingling of goals and plurality of goals. Every agreement is of a conditional and transitory character. The actors themselves have theories, drawn from their everyday experience, about the nature, scope, and probable success of negotiation processes. If this holds good even for relatively formal organizations, then it is all the more true of more loosely structured social formations. It is not the tracing out of static structures, but the reconstruction of reciprocal processes of definition extending over time that becomes, then, the central task for a sociology of organizations that is striving to be compatible with the premises of symbolic interactionism regarding social psychology and personality theory, and to regain thereby the possibility of achieving the more comprehensive goals of a transformation of pragmatism within sociology.

Such a sociology of organizations is, to be sure, only a first step along this path. The importance of negotiation processes in formal organizations is not merely asserted against an incorrect understanding of this social form; more far-reaching is the claim that almost all types of social order are misinterpreted if the role of negotiation processes is left out of consideration. Wherever neither absolute consensus nor pure force obtains, such processes can be found, and complete consensus and pure force are only limiting cases and not prototypes of social life (see Maines and Charlton 1985, p. 295).

The utilization of this insight, however, can take different directions. For example, one can attempt to distinguish the different dimensions of negotiation processes in order to become more sensitive to them in empirical studies. Anselm Strauss, in his book *Negotiations* (1979), has made an attempt to work out such a conceptual grid, although it is in many respects still very preliminary.[31] The dimensions he lists include the number of participants, their relevant experience, and whether they are speaking only for themselves or represent collectivities. He then points out that negotiations can be nonrecurring or can take place repeatedly, that they can recur at regular intervals or be ordered in determinate sequences. Further, the difference in power among the participating actors is significant. Other dimensions are the importance that the negotiation has for the participants, and that it does not have to be equally great for all of them; the visibility of the negotiation for other than the immediate partners in the negotiation; the number and complexity of the objects of the negotiation; and the options of the partners in the negotiation other than the implementation of consensual decisions, i.e. in case the negotiation is broken off.

This enumeration makes it clear that this approach is not concerned with asserting the existence of an ideal consensuality regarding social regulations in which power, conflict, and structural constraints play no role. That would be a gross misunderstanding. What is to be demonstrated is, rather, how the results of earlier actions must be taken into consideration even by the actor himself, both individually and collectively, both consensually and conflictually, and that this assimilation and assessment itself takes place under structural conditions which can, in their turn, be traced back to earlier negotiation processes and intended or unintended results of action.

A schema of the dimensions of negotiation processes is, at first, neutral with respect to the societal sphere in which these processes occur, as well as in relation to the question of the significance of these dimensions for the functioning of societies. A second direction in which the "negotiated order" approach has been elaborated can thus be characterized as the inclusion, in addition to the "professional organization," of other objects of research and the accomplishment thereby of the gradual enlargement of the approach's macrosociological capability.

Studies which are quite different from one another share this aim. The course followed by political decision-making, for example, almost literally forces itself on the attention of the researcher seeking an object for this approach (Hall 1972). Not only the formal and substantive determination of the relations among professional groups in existing institutions, but also the constitution of the structure of professions and of the system of societal division of labor in general are made an object of study by Eliot Freidson (1975–76). Some researchers, for example Harvey Farberman (1975) and Norman Denzin (1977b), have directed their attention to selected market phenomena and have shown that these remain incomprehensible without reference to the intermediation of negotiation processes. Gary Alan Fine and Sherryl Kleinman (1983) have extended symbolic interactionism's field of attention beyond small groups and organizations to encompass personal networks, to the investigation of which they have also made an original contribution.

Common to all these scattered undertakings is that they have yielded macrosociological studies or fragments of theory without lapsing into the naturalization of the processes investigated into a "biotic order." More than the theory of democracy in pragmatism's social philosophy, they insist not only on the normative but also on the empirical explosive power of an examination of the features of social life that appear under the conditions of democracy. For the most part, however, these studies are still only miniature portraits, not great tableaux of the present period treating matters of political and historical importance. Nonetheless, the threshold leading to a theory of society as a whole and to the understanding of forms of social integration, such as the market in which independence from collective decisions is institutionalized, has been crossed. Further progress along this path, however, cannot be made without confronting the great schools of theory on these topics. Yet it is to just these schools that the philosophical foundation laid by pragmatism, its extensively elaborated social psychology and microsociology, as well as the basic principles of the "negotiated order" approach, pose a theoretical challenge.

III An Assessment

An assessment of the theoretical fruits of the sociological school deriving from pragmatism and a contrast of this school with the other major currents of sociology at the present time cannot be succinctly formulated unless the many different problems addressed by the theories and research of the competing schools are restricted to a few fundamental questions. The most compelling suggestion on this point is to be found in the Parsonian tradition. According to this proposal, it is the questions of action and of social order as an ordered nexus of actions that make up the central and unavoidable metatheoretical problems of sociology.[32] These problems are metatheoretical because they do not concern the development of empirically tenable special theories for selected domains of phenomena, but questions dealing with the conceptual definition and description of the domain of sociology or the social sciences in general. These questions can be said to be unavoidable because, although not every sociological theory concerns itself with them explicitly, none can do without at least implicit assumptions about the nature of action and of social order. Metatheoretical reflection in this sense throws these more or less implicit assumptions into clear relief and requires their grounding. If one accepts this definition of the logical status of the theory of action and of social order, then the reality and the inherent possibilities of pragmatism can be related to competing or complementary schools of sociology on these two planes.

As it has been presented above, pragmatism's theory of action is radically different from the models of a sociological utilitarianism. In their exclusive recognition of rational action, these models are incapable of giving an account of activities deviating from this model of rationality other than as deficient modes of action. They produce a residual category of nonrational action which does not permit the reconstruction of the phenomenal diversity of action. The transcending of this utilitarian position, which is constitutive of sociology—implicitly in the works of the classical social theorists (Weber, Durkheim, and Pareto) and explicitly in the writings of Parsons—has continued to be shaped by the polemic with which it began. It is thus characterized by a concentration on the normative dimension, which certainly represents progress beyond utilitarianism but runs the risk of misunderstanding the role of norms in the dynamics of real action. In contrast, symbolic interactionism assumes neither the consistency nor the deterministic character of internalized norms. The great countertradition to academic sociology, Marxism, is incomprehensible, at least in its origin, without its foundation in its own theory of action, in the "expressionistic"[33] concept of work according to which work effects the embodiment of the worker's labor power and skills in the product of his work. However, many of those who contributed to the development of this tradition as a theory of society and history disregarded this foundation of Marxism. There has been hardly any elaboration of the notions of "praxis," of "activity," and of "labor" (or "work") nor a relating of them to the problems addressed by the sociological theory of action.

Even the most creative new approach to the sociological theory of action, which transcends utilitarianism, the normativist critique of utilitarianism, and traditional Marxism: Jürgen Habermas's theory of communicative action (1981), does not achieve a comprehensive revision of the sociological theory of action. The opposition of a communicative concept of rationality to the deficiencies of an instrumentalist understanding of rationality has the effect of excluding many dimensions of action which can be found in the history of social thought.[34] The unsolved problem in this connection is how the sociological theory of action can be integrated with the theoretical fecundity of pragmatism and the traditions of the philosophy of praxis, and with the expressionistic notion of work.[35] For the solution of this problem, pragmatism continues to be of central importance. For it has prepared the way not simply to take as a model for the sociological theory of action the purposively acting individual who has mastery over his own body and is autonomous in relation to his fellow human beings and to the environment, but instead to explain the conditions of the possibility of this type of "actor." For this clarification, the literature of symbolic interactionism supplies a wealth of material. Because pragmatism introduced the concept of action as a means to attain to a new view of the relationship between action and consciousness, that is, as a means to pass beyond and to supersede the philosophy of consciousness, it is also able to withstand the offensive of structuralism and poststructuralism, while recognizing some cogency in their arguments, and to safeguard the dimension of human action.[36]

On the level of the theory of social order, the theory of action of the pragmatist, or symbolic-interactionist, tradition compels a relativizing of utilitarian and functionalist models. A relativizing only, since the pragmatic usefulness and explanatory value of these models in many cases are not disputed but, rather, the claim made in sociology for their comprehensive validity. Substantively speaking, the only theory that will be able to avoid falling into functionalism is one which, in its theory of social order, takes collective action as its point of departure and develops a comprehensive typology of its forms, ranging from totemistic ritual to successful democratic self-government and ideal discourse. Sociological analysis is thereby centered on forms of collective processing of intentional and unintentional results of action, on the collective constitution of normative regulations and collective procedures for dealing with normative conflicts. In this regard, too, the tradition of symbolic interactionism offers important material in the categories of collective behavior and social movement, of the determination of social structures by negotiation, and of democracy as a type of social order. Often, though, these notions have been elaborated, in the manner of a "qualitative empiricism," in the investigation of objects of slight macrosociological relevance. The analytical richness of symbolic interactionism thus remains unutilized for a diagnosis of the present time that is politically oriented and that takes the era's historical development and context into consideration. This must change, if the tradition wants again to play the role that the social philosophy of pragmatism once, in its beginning, had for its own present.

Notes

1. I would like to thank Anselm Strauss for his helpful comments on the paper.

2. Exemplary statements of this position can be found in McPhail and Rexroat (1979) and Stryker (1980). For a discussion of Stryker's book, see Review Symposium, *Symbolic Interaction* 5 (1982), pp. 141–72.

3. See Lewis and Smith 1980. Several almost completely negative commentaries on this book have appeared which contain important arguments on the relation between

pragmatism and sociology. Some of these are Blumer (1983); Johnson and Picou (1985); Miller (1982); Rochberg-Halton (1983).

4. On Feuerbach, see Honneth and Joas (1988).

5. A very interesting account of the pragmatist theory of signs as it differs from the structuralist theory is given in Rochberg-Halton (1982).

6. Charles H. Cooley ("A social, or perhaps, I should say, a sociological pragmatism remains to be worked out") quoted in Jandy (1942, p. 110). On Cooley, see Mead's critique in Mead (1930).

7. See Mead (1934) and Joas (1985a). An important dissertation written under Mead's influence, which helps to understand the significance in contemporary sociology of the change of perspective proposed by Mead, is Bodenhafer (1920–21).

8. I have discussed the constitution of the body image in Joas (1983).

9. Since most of the standard accounts of pragmatism are not very helpful with regard to the questions of political theory and the possibilities of applying pragmatism in the social sciences, I call attention here to Rucker (1969) and White (1957).

10. On this point, see the outstanding article by Janowitz (1975–76).

11. On early American sociology, see Hinkle, (1963); (1980). On the independence of American sociology from the classical European social theorists, see Sutherland 1978.

12. Even in the recent writings of the authors of the first rank, such misinterpretations can be found: see Tenbruck (1985); Vidich and Lyman (1985).

13. On the reception of Simmel in the United States, see the comprehensive study by Levine et al. (1975–76).

14. The most important text by Parsons on this complex of themes is his study of Cooley (Parsons 1968b).

15. This thesis is advanced most strongly by Wilson (1968), from whom the quotation is taken.

16. The best historical account of the social-historical background of the developments mentioned here is given in Wiebe (1967).

17. On this topic, see Diner (1975). The most important accounts of the Chicago School are Bulmer (1984), Carey (1975), Faris (1967), and Fisher and Strauss (1978). Those interested in studying this subject further will find helpful the comprehensive bibliography by Kurtz (1984). A very brief but interesting account of a single, although important, aspect of the Chicago tradition is Farberman (1979).

18. A bibliography of Thomas's publications can be found in Janowitz (1966, pp. 307–10). There is no comprehensive biography of Thomas. Shorter accounts of his life that can be recommended are Janowitz's Introduction to the aforementioned edition of Thomas's writings (Janowitz: 1966, pp. vii–lviii), Coser on Thomas and Znaniecki (Coser 1977, pp. 511–59), Deegan and Burger (1981) and Zaretsky (1984).

19. It is well known that this work was practically written by Thomas.

20. Most of the important articles by Park have been published in the three-volume edition of his *Collected Papers* (1950–55). There is excellent secondary literature on Park. Outstanding is Matthews (1977), see also Coser (1977, pp. 357–84) and Turner (1967).

21. A comparison would have to make use of Durkheim's lectures on pragmatism, in addition to his sociology of religion (Durkheim 1955). Interpretations of those lectures are given in Joas (1985b; in this volume) and Stone and Faberman (1967).

22. For a summary, see Park (1936).

23. See the very good critical observations of Turner (1967, p. xxix).

24. For a critique of the race-relations cycle, see also the short report on the last years of Park's life after his departure from Chicago in Cahnman (1978).

25. See Wirth (1964; 1969); the former volume includes the famous and controversial paper "Urbanism as a Way of Life" (1964, pp. 60–83), first published in 1938 (Wirth 1938).

26. In addition to the general treatments of the Chicago School, see also Kuklick (1973) and Lengermann (1979).

27. Everett Hughes's shorter writings have been collected in *The Sociological Eye: Selected Papers* (1971). Two important interpretations of his work are Faught (1980) and Simpson (1972).

28. A good overview is given by Lauer and Handel (1977).

29. As Goffman's work cannot be explained by means of the premises of pragmatism, I only mention it here.

30. Examples of this research are Strauss et al. (1963) and Bucher and Stelling (1969).

31. In addition to Maines and Charlton (1985), for overviews see Fine (1984) and Maines (1977).

32. The clearest account of this position is to be found in Alexander (1982).

33. On this 'expressionist' tradition cf. Berlin (1980) and Taylor (1975).

34. For a critical examination of this theory of action, see Joas 1986 (reprinted in this volume). The two other most important new approaches in the theory of action at present are, in my opinion, Castoriadis (1987) and Giddens (1984). On both, see the chapters in this volume.

35. As an account of the different philosophical traditions that have elaborated the concept of action, Bernstein (1971) remains unexcelled.

36. Referring to the parallels between James and Nietzsche, Richard Rorty has made the following statement: "James and Nietzsche make parallel criticisms of nineteenth-century thought. Further, James' version is preferable, for it avoids the 'metaphysical' elements in Nietzsche which Heidegger criticizes, and for that matter, the 'metaphysical' elements in Heidegger which Derrida criticizes. On my view, James and Dewey were not only waiting at the end of the dialectical road which analytic philosophy travelled, but are waiting at the end of the road which, for example, Foucault and Deleuze are currently travelling" (Rorty 1982, p. xviii).

Bibliography

Alexander, J. 1982. *Positivism, Presuppositions, and Current Controversies,* vol. 1 of *Theoretical Logic in Sociology.* Berkeley and Los Angeles: University of California Press.

Anderson, N. 1923. *The Hobo.* Chicago: University of Chicago Press.

Becker, H. 1963. *Outsiders: Studies in the Sociology of Deviance.* London: Macmillan.

Becker, H. et al. 1961. *Boys in White.* Chicago: University of Chicago Press.

Berlin, I. 1980. *Against the Current.* London: Hogarth Press.

Bernstein, R. 1971. *Praxis and Action.* Philadelphia: Duckworth.

Blumer, H. 1928. "The Method of Social Psychology," Doctoral dissertation, University of Chicago.

———. 1938. "Social Psychology," in E. P. Schmidt (ed.), *Man and Society.* New York: Prentice-Hall, pp. 144–98.

———. 1939. "An Appraisal of Thomas and Znaniecki's 'The Polish Peasant in Europe and America,'" *Critiques of Research in the Social Sciences* I. New York: Transaction.

———. 1969. *Symbolic Interactionism: Perspective and Method.* Englewood Cliffs, N.J.: Prentice-Hall.

———. 1983. "Going Astray with a Logical Scheme," *Studies in Symbolic Interaction* 6: 123–38.

Bodenhafer, W. 1920–21. "The Comparative Role of the Group Concept in Ward's 'Dynamic Sociology' and Contemporary American Sociology," *American Journal of Sociology* 26: 273–314, 425–74, 583–600, 716–43.

Bogue, D. J. (ed.). 1974. *The Basic Writings of Ernest W. Burgess.* Chicago: University of Chicago Press.

Bressler, M. 1952. "Selected Family Patterns in W. I. Thomas's Unfinished Study of the 'Bintl Brief,'" *American Sociological Review* 17: 563–71.

Bucher, R. and Stelling, J. 1969. "Characteristics of Professional Organizations," *Journal of Health and Social Behavior* 10: 3–15.

Bulmer, M. 1984. *The Chicago School of Sociology: Institutionalization, Diversity, and the Rise of Sociology.* Chicago: University of Chicago Press.

Cahnman, W. J. 1978. "Robert E. Park at Fisk," *Journal of the History of the Behavioral Sciences* 14: 328–36.

Carey, J. T. 1975. *Sociology and Public Affairs: The Chicago School.* London: Sage.

Castoriadis, C. 1987. *The Imaginary Institution of Society.* Cambridge, Eng.: Polity Press.

Coser, L. 1977. *Masters of Sociological Thought.* New York: Harcourt, Brace, Jovanovich.

Deegan, M. J. and Burger, J. S. 1981. "W. I. Thomas and Social Reform: His Work and Writings," *Journal of the History of the Behavioral Sciences* 17: 114–25.

Denzin, N. 1977a. *Childhood Socialization: Studies in the Development of Language, Social Behavior, and Identity.* San Francisco: Jossey-Bass.

———. 1977b. "Notes on the Criminogenic Hypothesis: A Case Study of the American Liquor Industry," *American Sociological Review* 42: 905–20.

Dewey, J. 1927. *The Public and Its Problems.* New York: Henry Holt.

———. 1931. "The Development of American Pragmatism," in *John Dewey, Philosophy and Civilization.* New York: Minton, Balch, pp. 13–35.

———. 1934. *Art as Experience.* New York: Minton, Balch.

———. 1972. "The Reflex Arc Concept in Psychology," in *The Early Works,* vol. 5. Carbondale, Ill.: Southern Illinois University Press, pp. 96–109. First published 1896.

Diner, S. J. 1975. "Department and Discipline: The Department of Sociology at the University of Chicago 1892–1920," *Minerva* 13: 514–53.

Durkheim, E. 1955. *Pragmatisme et Sociologie.* Paris: Alcan.

Farberman, H. 1975. "A Criminogenic Market Structure: The Automobile Industry," *Sociological Quarterly* 16: 438–57.

———. 1979. "The Chicago School: Continuities in Urban Sociology," *Studies in Symbolic Interaction* 2: 3–20.

Faris, E. 1937. *The Nature of Human Nature.* Chicago: University of Chicago Press.

Faris, R. E. L. 1967. *Chicago Sociology 1920–32.* Chicago: University of Chicago Press.

Faught, J. 1980. "Presuppositions of the Chicago School in the Work of Everett Hughes," *The American Sociologist* 15: 72–82.

Fine, G. A. 1984. "Negotiated Orders and Organization Cultures," *Annual Review of Sociology* 10: 239–62.

Fine, G. A. and Kleinman, S. 1983. "Network and Meaning: An Interactionist Approach to Structure," *Studies in Symbolic Interaction* 6: 97–110.

Fisher, B. and Strauss, A. 1978. "Interactionism," in T. Bottomore and R. Nisbet (eds.), *A History of Sociological Analysis.* New York: Oxford University Press.

Freidson, E. 1970. *Profession of Medicine: A Study of the Sociology of Applied Knowledge.* New York: Harper and Row.

———. 1975–76. "The Division of Labor as Social Interaction," *Social Problems* 23: 304–13.

Giddens, A. 1984. *The Constitution of Society.* Cambridge, Engl.: Polity Press.

Glaser, B. and Strauss, A. 1967. *The Discovery of Grounded Theory: Strategies for Qualitative Research.* New York: Sociology Press.

Habermas, J. 1981. *Theorie des kommunikativen Handelns,* 2 vols., Frankfurt-on-Main. English translation, *Theory of Communicative Action.* Cambridge, Engl.: Polity Press, 1984.

Hall, P. M. 1972. "A Symbolic Interactionist Analysis of Politics," *Sociological Inquiry* 42: 35–75.

Hinkle, R. C. 1963. "Antecedents of the Action Orientation in American Sociology before 1935," *American Sociological Review* 28: 705–15.

———. 1980. *Founding Theory of American Sociology 1881–1915.* Boston: Methuen.

Honneth, A. and Joas, H. 1988. *Social Action and Human Nature.* Cambridge, Engl.: Cambridge University Press.

Hughes, E. 1971. *The Sociological Eye: Selected Papers of Everett Hughes.* Chicago: University of Chicago Press.

Jandy, E. C. 1942. *Charles H. Cooley: His Life and His Social Theory.* New York: Hippocrene Books.

Janowitz, M. (ed) 1966. *W. I. Thomas on Social Organization and Social Personality.* Chicago: University of Chicago Press.

———. 1975–76. "Sociological Theory and Social Control," *American Journal of Sociology* 81: 82–108.

Joas, H. 1983. "The Intersubjective Constitution of the Body Image," *Human Studies* 6: 197–204.

———. 1985a. *G. H. Mead: A Contemporary Re-examination of His Thought.* Cambridge, Engl.: Polity Press.

———. 1985b. "Durkheim and Pragmatism" (in this volume).

———. 1986a. "The Unhappy Marriage of Hermeneutics and Functionalism" (reprinted in this volume).

———. 1986b. "Giddens' Theory of Structuration," (reprinted in this volume).

Johnson, G. and Picou, J. S. 1985. "The Foundations of Symbolic Interactionism Reconsidered," in H. J. Helle and S. N. Eisenstadt (eds.), *Microsociological Theory: Perspectives on Sociological Theory,* vol. 2. London: Sage, pp. 54–70.

Kuklick, H. 1973. "A 'Scientific Revolution': Sociological Theory in the United States 1930–45," *Sociological Inquiry* 43: 3–22.

Kurtz, L. R. 1984. *Evaluating Chicago Sociology.* Chicago: University of Chicago Press.

Lauer, R. and Handel, W. 1977. *Social Psychology: The Theory and Application of Symbolic Interactionism.* Boston: Houghton-Mifflin.

Lengermann, P. 1979. "The Founding of the *American Sociological Review:* The Anatomy of a Rebellion," *American Sociological Review* 44: 185–98.

Levine, D. N. et al. 1975–76. "Simmel's Influence on American Sociology," *American Journal of Sociology* 81: 813–45, 1112–32.

Lewis, J. D. and Smith, R. L. 1980. *American Sociology and Pragmatism: Mead, Chicago Sociology, and Symbolic Interaction.* Chicago: University of Chicago Press.

Madge, J. 1962. *The Origins of Scientific Sociology.* New York: Free Press.

Maines, D. 1977. "Social Organization and Social Structure in Symbolic Interactionist Thought," *Annual Review of Sociology* 3: 235–59.

Maines, D. and Charlton, J. 1985. "The Negotiated Order Approach to the Analysis of the Social Organization," *Studies in Symbolic Interaction,* supplement 1, *Foundations of Interpretative Sociology,* edited by H. Farberman and R. Perinbanayagam, pp. 271–308.

Matthews, F. H. 1977. *Quest for an American Sociology: Robert E. Park and the Chicago School.* Montreal: McGill-Queens University Press.

McPhail, C. and Rexroat, C. 1979. "Mead vs. Blumer: The Divergent Methodological Perspectives of Social Behaviorism and Symbolic Interactionism," *American Sociological Review* 44: 449–67.

Mead, G. H. 1903. "The Definition of the Psychical," *Decennial Publications of the University of Chicago,* first series, vol. 3. Chicago: University of Chicago Press, pp. 77–112.

———. 1930. "Cooley's Contribution to American Social Thought," *American Journal of Sociology* 35: 693–706.

———. 1934. *Mind, Self, and Society,* edited by Charles W. Morris. Chicago: University of Chicago Press.

Miller, D. L. 1982. Review, *Journal of the History of Sociology* 4: 108–14.

Park, R. E. 1936. "Human Ecology," *American Journal of Sociology* 42: 1–15.

———. 1950–55. *Collected Papers,* 3 vols. Glencoe, Ill.: Free Press.

———. 1972. *The Crowd and the Public.* Chicago: University of Chicago Press. First published in 1904 as *Masse und Publikum: Eine methodologische und soziologische Untersuchung.* Bern.

Park, R. E. and Burgess, E. W. 1921. *Introduction to the Science of Sociology.* Chicago: University of Chicago Press.

Park, R. E. and Miller, H. A. 1921. *Old World Traits Transplanted.* New York.

Parsons, T. 1968a. *The Structure of Social Action,* 2 vols. New York: Free Press. First published 1937.

———. 1968b: "Cooley and the Problem of Internalization," in Albert J. Reiss (ed.), *Cooley and Sociological Analysis.* Ann Arbor: University of Michigan Press, pp. 48–67.

Peirce, C. S. 1934. "Some Consequences of Four Incapacities," in C. Hartshorne and P. Weiss (eds.), *Collected Papers,* vol. 5. Cambridge, Mass.: Harvard University Press.

Perinbanayagam, R. S. 1985. *Signifying Acts: Structure and Meaning in Everyday Life.* Carbondale, Ill.: S. Illinois University Press.

Rochberg-Halton, E. 1982. "Situation, Structure and the Context of Meaning," *Sociological Quarterly,* 23: 455–76.

———. 1983. "The Real Nature of Pragmatism and Chicago Sociology," *Studies in Symbolic Interaction* 6: 139–54.

Rock, P. 1979. *The Making of Symbolic Interactionism.* London: Rowman.

Rorty, R. 1982. *Consequences of Pragmatism: Essays 1972–1980.* Minneapolis: University of Minneapolis Press.

Rucker, D. 1969. *The Chicago Pragmatists.* Minneapolis: University of Minneapolis Press.

Shaw, C. 1930. *A Delinquent Boy's Own Story.* Chicago: University of Chicago Press.

Shibutani, T. 1961. *Society and Personality: An Interactionist Approach to Social Psychology.* Englewood Cliffs, N.J. Prentice-Hall.

Shils, E. 1970. "Tradition, Ecology, and Institution in the History of Sociology," *Daedalus* 99: 760–825.
Simpson, J. H. 1972. "Continuities in the Sociology of Everett Hughes." *Sociological Quarterly* 13: 547–59.
Stone, G. and Farberman, H. 1967. "On the Edge of Rapprochement: Was Durkheim Moving Towards the Perspective of Symbolic Interaction?," *Sociological Quarterly* 8: 149–64.
———. 1970 (eds.). *Social Psychology through Symbolic Interaction.* Waltham, Mass.: Ginn-Blaisdell.
Strauss, A. 1959. *Mirrors and Masks: The Search for Identity.* Glencoe, Ill.: Sociology Press.
———. 1979. *Negotiations.* San Francisco: Jossey-Bass.
Strauss, A. et al. 1963. "The Hospital and Its Negotiated Order," in E. Freidson (ed.), *The Hospital in Modern Society.* New York: Free Press of Glencoe, pp. 147–69.
Stryker, S. 1980. *Symbolic Interactionism: A Social Structural Vision.* Menlo Park, Calif.: Benjamin Cummings.
Sutherland, D. E. 1978. "Who Now Reads European Sociology? Reflections on the Relationship between European and American Sociology," *Journal of the History of Sociology* 1: 35–66.
Taylor, C. 1975. *Hegel.* Cambridge, Engl.: Cambridge University Press.
Tenbruck, F. H. 1985. "G. H. Mead und die Ursprünge der Soziologie in Deutschland und Amerika: Ein Kapital über die Gültigkeit und Vergleichbarkeit soziologischer Theorien," in H. Joas (ed.), *Das Problem der Intersubjektivität: Neuere Beiträge zum Werk G. H. Meads.* Frankfurt-on-Main, pp. 179–243.
Thomas, W. I. (ed.), 1909. *Source Book for Social Origins.* Boston: Badger.
———. 1923. *The Unadjusted Girl.* Boston: Little-Brown.
Thomas, W. I. and Znaniecki, F. 1926. *The Polish Peasant in Europe and America,* 2 vols. New York: Knopf.
Thrasher, F. 1927. *The Gang.* Chicago: University of Chicago Press.
Turner, R. 1967. "Introduction," in R. Park, *On Social Control and Collective Behavior.* Chicago: University of Chicago Press, pp. ix–xlvi.
———. 1970. *Family Interaction.* New York.
Vidich, A. J. and Lyman, S. M. 1985. *American Sociology: Worldly Rejections of Religion and Their Directions.* New Haven, Conn.: Yale University Press.
White, M. 1957. *Social Thought in America: The Revolt Against Formalism.* Boston: Oxford.
Wiebe, R. H. 1967. *The Search for Order 1877–1920.* New York: Greenwood.
Wilson, R. 1968. *In Quest of Community: Social Philosophy in the United States 1860–1920.* New York: Knopf.
Wilson, T. P. 1970. "Concepts of Interaction and Forms of Sociological Explanation," *American Sociological Review* 35: 697–710.
Wirth, L. 1938. "Urbanism as a Way of Life," *American Journal of Sociology* 44: 1–24.
———. 1964. *On Cities and Social Life: Selected Papers of Louis Wirth.* Chicago: University of Chicago Press.
———. 1969. *The Ghetto.* Chicago: University of Chicago Press. First published 1928.
Zaretsky, E. 1984. "Introduction" in W. I. Thomas and F. Znaniecki, *The Polish Peasant in Europe and America,* abridged ed. Urbana, Ill.: University of Illinois Press, pp. 1–53.

Pragmatism and Classical European Social Theory

2 Durkheim and Pragmatism: The Psychology of Consciousness and the Social Constitution of Categories

In the winter of 1913–14—after the publication of his last major work, *The Elementary Forms of the Religious Life,* and only a few years before his death—Emile Durkheim held lectures on "Pragmatism and Sociology." None of these lectures was published during his lifetime; indeed they did not appear until 1955, many decades after his death. They have been all but disregarded in the different strands which the reception of Durkheim's work has taken over the years. This is hardly surprising, considering that at the time these lectures were published pragmatism either was not highly regarded or was simply ignored, both in philosophy and in, particularly, sociology. This was true even on pragmatism's home territory, namely in the United States, and despite the constitutive role it had played during the hegemony of the Chicago School in sociology. Pragmatism fared no better in Europe, where its reception was burdened from the very beginning by a shortsighted identification of its underlying theses with those of the philosophies of life projected by Nietzsche and Bergson. For all the undeniable affinities between these discrete currents of thought, pragmatism was unhappily received because it accentuated aspects to which well-rehearsed critical arguments about the philosophy of life could easily be applied. This perhaps explains why so much more attention was devoted to the work of William James than to that of Charles Peirce, why familiarity with John Dewey's work was limited to his writings on education, and why George Herbert Mead was known only for his sociologically oriented social psychology.[1] Durkheim's relationship to pragmatism, then, was of little interest. The lectures must have given the impression that Durkheim was coming to terms with long outdated and largely forgotten philosophers who, although briefly relevant in their day[2] no longer merited any attention. Indeed, the motives for dealing with pragmatism which Durkheim himself listed at the beginning of his observations did not exactly focus on substantial questions. Here he talked of pragmatism as an armed struggle *against reason* which had to be resisted on three grounds. Firstly, and generally, pragmatism was dangerous because, more than any other doctrine, it was able to

Originally published in French, in *Revue française de sociologie* 25, 1984, pp. 560–81.

seek out the vulnerable points of rationalism, as it is commonly understood, and to make use of them for its own ends. Secondly, it was in the national interest to counteract an erosion of French culture, of which Cartesian thought was an essential component. And finally—an argument based on a philosophical interest in perpetuating the tradition that had persisted virtually throughout the history of philosophy—pragmatism threatened the belief that true knowledge is possible. As Durkheim saw it, pragmatism was a form of irrationalism and resembled ancient Greek sophistry. Its only benefit might consist in bringing salutary pressure to bear on philosophical thought and rouse it from the "dogmatic slumber" into which it had relapsed after Kant. Thus, Durkheim made it clear from the very beginning that his analysis was not intended as a discussion which weighed one approach against another, but rather as a "political" act in defense of a certain theory. It would therefore seem obvious that one should look for the deeper strategic motives behind Durkheim's stated objectives. Such an approach allows one to interpret the lectures on pragmatism globally as a hidden polemic against his rival, Georges Sorel, and as an act of resistance against the syndrome of decisionism, violence, and the immoralism of decadence.[3] However, the actual substance of Durkheim's line of argumentation is all too easily ignored if this view is taken.

In order to take the substance of his argument seriously and, consequently, raise the question as to the correctness of previous interpretations of the internal logic of Durkheim's work in the light of these late and, for the most part, completely disregarded lectures, we must first start by outlining an independent view of pragmatism that is not already prefigured by Durkheim. The chances of pursuing such a course seem favorable at present, for there are two senses in which one can say that pragmatism is currently undergoing a renaissance. Firstly, there is recognition of the radical degree to which pragmatism calls into question the Cartesian framework of modern philosophy, precisely without becoming irrationalistic in the process. Pragmatism not only challenges the role of philosophy as a fundamentalist discipline that consists primarily of epistemology, but also the dualist conception of mind as opposed to body, a mind which is itself an object of knowledge. Secondly, it becomes clear that pragmatism, in offering a constructive avenue of escape from the destruction of this Cartesian framework, develops a general theory of signs which nevertheless bears hardly any resemblance to the semiotic theory of French structuralism.[4] Now, if it is true that the pragmatist critique forces us to make far-reaching changes to our concept of mind or of consciousness, and if the theory of signs and of meaning generated by pragmatism provides the basis for its own specific conception of the social domain, then a critical discussion of these ideas on the part of a classical sociologist does indeed deserve our interest. The confrontation with pragmatism forces Durkheim to articulate himself at a level which is even more fundamental than that at which he proposes to overcome utilitarianism;[5] the conception of the symbolic developed in the sociology of religion is then not only reflected in the ideas of structuralism, but also in those of the sociological tradition which hinge on a concept of symbolically mediated interaction. Furthermore, these lectures on pragmatism may hold the key to answering the question of how Durkheim's ideas regarding the social constitution of categories—as expressed in the sociology of religion and in the essay, coauthored with Marcel Mauss, on primitive classification systems—show up against the background of a conception which shares Durkheim's underlying impulse, but leads to completely different solutions.

At first sight there appears to be a fundamental similarity between pragmatism and Durkheim's sociology. Durkheim's characterization of this common element is somewhat vague; as he puts it, they share an intimation of life and action, and they are both products of the same era. What Durkheim presumably has in mind is the tendency of both to seek a new and scientific approach to the key questions of philosophy—namely, to specify what can be known as true and what is morally good[6]—by treating them in a manner which is saturated in empirical evidence and which draws on historically and culturally variable forms of morality and worldviews. In more precise terms, this means that thc two join forces in opposition to epistemological empiricism and apriorism by invoking Kant's turn to the a priori conditions for the possibility of experience. At the same time, they attempt to take the deduction of such conditions beyond the domain of transcendental philosophy by inquiring how the individual intellect has to be equipped in order for any form of cognition to take place. This in turn transforms, however, the question of the constitutive conditions of cognition itself into the empirical question of how these conditions arise in the individual mind. Thus the problem of constitution remains, even though its transcendental-philosophical form and the guarantee of universal validity derived from this are both abandoned. One may deny the strictly Kantian charge that this amounts to throwing the basic Kantian heritage overboard. Yet, one is nevertheless bound to concede that the empirical recasting of the question as to what constitutes the conditions for cognition—be it via a natural history of human perception, a cultural history of culture-specific classification systems, or a developmental psychology of individual worldviews—

itself gives rise to the problem of finding new justifications for the universality of knowledge. This is a problem which arises for pragmatism just as it does for Durkheim's sociology. Against this background, how can the various individuals or the various cultures still come to an agreement and arrive at a truth that is valid for all? How can this truth still apply to the world? It can initially be assumed from the lectures on pragmatism that it was Durkheim's intention to arrive at such a foundation of truth. This is clearly at odds with the frequently articulated criticism leveled at Durkheim's theory of the social constitution of categories[7] for being epistemologically relativistic. Judging from the harshness of Durkheim's polemic against the dangers of relativism in pragmatism, it can be concluded that the criticisms raised against Durkheim in this regard apply only to the actual state of the solutions he developed, not to his underlying intentions.

Durkheim himself admits that the concept of truth used in pragmatism successfully criticizes a simple theory of reproduction or correspondence, and that the pragmatists were right to emphasize that truth is a product and therefore something malleable. In fact, the substance of Durkheim's program for a sociology which, rather than excluding questions that were traditionally treated philosophically, is instead characterized by an empirical approach to them shows an even greater affinity with the philosophy of pragmatism than Durkheim's own interpretation would have it appear. This becomes clear if one takes into account the manner in which Durkheim treats the representatives of pragmatism. In the preliminary remarks to his actual presentation Durkheim marks off the pragmatism which had then become topical from those forms promulgated by Nietzsche on the one hand and Peirce on the other. He correctly emphasizes that when Nietzsche talks of fictions that are necessary for life (or indeed survival) these are merely one aspect of a way of conceiving of the world. The other side of the same coin involves an adherence to a traditionally contemplative notion of truth (though it is only accessible from an elitist standpoint removed from the pressures of life). Durkheim excludes Peirce from his criticisms on the grounds that the latter, unlike James, retains the essential characteristics of the classical concept of truth. Thus, James, Dewey, and Schiller become the focus of Durkheim's critique. Yet in some respects even these writers display greater similarities to Durkheim than might be expected from his attitude toward them. It is surely unfair simply to dismiss William James as a utilitarian. Rather, his insistence on the link that exists between (religious) truth and the single individual deserves an interpretation in which he appears as a precursor of assumptions held by existential philosophy. Truth needs to be linked to the actor's problems in life in the sense of the existential questions they raise; it must not stand juxtaposed to them as mere insight into cold facticity. Durkheim's treatment of Dewey is even more strange. Although he mentions that Dewey distances himself from James, he trivializes the difference between the two thinkers. What is most striking, however,[8] is that Durkheim does not go into Dewey's manifold pedagogical and ethical writings at all and erroneously asserts that there is no connection between Dewey's ethical theory and his position regarding the concept of truth.

It is not possible here to clarify with philological tools whether such simple distortions in Durkheim's rendition of the pragmatists' ideas are attributable to a lack of knowledge or whether they are intentional. What emerges clearly however is Durkheim's rhetorical strategy of not accentuating the similarities but rather the differences between pragmatism and his own program of sociology. This should not cause us to overlook the features they have in common. But what exactly does Durkheim regard as the crucial difference? He draws the dividing line by means of differentiating between the individual and the social. Pragmatism, he claims, can only ground truth in the utilitarian considerations of individuals and therefore has to derive truth from the function it has in psychological gratification. As a consequence of this approach, pragmatism is then said to be unable to grasp precisely those decisive characteristics of truth which have been identified by the classical tradition. Truth, Durkheim says, is characterized by its compelling nature, by the power of its pure self-evidence to oblige us to accept it without the use of force. However, this is not to be understood on an individual basis, but only with regard to the collective. Pragmatism is therefore a *logical* form of utilitarianism and, he continues, merits the same criticisms that were raised against moral utilitarianism. Durkheim is thus able to establish a link to one of the key lines of argumentation in his program for a sociology.

This brings us to the heart of the problem. If "logical utilitarianism" is an accurate definition of pragmatism, then a critique of it does not conflict with the critique of utilitarianism on which the whole discipline of sociology is based. However, if pragmatism itself is to be understood as a critique of utilitarianism, albeit *not as a critique at the level of the conception of social order* but rather as a critique of the Cartesian assumptions which also underlie utilitarianism, then Durkheim's strategy of argumentation must run into difficulties. The thesis I wish to put forward is that pragmatism is above all a reflection on the fact that the subject is embedded in praxis and sociality prior to any form of conscious intentionality of action. In this reading, pragmatism thus undermines the conception of the individual who calculates in terms of utility at the *level of a theory of action.*[9] Because Durkheim does not see this and cannot see it for deep-seated systematic reasons,[10] he mixes up the lines of attack. It is not the shared opposition to utilitarianism, but rather the independence of consciousness from action which becomes his decisive battleground. He has to defend this, however, without contradicting his social theory of the constitution of categories. It is therefore not possible to answer the question whether Durkheim redeems his promise to reconstruct, rather than simply to defend, the "rationalism" of his tradition under the pressure of pragmatism. Nor is it possible to arrive at an adequate assessment of Durkheim's confrontation with pragmatism, if one simply takes it as read and merely inquires whether or not Durkheim provides an accurate analysis of pragmatism and whether his arguments apply to it. Rather, it is first necessary to make (1) pragmatism and (2) Durkheim's social theory of constitution respectively understandable as parallel projects. Then (3) the difficulties inherent in Durkheim's own program and (4) Durkheim's critique of pragmatism can be weighed up against each other. Finally, we shall investigate whether a consideration of the criticisms of the two programs can allow us to derive (5) a perspective which will permit the difficulties on both sides to be overcome.

1. Pragmatism is not a unified school grouped around a clearly identifiable key author. Its major representatives focused their attention on different subjects: Peirce concentrated on the logic of empirical-experimental research; James was interested in existential and religious questions which precisely cannot be solved scientifically; and Dewey and Mead both had an orientation toward politics and the social sciences. However, although these various domains of philosophical reflection contain differing definitions of the precise meaning of pragmatism, the connection between these thinkers is close enough to discern a uniform approach at a fairly general level.

Pragmatism begins by doubting the meaningfulness of Cartesian doubt.

> We cannot begin with complete doubt. We must begin with all the prejudices which we actually have when we enter upon the study of philosophy. These prejudices are not to be dispelled by a maxim, for they are things which it does not occur to us can be questioned. Hence this initial skepticism will be a mere self-deception, and not real doubt; and no one who follows the Cartesian method will ever be satisfied until he has formally recovered all those beliefs which in form he has given up. . . . A person may,

> it is true, in the course of his studies, find reason to doubt what he began by believing; but in that case he doubts because he has a positive reason for it, and not on account of the Cartesian maxim.[11]

It is precisely not the motive of pragmatism here to render thought uncritical, but rather to anchor it in such doubts as are motivated by reality. This means that not only science and philosophy but also everyday thought as a whole is related to the solution of actual problems in concrete life praxis. Doubt becomes necessary only when well-established certainties no longer stand the test of reality or when subjects raise objections to the certainties of other subjects. The purpose of this doubt is to bring about new certainties through creative problem solving. What these thinkers oppose is the "Cartesian" model of cognition oriented to the perception of objects and divorced from action, from communication between subjects and from the everyday, undoubted certainties. This radical shift in the way the problem is addressed is, furthermore, intended to permit a circumvention of the dualisms between perceiving and comprehending, facts and values, body and mind, individual and society which arise from the Cartesian approach. It is not possible here to elaborate on the details of how this is attempted and how successful these attempts are.[12] Nevertheless, mention must still be made of the path on which pragmatism advances to a theory of the sign. Pragmatism proposes that we are incapable of thinking without signs. The principle "is, that, whenever we think, we have present to the consciousness some feeling, image, conception, or other representation, which serves as a sign. . . . When we think, then, we ourselves, as we are at that moment, appear as a sign."[13] Armed with the idea of the sign-mediated quality of all knowledge, pragmatism sets out to repudiate all intuitionistic conceptions. Moreover, the particular nature of its theory of signs facilitates the transition from recognizing knowledge as sign-mediated to viewing it as socially determined. The sign is not conceived of as a bipartite relationship between an arbitrarily chosen vehicle of meaning and a conceptual content, but rather as a tripartite relationship between the qualitative specificity of the sign vehicle, the intended object, and an interpreting consciousness. This consideration of the qualitative specificity of the sign and the reference to intended objects marks a rejection of pure conventionalism in sign theory. Via the link with the interpreting consciousness, the sign becomes the vehicle of an intention which a subject wants to transmit to another subject or to itself. It is worthy of mention at this point that pragmatism is thus a theory of the constitution of knowledge in practical problem situations and that, at least in the form of its theory of signs, it also links the constitution of knowledge to sociality and to the conditions required for a consensus of the cognizant subjects.

2. The parallels between this and Durkheim's project become apparent if we take Durkheim's contributions to a "sociologie de la connaissance"—a sociology of cognition—as the point of comparison. This is not a sociology of knowledge which is interested in macrosocial complexes of interest groups and ideologies, but rather a theory of the social constitution of fundamental categories of cognition. It was not marginal to Durkheim's work but, certainly by the time of his reorientation toward a theory of religion, had come to stand alongside his theory of morality as an ongoing project. It is well known that the most important evidence of this is the essay written together with Marcel Mauss on "primitive classification systems," not to mention *The Elementary Forms of the Religious Life* itself, which was originally planned to be entitled "Les formes élémentaires de la pensée et de la pratique religieuse."[14] Here too, Durkheim attempts, by studying evidence from primitive cultures, to treat a problem empirically which, in the more complex form of modern culture, it is extremely difficult to address with such means. He sets out to demonstrate that not only the contents of knowledge but even the forms of cognition are socially constituted. The categories of space and time, power and causality, the person and the species, he claims, are all derived from social circumstances and are the model for perceiving and knowing the world as a whole. As he says elsewhere, "The space of the world was designed in a primitive manner after the model of the social space, i.e. according to the territory occupied by society and how society conceives of this; time expresses the rhythm of collective living; the idea of the species was initially only a different aspect of the idea of the human group; collective power and its effect on consciousness served as prototypes for power and causality, etc."[15] The essay on classification elaborates on the asserted isomorphism of social organization and logical structure by referring to examples taken from ethnological findings about Australian aborigines and Sioux as well as Zuñi Indians, as well as to Chinese thought. Durkheim, not content with the thesis of a structural isomorphism, proceeds to give it an unequivocally causal interpretation: "Now the classification of things reproduces this classification of men."[16] He admits that the classification systems, once they have emerged, exhibit a certain autonomy and a dynamic of their own, as well as the ability retroactively to affect and influence the cause that gave rise to them. However, it is social organization which Durkheim declares to be the cause of their origin as such.[17] This theory of

the *reproduction of social morphology in cultural systems of classification* is given a more refined form in his fully fledged sociology of religion. Here, the social morphology itself is seen to originate as religious group experience in collective ritual praxis. The decisive line of thought in Durkheim's sociology of religion with regard to the problems of a social theory of the constitution of categories is that the powers of the collective and its effects on the individual as experienced in "collective effervescence" can only be interpreted by the participating subjects as powers which are at work behind the observable things themselves and which prevail throughout the cosmos. In the religious group experience the reciprocal effect of the individual psyches is so intense that collective notions are established and these then exert their structuring power on the various perceptions in the individuals' everyday lives.

In other words, whereas pragmatism believed that the constitution of knowledge resided in practical problem situations, Durkheim clearly separates these off from religious experience. He draws a sharp distinction between, on the one hand, every form of knowledge aimed at facilitating action and, on the other, the wish to understand characteristic of religious cosmologies. This demarcation corresponds to the divide he sees between magic and religion, and between technology and science. In his theory of religion, however, he posits the collective *praxis* of ritual as the origin of categories. To summarize, pragmatism is a theory which, although geared primarily to the solution of problem situations involved in instrumental action, ultimately points to the dimension of sociality via the theory of signs. Durkheim's sociology entails a similar sequence, but here the progression is inverted: the orientation is toward the social dimension of a constitution of categories based on the model of social organization, yet which arrives at the practical constitution of categories in the form of ritual praxis.

3. Over the years, an exceptionally large number of objections have been put forward in criticism of Durkheim's conception. Many of them, however, are based on such a general level of doubt about the program of a "sociologie de la connaissance" that they have nothing to offer with regard to the difficulties inherent in Durkheim's program. Firstly, this is true of those criticisms which regard Durkheim's approach as nothing more than a simplistic circular argument. Durkheim's approach is deemed circular in one of two ways: either because as a sociologist he attempts to derive categories of knowledge with which he has always worked anyway,[18] or because he pinpoints social organization as the origin of classification systems which must always already have been used to classify social organization itself.[19] In the first objection the self-

reflexive or reconstructive process of forms of cognition which attempt to assure themselves explicitly of their own implicit assumptions is mistaken for circular logic. In the second case, a lack of clarity in the essay on primitive classification systems is rightly identified, but this was later overcome by the solution posited in the theory of religion, namely, the origin of collective consciousness in the collective "effervescence" of the ritual. Precisely this new solution is the target of criticism forthcoming from the camp of structural anthropology. Claude Lévi-Strauss regards Durkheim's theory of religion as nothing more than an "affective theory of the sacred." Lévi-Strauss views Durkheim's notion of ritual—which is not construed as an expression of previously conceived ideas but rather as a means of generating these ideas in the first place—as an unclear blend of the two poles of the Cartesian alternative: "In truth, the impulses and emotions do not explain anything; they are always a *result:* either of the power of the body or of the impotence of the mind. In both cases, they are effects but never causes. The causes can only be found in the organism, as only biology is capable of doing, or in the intellect, and this is the only path open to psychology and ethnology."[20] By emphasizing that it is not the emotions which produce rites, but ritual activities which engender emotions, he is out-trumping Durkheim with a distinction between the cognitive and the affective which the latter had avoided making precisely because he wanted to demonstrate that both were formed on the common basis of a special mode of social relationship.

A further criticism also remains on an entirely superficial level and fails to address the substance of the questions dealt with in Durkheim's theory. I am referring to the argument of how socially constituted categories could possibly be capable of grasping reality. Durkheim himself anticipated this criticism and asked how it is possible for socially constituted categories to be applied to nature in more than a merely metaphorical sense. His answer, however, is of only rhetorical value. He points to the fact that society is, after all, a part of nature and that, as a result, an isomorphism of forms is in a certain sense ontologically guaranteed.[21] Now this is completely unsatisfactory, both in view of the emergent properties of society which are emphasized to such a great degree in Durkheim's theory and also in view of the differences between the images of the world in various cultures.[22] On the other hand, it does not follow from the fact that Durkheim did not provide an adequate reply that his position has been proved false. For, if theoretical analysis of the world is *under*determined by empirical experiences, then standing the test of a comparison with reality is a necessary but not the decisive condition for a theory. The socially constituted classification systems would then come into contact with reality and would have to prove themselves in this testing ground; but there would be a broad spectrum of such proven conceptions, thus providing scope for the specific formation of classification systems.

The approach taken by empirical criticisms of Durkheim's program is completely different from that of these abstract, theoretical objections. They too, however, are only able to undermine the plausibility of Durkheim's theses from the outside. From the standpoint of cultural anthropology, for example, it is claimed that the social forms and classification systems can by no means be correlated as closely as Durkheim assumed. Rodney Needham emphasizes that different forms of classification can be found among similar social structures, and similar forms among very different types of societies, and that in some cultures several symbolic classification systems even coexist with one another.[23] The criticisms forthcoming from the standpoint of developmental psychology and socialization theory lie on a similar level. They argue that the presumed elementary classifications made by the individual, which Durkheim claims are made independently of collective notions, did not in fact develop without first being embedded in a social context: one need only think of the ability to distinguish between left and right, past and present, etc. Although such arguments cannot in themselves undermine Durkheim's systematic intention, they nevertheless have to be taken seriously if it is still to bear any weight.

It would seem to me that only two lines of argumentation strike at the core of Durkheim's program. One of them emphasizes the utilitarian compulsions of everyday life,[24] as opposed to Durkheim's concentration on the religious origin of classification. This tack can be taken by accentuating the necessities of social consensus in everyday material reproduction and by emphasizing the existence of shared experience in addition to the experience of the community itself. Another way in which this criticism has been raised is by referring to the question of how change in classification systems is dependent on experience, thereby highlighting the question of collective learning or cognitive creativity.[25] Durkheim himself naturally has an important reply in hand to meet these criticisms. In a footnote in the essay on classification, he already makes explicit reference to the existence of technological classifications: "It is probable that man has always classified, more or less clearly, the things on which he lived, according to the means he used to get them: for example, animals living in the water, or in the air or on the ground."[26] These classifications, he continues, were, however, not systematized in relation to one another. "But at first such groups were not connected with each other or systematized. They were divisions, distinctions of ideas, not schemes of classification."[27] Durkheim relates these to everyday practice and not to the comprehensive interpretative claims of religion or science. If this is taken seriously, then an essential idiosyncrasy of Durkheim's program becomes apparent, for understood in this way, the thesis of social constitution would be directed both against the constitution of categories in everyday *practice* and at the same time against their constitution in the practice of *everyday life.* We shall return to this point later.

Yet another question can be put to Durkheim which is aimed at a fundamental ambiguity in his discussion of social constitution.[28] The question is whether the theory of social constitution presupposes an originally clear-cut separation of the social from the nonsocial, or whether it conversely assumes that precisely these two domains were not separated originally. If the model contains the idea that an act of cognition is initially oriented exclusively toward the social and is then projected from this domain onto that of the nonsocial, then at first sight it would clearly seem logical to assume that the two were originally separated. On the other hand, it would surely be fruitless to attempt to provide empirical evidence to support this assumption. On the contrary: numerous examples[29] could be cited to show that in many primitive cultures this very distinction differed considerably from present-day notions, to the extent that it included both more and yet at the same time less. On the one hand, certain human beings were not accorded the status of subjects because they were aliens, impure, etc., while on the other, the dead, individual animals and plants were as a matter of course included in this domain. Even Durkheim must surely have thought along these lines, even though his formulations waver on this point. However, if we assume that the social and the nonsocial were originally indistinct from one another, then it becomes meaningless to speak in terms of a classification of the social which is merely transposed onto the nonsocial. This is particularly true of the theory of projection in the essay on classification, but it also applies to the theory of ritual in the sociology of religion, for then the participants in ritual can only be marked out as human beings and animate or inanimate objects from the standpoint of the scientific observer. However, if a social theory of constitution has to distinguish the boundaries of the social world at the level of the culture studied from those of its own social world, then it follows that at the very least the origin of the distinction between social and nonsocial can only be addressed by a theory which takes the entire domain of social life as embedded in nature as its point of departure.

Let us summarize what these considerations mean for a preliminary assessment of Durkheim's program. It initially appeared as if the presentation of the crucial differences between Durkheim's programmatic approaches and those of the pragmatists was primarily a matter of investigating the relationship between a social and a pragmatic theory of constitution. However, the examination of the difficulties inherent in Durkheim's program has meanwhile uncovered a new dimension, namely that of the relationship between the extra-ordinary sociality of ritual and the everyday sociality of social life. This may point the way toward a coherent assessment. However, it is first necessary to examine how the pragmatist program appears from Durkheim's point of view.

4. Durkheim's essay on "Représentations individuelles et représentations collectives," written in 1898, already evidences the preliminary elements of a debate with pragmatism, although these are reduced to a few points and are mainly implied rather than explicit. This text consists to a large extent of a polemic against William James's psychological theory of memory, and Durkheim's attack is directed primarily against reductionist theories which declare consciousness to be a mere epiphenomenon of physiological processes. Durkheim has a rigid alternative in mind: "We must choose: either epiphenomenalism is correct or else there is a memory that is a specifically mental phenomenon."[30] Because Durkheim from the outset rules out the existence of a third possibility in addition to physiological reductionism and the traditional notion of consciousness, he is totally unable to describe the specific contribution of James's works and is forced to declare him a covert reductionist. In view of James's self-interpretation, which states precisely the opposite, this is a highly risky strategy.[31] The criticisms which Durkheim levels against James are threefold. He uses all of them to challenge the thesis that consciousness is not a perpetual, constantly possible aspect of the actor, but is by contrast dependent on the momentary situation and is functionally interwoven into the solution of problems of action. He begins with the objection that limiting psychical life to the momentary conditions of lucid consciousness is tantamount to claiming that consciousness disappears without trace outside such phases. He emphasizes the influence of acquired behavioral habits, prejudices, and aspirations, and goes on to attempt to demonstrate the existence of associations of ideas in the style of traditional associative psychology in order thus to defend the notion of an autonomous logic of ideal contexts of meaning that cannot be reduced to physiology. Finally, Durkheim defends a specific concept of the subconscious as a domain of psychical phenomena which are not accessible to our ego. Regardless of the precise

nature of these phenomena, he claims, the existence of them is certainly conclusive evidence of a consciousness which extends beyond the consciousness of the moment.

Now, Durkheim's argumentation is undoubtedly oversimplistic. Although his reference to behavioral habits, thought constructs, and the unconscious is an appropriate line of defense against reductionist approaches, he fails to provide a sound counterargument to the programmatic anti-Cartesian interpretation of the psychical as a functional component of action situations rather than an independent domain of reality beyond the physical. Indeed, behavioral habits became the focus of precisely those psychological considerations that were influenced by pragmatism, inasmuch as the creative solution of the problem of action was seen as leading precisely to the acquisition of a more successful strategy which did not have to be acquired anew on each occasion. In becoming a new routine, however, this strategy does not remain in the bright light of consciousness, but is relegated through practice to the level of quasi-automatic skills. Whereas it may indeed be true that the autonomy of the mental constructs cannot be explained from an analysis of the individual action situations, the central status of sign theory in pragmatism is nevertheless an indication of the degree to which the latter was prepared to deal with this very subject. To do so, however, a more precise clarification of the function of signs was required, and especially that of symbols in the reflexive process of overcoming problems of action.[32] Finally, the reference to the unconscious indicates the presence of problems which were not solved constructively either by Durkheim or by the pragmatists. The distinction that is made in pragmatist lines of reasoning between ego-relatedness and the dependence of consciousness on the moment, however, at least provides a starting point for the incorporation of solutions developed elsewhere.

The lectures which Durkheim devoted to pragmatism a decade and a half later are partly a repetition of the level of criticism contained in his earlier essay, but they also introduce criticisms of a completely different nature. It is not necessary here to describe Durkheim's account of pragmatism, which is maintained up to the twelfth lecture. Suffice it to say that he concentrates on pragmatism's theory of truth, also touching on James's attempt at a metaphysics which instead of being monistic is "pluralist," as well as the latter's relativization of conceptual thought and the psychology of religion. However, what we must examine in detail are the grounds on which Durkheim refutes pragmatism.

The two characterizations supplied by Durkheim—which virtually amount to set formulas—concern the relationship, on the one hand, between body and consciousness, and, on the other, between the individual and the social. For Durkheim, as we know, a strict analogy obtains between these two questions and their solution: there are direct parallels between the proof that consciousness is not reducible to the body and the proof of the emergent properties of the social. With regard to the first question, Durkheim no longer polemically equates pragmatism and epiphenomenalism. The thrust of his criticism is now that pragmatism contains within it the unconscious contradiction of epiphenomenalism and idealism. He claims that despite pragmatism's denial of the existence of consciousness, its theory of truth puts forward an extreme form of constructivism.[33] As for the second question, Durkheim coins the (already mentioned) phrase that pragmatism is "logical utilitarianism": pragmatism holds that to be true which simply appears useful to the individual.[34] His overall assessment of pragmatism is therefore to see it not as a conception which accords action a pivotal position, but as an attack on the possibility of pure theory and logical discipline. "We can therefore conclude that pragmatism is much less of an undertaking to encourage action than an attack on pure speculation and theoretical thought. What is really characteristic of it is an impatience with any rigorous intellectual discipline. It aspires to 'liberate' thought much more than it does action."[35]

In direct opposition to the pragmatists' theory of action and their anchoring of consciousness in action, Durkheim raises the objection that many facts demonstrate an antagonism between thought and action. Thought tends much more often to hinder action than help it: this is true in the case of the pianist, for example, who must precisely not allow himself to focus his thoughts on the act of playing while playing, as this would distance him from it. Likewise but vice versa, action hinders thinking: we have to stop what we are doing and concentrate in order to be able to think clearly. Durkheim concludes from this that the alleged close relationship between thought and action does not exist and that consciousness, far from serving only practical purposes, is actually there precisely to serve requirements other than those of a practical nature.[36] But what, then, are the requirements for which consciousness is functional? Durkheim's answer is unequivocal: it serves self-knowledge, that is the individual's self-reflection, and thus creates a being which is fundamentally distinct from the organisms which are not capable of self-knowledge. "Consciousness is therefore not a function with the role of directing the movements of the body, but the organism knowing itself, and solely by virtue of the fact that the organism knows itself, we can say that something new occurs."[37] This consciousness arising from self-knowledge is, he claims, then capable of regulating its movements autonomously, of interrupting them and reproducing them at will.

Durkheim expressly accepts the emphasis which pragmatism places on the diversity of individual minds. His question, however, is how, in view of this diversity, one can still conceive of the possibility of propositions which are valid independently of individuals. Here he refers to the pragmatist formula of an ideal convergence of individual opinions "in the long run."[38] However, the only grounds he can find for the possibility of such a convergence consist either in the idea that purely individual experience nevertheless leads to those individuals who, disposing over superior experience, are granted authority, with others willingly placing their trust in them, or in the exigencies of collective action in which a uniform common interest wins out over individual considerations of personal benefit. Finding neither explanation convincing, he points out that in the first case only the authority is derived, not any evidence of "truth"; and that in the second case communal opinion wins out over individual truths only if, from the very beginning, it can force individuals to recognize its superior validity owing to its extra-individual origin. Durkheim, who in his theory of morality expanded the Kantian concept of duty to include the attractiveness of the moral norm, in his theory of truth now wants to supplement the pragmatist emphasis on the attractive and seductive character of truth by adding the characteristics of duty, namely its severity and resilience.[39] If the pragmatists' assumptions with regard to convergence were really true, this would necessarily be reflected in an increase in the degree of intersubjective agreement as history progressed. However, we are on the contrary able to detect an increasing degree of divergence: the original uniformity of thought has, according to Durkheim, become gradually ever more differentiated, and has culminated in the present-day claim to the right of individual freedom of thought. The crucial shortcoming of pragmatism is its failure to recognize the need for a self-understanding independent of individual practice. He continues by stating that this speculative need is an essential part of the mythical view of the world. It is also constitutive for modern science—which cannot be derived from purely technical demands, but only from a faith in nonpurposive research—and for all historiography, which has nothing to gain from overestimating the practical benefits of studying history. Durkheim approvingly quotes Fustel de Coulanges's statement that the greatness of historiography lies precisely in the fact that it serves no purpose.[40] Myth and science share the character of being collective systems of ideas. The difference lies in the different status of "représentations collectives" in relation to "représentations individuelles." "One might ask how individual minds can communicate. In two possible ways: either by uniting to form a single collective mind, or by communicating in one object which is the same for all, with each however retaining his own personality; like Leibniz's monads, each expressing the entirety of the universe while keeping its individuality. The first way is that of mythological thought, the second that of scientific thought."[41] Science, being an institutionalized form of search for suprapersonally valid truth, can thus become the model for a type of social order in which individual differences do not pose a threat, but rather of which they form a constituent factor. "Thus intellectual individualism, far from making for anarchy, as would be the case during the period of the domination of mythological truth, becomes a necessary factor in the establishment of scientific truth, so that the diversity of intellectual temperaments can serve the cause of impersonal truth."[42] In Durkheim's view it is therefore not individual arbitrariness which forms the basis and the bounds of individuation in society, but rather the existence of various tasks in a totality which is based on a division of labor.

Looking back from this end of Durkheim's line of reasoning, one might think that he was largely in agreement with pragmatism, if the latter is correctly understood.[43] The differences between the paths taken to reach this conclusion are, however, still so considerable that they must not simply be passed over. For Durkheim, pragmatism is a monism of action which proceeds from action just as one-sidedly as idealism takes thought as its starting point.[44] But even this reply contains the false Cartesian alternative of action as purely physical movement versus thought as a purely mental construct. It was against precisely this model that pragmatism had taken up the struggle, armed with a program which took the structure of action as the point of departure, for this was not guided by but nonetheless was dependent on reflection, and continued its struggle with the aim of gaining more complex models in the form of a gradual evolution of the structure of action. Durkheim's thesis of the antagonism of thought and action therefore only highlights problems which arise in the case of a reductionist theory of behavior ("behaviorism"), but not in that of the pragmatist theory of action. In the face of the feared irrationalist consequences of pragmatism, Durkheim withdraws to a traditionally Cartesian conception of consciousness. In so doing, he is inconsistent in two respects. On the one hand, he accepts the validity of questioning the functionality of consciousness in general, and thus does not construe consciousness as a self-evident fact or an inborn attribute of the human being. However, he does not answer the question by referring to the functionality required for the solution of problems of action, but instead refers to the functionality of consciousness for nonpurposive self-interpretation and self-knowledge. He consequently systematically excludes the possibility that self-reflection itself might result from the solution of a specific kind of problem of action. On the other hand, Durkheim's theory of the origin of "représentations collectives" in ritual is itself a theory of the constitution of categories in a type of social action. Finally, Durkheim truncates pragmatist ideas on the increase in intersubjective consensus, excoriating precisely the element of argumentative agreement. The higher degree of consensus in the mythical worldview is not a valid argument against the pragmatist thesis, since here it was merely a question of factual, not ideal, consensus "in truth." Although Durkheim also ends with science as the model for social order which promotes individuation, he treats it in a fundamentally ambiguous manner. It remains unclear whether the compulsion exerted by truth that is experienced by individuals results exclusively from the superiority of the argument or whether it is rather the social compulsion exerted by a powerful person or an institution.

5. This ambiguity can be taken as an opportunity to summarize the picture of the problematic of Durkheim's position as it emerges from an interpretation of his lectures on pragmatism, as well as the perspective it offers for a theory of the constitution of categories.

Antidualism was one of the leitmotifs of pragmatism; dualism is one of Durkheim's characteristic features. What does this mean? In particular, John Dewey and George Herbert Mead established a connection between the idea of a social order free of compulsion and the individual's power to control his own body free from domination. As they saw it, the Cartesian dualisms contained an element of domination. Their program was, therefore, to exclude this theoretically by demonstrating the function of consciousness in actions, the mediation of knowledge by signs, the function of self-reflexivity in situations of social interaction, and also the possibility of a social order that regulated itself via free communication. On all these levels, Durkheim's dualism led to different results. This has been described in detail with regard to the relationship of consciousness and action. The social is thought of as an addition to that which pertains to the organism—a position he most clearly defended in the late essay "The Dualism of Human Nature and Its Social Conditions."[45] This immediately raises two questions which should be answered with reference to empirical knowledge—an approach Durkheim generally took. Firstly, the question arises as to how Durkheim views the transition from animal, prehuman sociality to human sociality. After all, one must avoid projecting an individualistic egoism onto the behavior of animals. This comparison between animal and human permits a level of universal structures of human sociality which is lacking in Durkheim's program. Secondly, we should investigate the problem as to whether the subjectivity of the organism can logically be thought of before and without its social formation or whether, conversely, even physical needs should be thought of as arising from a socially constituted process of individuation. Particularly in primitive cultures, the individual is not initially perceived, either by the others or by himself, as an individualized body, but rather as a representation of mythical powers which he represents as an individual case, without thereby becoming a non-interchangeable individual.[46] In the development of children the elementary pre-given awareness of the body is acquired by the actor himself via an intersubjectively constituted body schema.[47] Durkheim's dualism occludes the possibility of thinking of sociality as a dimension of the solution to interpersonal conflicts of action, and leads him to posit a model of sociality that is at first purely mentalistic and is then limited to the extra-ordinary constitution of "représentations collectives," in opposition to a concept of action which he reduces to a narrowly utilitarian notion (including the ideas of order bound up with it). The divergence between Durkheim's and Dewey's ideas regarding democracy and the state—the former defending the strong state, the latter advocating an abrogation of such powers to society—could be used to show how this fundamental difference has political implications as well; or could it rather be that political considerations were the root of the divergence?[48]

With respect to a theory of the constitution of categories, the result of an interpretation of Durkheim's confrontation with pragmatism seems to be critical. Since Durkheim attempts to arrive at a social theory of constitution without a conception of everyday social interaction, his undertaking is burdened with insoluble paradoxes and flaws, and the constitution of socio-cognitive abilities is not explained. It would only be possible to fulfil his programmatic claims by means of a theory of the constitution of socio-cognitive abilities which also takes into account the foundations laid by the pragmatists for research into cognitive development as a solution to problems of action.[49] Yet this criticism also falls short of the mark. It sheds light only on the lack of a theory of symbolically mediated everyday interaction in Durkheim's conception. Durkheim's theory of the ritual is an attempt precisely to demonstrate the social constitution of categories in extra-ordinary interaction. The questions which overlap one another in Durkheim's work have to be kept separate in our critique. Even if, in opposition to Durkheim, we uphold the constitution of categories in what are in part anthropological and universal and in part historical and culturally specific structures of social interaction, we are nonetheless bound to agree with his thesis that comprehensive systems of interpretation only become viable through situations of "collective effervescence."[50] What remains of Durkheim's theory of a social constitution of categories and his critique of pragmatism, for all the deficiencies and untenable positions they contain and over and above their consequences for an interpretation of Durkheim's work, is therefore the compelling obligation to take the constitution of collective identities and their consequences seriously for both a theory of action and a theory of social order.[51]

Notes

1. The portrayals of pragmatism are often distorted to the point of caricature—even in the case of such important authors as Max Scheler, Max Horkheimer, and Georg Lukács. The characterizations range from a description of pragmatism as a particularly primitive form of empiricism, utilitarianism, or positivism through to pragmatism as the ideology of "big business" or of protofascist decisionism. (See the chapter "American Pragmatism and German Thought" in this volume).

2. Precise information on the contemporary French reception of pragmatism and on the relationship of Renouvier, Boutroux, and Bergson primarily to James can be found in Allcock, "Editorial Introduction to the English Translation," in E. Durkheim, *Pragmatism and Sociology* (Cambridge, Mass., 1983), pp. xxiii–xli.

3. This suggested interpretation stems from René König, "Drei unbekannte Werke von Emile Durkheim," in *Kölner Zeitschrift für Soziologie und Sozialpsychologie* 8 (1956): pp. 642–47; and his "Emile Durkheim," in Dirk Käsler (ed.), *Klassiker des soziologischen Denkens*, vol. 1 (Munich, 1976), pp. 312–64. Cf. also his book *Kritik der historisch-existenzialistischen Soziologie* (Munich, 1975). A large part of the literature on Durkheim either does not touch on the lectures on pragmatism at all or views pragmatism simply from Durkheim's point of view, as, unfortunately, does Steven Lukes, *Emile Durkheim: His Life and Work* (Harmondsworth, 1973). The works of Paul de Gaudemar ("Les ambiguités de la critique Durkheimienne du pragmatisme," in *La Pensée* 145 [1969], pp. 81–88), Gregory Stone and Harvey Farberman ("On the Edge of Rapprochement: Was Durkheim Moving towards the Perspective of Symbolic Interaction?" in *Sociological Quarterly* 8 [1967], pp. 149–64), and Edward A. Tiryakian ("Emile Durkheim," in T. Bottomore and R. Nisbet (eds.), *A History of Sociological Analysis* (New York, 1978), pp. 187–236) are the exception. The arguments formulated by Stone and Farberman are based on a thorough knowledge of pragmatism; they distinguish various tendencies in pragmatism and as a consequence stress—and to my mind this is an exaggeration—Durkheim's convergence with the nascent field of Symbolic Interactionism.

When Parsons wrote the chapters on Durkheim in *Structure of Social Action*—undoubtedly one of the key interpretations—he could not yet have been familiar with the lectures on pragmatism. What is all the more surprising is a footnote (Parsons, *The Structure of Social Action*, 1937, p. 440) in which he indicates that Durkheim's insight into the motivational force of ritual and his reference to the decision-making pressure in everyday action was not far removed from pragmatist lines of thought at the time.

4. On the renaissance of pragmatism, see the works of Karl-Otto Apel, Richard Bernstein, Jürgen Habermas, and Richard Rorty. On the difference between pragmatist and structuralist semiotic theory, see also Eugene Rochberg-Halton, "Situation, Structure, and the Context of Meaning," in *Sociological Quarterly* 23 (1982), pp. 156–80.

5. Parsons also recognized this in his study on Cooley: "In a more non-committal and perhaps less painstaking way than Freud, Weber, or Durkheim, James questioned the basic premises of the three systems which provided the starting points of this analysis—the Cartesian, the Utilitarian biological, and the idealistic. Of course, to question the Cartesian system was also to question the assumptions on which the two systems that followed it had been built." (Parsons, "Cooley and the Problem of Internalization," in A. Reiss (ed.), *Cooley and Sociological Analysis* (Ann Arbor, 1968), p. 59.) This insight is surprising inasmuch as Parsons still completely lacked any understanding of it at the time when he wrote *The Structure of Social Action.*

6. Aesthetics do not figure at all in Durkheim's work—but are a significant element in pragmatism. Cf. John Dewey, *Art as Experience* (New York, 1934).

7. Durkheim's use of the term "categories" is neither consistent nor completely faithful to Kant's model. For clarification, see Thomas F. Gieryn, "Durkheim's Sociology of Scientific Knowledge," in *Journal of the History of the Behavioral Sciences* 18 (1982), p. 127, note 41.

8. For evidence on the inaccuracy of this view, see Gérard Deledalle, "Durkheim et Dewey. Un double Centenaire," in *Etudes philosophiques, N.S.* 14 (1959), pp. 493–98 and Gaudemar (1969; see note 3).

9. The distinction between the level of a theory of action and that of a theory of order has been elaborated most clearly by Jeffrey Alexander, *Theoretical Logic in Sociology,* vol. 2, *The Antinomies of Classical Thought: Marx and Durkheim,* (Berkeley, 1982). See also vol. 1. However, even this new comprehensive interpretation of Durkheim has nothing to contribute to an interpretation of the pragmatism lectures.

10. Cf. the concluding section of the present essay.

11. Charles S. Peirce, "Some Consequences of Four Incapacities," in *Collected Papers,* vol. 5.264–5.317, here 5.265.

12. I have attempted to do so, using the example of George Herbert Mead, in my book *G. H. Mead. A Contemporary Re-Examination of His Thought,* tr. R. Meyer (Cambridge, Mass.: 1985).

13. Peirce, "Consequences . . . ," vol. 5.283 (p. 169).

14. Lukes, *Emile Durkheim . . . ,* pp. 407 and 459.

15. Durkheim, "Lévy-Bruhl, Les fonctions mentales dans les sociétés inférieures," in *Journal sociologique* (Paris, 1969), p. 680. The review was written 1909–10.

16. Durkheim (with Marcel Mauss), *Primitive Classification* (Chicago, 1963), p. 11. Originally written 1901–2.

17. Durkheim, ibid., p. 32. Durkheim gives a more precise definition of the model character of social organization at a later point: "We have seen, indeed, how these classifications were modelled on the closest and most fundamental form of social organization. This, however, is not going far enough. Society was not simply a model which classificatory thought followed; it was its own divisions which served as divisions for the system of classification. The first logical categories were social categories; the first classes of things were classes of men, into which these things were integrated. It was because men were grouped, and thought of themselves in the form of groups, that in their ideas they grouped other things, and in the beginning the two modes of grouping

were merged to the point of being indistinct." (Durkheim and Mauss, *Primitive Classification*, p. 82f.).

18. As Parsons did, in *The Structure of Social Action.* Parsons considered Durkheim's basic idea of sociological epistemology to be "completely untenable" (p. 443). He also reiterates this assessment and the warning against the dangers of relativism in his late retrospective of Durkheim's sociology of religion, "Durkheim on Religion Revisited: Another Look at the Elementary Forms of the Religious Life," in C. Y. Glock and P. Hammond (eds.), *Beyond the Classics? Essays in the Scientific Study of Religion* (New York, 1973), pp. 156–80; here, however, he reformulates Durkheim's thesis to make it appear as an assertion that society and culture were originally undifferentiated.

19. This is particularly clear in Rodney Needham, "Introduction," in Emile Durkheim and Marcel Mauss, *Primitive Classification* (Chicago, 1963), p. xxvii.

20. Claude Lévi-Strauss, *Le Totémisme aujourd'hui* (Paris 1962), p. 103.

21. Durkheim, *The Elementary Forms of the Religious Life* (London 1968), p. 18f., originally published in 1912.

22. Dominick La Capra, *Emile Durkheim: Sociologist and Philosopher* (Ithaca, 1972), p. 268, note 24, makes the following ironic criticism of Durkheim: "As a defense of the universal applicability and truth of categories which were presumed to be specifically social in origin, this piece of argument was unfortunately about as cogent as the idea that a photographer takes good photographs because he is himself photogenic."

23. Needham, "Introduction", p. xviff.

24. Peter M. Worsley, "Emile Durkheim's Theory of Knowledge," in *Sociological Review* 4 (1956), pp. 47–62.

25. See Edward L. Schaub, "A Sociological Theory of Knowledge," in *Philosophical Review* 29 (1920), pp. 319–39; Gérard Namer, "La Sociologie de la connaissance chez Durkheim et chez les Durkheimiens," in *L'Année sociologique* 28 (1977), pp. 41–77; Allcock, "Editorial Introduction . . ."

26. Durkheim and Mauss, "Primitive Classification" p. 81f., note 1.

27. Ibid.

28. This line of argumentation is not compiled from views expressed in the secondary literature, but rather comes from the author of this essay. Cf. also Lévi-Strauss, *Le Totémisme*, p. 142 ff., with reference to Rousseau.

29. Thomas Luckmann, "On the Boundaries of the Social World," in M. Natanson (ed.), *Phenomenology and Social Reality: Essays in Memory of Alfred Schütz* (The Hague, 1980), pp. 73–100; Jean Cazeneuve, "La Connaissance d'autrui dans les sociétés archaiques," in *Cahiers internationaux de sociologie* 25 (1958), pp. 75–99.

30. Durkheim, "Individual and Collective Representations," in *Sociology and Philosophy* (London, 1965), p. 10; originally written in 1898.

31. Cf. Mead's attempt "The Definition of the Psychical," in *Decennial Publications of the University of Chicago*, First series, vol. 3 (1903), pp. 77–112, which contrasts sharply with Durkheim's.

32. This problem provided an important impetus for the further development of pragmatist social theory.

33. Durkheim, *Pragmatism and Sociology* (Cambridge, 1983), p. 54.

34. Ibid., p. 72.

35. Ibid., p. 64.

36. Ibid., pp. 79–81.

37. Ibid., p. 82f.

38. Ibid., p. 75f.
39. Ibid., p. 74.
40. Ibid., p. 78.
41. Ibid., p. 88.
42. Ibid., p. 92.
43. Habermas makes this mistake (*The Theory of Communicative Action,* tr. Thomas McCarthy [Boston, 1985], vol. 2, p. 72, note 61) in his remark on the lectures on pragmatism. Habermas generally overestimates Durkheim's steps toward overcoming the philosophy of consciousness. A whole series of views on "représentations collectives" which had supposedly been overcome in the sociology of religion recur in these lectures. Cf. also note 51 below.
44. Durkheim, *Pragmatism . . . ,* p. 67.: "Everything is a product of certain causes. Phenomena must not be represented in closed series: things have a 'circular' character, and analysis can be prolonged to infinity. This is why I can accept neither the statement of the idealists, that *in the beginning there is thought,* nor that of the pragmatists, that *in the beginning there is action.*"
45. Durkheim, "Le Dualisme de la nature humaine et ses conditions sociales," in *La Science sociale et l'action* (Paris, 1970), pp. 314–32.
46. Cazeneuve, "La Connaissance . . ."
47. Joas, "The Intersubjective Constitution of the Body-Image," in *Human Studies* 6 (1983), pp. 197–204.
48. It would be necessary to draw up an account of Durkheim's conception of democracy and the state in the light of American authors of that period. In the absence of such an account, I recommend, as an enlightening comparison between Durkheim and Weber, this excellent work: Jeffrey Prager, "Moral Integration and Political Inclusion: A Comparison of Durkheim's and Weber's Theory of Democracy," in *Social Forces* 59 (1981), pp. 918–50. In this connection it would also be possible to clarify the ambivalences in Durkheim's concept of the division of labor which are occasion for the serious misinterpretation by Alexander, *Theoretical Logic.* On this point, see my essay on Alexander (in this volume).
49. On this, see more recent research in developmental psychology and socialization theory that draws on Mead and Piaget. See my essay on "Role Theories and Socialization Research" (in this volume).
50. This could provide one of the starting points for an analysis of Sorel. For now, only this much can be said: in Sorel's early conflict with Durkheim ("Les Théories de M. Durkheim," in *Le Devenir Social* 1 (1895), pp. 1–26 and 148–80), he argues a quasi-pragmatist line that science is founded in action. This is aimed at countering Durkheim's simple positivistic concept of causality as expressed in his *Rules,* where he questions the scientific nature of Marx's work. Even in his own book on pragmatism, i.e. as late as 1921, Sorel still refuses to allow his own antiscientism to be labeled a form of irrationalism or anti-intellectualism: "Owing to one of the anomalies of language so numerous in philosophy, one termed thereafter those doctrines anti-intellectual which wished to eradicate the confusions generated by *scientism* with a view to placing all confidence in the results of legitimate intellectual work" (Sorel, *De l'Utilité du Pragmatisme* [Paris, 1921], pp. 2–3).

The dividing line here would then run, if I see it correctly, not between rationalism and irrationalism, but between a scientistic confidence in the social-reformative impact of pure science on the one hand and, on the other, a reflection of the fact that science too is constituted in the actions and motives of social movements and classes.

What has already been neutralized in Durkheim's work into the scientific treatment of the social constitution of categories still reveals in Sorel's work its origin in the Enlightenment's critique of religion and ideology. Although quite distinct from the pragmatists owing to his completely different evaluation of democracy (and also of the Enlightenment), Sorel's authentic intellectual proximity to pragmatism enabled him to provide, both in his own works and indirectly via Labriola and Gramsci, an impulse toward a reconstruction of historical materialism in terms of the categories of praxis, an undertaking for which Durkheim had no understanding as long as he lived. (See Josep Llobera, "Durkheim, the Durkheimians, and Their Collective Misrepresentation of Marx," in *Social Science Information* 19 [1980], pp. 385–411.)

51. In his magnum opus, Habermas hints at such a possibility through his interpretation of Durkheim, just as he also hinders it with his conception of the dualism between "life-world" and "system." His work, an exceptional achievement despite all the problems involved, cannot be done justice here. Cf. my study (reprinted in this volume) "The Unhappy Marriage of Hermeneutics and Functionalism," in A. Honneth and H. Joas (eds.), *Communicative Action*, (Cambridge, 1991), pp. 97–118.

3 An Underestimated Alternative: America and the Limits of "Critical Theory"

Since the 1960s, the "Critical Theory" of the Frankfurt School has been accorded great attention, both in West Germany and, to an increasing extent, in the United States. It has been more than just a matter of having found the "letter in a bottle"—as Max Horkheimer and Theodor Adorno liked to call their theory. The genie in that bottle has, in fact, swollen to quite intimidating proportions. A widespread view today is that "Critical Theory" represents the very embodiment of a program of interdisciplinary social research—one that has a theoretical backbone, provides a diagnosis of our times, and at the same time contains motifs of a Western, non-Stalinist Marxism and of psychoanalysis (and, indeed, of the critique of reason, widely discussed today) that are truly worthy of preservation. Research into the history of science confirms almost no part of such a view. Instead it brings out how soon the program of an interdisciplinary social research was abandoned by the Frankfurt School and how little diagnosis of our time, close to the political reality of that period, was actually done.[1] In retrospect even the main representatives of the "Critical Theory" looked upon their work as a fragment if not as a failure; they surely did not consider it as an example for following generations. Nevertheless, the palliative image has increasingly assumed a life of its own and has evolved into a social fact that is now often taken as a point of orientation. Other Western approaches to Marxism having no or only a superficial contact with the Frankfurt School have been subsumed under the increasingly vaguely used label "Critical Theory." In Germany the oblique front line of the famous *Positivismusstreit* in the social sciences during the 1960s derived to a great extent from that palliative image. In the United States the elevation of "Critical Theory" has kept thinkers from drawing on American traditions and has confirmed the feeling of European theoretical superiority. A critique of this myth is of vital importance to my own work, for I think it highly important to make use of the motifs of the American pragmatist tradition in areas of philosophy and social science. Even those who locate themselves in the

Reprinted by permission from *Symbolic Interaction* 15, no. 3: 261–75. Copyright 1992 by JAI Press Inc.

ranks of "Critical Theory" can only gain from discussion with pragmatism, both in empirical and in normative respects.

The relation between the two scholarly traditions can best be investigated by establishing what image of America was prevalent in the Frankfurt Institute for Social Research after its emigration to New York. It is a pertinent question to what extent "Critical Theory" considered the details of American social and political life, or took into account American achievements in philosophy and the social sciences. In answering this question I shall not waste the reader's time with well-known facts of a more biographical than essential kind, such as, for example, the Frankfurt School's far-reaching self-isolation vis-à-vis the groves of American academia and its members' expressly nonconformist conduct and bearing as European academics. Incidentally, Paul Lazarsfeld, who had come to the United States only a few years earlier, mentioned sarcastically that in comparison to Adorno he felt like a member of the Mayflower Society.[2] More important than such anecdotes is an assessment of the members' writings. This has not been undertaken—as far as I know—until now, neither from this viewpoint regarding America nor with reference to the extensive review section in the School's periodical, the *Zeitschrift für Sozialforschung* (Studies in Philosophy and Social Science).

The basic theoretical assumption which the Frankfurt School members took with them when they emigrated can be roughly characterized as follows: liberal capitalism found itself ostensibly in an inexorable process of transition into monopolistic and state-regulated forms. They contended that as a result the liberal state was becoming transformed into its authoritarian counterpart and laws of a general nature were becoming subject to functional change and increasingly replaced by special regulations. These processes were accompanied by both the destruction of the conditions for true individuation and the increasing disintegration of all high culture in favor of commercial or propagandistic mass culture. The different levels of this diagnosis were interconnected via an unswerving functionalism. That is, cultural and psychological changes were, from the outset, interpreted as functional for the political, and these as functional for the economic centralization of domination. At least among the inner circle of school members, America and the experiences they had there after their emigration did not cause a revision of these assumptions. For them, America was capitalism in its purest form. Accordingly, the traits derived from the development of capitalism in Germany had to hold true with a vengeance for the United States. Each and every experience they underwent was but a confirmation of this pre-assumption: In the United States social research had, so they believed, become purely instrumental contract research, and philosophy nothing but a positivistic reduction of all questions to methodology; American social psychology merely promoted conformism; and mass culture represented decay and loss of the transcending powers of European high culture. Taken as a whole, the above made the society of the New Deal appear to be a nascent totalitarianism. Even the formulation, often used by the Frankfurt School members, that they were endeavoring to link European ideas and American methods is revealing, for it implicitly ignores the possibility of there being important American ideas. I wish to demonstrate here, if only briefly, the significance of these American ideas as an alternative to critical theory in some areas.

The positive myth of "Critical Theory" is complemented by the negative myth of the exclusively utilitarian and empirical character of American thought. Yet one encounters again and again in the various phases of American history an explicitly voiced search for new theoretical and practical patterns for forming communities. The forms of this search range from the fraternal and communal ideals of Puritanism, via a mysticism of nature, a longing for Catholicism, and utopian experiments, to the mystification of the colonial past or of the old conditions in the South. It is the classical republican tradition of America which is clearly the most important of these; this found at the end of the nineteenth century a new and contemporary expression in the philosophy of pragmatism, to the extent that ideals of communal self-administration formed the point of departure for a new understanding of the solutions to cognitive and moral problems. This philosophy initiated a "revolt against formalism"[3] in the whole area of the social sciences and in public discussion in the United States—though more in the form of exemplary studies than in theoretical syntheses. Nevertheless, it cannot be dismissed as merely social research which is reduced to methodological precision or disconnected from theoretical issues. One of the main objects of Horkheimer's criticism was precisely this pragmatism: not only in several of his essays but above all in his book *The Eclipse of Reason,* which appeared in German titled *Zur Kritik der instrumentellen Vernunft* ("On the Critique of Instrumental Reason").[4] He relies by and large, however, on the pertinent book by Max Scheler, in which pragmatism appears as a philosophy that reduces human life to labor and is therefore not adequate for a portrayal of what is authentically spiritual or personal.[5] In these works Horkheimer therefore continues the tradition of decades of arrogant and superficial German snubbing of the most ingenious stream of American thought. Scheler's interpretation suits Horkheimer's attempt to treat pragmatism throughout as the inconsistent brother of logical positivism. I shall not expand here on the fact that Horkheimer's presentation of logical positivism[6] was also utterly insufficient, and that the most important representative of an approach which emerged close to the positivistic circle but developed its own direction was not considered at all by the Frankfurt school: Ludwig Wittgenstein.

Horkheimer's conception is instilled with the following logic: he proceeds from a distinction between subjective and objective reason. A behavior is subjectively rational, he claims, which merely concerns itself with the choice of technically or economically suitable means to given ends. In the process, purposes themselves are placed in a realm not subject to reflection; thus, Horkheimer continues, the primacy of the self-preservation of the subject asserts itself unnoticed, in that no higher standards for purposes are taken to exist. Subjective or instrumental reason has become dominant ever since the beginning of modernity—in particular, however, since the Enlightenment's critique of religion and quite definitely following Hegel's death. Accordingly, Horkheimer judges it to have destroyed "objective reason," the knowledge of humankind's higher temporal goods above and beyond self-preservation and the calculation of utility. Yet, he asserts, such an objective reason clearly could not be restored in the guise of a new metaphysics. All the same, Horkheimer claims to be able to refer his own project, which he terms "dialectical," to this objective reason, to the rationality of ends themselves. In this context, the concept of "positivism" becomes a battle cry in the totalization of subjective reason. Under this term pragmatist thought is subsumed without much ado; empirical social research as a whole also falls more and more under the same verdict, without much consideration of its various forms or its possibly false self-understanding.

Adorno took a significantly more cautious approach toward such a stylization of "objective reason." He was well aware[7] that it would leave a dogmatic impression simply to contrast a "true" objective reason with a progressing subjectivation and instrumentalization of reason, and that it would not meet the rules of dialectical development and distinct negation to proceed in such a way. Thus, the dogmatism of "objective reason" did not appear in *The Dialectic of Enlightenment,* which was written by Adorno and Horkheimer together—though this fact was paid for by theoretical ambiguity. But Adorno also was sure that pragmatism and positivism should be viewed as totalizations of instrumental reason. Herbert Marcuse was a bit more open toward pragmatism in his reviews of John Dewey's books, published in *Zeitschrift für Sozialforschung.*[8] He did concede that Dewey rejected logical positivism himself, and that he did not plead for a value-free thinking in his theory of valuation. On the contrary, in fact Dewey made an effort to inquire into the possible rationality of values and, particularly, to find a new view of the constitution of values in human action. These constructive sides of Dewey's efforts, however, remained unnoticed by the representatives of the Frankfurt School. This is all the more amazing when one bears in mind that Dewey's conceptions were published in his great book on aesthetic experience and in his study on religious experience at the very same place and time Horkheimer and Adorno were working, in the middle of the 1930s at Columbia University in New York.[9]

This misreading of pragmatism can be shown most vividly with the use of the concept of "adaptation." The writings of the Frankfurt school members, e.g. Adorno's essay on Veblen, are riddled with polemics against the supposedly social-Darwinist and conformist character of the concept of "adaptation." First, they failed to recognize that the pragmatists made distinctions between very different kinds of adaptation; reaching from the passive "accommodation" to the given facts of environment, via active "adaptation," in the case of the transformation of the world into a life-serving environment, to the reconstructing of the whole personality in a religious experience ("adjustment"). But above all they failed to recognize that the pragmatists' concept of "adaptation" never meant routine and loss of subjectivity but practical innovation, *creative* solutions to real problems. "The pragmatic theory of intelligence means that the function of mind is to project new and more complex ends—to free experience from routine and from caprice. Not the use of thought to accomplish purposes already given either in the mechanism of the body or in that of the existent state of society, but the use of intelligence to liberate and liberalize action, is the pragmatic lesson" (John Dewey).[10] The classic sociological studies conducted by Thomas and Park—members of the Chicago School—accordingly concentrated precisely not on the adaptation of immigrants in the sense of their standardized Americanization, but rather on the creative reorganization of communal life, for example by the Polish peasants in Chicago,[11] and on the realization of democracy under conditions of ethnic and cultural heterogeneity. The main focus was not on the decay of community from some cultural-pessimistic perspective but rather on the gradual formation of new institutions. Dewey's theory of art and religion dealt with collective creativity in the constitution of ideal values and with individual creativity in the "abductive," not deductive, specification of these values as action goals. In the case of Dewey, quite the opposite of the instrumentalist misunderstanding of pragmatism is true. Here, it is not technical but rather *aesthetic* experience which is crucial because, by referring to it, Dewey was able to demonstrate the possibility both of a meaningful world that can be perceived sensuously and of creative attempts to imbue that world with meaning via the creative appropriation of the possibilities for ideality contained in the world. Whereas, in other words, the Frankfurt school members longed helplessly for some past notion of objective reason in their critique of instrumental reason or entangled themselves in the ambiguities of the concept of reason contained in the purported dialectic of Enlightenment, American pragmatism had grown beyond all such philosophies of history based on a metaphysics of reason and had developed a theory of the intersubjective constitution of values experienced as meaningful and binding.

This difference in social philosophy has a parallel on the level of political theory. In the latter case, the Frankfurt School's incorrect interpretations of America stemmed from a Marxist understanding of liberalism and democracy. These are conceived of in an orthodox Marxist manner as the superstructure of capitalism in the essays published prior to the Institute's emigration. In this reading, the transition from liberal to monopoly capitalism is accompanied by the emergence of the totalitarian state as the necessary pendant to the latter form—fascism is interpreted as the domination of monopoly capital. In his 1934 essay on "The Struggle against Liberalism in the Totalitarian Conception of the State" Marcuse provided what was in part a superb critique of the nascent national-socialist theories of law and the state; yet his main argument was that it was liberalism which "'engendered' from within itself the total-authoritarian state: as its own perfection at a more advanced stage of development."[12] All the elements of liberal democracy, such as freedom of speech and of the press and of publicity, tolerance, parliamentarism, and the division of powers, are expressly reduced to being functional components of competition capitalism. While in emigration, the Frankfurt School produced only very few concrete analyses of the trends of economic development in Western societies. Horkheimer and Adorno spoke quite globally of an "integral statism" that was forming, and later of the "administered world." Their originally positive points of reference—"planned economy" and "proletariat"—were unobtrusively dropped. The hopes connected therewith were abandoned and the hints about a subject of history and a reasonable social order were replaced by a deeply pessimistic vision of an enduring totalitarian dominance in which, above all, Jews would have to suffer as objects of power. Especially in Horkheimer's 1939 essay "Die Juden und Europa" ("The Jews and Europe"),[13] where he most significantly shifted his focus in this way, the diagnosis is repeated with a cutting ferocity: totalitarianism is seen as a result of capitalism, which had, out of necessity, to lose its liberalistic form. "The new Anti-semitism is the harbinger of a totalitarian order to which the liberal one has developed. It is necessary to go back to the tendencies of capital." Those who had not abandoned the hope "that somewhere the reform of Western capitalism takes place more smoothly than in Germany"[14] were rejected scornfully. Even the most horrifying consequences of National Socialism were taken as pieces of evidence for the unchanged validity of the Marxist critique of capitalism. This contained a covert political partisanship which led Marcuse even after the end of World War II to speak of the impending fascicization of the United States and the necessity of criticizing social democracy more strongly than the Soviet Union.[15] These pointers are naturally not intended as a political denunciation nor as an attempt to play down the dangers of a latent or manifest authoritarianism in the West, but are instead meant to demonstrate the inability of "Critical Theory" to do conceptual justice to the management of the deep economic and social crisis of the 1930s in the framework of societies with democratic constitutions. Admittedly, there were also different voices; Franz Neumann and Otto Kirchheimer differ from the School's inner circle both with regard to the analysis of Western democracies and in their diagnosis of National Socialism. It was above all Neumann who had always defended the political primacy of the maintenance of democracy.[16] In his critique of Carl Schmitt he had become aware of the problematic character of a Marxist-functionalist interpretation of parliamentarism and the constitutional state. Politically, he certainly sympathized with the line of American policy running from Wilson to Roosevelt; yet in theoretical terms he never overcame functionalism, but rather added to it proclamations of the intrinsic ethical value of democratic institutions, of the division of powers and the independence of the judiciary. But Neumann did not put the historical sources and the independent logic of these traditions into a consistent relation to the Marxist critique of liberalism. He never revised his thesis on the change in the function of law.

Such a Marxist-functionalist approach could not do justice to the American democratic tradition. If liberalism and democracy are equated with utilitarianism, this detracts precisely from the central battle line along which conflicts on America's understanding of itself have always been conducted. Since the eighteenth century, what must at least be termed tension has existed between the utilitarian and the republican-normativist poles of American thought. In the history of America the native sources have been exploited again and again to keep possessive individualism within reasonable limits. Examples are agrarian populism after the Civil War, progressive social reformative tendencies prior to World War I, and the New Deal. Social theorists as widely different from each other as John Dewey and Talcott Parsons are united in this battle against utilitarianism. Neither Parsons' epoch-making study of *The Structure of Social Action*[17] nor Dewey's political philosophy were even acknowledged by the Critical Theorists. Any permeation of politics with action theory had necessarily to collide with their Marxist-functionalist assumptions. However, Dewey's political thought proceeded precisely from processes of collective action and not from the State.[18] Such action encounters problems—so his argument runs—and has unintended or unanticipated consequences which the acting collective then has to process reflexively. Communication between all the participants plays a substantial role in this process of interpreting and evaluating consequences. Dewey's political program is aimed at recreating the endangered democratic public sphere by revitalizing community life even in the large cities, by preventing the development of expertocracy, by making the public sphere responsible for the host of unintended consequences industrial society produces, and by means of the publicity and freedom of research in the social sciences. It is not possible to assess this program adequately here. But it is vital to emphasize that, with its reduction of democracy to capitalism, the Frankfurt School obliterated one of the most important themes of today's discussion on theory in *the East and the West:* namely, the question as to the affinity or tension between these strands of modern social development.

In the area of social psychology, the American pragmatist tradition and the Frankfurt School also met head-on. Numerous studies were inspired by Cooley, Mead, and Dewey in which—by means of the concepts of role-taking, the self, the generalized Other and symbolic interaction—ego-development was shown to result from social interaction. Such research contrasted sharply with any behavioristic psychological reductionism and, in turn, inspired various attempts to integrate interactionist social psychology and psychoanalysis. With one exception, the Frankfurt School members—all of whom had been decisively influenced by psychoanalysis—reacted to this social-psychological correlate of the American democratic tradition by rejecting it in the sharpest of terms. Here the exception was Erich Fromm. Though he also had begun as a Marxist-functionalist and had tried to draw a line between libidinous and social structures he then became more and more skeptical about Freud's theory of drives. During his emigration he endeavored to integrate the interpersonal psychiatry of Harry Stack Sullivan and the cultural anthropology of

Ruth Benedict and Edward Sapir. This does not at all entail a consistent revision of the theory of drives. But Fromm, at least, parted company with the Marxist functionalism of his friends and this sufficed for them to excommunicate him from the circle on charges of revisionism. In 1936 Adorno scornfully advised him urgently to read Lenin in order to reacquaint himself with the significance of the avant-garde and dictatorship and arm himself for dealing with conformist dangers.[19] Fromm's rather more expressivist than interactionist turn was understood by Horkheimer and Adorno to indicate that he was prepared to conform to a social order which they saw as in need of a revolution. This they were obliged to think, for they had turned a blind eye to the idealizing contents of democracy. As a consequence, they considered the realm of intersubjectivity to comprise but conformity and conformism, and expected radical changes to be forthcoming from the untameable force of instinctual drives. Whereas, in the postwar years, Horkheimer returned to the Schopenhauerian pessimism of his early years, Marcuse honed his Freudianism to a more radical point, turning it into a justification for revolution based on a metaphysics no longer of reason but of instinctual drives. In his 1955 book *Eros and Civilization* he polemically attacked Sullivan and Fromm from this position.[20] While Fromm devoted his attention to the fate of human spontaneity in the society of the day, Horkheimer and Adorno could only perceive the destruction of all spontaneity. In 1940 they were to state that they witnessed "a change that makes men into mere passive centers of reaction, into subjects of 'conditioned reflexes', because they have left no centers of spontaneity, no obligatory measure of behavior, nothing that transcends their most immediate wants, needs and desires."[21] They thus took behaviorism as a description of facts, but regarded a psychology of creativity and interpersonality as merely some shrouding ideological disguise. No analysis could be further from the truth! This is for three reasons: First, it did not do justice to the reality of America, which, in Max Weber's words, was "not some formless sand heap of individuals, but a confusion of strictly exclusive, but voluntaristic associations."[22] Second, it also failed to deal appropriately with the dominant trend of the postwar era, in which ever more people adopted to an ever greater degree an understanding of themselves in terms of creative individuality. And third, the swiftness and falseness of this diagnosis indicates the lack of a social psychology within "Critical Theory" that could claim to do more than merely mediate directly between supposedly politico-economic laws and individual irrationality. Even the major study on the "authoritarian personality" was flawed, as Herbert Blumer emphasized, by the fact that in it psychological types were only correlated with political behavior, and the possible emergence of a social movement such as the Nazis was not analyzed in terms of action theory.[23] There were no conceptual means for the analysis of social processes in which people of different personality structures interact and join together to form groups or organizations. This deficiency holds also for the theory of socialization in its narrower sense as the study of the formative stage of personality structures. Above all, it is the feminist critique which in recent years has brought out the falsity of the orthodox psychoanalytical assumptions on the connection of gaining autonomy and the learning of the gender role.[24] But these assumptions formed the basis of the Frankfurt School's expositions on the dangers of a progressive weakening of paternal authority and its replacement by bureaucracy and culture industry. Especially the object relations approach—going back to Sullivan—stresses instead the importance of intersubjective perception and recognition for child development. Therefore it arrives at completely different theses: paternal authority does not simply disintegrate but is transformed into an increasing participation in child-rearing and into a greater autonomy of the maternal personality. "In any case, today both the real fathers and the ideal father as promoted by the media are much more devoted to parental obligations, beginning with the child's birth, than they were in the past."[25] Correspondingly there is no reason to talk of an increasingly colder family climate and about children being more open to manipulation.

Thus, the Frankfurt School members did not conceive of the mediation of social demands and the individual psyche in categories of a sociological theory of action. Instead, use was made of a theory of culture, which was, however, couched in ever narrower terms and soon focused solely on the autonomous, often esoteric artwork.[26] From the vantage point this offered, the members' critical gaze came to rest on the media and the contents of American mass culture. Adorno's pronouncements on jazz, on the reception of serious music on the radio, and on large sports meetings were devastating.[27] The only conclusion he came to in his studies was that the recipients were condemned in all of these areas to be but passive-unreflecting "newts," to use his term, as well as the prefiguration of a nascent totalitarianism. And he did not seem to be disturbed by the fact that totalitarianism tended to emerge in areas characterized by an absence of modern mass culture.[28] Empirically research into mass communications and cultural sociology would hardly have confirmed any of his analyses. I do not wish to minimize the possible problems of mass culture, but rather to ascertain that Adorno did not demonstrate these, preferring instead to prejudge them theoretically. Frankfurt School social theory did not permit the possibility of new media and popular culture having any positive effect in a democratic society in the first place.

One does not have to share Walter Benjamin's excessive utopian hopes for a cultural-revolutionary potential of the new technified art forms to see that the blueprint of Adorno's critique in each case was the high culture of a past epoch or the singularly perfect masterpiece and not the popular or mass culture of these times.[29] The contrast to America's own cultural criticism is obvious when Adorno sees in Veblen's polemical attacks against the conspicuous consumption of the "leisure class" nothing but an envy toward the last resorts against the forces of conformity. Bourgeois refinement determined to hope for a revolution which ends all exploitation uncomprehendingly confronts a, maybe, naive egalitarianism and adoption of a rural and urban "instinct of workmanship" in American thought.

Hence, the relationship between "Critical Theory" and America and its intellectual traditions remained unproductive throughout the various fields of thought. This was completely different in the cases of other emigrants–from Hannah Arendt to Alfred Schütz. But historical justice requires us to mention that their return to Germany led Horkheimer and Adorno to a revision in exactly the way one would have expected in connection with their emigration. In a kind of autobiographical retrospect in the text "Wissenschaftliche Erfahrungen in Amerika" ("Scientific Experiences in America"), Adorno speaks of the "absence of respect toward intellectuality"; and he explains that this enabled him to free himself from the German mandarins' belief in culture, that he could develop openness to Enlightenment and empirical research, and that he experienced in substantial democracy "a real humanitarian potential which could hardly be found in old Europe."[30] Among Horkheimer's and Adorno's projects for the translation of American books one finds the name of John Dewey; but the plan never came into existence. Nonetheless, this self-revision was only partial. In the same breath with Adorno's remarks on the democratic substance of America and, following from that, its possible immunity against totalitarianism, he again terms American society capitalism in its purest form. Moreover, his verdicts against the "positivism" of the various lines of thought remained unrevised. Also, Herbert Marcuse, who did not return to Germany, kept a hold on the stylization of "Critical Theory" as the only alternative to totalized positivism. More and more, this lonely feeling of theoretical superiority and intellectual mission became a barrier against the reception of intellectual trends. Whether in the cases of Wittgenstein or Dewey, Durkheim or Parsons, the Frankfurt

School members either rejected or did not respond to any of the great innovations of social theory in the twentieth century.

For these reasons, the achievement of Jürgen Habermas's opening up of the "Critical Theory" to these impulses cannot be overestimated. The ensuing difference resided not only in the various modifications but in a generally different attitude toward the construction of theory and the practice of research in the social sciences, as well as in Marxism. Reflections on the Frankfurt School's image of America may even appear superfluous to those who consider the work of Jürgen Habermas the successful synthesis of American and Frankfurt traditions. In a different place I have given extensive grounds why I would recommend caution with that claim, and I still see elements of pragmatism which transcend Habermas's achievements.[31] However sound Habermas's discussions of the works of Charles Peirce and George Herbert Mead may be, he never gave a full interpretation of his relationship to pragmatism. The most obvious gap relates to John Dewey, who is hardly ever mentioned. Habermas's early book *Strukturwandel der Öffentlichkeit,* which strongly calls Dewey to mind, nevertheless contains at the same time the perspective of the "administered world."[32] It was this heritage which led Habermas to his—critical—reception of Luhmann's systems theory and to the adoption of the thesis on the existence of normfree spheres of action as we find them in his main work, *Theory of Communicative Action.* The critique of Habermas's action theory comes from very different standpoints. For instance Arnason thinks that Habermas's action theory in its current form is narrowed by an anticipating adaptation to Luhmann's systems theory.[33] Because of this, he claims, Habermas's revisions in the field of a theory of history would result in a quasi-teleological framework which contains only the interaction of system logics and not the genuine openness of history. Alexander, on the other hand, objects that Habermas does not really unfold a theory of society on the basis of a non-instrumentalistic concept of action, but generates a residual category of noncommunicative action to propose a partially nonnormative description of modern life in the style of "Critical Theory."[34] Antonio sees a connection between the nonpragmatist quest for transhistorical normative reason in Habermas's work and his tendencies to an ethical formalism.[35] In summary, Habermas uses motifs from pragmatism only for an intersubjectivist continuation of the Weberian and Marxian theory of rationalization.

A theory of the creativity of action would correspond more closely to pragmatism and would replace the debates on the end of the individual with an inquiry into the social structures of individual creativity. I am thinking here of the whole spectrum from political and cultural participation, via "yuppified" creativity, to spontaneous violence as an expression of a blocked and submerged expressivity. An ethical reevaluation of primary bonding and empirical inquiry into the resources for community formation–such as has been conducted by Robert Bellah—would take the place of the *formal* universalism of discourse ethics.[36] Bellah perceives the potential that biblical and republican traditions offer for overcoming utilitarian and expressive individualism in private and professional, communal and national life in America. We must, by contrast, seek out via comparative analysis the German equivalents, and, by engaging in critical debate with the modish theses on individualization, assess the range of this potentiality. An inquiry into the extent to which societies make their own functional differentiation the object of democratic will formation would then replace a fixed demarcation of system and lifeworld.[37] In an age in which the question of the nature of democracy has proved to be the substantial axis of political debates throughout the world, it is absurd to neglect the theoretical and empirical instruments to be found in the history and present state of the American social sciences. In no other country has such a deep mark been left on thought by an understanding that views the reality of the day as that of a democratic society. In my opinion, the full impact of these conceptual instruments has not yet been felt.

Notes

1. Cf. above all Rolf Wiggershaus, *Die Frankfurter Schule. Geschichte-theoretische Entwicklung-politische Bedeutung* (München, 1986). My essay owes much to this excellent book. Rolf Wiggershaus has also commented upon an earlier version of this essay. I am grateful for his criticism and for the comments by Hans-Joachim Dahms (Göttingen) and Ricca Edmondson, Galway (Ireland).

2. Paul Lazarsfeld, "An Episode in the History of Social Research: A Memoir," in Donald Fleming and Bernard Bailyn, eds., *The Intellectual Migration: Europe and America 1930–1960* (Cambridge, Mass., 1969), p. 301.

3. This is the subtitle of a book by Morton White, *Social Thought in America* (Boston, 1947). Cf. also Darnell Rucker, *The Chicago Pragmatists* (Minneapolis, 1969).

4. Max Horkheimer, *The Eclipse of Reason* (New York, 1947).

C. Wright Mills had to write a confidential memorandum on the manuscript of this book for Oxford University Press. His evaluation is very close to mine. ("*But* frankly, I don't see any evidence that Horkheimer has really gotten hold of pragmatism except [1] in a rather vulgar form and [2] in the later pronouncements of the Partisan Review writers whom he belatedly attacks. Shouldn't he dignify the view enough to make evident his knowledge of more of its literature than such minor essays by followers . . . his remarks . . . certainly do not give one confidence that he knows the pragmatists whom he is attacking." See J. L. Simich and Rick Tilman, "Critical Theory and Institutional Economics: Frankfurt's Encounter with Veblen," in *Journal of Economic Issues* 14 [1980], pp. 631–48; here, p. 647.)

5. Max Scheler, *Erkenntnis und Arbeit: Eine Studie über Wert und Grenzen des*

pragmatischen Motivs in der Erkenntnis der Welt (Frankfurt, 1977). Originally published in M. Scheler, *Die Wissensformen und die Gesellschaft* (Leipzig, 1926).

6. Hans-Joachim Dahms, "Die Vorgeschichte des Positivismusstreits: von der Kooperation zur Konfrontation. Die Beziehungen zwischen Frankfurter Schule und Wiener Kreis 1936–1942," in *Jahrbuch für Soziologiegeschichte* 1990, pp. 9–78.

7. Adorno's letter to Löwenthal, June 3, 1945 (Wiggershaus, p. 371).

8. Herbert Marcuse, "Review of: John Dewey, Logic. The Theory of Inquiry, New York 1938," in *Zeitschrift für Sozialforschung* 8 (1939–40), pp. 221–28; and his "Review of: John Dewey, Theory of Valuation, Chicago 1939," in *Zeitschrift für Sozialforschung* 9 (1941), pp. 144–48; a much more extensive, but also more negative, interpretation of these reviews is to be found now in Hans-Joachim Dahms, *Positivismusstreit.* Ph.D. Dissertation (Göttingen, 1990), pp. 76–82.

9. John Dewey, *Art as Experience* (New York, 1934); Dewey, *A Common Faith* (New Haven, 1934).

There is now an excellent interpretation of Dewey's work from the perspective of his theory of aesthetic experience: Thomas Alexander, *John Dewey's Theory of Art, Experience and Nature: The Horizons of Feeling* (Albany, 1987).

10. John Dewey, "The Need for a Recovery of Philosophy," in Dewey et al., *Creative Intelligence* (New York, 1917), p. 63f.

11. Hans Joas, "Symbolic Interactionism," in Anthony Giddens and Jonathan Turner (eds.), *Social Theory Today* (Cambridge, 1987), pp. 82–115. Reprinted in this volume as "Pragmatism in American Sociology".

12. Herbert Marcuse, "Der Kampf gegen den Liberalismus in der totalitären Staatsauffassung," in *Zeitschrift für Sozialforschung* 3 (1934), pp. 161–95.

13. Max Horkheimer, "Die Juden und Europa," in *Zeitschrift für Sozialforschung* 8 (1939–40), pp. 115–37.

14. M. Horkheimer, p. 115: "Der neue Antisemitismus ist der Sendbote der totalitären Ordnung, zu der die liberalistische sich entwickelt hat. Es bedarf des Rückgangs auf die Tendenzen des Kapitals."; p. 116: "daß irgendwo die Reformierung des westlichen Kapitalismus glimpflicher sich abspielt als die des deutschen."

15. Wiggershaus, p. 432 and p. 435.

16. Franz Neumann, "Der Funktionswandel des Gesetzes im Recht der bürgerlichen Gesellschaft," in *Zeitschrift für Sozialforschung* 6 (1937), pp. 542–96.

For his experiences in America see Neumann, "Intellektuelle Emigration und Sozialwissenschaft," in Neumann, *Wirtschaft, Staat, Demokratie: Aufsätze 1930–54* (Frankfurt, 1978), pp. 402–23.

17. Talcott Parsons, *The Structure of Social Action* (New York, 1937).

18. John Dewey, *The Public and Its Problems* (New York, 1927).

19. Adorno's letter to Horkheimer, March 21, 1936 (cf. Wiggershaus, p. 184 and p. 299).

20. Herbert Marcuse, *Eros and Civilization* (Boston, 1955).

21. Adorno's proposal for Horkheimer's letter to Robert Hutchins (cf. Wiggershaus, p. 308).

A highly important text for any interpretation of Adorno's relationship to American culture and American cultural criticism is Theodor W. Adorno, "Veblen's Attack on Culture," in *Zeitschrift für Sozialforschung* (Studies in Philosophy and Social Sciences) 9 (1941), pp. 389–413.

22. Max Weber, "Die protestantischen Sekten und der Geist des Kapitalismus," in *Gesammelte Aufsätze zur Religionssoziologie I*, pp. 207–36; here, p. 215.

23. Herbert Blumer, "Collective Behavior," in Joseph B. Gittler (ed.), *Review of Sociology* (New York, 1957), pp. 127–58; here, p. 147.

24. Jessica Benjamin, "Die Antinomien des patriarchalischen Denkens: Kritische Theorie und Psychoanalyse," in Wolfgang Bonß and Axel Honneth (eds.), *Sozialforschung als Kritik* (Frankfurt, 1982), pp. 426–55.

25. J. Benjamin, p. 449.

26. Cf. Axel Honneth, *Kritik der Macht* (Frankfurt, 1985), pp. 11–111. This chapter is very important for the present essay, particularly its thesis of a sociological deficit in Horkheimer's original program and of Adorno's ultimate "repression of the social." The same is true for Honneth's brilliant elaboration of an idea originally presented by Jürgen Habermas: Honneth, "Critical Theory," in Anthony Giddens and Jonathan Turner (eds.), *Social Theory Today* (Cambridge, 1987), pp. 347–82.

My only objection to this essay is that Honneth exaggerates the differences between center and periphery of the Frankfurt School and hence claims ideas for Neumann and Fromm which I really cannot find elaborated in their writings.

27. Theodor W. Adorno, *Prismen* (Frankfurt, 1955).

28. Leon Bramson, *The Political Context of Sociology* (Princeton, 1961), p. 129.

Herbert Gans, "Popular Culture in America: Social Problem in a Mass Society or Social Asset in a Pluralist Society?," in Howard S. Becker (ed.), *Social Problems* (New York, 1966), pp. 549–620.

Adorno's views are seen with more sympathy by Douglas Kellner, "Kulturindustrie und Massenkommunikation: die Kritische Theorie und ihre Folgen," in Bonß and Honneth (see note 23), pp. 482–515; Martin Jay, "Adorno in Amerika," in Ludwig von Friedeburg and Jürgen Habermas (eds.), *Adorno-Konferenz 1983* (Frankfurt, 1983), pp. 354–87.

29. George Herbert Mead, "The Nature of Aesthetic Experience," in *International Journal of Ethics* 36 (1926), pp. 382–92.

30. Theodor W. Adorno, "Wissenschaftliche Erfahrungen in Amerika," in Adorno, *Schriften*, vol. 10.2 (Frankfurt, 1977), pp. 702–38: "Abwesenheit des Respekts vor allem Geistigen"; "Potential realer Humanität, das im alten Europa so kaum vorfindlich ist."

31. Hans Joas, "The Unhappy Marriage of Hermeneutics and Functionalism," in Axel Honneth and Hans Joas (eds.), *Communicative Action* (Cambridge 1991), pp. 97–118. Reprinted in this volume.

32. Jürgen Habermas, *Strukturwandel der Öffentlichkeit* (Neuwied, 1962). Now translated as *The Structural Transformation of the Public Sphere* (Boston, 1989). In an introduction to a new German edition (Frankfurt 1990, p. 30) Habermas now criticizes himself on this point.

33. Johann Pall Arnason, *Praxis und Interpretation* (Frankfurt, 1988).

34. Jeffrey Alexander, "Habermas' New Critical Theory: Its Promise and Problems," in *American Journal of Sociology* 91 (1985–86), pp. 400–24.

35. Robert J. Antonio, "The Normative Foundations of Emancipatory Theory: Evolutionary versus Pragmatic Perspectives," in *American Journal of Sociology* 94 (1988–89), pp. 721–48.

36. Robert Bellah et al., *Habits of the Heart* (Berkeley, 1985).

37. Hans Joas, "The Democratization of Differentiation," in Jeffrey Alexander and Piotr Sztompka (eds.), *Rethinking Progress* (London, 1990), pp. 182–201.

4 American Pragmatism and German Thought: A History of Misunderstandings[1]

Richard Rorty, an American philosopher who certainly cannot complain that his writings in Germany and the United States are not receiving their due attention, claims that Martin Heidegger, Ludwig Wittgenstein, and John Dewey are the three single most important twentieth-century philosophers (see Rorty 1979, p. 15) and describes his own philosophical approach as "neopragmatism." In Germany, Martin Heidegger's philosophical stature has only rarely been seriously called into question since the 1920s. Moreover, ever since the 1960s, Ludwig Wittgenstein has also been canonized in Germany in the manner afforded him at an earlier date in the English-speaking countries. Yet what of John Dewey? Who is John Dewey? In Germany he most certainly does not rank among the great names in philosophy, and at present I can see nothing to suggest that this situation will change in the near future, be it through Rorty's influence or otherwise. Indeed, there has been heated debate in the United States as to whether Rorty is justified, in the light of pragmatism's historical development, in labeling himself a pragmatist.[2] However, the question of Rorty's pragmatism has received virtually no attention in Germany. In fact, the label has been accepted uncritically, because in Germany pragmatism has remained probably the least known of the major modern philosophical currents. Since the language barrier was undoubtedly not a decisive factor in this case, we must look elsewhere for an explanation of this strange phenomenon in the relationship between German and American thought. The explanation put forward in this essay does not seek to reduce everything to one single factor. Rather, the intention is to offer a *history* of misunderstandings, deliberate distortions, and well-meaning incomprehension—and to show how these misunderstandings were compounded over generations. I shall recount this history in several chapters, resorting at times to anecdote.

Before I begin to tell the story, I should, however, mention which aspects will not be covered. I shall refrain from giving an account of the overall reception of William James's oeuvre—i.e., of those criticisms which go beyond treating James as a mere representative of pragmatism. In particular, I shall exclude the reception of his writings on general psychology and the psychology of religion. Nor shall I cover the temporary influence of John Dewey's writings on the theory of education, although in Germany they were instrumental in countering the idealist influence of "Bildung" and promoting the idea of practical, project-based learning, something which led to an understanding of the classroom as a cooperative community (see Bohnsack 1976). Finally, I shall only refer at a very indirect level to the fact that there were trends in German thought in the first half of the twentieth century—across the board of widely differing schools of thought; i.e., from neo-Kantianism to phenomenology to the philosophy of life—which could definitely be described as genuinely pragmatist (see Gethmann 1987). It is important to point this out, for it means that we can exclude there being any validity to the simplistic explanation that the misunderstanding of pragmatism resulted from some major implicit difference between German and American thought. In other words, these misunderstandings arose not only among positions which were irreconcilable with pragmatism, but also among positions which were similar to it. Indeed, there is evidence here of the influence of forces which can only be overcome by means of radical self-scrutiny.

The first chapter of my account could bear the title:

The Misunderstanding of Pragmatism as a Utilitarian Theory of Truth: The German Controversy on Pragmatism prior to the First World War

As is well known, the basic idea of pragmatism, namely that it is actions rather than consciousness which are the foundations of thought, was developed in the 1870s by a group of young thinkers in Cambridge, Massachusetts, and was first publicly voiced by Charles Peirce in 1878. His presentation received little attention, however. This was not to change until approximately twenty years later, when William James, an early member of the group around Peirce, returned in his lectures and writings to this basic idea and stated that it was Peirce who had first conceived of it. The breakthrough came in 1907 with the publication of William James's lectures on *Pragmatism,* which provoked unusually strong, not to say violent, reactions, not only in the United States but also in Europe. More appeared to be at stake here than simply an individual thinker or a new school of philosophy: the issue seemed to be an intellectual movement which reached far beyond the confines of the academic world. James's nimble, indeed sometimes careless, prose may have been well suited to attracting popular attention, but it also gave rise to objections from both opponents and potential allies of "pragmatism" alike. Even Peirce distanced himself from James and decided to describe his own thought henceforth as "pragmaticism," a name for his brainchild which he obviously believed was ugly enough to protect it from kidnappers. While James's book was thus by no means uncontroversial in the United States, in Germany it unleashed a veritable storm of protest, against which the few supporters of James were hardly able to make themselves heard.

James's book appeared in German in 1908, only one year after publication in the States. It had been translated by Wilhelm Jerusalem, the most steadfast of the early champions of pragmatism in the German-speaking world. Jerusalem had stumbled across pragmatism when searching for an ally in his battle against the a prioris of transcendental philosophy and found that it supported him in his demand that epistemology and logic should be founded on psychology. However, in Germany these ambitions were in themselves considered highly suspect. Indeed, the controversy over pragmatism was the main subject of debate at the 1908 World Philosophical Congress, which was held in Heidelberg, and the topic spawned a mass of essays in German journals in the years that followed.

What immediately strikes one about most of the pronouncements forthcoming in the framework of the controversy is that they show no willingness even to take James's arguments or the background to pragmatism into account. James's own statement of his intentions and the replies he penned to critics of pragmatism are largely ignored, although these were already included in the book *Pragmatism,* which contained the lectures of the same name. In fact, the commentators do not even make the effort to consult Peirce's work, despite the fact that James so clearly refers to it. Various spellings of the name Peirce (usually Pierce, though also Pearce) are to be encountered in articles at this time, suggesting that the critics lacked firsthand knowledge of his essays. A little detective work would undoubtedly soon reveal who copied from whom instead of referring back to the original source. Most of the participants in the debate radically narrowed down the field of discussion by viewing pragmatism as a new theory of truth, then accusing James of propagating a theory of truth which espoused the simplistic equation of truth with utility. The actor was entitled to regard as true that which was useful to him or which satisfied him emotionally. It was surely doubtful whether such a primitive philosophical position was even worthy of the term "philosophy," wrote Werner Bloch in 1913. Was it not sufficient merely to point to everyday phenomena, such as the detrimental effects of wishful thinking? Indeed, philosophy could surely not take seriously a theory which declared as true that which was useful. However, or so the critics continued, outside the domain of philosophy such an assertion had to be taken all the more seriously, since an attack on truth could only be interpreted as an assault on culture as a whole.

In fairness it should be said that William James was not entirely free of blame for the misunderstandings to which his work gave rise. Moreover, the fault lies not only in the laxity of his formulations. He had, for example, to a large extent blurred what was for Peirce the crucial distinction between the pragmatist maxim for clarifying meaning and a theory of truth. Peirce attached great importance to this distinction, on the one hand because it was only thus that all cognition could be linked to action, and on the other hand because he felt it necessary to preserve the ideal inherent in the concept of truth. Peirce did not develop a pragmatist theory of truth at all; rather, his was a consensus theory, i.e. a reconstruction of the concept of truth based on the idealized consensus of an unlimited community of researchers.

James's blurring of this distinction was compounded by further equivocations. He did not make it clear whether he understood the practical consequences of a proposition to be concrete individual actions or generalized rules and habits, nor what it was that distinguished practical consequences from effects which were subjectively experienced. Many of the points made by James were valid only if taken to mean unique, concrete psychological effects felt by individuals, rather than regularly occurring consequences. This was undoubtedly problematical in itself, yet there is nonetheless a vast difference between this observation and the assertion that James had equated subjective utility with ideal truth. James felt utterly misunderstood.[3] What he had conceived of as the awakening of a new feeling of creative freedom in the cognitive subject was flung back at him as the most reprehensible constriction of all cognition to direct utility in everyday life. Of his occasional use of the term "cash value" to describe the practical consequences by which the truth of a proposition could be verified, some critics even went so far as to charge that this was an involuntary confession of the spirit of commercialism behind his thought, which was said to be inimical to all philosophy and science.

Needless to say, some of the objections raised in the course of the German discussion had at least a rational core. Yet even these—as exemplified by Leonard Nelson's comments made at the World Congress—can be said to amount to a "petitio principii." Where pragmatism set out to overcome the philosophy of consciousness, these critics reconstructed the structure of pragmatism precisely within the framework of the philosophy of consciousness in order then to prove that pragmatism's assertions were untenable in terms of these premises. Where the pragmatist approach challenged the validity of any separation of psychology and logic, the critics arrogantly claimed that this separation could be taken as given. For the German opponents of pragmatism it was unthinkable that valid knowledge would still be possible if cognition were to be regarded as something based entirely on the achievements of concrete, organismic subjects. James's opponents simply ignored his detailed discussion of a concept of "reality" that regarded the latter not as a fixed entity divorced from action but as only being formed in the course of action. It is therefore striking that even those who put forward the more well-founded objections only believed it necessary to reply to individual points, rather than to counter James's theory as a whole.

The reason for this presumably lies in some self-confident assumption of the traditional superiority of German philosophy: the opponent was to be recognized, but should not, of course, be overestimated. The tone adopted was one of a condescension. The serious critics were obviously of the opinion that the Americans were simply not sufficiently well-versed in philosophy and that, although they had strayed up such garden paths as pragmatism, patient instruction would help them to find their way back to the straight and narrow. The less serious critics drew parallels between James and America which were even more direct than this reference to the lack of education in the New World. "We are encountering a new fad in philosophy, this time brought to us from across the ocean, from the land of the dollar, which must be regarded as the ideal of this philosophy. This philosophy degrades the truth to the level of expediency, just as, in days gone by, a similar way of thinking was imported to us from the land of the shopkeepers [i.e., Britain] preaching the reduction of morality to utility." (Gutberlet 1908, p. 437). This point of view took pragmatism to be a typical product of America—in other words, of a country in which the people are "degraded to the status of slaves of materialism, of industry, i.e. of dollars" (ibid., p. 445). Disreputable opportunism, relativism, and irrationalism are the typical epithets for pragmatism. Indeed, the fact that James and pragmatism were combated in the United States too by no means caused critics to falter in this identification of pragmatism with the dollar. Pragmatism, as G. H. Mead later concluded with irony,

> is regarded as a pseudo-philosophic formulation of that most obnoxious American trait, the worship of success; as the endowment of the four-flusher with a faked philosophic passport; the contemptuous swagger of a glib and restless upstart in the company of the mighty but reverent spirits worshiping at the shrine of subsistent entities and timeless truth; . . . a Ford efficiency

> engineer bent on the mass production of philosophical tin lizzies. (Mead 1938, p. 97)

An alternative to this interpretation of pragmatism as crass "Americanism" was offered by those critics who traced all the serious elements of pragmatism back to European sources. Fritz Mauthner saw pragmatism as evidence of the spread of Ernst Mach's ideas in America, and commented: "Pragmatism is another example of an ancient European craft which has been taken over by the Americans although it is held in less high esteem in Europe" (Mauthner 1910, p. 269). Georg Simmel is said to have called pragmatism "the part of Nietzsche which the Americans adopted."[4] In fact, however, despite a few individual contacts (see Thiele 1965), neither Mach nor Nietzsche were particular well-known or influential in the United States at this time (Müller-Freienfels 1913, p. 342).

The few positive reactions to James came from people who enjoyed themselves a marginal status in German academic philosophy. Wilhelm Jerusalem, the aforementioned translator of *Pragmatism,* was a high school teacher in Vienna, who tried in vain to persuade the academic world to take James's ideas seriously. He endeavored to do so by championing the insight that pragmatism focused on the problem of the essence and possibility of theoretical cognition itself, whereas the critics had hitherto failed to recognize this as the problem. Even relatively sympathetic commentators, such as Julius Goldstein and Ludwig Stein, still sprinkled their work with disclaimers in which they distanced themselves from certain aspects. Theodor Lorenz, himself a translator of James's writings who taught in England, was almost the only person to recognize the importance for pragmatism of the debate with Kant (well informed also: Waibel 1915). Lorenz regarded pragmatism as the attempt, influenced by modern psychology, to jettison the rationalist elements in Kant in order to achieve a new synthesis of Kant and Schopenhauer. These formulations were evidence of a profound understanding of the pragmatist problem, and they lent philosophical dignity in Germany to the pragmatists' ambitions. Yet such approaches were nevertheless still inextricably linked to the horizons of traditional German philosophical thought and were thus unable to go as far as to define the differences between the ideas fundamental to pragmatism and those of, say, Schopenhauer.

The most interesting case of a German critic who paid pragmatism its due at an early date was that of Günther Jacoby, a young lecturer at the University of Greifswald. Pragmatism was the subject of Jacoby's inaugural lecture, which was published in 1909. Jacoby was the only person who freed the debate on pragmatism from the confines of a theory of truth. "The aim of this paper is to divert attention from the debate on the pragmatist concept of truth and focus it on a discussion of the pragmatist concept of science" (Jacoby 1909, p. 3). He championed the cause of pragmatism almost as though it were a profession of faith. He dispensed with the most absurd misunderstandings on the part of his contemporaries and put forward the view that pragmatism was a suitable vehicle for drawing conclusions for modern philosophy from scientific thought. He meant this not in the sense that philosophy should be reduced to science, nor certainly in the sense of arbitrary relativism, but rather as recognition of the fact that the advance of science made a transformation of the absolutistic claims of philosophy both possible and necessary. This publication earned Jacoby the attention of William James and a visiting professorship at Harvard in 1910. However, although he lived and taught in Greifswald from that time until 1963, through all the twists and turns of German history, Jacoby is not known as a German pragmatist.

Even as early as the works which date from Jacoby's stay in America we can already detect a distinct change of tone, and by 1912 he seems to have completely lost interest in American philosophy. In that year he delivered a talk to a German-American audience published later as "William James's Attack on German Intellectual Life," in which he referred to the struggle surrounding pragmatism as a struggle for German national identity. James's admiration for the tradition of British empiricism and the skepticism James showed toward Kant and classical German philosophy were presented by Jacoby as a lack of understanding of German "nature." In this light, any remarks James made out of admiration for Germany were bound to seem like proof of the contention that the "inexhaustible power of the German people" was so great that even their enemies were forced to respect them. Jacoby attributed the difference between the Anglo-American and the German philosophical traditions to the difference between two ideals: that of the "gentleman" and that of the "personality." In order to characterize the "gentleman," as personified by James, Jacoby quoted from an American catalogue of "personal qualities having economic value." Thus even this young philosopher had abandoned his early, authentic understanding of pragmatism, and had gone over to interpreting this philosophical current in terms of national stereotypes—in other words, precisely the method of interpretation which he had initially and, still in his comparison of pragmatism with Vaihinger (1912c), vehemently rejected.

One final variation of the treatment of pragmatism was simply to portray it as a less polished version of the fictionalism developed by Hans Vaihinger and the German philosophy of life. (This was the tack taken, for example, by Rickert [Rickert 1920]). Both of these currents—Vaihinger's philosophy of the "as-if" no less than the German philosophy of life—were fundamentally influenced by Nietzsche. This would account for Simmel's totally erroneous conclusion that pragmatism resulted from the American reception of Nietzsche. It would have been more accurate to attribute the misunderstanding of pragmatism to the continued predominance of Nietzschean ideas in the German discussion. To German ears, James's reflections on the theory of truth must have sounded like a repetition of Nietzsche's subversion of the value of truth. To quote Nietzsche:

> The falseness of a judgement is to us not necessarily an objection to a judgement: it is here that our new language perhaps sounds strangest. The question is to what extent it is life-advancing, life-preserving, species-preserving, perhaps even more species-breeding; and our fundamental tendency is to assert that the falsest judgements (to which synthetic judgements *a priori* belong) are the most indispensable to us . . . To recognize untruth as a condition of life: that, to be sure, means to resist customary value-sentiments in a dangerous fashion; and a philosophy which ventures to do so places itself, by that act alone, beyond good and evil. (Nietzsche 1973, pp. 17–18)

Nietzsche doubts the value of truth and forces us to reflect on the tacit premises inherent in the will to truth. Vaihinger sets out to show the importance of fictitious assumptions in science, life, and our worldviews. However, what both men precisely do not do is to call into question the possibility of truth as something which corresponds to the facts. This explains why the German opponents of pragmatism were able to perceive this school as a gross exaggeration of a Nietzschean motif. Whereas Nietzsche, according to this interpretation, encourages us to cast doubts on an antiquated ideal, all that James offers is a shallow denial of the existence of ideals altogether.

The most interesting case of a German thinker who at least took account of this tension between the destruction and the revision of the ideal of truth was none other than Georg Simmel himself. In his 1895 essay "On a Relationship between the Theory of Natural Selection and Epistemology" he had himself described the crucial difference between, on the one hand, a utilitarian theory of truth that did not make use of a revised concept of truth, and on the other, the development of a completely new version of the concept of truth yielded by grounding all epistemology in the actions of the living human being. William James acknowledged this essay as an independent, albeit somewhat crude contribution to the development of pragmatism (see Perry 1936, p. 470). Yet Simmel too did not pursue this course further. For all the motifs borrowed from the philosophy of life, he later seemed to take for granted what was basically the rationalist-intellectualist position on the theory of truth. "Even so-called practical knowledge is of course also theoretical knowledge which is only subsequently used for practical purposes; yet, as knowledge, it remains part of an autonomous order, an ideal realm of truth" (Simmel 1918, p. 162). He is therefore no longer interested in pragmatism as a philosophy in itself, but merely as a phenomenon of modern culture, and here he uses the term "pragmatism" very broadly, not confining it to American authors. He could not resist the temptation to add that American pragmatism was the "most superficial and most limited" branch of this theoretical current. He considers that the cultural motif of pragmatism resides in the striving of modern individuality to dissolve all fixed forms and to return to creative life. What might manifest itself in an obsessive craving for originality could, he maintained, also lead to very serious corresponding phenomena in a wide variety of cultural spheres. According to Simmel, since cognition was seen as particularly autonomous from life, this was a provocation for the modern feel for life. Pragmatism expresses this by dissolving the subject into individual acts of life. In an obvious allusion to Henri Bergson, Simmel pointed out that the philosophy of life went even further, dissolving the object side as well. Thus Simmel regarded pragmatism as a symptom of the modernist abandonment of the principle of some overarching form, yet he was unable to detect in it the germ of what could lead to the development of new forms.

The vigorous controversy surrounding pragmatism prior to the First World War may have attracted attention to this school of thought, but did not gain it any influence. The reduction of pragmatism to a utilitarian theory of truth, or its interpretation as a crass version of the philosophy of life, meant that its profounder motifs remained undetected. Any better understanding of it was also impaired by the fact that these false interpretations were linked to a distinct tendency to be culturally condescending toward America, and by the reference to national stereotypes in order to express philosophical divergences. Those few thinkers who showed at least some indication that they had understood the full significance of pragmatism either found themselves preaching to deaf ears or changed their course. The First World War itself made it even more difficult to carry on a matter-of-fact debate with the thinkers who now belonged to the enemy. In the years leading up to the war, nationalist fever ran higher and higher, progressively undermining free intellectual exchange between nations; and the outbreak of war finally led to all sides indulging in unashamedly one-sided portrayals of the intellectual history of their enemies and interpreting their enemies' conduct during the war as a necessary consequence of some purportedly characteristic national way of thinking. Britain was the main target of German academic chauvinism, but was joined, by 1917 at the latest, by the United States. The main charges leveled against these countries were that they displayed a shopkeeper mentality and were moral hypocrites. In the United States too, numerous analyses of German intellectual history were published claiming that war was the direct natural culmination of such patterns of thought. John Dewey, the former Hegelian who had become a pragmatist, wrote an attack on German thought for its tendency to base itself on a prioris and for the strange coexistence of Kantian ethics and power-political realism. He attributed all these phenomena to the lack of a tradition of a political public sphere in Germany (see Dewey 1915). Although this work certainly deserved to be taken seriously, there were distinct signs that Dewey too was not entirely free of a tendency to indulge in polemical exaggeration. Even in the postwar years, emotions did not really cool down, nor was there a revision of the mutual stereotyping that had become common practice in the field of intellectual relations. We find only occasional evidence of a renewed study of pragmatism in Germany (e.g. Slochower 1927). In much work of the time the verdicts of the prewar period are simply taken up again. Nonetheless, the 1920s marked the start of a new chapter in the story, a chapter which bears the title:

The Hidden Pragmatism of Scheler and Heidegger

What is new about this chapter is the fact that the pragmatic motifs which had been developed autonomously in German thought before the First World War were now expanded by Max Scheler on the one hand and Martin Heidegger on the other to form a philosophy which could be characterized as hidden pragmatism. In Scheler's case, this development also led to an extensive study of pragmatism itself, namely *Erkenntnis und Arbeit* (Cognition and Work), published in 1926. Scheler intended it as a refutation of pragmatism, and for many years it was undoubtedly the most influential German text on the subject. Scheler's background may have been in phenomenology, but unlike Husserl he was not one to devote himself to the patient and ascetic study of the world as given for the cognizing subject. Instead, he sought to apply phenomenology to the whole range of relationships between man and world, thus giving phenomenology an anthropological turn. His central idea in this regard was to conceive of phenomenological reduction itself as an anthropological achievement. This was the clearest manifestation of man's capacity to distance himself both from the given conditions of his environment and from his own instincts and feelings. According to Scheler, it was this capacity which facilitated the factual accuracy of perception, the objectivity of cognition, and self-awareness. This shift of emphasis in phenomenology, together with his vast knowledge of the empirical sciences, enabled Scheler to become the founder of "philosophical anthropology" in Germany in the 1920s.

His confrontation with pragmatism stands in the context both of his anthropological studies and of his attempts to lay the foundations for a sociology of knowledge. His book begins as a severe criticism and a rejection of pragmatism, in which he perpetuates many of the motifs used by the prewar critics. Scheler too shows little concern for debating with the pragmatists, preferring to award points for their achievements and failings. The very title of the study is a clear expression of his underlying idea. "Cognition and Work" is intended to mean that pragmatism falsely universalizes a specific kind of knowledge, namely knowledge in connection with work. The links Scheler forges are not, however, supported by evidence. It is, of course, completely out of the question to suggest, as Scheler does, that Marx had any substantial influence on the pragmatists. Nor did any of the pragmatists attempt of their own accord to establish a connection between cognition and work. "Cognition and Action" would surely have been a more appropriate title for a study of pragmatism. Yet Scheler needs this relationship to "work" because it enables him not only to connect this study to his project of drawing up a "thorough synopsis of the history of science and philosophy *linked to the history of the technical forms of work*" (Scheler 1977, p. 5; my emphasis) but at the same time to show where pragmatism's limitations lie. For Scheler, the "knowledge of domination" or "knowledge of productivity" connected with work is only one of three types of knowledge. The other, superior forms are the knowledge of culture (*Bildungswissen*) and the knowledge of redemption (*Erlösungswissen*). In Scheler's view, pragmatism is a narrow epistemological theory confined to the lowest form of human knowledge, and as such it stands for the universalization of both technology and a calculating rationality in the modern world.

Now it is a relatively simple matter to uncover the distortions and injustices contained in Scheler's portrayal of pragmatism. (For a very good attempt, see Stikkers 1987.) All the pragmatists were themselves religious, or at least held religion in great respect, so they certainly cannot be accused of ignoring the "knowledge of redemption." Equally incomprehensible is Scheler's assertion (Scheler 1977, p. 59) that pragmatism set out to replace metaphysics with positivistic science. Clearly he wrongly equates pragmatism with positivism. A further untenable claim is that in pragmatism the power of imagination plays only a reproductive but not a productive role. In fact, James, for example, was particularly concerned to show the vital significance of imagination for human beings. The major part of Scheler's knowledge of pragmatism was obviously limited to James, and he compounded the latter's ideas with those of German contemporaries in a manner which left them far from clear.

Important though these flaws may be for the subsequent history of the German reception of pragmatism, they are nonetheless not the decisive feature of Scheler's book. For Scheler is at the same time severely critical "of all those who rejected pragmatism outright" (ibid., p. 17). Full of scorn, he distances himself from the typical rejection of the pragmatist approach. Countering the "la science pour la science" argument, which upheld the intrinsic value of acquiring knowledge, he remarks: "The auto-suggestions of scholarly vanity are no answer to a serious philosophical question" (ibid. p. 17). He therefore defends the way pragmatism tackles the issues and respects the degree of awareness and honesty with which the pragmatists abandon the contemplative theoretical self-conception of science. He sees this as a positive step because it is the only way to put an end to the illegitimate occupation of those places in the human intellect which were actually destined to harbor knowledge of culture and redemption (see ibid., p. 21). He gives an extensive account of the relative correctness of pragmatism, and thus of a "motoric" theory of human perception and emotions.

Despite the superficiality of his reception of American thought, Scheler thus elevates the discussion to a new level. He overcomes the reduction of pragmatism to a utilitarian theory of truth, replacing it with another reduction which is at least less restrictive. He thus defines pragmatism as an instrumentalistic conception of action and knowledge, yet is prepared to grant it validity provided that it is embedded in the framework of a personalistic metaphysics and a religious view of the world. As the subsequent history of German "philosophical anthropology" was to show, it was to prove possible to dispense with this metaphysical framework and Scheler's demand for an intuitive cognition of Being. Scheler's contribution therefore formed the basis for further development not only on the part of those who wished to interpret pragmatism and positivism as an expression of "instrumental reason," but also those who, on an anthropological level, stood for an openly declared pragmatism and not merely, like Scheler, for a limited, hidden version.

Nowadays, the idea of viewing Martin Heidegger in connection with hidden pragmatism will come as no great surprise. Several authors (Apel

1962, Sukale 1976, Rorty 1984; cf. the early American reviewers of Heidegger's book: von Wolzogen 1990a, p. 51f.) have already pinpointed correspondences between central Heideggerian concepts—such as "readiness-to-hand"—and the basic ideas of pragmatism, and also between the fundamental anti-Cartesian stance of *Being and Time* and Dewey's *Experience and Nature.* Gethmann even calls *Being and Time* "the earliest conception of consistent pragmatism in the German-speaking world" (Gethmann 1988, p. 143). If this view is correct—and I believe that it is—then it is of interest not only to compare these two forms of pragmatism, but also to investigate Heidegger's reception of American pragmatism. This poses some difficulties, as Heidegger did not usually disclose his sources.

As a student Heidegger seems to have dealt with James's psychology of religion at least indirectly and even with a few of Peirce's writings (see Heidegger 1911–12; von Wolzogen 1990b, p. 81, fn. 27). His knowledge of pragmatism may have been elaborated by listening to Emil Lask's lectures (see Gethmann 1988, p. 270, fn. 53). In a lecture on Aristotle in 1921–22, Heidegger refers to pragmatism in a manner which could certainly be described as sympathetic. The strong influence of Scheler on Heidegger prompted Jürgen Habermas to remark that Heidegger not only combines Dilthey with Husserl, but is also "able to take on the pragmatist motifs of a Max Scheler and apply them to overcoming through historicization the philosophy of the subject" (Habermas 1989, pp. 12f.). It is also possible to detect allusions to pragmatism in *Being and Time* itself. However, if we are to believe a source which has hitherto escaped attention, then the picture changes. In his unpublished autobiography (Baumgarten, undated), Eduard Baumgarten, a German expert on American philosophy, to whom I shall refer in more detail in the following section, records a profusion of condescending or positively hostile remarks by Heidegger on American pragmatism. Heidegger counters Baumgarten's enthusiasm for Dewey by declaring that the latter was not a philosopher in the sense of the great tradition of philosophy, and that American thought was "philosophically sub-standard." How are we to make sense of Heidegger's consistent pragmatism in certain individual respects in the light of this rejection of American pragmatism as a whole?

The answer to this question seems to lie in the fact that although Heidegger makes the turn toward pragmatism, he does not apply it to the relationship of philosophy to science and to politics itself. For him, the scope to which philosophy lays claim remains as wide as ever—there is no trace of the "democratic" modesty of the philosopher in recognition of the multiplicity of individual scientific disciplines and in recognition of the plurality of a nation's citizens, such as John Dewey's work embodies. His attempts to ground cognition itself in action are nonetheless grandiose—although he deliberately refrains from using the term "action," as he feels that this (see Heidegger 1977, p. 300) underestimates the passivity of resistances and reproduces the old division of theory and practice; he consequently prefers neologisms such as "being-in-the-world" and "care." Gethmann demonstrates how radical Heidegger's pragmatic thought was by referring to the latter's analysis of judgment and science, as well as by extending the question to ask whether there is some form of normativity inherent in action itself. However, even he comes to the conclusion that the solipsistic methodology of Heidegger's analysis of action, in which the experience of freedom is not itself constituted in an intersubjectively binding manner, results in the "concept of action in *Being and Time* not providing a possible means of access to the philosophical foundations of a republican-democratic understanding of politics" (Gethmann 1988, p. 170). Whatever our interpretation of the philosophical roots of Heidegger's biographical affinity to National Socialism, the fact remains that his "pragmatism" is found wanting at precisely the point at which American pragmatism establishes an inherent link to the idea of democracy.

Pragmatism as a Fascist Ideology of the Deed

Even today, Heidegger's affinity to National Socialism continues to be the subject of heated debate. A much less well-known fact is that it was American pragmatism, and not Heidegger's own version of a pragmatic philosophy, which was adopted as the ideology of a whole group of German intellectuals who sympathized with National Socialism, although it should be said that they did not go along with Nazism's worst, most primitive aspects, such as the ideology of race. For these intellectuals, pragmatism served the function of an activistic ideology. There was some precedence in fascism's appropriation of pragmatism: after all, Mussolini cited not only Georges Sorel—who had himself written a book on pragmatism—but also William James as important sources for his own ideas (see Perry 1936, p. 575). The two outstanding figures in this group of German intellectuals were Arnold Gehlen and Eduard Baumgarten—the former a pragmatist anthropologist, the latter a specialist in American intellectual history. Yet they were by no means the only ones to fit into this category. The assertion (Grathoff 1987, p. 134) that no relevant works on pragmatism were published in the German-speaking region during the Third Reich is thus quite absurd. No one in Germany up until that time had shown a better understanding of pragmatism than Baumgarten and Gehlen.

In his early idealist and existentialist writings, Arnold Gehlen (cf. Böhler 1973; Rehberg 1985), like many others, rejected pragmatism as a banal philosophy of adaptation. However, by 1935 at the latest, his opinion had completely changed. At this time, Gehlen began to develop his anthropology, which was finally presented in systematic form in 1940. This anthropology, following that of Scheler but radically breaking with the latter's residual metaphysics, is devised as an empirical philosophy of the human ability to act. This program is largely modeled on pragmatism, and, so it seems, particularly on John Dewey's book *Human Nature and Conduct.* Schelsky, who was influenced by Gehlen, wrote in 1941 that Dewey's anthropology was the first anthropology of any kind to take the unity of the act as its point of departure, and, instead of taking man as an amalgamation of various basic elements, to attempt to think of man reconstructively, starting from the conditions of the possibility of his highest cultural achievements. In order to realize this program, Gehlen draws on and condenses a wide range of information from the fields of biology, ethnology, and psychology. At the same time—and this is particularly evident in his postwar adaptation of George Herbert Mead, whose significance he was probably the first in Germany to recognize—he prunes pragmatism of its intersubjective-social aspects in order to be able to fit his anthropology of action into an authoritarian theory of the institution. Owing to this latent existence in Gehlen's anthropology, the influence of pragmatism in Germany had now become difficult to decipher.

The most remarkable case of a National Socialist adaptation of pragmatism is that of Eduard Baumgarten. He was a nephew of Max Weber, and for some time a friend and assistant to Martin Heidegger. During a six-year stay in the United States between 1924 and 1929, mainly in Madison, Wisconsin, he had acquired a more thorough knowledge of the history of American philosophy than anyone else in Germany. For a long time the only evidence of these prolonged studies was a sparse number of publications in journals. Then, in 1936, the first volume of his work *Die geistigen Grundlagen des amerikanischen Gemeinwesens* (The Intellectual Foundations of the American Polity) appeared, to be followed in 1938 by volume 2. Both volumes contained portraits of American thinkers. The first was devoted to Benjamin Franklin; the second to Ralph Waldo Emerson, William James, and John Dewey. Baumgarten explained this surprising combination by putting forward the bold assertion that by concentrating on these four he had dealt with the main figures of American pragmatism.

Needless to say, by including Franklin and Emerson in the circle of pragmatists he robbed American intellectual history of precisely its internal tensions, making it appear as a unilinear evolution, or a gradual emanation from some essentially American way of being. Baumgarten's motivation for not interpreting Franklin as a utilitarian could only have been to rebuff Weber's interpretation in his work on the Protestant ethic. Indeed, Baumgarten mentions in his autobiography that a positive critique of the motif of asceticism was one of the most important driving forces behind his work. It is also clear that, from a philological point of view, Emerson does not belong among the ranks of the pragmatists. Nonetheless, this classification does enable Baumgarten to arrive at some surprising insights into the differences between Emerson and continental European idealist-romantic currents which are often claimed to have influenced him. Yet what Baumgarten wrote on James, and particularly on Dewey, was infinitely superior to all previous German interpretations. The first time I read it, I therefore felt that the National Socialist objections to Dewey which were interspersed in the text must have been opportunistic gestures to appease the censors (in this way: Dahms 1987, p. 183 f.). However, a look at his preparatory publications and the framework in which the book was written soon showed this assumption to be false: when Baumgarten praises the spirit of pragmatism, he really does so from a National Socialist standpoint.

In order to be able to do so, he first has to reinterpret the meaning of the key concepts in the pragmatist tradition with their normative political contents, and those in American thought in general, in such a manner as to accommodate them to the profoundly anti-Western stance of the Nazis. The most important of these is the concept of democracy. In an essay written in 1934 entitled "Amerikanische Philosophie und deutscher Glaube" (American Philosophy and German Faith), he points out that in Germany democracy carries the stigma of decay and national weakness. "The concept of democracy in England and America is, by contrast, associated with memories of the nation's greatest glories. In those countries it is a concept of ascendancy, of strength, of enthusiasm" (Baumgarten 1934b, p. 98). He explicitly emphasizes Hitler's belief that true democracy meant a state based on a strong "Führer" legitimized by plebiscites. American individualism—as exemplified by the pioneer settler with axe in hand, out in all weather—is distinguished (in anti-intellectual manner) from the "self-opinionated virtuosity of the intellect" (ibid., p. 99). The Americans' liberalism, he claims, is not aimed at creating some arbitrary state of egoistic permissiveness, but is geared toward a system of unbureaucratic cooperatives. And pacifism in America has nothing in common with "ignominious defeatism." Even the much vaunted American spirit of tolerance has its limits, when "absolute faith in the highest value of American society" itself is at stake (Baumgarten 1938, p. xi). This admiration and sympathy for America is genuine, even though the praise has a sting in its tail.

Baumgarten associates his experience at the front during the First World War with the Americans' experience of the frontier, and sees Hitler's seizure of power in 1933 as the start of a new pioneer age. This enthusiasm, which is hard to bear, permeates the very language he uses. When portraying William James's achievements in the field of psychology, he repeatedly lapses into military metaphors culled from the First World War. The most horrifying formulation is to be found in his analysis of the necessarily selective nature of decisions: "Leadership for James means: allowing *one* party in life to gain victory by killing off the other party, or possibly *many* other parties" (Baumgarten 1938, p. 155). From around 1943 onward, Baumgarten began to campaign actively for an alliance of the Third Reich with Britain and the United States against Russia, emphasizing the affinity between National Socialism and the Anglo-Saxon traditions as demonstrated in his academic work. Even after 1945 he attributed Hitler's failure to the latter's lack of a technical understanding of the manner in which the principle of democracy functioned in society.

It is certainly not surprising that, in the international context of research on pragmatism, a book such as this should have sunk into oblivion. Baumgarten's perverse love of his subject, however, enables him to gain such a wealth of insights, particularly concerning anthropology and the theory of value, that even today parts of the book have yet to be matched by any other German thought on the subject.

His breadth of knowledge meant that he was the decisive figure who acted as a catalyst, conveying the ideas of pragmatism to fascist intellectuals. Gehlen had also studied his work. Indeed, the National Socialist reception of pragmatism can be detected in a variety of works. Helmut Schelsky, who wrote a knowledgeable review of Baumgarten's book in 1940, presented a *Habilitationsschrift* that same year on Thomas Hobbes, whom Max Scheler had already described as the "true grandfather of pragmatism" (Scheler 1977, p. 42). His entire analysis of Hobbes's anthropology is influenced by John Dewey's anthropology and the latter's study on Hobbes. He concurs with Dewey's decision to regard

Hobbes as a proto-pragmatist, and also accepts Dewey's thesis that an unresolved contradiction runs through Hobbes's work between the sovereign's absolute claim to power and the conception of scientific politics. Unlike Dewey, the "inveterate democrat," however, Schelsky sets out to resolve this contradiction in favor of the creative power of deeds by the state. In 1937, Hans Lipps, a friend and colleague of Baumgarten, member of the SS, presented a study on the parallels between pragmatism and existentialist philosophy. Gerhard Lehmann, too, seems to take for granted that pragmatism was an important influence on Heidegger, and praises Baumgarten's pioneering achievement in furthering the understanding of this, a "racially kindred" philosophy. He thus goes beyond the mere appropriation of pragmatism by the spirit of fascism by interpreting the similarities as a consequence of racial affinity. As a philosophy of action, pragmatism became caught up in the enthusiasm for decisiveness, action, and power which characterized National Socialist intellectuals. Its democratic ideal was redefined in terms of the ideology of a national racial community and derived from common ancient Germanic origins.

Exiled Intellectuals in the Grip of Prejudice

If even the intellectuals in the Third Reich were able to overcome the faults of the earlier German reception of pragmatism, how much better would those in exile have been able to do so. At least, this would seem to be the natural assumption to make about the pragmatism discussion among German intellectuals who had been forced to flee their country. Those intellectuals who had emigrated to America would seem to have had a particularly favorable opportunity either to make up for inadequacies in their knowledge of pragmatism or to revise the prejudices they may have brought with them. Yet, the extent to which this actually occurred is astonishingly slight. It is, of course, possible that the enthusiasm shown by individual Nazi intellectuals for pragmatism prompted emigrés to adopt a negative stance vis-à-vis the latter, but I believe that this can be ruled out. The fact is that only in a very few cases can traces of a more profound reception of pragmatism be discerned. Often there is no attempt at a really thoroughgoing discussion, even despite obvious affinities.

This applies, for example, to Ernst Cassirer (1944), who also draws on Dewey's work in his anthropology, yet fails to probe any deeper into the affinity between the semiotics of pragmatism and his own anthropology, which was geared toward investigating the human capacity for symbolization.

While in exile, Karl Mannheim came increasingly close to a pragmatist understanding of politics, but his untimely death prevented him from fully developing this nascent conception.

Hannah Arendt spent her time in exile in the United States acquiring a profound understanding of the specific nature of the American Revolution and American history. She therefore had every chance of developing a keen understanding of pragmatism, especially if one accepts that pragmatism is indeed a part of America's republican tradition. In the only piece of evidence which suggests a direct concern with the pragmatists—a review on Dewey—what predominates is, however, not endorsement, but rather the charge that Dewey is anachronistic. Arendt is distressed by the fact that Dewey's social critique is no longer appropriate to the new experience of totalitarianism. She simply cannot understand his polemic against laissez-faire society and the pathetic hopes he places in the enlightening role of social science, in view of the fact that "a glance at today's or yesterday's newspaper invariably teaches us that hell can be properly established only through the very opposite of laissez faire, through scientific planning" (Arendt 1946, p. 448). Despite the seriousness of this criticism, and despite Arendt's apparently very positive attitude toward Dewey's writings on the logic of science, she makes no attempt to appreciate Dewey's political philosophy in terms of its original experiential background.

In *The Principle of Hope*, Ernst Bloch provides one of the crassest examples of a Marxist analysis of pragmatism that takes on all the baggage of previous misunderstandings. In a passage of central importance to his argument, on Marx's Eleventh Thesis on Feuerbach, Bloch attempts to harden the contours of the Marxian understanding of the relationship between theory and practice by contrasting it to that of pragmatism. Marxism must be kept free of pragmatism because "the latter stems from a region which is utterly alien to Marxism, from a region which is hostile to it, intellectually inferior, ultimately downright disreputable" (Bloch 1986, p. 274). The subsequent description of pragmatism shows that Bloch too conceives of pragmatism as a theory of truth in which truth is synonymous with the "utility of ideas for business." Whereas James himself might still have had humane features, Bloch claims that "after James, pragmatism in America and in the whole of the world-bourgeoisie quickly showed itself for what it is: the final agnosticism of a society stripped of any will towards the truth" (ibid.). The transition from this "bustlers' ideology" to Nazi ideology was therefore, according to Bloch, only a logical progression. These are the same prejudices, coming this time from the Left, that were more likely to be draped in the colors of

German nationalism prior to the First World War. Just as in the polemic of those German professors, Bloch rushes to defend the rationalistic causal relationship between truth and utility against the assault of pragmatism: "In Marx a thought is not true because it is useful, but it is useful because it is true" (ibid., p. 277). In an article occasioned by the centenary of William James's birth in 1942, Bloch puts forward a somewhat more balanced view of pragmatism. Here he is concerned to draw attention to "a different side of William James." Yet even in this assessment, pragmatism is portrayed as irrationalism and decadence. In this text, Bloch also touches on James's notion of reality as something directed toward a horizon of possibilities, an idea which should have fitted in well with his own thinking. Yet Bloch is all too quick to attribute this to America as an erstwhile romantic country with wide open spaces and long clear roads, instead of taking account of the philosophical context of James's metaphysics and relating it to the theory of truth which he was combating.

Max Horkheimer's book *The Eclipse of Reason* is the most comprehensive attempt on the part of an exiled intellectual to come to terms with pragmatism. Another member of his school, Herbert Marcuse, also undertook a detailed analysis of several of John Dewey's writings. Yet anyone who expects to find an openness on the part of members of the exiled Frankfurt School to the thought and society of Franklin Delano Roosevelt's America is in for a disappointment. As I have analysed in detail elsewhere,[5] this was definitely not the case. Whatever the subject, be it political theory, social psychology, cultural theory or philosophy, the members of the Frankfurt School were mainly influenced by a Marxist functionalism which forced them to interpret the United States as the epitome of capitalism. In his study of pragmatism, Horkheimer approximates Scheler's position to such an extent that it almost appears doubtful whether he did any independent analysis of the American thinkers at all. Like Scheler, he perceives there to be an intimate connection between pragmatism and positivism, and regards both as expressions of a universalization of instrumental rationality. This critique, which remains unconvincing even when judged on its own terms, is linked to far-reaching political conclusions in which the universalization of instrumental rationality is held to play an important role in the imposition of modern totalitarianism.

Even Alfred Schütz, who had begun to concern himself with James long before his emigration and obviously founded his assessment of pragmatism on a wider base of knowledge, nevertheless remained strongly influenced by Scheler. His extensive study on James's concept of the "stream of thought" aims, above all, at pointing out similarities between

Husserl and James and the "extraordinary parallels between their theories of attention, of spatial and temporal perception, and of reality" (Schütz 1971b, p. 46). Schütz hopes to demonstrate to an American public that "phenomenology is not entirely foreign to this country." The thrust of this work is therefore not the significance of pragmatism but rather the proximity of James's psychology to Husserl's phenomenology. It is characteristic of Schütz that he ignores the fact that John Dewey abandoned precisely James's concept of "stream of thought" in favor of a circuit of action involving the organism and its environment. Where Schütz leans on the work of Dewey and Mead he does so without connecting them. Moreover, the fundamental criticisms which he levels against pragmatism are based on the tack Scheler took. Echoing the latter, Schütz ascribes to pragmatism the tendency to generalize the instrumental attitudes of everyday life and thus to suppress other forms in which reality may be constituted, such as through imagination or contemplation. "Pragmatism is therefore not a philosophy which deals with the totality of human existence, but rather a description of our life on the level of that which is taken unquestioningly to be reality" (Schütz 1971a, p. 169; for an excellent analysis of this, see Srubar 1988). It is extraordinary that such a sentence, which is nothing other than completely false, could nevertheless have been written after the publication of Dewey's *Art as Experience* in 1934.

In other words, a brief survey of some of the major German intellectual figures in exile shows that in most cases the mark made on their thought by the time spent in pre-Nazi Germany ran so deep that it continued to determine their relationship to pragmatism. It accounted both for their relative lack of interest in pragmatism and for the positions they took on the subject. Enthusiasm on the part of some National Socialist intellectuals and rejection on the part of the emigrés: to the pragmatists—assuming they were aware of the situation at all—it must have seemed as if the world had been stood on its head.

Misunderstandings Slowly Resolved

It was therefore not until the period after the Second World War that an opportunity arose to revise the prejudices which had become ever more deeply ingrained. This was made more difficult, however, by the fact that pragmatism had meanwhile itself lost its hegemony in the United States, having been marginalized in philosophy by logical positivism and an analytical philosophy of language. Despite the intensity with which the younger generation of academics in Germany had become receptive to Western thought, they therefore focused not on pragmatism but rather on these more recent, less controversial currents. The first works to be published showed no radical break with the tradition of German academic reception of pragmatism, still perpetuating many of the misunderstandings. As early as 1946, Schelsky wrote a paper in which he—like Baumgarten and others prior to 1945—used the example of pragmatism in order to play the Anglo-Saxon sense of freedom off against the French conception of republic and democracy. For a short time during 1949, a controversy surrounding Baumgarten's writings flared up in the pages of the American-oriented periodical *Der Monat,* only to subside again quickly. In East Germany, for the duration of the German Democratic Republic's existence, pragmatism continued to be written off as a typical expression of imperialism. Here, the situation was strongly influenced by Lukács's remarks in the introduction to *The Destruction of Reason* (1984) in which he attacks James for being a crass irrationalist subjectivist. In the German Democratic Republic, an assessment of pragmatism proper was never forthcoming: handbooks simply passed on a tradition of most vulgar prejudices. 1957 saw the translation of an unspeakable book on the subject by an American Stalinist named Wells.

Positive evaluations were presented to West German readers by individual emigrés, such as Siegfried Marck (1951) and particularly Ludwig Marcuse (1959), yet these men made little impact. The same is true of occasional dissertations (e.g. Schmidt 1959), despite their altogether solid foundations. The most significant evidence of progress in the reception of pragmatism was Jürgen von Kempski's slender volume on Peirce which appeared in 1952. Kempski—who also had a National Socialist past—had already called for a "retrial in the case of pragmatism" in Germany in 1937. Whereas the image of pragmatism had in the past so often been dominated by references to James's theory of truth, Kempski's postwar book was now the first ever serious attempt in Germany to revise this image by means of a careful reconstruction of Peirce's logic of abduction. There had already been a few isolated attempts in this direction before the war (cf. Scholz 1934; Burkamp 1938). Admittedly, even Kempski adjudged Peirce's misunderstandings of Kant to be systematic and not only philological flaws, as though this were a self-evident fact. Similarities between the Erlangen School of Constructivism and pragmatism appear to stem from Baumgarten's influence on Kamlah in their Königsberg years (Gethmann 1991, p. 68f.).

The real breakthrough which gave rise to a new German discussion of pragmatism did not therefore take place until the late 1960s. The main credit for this must be accorded to Karl-Otto Apel and Jürgen Habermas. And here my history ends, without explaining in detail how the misunderstandings that had been passed down from generation to generation were finally overcome. There can be no doubt that Karl-Otto Apel's comprehensive reconstruction of Peirce has set the standards for all present-day assessments of pragmatism. Jürgen Habermas, through his portrayal of Peirce in *Knowledge and Human Interests* and as a result of the major significance he attaches to George Herbert Mead in the development of his own theory of communicative action, has been responsible for drawing renewed attention to these two American thinkers. Further extensive studies have since appeared on Peirce and Mead, yet interest in James, which had been so great before the First World War, has not been rekindled.

The most spectacular feature of the present situation is, however, the continued ignorance of John Dewey's philosophy. To my mind, no other thinker of such intellectual stature has been so consistently neglected as Dewey. Even Apel and Habermas only mention Dewey's work in passing. Apel presumably considers that Peirce's ideas correspond more closely to his own project of a semiotic *transformation* of transcendental philosophy than those of John Dewey, who was more concerned to *overcome* transcendental philosophy, and whom Apel misleadingly treats as a relativist. However, in the field of social philosophy, it is Dewey more than the others who is a potential source of inspiration today. Which is why there is very definitely an open end to the story I have been relating here—and a moral.

Notes

1. It was necessary to collate a wide range of material as the basis of this essay in order to go beyond Oehler's important but all too brief observations (Oehler 1981) and in order to avoid the false conclusions drawn by Grathoff (1987). I am indebted to many colleagues for their suggestions regarding material, in particular James Campbell, Carl Friedrich Gethmann, Uwe Henning, Axel Honneth, Klaus Christian Köhnke, Karl-Siegbert Rehberg, Gerhard Schäfer, and Christoph von Wolzogen. I would like to thank Ronald Hermann for his help in tracing the material. I would also be grateful for suggestions as to further examples of the German reception of pragmatism which have so far escaped my attention.

2. I give a survey of this discussion, together with my own assessment, in my essay "The Creativity of Action and the Intersubjectivity of Reason" elsewhere in this volume. See particularly note 10 there.

3. Perry (1936, p. 468) cites the evidence of numerous letters which express this feeling of being misunderstood: "but the pragmatism that lives inside of me is so different from that of which I succeed in wakening the idea inside of other people, that theirs makes me feel like cursing God and dying."

4. This comment, made verbally, is quoted by Rudolf Pannwitz in K. Gassen and M. Landmann (eds.): *Buch des Dankes an Georg Simmel* (Book in Gratitude to Georg Simmel) (Berlin, 1958), p. 240.

5. See my essay "An Underestimated Alternative: America and the Limits of 'Critical Theory'" (in this volume). See there also references to the corresponding literature.

Bibliography

Apel, Karl Otto. 1962. "Wittgenstein und Heidegger: Die Frage nach dem Sinn von Sein und der Sinnlosigkeitsverdacht gegen alle Metaphysik," in Apel, *Transformation der Philosophie*, vol. 1, Frankfurt 1973, pp. 225–75.

———. 1967. "Der philosophische Hintergrund der Entstehung des Pragmatismus bei Charles Sanders Peirce," in Charles S. Peirce, *Schriften* I. Frankfurt, pp. 13–153.

———. 1970. "Peirces Denkweg vom Pragmatismus zum Pragmatizismus," in Charles S. Peirce, *Schriften* II. Frankfurt, pp. 11–211.

Arendt, Hannah. 1946. "The Ivory Tower of Common Sense: Review of 'Problems of Men' by John Dewey," *The Nation*, Oct. 19, 1946.

Baumgarten, Eduard. 1934a. "Die pragmatische und instrumentale Philosophie John Deweys," *Neue Jahrbücher für Wissenschaft und Jugendbildung* 9, pp. 236–48.

———. 1934b. "Amerikanische Philosophie und deutscher Glaube," *Zeitschrift für französischen und englischen Unterricht* 33, pp. 96–102.

———. 1936. *Benjamin Franklin. Die geistigen Grundlagen des amerikanischen Gemeinwesens*, vol. 1. Frankfurt.

———. 1936–37. "John Dewey," *Internationale Zeitschrift für Erziehung* 5, pp. 81–97, pp. 407–30; 6, pp. 177–200.

———. 1938. *Der Pragmatismus (R. W. Emerson, W. James, J. Dewey). Die geistigen Grundlagen des amerikanischen Gemeinwesens*, vol. 2. Frankfurt.

———. 1949–50. "James und die militärische Ausdrucksweise," *Der Monat* 2, pp. 327–28.

———. 1958. "Amerikanische Philosophie," in P. Hartwig and W. Schellberg (eds.), *Amerikakunde*. Frankfurt, pp. 162–99.

———. Undated. *Spielräume unter Hitlers Herrschaft*. Unpublished manuscript.

Bloch, Ernst. 1942. "Eine andere Seite bei William James," in Bloch, *Gesamtausgabe*, vol. 10 (*Philosophische Aufsätze zur objektiven Phantasie*). Frankfurt, 1969, pp. 60–65.

———. 1986. *The Principle of Hope*, tr. N. Plaice, S. Plaice, and P. Knight. Oxford: Blackwell, 1986.

Bloch, Werner. 1913. "Der Pragmatismus von Schiller und James," *Zeitschrift für Philosophie und philosophische Kritik* 152, pp. 1–41 and pp. 145–214.

Böhler, Dietrich. 1973. "Arnold Gehlen: Die Handlung," in J. Speck (ed.), *Grundprobleme der großen Philosophen: Philosophie der Gegenwart II*. Göttingen, pp. 230–80.

Bohnsack, Fritz. 1976. *Erziehung zur Demokratie. John Deweys Pädagogik und ihre Bedeutung für die Reform unserer Schule*. Ravensburg.

Boutroux, Emile. 1912. *William James*. Leipzig.

Brandenburg, Karl Heinz. 1942. *Kunst als Qualität der Handlung: John Deweys Grundlegung der Ästhetik*. Phil. dissertation. Königsberg.

Burkamp, Wilhelm. 1938. *Wirklichkeit und Sinn*, vol. 2: *Das subjektive Recht des Sinns über die Wirklichkeit*. Berlin.

Cassirer, Ernst. 1944. *An Essay on Man*. London.

Dahms, Hans-Joachim. 1987. "Aufstieg und Ende der Lebensphilosophie: Das philosophische Seminar der Universität Göttingen zwischen 1917 and 1950," in: Heinrich Becker et al. (eds.), *Die Universität Göttingen unter dem Nationalsozialismus.* München, pp. 169–99.

Dewey, John. 1915. *German Philosophy and Politics.* New York.

Eggenschwyler, W. 1913. "War Nietzsche Pragmatist?" in *Archiv für Geschichte der Philosophie* 26, pp. 35–47.

Elsenhans, Theodor (ed.). 1909. *Bericht über den III. Internationalen Kongreß für Philosophie in Heidelberg 1.–15. September 1908.* Heidelberg.

Engler, Ulrich. 1989. "Dewey und Heidegger: Wider den Primat des Kognitiven," in Clemens Bellut and Ulrich Müller-Schöll (eds.), *Mensch und Moderne.* Würzburg, pp. 355–71.

Gehlen, Arnold. 1940. *Der Mensch. Seine Natur und seine Stellung in der Welt.* Frankfurt, 1971.

Gethmann, Carl Friedrich, 1987. "Vom Bewußtsein zum Handeln: Pragmatische Tendenzen in der Deutschen Philosophie der ersten Jahrzehnte des 20. Jahrhunderts," in H. Stachowiak (ed.), *Pragmatik. Handbuch pragmatischen Denkens.* Hamburg, pp. 202–32.

———. 1988. "Heideggers Konzeption des Handelns in *Sein und Zeit,*" In A. Gethmann-Siefert and O. Pöggeler (eds.), *Heidegger und die praktische Philosophie.* Frankfurt, pp. 140–76.

———. 1991. "Phänomenologie, Lebensphilosophie und Konstruktive Wissenschaftstheorie: Eine historische Skizze zur Vorgeschichte der Erlanger Schule," in Gethmann (ed.), *Lebenswelt und Wissenschaft.* Bonn, pp. 28–77.

Goldstein, Julius. 1911. *Wandlungen in der Philosophie der Gegenwart.* Leipzig.

Gould, James. 1970. "R. B. Perry on the Origin of American and European Pragmatism," *Journal of the History of Philosophy* 8, pp. 432–50.

Grathoff, Richard. 1987. "Zur gegenwärtigen Rezeption von George Herbert Mead," *Philosophische Rundschau* 34, pp. 131–45.

Grünewald, Max. 1925. *Simmels Philosophie mit besonderer Berücksichtigung ihrer Beziehungen zum Pragmatismus.* Phil. dissertation. Breslau.

Gutberlet, C. 1908. "Der Pragmatismus," *Philosophisches Jahrbuch* 21, pp. 437–58.

Habermas, Jürgen. 1972. *Knowledge and Human Interests,* tr. J. Shapiro. Boston.

———. 1989. "Heidegger-Werk und Weltanschauung," in Victor Farías, *Heidegger und der Nationalsozialismus.* Frankfurt, pp. 11–45.

Heidegger, Martin. 1911–12. "Religionspsychologie und Unterbewußtsein," in *Der Akademiker* 4, no. 5, pp. 66–68.

———. 1977. *Sein und Zeit.* Tübingen. (English title: *Being and Time.* 1962. Tr. J. Macquarrie and E. Robinson. Oxford.)

Herms, Eilert. 1977. *Radical Empiricism: Studien zur Psychologie, Metaphysik und Religionstheorie William James'.* Gütersloh.

———. 1979. *Nachwort zu William James, Die Vielfalt religiöser Erfahrung.* Olten, pp. 481–521.

Husserl, Edmund. 1910–11. *Philosophie als strenge Wissenschaft.* Frankfurt, 1965.

Jacoby, Günther. 1909. *Der Pragmatismus: Neue Bahnen in der Wissenschaftslehre des Auslands.* Leipzig.

———. 1912a. "William James' Angriff auf das deutsche Geisteswesen," *Die Grenzboten* 71, pp. 109–15.

———. 1912b. "William James und das deutsche Geistesleben," *Die Grenzboten* 71, pp. 212-20.

———. 1912c: "Der amerikanische Pragmatismus und die Philosophie des Als Ob," *Zeitschrift für Philosophie und philosophische Kritik* 147, pp. 172–84.

Jerusalem, Wilhelm. 1908. "Der Pragmatismus: Eine neue philosophische Methode," *Deutsche Literaturzeitung* 29, no. 4, cols. 197–206.

———. 1910. Review of G. Jacoby, "Der Pragmatismus," *Deutsche Liteaturzeitung* 31, no. 13, cols. 789–92.

———. 1922. "Meine Wege und Ziele," In R. Schmidt (ed.), *Die deutsche Philosophie der Gegenwart in Selbstdarstellungen,* vol. 3. Leipzig, pp. 53–98.

Kempski, Jürgen von. 1937. "Der Pragmatismus," *Deutsches Adelsblatt* 55, cols. 1502–5; cols. 1542–44.

———. 1952. *Charles Sanders Peirce und der Pragmatismus.* Cologne.

Lehmann, Gerhard. 1939. Review of Baumgarten, *Internationale Zeitschrift für Erziehung* 8, pp. 65–67.

Leithäuser, Joachim. 1948–49. "William James und der Barwert der Philosophie," *Der Monat* 1, pp. 26–33.

Lipps, Hans. 1937. "Pragmatismus und Existenzphilosophie," in Lipps, *Werke,* vol. 5: *Die Wirklichkeit des Menschen.* Frankfurt, 1977, pp. 38–54.

Löffelholz, Thomas. 1961. *Die Rechtsphilosophie des Pragmatismus: Eine kritische Studie.* Meisenheim.

Lorenz, Theodor. 1908. "Der Pragmatismus," *Internationale Wochenschrift für Wissenschaft, Kunst und Technik* 2, cols. 943–90.

———. 1909. "Das Verhältnis des Pragmatismus zu Kant," *Kant-Studien* 14, pp. 8–44.

Lukács, Georg. 1984. "Über den Irrationalismus als internationale Erscheinung in der imperialistischen Periode," in Lukács, *Die Zerstörung der Vernunft.* Berlin, pp. 5–29. (English title: "On Irrationalism as an International Phenomenon in the Imperialist Period," in Lukács, *Destruction of Reason.* 1980. Tr. D. Fernbach. Atlantic Highlands, N.J.)

MacEachran, John. 1910. *Pragmatismus: Eine neue Richtung der Philosophie.* Leipzig.

Marck, Siegfried. 1951. *Der amerikanische Pragmatismus in seinen Beziehungen zum kritischen Idealismus und zur Existenzphilosophie.* Wilhelmshaven.

Marcuse, Ludwig. 1955–56: "Eine Theorie der Praxis: Amerikanischer und deutscher Pragmatismus," *Der Monat* 8, pp. 33–45.

———. 1959. *Amerikanisches Philosophieren. Pragmatisten—Polytheisten—Tragiker.* Hamburg.

Mauthner, Fritz. 1910. "Pragmatismus," in *Wörterbuch der Philosophie.* Munich.

Mead, George Herbert. 1938. *The Philosophy of the Act.* Chicago.

Müller, Gustav E. 1936. *Amerikanische Philosophie.* Stuttgart.

Müller-Freienfels, Richard. 1908. "William James und der Pragmatismus," in *Philosophische Wochenschrift und Literaturzeitung* 9, pp. 14–27.

———. 1913. "Nietzsche und der Pragmatismus," in *Archiv für Geschichte der Philosophie* 26, pp. 339–58.

Nietzsche, Friedrich. 1973. *Beyond Good and Evil,* tr. R. J. Hollingdale. Harmondsworth.

Oehler, Klaus. 1981. "Notes on the Reception of American Pragmatism in Germany, 1899–1925," *Transactions of the Charles Sanders Peirce Society* 17, pp. 25–35.

Perry, Ralph Barton. 1936. *The Thought and Character of William James,* 2 vols. London.

Rehberg, Karl-Siegbert. 1985. "Die Theorie der Intersubjektivität als eine Lehre vom

Menschen: G. H. Mead und die deutsche Tradition der 'Philosophischen Anthropologie,'" In. H. Joas (ed.), *Das Problem der Intersubjektivität.* Frankfurt, pp. 60–92.

Rein, E. 1910. *Erkenntnistheorie.* Leipzig.

Richey, Homer. 1935. *Die Überwindung der Subjektivität in der empirischen Philosophie Diltheys und Deweys.* Phil. dissertation. Göttingen.

Rickert, Heinrich. 1920. *Die Philosophie des Lebens.* Tübingen.

Rorty, Richard. 1979. *Philosophy and The Mirror of Nature.* Oxford.

———. 1984. "Heidegger wider die Pragmatisten," *Neue Hefte für Philosophie* 23, pp. 1–22.

Scheler, Max. 1977. *Erkenntnis und Arbeit: Eine Studie über Wert und Grenzen des pragmatischen Motivs in der Erkenntnis der Welt.* Frankfurt. (Identical to M. Scheler, 1960: *Werke,* vol. 8: *Die Wissensformen und die Gesellschaft.* Bern, pp. 191–382.)

Schelsky, Helmut. 1940. Review of Baumgarten, *Die Tatwelt* 16, pp. 27–30.

———. 1941. *Thomas Hobbes.* Berlin, 1981.

———. 1946. *Das Freiheitswollen der Völker und die Idee des Planstaates.* Karlsruhe.

Schlick, Moritz. 1918. *Allgemeine Erkenntnislehre.* Berlin.

Schmidt, Hermann. 1959. *Der Begriff der Erfahrungskontinuität bei William James und seine Bedeutung für den amerikanischen Pragmatismus.* Heidelberg.

Scholz, Heinrich, 1934. "Review of Charles Sanders Peirce," *Collected Papers I–II, Deutsche Literaturzeitung* 55, no. 9, cols. 392–95.

———. 1936. Review of Charles Sanders Peirce, *Collected Papers III–V, Deutsche Literaturzeitung* 57, no. 4, cols. 137–44.

Schütz, Alfred. 1971a. *Das Problem der Relevanz.* (English title: *Reflections on the Problem of Relevance.* 1970. New Haven.)

———. 1971b. "William James's Concept of the 'Stream of Thought' Phenomenologically Interpreted," in A. Schütz, *Collected Papers,* vol. 3. The Hague, pp. 1–14.

Simmel, Georg. 1895. "Über eine Beziehung der Selektionslehre zur Erkenntnistheorie," *Archiv für systematische Philosophie* 1, pp. 34–45.

———. 1918. "Der Konflikt der modernen Kultur," in G. Simmel, *Das individuelle Gesetz: Philosophische Exkurse.* Frankfurt, 1968, pp. 148–73.

Slochower, Harry. 1927. "Die Philosophie in den Vereinigten Staaten unter besonderer Berücksichtigung der Gegenwart," in *Reichls Philosophischer Almanach,* pp. 349–458.

Srubar, Ilja. 1988. *Kosmion: Die Genese der pragmatischen Lebenswelttheorie von Alfred Schütz und ihr anthropologischer Hintergrund.* Frankfurt.

Stein, Ludwig. 1908a. "Der Pragmatismus: Ein neuer Name für alte Denkmethoden," *Archiv für systematische Philosophie* 14, pp. 1–9; pp. 143–88.

———. 1908b. *Philosophische Strömungen der Gegenwart.* Stuttgart, pp. 33–75.

Stekeler-Weithofer, Pirmin. 1991. "Religionsphilosophie nach William James," in *Neue Zeitschrift für systematische Theologie und Religionsphilosophie* 33, pp. 74–87.

Stikkers, Kenneth. 1987. *Max Scheler and American Pragmatism.* Unpublished manuscript. Seattle.

Stumpf, Carl. 1928. *William James nach seinen Briefen. Leben—Charakter—Lehre.* Berlin.

Sukale, Michael. 1976. "Heidegger and Dewey," in M. Sukale, *Comparative Studies in Phenomenology.* The Hague, pp. 121–51.

Thiele, J. 1965. "William James und Ernst Mach: Briefe aus den Jahren 1884–1905," *Philosophia Naturalis* 9, pp. 298–310.

Troeltsch, Ernst. 1913. "Empirismus und Platonismus in der Religionsphilosophie: Zur Erinnerung an William James," in Troeltsch, *Gesammelte Schriften*, vol. 2. pp. 364–385.

Vaihinger, Hans. 1911. *Die Philosophie des Als Ob. System der theoretischen, praktischen und religiösen Fiktionen der Menschheit auf Grund eines idealistischen Positivismus.* Berlin.

Vollrath, Ernst. 1988. "Hannah Arendt und Martin Heidegger," in A. Gethmann-Siefert and Otto Pöggeler (eds.), *Heidegger und die praktische Philosophie.* Frankfurt, pp. 357–72.

Vorbrodt, G. 1913. "W. James' Philosophie," *Zeitschrift für Philosophie und philosophische Kritik* 151, pp. 1–27.

Waibel, Edwin. 1915. "Studien zum Pragmatismus," *Archiv für systematische Philosophie* 21, pp. 1–43.

Wartenberg, Gerd. 1971. *Logischer Sozialismus: Die Transformation der Kantschen Transzendentalphilosophie durch Charles S. Peirce.* Frankfurt.

Wells, Harry K. 1957. *Der Pragmatismus—eine Philosophie des Imperialismus.* Berlin.

Wolzogen, Christoph von. 1990a. "Die 'Sorge' des Philosophen: 'Sein und Zeit' im Echo seiner frühen Kritiken ab 1928," in *Seins-Verständnis: Zu Martin Heideggers "Sein und Zeit."* Materialien der Akademie der Diözese Rottenburg-Stuttgart, pp. 39–60.

———. 1990b. "Heidegger und die Mathematik: Zu einer unbekannten Quelle der Seinsfrage," in *Seins-Verständnis: Zu Martin Heideggers "Sein und Zeit."* Materialien der Akademie der Diözese Rottenburg-Stuttgart, pp. 61–85.

Pragmatism and Contemporary Social Theory

5 The Unhappy Marriage of Hermeneutics and Functionalism: Jürgen Habermas's Theory of Communicative Action

The thematic breadth of Jürgen Habermas's work is extraordinary, and his theoretical undertaking has been progressing with a high degree of internal coherence. In *The Theory of Communicative Action,* Habermas has attempted to use his impressive intellectual tools and the results of his theoretical endeavor to produce a systematic work which both clarifies highly abstract fundamental theoretical questions and offers handy formulas that give a diagnosis of the present era. The work's scope and the diversity of the problems treated in it make it difficult for anyone who wants to enter into dialogue with it to follow the author's course of argumentation with a critical eye, if only to come independently —and not seduced by the book's rhetorical persuasiveness—to agreement with it. For this reason, the discussion of Habermas's book at present is in the somewhat uncomfortable situation of being split between global appreciations of a defensive or critical nature, on the one hand, and the correction of errors of detail, on the other. But what is the significance of amending Habermas's reconstructions of the classical theories of philosophy and sociology, if it has no important consequences for the line of argument of the work as a whole? On the other hand, of what use are global generalizations about the work if they fail to capture the wealth of the book's various discussions? A typical expression of this dilemma, it seems to me, is the fact that many critics are inclined to see, very speculatively and arbitrarily, the cause of the defects of Habermas's vision in his fundamental theoretical positions, although the logical relationship between the components of the theory which are cited is by no means clear. Such an arbitrary, and therefore often erroneous, localization of theoretical weak points in his theory is indeed fostered by Habermas himself when he asserts, "in good Hegelian terms" (*The Theory of Communicative Action, [TCA],* vol. 1, p. xxxix), that there is an indissoluble connection between the formation of basic concepts and the treatment of substantive issues. The existence of such a connection will not be denied

Published as "The Unhappy Marriage of Hermeneutics and Functionalism," in *Communicative Action,* edited by A. Honneth and H. Joas (Cambridge, Eng./Cambridge, Mass.: Blackwell Press [Polity Press]/MIT Press, 1991), pp. 97–118. Reprinted by permission. (Originally published in German in 1986.)

here. However, a certain measure of doubt as to its inextricability does seem appropriate. Critical interpretations of sociological texts need not, by any means, assume a rigorous connection between the decisions regarding fundamental theoretical questions and the diagnosis of an historical period, which is always based on empirical information. Indeed, even between the solutions of different fundamental theoretical problems, tensions and ruptures can occur.

The following critical examination of Habermas's work takes as its starting point the conjecture that in this work, which claims to be completely coherent, we might find simply a "personal union" of theoretical positions. More concretely I would like to advance the thesis that Habermas's book treats three sets of questions, all of which are distinct from one another to such an extent that answering one set does not completely predetermine the solution to the others. These three sets comprise the two fundamental problems of sociology, namely the question of human action and that of the conditions of social order, and the question of the central problematics of society in contemporary capitalist democracies. Between the two metatheoretical problems and the empirical dimension there can exist no relationship of logical consequence. Admittedly, a certain conception of contemporary social problems has a motivating function for the posing and answering of metatheoretical questions, but the positing of a determinative relationship between the metatheoretical and substantive levels would make communication between different political-ideological positions inconceivable from the outset. But even between the two metatheoretical questions, a meaningful distinction can be made.

If one takes Habermas's theory as an example, this assertion means that between his theory's contribution to the theory of action, i.e., its taking account of communicative action, and its solution to the problem of social order by means of the duality of system and lifeworld, there lie conceptual and empirical steps which make it clear that other solutions as well to the problem of social order can certainly spring from the soil of communicative action.[1] The following exposition will therefore concentrate on examining Habermas's contribution to the theory of action independently from the contribution he makes to the theory of social order. With respect to the theory of action, it will be shown to what extent the introduction of the concept of communicative action in fact constitutes an advance for mainstream sociological theories of action; on the other hand, however, it will be shown to what extent that concept, like mainstream sociology, continues to ignore a plethora of pressing questions pertaining to the theory of action. As for the theory of social order, the examination of the concepts of lifeworld and system will undertake to demonstrate the indefensibility of Habermas's use of them and to explain how Habermas is led into his unfortunate joining together of hermeneutics and functionalism through the insufficient radicalness of his critique of functionalism and his concomitant failure to recognize the metatheoretical character of the theory of action. I will entirely pass over the more philosophical questions concerning his use of the notion of rationality, and thus questions about the normative implications of a critical theory of society. Concerning the issue of Habermas's diagnosis of the present era, I return to it briefly and only in so far as its plausibility is thrown into doubt when Habermas's broader theoretical grounds are thrown in doubt.

Habermas's most important insight with regard to the theory of action is that the specific structure of human communication is irreducible. As opposed to any reduction of human action which maintains that it is merely technical, instrumental, teleological, or oriented solely to success—whatever the counterconcepts might be, and no matter whether they are precise or imprecise—Habermas advanced the view that human beings can have dealings with one another without making each other into means for achieving individually predetermined ends, without closing themselves to the implicit or explicit demands of their fellow human beings for true knowledge, correct conduct, and authentic self-presentation. Since Habermas formulated the distinction between "labor" and "interaction" in the form of a radical dichotomy, and used this distinction in his critique of Marx's concept of labor, this idea has been hotly debated.[2] This discussion has made unequivocally clear that the distinction proposed by Habermas is defensible only as an analytical one. In every social activity, aspects of both types of action can be found; even for the acquisition of the abilities required for human commerce with things, elementary communicative abilities appear to be a prerequisite.[3] The heart of the distinction does not seem to me to be affected by such criticisms. At bottom, Habermas is directing attention to a fundamental difference in attitude among actors in social action-situations and those in nonsocial action-situations, although it is certainly true that even my counterpart in a social situation can in many ways be made into a mere object of my influence and of my will. The typology of action put forward in *TCA* (vol. 1, p. 384) consists in nothing else than a system of these three types of action: the instrumental, the strategic, and the communicative.

Just how meager this typology is can be shown by even a brief glance at Habermas's own theoretical development. If my own impression and

Thomas McCarthy's reconstruction of that development do not deceive me,[4] then opposition to a reduction of action to the "instrumental" was already a motive of Habermas's thought long before the concept of communicative action had assumed the role of a comprehensive counterconcept. At first, Habermas proposed a concept of praxis informed by the ancient Greek philosophy of praxis and by the early modern resistance to a theory of society influenced by the natural sciences. Even if there are good reasons for introducing the concept of communication or for making a triadic distinction between labor, work, and action, as Hannah Arendt does,[5] nevertheless one may ask whether the concept of communication is capable of assuming all the meanings previously carried by the notion of praxis in its fullest sense. For it could indeed be the case that there are more reasons for rejecting the limitation of the practical to the technical than can be derived from the concepts of communication and interaction.

This question becomes even more acute when it is raised not just with respect to the individual theoretical development of Jürgen Habermas, but with respect to the entire history of theory concerned with this matter. Even in classical antiquity, the ideas about praxis were developed, according to Rüdiger Bubner,[6] through the critique of the Sophists' attempt to apply the *techne* model of action to political action. In the eighteenth century, according to Isaiah Berlin and Charles Taylor,[7] an "expressionistic" countermodel of action as the expression of the actor was developed in opposition to utilitarian tendencies of Enlightenment. This model, which may not be confined to linguistic expression or to stylizing self-presentation, exercised widely ramified influences in post-Kantian German Idealism, in German Romanticism, and in the thought of Karl Marx, whose concept of labor is quite unsuited to serve as an example of the technicist-instrumentalist limitation of the concept of action. An important current of Marxist discussion in this century has concerned itself with the expressive moments of the concept of labor in Marx's early writings and with the constitutive significance of this concept for the critique of political economy. Pragmatism, with its emphasis on creative problem-solving, opposed to the instrumentalist reduction of action an alternative model of action, and was thereby led to reassess playful and artistic commerce with objects. Previously in intellectual history, play and art had, in the most diverse contexts, been presented as counternotions to instrumentalist reductionism. Durkheim, Parsons, and Gehlen, either within the framework of the theory of action or via a critique of utilitarian views on the social order, each elaborate a conception of "ritual" as a norm-constituting action as a counterconcept to the instrumentalist restriction of the concept of action. Habermas knows all this. The immediate purpose of the preceding enumeration is to call attention to the fact that a present-day theory of action must be capable of typologically reconstructing all the domains of these phenomena.

How little Habermas succeeds in this regard can also be illustrated by the typology of concepts of action which are widely used in the social sciences, and which Habermas himself presents in the context of his discussion of action's relations to the world and of its aspects of rationality (*TCA*, vol. 1, pp. 126ff.). Here he distinguishes the teleological or strategic models of action from norm-regulated, dramaturgical, and communicative action. Even a brief comparison of this typology with the concepts of action actually used in the social sciences and in philosophy suffices to show its serious defects. In the case of teleological action, Habermas makes no distinction between an action that accomplishes a previously set end and the type of action stressed by pragmatism and phenomenology, which finds its end within situations. Playful commerce with objects and situations as a type of action is also entirely absent from the typology. The description of norm-regulated action is oriented to the model of norm-observance, while symbolic interactionism and ethnomethodology by contrast emphasize the vague demarcation of behavior, the meaningfulness of which is situation-specific.[8] Consequently, interaction that is not normatively regulated, or is so only slightly, is lacking in Habermas's typology. The notion of dramaturgical action refers to the strategic presentation of oneself to a public. As a result, the truly expressionistic model of self-expression in actions performed without strategic intent is also lacking in the typology. The notion of communicative action appears at first (ibid., p. 128) to refer to the type of interaction that is normatively unregulated, or that regulates itself only in the immediate process of negotiations; later (ibid., p. 148) however, it is defined as that kind of action in which all "relations to the world" become reflexive. This inspection of Habermas's typology makes it impossible to deny that what we have here is neither a suitable précis of concepts of action currently employed nor even a comprehensive typology of a general theory of action, but rather a classification that aims from the start at Habermas's distinction—admittedly a convincing one—of various kinds of possible relations to the world. Thus, we can conclude that Habermas has not really attempted, from the standpoint of the theory of action, to do justice to the diversity of kinds of action, and accordingly has delivered only communication as such as the jam-packed residual category of noninstrumental action.

But the real point of this argument is something else: this relatively schematic construction of the theory of action allows Habermas to avoid making two distinctions, both of which would have significantly widened the field of problems at the level of the theory of social order, and would have placed theoretical obstacles in the way of the solution to those problems within the duality of system and lifeworld. Habermas, on the one hand, insufficiently separates the question of overcoming the philosophy of consciousness from the reduction of the paradigm of purposive activity and the turn to communicative action; on the other hand, he incorrectly identifies a typology of action with a typology of the different kinds of *coordination* of action.

I consider both the supplanting of the philosophy of consciousness and the integration of the concept of communicative action into the sociological theory of action to be of great importance, but I dispute the identity of these two feats. Historically, there has been a pragmatist critique of the philosophy of consciousness without a theoretical model of intersubjectivity, namely that of William James, as well as theoretical models of intersubjectivity based on the philosophy of consciousness, which were put forward by phenomenology and partly by Charles Cooley. Both strands are unquestionably joined together in the work of George Herbert Mead, but they nevertheless remain analytically distinct. A brief characterization of the fundamental premise of pragmatism's theory of action will make this point clear. This theory does not conceive of action as the pursuit of ends that the contemplative subject establishes a priori and then resolves to accomplish; the world is not held to be mere material at the disposal of human intentionality. Quite to the contrary, pragmatism maintains that we find our ends in the world, and that prior to any setting of ends we are already, through our praxis, embedded in various situations. There is an interplay between the manifold impulses of the actor and the possibilities of a given situation, which can be interpreted in various ways. Between impulses and possibilities of action, the actor experimentally establishes connections, of which, in any given instance, only one is realized; that one, however, is influenced in its particular manner of realization by the other possibilities that have been mentally played through. The course followed by an action then is not one that has been established once and for all time; rather, it must be produced over and over again by construction and is open to continual revision. A model of action that is in this sense nonteleological, that does not confine the situatedness of action to its conditions and means, raises the question of the conditions of the apparently self-evident schematization of natural totalities of action according to means and ends. John Dewey's view of the matter, for example, is that when the imprecise directedness with which customary actions are performed proves insufficient to overcome the resistance encountered in a particular situation, only then is the hitherto implicit intentionality of the action brought into the full light of consciousness and compelled to focus on the situation so as to make itself more precise.[9] Playful self-development and creative solution of problems, as used by the pragmatists, repudiate the primacy of an instrumentalist concept of labor for action just as radically as does the adducing of interaction and communication as kinds of action not accounted for by a model based upon labor.

What then would be the consequences if Habermas had clearly distinguished the two trains of reasoning which lead to the supersession of the philosophy of consciousness and to the emergence of the concept of communicative action? First, it would have been necessary to take into account, within the theory of action, nonteleological forms of dealing with objects in nonsocial situations. Second, and this is more important, the very way in which end- or success-oriented human action is viewed would change. It would become clear that the setting of ends is a self-reflective and therefore secondary presentation of an action in situations. On the level of the theory of action, a domain would thereby be brought into view, in which all action "has always been" embedded.[10] Focusing upon this "domain" permits a more radical refutation of the notion that individual actors enter into action-situations with preconceived intentions than is made possible by the thesis that meanings are linguistically constituted. It is in this domain that the actor's corporeality and prelinguistic sociality must be located. This domain has been examined from very different theoretical vantage points, and Habermas's theory of communicative action provides effective means for rejecting structuralism's claim on this "domain." But does his theory succeed in conceptualizing this domain as the lifeworld? If the lifeworld is supposed to be a correlate of communicative action, then there arises the problem that the "domain" under discussion here is the basis of all action, thus also of teleological action, no matter how it is defined.

Further consequences arise for the positions which Habermas allocates the classics within the history of theory; this, in turn, has indirect consequences for a substantive problem. I believe that Habermas rightly criticizes Weber, Lukács and Horkheimer/Adorno for the defects in their implicit or explicit theories of action, which arise from their deploying a philosophy of consciousness. However, because he does not make a clear-cut distinction between a nonteleological and a nonmonological interpretation of action, he has unnecessarily to expand a completely justified critique of Weber's concept of meaning, which is neo-Kantian and rooted in a philosophy of consciousness, by imputing a monological orientation in Weber's concept of action (*TCA*, vol. 1, pp. 280ff.). As for Parsons's work, Habermas finds it also to have foundations in the philosophy of consciousness (ibid., p. 239), yet does not see that these exist from the outset in a field of tension with other influences, initially brought to bear by Whitehead.[11] The most important consequence, however, concerns Emile Durkheim. At various points Habermas mentions Mead and Durkheim in the same breath as being the originators of the paradigm shift from purposive to communicative action. This classification unquestionably applies in the case of Mead's intersubjectivist pragmatism. However, with regard to Durkheim, it must be qualified to a great extent. Although it can indeed be concluded from his late sociology of religion[12] that he shifted to a theory of extra-ordinary, emotional, direct interaction, there is no basis whatsoever for claiming that Durkheim was at the same time or by virtue of that shift attempting to supersede the philosophy of consciousness. On the contrary: the lectures on pragmatism which he gave after the publication of *Elementary Forms of the Religious Life*[13] clearly show that Durkheim takes the offensive by positing central positions of the philosophy of consciousness against pragmatism. What links Durkheim to an intersubjectivistically oriented pragmatism is the attempt to forge a theory of the social constitution of categories of human knowledge. His first attempt—to be found in the famous essay, coauthored with Marcel Mauss, on primitive classification systems[14]—consists of a theory of the reproduction of social morphology in cultural systems of classification. He then refines this further in the mature sociology of religion. There, Durkheim is concerned with the emergence of social morphology itself out of the religious group experience in collective ritual praxis. He argues that the forces of the collective experienced in "collective effervescence" and the effects this has on the individual can be interpreted only by the participating subjects as forces which are at work behind the observable things themselves and prevail throughout the cosmos. In the religious group experience, the reciprocal effect of the individual psyches is intensified to such an extent that the connection to collective ideations ensues here, and these then exert their organizing power on the individual perceptions in the everyday world of the individuals. Whereas pragmatism, in other words, emphasizes the constitution of knowledge in practical problematic situations, Durkheim marks the religious experience sharply off from this. He distinguishes brusquely between all cognition directed toward enabling action and a desire to understand which is basic for all religious cosmologies. In his theory of religion, however, he designates the collective praxis of ritual to be the origin of categories. It can be shown that Durkheim's thesis on social constitution is directed against a constitution in everyday *practice* as well as a constitution in the praxis of *everyday* life. Precisely what Durkheim elaborates with regard to the extra-ordinary sociality of the ritual he then disputes with respect to the everyday reality of social life. If Habermas also wishes to include the everyday forms of action that are shot through with religion in his Durkheim interpretation, then he has good reasons for doing so, but he is violating the spirit of Durkheim's work. For the latter feared that such a theory could have irrationalistic consequences and instead defended a traditionally Cartesian concept of consciousness—before and after the shift in the theory of religion. Correcting Habermas's approach in this manner[15] is not only of interest in terms of the history of theory, because Habermas then sets out in a further step (*TCA,* vol. 2, p. 133) to fuse Durkheim's notion of a structural change in the collective conscience with a phenomenologically oriented investigation of the lifeworld. In so doing, he proposes that the analysis of the lifeworld be understood "as an attempt to describe reconstructively, from the internal perspective of members, what Durkheim called the *conscience collective*" (ibid., p. 133). If my reconstruction of Durkheim is accurate, this is an impossible undertaking. For the theory of collective conscience would then have to be regarded as a solution to a problem in the theory of social order that is possible only on the basis of a philosophy of consciousness, a solution that becomes untenable as soon as the switch is made to a nonteleological and nonmonological theory of action. On this terrain, the issue in the theory of social order and the question as to the nonconscious lifeworld background of all action would then have to be strictly separated from one another. I will return to this in detail.

As stated above, Habermas identifies in a misleading fashion a typology of action with the distinction among types of coordination of action. A number of Habermas's critics (Berger, Bader, Honneth)[16] have pointed out that in many formulations he connects too closely different types of action and different societal spheres of action, insofar as he speaks of subsystems of purposively rational or of communicative action. This is a valid criticism, since we must assume that every societal sphere of action exhibits a wealth of different types of action. In *The Theory of Communicative Action,* Habermas appears to want to avoid this problem by talking about types of coordination of action and by introducing on this level of his theory the distinction between success-oriented versus communicatively oriented action. However, since there is no typology adequate to the rich variety of the different kinds of action that correspond to the distinction among different forms of the coordination of action, and since to each of the societal domains and spheres of action only one principle of the coordination of action is ascribed, a linear relationship of correspondence among types of action, types of coordination of action, and societal domains is once again established. Once this relationship has been theoretically established in this manner, then of course no phenomena can block the progress of Habermas's argumentation, and he can shift back and forth between the different levels at will. When considered from the standpoint of the theory of action, this state of affairs is clearly problematic. However, the topic of the coordination of action leads to the second central metatheoretical problem of sociology, namely the question of social order.

Habermas's contribution to the solution of the problems posed by the theory of social order consists in his defense of two opposed conceptions of the theory of social order and in his attempt to join them by using empirical arguments. On the one hand, it is a matter of a type of social order that is supposed to correspond to communicatively oriented action and is represented as being intuitionally comprehensible and rooted in the actors' intentions. To refer to this type of social order, Habermas uses the concept of "lifeworld." The precise manner in which this concept is introduced into Habermas's argumentation will have to be treated later. However, according to Habermas, this concept alone is insufficient to solve the problems raised by a theory of social order, as it is constrained by the essential limits of any theory of action. An adequate theory of society must reach out beyond forms of sociality based on primary groups and beyond the intended results of action, and to do this it must critically draw upon functionalist systems theory. Habermas then elucidates the relationship between two models of social order, the "lifeworld" and "systems," in a quasi-empirical fashion, that is, first by means of an historical theory about the gradual uncoupling of the system from the lifeworld. Second, he analyses the present relationship among the societal spheres that supposedly correspond to these types of social order, and finally, he introduces a theoretical model, based on the media theory of functionalist theorists, concerning the interactions among these spheres and of the "mediatization," "instrumentalization," and "colonization" of the lifeworld through the imperatives of the system. In order to make perceptible the problems in Habermas's theory, which is sometimes developed at levels of abstraction so high that they make the reader's head spin, it is necessary to scrutinize in order: (1) Habermas's understanding of the status of the theory of action; (2) his interpretation and employment of functionalist systems theory; and (3) his introduction of the concept of the lifeworld into the argument. The problems that appear as we proceed along this path will give the reader an idea of just how infelicitous is the joining together of "lifeworld" and "system," of hermeneutic and functionalist conceptions of social order.

1. In many passages of his book, Habermas speaks of essential limits on what the theory of action can accomplish, and of the competition between approaches based on the theory of action and on systems theory as a competition between two different paradigms. This assertion seems to me to require critique, at least as a way of stating the matter; but the unsatisfactory formulation also reveals a questionable understanding of the problem. It is my thesis, that, with this formulation, Habermas confounds the distinction between the theory of action and the theory of social order with, on the one hand, the solution to the problem of social order provided by functionalist systems theory and, on the other hand, with the substantive question of the extent to which societal processes occur independently of the intentions of individual actors.

The theory of action does not per se compete with the theory of social order. It does not at all contain the empirical assumption that all results of action are covered by the intentions of the actors, or lie within the control and intuitive knowledge of the actors.[17] In fact, the theory of action directly compels us to pose the problem of social order. Every theory of action entails theoretical assumptions about the nature of social order that implicitly or explicitly correspond to it. This is true even of the poorest but very influential theory of action, namely utilitarianism, for which the corresponding model of social order is the market,[18] as well as of theories of action originating in ethnomethodology, which refer to the model of social order based on the fragile interaction among individual human subjects. It is not the case that the theory of action stands in a competitive relation to functionalist systems theory; rather, an anthropologically grounded theory of human action *and* of the basic structures of human sociality resists the unconsidered apprehension of the domain studied by the social sciences insofar as these use the categories of a systems theory that per se is not yet tailored to the specific characteristics of this domain. Functionalist systems theory is a proposal about how to solve the problems posed by the theory of social order that is, in relation to the social, still only metaphorical, but might prove to be fruitful after it has been made more specific. If functionalist systems theory should in fact turn out to be fruitful, then this will not be due to the essential limitations of what the theory of action can accomplish, but to its own possible superiority over other models of social order.

Like both Merton and Parsons,[19] Habermas adduces the problem of unintended results of action as an important reason for changing over to functionalist models of social order. This cannot be a compelling reason, since unintended results of action are made the focal point of attention in a large number of theoretical approaches, without leading these theories into functionalism. An example is the political theory of John Dewey,[20] for which the perception and the control of unintended results of group action constitute an important starting point. Some authors, for instance, Blau, Boudon, and others,[21] adduce the possibility of unintended results of action as evidence against functionalism, since from no perspective can all unintended results of action be interpreted as functional. This indicates that there is at least a problem in Habermas's distinction between two types of coordination of action. For he presents these types as the two members of a dichotomy in which coordination of action with reference to the intentions directing the action is opposed to coordination of action with reference to the results of action. Now all coordination of action with reference to intentions is extremely unstable, if retroactions of unintended or unanticipated results of action continuously occur that cannot be consensually interpreted within the framework of the actor's systems of meanings. Conversely, social integration effected by means of the results of action can mean not the interconnecting of the actors through all the results of action, but merely the definition of certain kinds of results that are recorded as legitimate.

The misleading restriction of the theory of action to "lifeworld" processes leaves its mark at many points in the reconstructions of the history of social theory. To my mind it is wrong, for example, to classify Weber simply as a theorist of action, while failing to consider the ideas which stem from a theory of social order contained in his work—"Some Categories of an Interpretive Sociology"[22] being but one obvious example. The charges against Weber's model of bureaucracy,[23] which Luhmann has assembled from developments in research on the sociology of organization, charges which Habermas repeatedly cites, do not in my opinion show limits of *the* theory of action *as such,* but rather flaws in the Weberian model of bureaucracies, and indicate the need to differentiate between the level of individual action and its rationalization and the rationalization of collective and organized action. Equally, I do not see the point of interpreting Marx's theory of value as an attempt to mediate conceptually between the level of systems processes ("accumulation of capital") and the dynamics of class conflict, since Marx devised the analysis of the value form as an attempt to develop systematically the central economic categories of a social theory meant to address capitalism from the perspective of collectively reversing the fact that social relations had gradually become independent; here Habermas is projecting on to Marx a distinction of his own which does not exist in this form in Marx's work.

However, I also have grave doubts as to whether the history of social theory in the late nineteenth century (*TCA*, vol. 2, p. 202) can be described in terms of the division between a German tradition of action theory and a tradition of an economic theory of social order.[24] However, I wanted to refer only briefly to this point; more detailed remarks will focus on the implications Habermas's view of the theory of action has for his interpretation of Mead and Parsons. The relativization of Mead's importance for social theory and the critique of the supposed "idealism" of his social theory at the end of the section devoted to Mead and Durkheim is as drastic in tone as Mead is central to Habermas's conception because of the "paradigm shift" from purposive action to communicative action. In his reconstruction of Mead, which on the whole is helpful and influenced by an analytical philosophy of language, Habermas limits Mead's conception of symbolically mediated interaction to the level of communication in signal language. This is a misunderstanding which can arise if one takes Mead's interest in the *origin* of human communication to be his sole interest. However, his works cover the entire spectrum ranging from the dialogue of significant gestures to complex scientific or public political discussions. The simpler forms are viewed not only as preliminary evolutionary stages, but rather also as forms of communication that are always given. The criticism that Mead does not elaborate the difference between the various forms or stages sufficiently is surely justified. As Mead sees it, a fundamental rupture occurs during the period of transition from animal to human in the structure of sociality, a rupture which from the very beginning results in the anthropological conditions for the possibility of an ideal social order, namely, that order which comes about via the institutionalization of discourses. This misunderstanding has to do with the general underestimation of Mead's achievements not only for action theory, but also for a theory of social order—one need only think of his emphatic concept of democracy. To this extent, it provides the basis for Habermas's polemic against Mead, namely that Mead was supposedly not aware of the one-sidedness of his communications-theoretic approach; Habermas claims this is already to be seen from the fact that only those social functions come into view in Mead's work that "devolve upon communicative action and in which communicative action also cannot be replaced by other mechanisms" (*TCA*, vol. 2, p. 110). Mead is accordingly judged to neglect the material reproduction of society and the securing of its physical maintenance and to occlude economics, warfare, and the struggle for political power from the theory. In general, Habermas says, Mead ignores the external restrictions (ibid., p. 108) on the development of communicative rationalization.

In my opinion, two distinctions have to be made if we are to assess this criticism of Mead.[25] We should distinguish, on the one hand, between a thematic and a systematic neglect of domains such as the economy, war, and politics. Thematically, it is true that in his essential contributions—but one also has to take into consideration his politico-philosophical reviews[26]—Mead concerns himself with problems other than the sociological analysis of the above-mentioned domains. Systematically, however, there is no basis for contending that his concepts of action and social order are too narrow in terms of communications theory. He does not place a naive trust in the development of communication. Rather, the problem as he sees it is how the economically advancing universalization of human social relations could be "compensated for" culturally and politically. The world market, for example, is in his view a case of advanced sociation to which as yet no forms of social integration correspond. It is precisely not the unleashed dynamics of communicative rationality, but rather complexes now independent and a reduction in their independence that form the level at which he addresses the problem. The second distinction I would like to call for concerns the meaning of the concept of a communicative theory of society. I think one should relate this exclusively to theories which at the level of action theory provide only models of communication and interaction, but should not link it to those which contain or normatively distinguish models of integration via unleashed communication at the level of the theory of social order. Habermas imputes to the concept of social integration a meaning of "life-worldly," interpersonal immediacy not to be found in Mead's work. He does not, therefore, take seriously enough the claim made by a conception in the context of a radical American democratism (or a Marxism given a normative twist) to render all structures of social action dependent on the result of collective will-formation. This is expressed crassly when Habermas (*TCA,* vol. 2, pp. 117f.) draws a parallel between the semanticization of "objective" meanings in the functional circuit of animal behavior and the understanding or the control of social processes by the members of society. Whereas in the one case it is indeed a question of the transition from animal to human behavior, in the other case it is a question of the collective mastery of the effects produced at any event by action. I see no point in embracing both the natural preconditions for human action and the gradual independence of social relations in the one concept of systemic interconnections; that would indeed be to render uncontrolled social developments natural in origin. Habermas is correct in declaring that the extent to which control is had over these developments is an empirical matter (ibid., p. 118); but, in accordance with his abbreviated understanding of action theory, he bundles this together with the metatheoretical decision for or against action theory.

Habermas's interpretation of the development of Talcott Parson's work is impressive owing to its ability to locate ruptures in the considerable continuity of this process—or so the self-stylizations and presentations of the Parsons orthodoxy would have it—and to uncover systematic problems generated by the dynamics of this development. The attempt to deploy in the theory an intrinsic meaning of cultural formations, without succumbing to some transcendentalization of culture (*TCA,* vol. 2, p. 231), and the magnificent interpretation of the anthropologizing esoteric late work of Parsons (ibid., pp. 375–84) are, to my mind, among the outstanding accomplishments of this part of Habermas's work. The Parsons interpretation as a whole, however, suffers from the conception of the status of the theory of action criticized above. In Habermas's view, the framework of Parson's action theory proved "too narrow for [him] to develop a concept of society from that perspective; thus he felt it necessary to represent complexes of action directly as systems and to convert social theory from the conceptual primacy of action theory over to that of systems theory" (ibid., p. 203). This proposition cannot be adhered to in this form if, as suggested here, one distinguishes the *problematics* of the theory of social order from systems theory's *proposal for a solution* and defines the status of the theory of action accordingly. For then it will be shown that in his *Structure of Social Action* Parsons quite clearly did already advocate not only a voluntaristic theory of action, but also a normativistic theory of social order. Moreover, the chapter in his early work on Pareto,[27] usually neglected in most interpretations of Parsons, contains an interesting attempt to present a concept of the system of action which does justice precisely also to the concatenation of utilitarian actions. Now, Habermas is not attacking the simple existence of attempts by the early Parsons to devise a theory of social order, but rather he is criticizing the supposed isolation of the concepts of action and of social order (ibid., pp. 208–9). In so doing, he proceeds from the notion that it would have been logical to "connect the concept of action with that of order so that they complemented one another at the same analytical level and thus yielded a concept of social interaction. The concept of *normative agreement* could have served as a bridge between the concepts of value-oriented purposive activity and an order integrating values with interests" (*TCA,* vol. 2, p. 213). Parsons, he claims, remains bound to his point of departure, namely the singular action of a single actor. Irrespective of whether this is true of Parsons's work,[28] Habermas's underlying assumption here does not seem tenable to me. It is admittedly correct to design from the very outset the concept of action with a view to the social embeddedness of action, as Mead attempted to do in his conception of the "social act" as a complex group activity. Yet, Habermas himself does not do this: although he takes the orientation toward interaction into account in introducing communicative action as a type, he nevertheless also develops this type in the context of the individual action of the individual actor. Even if group action or social interaction is made the point of departure at the level of the theory of action, I still do not see how this would solve the problem of the theory of social order itself. The problem of what unintended action sequences should be attributed to and how they are processed is, for example, just as much a problem as it ever was. I cannot see to what extent Parsons's later transition to a functionalist systems theory was *forced* upon him in any way by his original action-theoretic approach. The field of tension in which this theory of action becomes embroiled owing to Parsons's shift is, however, superbly analyzed by Habermas. Nevertheless, it would again seem to me that Habermas overdramatizes the results of his analysis by proposing that the harmonistic image of the present era outlined by Parsons can be traced directly back to the initial design of the theory. By contrast, it bears pointing out that Parsons arrives at appraisals that differ substantially from Habermas's (and mine), but not because his theory of modernization did not allow for a dissynchronous intensification in the four dimensions of adaptive capacity, inclusion, value generalization, and differentiation of media-controlled subsystems. Richard Münch's neo-Parsonian critique of Habermas on this point seems justified to me.[29] The potential for an analysis of the present era inherent in a trend toward "associationism" which Parsons asserts exists is equally not to be trivialized by pointing to individual harmonistic interpretations by Parsons.[30]

Now that we have elaborated Habermas's interpretation of the sociological classics, and this is indispensable if interpretation is as important for the development of systematic argumentation as it is in this thinker's case, let us once again call to mind what was first at issue here.

The foregoing reflection on the status of the theory of action was intended both to stress the inevitable existence of questions pertaining to the theory of social order in the fundamental problems of sociology and to refute the necessity of seeking answers to the theoretical questions of social order by way of functionalist systems theory. For the moment, all that is clear is that the theory of action entails the development of a typology of forms of communal and societal integration, and that the introduction of a theory of communicative action on the level of the theory of action compels the inclusion in such a typology of a type of social order that could be called a social order founded on discursively reached agreement. However, on this level it is still impossible to make any assertion about the normative precedence of this type over other types of social order, or about the empirical relationship among existing types of social order.[31]

2. Habermas gives the impression that the limitations of the theory of action make it necessary to have recourse to functionalist theories of systems. If we are not content to stop at phenomena that occur within the horizon of actors' intentions, or erroneously to explain macrosocial complexes of interrelations with reference to this model, then there seems to be no other choice than to analyze these nexuses according to the example given by systems theory. The only matter of dispute, then, is the claim of functionalist analysis to be exhaustive of the social totality. Habermas firmly rejects this claim, insisting on the constitution of systemic complexes of interrelations in lifeworldly nexuses of action. Let us examine more closely the procedure, the problems, and the motives of this critical examination and appropriation of functionalism, which is, however, no more than that.

To Habermas, the phenomenon of the interconnection of unintended results of action in the form of self-regulating societal mechanisms seems to be undeniable. He wants to free such mechanisms from the odium of being in their essence evidence of alienation. To this end he frequently emphasizes the problem-solving role of such mechanisms or media, which eases the burden on communication. In the sphere of rational economic activity, which is in conformity with the medium of money, and in the sphere of rational administration, which is in conformity with the medium of power, he sees successful forms for fulfilling societal tasks. In relation to these tasks, the demand for communicative regulation would be out of place, because it would never be capable of competing, from the standpoint of effectivity, with the other kinds of regulation proper to these spheres. The market, in particular, is presented as the prototype of a sociality that, while it is normatively constituted, is itself free of norms. Imperceptibly, Habermas glides from the existence of a type of social order that can be described only by using the means provided by functionalist systems theory to arguing for the indispensability of this kind of social order for the fulfillment of a particular societal task, namely that of material reproduction. "To be sure," states Habermas,

> the material reproduction of the lifeworld does not, even in limiting cases, shrink down to surveyable discussions such that it might be represented as the intended outcome of collective cooperation. Normally it takes place as the fulfillment of latent functions *going beyond the action orientations* of those involved. Insofar as the aggregate effects of cooperative actions fulfill imperatives of maintaining the material substratum, these complexes of action can be stabilized functionally, that is, through feedback from functional side effects. (*TCA*, vol. 2, p. 232)

Not only does Habermas functionalistically conceive of the unintended effects of action a priori as "latent functions" in this passage; in addition, he also gives a substantializing turn to the formalism of the systems model in the direction of material reproduction of a society.

Neither the one nor the other is self-evidently true. That the problem of unintended results of action does not compel one to have recourse to functionalism has already been stressed numerous times. It is also astonishing, in view of the pervasiveness in the social sciences of a normatively oriented functionalism that concentrates precisely on phenomena of "symbolic reproduction," that Habermas assigns to functionalism the task of explaining specifically material reproduction. This position contains at least a tendency toward reification of a principle of social order. This tendency is also revealed in Habermas's use of the concepts of system integration and social integration. This pair of concepts has become widely recognized and used following David Lockwood's critique of Parsons from a leftist perspective[32] and has become one of the focal points of the discussion of macrosociological theory. The distinction made by these two concepts in fact expresses the experience of the West European left that smoothly running economic reproduction by no means guarantees the socio-cultural integration of a society, and that economic crises do not necessarily trigger political or socio-cultural crises. With these concepts, Lockwood sought to go beyond the superficial critique of Parsons from the standpoint of the theory of social conflict, and to set against the notion of a system of values common to all the members of a society as a fundamental prerequisite of social order a completely different theoretical plane: that of the real interdependence of parts and domains of society. No matter how inexact this attempt to formulate an interesting idea might have been, it was clear that system integration and social integration referred to two dimensions of integration that are always present simultaneously and which do not belong to two distinct societal spheres. Habermas, in contrast, believes that a differentiation between system and lifeworld took place in the course of history; thus he arrives at the proposition that "societies are *systemically stabilized* complexes of action of *socially integrated* groups" (*TCA*, vol. 2, p. 152). The scope of societal integration is thus regarded, at least in modern societies, as fundamentally smaller than that of society in general, which embraces both system *and* lifeworld.

There is, however, a host of problems specific to Habermas's use of functionalist notions. I would like to call attention here especially to two difficulties. The first concerns the uncoupling from the lifeworld of subsystems of purposive rational action. Within the framework of a Weberian typology of action, this manner of formulation could still be considered to make a certain sense. But Habermas, in order to demonstrate the necessity of "going over" from the theory of action to systems theory, relies strongly on Niklas Luhmann's critique of Weber and the use of the concept of purpose at the level of system-rationality. Luhmann's critique, however, maintains that there is a rupture between the individual actor's end-oriented rationality of action and the functional rationality of social systems. Therefore, system-rationality does not at all require a rationality of action that is structurally analogous to it. The thesis that there are subsystems of purposively rational action is consequently untenable not only because it allows a societal domain to be based on a single type of action, but also because it assumes that a subsystem can be characterized by reference to the type of action dominant in it.[33] The second immanent difficulty reveals itself when one recalls the argument that Habermas himself used in some of his earlier writings to critique functionalism.[34] There he demonstrated that functionalist analyses in the social sciences encounter what he calls a problematic of the value that should be realized by a social system; this means, such analyses run into the fact that no self-evident, taken-for-granted guiding value is given beforehand to social systems—such as that of sheer self-preservation or of biological survival—but that this value can only be defined by the investigator. This insight ought to lead us to a distrust of any assumption of actually effective teleological tendencies in social systems. Of course, this line of reasoning can be extended beyond the decisionist positing of such guiding values by an investigator, to the question of the guiding values institutionalized in social systems. Then, however, with regard to functional interconnections it is again a matter of tendencies that, from the standpoint of such dominant "guiding values," are intended or at least acceptable. From this perspective, real processes that are functional in themselves are theoretically precluded. This is also true of material reproduction, implicit in which is, certainly, the task of self-preservation, but in a modified form. If this is so, then talk of system processes that are uncoupled from the lifeworld but which are nevertheless functional becomes meaningless.

In recent years, it has been above all Anthony Giddens who has championed—in contrast to Habermas—radical critique of functionalism which does not fall back into methodological individualism and which does not deny phenomena such as homeostatic processes, to the existence of which the programmatic adherents of functionalism like to call attention.[35] Such a radical critique of functionalism is aimed in the direction of a theory of collective action, the focus of which is the intended and unintended results of collective and individual action, and the collective constitution of normative regulations and collective procedures for dealing with normative conflicts. Classic expressions of this way of thinking point to social order resulting from negotiation processes and to the constitution of a collective will.[36] Habermas is unwilling to follow this route. He is forced to adopt a truncated version of the theory of action and to take recourse to functionalist lines of reasoning because he does not see the theory of action in relation to the task of describing collective actions, of describing the constitution of collective actors and identities. In my opinion, he has expressed his motives for not doing this most clearly in the speech he made in Stuttgart when accepting the Hegel Prize.[37] In his discussion of the question of whether complex societies are capable of developing a reasonable identity, he speaks of the two great, influential forms of collective identity in modern history: the nation-state and the political party. In order to judge the claim of these collective identities to rationality, he measures both of them by the standard of whether they embody goals that can be universalized. He adjudges that historically both have played such a role. In the current context, however, a nationalist consciousness means for him the danger of a particularist regression. He also regards the hopes set in the proletarian party as outmoded, after the historical experiences we have had with bureaucratized state parties and reformist parties integrated into the competitive political system of capitalist democracies. We shall not judge the factual basis of these assessments. What is clear, though, is that this judgment sends Habermas on a search for a structure of collective identity that is not very closely associated with the empirically available forms of partial collective identity. The explanation for Habermas's orientation, under Luhmann's influence, toward a functionalism that has been given a critical turn is to be found, in my view, in the above-mentioned assessments and in Habermas's suspicion that any theory centered on the constitution of collective actors promotes (a) the reification of organizations into collective subjects and (b) the assumption made by the philosophy of history that the history of humanity has a single persisting subject. This seems to be the crucial point from which Habermas is led into the dilemma arising out of the union of hermeneutics and functionalism.[38]

3. In Habermas's theory, the concept of the lifeworld fulfils simultaneously two tasks. It characterizes a type of social order and an epistemological position. Using concepts from the tradition of pragmatism and of sociology influenced by pragmatism, the type of social order in question is that called "democracy" or "negotiated order"; the epistemological theory is that theory according to which cognition is constituted in a "world that is there." I mention these concepts in order to point out that a theory can and must contain both kinds of concepts; they should, though, be clearly distinct from each other. In introducing the concept of the lifeworld into his argument, Habermas does not begin with theories of the constitution of cognition in contexts of everyday certainties of action and of social intercourse, theories that are not fundamentally transcendentalist from the outset like the one Mead develops in his later writings, or the theory of everyday life presented in the works of Lukács during his last period and in the writings of Agnes Heller.[39] He begins, rather, with the contributions made by phenomenology, which have been more influential in the social sciences. He criticizes their use of a model of individual perceptions taken from the philosophy of consciousness and attempts to transform that model in accordance with the theory of communication. This effort is influenced by the findings of analytical philosophy. If this transformation is successful, then we can "think of the lifeworld as represented by a culturally transmitted and linguistically organized stock of interpretive patterns" (*TCA*, vol. 2, p. 124). What the content of this lifeworld is, is of course unknown to the actors; it is merely background, which can become relevant or problematical, depending on the situation.

> From a perspective turned toward the situation, the lifeworld appears as a reservoir of taken-for-granteds, of unshaken convictions that participants in communication draw upon in cooperative processes of interaction. Single elements, specific taken-for-granteds, are, however, mobilized in the form of consensual and yet problematicizable knowledge only when they become relevant to a situation. (*TCA*, vol. 2, p. 124)

Up to this point I see no difficulty in principle in Habermas's procedure. This changes, though, with the next step. Habermas is unsatisfied with what he has achieved, inasmuch as the lifeworld concept of the theory of communication "still [lies] on the same analytical level as the transcendental lifeworld concept of phenomenology" (ibid., p. 135). This plane must be surpassed, however, says Habermas, if the goal is not to remain within the framework of epistemology, but to achieve a demarcation of the domain of investigation of the social sciences. Then, he continues, the lifeworld, which is conceived from the perspective of participants in action-situations, must be "objectivated." Habermas sees a first model for how this might happen in ordinary, everyday narrations, which can refer to the totality of socio-cultural facts without necessarily originating from the point of view of a participant in the narrated action. The crucial step, however, is the one that follows:

> This intuitively accessible *concept of the sociocultural lifeworld* can be rendered theoretically fruitful if we can develop from it a reference system for descriptions and explanations relevant to the lifeworld as a whole and not merely to occurrences within it. Whereas narrative presentation refers to what is innerworldly, theoretical presentation is intended to explain the reproduction of the lifeworld itself. (*TCA*, vol. 2,pp. 136–37)

The result of this attempt at objectivation is Habermas's contention that the lifeworld fulfils the functions of cultural reproduction, social integration, and socialization. In accordance with these functions that have been identified, Habermas distinguishes three structural components of the lifeworld: culture, society, and personality. By following Habermas in his train of reasoning, we have come to the very same result as Parsons, who at the beginning of the fifties presented his distinction among three levels of systems of action.[40] Still, we have arrived at it along a wholly different path.

Should this coincidence cause us to be skeptical? I think so. After the concept of the lifeworld has been appropriated for the theory of communication and reinterpreted accordingly, Habermas's daring construction presents us with two completely different ideas under the rubric of the objectivation of the participant perspective. The first idea has to do with an objectivation such as an ordinary storyteller or a historian undertakes. The storyteller tells of the knowledge and the action of other actors and objectivates this knowledge and action insofar as he places it within a context resulting from his understanding of the frames of reference within which he interprets the actions of others. He does not become an uncomprehending observer, but an interpretative reconstructor of the subjectively intended and "objective" meaning of the actions of others. Just as the totality of their lifeworldly background remains essentially noncognizable for the actors who are the object of the narration, so too does the lifeworldly background of the narrator remain essentially non-cognizable in its totality for him. Our narrator could become the object of narration for a second narrator, and so on, ad infinitum. This process would produce ever new "stories"; and these new stories would perhaps be ever more "objective," relative to the limited perspective of the original actors. However, in this process no plane would be reached that is essentially different from that of the reconstruction of the meaning of others' actions against the background of a lifeworld.

The other idea that Habermas links to the concept of objectivation does not have to do with the perspective of the storyteller or of the historian, but with the perspective of the epistemologist. The latter can make the mode of constitution of cognition itself, as it is performed by actors or narrators or historians, the object of his reflection. This is true, of course, even of the phenomenological theorist of the lifeworld. If phenomenology abandons its claim that the objects of cognition are transcendentally constituted, the result is an epistemological theory that attempts self-reflectively to bring into sight the preconditions of cognition. This effort yields corporeality, intersubjectivity, and the structuredness of knowledge as preconditions of all cognition. With regard to this objectivation, it is a matter of a self-reflective confirmation of the preconditions of cognition and action. This confirmation can only assume the character of a formal definition of such preconditions. For as soon as it tries to go beyond a formal definition of them, it becomes a particular theory, which necessarily arises upon a determinate lifeworldly foundation that as such is essentially noncognizable. It is, therefore, no accident that Habermas discovers as the structural components of the lifeworld precisely those dimensions which Parsons identified as the levels at which the concept of system is to be applied in the social sciences. However, no theory about changes of cultural reproduction, of social integration and of socialization can claim to have originated from an objectivation in principle of *the* lifeworld. It holds good also for the human being Jürgen Habermas that the lifeworld environing him, which forms the horizon of his cognition, cannot, in principle, be fully thematized or completely and clearly grasped. The discernment of structural components of the lifeworld therefore cannot smoothly pass over into propositions about the differentiation and structural rationalization of the lifeworld. The epistemologist's self-reflective certainty does not vouch for the empirical plausibility of his further conclusions. That does not mean that these conclusions are wrong; I am only stressing their complete theoretical independence, which, so it appears to me, Habermas conceals. If my reasoning is correct, then neither the objectivation of the lifeworld by the historian nor its objectivation by the epistemologist leads us to abandon the participant's point of view for that of the kind of observer who is posited by a functionalist systems theory. We remain, then, participant observers with respect to all socio-cultural processes, even at the highest levels of macrosocial complexes of relations. We are compelled neither by the alleged limitations of the theory of action, nor by the inevitability of functionalist analyses, nor by the theoretical sterility of the participant's perspective to grasp societal processes conceptually in any way other than in categories of action and of social order grounded in action. Action and social order can be normatively judged according to the degree of which the results of action and the effects of social order can be legitimated from the perspective of the individuals concerned and of course ourselves, that is, the degree to which those results and effects are rational when judged from that perspective.[41]

This critical examination of Jürgen Habermas's *Theory of Communicative Action* sought to call attention to difficulties in the fundamental theoretical argumentations presented in that work, and so to place in doubt the automatism with which a theory of communicative action yields the dualism of lifeworld and system, and the historical diagnosis that the present period is marked by a painless uncoupling of system and lifeworld, as well as by dangers of a "colonization" of the lifeworld. It would, of course, be inconsistent, after repeated declarations that argumentations on these different levels can be separated, now to draw substantive conclusions about the characteristics of the present era. The program that has been suggested, namely that of a more broadly based theory of action, of the drawing of a clearer distinction between the superseding of the philosophy of consciousness and the intersubjective turn, of a theory of social order centered on the constitution of collective actors—this program, too, yields no substantive conclusions. Such conclusions likewise could be no more than the speculative transferral of metatheoretical decisions into empirical assertions. On the other hand, it goes without saying that the way this program is structured is motivated by substantive empirical and normative premises. What this leads to has already been formulated by several authors:[42] they doubt the alleged ease with which the "monetary-bureaucratic" complex is uncoupled from the lifeworld; they criticize the lack of a dimension of "intra-systemic" problems and contradictions; they lament the defensiveness of an argumentation that no longer poses the question of democratic control of economy and state; they point out the hypostatization of "system" and "lifeworld" into the societal domains, of state and economy, on the one hand, and the public sphere and the private sphere (family, neighborhood, voluntary associations), on the other hand (vol. 2, p. 309); they find fault with the abstractness of a position that, while it correctly interprets capitalist modernization as one-sided rationalization, supplies no criteria with which meaningful degrees of differentiation could be established.[43] I find all these criticisms convincing, but I do not want to treat them here. The only question which a metatheoretically oriented critique should not, on principle, avoid answering is whether phenomena that are convincingly analyzed by the criticized theory could at all be understood also within an alternative theoretical framework. If we identify the autonomous rationalization of the lifeworld, the painless uncoupling of the monetary-bureaucratic complex from the lifeworld, and the "painful" colonization of the lifeworld as the three principal notions guiding Habermas's analyses of the problems of the present within the framework of the concepts "system" and "lifeworld," then, after the validity of a theory of society proceeding on these two levels has been placed in doubt, we can examine these notions separately with respect to whether they can be transferred into an alternative theoretical framework. I consider Habermas's explanations of an autonomous rationalization of the lifeworld in the dimensions of value-generalization, universalization of law and morality, and progressive individuation to be an important accomplishment. However, the stress Habermas places on the autonomy of these rationalization processes springs precisely from the pressure exerted against this direction by functionalist models. If one rejects these, however, then it is not the deductive definition of microsocial phenomena on the basis of macrosocial functions that guides us, but a reconstruction of the manner in which societal conditions that have become autonomous can as such issue from the complex of normative traditions and everyday actions, of concrete historical situations and actions, and do so in the face of possibilities of resistance to them that are produced, ever anew. The upside-down world of apparently autonomous social structures is then left behind, at least theoretically. The uncoupling of economic development and the governmental decision-making process from the results of the communication of society's members by means of the privatization of structurally crucial economic decisions and/or undemocratic political structures, as well as the repercussions of "thoroughgoing capitalization" and bureaucratization in all domains of society, do not require for their explanation the dualism of a theory based on "system" and "lifeworld." There remains, then, the thesis of the "painless uncoupling" of the processes of material reproduction. This uncoupling is presented by Habermas not as a matter of empirical fact, but as a theoretical inference drawn from the nature of the media of communication, money, and power. However, this uncoupling cannot be reconstructed in this fashion in a theoretical framework that refers all phenomena of social order to an actual or virtual collective will of society's members. In such a theoretical framework, "money" and "power" would remain at the same analytical level as the other media of communication of systems theory; that is, they would serve to ease the burden borne by communication among society's members, but they could not serve as a substitute for that communication without significant consequences. Surely, the thesis of the painless uncoupling of system and lifeworld cannot have been the cause of Jürgen Habermas's enormous theoretical effort.

Notes

1. For the foundational significance of the problems of action and social order, see especially Jeffrey Alexander, *Theoretical Logic in Sociology,* vol. 1: *Positivism, Presuppositions, and Current Controversies* (Berkeley, 1982). (The independence of the two problems from one another is discussed on pp. 117ff.) My approval of Alexander's formulation of this problem should not be construed as an expression of substantive agreement with his theoretical solutions. Cf. my discussion of his work in "The Antinomies of Neofunctionalism," *Inquiry* 31 (1988), pp. 471–94 (reprinted in this volume).

2. Jürgen Habermas, "Labor and Interaction: Remarks on Hegel's Jena Philosophy of Mind," in *Theory and Practice* (Boston, 1973), pp. 142–69.

3. Axel Honneth, "Arbeit und instrumentales Handeln" in Axel Honneth and Urs Jaeggi (eds.), *Arbeit, Handlung, Normativität: Theorien des Historischen Materialismus* 2 (Frankfurt, 1980), pp. 185–233. For the connection between communicative abilities and human commerce with objects from the standpoint of the theory of socialization, see the chapter entitled "Constitution of the Physical Object and Role-taking," in Hans Joas, *G. H. Mead: A Contemporary Re-examination of His Thought,* tr. Raymond Meyer (Cambridge, Mass., 1985).

4. Jürgen Habermas, "The Classical Doctrine of Politics in Relation to Social Philosophy," in *Theory and Practice,* pp. 41–81. Thomas McCarthy, *The Critical Theory of Jürgen Habermas* (Cambridge, Mass., 1978).

5. Hannah Arendt, *The Human Condition* (Chicago, 1970).

6. Rüdiger Bubner, *Handlung, Sprache und Vernunft: Grundbegriffe praktischer Philosophie* (Frankfurt, 1982), pp. 61ff.

7. Isaiah Berlin, *Against the Current: Essays in the History of Ideas,* edited by Henry Harding (New York, 1980). Charles Taylor, *Hegel* (Cambridge, 1975). Habermas rejects the significance of this concept of action, objecting to it on empirical grounds, which are as such also questionable, in his "A Reply to My Critics," in J. B. Thompson and D. Held (eds.), *Habermas: Critical Debates* (London, 1983), pp. 219–83.

8. On this point, cf. my definitions of the concept of role in "Role Theories and Socialization Research," in H. J. Helle and S. N. Eisenstadt (eds.), *Microsociological Theory* (Berkeley, 1985), pp. 37–53. Reprinted in this volume.

9. As one example among many, cf. John Dewey, "The Reflex Arc Concept in Psychology," in John Dewey, *The Early Works*, vol. 5 (Carbondale, 1972), pp. 96–109. From this viewpoint, cf. the excellent analysis in Eduard Baumgarten, *Die geistigen Grundlagen des amerikanischen Gemeinwesens*, vol. 2 (Frankfurt, 1938), pp. 282ff. One of the few sociologists who have taken up the critique of the teleological interpretation of action, although with a very different end in mind than the one pursued here, is Niklas Luhmann, *Zweckbegriff und Systemrationalität* (Frankfurt, 1973), pp. 18ff.

10. This is, in my opinion, the *theoretically* interesting theme of Ulrich Oevermann's repeated critique of Habermas.

11. Cf. Harald Wenzel, "Mead und Parsons," in Hans Joas (ed.), *Das Problem der Intersubjektivität* (Frankfurt, 1985), pp. 26–59.

12. Emile Durkheim, *The Elementary Forms of the Religious Life*, tr. J. W. Swain (London, 1976).

13. Emile Durkheim, *Pragmatisme et sociologie* (Paris, 1955).

14. Emile Durkheim and Marcel Mauss, "De quelques formes primitives de classification," in Emile Durkheim, *Journal sociologique* (Paris, 1969), pp. 395–461.

15. I have treated this question in detail in "Durkheim and Pragmatism" (in this volume).

16. Johannes Berger, "The Linguistification of the Sacred and the Delinguistification of the Economy," in Axel Honneth and Hans Joas (eds.), *Communicative Action* (Cambridge, 1991), pp. 165–80; Veit-Michael Bader, "Schmerzlose Entkoppelung von System und Lebenswelt? Engpässe der Theorie des kommunikativen Handelns von Jürgen Habermas," *Kennis en Methode* 7 (1983), pp. 329–55; Axel Honneth, *Kritik der Macht: Reflexionsstufen einer kritischen Gesellschaftstheorie* (Frankfurt, 1985).

17. Using the theory of action, it can be shown that human symbolizing operations make it possible for human beings to cooperate and to communicate without being present together in the same place at the same time.

18. This seems to me to be the point correctly made in the article by Alfred Bohnen, "Handlung, Lebenswelt und System in der soziologischen Theoriebildung: Zur Kritik der Theorie des kommunikativen Handelns von Jürgen Habermas," *Zeitschrift für Soziologie* 13 (1984), pp. 191–203.

19. Robert K. Merton, *Social Theory and Social Structure* (London, 1964); Talcott Parsons, *The Social System* (London, 1951), p. 30, n.5.

20. John Dewey, *The Public and Its Problems* (New York, 1927); and *Reconstruction in Philosophy* (New York, 1950).

21. See also Wolfgang van den Daele, " 'Unbeabsichtigte Folgen' sozialen Handelns: Anmerkungen zur Karriere des Themas" (and the other contributions on this topic), in Joachim Matthes (ed.), *Lebenswelt und soziale Probleme: Verhandlungen des 20. Deutschen Soziologentages zu Bremen 1980* (Frankfurt, 1981), pp. 237ff.

22. Max Weber, "Über einige Kategorien der verstehenden Soziologie," in *Gesammelte Aufsätze zur Wissenschaftslehre* (Tübingen, 1973), 4th ed., pp. 427–74. (Appeared in English as "Some Categories of Interpretive Sociology" in *The Sociological Quarterly* 22 [spring 1981], pp. 151–80.) Donald N. Levine has written an interesting essay from the standpoint of the rationality of types of order in Weber's theory, namely "Rationality and Freedom: Weber and Beyond," *Sociological Inquiry* 51 (1981), pp. 5–25.

23. Niklas Luhmann, "Zweck-Herrschaft-System: Grundbegriffe und Prämissen Max Webers," in Renate Mayntz (ed.), *Bürokratische Organisation* (Cologne, 1968),

pp. 36–55; and Luhmann's *Zweckbegriff und Systemrationalität* (Frankfurt, 1973).

24. In that case, Husserl would be an action theorist and utilitarianism or the subjective theory of value a theory of order in economics.

25. I go into Habermas's interpretation of Mead in more detail in my introduction to *Das Problem der Intersubjektivität*, pp. 7–25.

26. George Herbert Mead, *Selected Writings* (Indianapolis, 1964).

27. Talcott Parsons, *The Structure of Social Action* (1937; New York, 1968); here pp. 250ff.

28. In his late essay on Cooley, Parsons explains that the concept of action is to be introduced on an analytical level which presupposes neither the individual nor an acting collective as a reference. Talcott Parsons, "Cooley and the Problem of Internalization," in Albert Reiss (ed.), *Cooley and Sociological Analysis* (Ann Arbor, 1968), pp. 48–67.

29. Richard Münch, "Von der Rationalisierung zur Verdinglichung der Lebenswelt?," *Soziologische Revue* 5 (1982), pp. 390–97. Cf. also Münch, *Theorie des Handelns* (Frankfurt, 1982), and my discussion of this book, "Handlungstheorie und das Problem sozialer Ordnung," *Kölner Zeitschrift für Soziologie und Sozialpsychologie* 36 (1984), pp. 165–72.

30. This is true, for example, of Parsons's emphasis on the difference between professionalization and bureaucratization.

31. At this point, reflections about the consequences of discourse ethics for the judgment of the rationality of types of social order are called for.

32. David Lockwood, "Social Integration and System Integration," in G. Zollschan and W. Hirsch (eds.), *Explorations in Social Change* (Boston, 1964), pp. 244–57; Nicos Mouzelis, "Social and System Integration: Some Reflections on a Fundamental Distinction," *British Journal of Sociology* 15 (1974), pp. 395–409; Ramesh Mishra, "System Integration, Social Action and Change: Some Problems in Sociological Analysis," in *Sociological Review* 30 (1982), pp. 5–22.

33. Habermas himself uses such an argumentation against Horkheimer and Adorno (*TCA*, vol. 2, p. 490).

34. Jürgen Habermas, *On the Logic of the Social Sciences*, tr. Shierry Weber Nicholsen and Jerry A. Stark (Cambridge, Mass., 1989).

35. Anthony Giddens, "Functionalism: Après la lutte," *Social Research* 43 (1976), pp. 352–66. Extremely interesting from this standpoint is the controversy about Jon Elster's critique of functionalism in *Theory and Society* 11 (1982), pp. 453–539, with contributions from Jon Elster, G. A. Cohen, P. van Parijs, John E. Roemer, Johannes Berger and Claus Offe, and Anthony Giddens.

36. An exemplary presentation of the theory of "negotiated order" can be found in Anselm Strauss et al., "The Hospital and Its Negotiated Order," in Eliot Freidson (ed.), *The Hospital in Modern Society* (New York, 1963), pp. 147–69. For a review of the relevant literature, see David Maines, "Social Organization and Social Structure in Symbolic Interactionist Thought," *Annual Review of Sociology* 3 (1977), pp. 235–59. Also relevant to this topic are the political philosophy of Antonio Gramsci and the interesting attempt by Amitai Etzioni, *The Active Society* (New York, 1971).

37. Jürgen Habermas, "Können komplexe Gesellschaften eine vernünftige Identität ausbilden?," In Habermas and Dieter Henrich, *Zwei Reden* (Frankfurt, 1974), pp. 23–84, above all, pp. 57ff.

38. Perhaps I should make it clear that I am not condemning social-scientific func-

tionalism entirely. However, the relative success of its models can also be accounted for and appropriated within a different theoretical framework.

39. George Herbert Mead, *The Philosophy of the Act* (Chicago, 1938), pp. 26ff; Georg Lukács, *Die Eigenart des Ästhetischen,* 2 vols. (Neuwied, 1963); Agnes Heller, *Everyday Life,* tr. George Campbell (Boston, 1984). (See also my introduction to the German edition of Heller's work [Frankfurt, 1978], pp. 7–23).

40. Talcott Parsons and Edward A. Shils (eds.), *Toward a General Theory of Action* (New York, 1962); Talcott Parsons, *The Social System* (London, 1951).

41. Interesting objections to Habermas's introduction of the concept of the lifeworld into his argumentation can be found in Herbert Schnädelbach, "The Transformation of Critical Theory," in Axel Honneth and Hans Joas (eds.), *Communicative Action* (Cambridge, 1991), pp. 7–22.

42. See note 16. Also worth reading is Otto Kallscheuer, "Auf der Suche nach einer politischen Theorie bei Jürgen Habermas," in *Ästhetik und Kommunikation* 12 (1981), no. 45–46, pp. 171–82.

43. With regard to Habermas's interpretation of Marx, I should at least like to point out that, as a rule, Marx is not criticized for his lack of understanding of capitalism's civilizing role, as he is by Habermas, but rather for exaggerating that role.

6 Institutionalization as a Creative Process: The Sociological Importance of Cornelius Castoriadis's Political Philosophy

If it is not to lapse into academic sterility, sociological theory must continually debate the important public issues and approaches to social theory that arise outside its own boundaries. Otherwise, sociological theory is in danger of occupying itself with merely self-posed problems without hope of capturing the public's interest and risking a creeping loss of influence within the family of social- and human-scientific disciplines. The extraordinarily strong interest evinced in the writings of Jürgen Habermas and Anthony Giddens in recent American discussions of sociological theory testifies to a recognition by sociologists of this need to expand their inquiries, but it is also clear that this need cannot be fully satisfied by its own intellectual means and resources.

The publication of the English translation of a decade-old French book provides an occasion for calling attention to the work of a social theorist whose stature as a thinker is, without qualification, comparable to that of the aforementioned theorists, but whose work has heretofore gone almost unnoticed by sociologists. Certain of Cornelius Castoriadis's ideas have exercised a surreptitious influence through the writings of Alain Touraine, which, however, offer a wealth of empirical data at the expense of theoretical exactness. Cornelius Castoriadis is not a sociologist, and he is, moreover, quite skeptical about the sociological project insofar as it seeks to replace the old political philosophy with technical knowledge modeled on the positive sciences and oriented to immediate application. Castoriadis's entire personal history predisposes him for the role of a boundary crosser between the disciplines, between philosophy and science, and also between theoretical systematization and engagement in social movements.

Born in Greece in 1922, he joined the Greek Communist party as a young man and took part in the struggle against the occupying German army. Disappointed by the Stalinist character of that party, he switched, even before the end of the war, to the Trotskyist Fourth International, which for a time embodied for many European and American intellectuals the hope of a democratic and revolutionary socialism. How-

Originally published in English in the *American Journal of Sociology* 94 (1988–89), pp. 1184–99;

ever, soon after arriving in Paris, where he intended to study philosophy, he broke with this organization too. Together with a number of other, now-famous French intellectuals, he founded a political and theoretical journal, *Socialisme ou barbarie.* While professionally active as an economist, he published many analyses of capitalism, of the Soviet system, and of Marxism, using different pseudonyms. While the high intellectual quality of these articles is undeniable, it is also true that they were politically ineffectual for a long time and burdened by the radical Left's sectarian polemics. Castoriadis was one of the intellectual inspirations for the unexpected eruption of May 1968 in Paris. Even before this uprising, he had published a critical assessment of Marxism that was, for him, tantamount to a rupture with that theory. During this period, he changed professions and became a practicing psychoanalyst. But if this were all, I would not be discussing him here. Castoriadis withdrew from the fashionable intellectual movements of the time and worked for years on a new start in his own thinking, to build with laborious reflection the basis of an alternative theory on the ruins of a discredited Marxism.

Castoriadis's undertaking clearly differs in two respects from crucial features of the French zeitgeist after 1968. It is neither structuralist (or poststructuralist) nor liberal. Castoriadis's extensive work on a theory of language is intended primarily to engage structuralism at the very point on which this theory bases its scientific claims. He seeks a nonstructuralist theory of the sign and of the symbolical. But his trenchant critique of Marxism does not make him an uncritical champion of liberalism, as if the failure of Marxism "proved" that liberalism is the ideal or the only acceptable form of government (*Domaines de l'homme [DH]*, p. 106). The critical examination of psychoanalysis and the alternative theory offered by Castoriadis can be characterized negatively, first of all: he polemicizes against both Jacques Lacan's theory and the form of therapy Lacan advocated and practiced. Speaking positively, in the writings of this transitional period, Castoriadis subscribes to the tenets of a post-empiricist theory of science: "The illusions about successive approximations, about the accumulation of results, about the gradual and systematic conquest of a simple rational order pre-existing within the world are being dissipated" (*Crossroads in the Labyrinth [CL]*, p. xiv.) For Castoriadis, however, this recognition does not give carte blanche for relativism or for intellectual arbitrariness; rather, it poses afresh the problem of the history of science within the framework of scientific self-reflection and hence the problem of history in general.

Castoriadis's principal work, *The Imaginary Institution of Society,* now available in English, contains both the critical assessment of

Marxism that he developed in the 1960s and the most comprehensive and systematic presentation of his own theory that he has written to date. Since that work's original publication, however, a new collection of his essays has appeared in France, *Domaines de l'homme.* Here for the first time Castoriadis's philosophical writings are printed together with articles about the political events of the day. Complex and profound essays are intermingled with statements on more transient issues, wearying the reader with repetition. Even so, Castoriadis's writings make a favorable impression on the reader, who senses that they were written by a tenacious thinker whose intellectual projects are long term, who argues with exactitude, and who pays no heed to disciplinary boundaries. In the midst of the *industrie du vide,* as he calls it, that is rampant in Paris and elsewhere, Castoriadis champions an old-fashioned moral responsibility for the protection of authentic public discussion, not only against the state's attempts to influence it, but also against the deforming effects of commercialization, "contre le bluff, la démagogie et la prostitution de l'esprit" (*DH,* p. 25).

Now, in order to understand the forces motivating Castoriadis's own theory, it is necessary to examine his assessment and critique of Marxism. First, from the standpoint of the theory of action, he finds fault with Marx for ignoring the real activity of human beings and thereby becoming deterministic. According to Castoriadis, Marx's assertions are characterized by technological determinism, doctrinal economics, or quasi-utilitarianism. By positing an autonomous logic underlying the development of the forces of production, Marx fails to address the question of the social conditions required for the origin and choice of particular technologies and of the cultural response to, and processing of, these technologies. When Marx conceives of the economy as a closed system, he quickly encounters difficulties, which are immanent in that conception; the dominance of the law of value in the capitalist economy rests on a culturally influenced definition of value that is an object of controversy and struggle and that enters into the determination of the value of commodified labor power. By conceiving, in a quasi-utilitarian manner, of human action as arising solely from economic motives, he endangers the applicability of his theory beyond capitalism and contradicts the findings of economic anthropology. Castoriadis has given long and careful thought to the labor theory of value and, in a marvelous essay, "Value, Equality, Justice, Politics: From Marx to Aristotle and from Aristotle to Ourselves" (*CL,* pp. 260–339), he demonstrates that Marx continuously vacillated among three interpretations of capitalism within the framework of the labor theory of value.

It is not clear in Marx's analysis whether the capitalist economy actually transforms human beings and their diverse kinds of labor into something that is homogeneous and measurable, or whether that economy only makes visible something that has always been so but has remained hidden from human beings by their system of ideas, or, last, whether the qualitative sameness of "abstract labor" is only an appearance resulting from the reification effected by capitalism, an appearance that stems from the transformation of labor power into a commodity. This lack of clarity is an indication of a more fundamental ambiguity about why a particular value is a value. Had Marx clearly addressed this question, he would have had to abandon the hope of elaborating a science of capitalism's basic processes, independent of cultural preconditions. With this critique of Marx's labor theory of value, Castoriadis rejects the very heart of Marx's critique of political economy, the core of his scientific life's work. Castoriadis does not, however, reject it in favor of the marginalist revolution's subjectivist theory of value. For Castoriadis, this conception of the economy as a logic of the choice of means is vitiated by a fundamentally untenable view of the relationship of means and ends in social life. His critique differs from that of Habermas, who maintains that the conditions for the validity of this theory obtain only during a certain stage of liberal capitalism. Habermas concludes that, with the increasing prevalence of monopolies, economic intervention by the state, and the scientific organization of production, the possibilities of applying Marx's theory are also eliminated, and the whole "production paradigm" becomes obsolete. Since Castoriadis's critique is more immanent than that of Habermas, the significance of the concerns informing the labor theory of value and the "philosophy of praxis" are not lost if Marx's theory is not valid. These concerns, however, cannot be adequately expressed in the "production paradigm." The unresolved contradiction between Marx's deterministic reduction of human action and a practical philosophy of revolution is of crucial importance. For Castoriadis, a false scientistic ideal of theory is intrinsic to Marx's inconsistencies.

As an alternative to the positive sciences' conception of theory, not Marx but Aristotle is the decisive authority for Castoriadis's understanding of a practical philosophy. Using political thought (but also pedagogical and medical thinking), Castoriadis explains the nature of a nontechnical relation between knowledge and action. In all these domains, comprehensive knowledge does not assume the form of lawlike propositions employed to realize external and predetermined goals. Instead, nontechnical action bears its end within itself; the knowledge corresponding to it is always fragmentary and must rely on continuous expansion of itself within concrete action, without, however, ever becoming a theory *about* an object—"To think: to *elucidate,* not to 'theorise.' Theory is only one moment of elucidation, and always lacunary and fragmentary" (*CL,* p. 84). In this recourse to the origin of practical philosophy in the praxis of the Greek polis, Castoriadis differs from other critics of a latent positivism in Marx's thought, such as Lukács, Korsch, and Gramsci. In this regard, and in his fundamental reservations about the cognitive ideal of the social sciences, he resembles Martin Heidegger, Hans-Georg Gadamer, Joachim Ritter, Hannah Arendt, and, today, Alasdair MacIntyre. But none of these make such intense use in the theoretical model of practical philosophy as Castoriadis does of a moment that is present but marginalized in Marx's thought: the creative nature of "praxis."

In both his concept of labor and his historiographical analyses of the class struggles in France, Marx ascribed to human action a creative capacity, an ability to produce new objects or new social forms. Castoriadis does not try to trace the intellectual path along which Aristotelian practical philosophy became so transformed by German idealism and German romanticism that Marx was able to use it as the starting point of his own reflections. But because Castoriadis's own thinking straddles Aristotle and Marx, he is sensitive to the traces of a romantically transformed Aristotelianism in Marx's thought. Marx charges the concept of praxis with the meaning that classical philosophy counterposed to *techné:* "poiesis," which is not imitative but creative. Castoriadis takes this understanding of praxis further: "To do something, to do a book, to make a child, a revolution, or just doing as such, is projecting oneself into a future situation which is opened up on all sides to the unknown, which, therefore, one cannot possess beforehand in thought, but which one must necessarily assume to be defined in its aspects relevant to present decisions" (*The Imaginary Institution of Society [IIS],* p. 87). He vehemently opposes, though, the reduction of this possibility of creating new things or social forms to the contingency of unforeseeable events. Admittedly, contingency is one of the fundamental characteristics of historical processes, but it is not their distinguishing feature. In human history, the contingency of natural processes is mitigated because man "can provide new responses to the *'same'* situations or create new situations" (*IIS,* p. 44).

For sociological theory this means, first of all, that Castoriadis is working with concepts of the theory of action that cannot be made to fit the rigid dichotomy of theoretical models of rational action and their normative critique (see my critique of Jeffrey Alexander in this volume).

Castoriadis does not consider the goal-oriented, planned moment as the primary component of action because it constitutes only the technical moment of an activity that requires the setting of conditions, goals, and means. The implications of this position, however, extend further and lead to a questioning of the theoretical status of social-scientific theories in general. Just as the plan is but one moment of action, so too is the explanatory theory only a single moment of a historical self-reflection that expresses itself in science. Historical and social processes become intelligible only within the framework of practical intentions or of schemes of action; all metatheoretical categorial frameworks are themselves part of the history they set out to explain.

This idea was by no means foreign to Marx. He regarded his scientific labors as part of a praxis that would bring about a worldwide revolution. But he undercut this idea because, following Hegel's example, he considered it possible to anticipate the goal of human history. By holding this position, Marx joined his leanings toward a causally deterministic science of the historical with a teleological conception of history. Inasmuch as Marxism demands, writes Castoriadis, that "by asserting that everything must be grasped in terms of causation and at the same time that everything must be thought in terms of meaning, that there is but one immense causal chain which is simultaneously one immense chain of meaning, it exacerbates the two poles of the enigma to the point of making it impossible to think rationally about it" (*IIS*, p. 53). However, the historical character of human action, and knowledge of it, acquires its existential seriousness only when the openness of history, its always only partial rationality, and the irreversibility of human actions are recognized.

The driving force behind Castoriadis's penetrating critique of Marxism is his horror of the states that have elevated Marxism to an official ideology. In his eyes, his theory is not a rejection but a radicalization of Marxism: "Starting from revolutionary Marxism, we have arrived at the point where we have to choose between remaining Marxist and remaining revolutionaries" (*IIS*, p. 14). In Castoriadis's view, the deterministic versions of Marxism uphold bureaucratic claims to authority and domination. Whereas democratic institutions serve as a counterweight to this embodiment of formal rationality in capitalism, the social model represented by the Soviet Union is characterized by the total dominance of this one principle. The ideology of legitimation of "scientific socialism" is in and of itself undemocratic, since the claim to provide scientific answers to questions about political goals invalidates authentic decision making by the members of a society. In opposition to that ideology and its consequences, Castoriadis advocates forms of political self-organization, such as councils and models of industrial self-management, that have appeared only in isolated and short-lived instances. It is not my purpose to pass judgment on the political plausibility of this orientation but to cast light on the background of Castoriadis's theoretical innovations. For this orientation to the model supplied by revolutionary action gives him the strength to demonstrate the creativity that is proper to all action, just as Herder and German romanticism built on an examination of aesthetic praxis, pragmatists investigated experimental scientific praxis, and Marx reflected on materially productive praxis. This theory of action is the foundation of Castoriadis's political philosophy, which is built around the concept of the institution and also provides the basis for his efforts to elaborate an "ontology of indeterminacy." Creative action refers to the creation of institutions and to the world as a sphere of possibility for action.

The concept of the institution is one of the most important categories for both sociology and anthropology. It was given its most ambitious theoretical formulation in Durkheim's theory of religion, which Parsons tended to undermine by conceiving of institutionalization processes more as the realization of preexisting values than as the creation of new values. Castoriadis is clearly interested in the nonfunctionalist components of Durkheim's later theories. His theory of the institution is intended as a critique of the functionalist interpretation of institutions, which seeks to explain social phenomena by means of system imperatives yet is unable to state any stable human needs or system requirements. If, however, system imperatives themselves consist in cultural definitions, then the possibility of struggling over and arguing about these definitions within the framework of social systems must also be considered. These imperatives do not represent independent, nominal value but irreducible conceptions of a possible future. "The modern view of the institution," declares Castoriadis, "which reduces its signification to the functional aspect, is only partially correct. To the extent that it presents itself as *the* truth about the problem of the institution, it is only a projection. It projects onto the whole of history an idea taken not even from the actual reality of the institutions belonging to the Western capitalist world (which, despite the vast movement of rationalization, have never been and are still no more than partially functional), but from what this world *would like* its institutions to be" (*IIS*, p. 131).

Although one might wish that the critical examination of this view of the institution were broader and included an assessment of Talcott Parsons's enormous theoretical accomplishments, little can be added to Castoriadis's critique of structuralism. The reader senses the great influence of this school of thought in France. Inasmuch as structuralism apprehends only the symbolic dimension of the institution, it is a one-sided view of social phenomena that complements functionalism's one-sided understanding of them. In his essays, Castoriadis argues against the "structuralist ideology" and criticizes it for eliminating the meaning-producing accomplishments of the subject and therewith the subject's responsibility for and power over history. In contrast, *The Imaginary Institution of Society* presents a thoroughgoing and systematic alternative. Taking up reflections of Maurice Merleau-Ponty, Castoriadis denies structuralism's central argument, that linguistic theory has shown that meaning is the result of a combination of signs, merely the difference among the bearers of meaning. It is true that the relation between the signified and the signifier is not an empirical or a logical one; what is decisive, however, is that the relation of a sign to a meaning is the result of the institutionalization of a sign system and that sign systems must be understood together with their extrasystemic references to what is perceived and intended. The arbitrary character of the sign, to which structuralism attaches such importance, is retained, but it is accounted for by a process of institutionalization. In this way, Castoriadis reveals the meaning-originating accomplishments of the subject, behind structuralism's back, as it were.

For the determination of linguistic meaning is never completed but can be continued indefinitely. Every linguistic utterance becomes understandable only when placed in its proper context; this context comprehends both the sign system of the entire language and the complexes of affairs making up the universe. In "The Sayable and the Unsayable" (*CL*, pp. 119–44), Castoriadis explains, in reference to Merleau-Ponty, that structuralism should be understood as merely the reverse side of the phenomenological idea of a constitutive consciousness; in contrast, his own theory of language makes it possible to preserve subjectivity without making it all-important. In the language it shares with others, the subject is not obligated to make specific utterances but rather is aware—in Merleau-Ponty's words—of a "significative intention," "a void which is determined in the sense that the one who is about to speak knows that there is something other and more to be said than what has already been said, but knows nothing positive beyond that fact, beyond the fact that it is not said by what has already been said" (*CL*, p. 132). In language there is an interplay of individual signification and institutions that cannot be grasped with the typical theoretical models used by science to understand the social and the historical.

In his critique of the false theoretical ideals of the non-Marxist human and social sciences, Castoriadis repeats the stages of his critique of Marxism. The transfer into those sciences of physical or logical models can lead to a failure to grasp what is unique about human society and human history. These attempts to define society and history separately convince him of the fundamental falsity of such models. Also of importance for sociology, he objects (*IIS*, pp. 177ff.) to identifying the distinguishing features of human society with the emergence of supraindividual phenomena or with the primacy of the collectivity. Not collectivity and emergence but the specific structure of human collectivity *and* individuality is at issue. For history, this position entails a refusal of deterministic, predictive statements: "L'histoire est création du sens—et il ne peut pas y avoir d''explication' d'une création, il ne peut y avoir qu'une compréhension ex post facto de son sens" (history is the creation of meaning—there can be no "explanation" of a creation; there can be only a comprehension ex post facto of its meaning) (*DH*, p. 220). Thus the central idea of Castoriadis's theory of action, the creative dimension of action, reappears as the central determinant of the peculiarity of the social and the historical. Social reality is described as "the union *and* the tension of instituting society and of instituted society, of history made and of history in the making" (*IIS*, p. 108). What the false models fail to account for is precisely the creation of things that are radically new, a creation arising out of the inherent potentials of the imaginary. For Castoriadis, the imaginary is an ultimate determination; it cannot be accounted for by anything else, nor should it be confused with a copy of the perceived world, a mere sublimation of animal drives, or a strictly rational elaboration of the given. Thus, the title of Castoriadis's principal work, which may at first seem strange to the reader, becomes understandable: society is the result of an institutionalization process, and this process, because it arises from the imaginary, from the human capacity to conceive meaning, has an irreducibly creative dimension.

This insight can be pursued in a number of different directions. First, it can be applied empirically to the collective action of social movements that alter as well as produce institutions. This path has been followed by Alain Touraine, although not by Castoriadis himself, raising questions about the critical analysis of the present—the current significance of such social movements and the imaginary core of modern Western culture and of other cultures. In this connection, Castoriadis strongly suggests the central importance of rationality as an imaginary schema underlying the cultural dominance of technology, science, bureaucracy, and economic efficiency. However, he does not clearly differentiate his position from similar theoretical models such as that of Max Weber or from competing ways of thinking. Second, the cultural and intellectual history of this theory of creativity and of the social institution can be traced in the published fragments of the major study that he has announced. Perhaps the most impressive example is the study of the Greek polis and the "creation" of democracy (*DH,* pp. 261–306). In this essay, Castoriadis investigates the intertwined origins of democracy and philosophy, finding that they share a disavowal of mere social unrest and of myth. In the democracy of the polis, an institutionalization of the collective shaping of social institutions appears for the first time; in philosophy, inquiry into the truth and the ethical rightness of received ideas and beliefs.

In his principal work to date, however, Castoriadis follows a third path: the elaboration of an ontology of indeterminacy as a presupposition for creation. The starting point for this undertaking is Castoriadis's clear grasp of the problems posed for a philosophy of praxis or a theory of action when these rest on traditional metaphysical premises. How is intentional action possible if the world is a cosmos of endless, deterministic concatenations of causes and effects, or else a chaos that can acquire determinate form only through the imposition of human schematizations? For Castoriadis, the problems contained in the self-understanding of the social and natural sciences have their essential foundation in these sciences' unexamined dependence on an ontology of determinacy. In order to escape from this predicament, he broadens his theory of the interplay between that which has been instituted and the instituting agency into an ontology of "magma," of a fluid substrate of all determinate being. In doing so, he is not seeking to establish the exclusive, privileged status of this indeterminacy, as did Bergson and Heidegger; rather, he acknowledges the pragmatic necessity of determinacy for everyday action and speech. Using the Greek terms "legein" and "teukhein," Castoriadis investigates these islands of determinacy in an ocean of indeterminacy.

In this investigation, he persuasively demonstrates the inadequacy of the traditional mode of thinking, in particular through an examination of the phenomenon of time and of the experience of time. To sociologists, these problems might not seem to affect positive research. However, since the postempiricist turn of the theory of science, no scientist can permit him- or herself the luxury of indifference to the metaphysical implications of his or her methods. Furthermore, Castoriadis is able to explain the significance of his reflections for an adequate theoretical understanding of personality and of temporality. His reflections on these topics, are, I find, most similar to the late work of George Herbert Mead, which has also been little understood, and to the writings of John Dewey from the same time. For these American thinkers, too, the philosophy of action led to a theory of time and of nature as conditions of the possibility of action. Castoriadis's ontological enterprise is important for sociologists for a second reason. At the present time, at least in the Federal Republic of Germany, Niklas Luhmann's attempt to develop functionalist systems theory further, into a theory of "autopoiesis," on the basis of recent developments in the biological theory of cognition, is one of the most influential theoretical approaches. How else should the discussion of this approach, which, like that of Castoriadis, focuses on the self-origination of system structures, proceed than by reflection on the ontological premises that are implicit in Luhmann's program?

For Castoriadis, taking leave of Marxism does not mean taking leave of a concept of central importance at least for the young Marx: alienation. On the contrary. His theory of the institution leads directly to a concept of alienation: "Alienation occurs when the imaginary moment in the institution becomes autonomous and predominates, which leads to the institution's becoming autonomous and predominating with respect to society . . . in other words [society] does not recognize in the imaginary of institutions something that is its own product" (*IIS*, p. 132). Thus, it is not the nature of the institutions as such, but the relationship of a society to its institutions, that is of decisive importance for the question of alienation. With a pathos of enlightenment equal to that of Kant, Castoriadis counterposes to alienation the positive concept of autonomy. He uses the term in complete accordance with its etymological sense; autonomy means a society's or an individual's making the laws by which it is bound. In a reformulation of Freud's dictum, Castoriadis expresses the goal of autonomy thus: "Where No one was, there We shall be" (*CL*, p. 40). The project of autonomy is characterized by the practical dissolution of governance by others and of subjection to unrecognized mechanisms.

If this project is to be more than the proclamation of the values of the young Marx typical of humanistic postwar Marxism, then Castoriadis must answer several questions: In what kind of a relationship does individual autonomy stand to social autonomy? What are the consequences of the findings of psychoanalysis and of its program for our conceptions of individual autonomy? By what means can autonomy be gained and, speaking with Kant, the immaturity for which we are ourselves responsible be left behind?

Castoriadis's responses to the first and last of these questions undoubtedly make his task too easy. Social autonomy is brought about by revolution: "The socialist revolution aims at transforming society through the autonomous action of people and at establishing a society organized to promote the autonomy of all its members" (*IIS*, p. 95). However, as a result of his rejection of Marxism and, since 1968, his loss of belief in the historical mission of the working class, the identity of the actors who will carry out the revolution has become uncertain. Clinging to the act of revolution thus seems, at least prima facie, to be a remnant of his Marxism, and his overemphasis on it may be a response to accusations of accommodation and resignation. I will return to this point later. The way Castoriadis joins individual and social autonomy is similarly unsatisfactory. According to his theoretical model, individual autonomy is only possible within the framework of social autonomy. Habermas has correctly pointed out that Castoriadis oversteps the bounds of the Aristotelian concept of praxis when he gives it far-reaching implications that are consonant with the enterprise of the Enlightenment. Castoriadis supplies no arguments against elitist models of autonomy that are valid only for a particular individual or for the few, regardless of whether these models are of the Nietzschean or colonial sort. That is not to say that moral philosophy cannot demonstrate the necessity of linking individual and social autonomy. Rather, Castoriadis does not provide a convincing demonstration.

This criticism cannot be made of Castoriadis's discussion of individual autonomy in light of the recognition of the drive-based and corporeally conditioned nature of our egos, a recognition that has been asserted most consistently by psychoanalysis. Just as social autonomy was understood as a different relationship of society to its institutions, Castoriadis has developed a concept of individual autonomy not as completely conscious intentionality but as a changed relation between conscious and unconscious intentions. If, for Freud, the goal of psychoanalysis is expressed in the precept: "Where the id was, there the ego should come to be," then Castoriadis adds to the Freudian dictum the injunction: "Where the ego is, there the id should show itself."

When German romanticism turned away from Kant, the problem was raised of how to adhere to a concept of moral autonomy that might be achieved only at the cost of the imagination, which itself required freedom from the control of reason. Does moral autonomy necessarily imply a repressive relationship to oneself? Does self-control require self-repression, and does creativity demand renunciation of self-control? Within the psychoanalytic system of concepts, Castoriadis seeks to apprehend the conflict between drives and reality, which appears not to be susceptible to arbitration, in a manner different from that of Kant. He makes the imaginary reaction to, and processing of, both drives and reality a central theoretical concern. The imaginary accomplishments of the subject render moral autonomy possible, both in relation to reality and in relation to the drives. I can learn to accept statements about reality as true even if they contradict my own wishes. Similarly, I can learn to acknowledge my drives as they are even if I do not want to follow them. "An autonomous subject is one," declares Castoriadis, "that knows itself to be justified in concluding: this is indeed true, and: this is indeed my desire" (*IIS*, p. 104). This theoretical transposition, which has analogues in ego psychology and in the theories of the self proposed by psychoanalysis and symbolic interactionism, does not put forward the goal of an ideal person who has once and for all achieved control over himself and has silenced the voice of his unconscious, but rather of a person who has as open relation to and dealings with himself as with others, and who allows himself to be surprised over and over again by the unforeseeable wealth of his own fantasies and ideas.

This concept of moral autonomy, grounded in a way different from that in Kant's philosophy, is immanently tied to a theory of the human being's corporeality. If intentionality cannot be limited to the sphere of conscious intentions, but instead requires a new understanding of a person's relation to his unconscious and unexamined intentions, then the body as the locus of an unexamined involvement in the world must be considered part of our concept of action. Castoriadis does not pursue this insight to elaborate a theory of action from the standpoint of philosophical anthropology but develops, with exclusive reference to psychoanalysis, the basic outlines of a theory of socialization (*IIS*, pp. 273–339) that follows from his model of the imaginary. Since, for Castoriadis, the imaginary must not be understood causally, it cannot be a causal result of the activity of the drives. He thus inverts the relationship between drives and imagination because he does not regard fantasies as the expression or the compensatory satisfaction of drives but instead posits an originary imagination that is prior to the organization of the drives and that aids the drives to attain psychical representation. But how should we conceive of this originary imagination? In a radical manner, Castoriadis puts himself in the situation of the child before the differentiation of subject and object has taken place. In this situation, even the imagination is unable to make a mental representation of objects that satisfy needs and drives. Thus the imagination can originally apprehend only an undifferentiated unity of the child and the world, of subject and object, which is satisfying in itself. However, this state is one that is incapable of ever appearing as a mental representation: "What is missing and will always be missing is the unrepresentable element of an initial 'state,' that which is before separation and differentiation, a proto-representation which the psyche is no longer capable of producing, which has always served as a magnet for the psychical field as the presentification of an indissociable unity of figure, meaning and pleasure" (*IIS*, p. 296).

Castoriadis goes so far as to refer to this forever-lost state of unity as the primordial monadic state of the subject and identifies such phenomena as the wish for total union with another or the aspiration to total intellectual apprehension of the world with the longing to return to this primordial state. He develops a theory of socialization in which well-known theses of Freud are reformulated—for example, the stages of the adaptation of the psyche to social institutions and the psychical mechanisms such as projection and identification. Socialization, however, is never a social shaping of the inherent possibilities of the drives that may vary over an unrestricted range; it is, rather, a process of confrontation and conflictual interaction between the imaginative life of the individual and social institutions as the embodiment of collective mental representations. This confrontation, which constitutes the socialization process, is like the life of institutions in general, a process having unforeseeable results. Psychoanalysis is an elucidation not only "of the way in which the creations of society and history find analytic 'support' within the individual psyche, but of the psychic *sap* which the latter constantly supplies to the former" (*CL*, p. 95). The recognition of the *sociality* of the actor must not be paid for with the loss of the possibility of grasping the *creativity* of the individual imaginative life.

Castoriadis's reference to the "primordial monadic state" might give the impression that his conception of socialization lacks an adequate "mediation of individual and society," a criticism advanced by Habermas, adducing Mead as a counterexample. I consider this criticism misplaced, since Castoriadis does regard individuation as the result of socialization. He refuses only to derive the unconscious motivations and mental images of the individual from the social conditions of this socialization. If we consider that in his category of the "I" Mead, too, counterposed a biological root of spontaneity to the socially produced agencies of the "me" and the "generalized other," then there is no perceptible difference between Mead and Castoriadis on this point. It would be a Parsonian misunderstanding of Mead to strip the "I" entirely of the character of an extrasocial dimension that Mead, admittedly, conceives of as biological. Whereas Mead first accepts the premises of the psychology of instincts and then adopts Freudian ideas of the fundamental impulses to solidarity and aggression, Castoriadis develops his theory of the child's early experience of unity as the basis of the evolution of the drives. Unfortunately, Castoriadis himself almost forces his reader into this misunderstanding.

With his talk of the monad, as well as his explicit refusal of a biological basis of human social behavior and his belief in the presocial character of prehuman history (*IIS,* p. 205ff.), his argument in *The Imaginary Institution of Society* precludes the possibility of embedding his theory of socialization in a philosophical anthropology that recognizes the continuity and discontinuity of animals and human beings.

This weakness is directly related to a further difficulty. Castoriadis's theory of the psyche led necessarily to the idea of a "protorepresentation." On the other hand, his descriptions of the child's psyche recognize that in the early stages of our development, just as in the unconscious of the adult, we cannot even think of mental representations as separate from affects and intentions. Then, however, there is no "protorepresentation" but rather a "protoexperience" for which the categories of the later, more differentiated stages of psyche's development are not suited. However, Castoriadis does not develop a positive theory of the manner in which the child *practically* confronts and interacts with his world. He does not link the body of psychoanalytic knowledge with that gained by a developmental psychology that, like Piaget's, does not start from mental representations but from modes of behavior, sensory-motor circuits. Castoriadis's inability to relate prehuman and human sociality to each other has a parallel in his inability to treat the unity of mental representation, affect, and quasi intentionality that is characteristic of the young child's behavior as practical schemata rather than as some sort of "mental representation," a concept that belongs to the terminology of a mentalistic psychology of consciousness.

This is, certainly, not a superficial shortcoming. In contrast to Piaget and the pragmatists, Castoriadis does not develop a functional relation between mental representations and action. Unlike them, he does not interpret mental representations as the mediating link in problematic action situations. Undoubtedly, for Castoriadis every interpretation of the imaginary from the standpoint of function is a reduction. Yet the pragmatists did not believe that they were being reductionists when they rooted creative intelligence in the necessity of the human species to adapt to its environment. The problems of such adaptation are not given by nature but are mediated by cultural definitions; indeed, the solution of these problems is at the heart of the very creation that Castoriadis analyzes. The relation between an action problem and its solution does not have to be causal. Nor is it necessary to deny that there is any relation between a problem and its solution in order to oppose a falsely deterministic relation between them. Pragmatism may have falsely generalized the applicability of the experimental scientific method (its prototype of creativity) to encompass political and artistic creativity. Certainly, Marxism tied the creativity of action so closely to human beings' material life that only feeble traces of the liberating possibilities and power of production could still be detected. After Herder, the German tradition of the anthropology of expressivity was faced repeatedly with the problem of conceptualizing the self-expression of a being that is not teleologically defined. Castoriadis is right when he seeks to rise above narrow models of experimentation, production, and expression without abandoning the framework of a philosophy of praxis. But it cannot end well if the Gordian knot of these problems is severed with a single blow, for there then remains only the abstract idea of creation ex nihilo, an unaccounted-for conception, an ungroundable project.

Politically, the act of revolution seen as the autonomous self-institutionalization of a better society assumes ever stronger voluntaristic features in Castoriadis's writings. In bitter analyses of present-day Western societies, which are admittedly essayistic and lack empirical grounding for their conclusions, he sees an absence of creativity and of visions of the future and pervasive tendencies toward anomie. Counterposed to these pessimistic analyses there are only vague prospects for a better society. His critique of technology (*CL,* pp. 229–59) argues for its transformation into a means for the free unfolding of the potentials of individuals and groups. But the real problems begin only after proclamation of such a praiseworthy goal.

Castoriadis consciously does not link his demand for a radical equalization of income with the question of the productive efficiency resulting from differences in levels of income, since he is concerned to break symbolically with the ideology of "productionism." But one would really like to know how the masses of people might react to the possible loss of productive efficiency in their economy and to the consequent loss of income and Castoriadis's political assessment of these reactions. The vagueness of Castoriadis's program with regard to these "internal affairs" stands in contrast to the clarity and decisiveness of his analyses of "foreign affairs." In the latter, he, like many former Trotskyists, focuses his attention on the Soviet Union and on the armament policies and relative military strength of the Western and Eastern blocs. In 1981, he published a book in which he asserted that the Soviet Union was militarily superior to the West (quantitatively equivalent and strategically stronger) and, further, denied that the West enjoyed a superiority over the Soviet Union in military technology. His analyses reconcile these assertions with the indisputable economic inferiority of the Soviet Union by arguing that the Soviet Union is ruled by a "stratocracy"; that is, Soviet society is dominated not by the bureaucracies of the Communist party and the state but by its military-industrial complex. The political writings in his most recent collection of essays are full of passionate appeals for resistance to the Soviet Union. The declaration of martial law in Poland especially outraged him and led him to call for a total economic and cultural boycott of the government of—as Castoriadis refers to him—"Gauleiter" Jaruzelski.

This review is not the place to begin a political discussion with Castoriadis. However, the strident tones of his political statements, which he does not omit from his philosophical and scientific writings, provide an occasion for a few brief criticisms. Let me first call into question Castoriadis's assessment of Jaruzelski and also the thesis—which was published after Gorbachev had assumed office—of the essential incapacity of the Soviet Union to reform itself. The pathos of a call for a boycott is often a short-lived affair. Only the foreseeable consequences of a total demarcation between East and West in Central Europe are politically real. One of the lessons Germany has learned in the postwar era is that hostile and intransigent confrontation with the states in the Soviet sphere of power has not advanced the internal democratization of these states. "Transformation through rapprochement" was the slogan coined in the 1960s by Egon Bahr (Willy Brandt's adviser in matters of détente and disarmament) to express this recognition. Certainly, this strategy can also be wrong. If it is to be more realistic, then it must not be criticized as less ethical than a strategy of "combating totalitarianism." Castoriadis's military analyses are a rather sterile contribution to the discussion of the relative military superiority of the rival blocs and open no new prospects for Europe in the nuclear age. In this connection, the position of shared safety (or else shared destruction) is certainly more creative.

Speaking personally, I am deeply pained by the ostentatious indifference—despite his deep attachment to German thought—with which he describes the security interests of the Federal Republic of Germany as of no importance to NATO strategy (*DM*, p. 124). Thus Castoriadis's political worldview is composed of a utopian championing of revolution in the sphere of internal political affairs and of an aggressive, peace-threatening foreign policy toward the Soviet Union. Especially those who sympathize with his theoretical endeavors wish that Castoriadis had argued better on this topic. The linking of a new program of reform—motivated by the new social movements and joined to the interests of the traditional constituency of European labor parties—with policies of European and worldwide disarmament, of a shift to defensive armaments, and of joint security can also be understood as the political concretization of his theory of social autonomy.

It is, after all, not just the "revolution" that articulates autonomy politically. Many years ago, Mead described democracy as "institutionalized revolution," expressing the capacity for self-transformation that is associated with the idea of democracy. Etzioni's model of the active society is likewise an attempt to analyze, with sociological theory, the structures of a society that is institutionally creative and able to learn. In his political writings, Castoriadis both avoids and displaces the central problem posed by his theory of society, which is, after all, based on the philosophy of praxis: How can we continue to believe in, and strive to carry out, the project of autonomy when the myth of the revolution is dead?

Bibliography

Castoriadis, Cornelius. *Crossroads in the Labyrinth.* Cambridge, Mass.: MIT, 1984.

Castoriadis, Cornelius. *Domaines de l'homme: Les carrefours du labyrinthe II.* Paris: Seuil, 1986.

Castoriadis, Cornelius. *The Imaginary Institution of Society.* Cambridge, Mass.: MIT, 1987.

7 A Sociological Transformation of the Philosophy of Praxis: Anthony Giddens's Theory of Structuration

An unceasing stream of publications, which have attracted much attention, has made Anthony Giddens in recent years one of the best known authors participating in the international discussion of sociological theory. The debates on the theory of class, the appropriation of the work of the classical sociologists—Durkheim and Weber—for contemporary sociological theory, the critical examination of interpretative sociology, poststructuralism, and contemporary Marxism: these are all areas that can hardly be conceived of now without Giddens's contributions. Within the community of social scientists, the atmosphere of which is by no means free of envy and jealousy, such a degree of productivity draws to itself only too quickly the charge of superficiality. Theoretical openness to a great number of both historical and present-day approaches is dismissed too easily as eclecticism. In my opinion, the reproach of eclecticism can easily be rejected definitively at the latest since the publication of *The Constitution of Society.* What was for the greatest part only implicit in Giddens's first theoretical writings has become increasingly explicit and systematized since about 1976. His own theoretical approach announced itself then for the first time in the conclusions he drew from his study of functionalism and in his critique of interpretative sociology (Giddens 1977, pp. 96–134; Giddens 1976). Using an expression borrowed from the French, probably from Piaget, Giddens calls his approach a "theory of structuration." In his subsequent contributions, this theory was further elaborated and is presented in *The Constitution of Society* in a relatively systematic form. The charge of superficiality is surely to be accounted for by the fact that Giddens, faced with the necessity of doing justice to an extraordinary wealth of topics and competing approaches, occasionally gives the description of his positions priority over detailed grounding of them. The desire for more extensive argumentation is therefore certainly now and again legitimate. However, it cannot serve as an objection to Giddens's theoretical ideas, which are so original and rich in implications that they themselves should be at the center of an assessment of Giddens's work.

Published in English in *International Sociology* 2 (1987), pp. 13–26; © 1989 by Hans Joas. (Originally published in German, in *Zeitschrift für Soziologie* 15, 1986.)

These ideas could have reinvigorating effect, particularly in the discussion of sociological theory in the Federal Republic of Germany. Following the decline and atrophy of Marxism there, it can easily seem that everywhere in the Federal Republic, where sociological theory is not completely reduced to quantitative or qualitative empirical research, the publications of Habermas and Luhmann are regarded not just as the work of the two most important contemporary German theoreticians, but also as delimiting the range of logically possible theoretical positions. The generation that felt itself, in its adherence to Marxism, to be superior to all approaches employed by academic sociology, but that now has adopted an attitude almost of veneration toward one or both of the "grand masters," is particularly likely to fall prey to this impression. This is a state of affairs that cannot be productive.

A discussion of Giddens's sociological transformation of the philosophy of praxis must certainly begin by overcoming the reservations about this philosophy that exist among social scientists. I am referring here to the aversion to writings that, while remaining remote from empirical research, tend to champion, in a moralizing fashion, the program of a humanistic anthropology, and frequently do nothing more than repeat it. Even the most impressive works of adherents of the philosophy of praxis, whether those of the Budapest School or of Cornelius Castoriadis, remain at quite some distance from sociological questions in the narrower sense of an empirical analysis of society. Although Giddens's work admittedly does not match that of the aforementioned authors in philosophical depth, its sociological orientation nevertheless makes it deserving of the greatest attention. It merits careful consideration all the more inasmuch as Habermas, in his lectures on the discourse of modernity (Habermas 1985, especially pp. 95–103) has announced the end of just this philosophy of praxis, giving a mixture of metatheoretical and empirical arguments for his assertion, and has advanced the claim not only that his theory of communicative action defines more precisely than ever before a particular type of human praxis, but also that this theory takes the place of the philosophy of praxis as a whole.

Let us first ascertain how Giddens developed the basic outlines of his sociological transformation of the philosophy of praxis, and then ask where this approach, in its present state of elaboration, has weak points, and where it is open to attack.

The Genesis of the Theory of Structuration

Giddens has never attempted to conceal the fact that he is a leftist, nor his high opinion of the significance of Marx's work for the theory of society. From the start of his intellectual career, however, he has never allowed himself to be driven into adopting the opposition of Marxism and academic or "bourgeois" science that conceives of them both as mutually exclusive systems of thought competing with each other in a global fashion. This can be seen in his book *The Class Structure of the Advanced Societies,* in which the tension between the Marxist theory of classes and Weberian notions of social stratification is made productive for the analysis of present-day social problems. Incidentally the idea of the "structuration" of classes—directly by means of the production process and the mode of production or indirectly through intergenerational mobility—appears already in this work. However, Giddens's productive relationship to Marx and the classical sociologists becomes especially evident in his book *Capitalism and Modern Social Theory* and in his other interpretative studies of Durkheim and Weber. What Giddens proposes in these works is, in a certain sense, a countermodel to that presented in Parsons's *Structure of Social Action,* the work that laid the foundation for the "orthodox consensus" of the American-dominated sociology of the postwar era. Giddens acknowledges the epoch-making nature of the turning point in the history of social theory effected by Weber and Durkheim, but he denies that their theories can be regarded as the long-sought solution to a problem concerning the theory of social order that has existed since Hobbes, and that it is only with this generation of theorists and in the period from 1890–1920 that the new discipline of sociology begins. Giddens is interested not in the clear demarcation of sociology nor in the solution of theoretical problems on the supratemporal plane, but in the elaboration of an interdisciplinary social science and in firmly linking together metatheoretical and substantive questions. Against this background, he relates the generation of the classical sociological thinkers to the problems of liberalism at the end of the nineteenth century and in the early years of the twentieth century. In particular, Giddens has the merit of not carrying out his critical examination of the thought of the classical sociologists merely from abstract theoretical perspectives, and of never losing sight of the problems of the analysis of social realities, in the case of the assumptions regarding the character of "industrial society." Through his critical appropriation of the work of the classical authors in sociology, Giddens exposes the theoretical impulses, arising from the philosophy of praxis, to scrutiny in the light of the sociological theory of action.

In the late 1960s and the early 1970s, the "orthodox consensus" was called into question not only by Marxists and "conflict-theorists" inspired by Marxism, but also by that vaguely defined coalition of symbolic interactionists, phenomenologists, ethnomethodologists, and sociological hermeneuticists that practical researchers have often described as the interpretative approach, despite the fact that this homogenization of the various groups concerned makes more philosophically oriented sociologists a little uneasy. In 1976, in a book bearing the somewhat pretentious title *New Rules of Sociological Method,* Giddens presented a close, critical study of these theoretical currents. Having been instructed by the post-empiricist philosophy of the natural sciences, he could only agree with these approaches in their opposition to the misleading use of allegedly natural-scientific models for the domains studied by the cultural and social sciences. Of the contributions Giddens makes in this book, the one that has become best known is his notion of the "double hermeneutic," a term with which he characterizes the circumstance that the social sciences are not only confronted with the problem of interpretation within the community of scientists, but are moreover also faced with the problem of interpreting the actions and utterances of their "objects" of investigation. Thus Giddens shares with the interpretative approaches their emphasis of the subjectivity of social actors and of the reflexivity of sociology; but he finds it objectionable that in their fixation on problems of meaning and of normativity, these approaches too bear traces of the orthodox consensus. Not only for the problems posed for macrosociological theory, but also for the microsociological analysis of power phenomena, Giddens considers this foundation as still too narrow.

Giddens reacted once again with complete openness to an important change in the intellectual atmosphere with his critical study and appropriation of poststructuralism. Since the mid-seventies, the writings of Foucault and Derrida, as well as those of a large number of less significant French authors, have offered a starting point to many who are looking for an explanation of the loss of modernist illusions, or who, in some cases, are only seeking a justification for their rejection of their own leftist pasts. Giddens's study of structuralism and poststructuralism has had three noteworthy results for the development of his own theoretical approach. First, he accepts the structuralist arguments for a "decentering of the subject" as an antidote against the distressing consequences of the mentalistic philosophy of consciousness. He refuses, though, to convert the decentering of the subject into the elimination of the subject. The productive use of structuralism and poststructuralism therefore requires a theory of social structures that does not ignore the capacity of individual subjects for reflection and action, but that also does not conceive of structures on the model of macrosubjects. The second result of this theoretical dialogue that deserves mention is Giddens's search, under the influence of Heidegger, an influence that pervades French thought from

Castoriadis to Derrida, for a set of concepts that escapes the pitfalls of the philosophy of consciousness. This quest leads him to place the temporality (and the spatiality) of human existence and of all social phenomena at the heart of his approach. This is the point at which Giddens's attempt to elaborate a social theory—as it was first presented in *Central Problems in Social Theory*—began to overtax some sociologists' sympathetic interest in his enterprise. A third result can be seen in Giddens's new interpretation of the concept of power. He seeks to escape from the antithesis of power and freedom not by beginning with a definition of power as a difference in interactive possibilities for effecting one's will, but by beginning instead with the linking of power to the concept of action and to the transformative, world-changing character of all action. Very carefully, however, he demarcates this action concept of power from all Nietzschean echoes of an all-founding "will to power."

These rough characterizations describe important stages in the development of Giddens's theoretical framework. The basic features of it will not be explained in detail here. It must suffice to single out some points, by means of which the specifics of the "theory of structuration" can be better understood.

If one starts by considering that theory from the standpoint of the theory of action, then, first of all, Giddens's account of the relationship of intentionality and action has to be stressed. The concepts "praxis" and "action" are, to be sure, suited in principle to provide the impulse to surmount the dualisms of the philosophy of consciousness. Historically, however, they have often entered into association with ideas that subjected even action to the split between consciousness and the world, "I" and "you," body and mind. Action then appears to be merely the execution of pre-formed intentions, or of the realization of internalized values, or of the fulfilment of clearly determinate motives. Giddens avoids this false path with its many pitfalls by defining intentionality as the capacity for self-reflective control of ongoing behavior. Action is thereby conceived of as having a multiplicity of motives and determinations; it acquires a clear definition, unequivocal ends, only through the occurrence of problems in concrete situations, or through the social necessity of justifying an action. This understanding of action also removes the theoretical necessity to attribute one motive to every action. According to Giddens, only then can we understand a large part of human activity when we take into consideration the importance of the routinization of action. Further, the interpretation of intentionality as reflexivity requires a distinction between the clear consciousness found in the act of reflection and the sedimented certainties implicit in the course of the performances of action. By drawing a distinction between discursive and practical consciousness, Giddens expresses the difference, which has also always been of importance for pragmatism and phenomenology.

There is another false path that partisans of the philosophy of praxis have not always taken care to avoid. Sometimes, in the exuberance of their belief that they have demonstrated the creative and constitutive character of human action, they have ignored the limiting power of existing structures, or have simply ascribed them to an "alienated" state of society. The title of Giddens's book *The Constitution of Society* could also arouse the suspicion that its author conceives of society as originating from the constitutive accomplishments of subjects, with "constitution" suggesting a transcendental subject in the epistemological sense of term. That, however, would be a misunderstanding in two respects. Giddens's action-theory approach is not subject to the constraints of a Kantian epistemology; nor does it ignore the consequences of the fact that social structures are not constituted without presupposition, but in any given instance can only be transformed or reproduced. The chief problem of many discussions of the relationship between "action" and "structure" lies, in Giddens's view, in the one-sidedness of the conception of actions as *restricted* by structures. It is just this one-sidedness that gives rise to the sterile debates about the insurmountable opposition between approaches based on the theory of action and those based on structural theory, and also to the reifying identification, on the one hand, of action theory and microsociology, and of structural theory and macrosociology, on the other. In contrast, one of Giddens's central ideas is that of a "duality of structure," that is, of the twofold character of structures that make action both possible and restrict it, that are both the medium and the result of praxis. For this very reason, the processes of structuration occupy a central position in Giddens's theory, and his conception of the duality of structure promises to give a way out of the dilemma posed by the alternatives of voluntarism and determinism. If we compare Giddens's point of departure with Parsons's "action frame of reference," we arrive at an interesting finding. Whereas in the case of Parsons this action frame of reference contains, in addition to the actor, only the conditions and the means of action, as well as the actor's ends and norms, we find in the case of Giddens, leaving aside his different understanding of intentionality, two elements that Parsons does not mention, namely the unintended consequences of action and the unrecognized conditions of action. Of course, the unintended results of action were not a phenomenon unknown to the Parsonian tradition. Rather, they constituted one of the principal arguments for the usefulness of functionalist models. However, these models only imposed silence on what was in actual fact troubling about the unintended *consequences* of action. That functionalist models accomplished nothing more in this regard has been justifiably criticized again and again, especially by methodological individualists. In Giddens's theoretical framework, though, these ubiquitous unintended consequences of action become a component of a theory of structuration that specifically does not have a functionalist bias. The distinction between unrecognized and recognized conditions of action makes it clear how little Parsons, in his original model, took into consideration a cognitive dimension that is independent of normativity (Warner 1977–78). The fabric of spatiotemporally produced and reproduced actions is called by Giddens a "system"; from them he distinguishes the interrelational complexes of shared rules and apportioned resources, which, in his terminology, are designated "structures." The problem of social order, therefore, poses itself for him, in contrast to Parsons, not as one of social cohesion in spite of potentially or actually conflicting interests, but on a deeper level as the problem of the guaranteeing of social order through the transcending of narrow spatial and temporal limits. This production of social order, however, is not conceived of in the phenomenological sense as effected separately by individual subjects in their experience of the world. Instead, from the outset, it is embedded in a plexus of actions taking place in the world.

Giddens's approach acquires additional force from its rigorous opposition to two modes of thought that are widespread in sociology: functionalism and evolutionism. These two modes of thought are much more widespread than the readiness among sociologists to call themselves "functionalists" or "evolutionists" would lead one to believe. Giddens is undoubtedly right when he finds in much of Marxist literature functionalist and evolutionist modes of thought and reasoning. In his critical study of historical materialism, published so far in two works (Giddens 1981, 1985), he has subjected the latter to a severe critique, to the degree that it has yielded to the two tendencies that Giddens considers indefensible. In this critique, his attack on functionalism proceeds along two lines. On the one hand, it is directed against the possibility of functionalist explanations of social phenomena. Giddens forcefully denies this possibility, asserting that functionalist propositions can be considered admissible only as counterfactual statements about necessary conditions for possible consequences. The concept of reproduction is completely cleansed of all functionalist flavor by being defined as referring to the object of explanation and not the means of explanation. On the other hand, Giddens also doubts the meaningfulness of the essentialist manner of employing functionalist models. That does not mean that he simply denies the existence of, for example, homeostatic processes of self-regulation. But he does not believe that the requirements of a system that are necessary to make a functionalist model meaningful can be clearly ascertained in many domains. Thus the question of the existence of phenomena of self-regulation is at least not decided a priori on the metatheoretical plane. Rather, the question is treated as an empirical one, to which the answer is that there are "degrees of systemness." With his critique of evolutionist thinking, Giddens is aiming at nothing less than a "deconstruction" of all extant theories of social change, which he criticizes for having lost genuine historicity. Giddens's objections are thus directed against the attempts to elaborate a theory of history in general, and particularly against those approaches that accept biological models as exemplary for a theory of social evolution. This critique derives in part from the critique of functionalism, since in both cases the impossibility of formulating a version of the concept of adaptation that would be meaningful when applied to society was an obstacle to the transference of biological models into social theory.

Regardless of the degree to which this critique of functionalism and evolutionism might be convincing, one thing remains certain: as a mere rejection of existing theories, it is not yet capable of gaining victory as long as it does not at least point the way to alternatives. As long as this does not happen, the analytical tools provided by the functionalist-evolutionist mode of thinking will continue to hold their place in the everyday practice of the social sciences, because they at least make strong claims to explanatory power. Giddens sketches the basic features of such an alternative in *The Constitution of Society*, but also in his books on historical materialism. These features can be grouped under the headings of time and space, on the one hand, and of power, on the other. His extensive and penetrating consideration of the temporal and spatial aspects of social phenomena is achieved through an examination of microsociological phenomena, by incorporating the findings of the "time-geography school" and by making use of the theory of "time-space distanciation" according to which there are degrees of spatiotemporal organization of social systems. These steps bring the reification of time and the artificiality and commercialization of the use of space in the modern city into the theoretical field of vision. Giddens's theory of power first insists that phenomena of repression be investigated without being reduced to a dominant type. Giddens argues for the study of repression based on ethnicity and gender in addition to class-associated repression, and denies the possibility of understanding these as simply forms in which a type that is ultimately alone decisive finds displaced expression. In the same manner, military force and the structure of the national state are regarded as objects sui generis, in contrast to their economistic interpretations. The emphasis placed on the necessity of reflective self-control leads to recognition of the paramount importance of the control and storage of information for the power structure of social systems, from the origination of writing down to the present-day problems of the protection of private information. The definition of the concept of power from the standpoint of the theory of action is the point of departure for formulating the notion of a "dialectic of control"; that is to say, if all capability of action in social relations is power, then there is no absolute powerlessness of an actor; then even the most dependent and most oppressed can mobilize resources for controlling their situation and the reproduction of their social relations to the oppressors. Although he also gives a great deal of attention to the domains of social phenomena that have been brought to general awareness only by the skepticism of recent years regarding the ultimately beneficial nature of civilization, Giddens nevertheless resists a metatheoretically grounded pessimism about the nature and the inevitable course of human history.

Problems of the Theory of Structuration

It would be a miracle if in the case of such an ambitious and broadly conceived outline of a theory as the one presented by Giddens, there did not remain a plethora of internal problems of the theory's construction and of substantive difficulties in the theory's further elaboration. In what follows I will not deal with questions of the theory's application to contemporary or historical problems; instead, I will concentrate on basic theoretical questions within Giddens's field of reference. As these questions are considered, some open queries regarding Giddens's theory of time and power will become apparent.

As various of his critics have already noted, Giddens never bases his thinking on the writings of pragmatists and symbolic interactionists, even though this tradition has given a particularly strong emphasis to reflexivity in action and the problem of temporality in the context of the social sciences, and has done so in a fashion that, in fact, ought to be acceptable to Giddens. However, the turning point in his discovery of temporality appears to have been Martin Heidegger. This is not so odd as it might at first appear, since today it is no longer surprising if someone speaks of pragmatist elements in Heidegger's thought (Rorty 1984). The latter, however, are situated in a context so different from that of Giddens, and one that is so remote not only from pragmatism, but also from all empirical research on social phenomena, that the question immediately arises of what problems Giddens has brought upon himself by following this path to "temporality."

Heidegger was certainly not concerned with improving the extent to which, and the manner in which, science takes the temporal dimension into account. His intentions were also unlike those of Bergson; Heidegger was not undertaking a critique of culture that opposed subjectively experienced time to the physical measurement of time, and that finds its point of attack in the compulsion to spatialize time. He was concerned with much more. He interlinked an attempt to uncover the transcendental structures of a prereflexive understanding of the world with the claims of an ontology. Temporality was thereby discovered both as a dimension that is even more primordial than, and underlies the distinctions between, subject and object, and on the basis of which the natural-scientific schematization of time first arises, and—from the ontological standpoint—as an essential determination of being that is not to be surpassed by any dimension of the eternal. These two parts of Heidegger's investigation are also bound together by the recognition that only the radical acceptance of historicity and the uniqueness and limitedness of personal existence enables the individual to attain authenticity. Certainly a path is thus opened to the reconstruction of distinct individual "temporalities," as well as the prospect of a conception of history that is radically historical, that is not dependent on an encompassing philosophy of history or evolutionary theory. But the former path can only be continued by means of an anthropologization of Heidegger's analytics of being-there ("Dasein"), something that hardly accords with Heidegger's intentions. The last-mentioned prospect led, at least for Heidegger himself, to the concept of the history of being ("Seinsgeschichte), not to an improved version of the historical social sciences. There are, then, tensions that Giddens ought to carefully examine if he wants to include "temporality" in the core of his theoretical approach without following Heidegger in the aforementioned respects, or without being forced to reduce temporality to an objective dimension that is merely additionally to be taken into consideration.

According to a bon mot by Helmuth Plessner (1974, p. 24), Heidegger's philosophy takes only as much notice of human nature as is required for dying. That philosophy does not, then, provide a suitable basis for an anthropological grounding of the assumptions of the theory of action, or for an improved integration of temporality within the framework of this theory. In Giddens's work, the actor's corporeality is adduced at points that are of central importance for his strategy of argumentation: in the linking together of the everyday experience, the individual life span, and the "longue durée" of institutions (Giddens 1984, p. 35); and also in his transition to time-geography, when this transition is accounted for by the limitedness of the human lifetime and the indivisibility of the human body (Giddens 1984, p. 111). But these connections yield hardly any more than they do in Heidegger's philosophy. Thus the question can be posed whether this lack of an anthropological grounding has consequences for the architectonics of Giddens's approach, or merely constitutes a neglected field of topics for investigation.

It appears certain that such consequences can be ascertained in several respects. First of all, Giddens's definitions of the concepts in the theory of action are not, in general, developed from an analysis of the specific situation of human organisms in their environment. Many of these definitions are therefore ultimately imprecise in their demarcation of human action from animal behavior. This is true even for the definition of action as a causal intervention by corporeal beings in the flux of events. John Shotter has pointed out that it is also true of Giddens's description of the twofold character of social structures (1983). The reflexivity of human beings' control of their behavior must certainly be accepted as an anthropological determination of that phenomenon; but Giddens does not derive it from the structures of human sociality, neither from the development of individual capabilities in the domain of social cognition, nor from the social structures in which the capacity for action—in the sense of an assumption of the autonomy of individuals' actions—is either attributed or denied to individual human beings. It is connected with this shortcoming that, in my opinion, if no use is made of anthropological findings, then the internal elaboration of the concept of praxis can proceed only intuitively, or by means of definitional postulates. A point at which this fact becomes visible is the insufficient elucidation of the concept of production as a particular kind of action. Without such a clarification, however, the transference of the concept of exploitation to noneconomic phenomena is at least questionable. Because the constitution of all knowledge within the structure of the situations of organisms in environments is not elucidated in Giddens's theory, there can be no elucidation of the temporal dimension against the background of the practical embeddedness of the human being in his or her world. Giddens therefore takes recourse to Bergson's counterconcept to the conception of time in physics, to the French philosopher's concept of the "durée." Strictly speaking, this is an incorrect term in the framework of Giddens's theory. In his approach it cannot be a matter of a primacy of introspective experience of time, and certainly not of the contrasting of individual consciousness of time and "objective" time; it can be a matter only of the difference between schematizations of time differing from one culture to another and the time of physics. Thus it would be a matter of the difference that Evans-Pritchard sees between contextual time and time having no context (Matthes et al. 1985).[1]

This shortcoming could also be the reason why Giddens's work lacks an elaborated typology of culturally varying or developmentally succeeding forms of the structuration of time. The reader cannot but be astonished at the lack of this when first perusing Giddens's book. The inclusion of time-geography in Giddens's approach, regardless of how fruitful this notion might be, appears a logical lapse at this point in his theory. This notion does not make it possible to apprehend and describe culturally or individually different "temporalities"; rather, it employs an unequivocally objectivistic concept of time. For this purpose, of course, it would have been unnecessary for Giddens to draw either upon pragmatism or upon Heidegger's philosophy. Such an indefensible step can be taken only when the original motivation for treating the theme of time as the vehicle for going beyond the philosophy of consciousness is reduced to a mere defense of an additional dimension of social research.

As has already been observed, many studies on the theory of time have been, and continue to be, motivated by the protest, from the standpoint of a critique of culture, against spatialized time. These studies are opposed to a course of historical development that seems no longer to bring forth anything radically new, and that, while crushing historical creativity, threatens the feeling of personal, self-engendered continuity. This opposition underlies the rejection of the conception of time as an unlimited series of now-points and is implicit in the ideas about the recurrent emergence of the unexpected and the new, which compels us to make ever new reconstructions of the past and anticipations of the future. It is remarkable that, although he retains in his theory these connotations of cultural critique and speaks of the measurement of time as an expression of the commodification of time in modern society (Giddens 1981, p. 9), Giddens transforms the critique of the spatialization of time into the thesis that time *and space* have been neglected in society. Here too—as in the case of time-geography—the inclusion, for example, of human ecology approaches in Giddens's theory can only be useful; however, their logical integration with the approach of Giddens's theory as a whole is inadequate (Gross 1982). In this connection it also remains an open question whether we may really so quickly assume that the cultural dominance of the schematization of time that is proper to physics is the expression of a commodity character of time. If we take Mead's critique of Bergson seriously (Joas 1985, especially pp. 167–98), then it could be said that this form of temporality would be of central importance under all conditions of different kinds of complex cooperation, not only under those obtaining in capitalism. When reconstructing the genesis of the modern consciousness of time, we would then also have to draw a clear distinction between the recognition and general acceptance of the notion of time that is proper to physics and the recognition and general acceptance of the idea of historical uniqueness and the irreversibility of history.

This is, however, a question that cannot be pursued further here. The observation that was just made is important though, because it can establish the connection with an aspect of Giddens's theory that at first seems to be completely separate from his theory of temporality: Giddens's critique of evolutionism. As has already been set out above, he has rejected all forms of universal laws of social change. This liberation from evolutionist premises gives Giddens theoretical latitude to pursue productive ideas concerning the character of mechanisms of social change as being specific to particular epochs; a further effect is that the relationship between societies having different characters is brought into view in the concepts of "time-space edges" and "world-time," in a manner reminiscent of Trotsky's notions of the unequal and combined development of different countries. We thus have no objection, at first, to such a quasi-historicist skepticism about evolutionist arguments! Yet one can begin to reflect anew on this question when the origination of modern time consciousness in the eighteenth century, in the sense of historicity, is seen in its relationship with the philosophy of history. One need only think of Herder's innovative force in this respect. It then becomes apparent that, in addition to the alternatives of evolutionism and historicism, or episodism, which Giddens presents in his book, there is at least a third possibility that Giddens does not examine, even though the premise of this way of thinking is entirely compatible with the fundamental features of Giddens's enterprise. If self-reflexivity is not conceived of according to the model of an image reflected in a mirror, but—as in the case of Giddens—related to praxis and temporalized, then it means the actor's guidance of personal action is in accordance with future possibilities, in conditions that have been formed by the past. In this fashion, the concepts of self-identity and individual temporality can be joined together. Further, just as Giddens conceives of the storage and control of information on the basis of action problems of collective actors, the reconstruction of history should be conceived of as a collective attempt to interpret the past in the light of a projected future for the purpose of interpreting and controlling the present. Such a reconstruction of the past cannot, then, content itself with the episodism proposed by Giddens. Certainly, however, it inquires into the totality of history as preparation of a given present. This question does not imply any kind of teleological suppositions or assumptions regarding a linear upward development leading to the present day and to us. We agree with Giddens that such notions are to be unqualifiedly rejected. Nor does this point of view necessarily force us to adopt the dogmatic certainties of certain schools of Hegelians or Marxists, which are proof against modification by new experience. The attempts to learn from the philosophy of history without becoming dogmatic extend from Moses Hess to Maurice Merleau-Ponty. Jürgen Habermas has expressed this idea brilliantly, saying that: "Reason should not be regarded as something finished, as an objective teleology that manifests itself in nature or in history, nor as a merely subjective faculty. Rather, the structural patterns found in historical developments give enciphered pointers to the paths of unconcluded, interrupted, misled processes of formation going beyond the subjective consciousness of the individual" (Habermas 1985, p. 70). It is not at all necessary to consider Habermas's own program of a normative logic of development convincing in order to concede that he offers here an escape from the disintegration of historical analysis into segmental histories that are unconnected with each other. Giddens's critique of evolutionism has yet to confront the theses of such a modified philosophy of history. If that is done, it is possible that certain emphases would be changed in Giddens's critique of historical materialism too. For what argues against the weak version of evolutionary assumptions that E. O. Wright, in awareness of the problem at issue, proposes in his critique of Giddens's book on historical materialism (Wright 1983)?

For Giddens's theory of power, the ideas of Michel Foucault have played the decisive role, similar to that played by Heidegger's philosophy with respect to Giddens's theory of time. Giddens's aim is to learn from the empirical fruitfulness of an approach that permits the analysis of the immense wealth and diversity of strategies of power. In doing that though, he wants to avoid plunging into the Nietzschean abyss where power crushes all claims of reason. He succeeds to the extent that he ascribes to the dimension of "domination" a primacy equal to that of "signification" —the constitution of meaning—and of "legitimation." Power is thus fundamental, but is so only conjointly with the meaning-constituting and normative aspects of action. The problem that Giddens thereby burdens himself with, however, is that there is now no longer any kind of intrinsic connection between power and its justification. In this regard, Giddens is only being logically consequent when he denies the possibility of a society free from domination. But what, then, do the normative ideas brought forth by a long democratic tradition aim at? Fred Dallmayr (1982) has warned that Giddens's concept of action does not permit a distinction to be drawn between intentional and strategic action.[2] This objection which is, of course, inspired by Habermas's theory cannot be allowed for by a simple definitional supplement within Giddens's approach. For it requires the distinguishing of the various ways in which the character of power that is inherent in all action is brought to bear in particular situations. Again, Habermas's dichotomous distinction between strategic and communicative action does not offer the compelling solution. Nonetheless, Giddens is faced with the unsolved problem of better justifying the implicit normativeness of a theory that distances itself from the ideal of freedom from domination (Bernstein 1986).

Although the philosophy of praxis could traditionally be criticized for concentrating on the defense of normative postulates, the productive sociological transformation of that philosophy must not be purchased with the sacrifice of its normative orientation. However, it is not this orientation that determines the usefulness of a theory for purposes of social analysis. Both metatheoretically and substantively, the achievement of the "theory of structuration," even in its current state of elaboration, is already considerable.

Notes

1. This fact is probably linked to a certain excessiveness of Giddens's claims in relation to Freudian theory. The reconstruction of the "unconscious" in Giddens's approach has certainly only been begun. The assertion that Freud's psychical agencies (ego, id, superego) can be reconstructed with the conceptual triad of discursive consciousness, practical consciousness, and unconscious motives appears to be extremely problematical.

2. In addition to the studies by Shotter, Gross, Wright, and Dallmayr already mentioned, other important contributions to the discussion of Giddens's work are those by Callinicos (1985), Archer (1982), Habermas (1982), Layder (1986), Bernstein (1986), and Turner (1985–86).

Bibliography

Archer, M. 1982. "Morphogenesis versus Structuration: On Combining Structure and Action." *British Journal of Sociology* 33: 455–83.

Bernstein, R. 1986. "Structuration as Critical Theory." *Praxis International* 5: 235–48.

Callinicos, A. 1985. "Anthony Giddens. A Contemporary Critique." *Theory and Society* 14: 133–74.

Dallmayr, F. 1982. "Agency and Structure." *Philosophy of the Social Sciences* 12: 427–38.

Giddens, A. 1971. *Capitalism and Modern Social Theory.* Cambridge: Cambridge University Press.

———.1974. *The Class Structure of the Advanced Societies.* London: Hutchinson.
———.1976. *New Rules of Sociological Method.* London: Hutchinson.
———.1977. *Studies in Social and Political Theory.* London: Hutchinson.
———.1978. *Durkheim.* London: Fontana.
———.1979. *Central Problems in Social Theory.* London: Macmillan.
———.1981. *A Contemporary Critique of Historical Materialism,* vol. 1. London: Macmillan.
———.1982. *Profiles and Critiques in Social Theory.* London: Macmillan.
———.1984. *The Constitution of Society: Outline of the Theory of Structuration.* Cambridge, Engl.: Blackwell/Polity Press.
———.1985. *The Nation-State and Violence.* Cambridge, Engl.: Blackwell/Polity Press.
Gross, D. 1982. "Time-Space Relations in Giddens' Social Theory." *Theory, Culture and Society* 1: 83–88.
Habermas, J. 1982. "Reply to my Critics," in Thompson, J. B. and Held, D. (eds.), *Habermas—Critical Debates.* London: Macmillan, pp. 219–83.
Habermas, J. 1985. *Der philosophische Diskurs der Moderne.* Frankfurt: Suhrkamp.
Joas, H. 1985. *George Herbert Mead: A Contemporary Re-examination of His Thought.* Cambridge, Mass.: Polity Press/MIT Press.
Layder, D. 1985. "Power, Structure and Agency." *Journal for the Theory of Social Behavior* 15: 131–49.
Matthes, J. et al. 1985. "Gesellschaftliche Regelung von Zeitlichkeit im interkulturellen Vergleich." Unpublished manuscript. Erlangen.
Plessner, H. 1974. *Diesseits der Utopie.* Frankfurt: Suhrkamp.
Rorty, R. 1984. "Heidegger wider die Pragmatisten." *Neue Hefte für Philosophie* 23: 1–22.
Shotter, J. 1983. "Duality of Structure and Intentionality in an Ecological Psychology." *Journal for the Theory of Social Behavior* 13: 19–44.
Turner, J. 1985–86. "The Theory of Structuration." *American Journal of Sociology* 91:969–77.
Warner, R. S. 1977–78. "Toward a Redefinition of Action Theory: Paying the Cognitive Element its Due." *American Journal of Sociology* 83: 1317–49.
Wright, E. O. 1983. "Giddens' Critique of Marxism." *New Left Review* 138: 11–35.

8 The Antinomies of Neofunctionalism: A Critical Essay on Jeffrey Alexander

Since the beginning of the nineteen-eighties, a more or less homogeneous group of relatively young American sociologists has been energetically striving to provide for sociology a unitary and comprehensive theoretical framework by drawing upon the lifework of Talcott Parsons. Occasionally they have paused in their labors to cast nostalgic glances back at the decades immediately following the Second World War, when American sociology at least appeared to enjoy stability and consensus. In contrast, today a multitude of sociological currents vie with one another around a central domain consisting in theoretically penurious quantitative empirical research. One of the reasons these various currents present a picture of chaotic pluralism is that their competition hardly takes the form anymore of the refutation of each other's approach through reasoned argument, but expresses itself in rivalry for scarce resources and posts. However, attempts to achieve a new theoretical synthesis or to revitalize the Parsonian "orthodox consensus" have both encountered a plethora of difficulties. In addition to skepticism about the significance and possibility of general theory as such, there is the untroubled acceptance of the pluralistic coexistence of individual schools of sociology, as well as a conception of Parsons's work that consists of hearsay and a critique inherited from past generations of sociologists, a conception in which that work has been mutilated to the point of being unrecognizable.

The most spectacular attempt to overcome these difficulties has been made by Jeffrey Alexander. In his four-volume work *Theoretical Logic in Sociology* (Alexander 1982–83), he has undertaken to re-think, in a fashion corresponding to the present period, Parsons's first major theoretical work, *The Structure of Social Action.* Since its publication, Alexander's ambitious study has been continued in a history of sociology since 1945. In this history, Alexander describes the decay of Parsons's hegemony in sociology and interprets it from the standpoint of a self-critique of Parsonianism (Alexander 1987b). In a collection of articles he has edited, Alexander has promulgated the program of a neo-Parsonian school of social theory that he has christened "neofunctionalism" (Alexander

Reprinted by permission from *Inquiry* 31 (1988), pp. 471–94.

1985). In shorter writings, he has sought to show that there is a quite broad trend toward a Parsons renaissance (Alexander 1984, 1985–86), or to justify methodologically the linking of the elaboration of theory and the interpretation of the works of classical sociologists, which is characteristic of his multivolume work (Alexander 1987a). In a new collection of his own essays, Alexander (1988) attempts to verify and modify his theoretical approach by applying it to various empirical areas.

Alexander's theoretical offensive exhibits all the features of an intraprofessional political strategy. However, the same can be said of most of the reactions that greeted the appearance of Alexander's chef d'oeuvre. His ambitious and far-reaching attempt to mount the throne that has stood unoccupied since Parsons's fall necessarily provoked all kinds of opposition. At the same time, hardly any work of sociological theory, especially one by a young and previously not well-known author, had been so showered with laurels before its appearance.

In the first round of criticism, in reaction against the panegyrical tone of the advance notices of Alexander's work, scathing doubts about the usefulness and originality of the entire undertaking were voiced, and derivations from Parsons with respect to style and content were sneeringly pointed out. In a second wave of responses, there were some broad and penetrating critiques of Alexander's procedure and of his interpretations of sociological classics (Burger 1986; Collins 1985; Porpora 1986; Turner 1985). However, the decisive substantive question, to what extent do Jeffrey Alexander's writings constitute a theoretical advance in sociology?, was, for the most part, touched upon only marginally. Attractive though it might be to examine the debate about an alleged Parsons renaissance as a case study of conflicts having to do with intraprofessional politics, another path will be followed here. It shall be shown that, while meritoriously defending the necessity of a new theoretical synthesis in sociology, Jeffrey Alexander partially deprives himself of the means of attaining the goal he has set himself. His advance to recognition of the necessity of a comprehensive and synthetic sociological theory is obtained at the price of a closing-off of his enterprise to the present-day possibilities and necessities of such a theory. That this is so shall be shown through examination of the fundamental features of Alexander's theoretical framework, of his interpretation of major social theorists, and of the way he has tailored his history of postwar sociology.

Alexander's theoretical framework can be described most easily by comparison with the guiding model he follows in his four-volume study, to wit Parsons's *Structure of Social Action* (Parsons 1937). In this work Parsons had sought to find a way out of the conflict between the two most important contemporary American schools of economics: that holding to the neoclassical theory of marginal utility, and the institutionalist school. The neoclassical school, using a theory of rational action, had achieved impressive progress toward an empirical quantitative and theory-guided investigation of a particular part of social life. On the other hand, the institutionalist school, like the historical school of German political economy, accorded better with the felt need for an embedding of economic phenomena in the historical and social totality. This methodological controversy among the economists was of central importance for sociology inasmuch as at first glance the area of inquiry to which sociology laid claim overlapped at least partially with that of the historicist and institutionalist schools of economics. But if sociology wanted to avoid falling prey to these schools' lack of theory, then it had to combine their comprehensive determination of their object of investigation with the neoclassical schools' orientation and commitment to theory. Part of this undertaking was the task of supplying sociology with a basis that was analogous to, but different from, the theory of rational action, that is, the task of demonstrating the limits of the theory of rational action while at the same time positively analyzing the sphere of nonrational action that was not dealt with by economic theory. Max Weber had already sought to address these problems with his efforts to define categories of action in the famous section entitled "Basic Sociological Categories" at the beginning of *Economy and Society.*[1] For the development of Parsons's thought prior to the composition of his first major work, and also for the argumentation in this work, this situation then was of crucial importance. Parsons also recognized the more comprehensive, cultural significance of this scientific problematic as a controversy about the range and the limits of the entire utilitarian moral and social philosophy, as well as—even more generally—of a liberal capitalist economy. Parsons began his book with preliminary methodological discussions having as their principal goal the exposition of the "analytical" status of the theory of rational action and of possible analogous constructs, and the prevention thereby of misconstruals of that theory as maintaining ontologically or empirically the actual rationality of social action.

The heart of Parsons's work, though, consisted of widely inclusive interpretations of the writings of Alfred Marshall, Vilfredo Pareto, Emile Durkheim, and Max Weber. These interpretations were given coherence by the "convergence thesis," according to which it was demonstrable that from the standpoint of a sociological theory of action there was a convergence between, on the one hand, immanent attempts to go beyond utilitarianism in the thought of Marshall and Pareto and, on the other hand, the founding of sociology in the works of Durkheim and Weber, which was detaching itself in the one instance from positivism and in the other from idealism. For Parsons, this convergence was virtually empirical proof of the correctness of the theory emerging out of the writings of these thinkers, since the agreement among them could not be taken simply as the expression of a common ideological ground, seeing that they did not reciprocally influence one another and were working in nationally very different intellectual and theoretical milieus. Rather, their agreement was to be regarded as like a "multiple discovery" in empirical research, that is to say, as the simultaneous solution by a number of independent investigators of a received theoretical problem. This solution consisted in the demonstration of the normative dimension of social order and in the development of the categorial framework of a "voluntaristic" theory of action, the latter being closely linked with the former.

Now, how does Alexander modify Parsons's theoretical framework in the organization of his own study? Corresponding to Parsons's early methodological chapters we have the first volume of Alexander's work, which proclaims, against the backdrop of the long road of reflection traveled by the post-empiricist or "post-positivist" theory of science, the autonomous elaboration of sociological theory that cannot be reduced either to the findings of empirical research or to worldviews, and which gives this proclamation concrete form by naming the two fundamental problems of such a theory, to wit, "action" and "social order." The present-day theory of science has made Alexander's task easier. In contrast, Parsons gained a certain degree of imperviousness to the pressure of logical positivism only by using the philosophy of science of the late Whitehead. Alexander's propinquity to Parsons is undeniably conjoined with a greater explicitness of argumentation than Parsons himself could attain.

The subsequent volumes give extensive interpretations of the work of Marx, Durkheim, Weber, and Parsons himself. In them, however, the connection with the economic controversy that was the informing center of Parsons's book has become unrecognizable. Parsons's examination of the leading theorist of marginal utility, Alfred Marshall, has no parallel at all in Alexander's study; nor has that of the thought of Vilfredo Pareto, who evolved from an economist into a sociologist. From the formal standpoint, the work of these two theorists is replaced in Alexander's study by the work of Karl Marx, which appeared in Parsons's theoretical interpretation of social theory only briefly and in a very contradictory fashion, once as part of the utilitarian tradition and again as part of the idealist tradition. The discussion of Weber and Durkheim in Parsons's book is paralleled by an examination of their thought in Alexander's work. Of course, the latter consideration of these two undisputed classics of the sociological discipline could be based on a much more advanced state of the knowledge of their oeuvres and their theories than was available to Parsons. The most extensive volume of Alexander's work deals with Parsons himself as a classic. These differences between the content and organization of Parsons's and Alexander's studies might seem at first to be of less significance than they in fact are. For in eliminating the intraeconomic controversies that formed the backdrop of Parsons's study, Alexander also eliminates the "clamp" that held Parsons's monographic interpretations together, namely, the convergence thesis. Alexander declares that this thesis is false not because, with regard to theoretical questions posed by the social sciences, a simultaneous transformation of many different schools can still be construed as the expression of circumstances that are typical of an epoch, and need not be construed simply as positive scientific progress, which is what one would have expected; but rather because he considers the thesis to be in point of fact wrong. Recognizing the convergence of Weber's theory of legitimacy and charisma with Durkheim's notion of the sacred was, Alexander concedes, a pathbreaking theoretical achievement on the part of Parsons. On the whole, however, the assertion that there is a real convergence among the theories he examined was untenable, and resulted only from the tacit revisions that Parsons made of the weak points in the analyses and arguments of the major social theorists whom he treated, weaknesses that he intuitively perceived.

But what holds Alexander's interpretations of the different theorists together, if the convergence thesis is invalid? The principle of Alexander's general construction of social theory consists in the conflict between sociological idealism and sociological materialism, and in the surmounting of this conflict in a "multidimensional," "synthetic" approach. For him, the theories of Marx and Durkheim are mutually exclusive in their one-sidedness. The sociological materialism of the one, which systematically precludes the adequate theoretical apprehension of the normative and the cultural, has its counterpart in the sociological idealism of the other, who, admittedly, supplied the decisively important components of a theory of normativity, but did not convincingly integrate the normative into the world of means and conditions. Alexander undertakes to trace out the development of both thinkers, using this guiding thread. In following their intellectual evolution, he sees both of them caught up in a conflict between the two aforementioned opposed positions. Further, he analyzes the theoretical contributions of the more important Marxists and Durkheimians in order to show that these result from the disciples' efforts to solve the problems ensuing from the one-sidedness of their masters. The interpretations of Max Weber in Alexander's third volume serves the purpose of presenting the classical attempt to find an escape from this antinomy. However, long stretches of the discussion in this volume are devoted to critically pointing out deviations by Weber from the ideal of a "multidimensional" synthesis. It was, asserts Alexander, Parsons who first provided the conceptual bases of such a comprehensive theory, but certainly not without minor errors and some instances of theoretical recidivism.

Through this modification of the general framework, Alexander skillfully avoids the various criticisms that were leveled at Parsons's convergence thesis. With his discussion of Marx, he also fills up the most obvious lacuna in Parsons's efforts to work out the historical background of his theoretical enterprise. His strategy is not without its problems, though. For the new interpretation is persuasive only if the concepts of sociological idealism and materialism do in fact refer to centrally important problems of social theory and of the major social theorists Alexander treats, and if Weber's and Parsons's bodies of thought can reasonably be construed as efforts to achieve a synthesis of the theories of Marx and Durkheim. However, that is not at all self-evident. Even before examining the plausibility of his individual interpretations of the seminal social theorists he discusses, I would like to call into question, in at least three regards, Alexander's general framework of interpretation.

1. Today, the eternal struggle between idealism and materialism is considered to be an adequate description of the foundation of the history of philosophy only in the textbooks of Marxism-Leninism. Admittedly, Alexander is not talking about the conflict between opposed epistemological positions, but about sociological approaches. In the context of his discussion, sociological materialism refers to a whole family of approaches such as economism, utilitarianism, hedonism, behaviorism, Darwinism, and Machiavellianism, which have in common an insufficient reflection on the normativity that underlies human action. They all view the process of setting goals as a merely technical assessment and utilization of external conditions (I, 74). In contrast, sociological idealism consists in one-sidedly directing attention to the normative dimensions of society at the expense of the restricting conditions in action-situations. Sociological idealism does, certainly, have the merit of insisting on the irreducibility of the normative character of human action.

The choice of the terms of materialism and idealism to designate this set of problems is clearly not a happy one. For what Alexander obviously has in mind is, rather, the opposition between a Kantian and a utilitarian conception of morality and sociality. If the opposition in question had been described in the latter categories, then it would have been immediately clear that this characterization of the fundamental problem of the sociological classics permits a correct analytical reconstruction of their thought only insofar as they were in fact caught up in the tension between these opposed conceptions. With regard to Weber and Parsons, one can be more optimistic about the likelihood that this is so than for Marx and Durkheim. To be sure, it can be ascertained that all four thinkers stood in a complexly critical relationship with classical political economy and neoclassical economics, to Spencer's sociology, and to utilitarian moral philosophy. Parsons himself gave impetus to the talk of a Kantian core in his thought, although there are grounds for believing that he was retrospectively revising his intellectual evolution when he did so (Joas 1984).

For Weber and Durkheim, the contemporary neo-Kantianism as represented by the work of Rickert and Renouvier was certainly not without formative significance. However, a much more important question is whether the critical examination of and engagement with the thought of Nietzsche (in the case of Weber) and the theories of Bergson (in the case of Durkheim) were not of considerably greater importance. And to understand Marx, not only is it necessary to be familiar with Kant's philosophy; one must also know the convoluted history of post-Kantian German idealism, German Romanticism, and the works of the Left Hegelians. This is not to say that Alexander is unaware of the importance for the social theorists he discusses of Hegel and Feuerbach, of Nietzsche and of *Lebensphilosophie.* He speaks of them here and there in his interpretations. Rather, the point is that the categories out of which he constructs his interpretative framework, and according to which he organizes his study, do not permit presentation of the field of problems within which the founding theorists of modern sociology pursued their reflections. Alexander gives his exposition of the ideas of these theorists in an interpretative framework that is conceptually too exiguous to achieve an understanding of the complex of problems that they were concerned with.

This shortcoming would have no serious consequences if it were a matter of philosophical backdrops having no bearing on the construction of sociological theory. Perhaps Alexander thinks that is so. Even then, though, it would be a grave failing to overlook the fact that in relation to the philosophical problems dealt with in the works of the sociological classics, Alexander's construction is insensitive and unjustified. This criticism, incidentally, also holds good with regard to the philosophical problems of the present time. Let us illustrate this with a single example. Following Wittgenstein, there came about an intrinsic linking together of linguistic theory and the theory of action, as had happened much earlier under the influence of pragmatism. This connection is one that cannot simply be ignored by any contemporary attempt to elaborate a sociological theory of action. Alexander's construction, however, like that of Parsons, remains completely unaffected by the link established between the two theories. Let us not forget what Charles Taylor, in particular, has so persuasively pointed out, namely that even during Kant's lifetime, reflection on language and the problem of linguistic meaning, as pursued in the thought of Herder and Wilhelm von Humboldt, added to Kantian autonomy and utilitarianism a new path for reflection to explore. Especially in the German history of ideas, the exploration of this new path proved to be extremely fruitful, as it led, on the one hand, to Karl Marx and on the other to hermeneutics and philosophical anthropology (Taylor 1986).

2. However, examination of a second set of themes demonstrates that Alexander's theoretical construction and his failure to subject its principles to philosophical scrutiny were not at all without significant consequences. In Parsons's theory, the centrally important position of the problem of a theory of action conceived of as an alternative to the theory of rational action, and of the problem of social order which cannot be solved with the means provided by a theory of rational action, is quickly justified. In Alexander's interpretation of social theory, no sufficient argument is given for the assertion, which he makes very forcefully, that the problems of action and social order are the key problems of any and every sociological theory. His most recent book, though, supplies in passing an argument for the thesis advanced in the earlier work. According to that argument, the endeavor to achieve integration of individual freedom and social order is a typically modern, typically Western cultural problem. This claim sounds plausible and is entirely compatible with Parsons's goals; it leads to difficulties, however, insofar as the problem thereby becomes relativized with respect to its cultural significance and can no longer be understood self-evidently as a universal, purely theoretical central problem. Further, Alexander's assertion makes inescapably clear the need to think about freedom, individualism, and social order within a wider horizon of reflection than that delimited by the conflict between autonomous morality and the egoistical calculation of benefits.

As I have remarked, however, the aforesaid argument is advanced only as a digression. Admittedly, Alexander gives extensive and detailed explanations of the embeddedness of science in a "metaphysical" and an "empirical" environment, and of the various "components" of the domain lying between these two poles, which he calls the "scientific continuum." The purpose of these explanations is to distinguish different levels of scientific argumentation in a way that prevents the erroneous location of arguments and in particular enables a level of most general presuppositions to be identified. He intends thereby to make possible the explicit discussion of presuppositions. In light of his project, it is astonishing that he does not undertake to lay bare his own presuppositions, which are indeed implicit in the plan of his theoretical construction and in the most general schemata of his argumentation. The assertion that action and social order are the two central problems of sociological theory is as little thoroughly grounded as is the distinction between the principal types of theory of action (rational-instrumental versus nonrational-normative) or of the theory of social order (individualistic-emergent versus collectivistic-sui generis). Yet nothing would have been of greater importance for the persuasiveness of Alexander's argumentation than not simply *positing* these crucial distinctions and then schematically applying them, but grounding them at the start in relation to the kind of problems that sociology is currently concerned with and to those that are constitutive of sociology itself. Are the distinctions Alexander draws at all appropriate, then, to the problems dealt with in the works of the sociological classics, or do they rather constitute an artificial schema, a kind of mill through which everything is forced without regard to the losses that thereby occur?

There is a direct connection between this remarkable lacuna in Alexander's argumentation and a further problem. Like Parsons, Alexander places great emphasis upon the *analytical* status of theoretical abstractions; this was mentioned briefly above in the description of theories of rational action. But Alexander tells us nothing about how arguments can be made on this analytical plane. There must, however, be rational reasons for determining the directions in which a metatheoretical frame of reference, conceived of as analytical in nature, may and may not in fact be further developed. If emphasis of the analytical character of a particular theory only serves to ward off criticisms of it, then there is the danger that a specific metatheory might simply make itself proof against criticism. If I understand the matter correctly, there are only two ways in which an analytical metatheoretical argumentation can be grounded. There can be pragmatic reasons for making a certain abstraction—that of *homo oeconomicus*, for example—without claiming that this abstraction has any kind of reality. On the other hand, there can be ontological reasons why a certain abstraction corresponds best to the essence of the human being in general, or to the human being of the bourgeois era, or to anything like that. In the one case, the tasks and the division of labor of the various sciences, in the other case, anthropological assumptions or historical ideal types supply the justification for particular analytical abstractions. If this is correct, then there are only two possible ways of grounding a sociological theory of action. First, the theory can be grounded by means of the pragmatic usefulness of its particular analytical abstraction. Parsons probably had this kind of argument in mind when he advanced his thesis that sociology was the special discipline for the investigation of normative social integration; Alexander, however, explicitly does not take over this definition of the task of sociology. The second possibility is that anthropological assumptions about the distinctive features of human action—either in comparison with animal behavior, or with respect to the traits of historically dominant types of action—permit the grounding of the chosen apparatus of categories. Of this second kind of grounding too, however, there is no trace in Alexander's work. Because both possible ways of grounding a sociological theory of action are lacking, Alexander's fundamental conceptual distinctions have no basis. What could still be easily understood in Parsons's writings in light of their relation to the controversy about methods in economics is present in Alexander's study merely as a reminiscence. He does not undertake to think through the competing abstractions of human action—the rational versus the nonrational model—and to examine closely the constitution of the distinction between them. Instead, he merely proclaims that social theorists have the task of simultaneously taking into consideration both types of action. In doing that, however, he has not even begun to carry out the task of developing a satisfactory conceptual apparatus for a theory of action.

Thomas Burger has pointed out that a conceptualization that seeks to probe beyond abstractions is essentially different from the simultaneous empirical taking into consideration of different dimensions of influence on the object of investigation (Burger 1986, p. 278). This seems to me a crucially important point for the assessment of Alexander's claim that he has elaborated a multidimensional and synthetic theory. In his critique of other theories, Alexander can, certainly, demonstrate from his standpoint that the ignoring of a particular dimension *can* and in fact often does have harmful consequences for a social theory. But also he can not preclude that the neglect of a certain dimension (whether the "normative" or the "material" one) may have no consequences for the purposes of a particular empirical explanation, inasmuch as the dimension in question can in fact be ignored without practical consequences. If he were to derive from his claim to have elaborated a multidimensional theory the positive assertion that all dimensions must always be equally important empirically, this would be a false concretization of the analytical multidimensionality of his theory. Moreover, it is impermissible to draw any positive empirical conclusion from the metatheory proposed by Alexander. The theoretical construction presented to us as a synthesis is, therefore, from the practical viewpoint only an empty "not only this, but also that."

3. In yet a third respect, Alexander's theoretical construction, in which the theory of action has been accorded such a centrally important place, proves to be insufficient precisely with regard to the requirements of a theory of action. Its shortcomings have to do with the status of general social theory and with the "scientific continuum." Many of Alexander's critics have passed trenchantly negative judgment on just this part of his undertaking and on the first volume of his *Theoretical Logic* in its entirety. If one judges Alexander using the yardstick provided by the body of theoretical writings that serves him as the basis of his own thinking, then this text certainly does not come out well; however, if one measures what Alexander offers here against the level of epistemological reflection generally found among practicing social researchers, then his text unquestionably makes a useful contribution to sociology's reflection upon itself from the perspective of the theory of science. Various critics have maintained that Alexander emphasizes more strongly the relative autonomy of fundamental theoretical premises vis-à-vis empirical research and experiential knowledge than the reverse relationship, namely that facts, too, while their formulation is guided by theory, may be commonly recognized in competing theories. By doing so, these critics continue, Alexander runs the danger of falling prey to a kind of theoretistic determinism. Correct as this objection is, it nevertheless seems to me that it does not address the salient point with regard to Alexander's construction of the "scientific continuum." He does not interpret the situation of cognition between metaphysical apprehension of the world and knowledge gained from everyday experience as itself an action-situation! Like Parsons before him, Alexander fails to grasp pragmatism's basic idea, that cognition is situated in problematic action-situations. His concept of action exhibits no intrinsic relation to a concept of knowledge. Because of that fact, however, within Alexander's theoretical framework the relationship between (metaphysical) appre-

hension of the world and knowledge gained from practical experience becomes one of super- or subordination, and not—as in Toulmin's work (Toulmin 1972)—a relationship of reciprocal intermeshing. Alexander does not conceive of the thinking that produces social theory as the practical self-reflection of actors and thus fails to perceive a new kind of grounding for the central position in social theory of the category of action. If cognition is necessarily tied to action, then every scientific theory must ultimately reflect upon and identify its locus in human action.

With that conclusion, an interim result becomes apparent. Recognition must admittedly be accorded to Alexander for championing the importance of general sociological theory and in particular the significance of the theory of action and social order. Yet he has contributed nothing really new with regard either to the historical analysis of the genesis of the sociological theory of action, or to the internal elaboration of that theory, or to the reflexive examination of the scientific status of this theory. Let us, therefore, redirect our attention to the field at which the greatest part of Alexander's endeavors was obviously aimed: to his interpretations of the thought of the sociological classics. In this domain, there can be no doubt about the fundamentality and the principled nature of his work. The argumentation is always clear and just; the overview he gives of both primary and secondary literature is impressive. It is certainly necessary that theoretical argumentation and interpretative scrutiny and criticism be linked together. From the standpoint of sociology, the purely historical study of the founders of sociology would indeed be irrelevant; purely theoretical argumentation would become fatally entangled in its hypercomplexity without the focus given to it by its connection to the sociological classics. Thus it is not this link itself that is in question, but solely whether Alexander has successfully established and maintained it. It is, generally, a question of whether the metatheoretical framework employed by Alexander is hermeneutically supple enough to not only delineate individual problem areas, but also to link together, on the one hand, the tasks set themselves by the theorists being interpreted, and on the other hand the orientation of the interpreter's own inquiry by showing the historical continuity between the former and the latter (*wirkungsgeschichtlich,* as Gadamer uses this word). The successful establishment of such a connection determines whether a theorist's body of work appears as a tangle of contradictory responses to the interpreter's questions, or whether the interpreter succeeds, within the horizon of his own inquiry, in understanding the questions posed by a particular theorist and the answers the theorist gives to them; also in comprehending the reasons for a possible vacillation on the theorist's part or for internal contradictions of his theory; perhaps even in analyzing the problems resulting from the theorist's attempt to solve the principal problems with which he is concerned, and by so doing in actually understanding a thinker better than he was able to understand himself. By choosing the quotation from Schleiermacher as the epigraph of his volume on Weber, Alexander has signaled that he has adopted—justifiably—this hermeneutic goal. Questions of influence or of dating and periodization thereby acquire a theoretical worth that transcends the domain of mere philological fact.

In posing and answering such questions, however, Alexander treats particulars in a quite cavalier manner. Again and again he annoyingly asserts the existence of developments that he cannot prove philologically, and that he quickly isolates from the exigencies of empirical hermeneutic investigation by declaring them to be purely metatheoretical matters. Not all possible technical errors committed by Alexander in the execution of his undertaking are, however, of theoretical interest here, but only such interpretative problems as can be shown to arise out of problems inherent in his metatheoretical framework. The remainder of this essay, therefore, shall be devoted almost exclusively to the examination of these.

Alexander's interpretation of Marx joins together the characterizations of the latter's thought given by Parsons, who did not, however, elucidate the relationship between them. According to Alexander, Marx's thought has its origins in a normative idealism, and his earliest writings are incomprehensible without the conflict between a universalistic ethics and the existing institutionalized norms. The rupture in the evolution of his thought, however, consists in the alleged recognition of the powerlessness of a moral critique of the existing socio-economic order and in the adoption of the view that the elaboration of a theory adequate to the age of alienation, that is, of capitalism, had to begin not from an anthropology of the free human being who expresses and objectifies himself (in his actions and in his works), but from the model of the utilitarian-egoistical action of competing individual subjects, which had been formulated by classical political economy. The debate about a rupture in the development of Marx's thought is thus broadened through the addition of yet another position: Alexander places the break at an earlier date than anyone else, in the years 1842–43. In his opinion, the *Paris Manuscripts* are no longer writings of the early Marx, but already part of his transition to a pure utilitarianism, which was concluded by 1845. The manuscripts are, to be sure, still marked by an ambivalence on their author's part. As

Alexander sees the rupture in Marx's theoretical development, then, it coincides with the latter's study and appropriation of political economy. From the theoretical standpoint, this means that Marx did not surmount utilitarianism, but on the contrary accepted it completely, merely relativizing its validity historically. This thesis, which constitutes the core of Alexander's interpretation of Marx, is particularized inasmuch as he maintains that Marx adopted only the utilitarian theory of action, and not the utilitarian theory of social order. With respect to the theory of social order, Marx directly opposes the utilitarian theory with his insistence on the class character of the structure of existing social formations. In this basic theoretical structure of Marxism, says Alexander, is rooted its systemic inability to go beyond an instrumentalist theory of the state and a functionalist reduction of law, ethics, and ideas.

There can be no doubt that Alexander has put his finger on a problem that has also been noted by other critics of Marxism and raised as a question in discussion among Marxists. The question is: How can a critique of political economy that is in point of fact founded on utilitarian premises be joined with Marxism's theory of revolution or, more generally, with its political sociology if the foundations of both components of Marxist theory in a theory of action are not referred to each other from the outset? Alexander champions with great radicalism the thesis that Marx's systematic theory is utilitarian in character. His position on this matter enforces a salutary clarification about Marx, as it closes off favorite escape routes. Alexander does not accept the claim that Marx's factual research is superior to his interpretations of his methodology, since the criticism that Marx's work is utilitarian is true precisely of his factual research. He accords no importance to references to Marx's general view of life, nor to his political journalism, nor even to his historiographical writings, for while these are certainly an expression of Marx's tacit knowledge and his undeniably great learning and acumen, they are not expressions of the systematic results of his conceptual system. Finally, he discounts references by Marx to cultural elements as an argument against his interpretation of Marxism, regarding them rather as evidence for its correctness inasmuch as in every theory whatever has been systematically excluded from it usually manifests itself in the form of residual categories. All of this must be taken extremely seriously. Nevertheless, two objections can be made to Alexander's interpretation of Marx's thought that can call parts of it seriously into question.

1. The first objection concerns the peculiarities of Marx's critique of political economy in comparison with classical political economy in

general. Alexander's reconstruction of Marx's critique recognizes its differences from utilitarianism only on the plane of the theory of social order. Opposed to this view, however, is the fact that Marx's specific version of the labor theory of value with all its implications, from the theory of surplus value to the law of the tendential fall of the rate of profit, remains incomprehensible if its grounding in the non-utilitarian, but rather "expressivistic" concept of labor—to adopt Charles Taylor's term—is not seen. If this is true, then a completely different strand of the theory of action than the utilitarian one is still of decisive importance in the work of the late Marx, and the significance of the anthropology of praxis cannot be reduced to that of a normative background of a theory formulated in different categories. This observation is not intended to contradict the assertion that Marx did not himself work out and clearly define this basic concept of his theory, and that he did not take it seriously especially in its importance for the analysis of the consciousness and the political activity of wage laborers. It is to this domain that the second objection is directed.

2. Alexander's argumentation presupposes that only the critique of political economy is to be regarded as the scientific part of Marx's oeuvre, and that this critique must also be considered as a theory of society as a whole. In the identification of *Capital* with Marx's theory of society, Alexander is as peremptory as the driest exegetes of that work were during the heyday of seminar Marxism in West Germany in the 1970s. This identity is not self-evident, though, and its assertion raises the question of the status of the critique of political economy in a social theory. Correct as it is that Marx's critique of political economy does not content itself with the status of a disciplinal economics—and in this respect, incidentally, it is just like classical political economy—it would be just as wrong to simply declare that critique to be a comprehensive sociology. If it were such, then only the status of quasi-functionalist "derivations" would be possible for a theory of the state, of law, of the family, and of art. In contrast, if one sees in *Capital* the ascertaining and description of certain developmental tendencies at a high level of abstraction, then the relationship of these tendencies to others has not at all been established by the analysis presented in that work. Alexander's interpretation projects the problems that the sociological classics were concerned with in the generation of Max Weber, Emile Durkheim, and Vilfredo Pareto back onto Marx, during whose time a scientized economics was supplemented solely by a political philosophy, both in Marx's thought and in the works of the thinkers whom Marx criticized.

However, the key to understanding the traditions of this political philosophy is not provided by the conflict between utilitarianism and normativism. These traditions go back to the practical philosophy of Aristotle and undergo diverse transformations in the reaction to the utilitarian and materialist tendencies of the Enlightenment. Herder's and Humboldt's expressivist anthropology, Fichte's theory of interpersonality, Hegel's efforts to charge practical philosophy with the pathos of the freedom of transcendental philosophy's conception of natural law, Feuerbach's anthropological materialism—all of these are forms of thinking which in their development either bypassed Kant or incorporated his theories but went beyond them. In Parsons's introductory remarks to his interpretation of Weber the account given of German idealism was wholly inadequate. He erroneously projected onto all of German idealism historicism's tendency to interpret social phenomena as the emanation or expression of cultural plexuses of meaning. By doing so he failed to grasp in particular the significance of the expressivist model of human action, because he rejected—correctly—the interpretation of human activities as the expression of an "objective spirit," but explored not at all the possibilities implicit in the interpretation of activities as the expression of the actor. In dealing, in contrast admittedly to Parsons, with Marx at length and in detail but, in his turn, perpetuating Parsons's insufficient attention to the path of philosophical development that led to Marx, Alexander's detailed treatment of the latter constitutes only a small advance. If Hegel's influence on Marx is to be considered of little moment—as Alexander maintains—then there nevertheless remains the question whether Alexander's schema is unable to comprehend Hegel's theory. This is not the place to expound upon the history of German idealism from the viewpoint of the theory of action. It is, however, important to stress that the central concept of German idealism, "spirit," cannot be reconstructed as a "normative dimension," but rather is a specific form of descriptive designation of the *creativity* of human activity. In Marx's writings there are at least two models of action that cannot be described either as utilitarian or as normativist (Honneth and Joas 1987). The expressivist concept of labor has already been mentioned; Marx makes clear, especially in his early writings, that for him human labor is not merely a process of productive expenditure of efforts, but is also to be regarded as an expressive event, through which the human being seeks to realize himself. Capitalism becomes the target of Marx's critique precisely because, structurally, it makes difficult or impossible this self-realization, that is, the recognition by the working subjects of themselves in their own products. In addition to this expressivist model of labor, the problems of which cannot be discussed here, there is a model of collective action, to be found especially in Marx's historical writings. It must be emphasized that this model does not include only the *normative* dimensions of the class struggle, but ascertains and describes the *creative* and *norm-establishing* achievements of social groups. The class struggle as it appears in Marx's thought is not to be understood according to the schema of utility-oriented action guided by self-interest, since Marx declares that the concerns of utmost importance to the proletariat are self-realization and self-determination. In saying this I do not at all mean to assert that Marx's attempts to solve the problems inherent in his action-theoretical concepts are themselves unproblematical. The synthesis of expressivist anthropology and utilitarianism is equally unstable in both instances, in the concept of labor and in that of class struggle. Furthermore, the relationship between the interpretation of history from the perspective of political economy and that centered in class struggles has never been truly clarified, as Castoriadis, in particular, has shown (Castoriadis 1987; see also Berki 1979). Alexander's action-theory schema, however, contains no possibility at all of even acknowledging the existence of these problems.

The basic theme of Alexander's interpretation of Durkheim is the search for a concept of social order that is compatible with the individual's freedom of will. It is Alexander's goal to trace out, in a more detailed manner than Parsons, the sinuous evolution of Durkheim's solution of the problem of social order, that is to say, the development of his recognition of the sociality of the actor. He presents in a nuanced fashion the various intellectually tested approaches proposed in Durkheim's early writings, as well as the French sociologist's steps toward a theory of "emotional" and not "instrumental" interaction that accompanied his sociological investigations of religion. In contrast to Parsons, Alexander is not of the opinion that Durkheim was en route from positivism to idealism, but instead from a normativist early stage, through a materialist middle stage, to his late work that was becoming ever more normativist or idealist. The most pronounced difference of Alexander's interpretation from Parsons's does not result from the former's more intense and extensive consideration of Durkheim's early writings, but is to be found rather in his interpretation of Durkheim's study of the division of labor, which is diametrically opposed to that of Parsons. From Parsons to Giddens, in almost all of the literature on Durkheim, that book has been regarded as the classic critique of utilitarianism because it demonstrates the noncontractual presuppositions of contracts and the moral foundation even of modern society. In Alexander's view, this is not true, and the misinterpretation arises out of the reading of the first part of the book in isolation from the rest of it. According to him, Durkheim formulates, rather, a theory of the progressive elimination of this moral basis of society and thus is treading the road back to Spencer or to a Marx who is understood as a utilitarian. In this regard, says Alexander, it is a question especially of Marx, inasmuch as Durkheim's theory of the forms of solidarity directly corresponds to Marx's historical relativization of utilitarianism. In Alexander's exposition of this bold thesis there are immanent difficulties that give grounds for caution, according to the experiential rules of hermeneutics. Alexander's thesis requires that he assume an extreme degree of internal inconsistency in Durkheim's study of the division of labor, theoretical vacillations in the French thinker's next stage of intellectual development, and regular diversionary maneuvers in his next book, *Rules of Sociological Method.* Could not these difficulties be an indication that, even in the case of Durkheim, the problems that are at issue can simply not be grasped theoretically within the framework supplied by the opposed categories of normativity and utilitarianism? This suspicion is further strengthened if one takes advantage of the opportunity to introduce into evidence works of Durkheim that Parsons could not have been acquainted with, as they were published only posthumously, but that shed light on Durkheim's intellectual evolution after the conclusion of his book on the theory of religion. The works in question are Durkheim's lectures on "Pragmatism and Sociology." These lectures, which Alexander does not discuss at all, can show how little able a category such as "sociological idealism" is to grasp descriptively Durkheim's halfhearted attempt to reformulate Cartesianism in response to the pragmatist critique of it (Durkheim 1983).

An alternative interpretation of Durkheim, as previously in the case of Marx, can only be sketched here in order to demonstrate how necessary it is to employ a broader metatheoretical framework than Alexander's. I do not believe that we correctly understand Durkheim's study of the division of labor if we see in it either the positivist demonstration of the automatic origination of moral integration through physical interaction, as Randall Collins does, or the merely abstract, quasi-utilitarian hope that instrumentally oriented actions might somehow contain their own morality, as Jeffrey Alexander does. Rather, it seems to me that in this work Durkheim wanted to advocate an idea for the clear formulation of which he lacked the conceptual tools. This idea was that of an ethics of cooperation, that is, of a morality that can grow out of the experiences and requirements of cooperation among actors having equal rights through the self-reflection of the cooperating actors. Such a cooperative ethics would be neither a causal result of cooperation nor a merely pious accompaniment to an exchange economy. However, Durkheim was unable to formulate this idea more clearly because, first, he lacked the conceptual tools that have been fashioned by developmental psychology and the theory of socialization, and which he needed in order to describe the genesis of a cooperative ethics, as Piaget did in his early masterwork on the development of moral judgment in the child (Piaget 1932). For this reason there is a yawning gap in his account between the demonstration of the frequency of instances of cooperation and the asserted origination of a cooperative ethics. The other reason why Durkheim was incapable of formulating more clearly the idea of an ethics of cooperation lies in a profound ambiguity implicit in his concept of the division of labor, which Alexander fails to notice. Durkheim does not distinguish between the antagonistic division of labor proper to the market and the nonantagonistic division of labor in organized cooperation. Durkheim's thesis of an ethics that arises out of the very division of labor can be reasonably defended only for an ethics that results from egalitarian cooperation. The modern society of capitalist industrialization, which Durkheim undertook to analyze, is not, however, characterized simply by the propagation of such cooperative relationships, but by the liberation of the processes of the market economy and, as Marx would have said, their contradictory union with an extension of hierarchical cooperation within firms. Thus Durkheim necessarily becomes entangled in contradictions when he expects a new morality in this new society, while in point of fact ascertaining the existence chiefly of tendencies leading to anomie. The interpretation of these phenomena as transitional ones is an evasion. Alexander grasps only one possible meaning of the division of labor in his interpretation of Durkheim's investigations: the kind of interconnectedness of individual, utility-oriented actions that is proper to the market economy. If this is what one understands, then, naturally the path leading to the notion of an ethics of cooperation is completely closed, and Durkheim's theory must be interpreted as resembling the position of classical utilitarianism that social integration of individuals is accomplished through the market. On the contrary, however, the question Durkheim posed was that of *the origination of a new ethics.* In the further course of the evolution of this thinking, Durkheim did not succeed in solving the problems that have been mentioned, but he modified his formulation of the problem. His conviction became ever stronger that such an ethics of cooperation is in itself too weak if it only grows out of cooperation; it must itself be institutionalized. This conviction led him to inquire into the genesis of institutions. He answers this question with his theory of ritual and of collective effervescence. I therefore propose that Durkheim's development be regarded as the evolution of the question of the origin and creative production of institutions and worldviews. But even with the most mature variant of this question Durkheim does not succeed in linking recognition of the importance of extraordinary collective interaction with a theory of everyday social interaction. Alexander does indeed note that Durkheim's concept of action contains utilitarian residues, and that in his thought the social is separated from action. Durkheim's concept of personality combines a substantialized biological individual with a social concept of personality structure. In this connection Mead's thought, which assumes the social shaping of biological impulses, is much more radical. If, then, it were only a matter of demonstrating the social character of the person, Durkheim would not be the crucial theorist. But he is of decisive importance precisely for the concern that can be designated only with difficulty within Alexander's metatheoretical framework, namely the production of institutions and worldviews in processes of collective action.

If my examination of Alexander's interpretations of Marx and Durkheim was mainly critical, this will not be so in my discussion of his treatment of Weber and Parsons. In his study of the former Alexander refrains from all philological assertions about Weber's intellectual development. He perceives, rather, a permanent tension in Weber's work that gives very different characters to the various parts of that work. This tension is, once again, that between normativism and utilitarianism, but in Weber's case these determinations prove to be quite helpful. In Alexander's view, Weber is intent on theoretically apprehending "ideas" and "interests" in an integrated fashion. This integration, Alexander says, is exemplarily successful in some parts of Weber's oeuvre, such as the theory of social classes and the sociology of the city. In other parts, like the comparative studies of economic morality and the religion of the world, the results in this regard are of extremely uneven quality. The negatively judged study of China is counterposed to the investigation of ancient Judaism, its positively assessed counterpart. It is of critical significance, though, that it cannot be a matter in this respect of unimportant deficiencies in the working out of details, since in a principal part of his work, Weber proceeds in a consistently reductive manner, namely in his analysis of modernity. "Multidimensional" though the analysis of modernity's genesis might be, this state of affairs changes programmatically when it comes to the presentation of that analysis. Whether it is a matter of the sociology of law or of social stratification, of the sociology of bureaucracy or of democracy—everywhere the one-sided emphasis on utilitarian features of modernity prevails and leads to empirical weaknesses in Weber's investigations. Alexander rightly rejects as a possible explanation for this the contention that this emphasis by Weber on utilitarian features is in fact an expression of the essence of this modern society, for Weber's procedure metatheoretically decides in advance what should be proved empirically. For long stretches Alexander's argumentation resembles Jürgen Habermas's even more subtle reasoning in the chapter on Weber in his *Theory of Communicative Action* (Habermas 1981) and differs strongly from the picture of Weber given by Parsons. Alexander demonstrates extremely well the internal ambiguity of Weber's concept of purposive rationality and thereby the lack of clarity of the typology of action that is dependent on this concept. He perceives Weber's vacillation between a utilitarian interpretation of purposive rationality and a pragmatist version of it in which even goals or purposes are pondered in relation to the givens of the particular situation. If, however, this category and Weber's theory of action are ambiguous, then this fact has consequences for the concept of rationality, which plays such a central role in Weber's historical analyses. Is, then, the modern period the age of unconstrained individual action guided by utility, or of a heightened, pragmatically reasonable autonomy of action? What, then, is in fact to be understood by a process of rationalization?

I consider these questions, which Alexander poses, as justified and extremely important. It could, though, be the case that Alexander's schema of categories is, again, inadequate to answer them. For that schema contains only a, as it were, Kantian concept of moral autonomy. Weber's worldview, however, was informed much more strongly by the features of the Nietzschean theory of personality oriented to creativity, that constituted an aesthetics of genius (Hennis 1987). As he stripped Marx's concept of class struggle of its non-utilitarian traits, Alexander does not recognize, in Weber's case, the features of the concept of power deriving from Nietzsche and therefore interprets Weber's contentless concept of power (III, 92) as though it were utilitarian in nature. The formative influence on Weber's thought from Nietzsche on the one side and from the historical school of German political economy on the other is certainly not adequately captured and described with the concepts of "sociological idealism" and "normativism." The question of the very great influence on Weber's theory of the modern era exercised by this background, by the possibilities for the powerful unfolding of great individuals responsible only to themselves, cannot be pursued here. Here Alexander's schema once again painfully pinches the object of analysis, but this time with palpably smaller losses from the friction than in the cases of Marx and Durkheim.

The critical examination of Parsons in the fourth volume of Alexander's study is clearly the most successful part of the whole enterprise. In his penetrating study of Parsons's writings and his perusal of the critical literature on Parsons, Alexander has carried out an enormous accomplishment. As a self-critical reform of the Parsons school, this volume, taken by itself, would surely have been received as positively as the announcements claimed that the entire work would be. Without leaving the least doubt about his admiration for the man's lifework, Alexander is by no means forbearing in his criticism of Parsons for failing to attain his self-set goals. This holds true on both the methodological and substantive levels, for the theory of socialization as well as for Parsons's political moderation in the postwar United States.

Alexander's most important theoretical emendation of Parsons's theory is surely that he frees the famous AGIL schema of the exchange relations obtaining between functional subsystems from its functionalist reading. For Alexander, this model is untenable as a functionalist model of society: it merely formulates on the metatheoretical level a taxonomy of analytic abstractions. This cannot be dealt with in greater detail here. Rather, we can simply ask whether even here problems of interpretation result from Alexander's approach. I see one such problem that is of capital importance. Parsons's theory has no means for conceptually grasping and describing the historically contingent creative production of institutions and worldviews. All the processes that his theory recognizes and describes are concerned with the internalization or institutionalization of preconstituted values or the generalization, modification, or specification of such values. What is excluded from Durkheim's theory of institutions, from Marx's concepts of labor and class struggle, and from Weber's concept of power, or else subsumed under normativity, namely the creativity of individual or collective action, finds no possibility of recognition and inclusion in Parsons's theory and in the immanent critique of that theory.[2] This assertion is itself, admittedly, no immanent argument against that theory.

Jeffrey Alexander has added to his scrutiny and critique of the sociological classics an account of the history of sociology after 1945. Whereas the style of his four-volume work was often clumsy, and his argumentation in it encumbered with countless quotations and extensive references to the secondary literature, his book on the history of sociology travels with much lighter baggage. It originated from lectures, and this form has been retained. It is incomparably more readable and exciting than the multivolume study. Following an outstanding account of Parsons's body of theory and of the necessary revisions of it—a popular version, so to speak, of the fourth volume of *Theoretical Logic*—Alexander presents postwar sociology according to a simple plan. He considers the different schools that have been battling with one another since the 1960s and have destroyed the hegemony of Parsons's theory, none of them, however, having succeeded in establishing its own hegemony, each being a one-sided emphasis on an aspect inadequately treated in Parsons's theory and now treated by the school in question with an exclusiveness that makes a "synthetic" theory impossible. Alexander is helped in holding to this view of matters by the fact that he regards only a small number of logically possible combinations of metatheoretical elements as at all conceivable, and at the same time believes that he has identified these combinations in the schema of the two types of action and the two types of social order that we are familiar with from *Theoretical Logic.* Thus he can easily classify (according to his schema) the conflict theory of Rex, Homans's exchange theory, the symbolic interactionism of Blumer and Goffman, Garfinkel's ethnomethodology, Geertz's cultural sociology, and Critical Theory as represented by the work and ideas of Marcuse. Refracted through the prism of Alexander's schema, conflict theory proves to be a rationalist theory of action and a collectivist theory of social order. In contrast, exchange theory combines a rationalist theory of action with an individualist theory of social order, while symbolic interactionism is a combination of an individualist theory of social order with a nonrational, normativist model of action. And so forth.

Once again Alexander expends little effort on justifying the schema he employs. Once again it is very unclear how far he wants to consider these schools of theory in their difference from Parsons, and how far he is claiming that critical confrontation and conflictual interaction with Parsons's theory, the severing of the umbilical cord tying them to a mother-theory, is in fact constitutive for the development of these theories. We must, therefore, once again ask ourselves how convincing the interpretations made with Alexander's schema are.

When one begins to examine those interpretations, what strikes one most powerfully has nothing to do with the restrictive nature of the schema, but has everything to do with the forms of theory he considers. Alexander's account of the development of sociology after 1945 is shamelessly americacentric. We hear literally not one word about sociological theorists or about authors who are not sociologists but who are of central importance for the present-day discussion of social theory such as Pierre Bourdieu, Cornelius Castoriadis, Michel Foucault, and Alain Touraine in France; Norbert Elias, Arnold Gehlen, Niklas Luhmann, and Helmuth Plessner in the Federal Republic of Germany; Anthony Giddens's theory is dealt with on half a page; likewise that of Jürgen Habermas. In my opinion, it would have been more honest to say that this book presented a history of *American* sociological theory from 1945 *up to about 1970.* Neither the present-day American nor the European discussion and debate about social theory is presented and examined in an even approximately adequate manner. Thus the truly exciting question of how the theories of these authors would be analyzed according to Alexander's schema cannot be posed at all.

When one considers the theorists and theories treated in this book, it quickly becomes apparent that here, too, the capacity of Alexander's interpretative schema to comprehend theories is greatest when it comes to "renegade" students of Parsons (such as Garfinkel and Geertz), or when the theories in question were actually developed through confrontation and critique of Parsons's theory. When Alexander attempts to give accounts of theories that are independent of the problems that Parsons was concerned with, the results are in part, caricatures. The expositions given of the work of Peirce, Husserl, and Merleau-Ponty, for example, are completely unreliable, while the limiting of Critical Theory to Marcuse's work is indefensible. Of such theorists, the one who is dealt with most successfully is George Herbert Mead. In contrast, the critical discussions of Rex, Homans, Blumer, Garfinkel, and Geertz are worth reading.

After examining the studies by Alexander discussed here, one is left with the impression that this author is extraordinarily well read and adept at analytical argument; that he has been willing to reflect on the problems of human action and of social order in a scientific environment which is certainly not sympathetic to theory, but that he has not had the courage really to engage with the actual diversity of present-day thought nor with its wealth of varied historical roots and intellectual ancestry. The opening for development of theory that Alexander creates is immediately closed by a schematic limitation of theoretical possibilities. Where unsolved problems in the theoretical apprehension of human action reveal themselves, they are often covered over by his schema. In the form given it in his studies, neo-Parsonianism can, certainly, make itself heard as yet another voice in the chorus of sociological schools. To become the generally accepted framework of sociology, however, it would first have to heighten its capability to take seriously the different sociological positions that are now really competing with one another. Until it has done so, there will be no basis for proposing that it is able to compete with the efforts made by Habermas and Giddens to achieve a synthesis of social theory.

Notes

1. Pursuing ideas advanced by Göran Therborn, Simon Clarke (1982), in particular, has identified and described this historical background of modern social theory. These findings have recently been applied to the interpretation of Parsons by Charles Camic (1987), obviously following suggestions by Donald Levine. In my opinion this excellent essay has only one weakness: it underestimates the importance of Whitehead for Parsons's methodological consciousness (see Wenzel 1985).

2. In an essay written together with Paul Colomy (Alexander 1988, pp. 193–221) Alexander takes one step forward in this respect. He attempts there a synthesis of a revised functionalist theory of differentiation and a symbolic interactionist theory of collective behavior. His action-theoretical conceptual apparatus is also opened toward "inventive" components of action. A critical discussion of these indicators of further development in Alexander's work does not take place here; it would have to point out the problematic character of his sustained primacy of the theory of differentiation.

Bibliography

Alexander, Jeffrey. 1982–83. *Theoretical Logic in Sociology.* 4 vols. (vol. 1: *Positivism, Presuppositions, and Current Controversies;* vol. 2: *The Antinomies of Classical Thought: Marx and Durkheim;* vol. 3: *The Classical Attempt at Theoretical Synthesis: Max Weber;* vol. 4: *The Modern Reconstruction of Classical Thought: Talcott Parsons*). London: Routledge.

———1984. "The Parsons Revival in Germany," *Sociological Theory* 2:394–412.

———1985. "Introduction," in J. Alexander (ed.), *Neofunctionalism.* London: Sage, pp. 7–18.

———1986. "Habermas's New Critical Theory: Its Promise and Problems," *American Journal of Sociology* 91 (1985–86): 400–24.

———1987a. "The Centrality of the Classics," in A. Giddens and J. Turner (eds.), *Social Theory Today.* Cambridge, Engl.: Polity Press, pp. 11–57.

———1987b. *Sociological Theory Since 1945.* London: Hutchinson.

———1988. *Action and Its Environments.* New York: Columbia University Press.

Berki, R. N. 1979. "On the Nature and Origins of Marx's Concept of Labour," *Political Theory* 7:35–56.

Burger, Thomas. 1986. "Multidimensional Problems," *Sociological Quarterly* 27:273–92.

Camic, Charles. 1987. "The Making of a Method: A Historical Reinterpretation of the Early Parsons," *American Sociological Review* 52:421–39.

Castoriadis, Cornelius. 1987. *The Imaginary Institution of Society.* Cambridge, Mass.: MIT Press.

Clarke, Simon. 1982. *Marx, Marginalism, and Modern Sociology.* London: Macmillan.

Collins, Randall. 1985. "Jeffrey Alexander and the Search for Multidimensional Theory," *Theory and Society* 14:877–92.

Durkheim, Emile. 1983. *Pragmatism and Sociology.* Cambridge, Engl.: Cambridge University Press.

Habermas, Jürgen. 1981. *Theorie des kommunikativen Handelns,* 2 vols. Frankfurt: Suhrkamp.

Hennis, Wilhelm. 1987. "Die Spuren Nietzsches im Werk Max Webers," in W. Hennis, *Max Webers Fragestellung.* Tübingen: Mohr, pp. 167–91.

Honneth, Axel, and Joas, Hans. 1987. "War Marx ein Utilitarist? Für eine Gesellschaftstheorie jenseits des Utilitarismus," in H. Steiner (ed.), *Karl Marx und Friedrich Engels—ihr Einfluß und ihre Wirksamkeit in der Geschichte und Gegenwart der soziologischen Theorie.* Berlin (DDR), vol. 1, pp. 148–61.

Joas, Hans. 1984. "Handlungstheorie und das Problem sozialer Ordnung: Zur 'Theorie des Handelns' von Richard Münch" *Kölner Zeitschrift für Soziologie und Sozialpsychologie* 36:165–72.

Parsons, Talcott. 1937. *The Structure of Social Action.* New York: Free Press.

Piaget, Jean. 1932. Le jugement moral chez l'enfant. Paris: Alcan.

Porpora, Douglas. 1986. "A Response to Jeffrey Alexander's 'Theoretical Logic in Sociology' Concerning the Alleged Unidimensionality of Marxian Theory," *Sociological Quarterly* 27:75–90.

Taylor, Charles. 1986. *Philosophical Papers,* 2 vols. Cambridge Engl.: Cambridge University Press.

Toulmin, Stephen. 1972. *Human Understanding,* vol. 1: *The Collective Use and Evolution of Concepts.* Princeton: Princeton University Press.

Turner, Stephen. 1985. "Review of Jeffrey Alexander," *Philosophy of the Social Sciences* 15:77–82, 211–16, 365–68; 512–22.

Wenzel, Harald. 1985. "Mead und Parsons: Die emergente Ordnung des sozialen Handelns," in Hans Joas (ed.), *Das Problem der Intersubjektivität.* Frankfurt, Suhrkamp, pp. 26–59.

9 Role Theories and Socialization Research

Introduction

It has become commonplace to begin papers on role theory with a reference not only to the frequent use in the social sciences of role theory concepts but also to their confusing ambiguity. This seems to indicate that purely definitive attempts at clarification as well as global attacks on role theory have not been particularly successful up to now. Behind the disparate and disputed terminology there seems to be a social reality that presses to be treated in role theory terms. But what exactly is the nature of this theory? Does it actually encompass certain basic anthropological structures of social action, or is it just the ideological expression of historical facts in capitalist society, or do we have in it simply an efficient instrument with which to formulate sociopsychological laws? What is meant by a clarification and definition of role theory depends on how this question is answered. The order of the day is, in the first case, the shaping of role theory within an overarching anthropological theory of human action competence and intersubjectivity; in the second, the improvement of the ideologically critical evidence of its historical roots; and, in the third case, the scientific clarification of role theory propositions as a preliminary to the transparent formation of hypotheses. In this debate it seems inappropriate to proceed simply by taking an a priori decision before discussing the different positions. As a result, the history of the development of role theory will be reconstructed in brief to prepare the ground for a reasoned definition of the key concepts. The particularly interesting question of the position of role theory in socialization research can only be dealt with summarily in the following section, since various phases in the development of the child and the adolescent and the inner structure of all socializatory stages are accessible to treatment in role theory terms. Consequently, only one dimension—the development of role-taking ability—will be singled out for detailed treatment, since it does not represent a mere application of role theory but discusses the ver-

An earlier and shorter version of this was published in *Micro-Sociological Theory,* vol. 2 of *Perspectives on Sociological Theory,* edited by H. J. Helle and S. Eisenstadt (London: Sage Publications, 1985), pp. 37–53. Reprinted by permission.

ification by socialization theory of the key concept of role-taking itself. This is also an appropriate way of showing that role theory—whether it wants to or not—emerges at a point at which the grounding of socialization research in social theory and the relationship between individuality and sociality have become problematical.

A Historical Reconstruction of the Development of Role Theory

George Herbert Mead

The works of George Herbert Mead (1934, 1964) have, undeniably, been the most important source for the emergence and development of role theory. Mead introduces the concepts of "role" and "role-taking" within the framework of an anthropological theory of a specifically human form of communication. Human communication is, according to Mead, principally superior to animal forms of communication in that it operates through "significant symbols." By this is meant that people are able to react to their own gestures and utterances in a way that is anticipatory and thus inwardly represents their fellow actors' possible responses. This makes it possible for their own behavior to be oriented toward the potential reactions of other actors. As these actors, too, are principally in possession of this ability, common collective action oriented toward a common binding pattern of mutual behavior expectations becomes a possibility. Mead believes that he has, with this theory of communication, revealed the fundamental feature of human sociality. In human society, individual, non-naturalistically determined behavior develops and is integrated into a group activity via mutual behavior expectations. As a pattern of sociality, this differs fundamentally from that of a system of strict division of labor guaranteed through biological specialization in anatomical structure or the differentiation of hereditary patterns of behavior. The regulation of communal life through rigid instinctive forms of behavior that only the acquisition of status in a unilinear dominance hierarchy can modify is a principle of the vertebrate world that has also been overcome in human beings. Although *traditions* occur in social groups of primates, they remain severely limited, owing to the fact that they do not become objectified. The motive for the anthropological elaboration of a pattern of sociality based on the idea of an identity of meaning constituted collectively and through action can be found in Mead's theoretical and political biography as a radical democratic intellectual. Mead's scientific conception can be subsumed under three fundamental headings (Joas 1985, p. 33): confidence in the emancipatory prospects of scientific rationality, a striving to root "mind" or "spirit" in the human organism, and the attempt to elaborate a theory of intersubjectivity that would conceive of the self as socially originated. The concept of role is introduced by Mead in a model of practical communication and collective self-determination and describes expectations toward a fellow actor's behavior in an interactive context; "taking the role of the other" is the anticipation of alter's behavior in a specific situation.

The possibility of a communication through the inner representation of alter's behavior leads to the formation of different instances in the personality structure of the individual. This is because the individual observes and estimates his or her own behavior similarly to the way that he or she sees the behavior of partners. The individual is able to look to himself/herself from the perspective of the other. Alongside the dimension of impulses there is now an instance to evaluate those impulses, an instance which arises out of the expectations of the reactions caused by the manifestations of these impulses. In this context Mead speaks about "I" and "me." For Mead the concept of the "I" designates not only the principle of spontaneity and creativity, but also the endowment of the human being with impulses, since he sees man as a being with a "constitutional surplus of impulses" (Gehlen). This surplus of impulses exceeds all the possible limits of the impulses' satiation, expands into the realm of imagination, and social norms can only channel it. "Me" refers to my own mental presentation of alter's image of me, or, on a more primitive level, to my internalization of his expectations of me. The "me" as a precipitate within me of a person who serves as a standard of reference for me is as well an instance of judgment for the structuration of spontaneous impulses as an element of my emerging self-image. As I face several different reference persons who have significance for me, I acquire several different "me"s. These have to be synthesized to make a consistent self-image possible. A successful synthesis generates the "self," as a unitary self-evaluation and as an orientation for action, which is at the same time flexible and open to communication with more and more partners. Simultaneously, a personality structure develops which is stable and certain of its needs.

Mead's ideas about the development of the self can be found *in nuce* in his theory of children's play. Therein, he draws a line between "play" and "game." "Play" means the child's playful interaction with an imaginary partner in which the child mimes both parts of the interaction. Thereby the capacity for anticipation of behavior is given practice: alter's behavior is represented directly, i.e. via imitation, and is complemented by the child's own behavior. The child has reached this stage as soon as it is able to interact with any single reference person whatever, and to take alter's viewpoint; that means, when the reference person with a cathectically high significance is no longer the solely important one. This stage of development is followed by the attainment of the ability to participate in "games," i.e. group activities. In "games" it is not sufficient to anticipate the behavior of one single partner; now it becomes necessary that the behavior of all partners can be taken as the guideline for the child's action. These others are not at all unconnected parts; they have functions within groups, whose activities are directed to goals through division of labor. The individual actor has to orientate himself to a goal that is valid for all the actors concerned, and which Mead calls, trying to express its psychological bases, the "generalized other." In the case of games the "generalized other"'s expectations of behavior are the rules of the game, in general it means norms and values of a group; they are differentiated in a specific way to take into account the specific positions in the group and specific situations. The orientation to a particular "generalized other," however, reproduces on a new plane the same restriction which the orientation to a particular concrete other has. Thus follows the problem of an orientation to an ever more universal "generalized other."

It becomes clear that the way in which Mead uses the concept of role-taking has major ramifications for a theory of socialization and, in addition to that, for ethics and political theory. Role-taking involves not only a delineable sector of the communicative abilities but is related by Mead to general cognitive, to motivational and to moral development. The development of communicative abilities becomes a condition for cognitive progress inasmuch as it is the development of role-taking ability that allows an actor to assume a reflexive attitude toward him- or herself and substantial cognitive achievements presuppose just such an attitude. Mead's elaboration of this idea, particularly the problem of the constitution of the permanent object, is contained in works that are little known and poorly understood. He puts forward a theory of the social constitution of the development of general intelligence (Joas 1985, pp. 145 ff.). Its ethical implications are expounded at the individual level as universal role-taking ability and performance and, at the societal level, in a concept of an ideal society with a universal capacity for communication. While all this frequently has a speculative and fragmentary quality and is in parts incomplete, Mead has provided future role theory and research into the development of role-taking ability with a sociophilosophical framework and daring hypotheses. This should be remembered along with the elementary version of role-taking as a precondition for the use of significant symbols and, consequently, for all typically human communication.

Talcott Parsons

Mead's theory is only one of the sources out of which Talcott Parsons developed his comprehensive theory of the integration of socialization into the functioning of social systems. Even those parts of Parsons's work which deal immediately with the category of role do not refer to Mead as their only source. It is instructive to see how Parsons takes recourse to Ralph Linton's (1945) cultural anthropological conception as well as to Mead. Linton stressed the structural independence of (primitive) societies from distinct individuals: he sees a conflict between a static structure, which has defined places ("status") for individuals, and the actor's actions, which can only be thought of as execution of the pressures of the static structure. The coexistence in his work of Mead's and Linton's conceptions is typical of Parsons. In his reception of Mead he loses the emphasis on the collective self-determination; he is only interested in the aspect of a system of norms and values which has become "objective" for the individual actors and their behavior. Thereby, Parsons adopts Mead's ideas of the reciprocity of expectations and of the relative independence of meaningful patterns. But he cuts off the ties between the interaction which generates these norms and values and the norms and values themselves.

For Parsons, interaction is the mutual relation of the action of two actors, of whom each one needs the other to realize his/her needs. It is this mutual gratification that leads to the common interest in the maintenance and stabilization of the relationship. The stabilization enables the production of a fixed pattern for the complementary orientation of the acting individuals. A social institutionalization of certain norms allows the transgression of the framework of a system with only two interaction partners. Now, immediate mutual gratification is unnecessary; rather, a universally guaranteed conformity toward a common value system takes care of the equal distribution of gratifications. The interest in gaining gratifications, the avoidance of frustration, and the necessity of stabilizing the value system support each other. Thus, as a model, the institutionalized normative expectations of behavior and the need-dispositions and the motivations of the actors coincide in such a way that an action can be expected that is in conformity with the norms and, by that, satisfactory. And from that follows, at the same time, the stability of the social system.

Parsons's theory contains very different definitions of role: as an organized sector of the actor's orientation, as a set of the interactive partners' expectations, as a specific demand on behavior, which is functional for the stability of the value system. These definitions are in no way contradictory but show the different functions of role as Parsons sees them. Roles have the function of orientation and motivation for the single actor and an integrative function for the social system. Just like the values are to be seen as elements of the value system and the need-dispositions as elements of the personality system, so Parsons understands this unity which derives from values, refers to interactions, and is grounded in need-dispositions as an element of the social system. This unity he calls "status" or "role," depending on whether the structural or the functional aspect is in the foreground. It is impossible here to describe at length Parsons's theory, which is truly rich in its ramifications and recently vividly discussed again, but it must be said that he attempts to integrate systematically a theory of social systems with a socialization theory. He has a differentiated model of maturation phases of the organism, which are understood psychoanalytically. The phases follow each other systematically step by step and cause an increasing integration into comprehensive social systems and an internalization of the societal value system.

Receptions and Falsifications of the Classical Approaches

As an examination of Parsons's reception of Mead shows, the critical element in his scheme is the question of the autonomy and uniformity of a society's value system. This question arose during the period of Parsonian domination in American sociology, chiefly in the light of empirical research into role conflict (Handel 1978–79). By this was meant inter-role conflict, i.e. a conflict in the individual's orientation toward two simultaneously occurring, possibly contradictory, roles. The Parsons school initially assumed that conflicts of this kind have to be solved by a clear-cut decision for one of the roles. Merton's (1957) list of mechanisms with which such inter-role conflicts can be handled represented a significant differentiation. He had in mind a clear-cut spatial and temporal separation of the modes of behavior demanded by the various roles, or the sequentialization of mutually exclusive roles. While inter-role conflicts involved the problems of the individual in coming to terms with his or her various roles, the topicalization of *intra*-role conflicts posed an even greater threat to the construct of Parsonian theory. The assumption of a normative consensus as a prerequisite for the successful functioning and stability of the social system was threatened if it was not only possible for various roles to be in situational contradiction but also that one and the same role could itself contain this contradiction. Merton also suggested a number of mechanisms for the resolution of this type of role conflict, which consists of the contradiction in the expectations toward one and the same role as a result of alter's varying roles. The varying sanctional power available to those in alter's roles, the limiting of reference to these and similar features produce societal mechanisms for dealing with role conflict. One immediately notices that Merton's conception was only a liberalization of Parsons's theory and not a fundamental transformation. It was precisely the dimension of the individual actor's action competence that was not yet attained with an examination of the mechanisms provided by society—i.e. structurally—for dealing with role conflict. Questioning the normative consensus in no way indicated another medium for the integration of social systems. It was only logical for Merton to demand just a toning down of Parsons's claim to theoretical comprehensiveness and the acceptance of middle-range theories. However, this lost sight of Parsons's highly fertile ambition—the systematic incorporation of socialization into a theory of society—and left the door wide open for the concept of role and a few associated concepts, such as role conflict and role-taking, to be used in isolation from all theories of society, as well as added the danger that they would become uncritically accepted sociological jargon.

It was in this diluted form, far removed from Mead and Parsons, that role theory terminology reached Germany. Dahrendorf's *Homo Sociologicus* (1959) represented an attempt to catch up with developments in American sociology, from which Germany had been cut off through Nazism and war. What Dahrendorf did, however, was to present a catalogue of role theory concepts without the underlying theory. In its place came a superficially speculative discussion of the theatrical metaphor and the question of human freedom given the universality of roles. There was no mention of the question of the systemic structure of society—this being a codeterminant of the expectations toward the individual actor—nor of needs and motivations as a basis of action. In their place came the statics of a mesh of positions and the abstraction of a universal motivation toward the avoidance of sanctions.

Dahrendorf's book triggered off a host of contributions to a debate that is still not quite over. Contemporary replies particularly worth mentioning came from Bahrdt, Claessens, and Tenbruck. While Bahrdt (1961) quite rightly insisted on the necessity of creative performance on the part of the individual actor (something that had disappeared in Dahrendorf's model of conformity), Claessens (1963) did the same for the dimension of rational justification. Tenbruck (1961) alone criticized Dahrendorf's approach extensively from his knowledge and understanding of Parsons and pointed out his total neglect of the fields of internalization and the formation of a systemically adequate personality structure. In doing so, his position was that of orthodox Parsonianism. Later I pointed out the epistemological untenability of the "Homo Sociologicus" myself. I see it as a self-misunderstanding of a normative-analytical approach (Joas 1973, pp. 20 ff.).

In this diluted version, which can be found in Dahrendorf and, partially, in American sociology as well, there was nothing left from Parsons's and Mead's concepts of action. Therefore it could happen that the concept of role became a victim of behavioristic and neobehavioristic attempts. Already Parsons had not been totally consistent in his relation to Tolman (Parsons/Shils 1951). This loss of the critical potentiality of the role concept against behaviorism especially applies to experimental social-psychological research. The most striking attempt to subsume role theory under a general theory of behavior was made by Opp (1970; see Joas 1973, pp. 22 ff.). The work of Wiswede (1977), though it is less dogmatic and systematizes a wealth of social-psychological research, shows nonetheless a fundamental misunderstanding of the epistemological status of the role concept. Solely the works of Waller (1971, 1973, and above all 1978) differ from these attempts to subsume role theory, although Waller also has a background in learning theory. This author elaborates on the differences between the basic approaches in such a fruitful and differentiated way that he reaches a level of mutual critique and supplementation of these approaches.

Developments and Innovations of Symbolic Interactionist, Phenomenological, and "Critical" Kind

Role theory developed along other paths. In the United States, criticism of the form in which role theory had become established drew mainly on Mead. In two perceptive essays (1955–56, 1962) Ralph Turner, one of the leading representatives of the symbolic interactionist school, criticized conventional role theory's assumptions on interaction and personality theory. His concept of "role standpoint" allowed a clear distinction to be made between cognitive role-taking and an identification with the identities and intentions of other actors: anticipating alter's behavior does not imply a readiness to behave conformistically. Turner's concept of "role making" is even more important. Its principal meaning is the active definition of social relations through mutual consideration of the claims and expectations actors have toward each other. Turner, like Mead, sees this situation of the interactive emergence of common meanings and a process of flexible interaction not as a problematic limiting case of extreme instability but as a feature of all routine interaction that never completely disappears from even the most formalized and highly institutionalized social organizations. Social relations are not to be thought of as immutably stabilized patterns of expectations, nor role enactment merely as the practical realization of prescriptions; the definition of the relation and the development of the action plan themselves call for active and creative efforts for interpretation and design.

Another dimension that could only with the greatest difficulty be given a place in dominant role theory was developed by Erving Goffman, an author loosely connected with symbolic interactionism. Goffman (1961) elaborated the phenomenon of "role distance," with which he described two things. On the one hand he meant public signalization by the actor of a differentiation between himself and his role with the aim of articulating the difference between his image of himself and his implied role identity, and, on the other hand, a "sovereign" distancing demanded by the role itself from its obligations. What these two definitions had in common was that they obviously did not assume, as did Parsons, "unconscious" conformity with role expectations as a result of actors' prior internalization of the associated value orientations, but rather the possibility of distance as a structural component of the role or as the actor's own creation. Goffman's blurring of the difference between the two meanings shows that he did not unequivocally belong either to the structural-analytical or to the interactionist camp, and that he did not clarify the relationship between the two approaches. Gouldner, who presented a third, influential critique (1960), demonstrated that Parsons had failed to distinguish sufficiently between the complementarity of behavioral expectations and the reciprocity of gratifications. If this distinction is introduced it can be seen that general norm-conformity in no way guarantees the equal distribution of gratifications. This would apply only if authority was not a factor in the determination of norms. Consequently, the question of the unequal satisfaction of needs can again be discussed within a theory of society.

In postulates that were as concise as they were precise, Jürgen Habermas (1973a, written 1968) drew together these various strands of criticism. His postulates attained an extraordinary influence in German socialization research and educational thinking and were the subject of much debate, no doubt because they were seen as formulating a concept of emancipation that could be utilized pedagogically. Drawing on Gouldner he put forward a repression theorem in place of the integration theorem in Parsons's theory of motivation; drawing on Goffman, a distance theorem in place of the conformity theorem; and drawing on Turner, a discrepancy theorem in place of the identity theorem with its assertion of a congruence of role definition and role interpretation. These three theorems formulate

> three dimensions of possible degrees of freedom of action . . . We can introduce the three neglected dimensions in order to distinguish institutions (role systems) according to the degree of their repressivity, the degree of their rigidity and the nature of the behavioral control imposed by them. As we interpret the primary socialization process as the acquisition of basic role-playing qualifications, at the personality structure level the same dimensions can serve to express basic qualifications not covered by the normal concept of role learning. (Habermas 1973a, pp. 127f.)

And Habermas develops the basic qualifications of frustration tolerance, controlled self-presentation, and the flexible superego formation and brings them together in a concept of ego identity signifying the capacity actively to restructure one's own ego.

Krappmann (1971a) took Habermas's suggestions a comprehensive step further. Habermas himself returned to role theory mainly in connection with his attempts to work out a logic of the development of moral consciousness and role competence and to present it as an ontogenetic counterpart to a theory of social evolution (Habermas 1973a, 1973b, 1976). Two of his collaborators developed a theory of adolescence crisis in this context, by which they tried to examine the present state of youths in a social-psychological way (Döbert/Nunner-Winkler 1975). Dreitzel (1972) put forward his own extensive model of a "critical" role theory. He also referred to the American developments mentioned by Habermas, placed particular stress on the dimension of needs and their repression and saw his own study as a preliminary to an analysis of the sociogenesis of behavioral maladjustment. Its shortcomings are the lack of clarity of its conceptual borrowing from Alfred Schütz's phenomenological sociology and the fact that, influenced by Plessner's anthropology (1974), it sees only a balance between individuation and sociality, unlike Mead and Habermas, who take the radical view that individuation is itself a product of socialization.

Responding sensitively to current social changes Ralph Turner again put forth important studies on role theory in later writings. In one of his essays (1978–79) Turner introduces differentiations in the idea of an internalization of roles with the concept of "role-person-merger." Therewith, he both criticized Parsons and the idea of totally explicit self-images. Another essay deals with what is called in Germany *Individu-*

alisierung (individualization): Turner claims that there is a trend from an institutionally mediated to an immediate way of self-experience and self-assurance. He sees a decrease of the traditional inner-directed but no increase of the conformist other-directed type. He tries to put this form of immediate-impulsive "individualization" which escapes psychological concepts in a sociological framework, and he attempts to show it as a new mode of social control via diffusion.

In Germany role theory came under a broad attack from the perspective of an ideology critique. It started with Claessens's thesis—which was poorly verified—that role theory was the product of a specific ideology of a higher educated class. This critique was carried on by Furth, Haug, and Willms to the doubtless most profound work of this approach by Kirchhoff-Hund. Although the latter book contains a striking and devastating critique of its predecessors, it shares two shortcomings with those: In the first place, legitimate objections to one strain of role theory are generalized and used against all of them without much ado. (Thus, Haug addresses only the epigonal German discussion while Kirchhoff-Hund has a remarkable critique of Parsons but is utterly wrong about Mead). Secondly, there are no hints toward an alternative conception of action theory in these authors. Kirchhoff-Hund replaces the concept of interaction competence by a concept of working abilities. That has a lack of utopianism which is odd, and it is blind to the specific autonomous structures of numerous spheres of society.

In Eastern Europe, but also increasingly in the West, the literature relating to Marxism has recently rediscovered the important work of the Soviet psychologist Lew Vygotsky (1962, 1978). Without any mutual influences, Vygotsky's work is in many respects surprisingly close to Mead's communication theory. However, of the "activity theoretical" approach, which is based on Vygotsky, it has to be asked whether that approach succeeded in analyzing the intersubjective aspects of action and in avoiding the restriction of the manifold types of human action to instrumental action as consequently as did the tradition of symbolic interactionism.

The 1980s saw two major developments within symbolic interactionism in the field of role theory. Firstly, there were qualitative studies on role-taking behavior of children in natural settings (e.g. Mandell 1984). These studies emphasized the importance of the situation of action, familiarity, and affective relations for role-taking. But most of these studies are purely descriptive, and it is hard to integrate them theoretically. A frequent shortcoming is a complete lack of competence theoretical considerations.

The other development shows an increasing rediscovery of the macrosociological content of the basic categories of symbolic interactionism (Callero 1986; Joas 1987). This has to be seen in a context with a more general development in theory, which tries to transcend the microsociological restriction of findings of role theory and to save them for macrosociological considerations. Schulte-Altendorneburg (1977) already had this context in mind when he connected role theory and theory of democracy in his meritorious work. An important assumption for that is to avoid the psychologistic misreading of Mead and his school. It should neither be considered as astructural and contrasted with a structural approach which is deemed to be the truly sociological one nor be subsumed to a structural approach as a mere complement. Thus the problem is how to develop an interactionist concept of structure and to use it in analyses which consider society as a whole.

In the 1980s the debates on role theory were on the wane. In Germany the interest in ideology critique and epistemological critique against role theory decreased. In the United States the gap between interactionist and structurally orientated approaches has been narrowed from both sides (see also Stryker/Statham 1985). Generally speaking, one can claim that the decrease of interest in role theory was not due to falsifications of its assumptions but, to the contrary, because these assumptions have increasingly become a matter of course in the body of sociological knowledge. This is true both for the particular field of socialization research and for the general development of theory, wherein tendencies toward a new synthesis and a certain consolidation are increasingly replacing paradigmatic conflicts.

The Status of Role Theory and Its Fruitfulness in Socialization Research

Definition of the Role Concept

This brings us to the question of role theory's status, a question that can be answered now that we have reconstructed the history of role theory. Role theory should not be interpreted as a theory in the sense of a systematic body of hypotheses on empirical regularities; it therefore does not contain ready answers on the processes of socialization. Rather, it should be regarded as a metatheoretical scheme for the conceptual structuring of an area of study within the social sciences. As such its job is to provide a conceptual framework for the formulation of fields of empirical research. However, the choice of this metatheoretical scheme cannot be a random one; the scheme itself requires empirical, i.e. anthropological, justification. Role theory and the general theory of action, of which it is a part, should thus be seen as a reconstruction of the basic features of the interaction competence of actors and of the basic features of interactive systems of action (Joas 1973; pp. 91 ff.; Döbert, Habermas, and Nunner-Winkler 1977, pp. 27f.). Anthropological justification does not mean the premature dehistoricization of historically specific contexts but has its roots in the phylogenetic emergence of the prerequisites for all human history and sociality.

On the basis of the above definition of the status of role theory we can now move on to the question of an appropriate definition of the role concept. The problem here is as follows: on the one hand, a kind of minimal consensus has developed among the competing schools of thought summed up by the often heard formula: "Social roles are clusters of normative behavioral expectations directed at the behavior of position-holders." On the other hand, it has been shown that Mead, symbolic interactionism, and all "critical" role theory take a more fundamental approach, namely the need—in any interaction—for role-taking in the sense of situationally specific anticipation of alter's behavior. How can the two definitions be linked in a way that is consistent?

A first step toward closing the gap is the introduction of the concept of situation and with it the need for norms to be interpreted. Roles then become *situationally specific* normative expectations toward position-holders. The problem, however, is the concept of position. The questionableness of Parsons's interaction model would, in a way, just go through a terminological shift if the strict concept of position, rooted as it is in structures, were to be weakened and generalized on to all interactive situations. For this reason, a reverse introduction of the concept from the unstructured interactive situation itself is to be recommended. Turner (1955–56, p. 317) interprets role as a "meaningful unit of behavior," although he, too, maintains the reference to a vague concept of position. Waller (1978, p. 57) very convincingly describes roles as "meaning categories of social action . . . through which social situations, persons, patterns of action and their underlying motive structures are placed in normative relation to one another." In this definition of role there is no reference to positions and yet no confusion between role and mere expectation of particular features or modes of behavior. *Role is thus the normative expectation of situationally specific meaningful behavior.*

This expectation can become reflexive in two ways. First, the individual acquires the ability to see a situation not only in his or her own immediate perspective, and not only, through role-taking, in alter's perspective but to adopt a third perspective in which the context of both actors is reconstructed as an objective one. This is what Mead had in mind with his idea of taking the role of the "generalized other." Second, the extent to which interaction is structured through predefined expectations toward actors can be such that they act as if they were under a quasi-causal constraint that is independent of their intentions. This state of the value system becoming autonomous in formalized, e.g. bureaucratic, institutions is what Parsons seems to have had in mind. The question is not so much whether or not this actually occurs but how norms and values that have become autonomous react to problematization and to attempts at change by the individuals subsumed under them. Shibutani (1961, p. 47) is quite clear on this point:

> Some social psychologists have spoken of behavior as being "determined" by roles, as if the latter existed independently of human conduct and forced men into some mould. Roles, however, exist only in the behavior of men, and the patterns become discernible only in their regularized interaction. Roles are models of conduct which constitute the desired contribution of those participating in group activity. But even in stable societies men are not automatons, blindly acting out conventional roles. The very fact that deviation is possible indicates that such models do not "cause" behavior.

This is the only way that a non-subject-free concept of transpersonal action structures can be introduced analytically and normatively.

The Meadian concept of role-taking has come to be of crucial importance in this definition of the role concept. This being so, a number of widespread misconceptions needs to be dealt with. In a useful clarification, Lauer and Boardman (1970–71) systematize these misconceptions and point out a genetic connection between role-taking in the strict sense and other meanings. They distinguish three dimensions that role-taking can exhibit. It can (1) be reflexive or not. This preserves Mead's reference to direct complementary reactions in gestural communication and introduces the concept of role before the higher level of cognitive development at which role-taking is always reflexive. Role-taking can (2) be appropriative or not, that is to say it can or cannot lead to an adoption of alter's standpoint, which ego has understood cognitively. It is in this dimension that the distinction between identification, imitation, and role-taking is located. Finally, role-taking can (3) be synesic or not. By this Lauer and Boardman mean aesthetic, therapeutic, and emotional-expressive forms of behavior. Role-taking as such is not identical with affective empathy, nor even with emotional sympathy, and is not to be confused with mimetic "playing-at-a-role" (Coutu 1951). These are demarcations of definition. Investigation of the relations between the phenomena thus distinguished, and of their development, is an important theoretical and empirical task.

Role Theory in Socialization Research—Stimulations and Achievements

Socialization research is, with the sociology of organizations, the main field of empirical application of role theory. It achieved this key position following the passing of the hegemony of psychoanalytical/cultural anthropological and behavioristic/learning theory approaches. As there is not enough room here to outline the findings of the various schools and currents within role theory in the numerous divisions of socialization research, only a few essential details will be mentioned.

There is no theory of socialization as such associated with role theory in its reduced form, e.g. as in Dahrendorf. Dahrendorf's assumptions in fact replace the question of the development of specific motivations and cognitive abilities. Where Dahrendorf's ideological overtones are missing, a number of fields do indeed become accessible. Topics frequently discussed include the acquisition of the fundamental gender and age roles, the structure of anticipatory socialization, the inner social structure of basic institutions of socialization such as the family and the school class, and the personality structure of socialization agents (synopsis in Sewell 1970). However, there are two obvious problems here. First, the naive kind of role theory research tends to simplify the acquisition of roles in a way that gravitates toward positions. This means that what is examined is not the development of role-taking ability itself, but solely the development of the discrimination of positionally specific characteristics and the formation of stereotypic, role-conforming modes of behavior.

This ignores the problems involved in the transformation of such stereotypes into situationally specific behavior (see also Waller 1978, pp. 40 ff.). Second, the linkup with a comprehensive theory of socialization in the Parsonian sense is often rather tenuous. Though in no way able to match Parsons's distinctions, Brim's model is often cited as a point of reference. In it socialization is seen as role learning in a sense that makes personality seem to be merely a "learned repertoire of roles" (Brim 1960, p. 141) and trans-situational consistence in behavior to be insufficient flexibility and thus deficient socialization. What we encounter here in its crude form is also a critical question in Parsons. He, too, as Geulen (1977, p. 156) aptly puts it, "does not see socialization as a societally mediated genesis, formulated in psychological categories, of the subject itself but as societal programming of the action decisions of a subject otherwise assumed to be complete." Mead's crucial dimension of the formation of the self as the core of the socialization process is, therefore, not reflected in Parsons's model of socialization, a deficiency that remains even after a later, explicit examination of this question (Parsons 1968).

The Meadian tradition of role-theoretical socialization research can point to its achievements in four fields. The social genesis of the self (1) constitutes a major topic. This requires (2) the inclusion of motivation theory and sections of the psychoanalytical tradition as well as Parsons's work, but also a reference to dimensions of cognitive development, to an examination of the development of communicative abilities, and to the relations between these dimensions. Consideration of the open and process-like character of interaction has led to a different analysis of the inner structure of socialization agencies. Attention is focused more on the dynamics of mutual processes of definition than on static structural factors (3). Through a loosening of the reference to an irrevocably complete personality structure, socialization research has been extended beyond the fields of childhood and adolescence to (4) an investigation of professional socialization and lifelong personality changes. Vital pioneer work was undertaken here by symbolic interactionists (Becker, Strauss, and Hughes). It cannot be denied that these new lines of research have not yet taken on the categorical solidity of Parsons's work and that the models of the development of the action competence of the subject are often insufficiently grounded in general social theory.

Theories and Research on the Development of Role-Taking Ability

Conceived as a specifically anthropological feature by Mead, role-taking ability is at least mentioned in other role theories. A discussion of its development is of more fundamental importance than the question of the contribution of role theory approaches to our understanding of specific problems. In a certain sense this makes the core of role theory itself accessible to empirical validation in spite of its "metatheoretical" status. Furthermore, a clear distinction between role-taking ability and the stages of its development means that a distinction is made, at least in principle, between levels of competence and performance as far as social learning is concerned even though this poses a number of difficult problems. Finally, a discussion of this kind inevitably produces a more precise statement of views on the relationship between cognitive and communicative development.

It will be obvious that those currents within role theory that give only very implicit consideration to active communicative performance have little to contribute to the genesis of role-taking ability. It is less obvious why the symbolic interactionist school provided so few impulses for research of this kind, given that Mead's original model decidedly pursued a genetic explanatory strategy. The reasons for this are many and the fact that the approach has not spread particularly far is only one of them; it was not as if authors had not been soon aware of the problem (Cottrell 1950). Certain conceptual reinterpretations of Mead's initial conception played a part, as a self-critical retrospective in the symbolic interactionist tradition demonstrates (Sherohman 1977). The subject of the majority of studies was not role-taking ability but accuracy, which meant that anthropological themes were hurriedly translated not into universalistic questions of developmental psychology but into questions of differential psychology. The results of accuracy surveys were frequently interpreted as indicating ability levels, an inadmissible step because of the countless components of substantive nature in the index of accuracy—actors' common culture, for example—which as such have nothing to do with role-taking competence. Role-taking ability is just one of several sources of the accuracy of role-taking. Another misleading operationalization is the investigation of only the anticipation of certain attitudes in another actor and not of role-taking ability. This type of operationalization dissolves the context of a shared situation that practically forces actors to coordinate their behavior and replaces this role-taking situation by test situations in which individuals are questioned about their context-free assessments of fictitious alters.

Other schools of experimental psychology are also characterized by these deficiencies of symbolic interactionist work. A decisive change did not occur until the meeting of the Meadian and Piagetian traditions, something that did not apply to Piaget himself. It is a well-known fact that in his lifetime of work Piaget neglected the dimension of the child's early social behavior. This neglect resulted in a tendency to operationalize role-taking with regard to the coordination of perspectives toward nonsocial contexts. Apart from forerunners such as Feffer and parallel developments such as that of Kerckhoff, the pioneer work in empirical research was done by Flavell and colleagues (1968). Flavell introduces his own research program with an interesting critique of Mead, whom he accuses of not giving sufficient consideration, in his concept of communication, to the problems of inter-individual heterogeneity.

> The two-year-old who looks at his mother, points to the household pet, and says "Doggie" has met at least the minimal require-

> ments for Mead's acquisition. The ten-year-old who can picture to himself how an object in front of him appears to a friend standing on the opposite side of it, and who simplifies his message when explaining something to his three-year-old brother—he is well on the way to acquiring the kind of skills we have in mind. Mead defines a significant symbol as a gesture which arouses the same response in both A and B; what he does not deal with is how A acquires the ability to discern B's qualities as a respondent generally, and in particular how he acquires the ability to select those gestures which will, in fact, arouse the same response in B. (Flavell 1968, p. 16)

It is ironic that Flavell's step toward a treatment of this question and his quite justified pointer to the general character of Mead's comments should be marked by a profound lack of understanding of Mead's conception of language. What Flavell says about egocentric communication shows that his starting point is an initially nonsocial inner language that only secondarily becomes socially oriented for communication purposes. But in doing so he destroys the continuity that can be seen in the Meadian tradition between the earliest form of role-taking and subsequent communicative and cooperative ability. The importance of the dimension of cognitive development is then emphasized instead of this continuity, and this is what characterizes Flavell's operationalizations. His test situations favor linguistic communication to the detriment of mime or gesture and ignore the possibility of emotional involvement in the set tasks.

Flavell's pioneer work was taken considerably further by Selman (1971a, 1971b, 1974, 1980). The merits of Selman's work are that the form of interactions is indeed made the method of research and that, drawing on Kohlberg, the development of role-taking ability is related not only to cognitive but to moral development in particular. His differentiated models of phases of development in early and middle childhood should also be mentioned. However, his dating of early childhood (beginning at the age of three) shows that he, too, feels there can be no meaningful discussion of the child's social interaction at a considerably earlier age in terms of the theory of role-taking. The focal question in Selman's studies has been brilliantly defined by Keller (1976, p. 65) as the genetic priority of cognitive operations. While not assuming a determinative connection between cognitive and social abilities, Selman does refer to the cognitive dimensions as a necessary if not sufficient prerequisite for the development of social abilities. This precludes any reverse effect.

Habermas, Döbert, and Nunner-Winkler, who draw on Piaget but above all on Kohlberg and Selman, are surprisingly uncritical as regards internal problems in the works and theoretical approaches of these three authors. In fact, they absorb the problems in question unaltered, increasing the claim to general validity even further. Keller (1976) and Waller (1978), both excellent pieces of work, are the two most important critical contributions and relatively extensive models. Keller identifies the principal shortcomings in previous analyses:

> Obviously, in all these previous operationalizations of role-taking, abstract formal thought processes are demanded which are alien to the child's world in as much as relations or identifications with those acting are not available. The child is therefore expected to supply a trans-situational generalization. Role-taking would then be acquired in a particular experiential situation highly motivational in content and could be performed initially in similar situations as an "act of social-cognitive achievement". It is only later that this ability is separated from the context of its genesis by means of generalizing abstraction and becomes available regardless of situation. (Keller, 1976, pp. 152f.)

Her emphasis is on the social background to the development of role-taking ability and primarily on parent-child interaction. Waller, who bases his argument on other theoretical traditions, comes to the similar conclusion that social-cognitive structures have to be deduced from social experience. Though his concept of role-taking is not as profound as Mead's, which is the one adopted by Keller, he does place greater stress on interaction between children.

This emphasis on the real interaction between children has more and more prevailed in the social-cognitive developmental psychology (representative works by Damon 1977 and Youniss 1980). The study of child interaction in "naturalistic settings" brings psychological research closer to the sociological tradition of symbolic interactionism. The reinforced attention to conditions of performance in social-cognitive developmental psychology encounters—at least at some points, and theoretically—a similar movement toward competence theories on the side of symbolic interactionism. Thus, Schwalbe (1987, 1988) distinguished between role-taking ability and the motivation for role-playing. Moreover, he described different dimensions in role-taking ability (range, depth, accuracy). It is on the basis of these differentiations that reasonable studies on the conditions of development and the conditions of performance of the role-taking ability become possible. With these works a suitable approach emerges for an empirically and conceptually precise treatment of the development of social and communicative abilities: an approach that will prevent this field from turning into a new version of the sociolinguistically outmoded "deficit hypothesis" as a result of an overestimation of the cognitive-linguistic dimension and a neglect of cultural and subcultural typicalities. Premature talk of degrees of competence in role-taking ability may be the product of inadequate "role-taking" by the researcher where other cultures and classes are involved. On the contrary, the approach at sight allows the improvement of the action theoretical foundations of social theory by confronting them with the problems of developmental psychology, and the carrying of the question of the constitution of the categories of human cognition up to an empirical treatment.

Bibliography

Bahrdt, H. P. 1961. "Zur Frage des Menschenbildes in der Soziologie," *Europäisches Archiv für Soziologie 2:* 1–17.

Bertram, H. and B. 1974. *Soziale Ungleichheit, Denkstrukturen und Rollenhandeln: Ein empirischer Beitrag zur Diskussion über soziokulturelle Determinanten kognitiver Fähigkeiten.* Weinheim: Beltz.

Brim, O. G. 1960. "Personality Development as Role-Learning," in J. Iscoe and H. W. Stevenson (eds.), *Personality Development in Children.* Austin, Tex.: University of Texas Press, pp. 127–59.

Callero, P. L. 1968. "Toward a Meadian Conceptualization of Role," *Sociological Quarterly* 27:343–58.

Cicourel, A. V. 1970. "Basic and Normative Rules in the Negotiation of Status and Role," in H. P. Dreitzel (ed.), *Recent Sociology No. 2, Patterns of Communicative Behavior.* London: Macmillan, pp. 4–45.

Claessens, D. 1963. "Rolle und Verantwortung," *Soziale Welt* 14:1–13.

———1970. *Rolle und Macht.* München: Juventa.

Cottrell, L. S. 1950. "Some Neglected Problems in Social Psychology," *American Sociological Review* 15:705–12.

Coutu, W. 1951. "Role-Playing vs. Role-taking," *American Sociological Review* 16: 180–87.

Dahrendorf, R. 1959. *Homo Sociologicus: Ein Versuch zur Geschichte, Bedeutung und Kritik der Kategorie der sozialen Rolle.* Köln/Opladen: Westdeutscher Verlag.

Damon, W. 1977. *The Social World of the Child.* San Francisco: Jossey-Bass.

Denzin, N. K. 1977. *Childhood Socialization: Studies in the Development of Language, Social Behavior, and Identity.* San Francisco: Jossey-Bass.

Döbert, R. and Nunner-Winkler, G. 1975. *Adoleszenzkrise und Identitätsbildung: Psychische und soziale Aspekte des Jugendalters in modernen Gesellschaften.* Frankfurt: Suhrkamp.

Döbert, R., Habermas, J. & Nunner-Winkler, G. 1977. "Zur Einführung," in R. Döbert, J. Habermas, and G. Nunner-Winkler (eds.), *Entwicklung des Ichs.* Köln: Kiepenheuer und Witsch, pp. 9–30.

Dreitzel, H. P. 1972. "Soziale Rolle und politische Emanzipation: Sechs Thesen gegen Peter Furths melancholische Kritik am Rollenbegriff," *Das Argument* 14, no. 71: 110–29.

———.1972. *Die gesellschaftlichen Leiden und das Leiden an der Gesellschaft: Vorstudien zu einer Pathologie des Rollenverhaltens.* Stuttgart: Enke.
Edelstein, W. and Habermas, J. (eds.). 1984. *Soziale Interaktion und soziales Verstehen: Beiträge zur Entwicklung der Interaktionskompetenz.* Frankfurt: Suhrkamp.
Edelstein, W. and Keller, M. (eds.), 1982. *Perspektivität und Interpretation: Beiträge zur Entwicklung des sozialen Verstehens.* Frankfurt: Suhrkamp.
Flavell, J. H. et al. 1968. *The Development of Role-Taking and Communication Skills in Children.* New York: Wiley.
Furth, P. 1971. Nachträgliche Warnung vor dem Rollenbegriff. *Das Argument* 13, no. 66: 494–511.
Gerhardt, U. 1971. *Rollenanalyse als kritische Soziologie.* Neuwied/Berlin: Luchterhand.
Geulen, D. 1977. *Das vergesellschaftete Subjekt: Zur Grundlegung der Sozialisationstheorie.* Frankfurt: Suhrkamp.
Geulen, D. (ed.) 1982. *Perspektivenübernahme und soziales Handeln: Texte zur sozial-kognitiven Entwicklung.* Frankfurt: Suhrkamp.
Goffman, E. 1961. "Role-Distance," in E. Goffman, *Encounters: Two Studies in the Sociology of Interaction.* Indianapolis: Bobbs-Merrill, pp. 85–152.
Gouldner, A. 1960. "The Norm of Reciprocity: A Preliminary Statement," *American Sociological Review* 25: 161–78.
Gross, N. et al. 1966. "Role Conflict and Its Resolution," in B. J. Biddle and E. J. Thomas (eds.), *Role Theory. Concepts and Research.* New York: Wiley, pp. 287–96.
Grunt, M. 1977. "Individueller Handlungsspielraum: Eine rollentheoretische Interpretation," *Soziale Welt* 28: 133–43.
Habermas, J. 1973a. "Stichworte zur Theorie der Sozialisation," in Habermas, *Kultur und Kritik.* Frankfurt: Suhrkamp, pp. 118–94.
———. 1973b. "Notizen zum Begriff der Rollenkompetenz," In Habermas, *Kultur und Kritik.* Frankfurt: Suhrkamp, pp. 195–231.
———.1976. "Moralentwicklung und Ich-Identität," In Habermas, *Zur Rekonstruktion des Historischen Materialismus.* Frankfurt: Suhrkamp, pp. 62–92.
Handel, W. 1978–79. "Normative Expectations and the Emergence of Meaning as Solutions to Problems: Convergence of Structural and Interactionist Views," *American Journal of Sociology* 84: 855–81.
Haug, F. 1971. *Kritik der Rollentheorie und ihrer Anwendung in der bürgerlichen deutschen Soziologie.* Frankfurt: Fischer.
Heiss, J. 1981. "Social Roles," in M. Rosenberg and R. Turner (eds.), *Social Psychology: Sociological Perspectives.* New York: Basic Books, pp. 94–129.
Hilbert, R. 1981. "Toward an Improved Understanding of 'Role.'" *Theory and Society* 10: 207–25.
Jackson, J. A. (ed.) 1972. *Role.* Cambridge, Engl.: Cambridge University Press.
Joas, H. 1973. *Die gegenwärtige Lage der soziologischen Rollentheorie.* Wiesbaden: Akademische Verlagsanstalt.
———.1985. *G. H. Mead: A Contemporary Re-examination of His Thought.* Cambridge, Mass.: Polity/MIT.
———.1987. "Symbolic Interactionism," in A. Giddens and J. Turner (eds.), *Social Theory Today.* Cambridge, Engl.: Polity Press, pp. 82–115. Reprinted in this volume as "Pragmatism in American Sociology."
Keller, M. 1976. *Kognitive Entwicklung und soziale Kompetenz: Zur Entstehung der*

Rollenübernahme in der Familie und ihrer Bedeutung für den Schulerfolg. Stuttgart: Klett.

Keller, M. and Reuss, S. 1984. "An Action-Theoretical Reconstruction of the Development of Social-Cognitive Competence," Human Development 27: 211–20.

Kerckhoff, A. C. 1969. "Early Antecedents of Role-Taking and Role-Playing Ability," Merrill-Palmer Quarterly 15: 229–47.

Kirchhoff-Hund, B. 1978. *Rollenbegriff und Interaktionsanalyse: Soziale Grundlagen und ideologischer Gehalt der Rollentheorie.* Köln: Pahl-Rugenstein.

Krappmann, L. 1971a. *Soziologische Dimensionen der Identität: Strukturelle Bedingungen für die Teilnahme an Interaktionsprozessen.* Stuttgart: Klett.

———.1971b. "Neuere Rollenkonzepte als Erklärungsmöglichkeit für Sozialisationsprozesse," *betrifft erziehung* 4, no. 3: 27–34.

———.1985. "Mead und die Sozialisationsforschung," In H. Joas (ed.), *Das Problem der Intersubjektivität: Neuere Beiträge zum Werk G. H. Meads.* Frankfurt: Suhrkamp, pp. 156–78.

Lauer, R. H. and Boardman, L. 1970–71. "Role-Taking: Theory, Typology, and Propositions," *Sociology and Social Research 55:* 137–48.

Lempert, W. 1973. "Soziale Rolle und berufliche Sozialisation: Zur berufspädagogischen Verwendung einer soziologischen Kategorie," *Die deutsche Berufs- und Fachschule* 69: 671–87.

Linton, R. 1945. *The Cultural Background of Personality.* New York: Appleton-Century.

Maccoby, E. 1959. "Role-Taking in Childhood and its Consequences for Social Learning," *Child Development 30:* 239–52.

Mandell, N. 1984. "Children's Negotiation of Meaning," *Symbolic Interaction* 7: 191–212.

Mead, G. H. 1934. *Mind, Self and Society.* Chicago: University of Chicago Press.

———.1964. *Selected Writings,* edited by A. Reck. Indianapolis: Bobbs-Merrill.

Merton, R. K. 1957. *Social Theory and Social Structure.* Glencoe: The Free Press.

Miller, D. L. 1981. "The Meaning of Role-Taking," *Symbolic Interaction 4:* 167–75.

Opp, K. D. 1970. *Soziales Handeln, Rollen und soziale Systeme: Ein Erklärungsversuch sozialen Verhaltens.* Stuttgart: Enke.

Parow, E. 1973. *Die Dialektik des symbolischen Austauschs: Versuch einer kritischen Interaktionstheorie.* Frankfurt: Europäische Verlagsanstalt.

Parsons, T. 1951. *The Social System.* London: Routledge.

———.1968. "The Position of Identity in the General Theory of Action," in C. Gordon and K. J. Gergen (eds.), *The Self in Social Interaction.* New York: John Wiley, pp. 11–24.

Parsons, T. and Bales, R. F. 1955. *Family, Socialization and Interaction Process.* Glencoe: The Free Press.

Parsons, T. and Shils, E. A. (eds.) 1951. *Toward a General Theory of Action.* New York: Harper.

Plessner, H. 1974. "Soziale Rolle und menschliche Natur," in Plessner, *Diesseits der Utopie: Beiträge zur Kultursoziologie.* Frankfurt: Suhrkamp, pp. 23–35.

Popitz, H. 1967. *Der Begriff der sozialen Rolle als Element der soziologischen Theorie.* Tübingen: Mohr.

Schulte-Altendorneburg, M. 1977. *Rollentheorie als Soziologie der Herrschaft.* Frankfurt: Campus.

Schwalbe, M. L. 1987. "Mead among the Cognitivists: Roles as Performance Imagery," *Journal for the Theory of Social Behavior* 17: 113–33.

———.1988. "Role-Taking Reconsidered: Linking Competence and Performance to Social Structure," *Journal for the Theory of Social Behavior* 18: 411–36.

Selman, R. 1971a. "The Relation of Role-Taking to the Development of Moral Judgment in Children," *Child Development* 42: 79–91.

———.1971b. "Taking Another's Perspective: Role-Taking Development in Early Childhood," *Child Development* 42: 1721–34.

———.1980. *The Growth of Interpersonal Understanding.* New York: Academic Press.

Selman, R. and Byrne, D. 1974. "A Structural-Developmental Analysis of Levels of Role-Taking in Middle Childhood," *Child Development* 45:803–06.

Sewell, W. H. 1970. "Some Recent Developments in Socialization Theory and Research," in G. P. Stone and H. A. Farberman (eds.), *Social Psychology through Symbolic Interaction.* Waltham, Mass.: Xerox College Publishing, pp. 566–83.

Sherohman, J. 1977. "Conceptual and Methodological Issues in the Study of Role-Taking Accuracy," *Symbolic Interaction* 1: 121–31.

Shibutani, T. 1961. *Society and Personality: An Interactionist Approach to Social Psychology.* Englewood Cliffs, N.J.: Prentice-Hall.

Stryker, S. and Statham, A. 1985. "Symbolic Interaction and Role Theory," in G. Lindzey and E. Aronson (eds.), *Handbook of Social Psychology.* New York: Random House, pp. 311–78.

Stryker, S. 1970. "Die Theorie des Symbolischen Interaktionismus: Eine Darstellung und einige Vorschläge für die vergleichende Familienforschung," in G. Lüschen and E. Lupri (eds.), *Soziologie der Familie* (Sonderheft 14, *Kölner Zeitschrift für Soziologie und Sozialpsychologie*), pp. 49–67.

Tenbruck, F. H. 1961. "Zur deutschen Rezeption der Rollentheorie," *Kölner Zeitschrift für Soziologie und Sozialpsychologie* 13: 1–40.

Thomas, D. L., Franks, D. D. and Calonico, J. M. 1972. "Role-Taking and Power in Social Psychology," *American Sociological Review* 37:605–14.

Turner, R. H. 1955–56. "Role-Taking, Role-Standpoint, and Reference-Group Behavior," *American Journal of Sociology* 61:316–28.

———.1962. "Role-Taking: Process Versus Conformity," in A. M. Rose (ed.), *Human Behavior and Social Processes.* London: Routledge, pp. 20–40.

———.1975–76. "The Real Self: from Institution to Impulse," *American Journal of Sociology* 81: 989–1016.

———.1978–79. "The Role and the Person," *American Journal of Sociology* 84: 1–23.

———.1985. "Unanswered Questions in the Convergence between Structuralist and Interactionist Role Theories," in H. J. Helle and S. N. Eisenstadt (eds.), *Micro-Sociological Theory: Perspectives on Sociological Theory,* vol. 2. London: Sage, pp. 22–36.

Van de Voort, W. 1975. "Die Bedeutung von Vorformen des kommunikativen Handelns für die Entwicklung der vorsprachlichen Intelligenz beim Kinde," in A. Leist (ed.), *Ansätze zur materialistischen Sprachtheorie.* Kronberg: Scriptor, pp. 206–33.

———.1977. *Interaktion und Kognition: Die Bedeutung der sozialen Interaktion für die Entwicklung der kognitiven Strukturen nach Jean Piaget.* Ph.D. Dissertation. Frankfurt.

Vygotsky, L. S. 1962. *Thought and Language.* Cambridge, Mass.: MIT Press.

———.1978. *Mind in Society: The Development of Higher Psychological Processes.* Cambridge, Mass.: Harvard University Press.

Waller, M. 1971. "Die Entwicklung der Rollenwahrnehmung: Ihre Beziehung zur allgemeinen kognitiven Entwicklung und sozialstrukturellen Variablen," *Zeitschrift für Sozialpsychologie* 2: 343–57.

———.1973. "Zur Kritik der rollentheoretischen Orientierung der psychologischen Sozialisationsforschung," in H. Walter (ed.), *Sozialisationsforschung,* vol. 1. Stuttgart: Fromann-Holzboog, pp. 213–42.

———.1978. *Soziales Lernen und Interaktionskompetenz: Die Ausbildung von Verhaltenserwartungen und die Konstruktion von Regeln interpersonalen Verhaltens beim Kinde.* Stuttgart: Klett.

Willms, B. 1970. "Gesellschaftsvertrag und Rollentheorie," *Jahrbuch für Rechtssoziologie und Rechtstheorie* 1: 275–98.

Winnubst, J. A. M. and ter Heine, E. J. H. 1985. "German Developments in Role Theory 1958–1980," *Sociology 19:* 598–608.

Wiswede, G. 1977. *Rollentheorie.* Stuttgart: Kohlhammer.

Youniss, J. 1980. *Parents and Peers in Social Development: A Sullivan-Piaget Perspective.* Chicago: University of Chicago Press.

Conclusion: The Creativity of Action and the Intersubjectivity of Reason—Mead's Pragmatism and Social Theory[1]

Pragmatism and sociology are children of the same epoch. That was the assertion made by Emile Durkheim, the French founder and classical theorist of sociology, in a series of lectures on the relationship between the two intellectual movements that he delivered shortly before the outbreak of the First World War, during which his life came to its end.[2] By that comment he meant more than the trivial fact that the representative philosophy of the United States of America originated in the same period in which sociology made the transition from being an idea of academic outsiders and of social reformers to being an institutionalized academic discipline. Rather, he saw in both enterprises the same spirit at work, a spirit that was striving to formulate in a new fashion philosophical problems with a long tradition and to find a solution for them through a changed relationship to the methods of empirical science. It is true that for Durkheim pragmatism, which in his eyes was represented chiefly by William James, was an irrationalist attack on rationality that had to be warded off by sociology for the sake of reason and of rationalist French culture. While holding that position, however, he did not regard sociology itself as a simple continuation of previous traditions of thought, but as "reconstructed rationalism." In Durkheim's opinion, sociology and pragmatism had both made a break with the older philosophy; his own program of sociology, though, was intended also to circumvent the dangers that pragmatism engendered. Sociology was thus not just an empirical discipline, but in Durkheim's view also a specific *philosophical project.*

It remains in the interest of both sociology and philosophy to recall this view of sociology as a philosophical project. To be sure, sociology has never succeeded in univocally defining its own proper tasks in relation to other sciences and to the sphere of public political discourse and activity. Consequently, it has been compelled to engage again and again in reflections on the status of its scientific character. Nevertheless, its efforts were aimed at attaining a stable self-confidence by means of its break with philosophy and through the exemplary nature of its empirical re-

Reprinted by permission from *Transactions of the Charles Sanders Peirce Society* 16 (1990), pp. 165–94.

search. Philosophy, on the other hand, generally makes use of sociology only as a source of information that serves to illustrate philosophical arguments, or it develops norms of methodology and of the theory of science that it seeks to make binding on sociology as well. Sociology is often apologetic that it does not only investigate facts, but also studies texts; that it is concerned not just with empirical research, but also with the interpretation of its classical theorists. For its part, philosophy seldom recognizes that the work of the sociologists can be of direct significance for its own questions. As a result, social theory falls between two stools. For the sociologists it is not sufficiently empirical; for the philosophers, it is an unfamiliar language game. Thus the fundamental impulse of Durkheim and other classic figures not to positivistically silence the problems of epistemology, of moral philosophy, of political philosophy, and even of religion, but rather to reformulate them in a new way, has not been taken up by many successors.

These are necessary preliminary reflections for an attempt to give an account of the significance for social theory of the pragmatist George Herbert Mead. I maintain that this significance consists not only in the fact that Mead made certain positive contributions to sociology's theoretical arsenal, although that is certainly the case. It is well known that he elaborated the basic outline of an anthropological theory of communication and of a theory of the development of the self. But I have in mind something else, something greater. I believe that in its entire conceptual orientation, Mead's theory constitutes an enterprise that has great philosophical relevance and importance today, at a time of a renaissance in many respects of pragmatism. I also believe that Mead's work makes it possible, through a modification of sociology's fundamental notions, for that science to connect itself once again to the impulses that at one time gave it vitality and certainty about its future. In the present context, of course, only portions of Mead's theory can be dealt with. In my exposition of the foregoing thesis, I will concentrate—after a short retrospect—on three problem areas that are of special philosophical interest: (1) the problem of action, (2) the problem of normativity, and (3) the problem of the logical character of a science of social phenomena. Discussion of these three problem areas here requires that their interconnectedness be made clear. Mead developed a theory of action in which the creativity of action stands in the foreground. His theory of normativity is an attempt not to mask the dimension of creative solution of moral problems in action by stressing the intersubjective validity of norms. His conception of science of social phenomena is not an instance of scientism, but rather the attempt to conserve the legacy of practical philosophy under the conditions obtaining in a scientific-technical civilization. To understand Mead's efforts in all three areas, and his work in its entirety, it is necessary to grasp the central importance in his thought of the tension between the creativity of action and the communicative character of human sociality.

The history of the influence of Mead's thought has been affected especially strongly by the division between philosophy and sociology. In philosophy, Mead remained, even in the circle of the pragmatists, a marginal figure; the literature on his work cannot be compared even quantitatively with that on Peirce, James, or Dewey. In sociology, on the other hand, Peirce, James, and Dewey are almost unknown, while Mead has risen to the rank of a classical theorist, something that he certainly never dreamed of becoming. This canonization, however, went hand in hand with a highly selective reception of his work, with an indifference or skepticism regarding any of Mead's writings that could not be considered part of his empirically usable social psychology.

With regard to their philosophical importance the other principal sociological theorists have not been treated much better. In Max Weber's case, the influence of neo-Kantianism has, it is true, been examined and discussed again and again; however, the importance of Nietzsche for Weber's thought frequently remained unnoticed, even though we cannot understand Weber's image of the human being at all if we do not take Nietzsche into consideration. It is not too much to say that large parts of Georg Simmel's work belong to *Lebensphilosophie*; his sociological writings are only parts of a primarily philosophical oeuvre. Emile Durkheim's dependence on the French neo-Kantianism of a Renouvier and a Boutroux, as well as the concealed debate with Bergson in his work, have remained almost entirely unstudied. Talcott Parsons's debt to Whitehead is largely unknown. The significance of pragmatism for early American sociology is generally seen only in the pressure it exerted to engage in empirical research and to deal "pragmatically" with social problems, and not in the basic theoretical framework that pragmatism bestowed on the Chicago School of sociologists. Instead of directing its attention to the philosophical problems from which the classical sociological thinkers began the project of sociology, this discipline has fabricated a mystical prehistory for itself. In its most recent—neofunctionalist—form, this prehistory is to be found in the eternal conflict between idealism and materialism, a conflict from which escape is to be achieved by means of a multidimensional orientation of theorizing; that is, by taking both ideal and real factors into account in a balanced fashion. Philosophically speaking, that is quite insubstantial fare. However, without a grasp of the philosophical roots of classical sociology, it is hard to understand the claim that Mead is important. This assertion is easier to comprehend if it is formulated as the superiority of pragmatism over the contemporary European intellectual currents of *Lebensphilosophie,* neo-Kantianism, and Marxism. We might ask ourselves: How would sociology have developed if the philosophy of pragmatism had shaped, comprehensively and lastingly, its theoretical foundations? What could we expect if sociology reformed itself in accordance with the principles of pragmatism?

Retrospect

As the questions asked here first arose in the context of a new edition of my book on Mead—essentially unchanged from the first edition—it may be appropriate to look back at first and point out how far my perspectives have changed since I finished this book. The fundamental motivation has not changed. The thinking of Mead and of other pragmatist philosophers still seems to me to be unavoidable if one really wants to get out of the aporiae of specifically German intellectual traditions as well as those of Marxism. Whereas I was—at the time of writing the book—quite clear about the fact that every dealing with pragmatism in Germany touched the problem of the relationship between democratic ideals and German history, the exact relationship between Marxism and pragmatism in general and for my personal convictions had remained quite unclear. In the meantime I tend to agree with certain American reviewers who interpreted this book as a document of the German left in its quest for a non-Marxist foundation or who referred it to the debates on the perspectives of democratic socialism. The self-confidence with which Mead's certainly problematical attitudes during the First World War were criticized then from the standpoint of a Marxist theory of imperialism has not been sustained. This one point is mentioned because it is symptomatic of a deeper change in my views: I no longer believe that Marxism should be seen as a theory which is simply in need of an additional foundation by pragmatist elements and a solution of inherent problems of the mediation of base and superstructure by the integration of interactionist social psychology in order to be developed into a scientifically informed diagnosis of the time. The reasons and motives for this change come from topics and fields which appear only marginally in my Mead book; that is why this change of perspective does not force any major modification of the interpretations contained in it. Hopefully one does not have to add that this change should not be seen as a fashionable retreat and that for me the contributions of Marx and Engels and of many thinkers from the labor movements still are essential elements of any acceptable social theory.

The objections raised against the book on Mead[3] did not—I am happy to say—refer to this part of the background of my interpretations. I want to mention two of these objections briefly and then emphasize another. Several reviewers pointed out that the sharp contrast between pragmatism and phenomenology which I drew referred exclusively to the differences between Mead and Husserl. Undoubtedly, my presentation disguised the fact that there are so-called social phenomenological approaches which come quite close to Mead's pragmatism by immanent improvements and transformations of Husserl's phenomenology. In my eyes this is somewhat true for Max Scheler and Helmuth Plessner, and much more so for the brilliant writings of Maurice Merleau-Ponty. Werner Bergmann and Gisbert Hoffmann have compensated for this lacuna in my book insofar as they take into consideration the internal plurality within the phenomenological tradition by comparing Mead not only with Husserl but also with Schutz, Gurwitsch, Heidegger, Sartre, and Merleau-Ponty. Another obviously justified objection came from Dénes Némedi; that my claim to have demonstrated the internal connection of instrumental and communicative action in a theory of the constitution of the physical thing is restricted in this form to a very elementary level of infantile development and that the intersubjective constitution of instrumental action on more advanced levels of development is not yet really proved by this step. From this objection, however, one can draw two clearly distinct conclusions. One would be to say that the importance of the prelinguistic roots of cognitive development is only minor in the phases that occur after the acquisition of one's native tongue;[4] the other would consist in the assumption that the analysis of the constitution of the physical thing leads us to take seriously the corporeal and the intersubjective constitution of cognitive achievements beyond simpleminded language-centered approaches and thus even develop a changed understanding of linguistic meaning.[5]

The most important objection of an immanent kind was raised by Gary Allan Cook and by Dmitri Shalin. Both of them pointed out that my interpretation of Mead suffered from an insufficient appreciation of the importance of John Dewey. Their objection may appear initially as an arbitrary complaint about the omission of one classic figure. They do not complain, for example, about the omission of Peirce or James, though in the case of either one a more profound treatment would certainly have been possible. But I do not see how such a fuller examination of either

Peirce or James would have influenced my general argument. In the case of John Dewey things are different. First, I still think it is correct to say that Mead was the more original and the more profound thinker with regard to an "intersubjective" foundation and in his definition of the psychical; but it is wrong to reduce Dewey's own orientation to a concept of specifically human communication simply to Mead's influence and to overlook how deeply it was already grounded in Dewey's early idealist writings. Second, my limited knowledge of Dewey's extensive life's work brought about obvious difficulties in the interpretation of Mead's "metaphysical" later work. I still maintain, however, that the unity of Mead's work should not be sought in this late metaphysics of sociality and that neither in Mead's nor in Dewey's thinking is metaphysics directed against or proceeding without science. Both of them wanted to defend the legitimacy of those questions to which there is no scientific solution against any positivist inhibition of thinking about metaphysical problems. Out of my own discomfort with every version of metaphysics I found too simple a way out by merely dealing with consequences of Mead's "naturalistic metaphysics" in the field of socialization theory and developmental psychology. This is not wrong in itself, but it is highly selective; one should add that the relationship between Dewey's important work *Experience and Nature* and Mead's approach is not adequately dealt with if one merely mentions the existence of divergences. Third, and finally, I did not see in my reception of Mead those areas in which Dewey is clearly superior to Mead. If one's interest is directed mainly toward a theory of intersubjectivity, Mead certainly is the more important author. But if the "practical" moment in my formula "practical intersubjectivity" is to be taken seriously, then Dewey's much better and more comprehensively elaborated pragmatism is essential. I will come back to this point. Had Dewey's extreme importance been as clear to me then as it is today, I might have abandoned my task in advance because of the almost complete lack of a Dewey reception in Germany. But today the general overshadowing of Dewey by Mead, from which I personally benefited, can be removed by the increased familiarity with Mead to which I have myself contributed.

A brief report on Mead research since finishing my book on Mead was given in another place (Joas 1985). On Mead's biography there is still the unfinished research being carried on by Cook and by Orbach; the most important publication is Shalin's essay on Mead's political biography. Fruitful attempts were undertaken to determine the relationship between Mead and other partly similar schools of thought. The relationship to social phenomenology was already mentioned; there are also now thorough, although not final studies on psychoanalysis (Weiss, Busch), on philosophical anthropology (Rehberg), and on Vygotsky (Glock, Valsiner/van der Veer). There is presently stronger interest in the relationship between Mead and the existentially transformed phenomenologies of Heidegger (Tugendhat, Malhotra) and Sartre (Aboulafia). I tried myself to contribute to placing Mead in the context of the Chicago School of sociology and the tradition stemming from there—when the smoke of the Lewis/Smith controversy had vanished (in this book pp. 14–51). After the death of Herbert Blumer, who had formed the symbolic interactionist approach out of parts of Mead's work, the historicizing interest in sociology seems to be turning toward him at the moment. A few years ago the most important attempts in the theory of action and of social order, for example, Jeffrey Alexander's and Richard Münch's, like Talcott Parsons's before them, did not try to come to terms with pragmatism; because of that, Jürgen Habermas's step in his *Theory of Communicative Action* to admit Mead to the small circle of sociological classics appeared to be the sole exception. This situation has changed insofar as more and more authors with comprehensive theoretical ambitions feel today the necessity to reflect upon and publicly declare their relationship to Mead. Thus Alexander has accepted Mead's challenge; most recently Randall Collins, one of the main proponents of a conflict approach in sociology, attempts a synthesis of Mead's theory of mind with his own theory of interaction ritual chains. A common feature of all these attempts—Habermas's renewed effort after the *Theory of Communicative Action* in a long essay on Mead included—is, however, that they more or less openly suggest that everything worthwhile in Mead's work is already contained in the favored approach. But only in the case of Habermas could one argue that Mead was in fact a central influence in the formation of his thinking. Even Habermas does not take into consideration the whole pragmatist framework of Mead and Dewey. In his theory the notion of action in the sense of common traits of instrumental, respectively strategic and communicative, *action* remains quite unclear. This goes hand in hand with a closure toward the anthropological elaboration of the concept of action and with a tendency toward a functionalist model of society. This judgment was my motive years ago to talk about a theory of "practical intersubjectivity"—in distinction to Habermas's concept of intersubjectivity, which is narrowed down to linguistic forms. But only after a very long study of the typical classics of the sociological theory of action (Weber, Durkheim, Parsons) do I feel able now to describe historically and systematically the relationship between pragmatism and the action-theoretical reflections of the founders of sociology.[6] In the following only the main thrust of these ideas can be delineated.

The Problem of Action

Today, "action" is a central concept of philosophy and of almost all the sciences that concern themselves with human beings. However, by no means has an integration of the action theories of the different disciplines been achieved. In order to understand the sociological theory of action, it is necessary to see it in its derivation from the guiding model of the economic theory of rational action. In the so-called marginalist revolution, the discipline of economics abandoned its aspiration to provide a comprehensive social theory, and developed instead a strict theoretical model of rational action derived from the essential elements of a utilitarian philosophy that were already implicit in classical economic theory. This model of rational action provided a new and very promising approach to solving problems that had to do with the decisions of individual participants in the market and with the resulting aggregation of such decisions and their consequences. However, the logical status of such a theory of rational action as a theory of the relation between ends of all kinds on the one hand and, on the other, scarce goods and resources that could be employed in a number of different ways remained unclear and a matter of controversy. Is such a theory an empirical assumption about human action that might be grounded with the aid of a hedonistic psychology; or does it represent a historically determinate ideal type of action? Should we interpret this theory normatively to mean that anyone who wants to act rationally must act in accordance with its findings and dictates; or is the theory nothing more than an elucidation of options for action that allows one to avoid undesired consequences of action, without necessitating the choice of a particular goal or mode of action? No matter how these questions were answered, for the European sociologists of the discipline's earliest years, the theory of rational action was generally regarded as a guiding model, a standard that had to be met if theory-guided empirical research which also permitted preservation of the individual's freedom of choice, in opposition to deterministic conceptions of human activity, was to be possible. The individual's freedom of choice was in any case implicit in the approach provided by the theory of action.

The assertion that the economic theory of rational action was an exemplary model for the nascent discipline of sociology should not, however, be taken to mean that sociology simply took over that theory from economics. The usefulness of the theory was accepted for the purposes of economics; at the same time, though, sociology claimed that the tasks and objects of investigation that such an economics refused to take over from an older economic theory and political philosophy fell within its own province. Sociology was to be responsible for the study of those dimensions of social integration that were not dealt with conceptually by the newer form of economics, and it was to investigate those dimensions with the means supplied by a theory of action that also took into account particularly nonrational forms of action. Sociology therefore had a fundamental need of a theory of action that defined different types of action on the basis of their specific difference from rational action. It required a theory of society as a complex of interrelated actions that was more than the unintended interconnecting of self-interested actions. It is for this reason that the dimension of normative agreement among the members of society played such an important role for sociology.

Just as fixation upon an adversary affects an individual as profoundly as does emulation of a guiding model, so too has the sociological theory of action been deeply influenced by the theory of rational action. This is so because it identifies and descriptively defines types of action as gradations of deviation from the concept of complete rationality, and not in their phenomenal peculiarity. This state of affairs can be demonstrated most impressively using the example of Vilfredo Pareto's terminology. In addition to a concept of logical action, which encompasses rational action also in noneconomic areas, Pareto's system of terminology has only a single collective designation for all other action, that of nonlogical action. This terminology thus offers only a negatively defined residual category for all the forms of action that Pareto himself recognizes as empirically preponderant.

Max Weber's set of distinctions, which has become classic in sociology, consists of four types of action. It can be shown that the typological principle behind these distinctions is the gradual abandonment of the rationalization of more and more dimensions of action.[7] Thus only purposively rational action satisfies the conditions for being completely action. In value-rational action, consideration of the consequences of action is omitted; in affectual action, consideration of values, and in traditional action, consideration even of ends. The ideal remains, then, an action that rationalizes ends, values, and consequences of action.

Durkheim shifts the problem out of economics into psychology. Since he, unlike Weber, does not deny the possibility that psychology might supply a foundation for the theory of marginal utility in order to be able to hold on to this economic theory, the refutation of a hedonistic psychology becomes of paramount importance for him. The similarity between

Durkheim and Kant is strongest, insofar as Durkheim, in an absolute dualism, opposes to the assumptions of hedonism the necessity of moral obligations to insure the maintenance of a social order.

However, even in Weber's work, which teems with inconsistencies, the traces of Kant's philosophy can be found in the distinction between purposive rationality and value-rationality of action, as well as in the distinction—linked with the aforementioned one—between an ethics of responsibility and an ethics of conviction. As a safeguard against the utilitarian dangers of the theory of rational action, the founding theorists of sociology have recourse to Kant and his notion of free, moral action. That is, certainly, not the whole of the matter, but what I have said should suffice for the moment to show the original scope of sociological thinking about action.

Now, in pragmatism matters stood very differently. The pragmatist philosophers shared with the early sociologists a deep skepticism about the pathos of a laissez-faire liberalism, a pathos that was generally associated with the marginalist economics of the time. However, the economists who were influenced by pragmatism, like Veblen and Cooley, did not accept the theoretical model of rational action as either an historical ideal type or a psychological assumption. They found the possibility for making this refusal in the theoretical model of action proposed by pragmatism, and they thereby escaped from the dilemma of having to choose between the alternatives of utilitarianism or Kantianism. The course of the history of ideas did not at all force reflection on action into the apparent exclusivity of these alternatives. Even the philosophical concepts of classical antiquity that were referred to action pointed in completely different directions than these two philosophies. The situation-directed astuteness implicit in the concept of "praxis" and the artisanal or poetic creation of something new that is at the heart of the notion of "poiesis" are difficult to apprehend with either utilitarian or Kantian concepts. In the thought of Herder, Wilhelm von Humboldt, and German Romanticism, the reaction against the Enlightenment led to an anthropology of expressivity that allowed the interpretation first of language and art, then of all human action as the self-expression of a human person. The history of the influence exerted by this intellectual innovation is extremely ramified. It includes not only Hegel's notion of mind or spirit and Marx's concept of labor, but also Dilthey's hermeneutics and Helmuth Plessner's anthropology. In these theories, action is interpreted in each instance using certain fundamental forms of action that make perceptible the creative character of human action.

The pragmatism that arose in the United States constitutes an entirely original and autonomous way of interpreting the creativity of action. For pragmatism, the guiding metaphor is neither poetic expression nor material production nor revolutionary transformation of society, but instead the creative solution of problems by an experimenting intelligence. Let us try to grasp more clearly the power and the inherent possibilities of this fundamental idea by examining Mead's writings.

Mead's early thought operated in the field of intellectual tension generated by the poles of a naturalized Hegelianism and functionalist psychology. Even before he had unequivocally assigned himself to the school of pragmatism, the problem of the relationship between action and consciousness was a central concern for Mead; the interpretation of consciousness as a phase of action that is functional for the successful continuation of the action made it possible for him to link his ideas to Darwin's insights and also to entertain the hope of transcending the Cartesian dualisms. It was not the relationship between utility-oriented or moral individual action and social order, but rather the relation between action and consciousness, that moved Mead's thought forward. The terminology of a naturalistic psychology used in his early work might well hide the fact that Mead is attempting here to formulate the idea of creative subjectivity.

This approach completely changes the meaning of intentionality, inasmuch as here action is no longer understood as the realization of ends set beforehand, in contrast to the theories of rational action and their transformation in the sociological theory of action. For the pragmatists, the setting of ends is not an act of consciousness that takes place outside of contexts of action. Rather, the setting of an end can only be a result of reflection on resistances encountered by the variously oriented behavior of a life form whose world is always already schematized in a practical manner prior to all reflection. If it proves to be impossible to follow simultaneously all the different impulses or compulsions directing our action, then the selection of a dominant motivation can occur that will, as an end, dominate all the others or allow them to come into play only secondarily. Such a clear orientation to a single end is, however, by no means the normal case. By its nature, action is only diffusely teleological. Even perception is shaped by our capacities for, and possibilities of, action. Only when constrained either by himself or by something external to himself does the actor narrow down the wealth of his impulses and his sensibility to a single clear line of action. In the case of action problems, connections are experimentally established between impulses and possibilities of action, connections of which only one is realized. The particular mode of realization of this one connection, however, is influenced by the other possibilities that have been imaginatively played through. Further, the course followed by an action is by no means set once and for all. On the contrary, what typically happens is continuous revision and constant reconstructive generation of the course that action is to follow. Again and again, Mead and Dewey explain their theory of action using as their principal examples experimentation and play or art. The play of children, which both theorists placed at the center of their efforts to achieve pedagogical reforms, served them as a theoretical model of an action in which there is only slight pressure to establish unequivocalness of the ends of the action. The experiment was for them the clearest, most evident case of an overcoming of action problems through the invention of new possibilities of action. For Mead and Dewey, the capacity of invention, that is creativity, had as its precondition the self-aware employment of and disposal over the form of action known as play, the conscious "playing through" in imagination of alternative performances of action.

When the central position of the creativity of action in this theory is not recognized, then well-known parts of Mead's framework remain unintelligible. Thus numerous misunderstandings have long existed about Mead's concept of the "I" and human spontaneity and creativity which are opposed to all social norms and expressed in this notion. Concerning these misunderstandings Mead is actually not without guilt because he in fact did not clearly distinguish the different stages of the activity of the "I" from mere impulsivity to creative productivity. Similarly—what I already pointed out in my book—Mead's model of the phases of the act is somewhat irritating insofar as it seems to aim at the activities of single individuals directed to the satisfaction of their needs. From other parts of his work we can learn, however, that Mead has in mind the achievement of collectively constituted goals in coordinated activities. A total dissolution of these misunderstandings and of any trace of a suspected biological or instrumentalist reductionism is possible only when the full meaning of the notion of experience—which is not restricted to its cognitive dimension—is grasped. Unfortunately, in my book I mentioned Mead's important article on "The Nature of Aesthetic Experience" only at the end as a document of his cultural critique in the late writings. It is probable that the importance of this text, which goes far beyond that, can only be detected when it is seen as a preliminary step on the way to those texts extremely important in Dewey's later work: namely, the books on art and on religion. In these writings it comes out that Mead's and Dewey's theory did not only leave behind the idea of originally isolated individuals, but also the restriction of communication to the coordination toward fixed goals. The point is rather the collective creativity in the constitution of ideal values and the individual creativity in the "abductive" and not deductive specification of these values to concrete ends of action. Aesthetic experience attains a central place because in it the possibility of a meaningful world which is sensually experienceable can be demonstrated. Art is the creative attempt to make the world meaningful by a creative appropriation of possibilities of ideality contained in the world. Action can only be satisfying in itself and not at eternally receding endpoints when its meaning is permeated by ideal meaning. The emphatic notion of democracy which Mead and Dewey used during their whole life expresses the ideal of a social order and of a culture in which the collective formation of common life processes approaches this ideal of an experienceable meaning. To understand Mead, this is a necessary precondition; an elaborated version of these background ideas can only be found, however, after Mead's death, in Dewey's work.[8]

Hence pragmatism's theoretical model of action does more than give access to new phenomena of action, phenomena which can be grasped only in a highly unsatisfactory fashion in the theories informed by the idea of rational action. It also compels one to consider familiar phenomena in a new light. On the basis of pragmatism, purposively rational and value-rational action too can no longer be defined as they had been in Weber's theory of action and made into the central axis of a typology of action. Instead of positing rational action as a type and defining other types of action as deficient modes of action, it is also possible to make explicit the presuppositions implicit in the idea of rational action. It is possible to make the human being who acts in a goal-directed manner, has control over his body, and is autonomous in relation to his fellows and his environment not simply the guiding model for the theory of action, but instead to work out the conditions of the possibility of this type of "actor" in a comprehensive reconstruction. I maintain that we have grasped the internal coherence of some parts of Mead's work if we understand them as fragments of such an undertaking. If this is correct, then the steps that Mead took toward a "social" or "intersubjective" turn of the fundamental pragmatist model of action are an important component, but only one component, of this enterprise. The theory of the individual's sociality that is elaborated in Mead's theory of the self, of communication, and of self-reflection shows then that the interrelation among individual human beings does not consist only of interconnection of their utility-oriented actions or in a normative consensus. From the standpoint of the theory of action, the conditions of the autonomy of rational actors are thereby illuminated. Beyond that, Mead's theory of the constitution of the body image, of the physical object, and of subjective temporality provide clarification of the conditions for the givenness of the body for the actor, while his theories of the psychical and of creativity show what the conditions of goal-directed action are.

Once one has been sensitized by pragmatism to those features of the concept of action that cannot be captured by the simple alternatives of rational action and normative obligation, then various germs of an apprehension of the creative moments of action can also be found in the writings of the founding theorists of sociology. In Durkheim's work, these are to be found in his theory of ritual, in which he describes in particular a state of collective excitation called effervescence, the personality-transforming effects of which are ascribed by the participants not to their joint activity, but to the place, the time, or to the occasion of their assembly and to sources of power situated outside the collective. In Weber's thought, we find, especially in his theory of charisma, the idea of the origination of new institutions through the creativity and the emotional power of the exceptional and highly gifted individual. However, one can infer *ex negativo,* from his critical scrutiny of his era and in particular from his critique of the pervasive bureaucratization of all spheres of life, that the yardstick of this critique is a conception of creativity that became increasingly impossible in the modern period after the end of the heroic age of the bourgeoisie. In regard to Simmel's writings, it has seldom been noted that he—for example, in his monograph on Rembrandt—continuously pursued the analysis of creativity in addition to his analysis of the rationalizing tendencies of modern culture. Therefore, when one considers not just the definition of action in the works of these thinkers, but also their substantial analyses, then, from the vantage point afforded by pragmatism, elements in these writings become visible, elements of which the tradition of sociological theory has heretofore made little use. But they were the points of departure for the classics' attempts to find a way out of the cultural crises of their present. This assertion cannot be developed at greater length here. But the observations that I have made can lead to the conjecture that the limits of the usual sociological model of action are overstepped precisely when it is no longer just the problem of the social order in the sense of a normative consensus of society's members, but a matter rather of the engendering of institutions or of the genesis of culture.

Normativity

An examination of Mead's ethical writings will demonstrate most clearly that he recognized and went beyond these limits. As early as 1901, in an essay about a contemporary critique of Hegel, Mead declared that in his view the most important part of Hegel's legacy lies in his recognition of the "synthesizing," that is, creative accomplishments, of the ego, and that in his belief this fact can be grasped most directly through study of the resolution of moral problem situations. Mead's critique of Kant's ethics contains the original argument that the procedure of self-examination which is inherent in the categorical imperative loses its value when it is not a matter of determining duty itself, but a matter of resolving a conflict between different duties or of establishing the constructive manner of fulfilling one's duty. The question of the right way to fulfil one's duty, of the way that is not pregiven but rather must be creatively discovered, bursts asunder the framework of a Kantian ethics of conviction, without thereby setting forth upon the road leading back into utilitarianism. Mead speaks of the application of the experimental method to the problems of ethics. This assertion must not be understood as the expression of the naive belief that moral problems are to be decided or solved by means of the empirical knowledge of scientists conducting experimental research. Rather, Mead means that the solution of moral problems requires creative intellectual accomplishments and the taking into account of all the values that are relevant in the situation in question. When the paths leading to the solution of moral problems are irremediably risky, then ethics is impossible without factual knowledge; when mere ethics of conviction has been surpassed, then experimental reflection on the consequences of one's own alternatives of action belongs to the very core of morality. Mere good will with no concern for acquiring the ability to carry out one's will is futile and of no moral worth. Mead's requirement that all values be taken into consideration, which he makes in explicit parallel to his demand that scientists take all facts into consideration, is aimed beyond the dimension of the creativity of action to the dimension of intersubjectivity, where Mead's theory has made such important contributions. But I am not concerned here with these contributions. Just like Kantian ethics, an intersubjective ethics can also ignore the creative solution of moral action problems and concentrate on consensual agreement, for example, discursive agreement about morally appropriate action. In contrast, a pragmatist ethics places itself in the situation of the actor, who has been set the practical problem of mediating between the values he holds and the givens of a particular situation. Since in Mead's theory of action the setting of an end does not occur prior to or independently of the particular situation in which the end will be pursued, the setting of an end is intermeshed with the existence of available means for achieving the end. Therefore, ethics does not elucidate the validity of the ultimate values, but instead attempts to reconstruct empirically the procedure for resolving situations requiring moral decisions in such a way that in it a procedure becomes recognizable that can itself serve as a basis for its own self-perfecting.

When I wrote the chapter on ethics in my book on Mead, I emphasized very strongly the fundamental difference between pragmatist ethics on the one hand and universalist Kantian ethics and Apel's or Habermas's discourse ethics on the other. I did this because in these latter ones it is unequivocally the problem of the justification of norms, and not the problem solution of moral actors themselves, which is crucial. Other writers, especially Gary Allan Cook, have also stressed in their more recent interpretations that Mead's point of departure lay in the inadequacy of conventional moral definitions of situations and in the solution of moral problems—and not in the clarification and normative foundation of abstract ethical principles. Now, this simple opposition of pragmatist and discourse ethics certainly has to be superseded, be it merely for the immanent reason that Mead undoubtedly defended a universalistic claim for his ethics. A universalistic pragmatist ethics means then that the practical solution of moral action problems must itself be evaluated from a universalistic viewpoint.

This whole topic has won considerably pressing importance because of the broad offensive of conservative and progressive versions of neo-Aristotelianism in ethics—influenced by writers like Hannah Arendt and Alasdair MacIntyre. In these approaches the practical power of judgment, the ability to *apply* norms in a situationally adequate manner is played off against the dimension of *justifying* norms in various ways. The claimed universalism of Kantian ethics is mostly repudiated there as an unpracticable or even obnoxious rigorism. Now pragmatist ethics is distinguished from Aristotelian ethics in spite of the common interest in the situatedness of action problems because it is not only interested in the *application* of pregiven normative rules, but in the *construction* of new possibilities for moral action. The emphasis in pragmatism is on the creative character of application or on the creative character of the solution of moral problems which can no longer be called "application." Even the cosmological Achilles' heel of modern versions of Aristotelian ethics is here successfully avoided by pointing to the creative transformation of the cosmos by the moral praxis of men. But this is not yet sufficient to justify its universalistic claims. At this point the proponents of discourse ethics, by self-critically revising their program, come to meet pragmatist ethics halfway.[9] Habermas has frankly admitted the existence of this problem in several places. Albrecht Wellmer has submitted a far-reaching and ambitious attempt to synthesize Kant and Aristotle in his own way and thus to retain discourse ethics in a comprehensive understanding of "application situations." Klaus Günther has undertaken what is most convincing in my eyes; namely, to clearly distinguish between the dimensions of foundation and application of norms and to reflect on the relationship between these dimensions. He develops the idea of a principle of impartial application of norms and therewith expresses very well the fact that the dimension of application or of the constructive production of moral hypotheses is itself open to discursive examination. At least when it attempts to think of an idealized "mankind" beyond every reference to a concrete "generalized other," however comprehensive that may be, pragmatist ethics has to agree that there is the possibility and the necessity to justify the standards of creative problem solution.

This clearly opens up the perspective of an integration of pragmatist and discourse ethics. It is no objection against such a perspective when one points out that—of course—the demonstration of the possibility of discourses for the justification of application solutions is something different from the analysis of the creative process of finding such solutions. It would no longer be a contradiction, but a relation of complementarity and division of labor that exists between the analysis of justification and the analysis of the genesis of new validity claims. Both types of analysis have their own right in the field of ethics as this is true for the distinction of a "context of justification" from a "context of discovery" in the analysis of scientific propositions. A special point of this integration of pragmatist and discourse ethics lies in the fact that in this way Klaus Günther, for example, finds himself compelled to distinguish the situatedness of action from its intersubjective character as two clearly distinct but equally original sides. I see in this a confirmation of my insistence that there is not—as in Habermas—one sole theoretical step that leads "from instrumental to communicative action." It is rather at first the properly action-theoretical step of a nonteleological interpretation of the relation of action and situation, then the introduction of a communicative dimension in the constitution of meaning and validity. Mead and Dewey always criticized Kantian and utilitarian ethics as involving a wrong concept of action; they did not mean by that the neglect of communication and discourse, but the rupture between motive and object. If this whole argument is true, then the importance of pragmatism not only in social theory but also in ethics consists in its insistence on a totally new approach in the theory of action, not only in a new understanding of communicative action.

Accordingly, for Mead social order is not to be found in normative consensus, but in the capacity of a collective to successfully solve its problems. Since there is no unequivocal criterion for the success of problem solving other than that of those concerned with and affected by the problem, this reflection naturally leads back to the consensus of society's members in the assessment of the various putative solutions of a particular problem. It is not, however, a matter of consensus that can become stabilized in itself, but of an intermediary phase in the continuous cropping up of unanticipated problems and of their creative and risky resolution. The sociologists of the Chicago School, which was inspired by pragmatism, gave this idea the name of "social control." This term is tantamount in meaning to societal autonomy, and is the parallel concept to the Chicago School's notion of the self-control of the individual, a concept that refers to the personality structure of the creative personality. In the personality theory of William Isaac Thomas, the leading representative of this school up to the end of the First World War, the creative personality is the normative type of personality, which, in contrast to the rigid personality of the "Philistine" and the diffuse personality of the "Bohemian," possesses the capacity for self-guidance, although always less than complete, of its own development. In sociology, the distinction between a creative sociality and normativity makes it possible to conceive of society not just as an agency of restraint, of compulsion, or of obligation in relation to the individual, but to conceive of it also as a source of inspiration, of an expansion of the self, and of a liberation and intensification of hidden personal energies. This distinction makes it possible to grasp the dynamics of interpersonal interactions and of the intrapersonal relation to internalized norms and socialized drives. Human action is neither the realization of norms nor the fulfillment of drives: the individual is engaged in a continuous process of drawing boundaries and of opening them vis-à-vis other individuals and the collectives with which he is associated. Out of this "magma" of sociality—to borrow an expression from Cornelius Castoriadis—there arise, by means of creative accomplishments of human action, the norms, values, cultural works, and institutions that are accepted and operative in a given society.

Social Science and Practical Philosophy

Both sociology and pragmatism claim to be sciences of human action, or to provide the bases for such a science. However, the great differences between their understandings of what action is raise the question of the difference in the conceptions of the nature of scientific investigation of human action that were linked with the differing approaches to developing a theory of action. The early sociology of Comte and Spencer, a sociology that was not yet informed by a theory of action, saw scientific gain rather than a problem in a transfer to sociological research of the methods of the natural sciences, as they were understood at the time. Everything that was once part of practical philosophy could, if understood in this way, be robbed of its normative claims, and each separate part of practical philosophy could be made the object of study of an empirical discipline. The opposition by the German hermeneutical and historical tradition to such a natural science of the social is in agreement with its adversary on one point: historicism too cuts through its connection with the normative claim of practical philosophy by providing justification solely for the positive investigation of historically and culturally relative normative interpretation of reality. In both cases, the tie between a normatively substantive reflection on the ends of human action and scientific study of that action is severed.

Caught in this dilemma, the classical theorists of sociology proposed various solutions that were, however, all unable to achieve stable results. Neither Durkheim, nor Weber, nor Parsons joins sociology as a theory of action to a determination of the practical character of a science of social action. This same tension between "science" and "action" can also be discerned in pragmatism. There, however, the tension is not resolved through recourse to a theoretical model of action that satisfies the requirements of a scientific method, as is the case with the theory of rational action. Rather, in pragmatism the path of resolution of this tension leads in the opposite direction, to reflection upon the methods of science, in order to elucidate the practical character of those methods on the basis of the pragmatist theory of action. The unexamined general acceptance of a scientistic understanding of scientific methods led to continuous misunderstanding of pragmatist theorists and to the disastrous response that their writings received, for example, in Germany. No matter whether one inquires of the phenomenologist Max Scheler or of the "critical theorist" Max Horkheimer, one finds that pragmatism is regarded as merely a variant of a positivistic faith in the scientific solvability of moral and political problems.

Mead's own writings, however, show that the opposite was true. By conceiving of science as the type of systematized solution of cognitive action problems, pragmatism makes evident the practical foundation of all science. Neither a specific system of propositions, nor a method that can be described univocally, but rather the relatively most successful procedure for solving specific problems of cognition—that is what science is. Science and ethics or politics cannot be sharply distinguished from each other, but are just as intermeshed with one another as are the search for suitable means and reflection on the appropriateness of ends in practical situations in the pragmatists' theory of action. Ethical or political problems are not reduced to scientific problems. But it is also true that the success of the sciences in the solution of certain problems forbids a simple return to the old unity of practical philosophy. In a civilization shaped by science and technology, the way that practical problems of all kinds are dealt with must be oriented to the level that has been reached by the creative praxis of experimentation and research and by intersubjective discussion and argument in science. Not the imposition of scientific rules on the solution of practical problems, but the attainment of the sciences' level of rationality in the solution of practical problems, is what pragmatism calls for as a norm.

It is well known that Dewey insisted that his goal was not to make intelligence practical, but to make praxis intelligent. The development of the social sciences constitutes a step toward this higher level of rationality. From the pragmatist perspective, the social sciences are to aid human communities precisely in the improvement of their possibilities of collective action, and, in a world destitute of metaphysical certainty, they make a crucially important contribution to the solidarity of a community of human beings who collectively recognize and discuss their earthly problems and creatively solve them. On this view, the social sciences are not a substitute for practical philosophy, but become a moment of a new form of practical philosophy that is suited to our age.

During the passing decade of the eighties pragmatism, however, did not come into the headlines of philosophic debates as a modern type of practical philosophy which proceeds in close relationship to the social and natural sciences, but in the spectacular and brilliantly formulated way in which Richard Rorty declared his farewell to the sterility of the academic execution of analytic philosophy. For Rorty John Dewey is, together with Martin Heidegger and Ludwig Wittgenstein, one of the philosophical heroes of our century; in several places one can hear of a movement of "neopragmatism" deriving itself from Rorty. The American experts on historical pragmatism reacted to Rorty's use of Dewey—Mead is ignored by Rorty—and of the label "pragmatism" with many convincing objections. Rorty himself retreated very far in direct controversy,[10] but not in his writings in general. The debate about Rorty is very instructive for a contemporary understanding of pragmatism. The most important question hereby is whether one has to draw the same conclusions as Rorty does from his criticisms of contemporary philosophy.

There is no doubt that Rorty's critique of academic and professional philosophy—particularly in English-speaking countries—hits its target.

His critique has been substantiated by deep-reaching changes within the analytic tradition which have led to a rediscovery of pragmatist motives. Moreover, Rorty is not alone in considering Dewey as not simply a part of the pragmatist school, but as a clear contemporary of Heidegger and Wittgenstein, simply because of his differences from Peirce. From a totally different position Stephen Toulmin had presented the same insight; Ernst Tugendhat on his part has attempted a sort of mutual correction of Heidegger and Mead. Michael Sukale has examined the parallels of Heidegger's *Being and Time* and Dewey's "metaphysical" principal work *Experience and Nature.*[11] It is quite ironic that Rorty presents Dewey's philosophy to an astonished public not as the prototype of a naive belief in science, but as the case of a postmodern deconstructionist *avant la lettre.* Rorty's provocative formula for his own preferences is "postmodern bourgeois liberalism." Were Dewey and Mead "postmodern bourgeois liberals"?

Even a cursory inspection of their writings shows that Rorty's reference to Dewey is not well grounded. Essential parts of Dewey's theory and of the influences on him are completely lacking; for example, the importance of Darwin and of experimental psychology, the whole framework of the conditions of problem situations which make creativity necessary and which allow for learning processes by a progressive appropriation of the world. With regard to politics the truly radical element of Dewey and Mead is lacking in Rorty; namely, the permanent critique of the degree to which democratic ideals are realized in the existing political institutions and their impulse toward social equality which is a precondition for the improvement of institutions and for true democracy. All this shows that it is not only the contents, but also the status of philosophy which is different in Dewey and Mead from Rorty's views; in Campbell's formulation reconstruction *in* philosophy is for them only a preliminary stage for social reconstruction *by* philosophy. It is exactly this contribution of philosophy and the sciences to changing the social order which Rorty wants to exclude. He pleads for an end to the spirit of seriousness and for a new spirit of flexibility, imagination, creativity, and nonprofessionality. A playful commerce with the stocks of knowledge is to replace the orientation toward social reform as much as tolerant conversation the search for *the* correct method. What is striking in all these arguments and pleas is how dualistically—and not synthetically—Rorty proceeds. The way out of the blind alley of watertight professionalization and total belief in methods is for him free play and a complete retreat from professionalism. Democratic institutions are taken as such and not considered in their tension with their own legitimation. The mediation of natural contexts of conditions with human creativity—which Dewey and Mead undertook to show—is not recognized by Rorty. The destruction of a misleading objectivist self-understanding of philosophy and the sciences is seen as a final farewell to all claims to objective validity and not as the precondition for the development of a more adequate understanding which then makes possible the rationality of ethical and aesthetical values. In Rorty's neopragmatism there happens the "Heideggerization" of American thinking, whereas the more recent German studies on pragmatism by Apel and Habermas and also my book on Mead make the contrary attempt to free German thinking from its Heideggerian and other aporiae, by making it more "pragmatic."[12] The debates on the interpretation of pragmatism delineate an area which has an importance for understanding our present similar to that of the international discussion on Heidegger. If Dewey's assumption is correct that classical metaphysics is a result of the attempt to dispel the risky character of everyday life by a philosophy of necessity and atemporal stability,[13] then the rising power of mankind and the domination of nature are a historical precondition for the rollback of this metaphysics. The unintended consequences of this domination of nature which we contemporaries experience so intensely are able, however, rapidly to deprive one of the courage of this insight. Then there arises a *secondary* covering up of the natural conditions and potentials of human creativity and the dangers of the human condition. Against such a secondary covering up, as it happened prototypically in Heidegger's philosophy, we have the project of pragmatism inspired by John Dewey and George Herbert Mead.

Notes

1. The present essay was originally written in response to an invitation to present a paper on Mead as an "Invited Speaker" at the Eastern Division meetings of the American Philosophical Association in New York in December of 1987. This shorter version was translated by Raymond Meyer. The contributions to the discussion there, particularly the comments by James Campbell and the remarks by Richard Bernstein and Thomas McCarthy, led to certain corrections and additions. James Campbell and Gary A. Cook helped me to improve the English style of this manuscript.
2. Emile Durkheim, *Pragmatism and Sociology* (Cambridge, Mass., 1983).
3. From the reviews of my book I have found the following most helpful:

    Gary Allan Cook, *Transactions of the Charles Sanders Peirce Society* 22 (1986), pp. 338–43.

    David Maines, *American Journal of Sociology* 93 (1987–88), pp. 198–201.

    Dénes Némedi, *European Sociological Review* 2 (1986), pp. 240–42.

Karl-Siegbert Rehberg, "Sozialphilosophie und Theorie der Intersubjektivität, Zur neueren deutschen Mead-Literatur," *Philosophischer Literaturanzeiger* 38 (1985), pp. 70–83.

Dmitri Shalin, *Symbolic Interaction* 9 (1986), pp. 273–76.

Alan Sica, *Telos*, no. 66 (1985–86), pp. 143–53.

Dennis Smith, *The Sociological Review* 34 (1986), pp. 675–78.

Ilja Srubar, *Kölner Zeitschrift für Soziologie und Sozialpsychologie* 35 (1983): pp. 795–97.

Unhelpful, and in part misleading, is Richard Grathoff, "Zur gegenwärtigen Rezeption von G. H. Mead," *Philosophische Rundschau* 34 (1987), pp. 131–45.

I have developed the research on Mead further in: Hans Joas (ed.), *Das Problem der Intersubjektivität* (Frankfurt: Suhrkamp, 1985).

These texts and the new German edition of the book on Mead contain all the bibliographical references for the following remarks.

4. This is how I understand Jürgen Habermas's remark in the essay "Metaphysik nach Kant," in his book *Nachmetaphysisches Denken* (Frankfurt, 1988), p. 34, n. 17.

5. See Mark Johnson, *The Body in the Mind, The Bodily Basis of Meaning, Imagination, and Reason* (Chicago, 1987).

6. This is a reference to a book recently published in German (*Die Kreativität des Handelns*, Frankfurt 1992). In a series of articles I have attempted to delineate its program in contrast to the main approaches for a theory of action today—see the chapters on Habermas, Castoriadis, Giddens, and Alexander in this volume.

7. Cf. Wolfgang Schluchter, *Die Entwicklung des okzidentalen Rationalismus* (Tübingen, 1979), p. 192.

8. George Herbert Mead, "The Nature of Aesthetic Experience," *International Journal of Ethics* 36 (1925–26), pp. 382–93. John Dewey, *Art as Experience* (New York, 1934); *A Common Faith* (New Haven, 1934). See also the excellent book by Thomas M. Alexander, *John Dewey's Theory of Art, Experience and Nature: The Horizons of Feeling* (Albany, 1987).

9. Jürgen Habermas, "Moralität und Sittlichkeit: Treffen Hegels Einwände gegen Kant auch auf die Diskursethik zu?," in Wolfgang Kuhlmann (ed.), *Moralität und Sittlichkeit: Das Problem Hegels und die Diskursethik* (Frankfurt, 1986), pp. 16–37; Albrecht Wellmer, *Ethik und Dialog: Elemente des moralischen Urteils bei Kant und in der Diskursethik* (Frankfurt, 1986); Klaus Günther, *Der Sinn für Angemessenheit: Anwendungsdiskurse in Moral und Recht* (Frankfurt, 1988).

10. Richard Rorty, *Philosophy and the Mirror of Nature* (Princeton, 1979); *Consequences of Pragmatism* (Minneapolis, 1982). "Postmodernist Bourgeois Liberalism," in Robert Hollinger (ed.), *Hermeneutics and Praxis* (Notre Dame, 1985), pp. 214–21. Some of the most important critical studies of Rorty are: Garry Brodsky, "Rorty's Interpretation of Pragmatism," *Transactions of the Charles Sanders Peirce Society* 18 (1982), pp. 311–37; John J. McDermott, Ralph Sleeper, Abraham Edel, and Richard Rorty, "Symposium on Rorty's *Consequences of Pragmatism, Transactions of the Charles Sanders Peirce Society* 21 (1985), pp. 1–48; Richard Bernstein, "Philosophy in the Conversation of Mankind," in his *Philosophical Profiles* (Philadelphia, 1986), pp. 21–57; James Campbell, "Rorty's Use of Dewey," *Southern Journal of Philosophy* 22 (1984), pp. 175–87; Thomas Alexander, "Richard Rorty and Dewey's Metaphysics of Experience," *Southwest Philosophical Studies* 5 (1980), pp. 24–35; Cornel West, "The Politics of American Neo-Pragmatism," in John Rajchman and Cornel West (eds.), *Post-Analytic Philosophy* (New York, 1985), pp. 259–75; Richard Bernstein, "One Step

Forward, Two Steps Backward: Richard Rorty on Liberal Democracy and Philosophy," *Political Theory* 15 (1987), pp. 538–63 (with a rejoinder by Richard Rorty: "Thugs and Theorists: A Reply to Bernstein, pp. 564–80). Other excellent studies of Rorty's analysis of the status of philosophy, which do not center on the accuracy of his interpretation of pragmatism, are: Jürgen Habermas, "Die Philosophie als Platzhalter und Interpret," in his *Moralbewusstein und kommunikatives Handeln* (Frankfurt, 1983), pp. 9–28, and Kai Nielsen, "Scientism, Pragmatism, and the Fate of Philosophy," *Inquiry* 29 (1984), pp. 277–304.

11. To see how differently the relationship between Heidegger and pragmatism can be interpreted, cf. Michael Sukale, "Heidegger and Dewey," in his *Comparative Studies in Phenomenology* (The Hague, 1976), pp. 121–51; Richard Rorty, "Heidegger wider die Pragmatisten," *Neue Hefte für Philosophie* 23 (1984), pp. 1–22; and Stephen Toulmin, Introduction to John Dewey, *The Later Works*, vol. 4 (Carbondale, Ill., 1984), pp. vii–xxii.

12. On the history of the German reception of pragmatism see the chapter "American Pragmatism and German Thought" in this volume.

13. John Dewey, *Experience and Nature* (New York, 1958).

Subject Index

Name Index

SIGNIFICANT CHANGES TO THE

CALIFORNIA BUILDING CODE

2013 EDITION

Significant Changes to the California Building Code 2013 Edition

International Code Council and California Building Officials

ICC Staff:

Executive Vice President and Director of Business Development: Mark A. Johnson

Senior Vice President, Business and Product Development: Hamid Naderi

Vice President and Technical Director, Education and Product Development: Doug Thornburg

Director, Project and Special Sales: Suzane Nunes

Senior Marketing Specialist: Dianna Hallmark

CALBO Staff:

Executive Director: Matthew Wheeler

Director of Training and Communications: Doug Nisenson

Director of Government and Public Affairs: Kelly M. Sherfey

ISBN: 978-1-60983-500-2

Cover Design: Lisa Triska

Project Editor: Mary Lou Luif

Project Head: Steve Van Note

Publications Manager: Mary Lou Luif

Errata on various ICC publications may be available at www.iccsafe.org/errata.

First Printing: September 2013

PRINTED IN THE U.S.A.

37474 - T014998

Contents

Preface

The purpose of *Significant Changes to the California Building Code 2013 Edition* is to familiarize building officials, fire officials, plans examiners, inspectors, design professionals, contractors, and others in the construction industry with many of the important changes in the *2013 California Building Code* (CBC). This publication is designed to assist those code users in identifying the specific code changes that have occurred and, more important, understanding the reason behind the change. It is also a valuable resource for jurisdictions in their code adoption process.

Only a portion of the total number of code changes to the CBC are discussed in this book. The changes selected were identified for a number of reasons, including their frequency of application, special significance, or change in application. However, the importance of those changes not included is not to be diminished. The *2012 International Building Code®* (IBC®) is the basis for the CBC. Further information on all code changes can be found in the *Code Changes Resource Collection*, available from the International Code Council® (ICC®). The resource collection provides the published documentation for each successful code change contained in the 2012 IBC since the 2009 edition.

This book is organized into seven general categories, each representing a distinct grouping of code topics. It is arranged to follow the general layout of the CBC, including code sections and section number format. The table of contents, in addition to providing guidance in use of this publication, allows for quick identification of those significant code changes that occur in the 2013 CBC.

Throughout the book, each change is accompanied by a photograph, an application example, or an illustration to assist and enhance the reader's understanding of the specific change. A summary and a discussion of the significance of the changes are also provided. Each code change is identified by type, be it an addition, modification, clarification, or deletion. The code change itself is presented in a format similar to the style utilized for code-change proposals. Deleted code language is shown with a strike-through, whereas new code text is indicated by underlining. As a result, the actual 2013 code language is provided, as well as a comparison with the 2010 language, so the user can easily determine changes to the specific code text.

As with any code-change text, *Significant Changes to the California Building Code 2013 Edition* is best used as a study companion to the 2013 CBC. Because only a limited discussion of each change is provided, the code itself should always be referenced in order to gain a more comprehensive understanding of the code change and its application. The commentary and opinions set forth in this text are those of the authors and do not necessarily represent the official position of the ICC. In addition, they may not represent the views of any enforcing agency, as such agencies have the sole authority to render interpretations of the CBC. In many cases, the explanatory material is derived from the reasoning expressed by the code-change proponent.

Comments concerning this publication are encouraged and may be directed to the ICC at significantchanges@iccsafe.org.

About the California Building Code®

Building officials, design professionals, and others involved in the building construction industry recognize the need for a modern, up-to-date building code addressing the design, construction and installation of building systems through requirements emphasizing performance. The *International Building Code* (IBC), 2012 edition, is the basis for the 2013 *California Building Code* (CBC) and is intended to meet these needs through model code regulations that safeguard the public health and safety in all communities, large and small. The IBC is kept up to date through the open code-development process of the International Code Council (ICC). The provisions of the 2009 edition, along with those code changes approved through 2010, make up the 2012 edition. The ICC, publisher of the IBC, was established in 1994 as a nonprofit organization dedicated to developing, maintaining, and supporting a single set of comprehensive and coordinated national model building construction codes. Its mission is to provide the highest quality codes, standards, products, and services for all concerned with the safety and performance of the built environment.

The CBC is one in a family of California building codes (California Code of Regulations, Title 24) that are published on a triennial basis. This comprehensive building code establishes minimum regulations for building systems by means of prescriptive and performance-related provisions. It is founded on broad-based principles that make possible the use of new materials and new building designs. The California Building Standards Commission (CBSC) is responsible for the administration of each code cycle, which includes the proposal, review and adoption processes. Supplements and errata are issued throughout the cycle.

Acknowledgments

A special thank you is extended to Scott Stookey, former Senior Technical Staff with ICC for his assistance with the fire protection portions of this text. Thanks also to ICC staff members Alan Carr, Kim Paarlberg, Bill Rehr, and Kermit Robinson and to Stuart Tom, P.E., building official of Glendale, California for their valued review and input.

About the Authors

Douglas W. Thornburg, AIA, CBO
International Code Council
Vice President and Technical Director of Product Development and Education

Douglas W. Thornburg is the Vice President and Technical Director of Product Development and Education for the International Code Council (ICC), where he provides leadership in technical development and positioning of support products for the council. In addition, Doug develops and reviews technical products, reference books, and resource materials relating to construction codes and their supporting documents. Prior to employment with the ICC in 2004, he spent nine years as a code consultant and educator on building codes. Formerly Vice-President/Education for the International Conference of Building Officials (ICBO), Doug continues to present building code seminars nationally and has developed numerous educational texts and resource materials, including *the International Building Code Handbook*. He was presented with ICC's inaugural Educator of the Year Award in 2008, in recognition of his outstanding contributions to education and professional development. A graduate of Kansas State University and a registered architect, Doug has more than 30 years of experience in building code training and administration, including 10 years with the ICBO and 5 years with the City of Wichita, Kansas. He is certified as a building official, building inspector, and plans examiner, as well as in seven other code enforcement categories.

John R. Henry, P.E.
International Code Council
Principal Staff Engineer

John R. Henry is a Principal Staff Engineer with the International Code Council (ICC) Business and Product Development Department, where he is responsible for the research and development of technical resources pertaining to the structural engineering provisions of the *International Building Code* (IBC). John also develops and presents technical seminars on the structural provisions of the IBC. He has a broad range of experience that includes structural design in private practice, plan-check engineering with consulting firms and building department jurisdictions, and 14 years as an International Conference of Building Officials (ICBO)/ ICC Staff Engineer. John graduated with honors from California State University in Sacramento with a Bachelor of Science Degree in Civil Engineering and is a Registered Civil Engineer in the State of California. He is a member of the American Society of Civil Engineers (ASCE) and the Structural Engineers Association of California (SEAOC) and is an ICC Certified Plans Examiner. John has written several articles on the structural provisions of the IBC that have appeared in *Structure Magazine* and *Structural Engineering and Design* magazine's Code Series. He is also the coauthor of the *International Building Code Handbook*.

Jay Woodward
International Code Council
Senior Staff Architect

Jay is a senior staff architect with the ICC's Business and Product Development department and works out of the Lenexa, Kansas, Distribution Center. His current responsibilities include serving as the Secretariat for the ICC A117.1 standard committee and assisting in the development of new ICC publications.

With more than 28 years of experience in building design, construction, code enforcement, and instruction, Jay's experience provides him with the ability to address issues of code application and design for code enforcement personnel as well as architects, designers, and contractors. Jay has previously served as the Secretariat for the ICC's *International Energy Conservation Code* and the *International Building Code's* Fire Safety Code Development committee.

A graduate of the University of Kansas and a registered architect, Jay has also worked as an architect for the Leo A. Daly Company in Omaha, Nebraska; as a building Plans Examiner for the City of Wichita, Kansas; and as a Senior Staff Architect for the International Conference of Building Officials (ICBO) prior to working for the ICC. He is also author of *Significant Changes to the A117.1 Accessibility Standard 2009 Edition.*

Paul D. Armstrong, P.E., CBO
CSG Consultants, Inc.
Southern California Regional Manager

Mr. Armstrong is the Southern California Regional Manager for CSG Consultants, Inc. He has worked for a number of private municipal consulting firms and in that capacity served as the Building Official for the City of El Monte. Prior to working for private firms, he worked for 14 years for the International Code Council and the International Conference of Building Officials, ending his time as the initial ICC Vice President of Architectural and Engineering Services. He also served as the drafting secretariat for the *2000 International Residential Code.* He represented the model code organizations to many federal, state and local agencies and is a recognized lecturer on many code-related topics. Mr. Armstrong graduated from California State University at Long Beach and is a Professional Engineer in the State of California and a Certified Building Official.

About the ICC

The International Code Council is a member-focused association. It is dedicated to developing model codes and standards used in the design, build and compliance process to construct safe, sustainable, affordable and resilient structures. Most U.S. communities and many global markets choose the International Codes. ICC Evaluation Service (ICC-ES) is the industry leader in performing technical evaluations for code compliance fostering safe and sustainable design and construction.

Headquarters:
500 New Jersey Avenue, NW, 6th Floor
Washington, DC 20001-2070

District Offices:
Birmingham, AL; Chicago, IL; Los Angeles, CA

1-888-422-7233
www.iccsafe.org

About the California Building Officials (CALBO)

Founded in 1962, California Building Officials (CALBO) represents local city and county governments throughout the entire state of California. As a nonprofit 501(c)6 organization, CALBO is dedicated to promoting public health and safety in building construction through responsible legislation, education and building code development. CALBO members are primarily responsible for enforcing building code requirements in an estimated 95 percent of the buildings constructed in the state. CALBO ensures that proper public health and structural safety requirements, codes and standards are adhered to within the built environment. The organization protects the citizens served and the overall safety of the public.

www.calbo.org

PART 1

Administration

Chapters 1 and 2

- **Chapter 1** Administration
- **Chapter 2** Definitions

The provisions of Chapter 1 address the application, enforcement, and administration of subsequent requirements of the code. In addition to establishing the scope of the *California Building Code* (CBC), the chapter identifies which buildings and structures come under its purview. A building code, as with any other code, is intended to be adopted as a legally enforceable document to safeguard health, safety, property, and public welfare. A building code cannot be effective without adequate provisions for its administration and enforcement. Chapter 2 provides definitions for terms used throughout the CBC. Codes, by their very nature, are technical documents, and as such, literally every word, term, and punctuation mark can add to or change the meaning of the intended result. ■

110.3.4, 110.3.10

Frame and Final Inspections

202

Definitions—Group I-3 Occupancies

110.3.4, 110.3.10

Frame and Final Inspections

CHANGE TYPE: Addition

CHANGE SUMMARY: Moisture content verification has been added to the frame inspection requirements. Placement of a maintenance manual in the building is required at the time of final inspection. These new provisions come from the CALGreen requirements.

2013 CODE: **110.3.4 Frame Inspection.** Framing inspections shall be made after the roof deck or sheathing, all framing, fireblocking and bracing are in place and pipes, chimneys and vents to be concealed are complete and the rough electrical, plumbing, heating wires, pipes and ducts are approved..

110.3.4.1 (HCD 1) Moisture Content Verification. *Moisture content of framing members shall be verified in accordance with the California Green Building Code (CALGreen), Chapter 4, Division 4.5.*

110.3.10 Final Inspection. The final inspection shall be made after all work required by the building permit is completed.

110.3.10.1 Flood Hazard Documentation. (No change to text)

110.3.10.2 (HCD 1) Operation and Maintenance Manual. *At the time of final inspection, a manual, compact disc, web-based reference or other media acceptable to the enforcing agency shall be placed in the building in accordance with the California Green Building Code (CALGreen), Chapter 4, Division 4.4.*

CHANGE SIGNIFICANCE HCD has included pointers to mandatory CALGreen Code requirements in this code to enhance user convenience and familiarity. These mandatory pointers are excerpts to code sections in CALGreen. Users should consult the actual code text in CALGreen for complete requirements.

The moisture content verification inspection in Section 110.3.4.1 intends to reduce the probability of mold and mildew growth and as a result improve indoor air quality.

The intent of the operation and maintenance manual in Section 110.3.10.2 is to encourage the proper maintenance and performance of the systems built into the building after the certificate of occupancy is issued.

202

Definitions — Group I-3 Occupancies

CHANGE TYPE: Addition

CHANGE SUMMARY: New definitions and modification to existing definitions related to Group I-3 occupancies are the result of the California State Fire Marshal's Group I-3 Task Force recommendation.

2013 CODE: **CELL** ~~**(Group I-3 occupancy**~~ *(Detention or correctional facility)* ~~A room within a housing unit in a detention or correctional facility used to confine inmates or prisoners. Cell~~ [SFM]. A sleeping or housing unit in a detention or correctional facility for the confinement of not more than two inmates or prisoners ~~A housing unit in a detention or correctional facility for the confinement of not more than two inmates or prisoners~~.

COURTROOM DOCK. *Courtroom dock shall mean an area within a courtroom where persons may be restrained and are awaiting court proceedings.*

COURTHOUSE HOLDING FACILITY [SFM]. *Courthouse holding facility shall mean a room, cell, cell complex or building for the confinement of persons for the purpose of a court appearance for a period not to exceed 12 hours.*

Temporary holding room.

DETENTION ELEVATOR [SFM]. *Detention elevator shall mean an elevator which moves in-custody individuals within a secure and restrained environment.*

DETENTION TREATMENT ROOM. [SFM]. *Detention treatment room shall mean a lockable room or rooms within Group I-3 occupancies used for recreational therapy, group rooms, interdisciplinary treatment team rooms, and interview rooms not classified solely as a Group I-2 occupancy*

RESTRAINT. [SFM] *shall mean the physical retention of a person within a room, cell or cell block, holding cells, temporary holding cell, rooms or area, holding facility, secure interview rooms, courthouse holding facilities, courtroom docks, or similar buildings or portions thereof by any means, or within the exterior walls of a building by means of locked doors inoperable by the person restrained. Restraint shall also mean the physical binding, strapping or similar restriction of any person in a chair, walker, bed or other contrivance for the purpose of deliberately restricting the free movement of ambulatory persons.*

Restraint shall not be construed to include nonambulatory persons nor shall it include the use of bandage material, strip sheeting or other fabrics or materials (soft ties) used to restrain persons in hospital-type beds or wheelchairs to prevent injury, provided an approved method of quick release is maintained.

Facilities employing the use of soft ties, however, shall be classified as a building used to house nonambulatory persons. Restraint shall not be practiced in licensed facilities classified as Group R-2.1, R-3.1 and R-4 occupancies unless constructed as a Group I-3 occupancy. For Group I-3 Occupancies, see Section 408.1.1.

SECURE INTERVIEW ROOMS: *A lockable room used to hold and interview detainees for further processing.*

TEMPORARY HOLDING CELL, ROOM or AREA. [CSA and SFM] *Temporary holding cell, room or area shall mean a room for temporary holding of inmates, detainees, or in-custody individuals for less than 24 hours.*

TEMPORARY HOLDING FACILITY [SFM] *A building or portion of a building, operated by law enforcement personnel, with one or more temporary holding cells or rooms.*

TENABLE ENVIRONMENT [SFM] *Tenable environment shall mean an environment in which the products of combustion, toxic gases, smoke and heat are limited or otherwise restricted to maintain the impact on occupants to a level that is not life threatening.*

CHANGE SIGNIFICANCE: The I-3 Occupancy Codes Task Group reviewed a number of definitions related to Group I-3 occupancies. The definition of "cell" was changed to more accurately reflect conditions already in practice throughout the state. The previous definition did not adequately define "cell" as used within the content California Code of Regulations, Title 15, entitled "Crime Prevention and Corrections." For example, Section 3269, Inmate Housing Assignments, provides operational expectations that all inmates are housed in a double cell. Single cell housing status may be considered for those inmates who demonstrate a history of in-cell abuse, significant in-cell violence towards a cell partner, verification of predatory behavior towards a cell partner, or who have been victimized in-cell by another inmate.

The Administrative Office of the Courts advised SFM that the current common term for the area within a courtroom where persons may be restrained and are awaiting court proceedings is "courtroom dock." The definition was added to reflect common practice throughout the state.

The addition of the term "courthouse holding facility" differentiates between temporary holding rooms, temporary holding cells, and cells where persons are kept for less than 24 hours, and housing cells within jails and prisons.

The addition of the term "detention elevator" differentiates it from passenger or freight elevators and provides for appropriate fire, life safety and security regulations.

"Detention treatment rooms" in detention areas are defined to allow for special circumstances which exist when persons are systematically escorted and locked in rooms with doors equipped with paracentric (security bolt) hardware which are incompatible with closers and self-closing devices.

The revision to the definition of "restraint" makes it clear that the term is applied in the same fashion to a number of similar areas including holding cells, temporary holding areas adjacent to courtrooms and courtroom docks.

The addition of the terms "temporary holding cell, room or area" and "temporary holding facility" differentiates between temporary holding areas where persons are kept for less than 24 hours and housing cells where persons sleep overnight or reside.

The term "tenable environment" helps to quantify requirements found in Sections 408.9 and 909. This definition is in-line with nationally recognized codes and standards. [From NFPA 92B – Smoke Management Systems in Malls, Atria, and Large Spaces.]

PART 2

Building Planning

Chapters 3 through 6

■ **Chapter 3**	Use and Occupancy Classification
■ **Chapter 4**	Special Detailed Requirements Based on Use and Occupancy
■ **Chapter 5**	General Building Heights and Areas
■ **Chapter 6**	Types of Construction

The application of the *California Building Code* to a structure is typically initiated through the provisions of Chapters 3, 5, and 6. Chapter 3 establishes one or more occupancy classifications based upon the anticipated uses of a building. The appropriate classifications are necessary to properly apply many of the code's nonstructural provisions. The requirements of Chapter 6 deal with classification as to construction type, based on a building's materials of construction and the level of fire resistance provided by such materials. Limitations on a building's height and area, set forth in Chapter 5, are directly related to the occupancies it houses and its type of construction. Chapter 5 also provides the various methods available to address conditions in which multiple uses or occupancies occur within the same building. Chapter 4 contains special detailed requirements based on unique conditions or uses that are found in some buildings. ■

303.1.3

Assembly Rooms Associated with Group E Occupancies

303.3

Occupancy Classification of Casino Gaming Floors

303.3, 306.2

Occupancy Classification of Commercial Kitchens

TABLE 307.1(1), SECTION 307.4

Facilities Generating Combustible Dusts

308.5

Institutional Group I-3 Occupancies

403.3, 403.5

High-Rise Buildings—Fire and Smoke Protection

403.6.1

High-Rise Buildings—Fire Service Access Elevators

406.4

Public Parking Garages

406.5.2.1

Open Parking Garages—Openings below Grade

407, 408

Group I-3 Occupancies

410.6.3, 202

Technical Production Areas

412.4.6.2

Aircraft Hangar Fire Areas

420.7

Construction Waste Management for Group R Occupancies

503.1

Building Height and Area Limitations—Solar Photovoltaic Systems

505.2.2

Mezzanine Means of Egress

507.1

Unlimited Area Buildings—Accessory Occupancies

509

Incidental Uses—General Provisions

509

Incidental Uses—Separation and Protection

TABLE 509

Incidental Uses—Rooms or Areas

602.1

Fire-Resistance Rating Requirements for Solar Photovoltaic Systems

303.1.3

Assembly Rooms Associated with Group E Occupancies

CHANGE TYPE: Clarification

CHANGE SUMMARY: The allowance for a Group E classification of accessory assembly spaces in school buildings has been clarified so as to not confuse the provision with the mixed-occupancies requirements dealing with accessory occupancies as regulated by Section 508.2.

2013 CODE: 303.1 Assembly Group A. Assembly Group A occupancy includes, among others, the use of a building or structure, or a portion thereof, for the gathering of persons for purposes such as civic, social, or religious functions; recreation; food or drink consumption; or awaiting transportation.

~~**Exceptions:**~~

~~**1.**~~ **303.1.1 Small Buildings and Tenant Spaces.** A building or tenant space used for assembly purposes with an *occupant load* of less than 50 persons shall be classified as a Group B occupancy.

~~**2.**~~ **303.1.2 Small Assembly Spaces.** The following rooms and spaces shall not be classified as Assembly occupancies:

1. A room or space used for assembly purposes with an *occupant load* of less than 50 persons and accessory to another occupancy shall be classified as a Group B occupancy or as part of that occupancy.

~~3.~~2. A room or space used for assembly purposes that is less than 750 square feet (70 m^2) in area and accessory to another occupancy shall be classified as a Group B occupancy or as part of that occupancy.

International Code Council®

High school gymnasium/auditorium.

~~4.~~ **303.1.3 Associated with Group E Occupancies.** ~~Assembly areas that are accessory to Group E occupancies are not considered separate occupancies except when applying the assembly occupancy requirements of Chapter 11.~~ A room or space used for assembly purposes that is associated with a Group E occupancy is not considered a separate occupancy.

~~5.~~ **303.1.4 Accessory to Places of Religious Worship.** Accessory religious educational rooms and religious auditoriums with occupant loads of less than 100 are not considered separate occupancies.

CHANGE SIGNIFICANCE: Where persons gather for civic, social, or religious functions; recreation; food or drink consumption; and similar activities, the function is considered "assembly" in nature. Classification as a Group A occupancy is typically warranted, unless the space is relatively small or the occupant load is relatively low. In addition, assembly spaces—such as gymnasiums and auditoriums—directly related to Group E educational occupancies are not generally classified as Group A occupancies but rather as simply portions of the Group E building. The allowance for the Group E classification of "accessory" assembly spaces in school buildings has been clarified by modifying the code to address "associated" assembly spaces so as to not confuse the provision with the mixed-occupancies requirements dealing with accessory occupancies as regulated by Section 508.2. The application of the provision continues to be appropriate to those assembly areas of school buildings—such as gymnasiums and auditoriums—that are primarily an extension of the educational function.

The reference to Chapter 11 was also removed as it was deemed unnecessary in the application of accessibility provisions as they apply to assembly areas. The accessibility requirements for fixed-seating facilities, dining areas, and other assembly seating areas are based on the general function of assembly activities and not tied to an occupancy classification. In addition, the assembly means of egress provisions of Section 1028 are also identified as applicable to assembly spaces within Group E occupancies. A number of other text changes were made throughout the code to focus on the use of the space for assembly purposes, rather than the occupancy classification.

303.3

Occupancy Classification of Casino Gaming Floors

CHANGE TYPE: Addition

CHANGE SUMMARY: The classification of a casino gaming floor is now specifically identified as a Group A-2 occupancy.

2013 CODE: **303.3 Assembly Group A-2.** Assembly uses intended for food and/or drink consumption including, but not limited to:

Banquet halls

Casinos (gaming areas)

Night clubs

Restaurants, cafeterias, and similar dining facilities (including associated commercial kitchens)

Taverns and bars

CHANGE SIGNIFICANCE: Assembly uses classified as Group A occupancies are further subclassified into one of five occupancy groups. Many assembly uses are specifically identified as to which classification they most typically belong through the listing of various uses found within each subclassification. Casino gaming floors have traditionally been considered as Group A occupancies where the occupant load is 50 or more persons; however, there has been disagreement over the specific classification of such uses as they previously have not been listed in the code. The classification of a casino gaming floor is now specifically identified as a Group A-2 occupancy.

Assigning an occupancy group to a casino gaming floor has varied due to the lack of any specific mention as to its proper classification. Although the degree of hazard has caused some to historically classify the use as a Group A-2 occupancy, the lack of a specific mention often resulted in applying the default provisions associated with Group A-3 occupancies. And although a casino gaming floor does not seem to fit into a classification reserved for food and/or drink consumption, it has been determined that there are similar hazard characteristics with other uses classified as Group A-2. There are distracting lights, sounds, decorations, and, in many

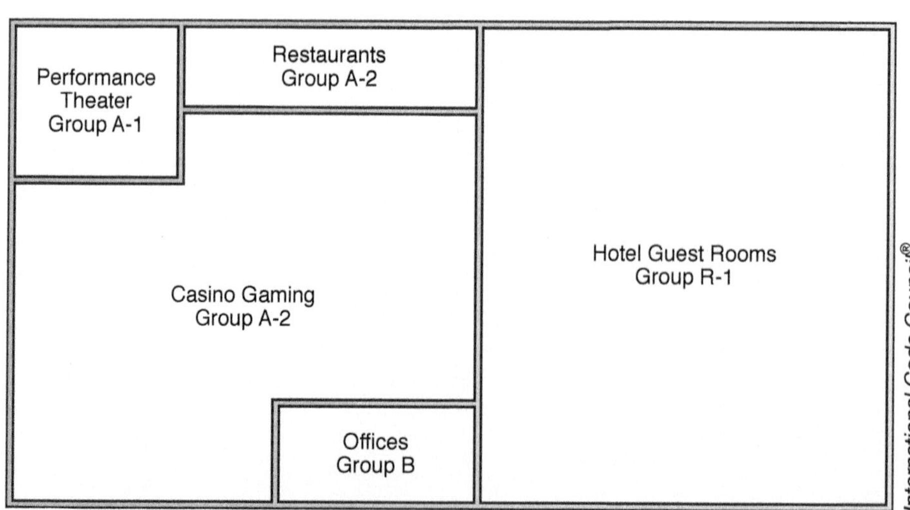

Classification of casino and related uses.

cases, alcoholic beverages are being consumed. Due to the various distractions, it is possible that the occupants will become disoriented and confused in an emergency situation and have difficulty locating the means of egress.

Classification of a casino gaming floor as a Group A-2 occupancy allows for application of the necessary provisions to address the expected hazards. It should be noted that small casino gaming facilities may be classified as Group B where they meet the conditions of Section 303.1.1 or 303.1.2. It is also important to note that the Group A-2 classification is limited to the gaming areas only. Other areas in a casino that may be associated with the gaming activities—such as restaurants, theaters, guest rooms, and administrative areas—are to be classified based upon their own individual function.

303.3, 306.2

Occupancy Classification of Commercial Kitchens

International Code Council®

Commercial kitchen.

CHANGE TYPE: Clarification

CHANGE SUMMARY: The appropriate occupancy classification of a commercial kitchen has been clarified based upon the kitchen's relationship, or lack of a relationship, to dining facilities.

2013 CODE: **303.3 Assembly Group A-2.** Assembly uses intended for food and/or drink consumption including, but not limited to:

Banquet halls
Casinos (gaming areas)
Night clubs
Restaurants, cafeterias, and similar dining facilities (including associated commercial kitchens)
Taverns and bars

306.2 Moderate-hazard Factory Industrial, Group F-1. Factory industrial uses which are not classified as Factory Industrial F-2 Low Hazard shall be classified as F-1 Moderate Hazard and shall include, but not be limited to, the following:

Food processing and commercial kitchens not associated with restaurants, cafeterias, and similar dining facilities.
(no changes to other uses on the list)

CHANGE SIGNIFICANCE: Commercial kitchens have historically been characterized as two different types, those that are directly associated with a restaurant or similar dining facility and those that are independent of any related dining area, such as a catering business. The appropriate occupancy classification of commercial kitchens has been clarified through text changes in three different areas of the code.

In Table 508.4 regulating separated occupancies, footnote d has been eliminated to help provide clarity to the classification of a commercial kitchen. The past presence of the footnote eliminating any required fire separation between a commercial kitchen and the restaurant seating area that it serves often led to a conclusion that the commercial kitchen needed to be classified differently than the associated dining area. It was occasionally assumed that if they were intended to both be classified as the same occupancy, that of the restaurant seating area, then there was no relevance to the footnote. However, common practice has always been to include the kitchen area as an extension of the restaurant seating area, causing both spaces to be considered as Group A-2, or Group B for smaller restaurants. In order to clarify the appropriate occupancy classification of the associated kitchen, the footnote has been deleted.

To further identify the classification of the two types of commercial kitchens, additional language has been added to the code listings of those uses classified as Group A-2 and Group F-1 occupancies. Commercial kitchens associated with restaurants, cafeterias, and similar dining facilities are now considered as a portion of the Group A-2 occupancies classification. Extending this concept, a kitchen associated with a small

Group B restaurant would simply be classified as a portion of the Group B occupancy. Although a commercial kitchen does not pose the same types of hazards as an assembly use, the allowance for a similar classification has generally been considered as an appropriate decision. Where the commercial kitchen is not associated with a dining facility, such as a catering business, the kitchen is to be classified as a Group F-1 occupancy in the same manner as any other food processing operations.

Table 307.1(1), Section 307.4

Facilities Generating Combustible Dusts

CHANGE TYPE: Modification

CHANGE SUMMARY: In the determination of occupancy classification for a facility where combustible dusts are anticipated, a technical report and opinion must now be provided to the building official that provides all necessary information for a qualified decision as to the potential combustible dusts hazard.

2013 CODE:

TABLE 307.1(1) Maximum Allowable Quantity Per Control Area of Hazardous Materials Posing a Physical Hazard

			Storage[b]			Use-Closed Systems[b]			Use-Open Systems[b]	
Material	Class	Group When the Maximum Allowable Quantity is Exceeded	Solid pounds (cubic feet)	Liquid gallons (pounds)	Gas cubic feet at NTP	Solid pounds (cubic feet)	Liquid gallons (pounds)	Gas cubic feet at NTP	Solid pounds (cubic feet)	Liquid gallons (pounds)
Combustible Dust	N/A	H-2	Note q	N/A	N/A	Note q	N/A	N/A	Note q	N/A

q. Where manufactured, generated or used in such a manner that the concentration and conditions create a fire or explosion hazard based on information prepared in accordance with Section 414.1.3.

(no changes to remainder of table and footnotes)

307.4 High-hazard Group H-2. Buildings and structures containing materials that pose a deflagration hazard or a hazard from accelerated burning shall be classified as Group H-2. Such materials shall include, but not be limited to, the following:

> Combustible dusts where manufactured, generated, or used in such a manner that the concentration and conditions create a fire or explosion hazard based on information prepared in accordance with Section 414.1.3.
>
> (no changes to other materials on list)

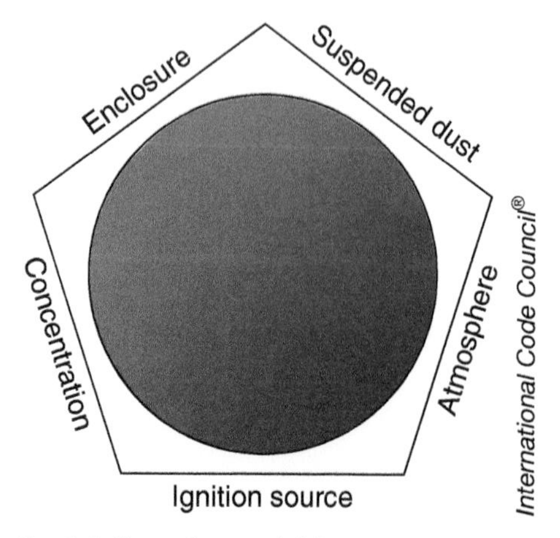

Dust deflagration variables.

CHANGE SIGNIFICANCE: Combustible dusts are considered as finely divided solid material that is less than 420 microns in diameter which, when dispersed in air in the proper proportions, could be ignited by a flame, spark, or other source of ignition. Examples include organic materials such as wheat flour or corn meal in a food manufacturing plant, pharmaceuticals, wood flour produced during sanding operations in a furniture manufacturing plant, or powdered plastics in a manufacturing environment. The hazard presented by uncontrolled combustible dusts is so great that classification as a Group H-2 occupancy occurs where the concentration and conditions under which the dusts are manufactured, generated, or used are such that a fire or explosion hazard is created. Reference is now made to Section 414.1.3, which requires a technical report and opinion be provided to the building official that provides all necessary information for a qualified decision as to the potential combustible dusts hazard.

A comprehensive discussion on the evaluation of combustible dusts hazards can be found in the *Significant Changes to the International Fire Code*, 2012 Edition, authored by Scott Stookey.

308.5

Institutional Group I-3 Occupancies

CHANGE TYPE: Addition/Modification

CHANGE SUMMARY: Definitions and conditions for secure interview rooms and temporary holding facilities have been added to the CBC as part of the California State Fire Marshal's Task Force recommendations for Group I-3 Occupancies.

2013 CODE: **~~308.4~~ 308.5 Institutional Group I-3.** This occupancy shall include buildings *or portions of buildings* and structures that are inhabited by *one or more persons* who are under restraint or security. An I-3 facility is occupied by persons who are generally incapable of self-preservation due to security measures not under the occupants' control, *which includes persons restrained.* This group shall include, but not be limited to, the following:

Correctional centers
Courthouse Holding Facility
Detention centers
Detention Treatment Room
Jails
Juvenile Halls
Prerelease centers
Prisons
Reformatories
Secure Interview Rooms
Temporary Holding Facility

Temporary holding cell.

Buildings of Group I-3 shall be classified as one of the occupancy conditions indicated in Sections ~~308.4.1~~ 308.5.1 through ~~308.4.5~~ 308.5.8 (see Section 408.1).

308.5.1 Condition 1 through 308.5.5 Condition 5. (No change to text)

308.5.6 Condition 6. *This occupancy condition shall include buildings containing only one temporary holding facility with five or less persons under restraint or security where the building is protected throughout with a monitored automatic sprinkler system installed in accordance with Section 903.3.1.1 and where the temporary holding facility is protected throughout with an automatic fire alarm system with notification appliances. A Condition 6 building shall be permitted to be classified as a Group B occupancy.*

308.5.7 Condition 7. *This occupancy condition shall include buildings containing only one temporary holding facility with nine or less persons under restraint or security where limited to the first or second story, provided the building complies with Section 408.1.2.6. A Condition 7 building shall be permitted to be classified as a Group B occupancy.*

308.5 continues

308.5 continued

308.5.8 Condition 8. *This occupancy condition shall include buildings containing not more than four secure interview rooms located within the same fire area where not more than six occupants under restraint are located in the same fire area. A Condition 8 building shall be permitted to be classified as a Group B occupancy, provided the requirements in Section 408.1.2.7 are met.*

CHANGE SIGNIFICANCE: These new occupancy classifications and conditions are necessary for two uses that currently are used in law enforcement buildings but do not meet the definitions of other conditions listed in the model code or CBC. These technically employ the use of restraint (locked doors) and therefore are I-3 occupancies, but fall well below the security and danger levels described in the other conditions. As temporary rooms for interviews or staging, which are continuously observed by law enforcement personnel, they should not be held to the type of restrictive construction required for other I-3 conditions. These newly defined uses should be allowed in sheriff's offices, police stations, border patrol buildings, FBI office, DEA, etc., which are B occupancies. The inclusion of a small number of lockable rooms which are under supervision should not require the entire building to meet I-3 conditions. The alternative would be to handcuff or shackle detainees to a desk or bench which would be more risk to life safety. These code additions allow CSA and the SFM to regulate a use which already is in practice. Since these requirements are in addition to the regulations in Section 1231, these specific definitions do not conflict with Section 1231.1. Section 1231.2.2 requires bunks for inmates held for more than 12 hours. Section 1231 may not apply to facilities operated by Federal law enforcement located in leased buildings such as those by the FBI or DEA and CBP and ICE.

403.3, 403.5

High-Rise Buildings—Fire and Smoke Protection

CHANGE TYPE: Modification

CHANGE SUMMARY: The code now requires the connection of the fire sprinkler system to a minimum of two combination standpipe system risers or sprinkler system risers on each floor for super high-rise structures to minimize the risk of sprinkler system failure on every floor of the building. For the water supply to fire pumps, connection to two separate water mains is no longer required for high-rise buildings that do not have an occupied floor more than 120 feet above the lowest level of fire department vehicle access. Redundant fire pump systems are required for high-rise buildings with an occupied floor more than 200 feet above the lowest level of fire department vehicle access. Smokeproof enclosures are no longer required for exit enclosures serving three or less adjacent floors where one of the floors is the level of exit discharge

2013 CODE: 403.3.1 Number of Sprinkler System Risers and System Design. Each sprinkler system ~~zone~~ serving a floor in buildings that are more than 420 feet (128 000 mm) in building height shall be ~~supplied by no fewer than~~ *connected to a minimum of* two *sprinkler* risers *or combination standpipe system risers located in separate shafts. Each sprinkler system shall be hydraulically designed so that when one connection is shut-down, the other connection shall be capable of supplying the sprinkler system design demand.* ~~Each riser shall supply sprinklers on alternate floors. If more than two risers are provided for a zone, sprinklers on adjacent floors shall not be supplied from the same riser.~~

403.3.1.1 Riser location. (No change to text)

Sprinkler riser room.

403.3.2 Water Supply to Required Fire Pumps. Required fire pumps shall be supplied by connections to a minimum of two water mains located in different streets. Separate supply piping shall be provided between each connection to the water main and the pumps. Each connection and the supply piping between the connection and the pumps

403.3, 403.5 continues

403.3, 403.5 continued

shall be sized to supply the flow and pressure required for the pumps to operate.

Exceptions:

1: Two connections to the same main shall be permitted provided the main is valved such that an interruption can be isolated so that the water supply will continue without interruption through at least one of the connections.

2: *High-rise buildings not having an occupied floor more than 120 feet above the lowest level of fire department vehicle access where a secondary water supply is provided in accordance with Section 903.3.5.2.*

403.3.2.1 Fire Pumps: *Redundant fire pump systems shall be required for high-rise buildings having an occupied floor more than 200 feet above the lowest level of fire department vehicle access. Each fire pump system shall be capable of automatically supplying the required demand for the automatic sprinkler and standpipe systems.*

403.3.3 Fire Pump Room Fire pumps shall be located in rooms protected in accordance with Section 913.2.1.

403.3.4 Fire Pumps. *See Section 913.6.*

403.5.4 Smokeproof Exit Enclosures. *Every exit enclosure in high-rise buildings shall comply with Sections 909.20 and 1022.9.* Every required level exit stairway in Group I-2 occupancies serving floors more than 75 feet (22 860 mm) above the lowest level of fire department vehicle access shall comply with Sections 909.20 and 1022.9.

Exception: *In high-rise buildings, exit enclosures serving three or less adjacent floors where one of the adjacent floors is the level of exit discharge.*

CHANGE SIGNIFICANCE: In the previous edition, Section 403.3.1 required the fire sprinkler system risers serving each floor of buildings taller than 420 feet in height to be supplied from one of the standpipe system risers located in each stair shaft. Additionally, it required that each standpipe system riser supply the sprinkler system on alternate floors. There were concerns that failure of either standpipe riser would impair the operation of the sprinkler systems on half the floors of the building.

SFM proposed this amendment to Section 403.3.1 requiring the connection of the fire sprinkler system to a minimum of two combination standpipe system risers or sprinkler system risers on each floor which will significantly minimize the risk of sprinkler system failure on every floor in super high-rise structures. The cost of this additional requirement is minimal for the significant increase in the enhanced level of reliability of the automatic sprinkler system.

SFM proposed the amendment to Section 403.3.2 because all high-rise buildings in California require a secondary on-site water supply (CBC 903.3.5.2). The additional reliability of connecting the sprinkler system supply to two separate water mains in different streets does not appear to be necessary for high-rise buildings under 120 feet in height that pose a

403.3, 403.5 continues

403.3, 403.5 continued

lesser risk than taller high-rise buildings. The 120-foot threshold for fire service access elevators and redundant fire pump systems was chosen. This amendment will result in significant construction cost savings for buildings in this category.

A new Section 403.3.2.1 has been added to require a redundant fire pump for buildings with an occupied floor more than 200 feet above the lowest level of fire department vehicle access. Initially the SFM High-rise Task Force proposed recommendations for 120 feet. However, during the Building Standards Commissions Code Advisory Committee hearing for the SFM rulemaking package, further study was requested to determine if the 120 feet should be revised to 200 or 225 feet. The SFM reviewed local enforcing agencies ordinances that require redundant fire pump systems for high-rise buildings and revised the height trigger to not place a more restrictive provision beyond what is currently implemented by local enforcing agencies.

The following are examples of several local enforcing agencies' requirements/triggers:

- Glendale: all high-rises
- Los Angeles City: 150 feet
- Orange County Fire Authority: 15 stories (approximately 135 feet to 195 feet)
- Sacramento: all high-rises
- San Francisco: 200 feet

Additionally, NFPA 20 – 2013 edition that is proposed to be adopted indicates that "most urban fire departments have the capability of getting sufficient water at sufficient pressure up to the top of a 200-foot tall building." (See Annex A, Section A.5.7.)

Furthermore, fire departments in most California cities are capable of providing water to that height through their pumping apparatus, which can conservatively supply 250 psi. 225 feet equates to roughly 150 psi including friction loss and static pressure, which would leave roughly 100 psi at the roof for hose streams, which complies with NFPA and CBC requirements. The 200 foot is chosen instead of 225 foot, as this is a little more conservative. This still allows individual cities to retain their existing ordinance for a lower trigger height.

The new Section 403.3.2.1 requires redundant fire pump systems for high-rise buildings having an occupied floor more than 200 feet above the lowest level of fire department vehicle access. This amendment intends to ensure that adequate water is available for the building automatic sprinkler system and the fire department standpipe system provided for the fire department to fight fires on upper floors of high-rise buildings that are greater than 200 feet tall (about 16 to 22 stories). This amendment also requires each fire pump system to independently serve the required design demands for both the automatic sprinkler and standpipe systems in the building.

The failure of a fire pump will significantly impair the water supply to the water-based fire protection systems in a building. In the case of a fire pump failure in buildings greater than 200 feet in height, the public water supply will most likely not be adequate to supply the automatic sprinkler and standpipe systems above that height. A redundant fire

403.3, 403.5 continues

pump system greatly increases the reliability of the water-based fire protection systems when any one of the fire pumps may be out of operation for repairs or maintenance or is otherwise inoperable or fails.

The SFM proposed the amendment to Section 403.5.4 to allow exit enclosures which serve three or less adjacent floors to be exempt from the smokeproof enclosure requirements where one of the floors is at the level of exit discharge. For example, a building with two basement levels and the lobby at grade level, or a building with a mezzanine and a second floor with a lobby at the level of exit discharge would qualify for this exception. One of the floors must be at the exit discharge level because it offers a higher degree of safety for means of egress.

Previously, all exit enclosures in a high-rise building were required to be smokeproof enclosures. This included an enclosed interior ramp on the ground level of the building, or an exit stair from the basement to the exterior with a door at the basement and the only other door discharging to the exterior. There is a minimum benefit in providing such enclosures as smokeproof. This modification to the existing language will result in significant construction cost savings and will not impact fire and life safety in high-rise buildings.

403.6.1

High-Rise Buildings—Fire Service Access Elevators

CHANGE TYPE: Modification

CHANGE SUMMARY: The minimum number of fire service access elevators required in applicable high-rise buildings has been increased from one to two where multiple elevators are provided in the building.

2013 CODE: 403.6.1 Fire Service Access Elevator. In buildings with an occupied floor more than 120 feet (36 576 mm) above the lowest level of fire department vehicle access, no fewer than ~~one~~ two fire service access elevators, or all elevators, whichever is less, shall be provided in accordance with Section 3007. Each fire service access elevator shall have a capacity of not less than 3500 pounds (1588 kg).

CHANGE SIGNIFICANCE: To facilitate the rapid deployment of firefighters, Section 403.6.1 of the 2010 CBC introduced a new requirement for a fire service access elevator in high-rise buildings that have at least one floor level more than 120 feet above the lowest level of fire department

403.6.1 continues

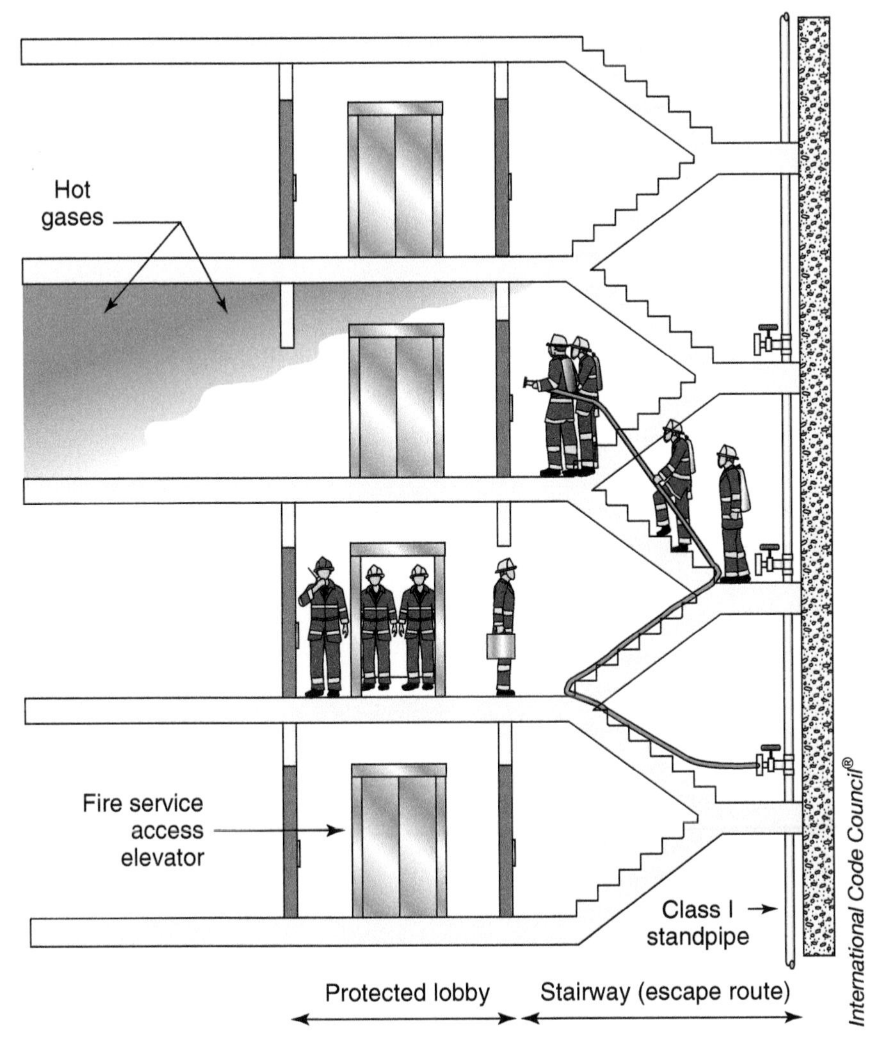

Fire service access elevator.

403.6.1 continued

vehicle access. Usable by firefighters and other emergency responders, the specific requirements for this type of elevator are set forth in Section 3007. A fire service access elevator has a number of key features that will allow firefighters to use the elevator for safely accessing an area of a building that may be involved in fire or for facilitating rescue of building occupants. The minimum number of fire service access elevators required in applicable high-rise buildings has been increased from one to two, except for those buildings that are provided with only a single elevator.

The mandate for a second fire service access elevator is based on information that indicates at least two elevators are necessary for firefighting activities in high-rise buildings. In addition, past experience has shown that on many occasions elevators are not available due to shutdowns for various reasons, including problems in operation, routine maintenance, modernization programs, and EMS operations in the building prior to firefighter arrival. A minimum of two fire service elevators provided with all of the benefits afforded to such elevators better ensures that there will be a fire service access elevator available for the firefighters' use in the performance of their duties.

406.4

Public Parking Garages

CHANGE TYPE: Clarification

CHANGE SUMMARY: Those parking structures that fall outside of the scope of Section 406.3 regulating private parking garages are now identified as public parking garages.

2013 CODE: **~~406.2.1 Classification~~ 406.4 Public Parking Garages.** Parking garages other than private parking garages, shall be classified as public parking garages and shall comply with the provisions of Sections 406.4.2 through 406.4.8 and shall be classified as either an open ~~as defined in Section 406.3,~~ parking garage or an enclosed parking garage ~~and shall meet appropriate criteria of Section 406.4~~. Open parking garages shall also comply with Section 406.5. Enclosed parking garages shall also comply with Section 406.6. ~~Also~~ See Section 510 for special provisions for parking garages. ***(DSA-AC & HCD 1-AC)*** *The clear height of vehicle and pedestrian areas required to be accessible shall comply with Chapter 11A or Chapter 11B, as applicable.*

CHANGE SIGNIFICANCE: Parking garages, as well as other types of structures where motor vehicles are involved, present some unique characteristics that are addressed through the special provisions of Section 406. The sizes and operations of parking garages vary significantly, and such differences are uniquely regulated. The varying requirements have now been reformatted to allow for the provisions to be more clearly applied to the correct situation. In addition, the descriptions of the various types of parking garages have been clarified for consistency purposes.

There are fundamentally two types of parking garages regulated by the CBC: private garages and public garages. Although there is no specific definition for either type of garage, the basis for both classifications is Section 406.3 addressing private garages and carports. Those parking structures that fall outside of the scope of Section 406.3 are now

406.4 continues

International Code Council®

Public parking garage.

406.4 continued considered as public parking garages. The primary difference between private and public garages is the size of the facility, rather than the use. Strictly limited in permissible height and area, private parking garages are typically not commercial in nature. They generally serve only a specific tenant or building and are not open for public use. It is important to note that there is no implication that public parking garages must be open to the public, as they are only considered public in comparison to private garages. A public parking garage is then further characterized as one of two types—either an enclosed parking garage or an open parking garage—and regulated accordingly.

406.5.2.1

Open Parking Garages—Openings below Grade

CHANGE TYPE: Addition

CHANGE SUMMARY: A clear horizontal space, whose minimum distance is based on the depth of the open parking garage's exterior wall openings, must now be provided adjacent to any such openings located below grade.

2013 CODE: **~~406.3.3.1~~ 406.5.2 Openings.** For natural ventilation purposes, the exterior side of the structure shall have uniformly distributed openings on two or more sides. The area of such openings in exterior walls on a tier shall be not less than 20 percent of the total perimeter wall area of each tier. The aggregate length of the openings considered to be providing natural ventilation shall be not less than 40 percent of the perimeter of the tier. Interior walls shall be not less than 20 percent open with uniformly distributed openings.

> **Exception:** Openings are not required to be distributed over 40 percent of the building perimeter where the required openings are uniformly distributed over two opposing sides of the building.

406.5.2.1 Openings below Grade. Where openings below grade provide required natural ventilation, the outside horizontal clear space shall be one and one-half times the depth of the opening. The width of the horizontal clear space shall be maintained from grade down to the bottom of the lowest required opening.

CHANGE SIGNIFICANCE: The overall fire hazards in a parking garage are relatively low. Because permanently open exterior walls provide sufficient natural ventilation and permit the dissipation of heated gases, open parking garages are viewed as an even lesser hazard because they do not need to rely on mechanical ventilation. As such, a number of code benefits are afforded to open parking garages, including increased allowable heights and areas. There are situations where the required exterior openings of open parking garages are located below the surrounding grade. Previously, no minimum exterior clearance has been mandated between the required openings and adjacent retaining walls or similar enclosures. This has resulted in conditions where the exterior openings were

406.5.2.1 continues

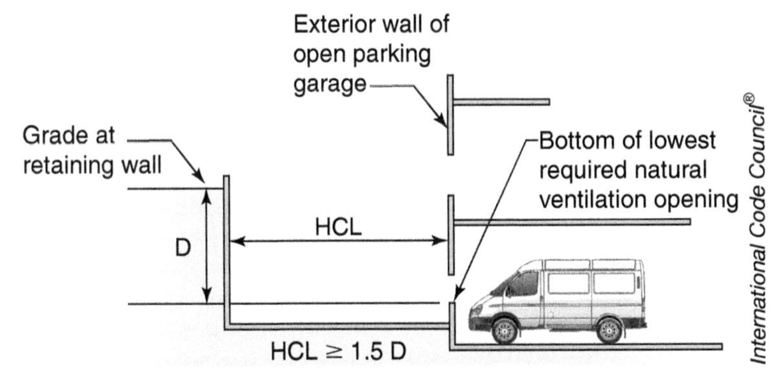

Parking garage openings below grade.

406.5.2.1 continued

relatively ineffective for ventilation purposes. A new provision mandates that a clear horizontal space be provided adjacent to the garage's exterior openings that allows for adequate air movement through the opening. The dimensional requirements are based upon the provisions of Section 1203.4.1.2, which address openings below grade when such openings are used for the required natural ventilation of a building's occupied spaces.

Where openings in the exterior wall of an open parking garage are located below grade level, some degree of clear space must be provided at the exterior of the openings. As the distance of the openings below the adjoining ground increases, the minimum required exterior clear space also increases proportionately. The horizontal clear space dimension, measured perpendicular to the exterior wall opening, must be at least one and one-half times the distance between the bottom of the opening and the adjoining ground level above. The extent of the required clear space allows for adequate exterior open space to meet the intent and dynamics of natural ventilation requirements for open parking garages.

CHANGE TYPE: Modification

407, 408

Group I-3 Occupancies

CHANGE SUMMARY: Changes to the fire-safety and egress provisions for Group I-3 occupancies are the result of the recommendations by the CA State Fire Marshal's Group I-3 Task Force. Fire resistance requirements are somewhat less restrictive and travel distances have increased for certain less hazardous areas, such as staff areas and temporary holding areas.

2013 CODE: 407.2.2 ~~Care providers~~' Nurses' Stations. Spaces for doctors' and nurses' charting, communications and related clerical areas shall be permitted to be open to, *or located within,* the corridor *provided the required construction along the perimeter of the corridor is maintained* ~~when such spaces are constructed as required for corridors~~. *Construction of nurses' stations or portions of nurses' stations, within the envelope of the corridor, is not required to be fire-resistive rated.* *Nurses' stations in new and existing facilities see the California Code of Regulations, Title 19, Division 1, Chapter 1, Subchapter 1, Article 3, Section 3.11(d) for storage and equipment requirements.*

In detention or secure mental health facilities, the provisions above apply to enclosed nurses' stations within the corridor.

407.3.1.1 Swing of Corridor Doors. *Corridor doors, other than those equipped with self-closing or automatic-closing devices, shall not swing into the required width of corridors.*

> ***Exception:*** *Doors may swing into required width of corridors in I-3 facilities as long as 44 inches clear is maintained with any one door open 90 degrees and clear corridor widths required in Chapter 12 can be maintained with doors open 180 degrees.*

Doors swinging into corridor.

~~**408.1.2.2 Cells with open bars.** In buildings protected throughout by an automatic sprinkler system and automatic fire detection system, corridor doors or walls of cells and dormitories, may be of open bars, perforated metal, grilles, or other similar construction.~~

408.1.2.2 Intervening Spaces. *Common rooms and spaces within Group I-3 occupancies can be considered an intervening space in accordance with Section 1014.2, and not considered a corridor, when they meet any of the following:*

1. *The inmate and/or staff movement within cell complexes, medical housing wings, and mental health housing wings of Type I construction.*
2. *Areas within any temporary holding area of non-combustible construction.*
3. *Areas within secure mental health treatment facilities of non-combustible construction.*

407, 408 continues

407, 408 continued

408.1.2.3 Courthouse Holding Facilities. *Group I-3 courthouse holding facilities shall be considered a separate and distinct building from the remaining courthouse building for the purpose of determining the type of construction where all of the following conditions are met:*

1. *2-hour fire barriers in accordance with Section 707 and 2-hour horizontal assemblies in accordance with Section 711 are provided to separate the courthouse holding facility from all other portions of the courthouse building.*

2. *Any of the structure used to support courthouse holding facilities meets the requirements for the Group I-3 portion of the building.*

3. *Each courthouse holding facility located above the first story is less than 1,000 square feet in area, and is designed to hold 10 or less in-custody defendants.*

4. *Courthouse holding facilities located above the first story containing an internal stairway discharging to the main courthouse holding facility at the first story or basement.*

5. *Additional exits from the courthouse holding facility located above the first story shall be permitted to exit through the courtrooms.*

6. *The main courthouse holding facility located on the first story or basement has at least one exit directly to the exterior and additional means of egress shall be permitted to pass through a 1-hour corridor or lobby in the courthouse building.*

408.1.2.4 Horizontal Building Separation for Combined Group I-3/ Group B Occupancy.

A Group B Administration building one story in height shall be permitted to be located above a Group I-3 (or Group I-3/I-2) housing/treatment building which is one story above grade and shall be classified as a separate and distinct building for the purpose of determining the type of construction, and shall be considered a separate fire area, where all of the following conditions are met:

1. *A 3-hour floor-ceiling assembly below the administration building is constructed as a horizontal assembly in accordance with Section 711.*

2. *Interior shafts for stairs, elevators, and mechanical systems complete the 3-hour separation between the Group B and Group I-3 (or Group I-3/I-2).*

3. *The Group I-3 occupancy (or Group I-3/I-2occupancies, correctional medical and mental health uses) below is minimum Type I-B construction with 2-hour fire-resistive-rated exterior walls.*

4. *No unprotected openings are allowed in lower roofs within 10 feet of unprotected windows in the upper floor.*

5. *The Group B building above is of non-combustible construction and equipped throughout with an approved automatic sprinkler system in accordance with Section 903.3.1.1.*

6. *The Group B occupancy building above has all required means of egress capable of discharging directly to the exterior to a safe dispersal area.*

408.1.2.5 Temporary Holding Area. *In buildings protected with automatic sprinklers, corridors serving temporary holding rooms shall be 1-hour fire-resistance rated when the temporary holding occupant load is greater than 20.*

408.1.2.6 Temporary Holding Facilities. *Temporary holding facilities with nine or fewer persons under restraint may be classified as Group B when located in a building complying with all of the following conditions:*

1. *The building shall be protected throughout with a monitored automatic sprinkler system installed in accordance with Section 903.3.1.1.*

2. *The building shall protected with a automatic fire alarm system with notification appliances throughout the holding facility in accordance with Section 907.2.*

3. *The building shall be constructed of Type I, IIA, IIIA or VA construction.*

408.1.2.7 Secure Interview Rooms. *Secure interview rooms used for law enforcement shall be permitted to be locked, and shall not be classified as Group I-3 occupancies where all of the following conditions are met:*

1. *A monitored automatic sprinkler system shall be provided throughout buildings and portions thereof including secure interview rooms. The automatic sprinkler system shall comply with Section 903.1.1.*

2. *Secure interview rooms shall be located in non-combustible construction.*

3. *Secure interview rooms shall have glazed or barred openings with direct, continuous observation from law enforcement personnel who have a means to open the secure interview room.*

4. *Not more than six occupants in secure interview rooms shall be located in the same fire area.*

407, 408 continues

407, 408 continues

5. *An automatic smoke detection system shall be installed within secure interview rooms and mechanical and electrical rooms.*

408.2 Other Occupancies. (No change to text)

Exceptions:

1. and 2. (No change to text)

3. *For the purpose of occupancy separation only ~~prisoner docks~~ courtroom docks that are directly accessory to courtrooms need not be separated from a courtroom.*

408.2.1 Correctional Medical and Mental Health Uses. *Where a Group I-2 occupancy in accordance with Section 308.4 and a Group I-3 occupancy occur together in buildings or portions of buildings, the following sections of 407 shall apply: 407.2.1; 407.2.2; 407.2.3; 407.3.1; 407.3.1.1; 407.4; 407.10.2.*

408.3.10 Travel Distance. *The travel distance may be increased to 300 feet for portions of Group I-3 occupancies open only to staff or where inmates are escorted at all times by staff.*

408.3.11 Number of Exits Required. *In temporary holding areas of noncombustible construction, a second means of egress is required when the occupant load is greater than 20.*

408.6.1 Smoke Compartments. The maximum number of residents in any smoke compartment shall be 200. The travel distance to a door in a smoke barrier from any room door required as exit access shall not exceed 150 feet (45 720 mm). The travel distance to a door in a smoke barrier from any point in a room shall not exceed 200 feet (60 960 mm).

Exception: *The travel distance may be increased by 50 feet from areas open only to the staff.*

408.9 Windowless Buildings. For the purposes of this section, a windowless building or portion of a building is one with nonopenable windows, windows not readily breakable or without windows. ~~Windowless buildings shall be provided with an engineered smoke control system to provide a tenable environment for exiting from the smoke compartment in the area of fire origin in accordance with Section 909 for each windowless smoke compartment.~~

408.9.1 Smoke Venting. *Windowless buildings containing use conditions 3, 4 or 5 shall be provided with an engineered smoke control system in accordance with Section 909, windows or doors, smoke vents, or equivalent means to provide a tenable environment for exiting from the smoke compartment in the area of fire origin. If windows or doors are used to meet this section at least two windows or doors to the exterior must be* *provided at or above the highest occupied level in each smoke compartment, and the windows or doors must be operable or readily breakable and arranged to manually vent smoke.*

Exceptions:

1. *Local adult detention facilities, CDCR, and CDCR mental health housing facilities shall be exempt from this section when they meet each of the following criteria:*
   1.1. *Are Type I-B or I-A construction.*
   1.2. *Are protected with sprinklers throughout in accordance with Section 903.1.1.*
   1.3. *Include a fire alarm system with smoke detection in accordance with NFPA 72 in the dayroom and/or corridor serving as exit access from the cells, reporting to a 24 hour central control at the institution.*
   1.4. *Include at least one exit from each housing unit that discharges directly to the exterior.*
   1.5. *The building is divided into at least two smoke compartments per Section 408.6.1.*
   1.6. *Staffing in the institution is sufficient to evacuate inmates from the smoke compartment 24 hours per day, as approved by the Enforcing Agency or the facility is provided with gang or electric locks.*

2. *No venting or smoke control is required when an engineering analysis shows an acceptable safe egress time compared to the onset of untenable conditions within a windowless building or portion of a windowless building and approved by the enforcing agency.*

CHANGE SIGNIFICANCE: In Group I-3 occupancies where glazing separates nurses' stations from the corridor due to security requirements, the addition of glazing should not require the walls surrounding such a nurses' station (which may be located entirely within a rated corridor) to be rated. Section 407.2.2 does not require fire-resistant-rated walls and glazing enclosing a nurses' station within a corridor of a secure facility.

Section 407.3.1.1 provides challenges for doors in detention and secure mental health facilities for the following reasons:

- closers are not safe in secure environments
- doors must swing out of rooms (to avoid the potential for barricades)
- doors should not be located in alcoves (to maximize visual control)
- Section 1227.5.1 requires 8'-0" clear corridors

Inmates are moved one at a time in these secure facilities eliminating the possibility of bed movement conflicting with others in the corridor and it is appropriate to ease the requirements for 8-foot corridors.

Section 1018 requires a corridor whenever the occupant load is 6 or more. This does not consider the concept of intervening spaces. Table 1018 references Section 408.1.2.2 which which now clarifies that common areas are not considered a corridor. This is consistent with Group B

407, 408 continues

407, 408 continues

occupancies with open areas containing cubicle work stations without establishing a corridor. Likewise, corridors should not automatically be required in I-3 occupancies when the occupant load is greater than 6. Just like dayroom space in cells is not required to be rated (the dayroom is essentially an intervening space) circulation in housing wings should not be required to be rated which is why open barred fronts are allowed. As long as there is a clear and discernable path to an exit, the circulation should be considered an intervening space until it discharges into a collector corridor or leads to the exterior.

For small courthouses, construction type is driven by the Group I-3 occupancy, which typically only occupies less than 10 percent of the overall area of the building. It is unreasonable to require a very small portion of the building to dictate the construction of the entire building, and as good stewards of public monies, we should allow for exceptions for courthouse facilities. This change to Section 408.1.2.3 still requires the I-3 portion to be constructed in a manner consistent with what is required for that occupancy.

Administration space and inmate treatment space have different building requirements and ideally would be constructed next to one another. But space limitations are requiring them to be stacked. Administration areas above Type I detention occupancies (similar to podium construction), when separated by 3-hour horizontal construction, are now allowed by Section 408.1.2.4 to be of less restrictive construction provided independent free egress is allowed for the administration area. This arrangement provides a higher degree of fire and life safety than requiring the administration area to fall within the I-3 requirements and exit into locked portions of the building below. This configuration provides separate and distinct emergency egress for non law enforcement support and professional staff, improving egress times and allows correctional staff to focus on inmate evacuation.

There is a difference in fire risk between temporary holding rooms where persons are kept for less than 24 hours, and housing cells where persons sleep overnight or reside. The change to Section 408.1.2.5 differentiates the level of protection based on this distinction. Temporary holding rooms, including courthouse holding areas, have far less combustible content and sources of ignition and should not be held to the same restrictions as I-3 sleeping areas. Occupants of these spaces are there for limited periods of time. These spaces impose lower risk than housing units because occupants cannot accumulate or store combustibles. Temporary holding area is generally an incidental use that is provided with a 2-hour occupancy separation as required by the code. Therefore, a fire-resistance rating is not necessary for corridors serving a temporary holding occupancy with an occupant load of 20 or less due to the presence of lower fire load, incidental use, supervision, and occupancy separation.

The code change to Section 408.1.2.6 addresses temporary holding facilities that include up to 9 restrained occupants within the building such as may occur at ports of entry into the United States, police substations and certain court facilities. Since no sleeping will occur, smoke control should not be required. Furthermore requiring non-combustible fire-resistive construction throughout is overly restrictive. Requiring at least fire-resistant construction will allow locations on the second floor. The requirements allow for a level of defend-in-place protection as is assumed in most institutional occupancies and provides for notification, fire suppression and construction. The limited number of restrained supervised individuals will allow for timely evacuation of individual detainees held by members of law enforcement. While not limiting the number of rooms and restrained persons in a building, this change limits the number of restrained occupants in fire areas and therefore requires fire barriers and horizontal assemblies to include more than 6 restrained occupants or 4 interview rooms in a temporary holding facility.

To achieve court mandates, California is tasked with constructing sub-acute medical and mental health care facilities (I-2 occupancies) for patient-inmates within the California state prison system (I-3 occupancies). The revision to Section 408.2.1 clarifies the specific provisions that are necessary to facilitate inmate care while maintaining a secure environment.

The change to Section 408.3.10 permits staff areas such as storage, control rooms, tunnels and officer areas to have a 300-foot travel distance, similar to Group B office areas. Section 408.3.11 permits a single means of egress to serve up to 20 occupants in temporary holding areas. Other Group I-3 occupancies set the threshold at 10 occupants.

Staff areas in Group I-3 occupancies such as storage, control rooms, tunnels and officer areas have a similar or smaller fire load than Group B office areas which are permitted a greater travel distance. The increase of 50 feet for travel distance in Section 408.6.1 recognizes that staff in an institution should be moving at faster speeds than the average person and can travel the extra 50 feet safely.

Section 408.9 now provides exceptions to the smoke control requirements based on a number of specific conditions. Operable windows pose a security threat in Group I occupancies and provide limited benefits to fire and life safety because they must be manually operated. However, there is a need to address the tenability of areas where inmates might be asleep and their escape is delayed by the need to unlock their cells. The new language clarifies the intent of code by limiting the requirement to overnight sleeping areas where inmates are locked in their cells, and provides exceptions for commonly built housing types.

410.6.3, 202

Technical Production Areas

Technical production area.
(© iStockphoto/hsvrs)

CHANGE TYPE: Clarification

CHANGE SUMMARY: Outdated terminology, such as fly galleries, gridirons, and pinrails, has been replaced by the general and comprehensive term "technical production area," and the special means of egress provisions for such areas have all been relocated to Section 410.

2013 CODE:

SECTION 410
STAGES, ~~AND~~ PLATFORMS, AND TECHNICAL PRODUCTION AREAS

410.2 Definitions. The following ~~words and~~ terms ~~shall, for the purposes of this section and as used elsewhere in this code, have the meanings shown herein~~ are defined in Chapter 2:

~~**FLY GALLERY.** A raised floor area above a stage from which the movement of scenery and operation of other stage effects are controlled.~~

~~**GRIDIRON.** The structural framing over a stage supporting equipment for hanging or flying scenery and other stage effects.~~

~~**PINRAIL.** A rail on or above a stage through which belaying pins are inserted and to which lines are fastened.~~

PLATFORM (definition moved to Chapter 2 with no change)

PROSCENIUM WALL (definition moved to Chapter 2 with no change)

STAGE (definition moved to Chapter 2 with no change)

TECHNICAL PRODUCTION AREA

202 Definitions. TECHNICAL PRODUCTION AREA. Open elevated areas or spaces intended for entertainment technicians to walk on and occupy for servicing and operating entertainment technology systems and equipment. Galleries, including fly and lighting galleries, gridirons, catwalks, and similar areas are designed for these purposes.

410.6.3 Technical Production Areas. Technical production areas shall be provided with means of egress and means of escape in accordance with Sections 410.6.3.1 through 410.6.3.5.

410.6.3.1 Means of Egress. No fewer than one means of egress shall be provided from technical production areas.

410.6.3.2 Travel Distance. The length of exit access travel shall be not greater than 300 feet (91 440 mm) for buildings without a sprinkler system and 400 feet (121 900 mm) for buildings equipped throughout with an automatic sprinkler system in accordance with Section 903.3.1.1.

410.6.3.3 Two Means of Egress. Where two means of egress are required the common path of travel shall be not greater than 100 feet (30 480 mm).

> **Exception:** A means of escape to a roof in place of a second means of egress is permitted.

410.6.3.4 Path of Egress Travel. The following exit access components are permitted when serving technical production areas:

1. Stairways
2. Ramps
3. Spiral stairways
4. Catwalks
5. Alternating tread devices
6. Permanent ladders

410.6.3.5 Width. The path of egress travel within and from technical support areas shall be a minimum of 22 inches (559 mm).

CHANGE SIGNIFICANCE: Many auditoriums and performance halls, as well as other types of entertainment and sports venues, are provided with elevated technical support areas used for lighting, sound, scenery, and other performance effects. Such areas may or may not be associated with a stage but are typically an integral part of the production. These spaces are generally limited in floor area, and access is always restricted to authorized personnel. Special means of egress provisions have always been provided that recognize the uniqueness of these areas. In the establishment of these means of egress requirements, outdated terminology—such as fly galleries and gridirons—has now been replaced by the general and comprehensive term "technical production area." In addition, the special means of egress provisions for such areas have all been relocated to Section 410 and revised to eliminate any conflict with Chapter 10.

The new term "technical production areas" is intended to encompass all technical support areas, regardless of their traditional name. These areas are typically used to support entertainment technology from above the performance area. As a result of the new comprehensive definition, the defined terms of "fly gallery" and "gridiron" have been deleted. In addition, the title of Section 410 has been revised to "Stages, Platforms, and Technical Production Areas" in order to recognize that these areas may not necessarily be associated with a stage or platform, such as at sports arenas, and may be considered as stand-alone building elements.

Means of egress provisions relating specifically to technical production areas have previously been located in both Section 410 and in Chapter 10. In addition, the provisions were in conflict with one another and inconsistent in terminology. All of the means of egress requirements relating to technical production areas that modify the general provisions of Chapter 10 are now located in Section 410.6.3. The provisions reflect the special allowances for minimum number of means of egress, maximum travel distance, allowable exit access components, and minimum travel path width.

410.6.3, 202 continues

410.6.3, 202 continued

A related modification was made to the minimum required number of exits or exit access doorways required from a stage. Previously, a minimum of one means of egress was required from each side of the stage. This requirement is now only applicable where two or more exits or exit access doorways are required by Section 1015.1 based upon occupant load and common path of egress travel. It was determined that a stage was no different from other spaces in the building regarding the threshold at which two means of egress are required.

412.4.6.2

Aircraft Hangar Fire Areas

CHANGE TYPE: Modification

CHANGE SUMMARY: Spaces ancillary to the aircraft servicing and storage areas of an aircraft hangar need no longer be included in the fire area size when determining fire suppression requirements.

2013 CODE: 412.4.6.2 Separation of Maximum Single Fire Areas. Maximum single fire areas established in accordance with hangar classification and construction type in Table 412.4.6 shall be separated by 2-hour fire walls constructed in accordance with Section 706. In determining the maximum single fire area as set forth in Table 412.4.6, ancillary uses which are separated from aircraft servicing areas by a fire barrier of not less than one hour, constructed in accordance with Section 707 shall not be included in the area.

CHANGE SIGNIFICANCE: In order to minimize the fire hazards associated with aircraft hangars, fire suppression is required based upon the criteria of Table 412.4.6. The table determines the hangar classification (Group I, II, or III) to which the fire suppression must be designed in accordance with NFPA 409, *Aircraft Hangars*. The classification is based upon the hangar's type of construction and fire area size. Fire area size is based on the aggregate floor area bounded by specified fire walls that have a minimum 2-hour fire-resistance rating. For the purposes of hangar classification, ancillary uses located within the fire area are no longer required to be included in the fire area size provided they are separated from the aircraft serving area by minimum 1-hour fire barriers.

Many times there are ancillary areas associated with an aircraft hangar, such as offices, maintenance shops, and storage rooms. Unless located in a fire area different from that of the aircraft storage and servicing area, the floor area of such ancillary areas has previously been included in the hangar fire area and included in the application of Table 412.4.6. Because the fire suppression requirements of NFPA 409 are primarily for the protection of aircraft within the storage and servicing

412.4.6.2 continued

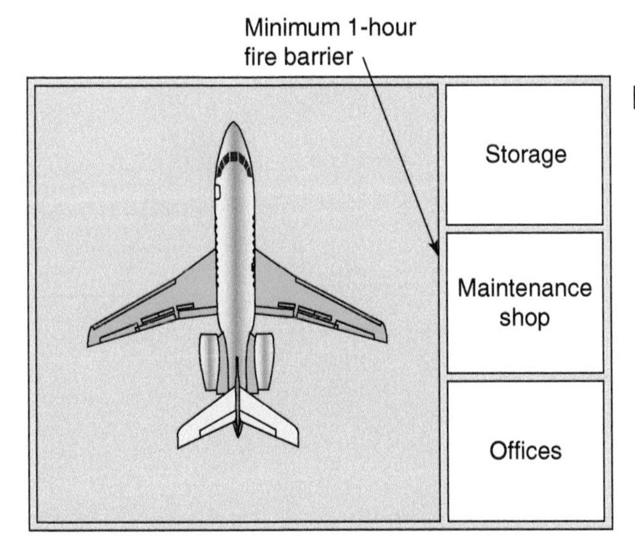

Aircraft hangar fire area.

412.4.6.2 continued

area, inclusion of the floor area of the ancillary spaces into the fire suppression criteria was thought to be inappropriate. The fire protection requirements in the ancillary areas are considered to be less extensive than those required for the aircraft servicing and storage areas. Therefore, their inclusion in the application of Table 412.4.6 for fire area size has been eliminated where a limited degree of fire separation is provided.

In order to be exempted from the fire area calculation within the aircraft hangar, it is necessary that the ancillary areas be separated from the aircraft storage and servicing areas by minimum 1-hour fire barriers. The 1-hour requirement intends to provide an acceptable fire separation without the creation of additional fire areas that would require separation by minimum 2-hour fire walls.

420.7

Construction Waste Management for Group R Occupancies

CHANGE TYPE: Addition

CHANGE SUMMARY: The CALGreen requirements for construction waste reduction for Group R residential occupancies are now included in the CBC.

2013 CODE: **420.1 General.** Occupancies in Groups R-1, R-2, R-2.1, R-3, R-3.1 and R-4 shall comply with the provisions of this section and other applicable provisions of this code.

420.7 (HCD 1) Construction Waste Management. *Recycle and/or salvage for reuse a minimum of 50 percent of the nonhazardous construction and demolition waste in accordance with the California Green Building Code (CALGreen), Chapter 4, Division 4.4.*

Material waste on jobsite.

CHANGE SIGNIFICANCE: HCD has included pointers to mandatory CALGreen Code requirements in this code to enhance user convenience and familiarity. These mandatory pointers are excerpts to code sections in CALGreen. Users should consult the actual code text in CALGreen for complete requirements.

Construction waste makes up approximately 27 percent of all waste in landfills. The provisions of Section 420.7 intend to reduce that amount and encourage material efficiency during the construction process for Group R residential buildings.

503.1

Building Height and Area Limitations—Solar Photovoltaic Systems

CHANGE TYPE: Addition

CHANGE SUMMARY: With certain limitations, solar photovoltaic systems are permitted to exceed the height limitations in Table 503 and are not counted as an additional story or floor area.

2013 CODE: **503.1 General.** The building height and area shall not exceed the limits specified in Table 503 based on the type of construction as determined by Section 602 and the occupancies as determined by Section 302 except as modified hereafter. Each portion of a building separated by one or more fire walls complying with Section 706 shall be considered to be a separate building.

Solar PV panels.

Exceptions:

1. [HCD 1] Limited-density owner-built rural dwellings may be of any type of construction which will provide for a sound structural condition. Structural hazards which result in an unsound condition and which may constitute a substandard building are delineated by Section 17920.3 of the Health and Safety Code.

2. Other than structural requirements, solar photovoltaic panels supported by a structure with no use underneath shall not constitute additional story or additional floor area and may exceed the height limit when constructed on a roof top of a building provided the following conditions are met:

1.1. For all occupancies, the highest point of the structure/panel shall meet the lower of the two values below:

1. 3 feet above the allowable building height per this code.

2. 3 feet above the roof of the building immediately below.

2.1. For installations on flat roofs in other than Group R-3 and R-4 occupancies, the highest point of the structure/panel shall meet the lower of the two values below:

1. *10 feet above the allowable building height per this code.*
2. *10 feet above the roof of the building immediately below.*
3. *Other than structural requirements, solar photovoltaic panels supported by a structure over parking stalls shall not constitute additional story or additional floor area and may exceed the height limit as specified in Exception 2 (above) when the following conditions are met (see Figure 5-1):*
   1. *The area within the perimeter of the photovoltaic array has a maximum rectangular dimension of 40 feet by 150 feet.*
   2. *The distance between solar photovoltaic array structures is a minimum of 10 feet clear.*
   3. *The driveway aisle separating solar photovoltaic array structures has a minimum width of 25 feet clear.*
   4. *Solar photovoltaic array structure is used only for parking purposes with no storage.*
   5. *Completely open on all sides (other than necessary structural supports) with no interior partitions.*

CHANGE SIGNIFICANCE: Previously, rooftop solar structures were occasionally interpreted as creating an additional story of the building, as an increase to the overall building height or as an increase to the floor area of the building (when there was a use underneath such as solar carports). As a result, solar installations might not have been allowed in buildings that were built to the maximum height, story or floor area. The code revision provides exemptions for photovoltaic systems from these code restrictions.

The new Exception 2 allows solar PV systems to be installed above the maximum building height specified by Table 503 with certain limitations. This circumstance is especially common in existing buildings. The added height also makes it practical for PV panels to be installed above the roof with the required tilt angle and be at a height that avoids interference with vents and equipment on the roof.

The new Exception 3 allows solar PV panel installations over parking stalls to be installed without being considered a story or floor area. The previous provisions were sometimes interpreted as prohibiting solar PV systems from being installed on buildings that had the maximum number of stories or floor area, which is especially common in existing buildings. The exception requires minimum spacing between solar PV panel structures to allow fire access and provide a fire break.

505.2.2

Mezzanine Means of Egress

CHANGE TYPE: Modification

CHANGE SUMMARY: The specific provisions for mezzanine means of egress have been deleted and replaced with a general reference to Chapter 10.

2013 CODE: ~~**505.3**~~ **505.2.2.** The means of egress for mezzanines shall comply with the applicable provisions of Chapter 10. ~~Each occupant of a mezzanine shall have access to at least two independent means of egress where the common path of egress travel exceeds the limitations of Section 1014.3. Where an unenclosed stairway provides a means of exit access from a mezzanine, the maximum travel distance includes the distance traveled on the stairway measured in the plane of the tread nosing. Accessible means of egress shall be provided in accordance with Section 1007.~~

> **Exception:** ~~A single means of egress shall be permitted in accordance with Section 1015.1.~~

CHANGE SIGNIFICANCE: Defined as "an intermediate level or levels between the floor and ceiling of any story," a mezzanine must also comply with the special conditions established in Section 505. By virtue of the conditions placed on such elevated floor levels, a mezzanine is not considered to create additional building area or an additional story for the purpose of limiting building size. In addition, a relaxation of the means of egress requirements has previously been granted in regard to the minimum required number of independent egress paths from the mezzanine. This special allowance for mezzanine means of egress has been deleted and the provisions have been replaced with a general reference to Chapter 10. As a result, the means of egress requirements for a mezzanine are consistent

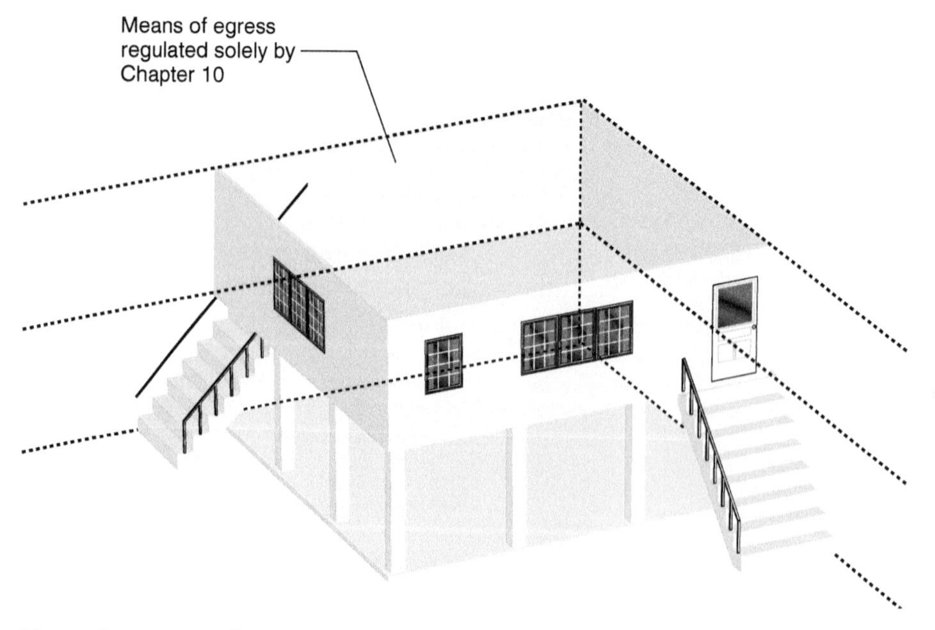

Mezzanine means of egress.

with those for other portions of the building regulated as the exit access. The consideration of an elevated floor level as a mezzanine no longer provides any special allowances for means of egress purposes.

The inclusion of specific mezzanine means of egress provisions caused inconsistent application in two ways. One, the incomplete statement of certain means of egress design requirements erroneously alluded to the notion that any provisions that were not stated did not apply. The new reference to Chapter 10 clarifies that mezzanines must comply with the general means of egress provisions as applicable. Secondly, the provision addressing required access to at least two means of egress did not indicate required compliance with the occupant load limitations of Table 1015.1. It was often assumed that a single means of egress was permitted as long as the common path of egress travel was compliant, regardless of the mezzanine's occupant load. This confusion has also been addressed through the blanket reference to Chapter 10.

507.1

Unlimited Area Buildings—Accessory Occupancies

CHANGE TYPE: Clarification

CHANGE SUMMARY: The allowance for occupancy groups not specifically scoped under the unlimited area building provisions of Section 507 to be located in such buildings under the accessory occupancies provisions of Section 508.2 is now contained within the code text.

Example:

Given: A 120,000 square-foot retail sales building housing a 1,080 square foot cafe with an occupant load of 72 persons. The building is fully sprinklered, is of Type IIB construction, and qualifies for unlimited area under the provisions of Section 507.

Determine: How the accessory occupancy provisions of Section 508.2 are applicable to the unlimited building provisions of Section 507.

1. Is the accessory occupancy subsidiary to the building's major occupancy?

   Yes, the cafe is intended as an extension of the sales function if they are part of the same tenant.

2. Is the accessory occupancy no more than 10% of the floor area of the story?

   Yes, 10% of 120,000 sq. ft. = 12,000 sq. ft. maximum; the cafe is 1,080 sq. ft.

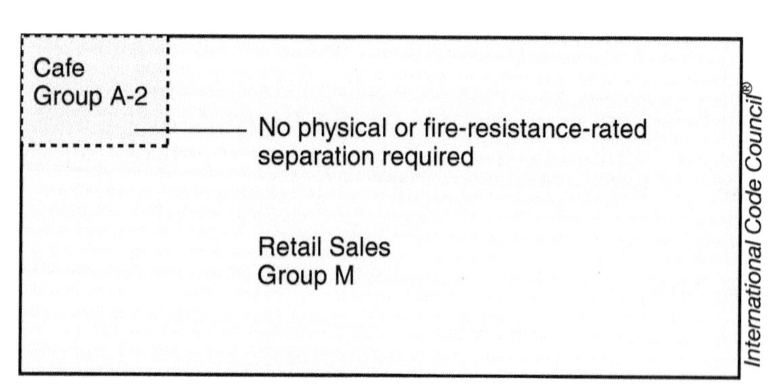

Accessory occupancy in unlimited area building.

3. Is the accessory occupancy no larger than the tabular values in Table 503?

   Yes, the tabular value for a Group A-2 of IIB construction is 9500 sq. ft.; the cafe is 1,080 sq. ft.

4. What is the occupancy classification of the cafe?

   Group A-2, based on the individual classification of the use.

5. How are the other requirements of the IBC applied?

   The provisions for each occupancy are applied to only that specific occupancy.

6. What is the allowable height and area of the building?

   The building's allowable height and area are based on the major occupancy involved, in this case it is Group M. Based upon the criteria of Section 507, the building is permitted to be unlimited in area and limited to two stories in height.

7. What is the allowable height for the lunchroom?

   Two stories, based on Table 503 for Group A-2 in a Type IIB building.

8. What is the minimum required separation between the cafe and the manufacturing area?

   There is no fire-resistive or physical separation required due to compliance with the provisions of Section 508.2 for accessory occupancies.

2013 CODE: **507.1 General.** The area of buildings of the occupancies and configurations specified ~~here~~in Sections 507.1 through 507.12 shall not be limited.

> **Exception:** Other occupancies shall be permitted in unlimited area buildings in accordance with the provisions of Section 508.2.

CHANGE SIGNIFICANCE: In other than Type I construction, buildings are typically limited in allowable floor area based on occupancy classification and type of construction. However, Section 507 permits a variety of buildings to be unlimited in floor area where specified safeguards are present. Historically, structures constructed under the provisions for unlimited area buildings have performed quite well in regard to fire and life safety. In general, only those occupancies and configurations that are specifically identified in Section 507 are subject to the unlimited area allowance. A commonly applied method of allowing occupancy groups not specifically mentioned in Section 507 to be located in such buildings under the accessory occupancies provisions of Section 508.2 is now contained within the code text.

As an example, Group I occupancies are not mentioned in Section 507 as an occupancy group permitted to use the unlimited area building allowance. If the Group I complies with the provisions of Section 508.2 as an accessory occupancy, it is permitted to be located in an unlimited area building complying with Section 507. The basis for this allowance is found in Section 508.2.3 which indicates that the allowable area for an accessory occupancy is to be based upon the allowable area of the main occupancy. If the main occupancy is permitted by Section 507 to be in an unlimited area building, the accessory occupancy also enjoys the same benefit.

509

Incidental Uses—General Provisions

CHANGE TYPE: Clarification

CHANGE SUMMARY: The concept of incidental uses has been clarified by eliminating the previous relationship with the mixed-occupancy provisions.

2013 CODE: **~~508.2.5~~ 509.1 ~~Separation of Incidental Uses~~. General.** ~~The incidental accessory occupancies listed in Table 508.2.5 shall be separated from the remainder of the building or equipped with an automatic fire-extinguishing system, or both, in accordance with Table 508.2.5.~~ Incidental uses located within single occupancy or mixed occupancy buildings shall comply with the provisions of this section. Incidental uses are ancillary functions associated with a given occupancy that generally pose a greater level of risk to that occupancy and are limited to those uses listed in Table 509.

> **Exception:** Incidental ~~accessory occupancies~~ uses within and serving a dwelling unit are not required to comply with this section.

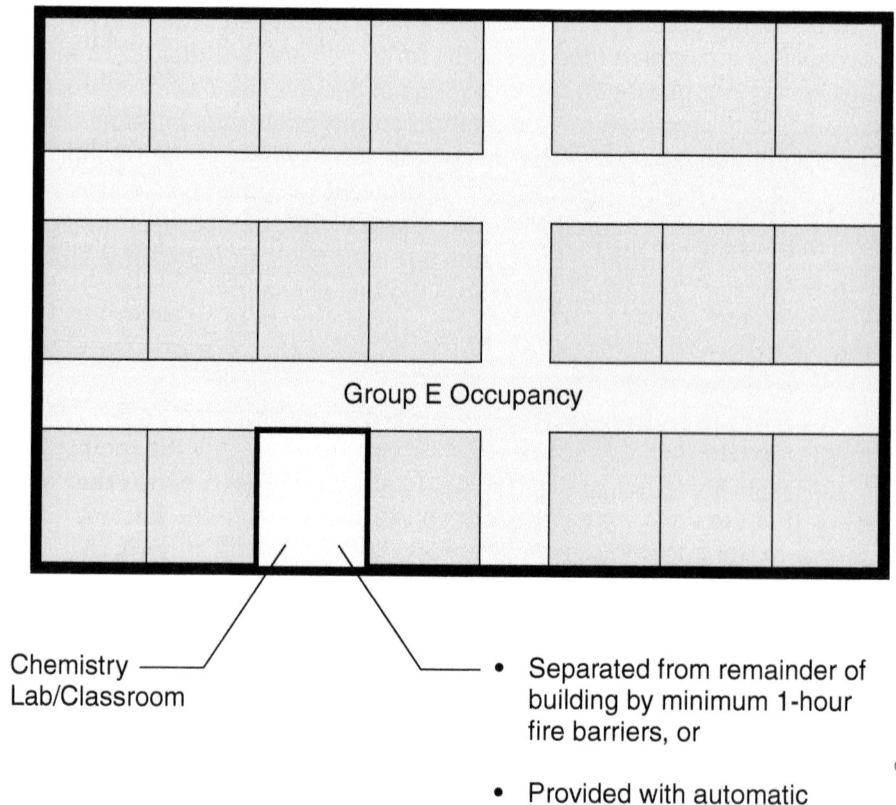

School lab/classroom regulated as incidental use.

509.2 Occupancy Classification. Incidental uses shall not be individually classified in accordance with Section 302.1. Incidental uses shall be included in the building occupancies within which they are located.

509.3 Area Limitations. Incidental uses shall not occupy more than 10 percent of the building area of the story in which they are located.

CHANGE SIGNIFICANCE: There are occasionally one or more rooms or areas in a building that pose risks not typically addressed by the provisions for the occupancy group(s) under which the building is classified. However, such rooms or areas may functionally be an extension of the primary use. These types of spaces were previously considered in the 2010 CBC to be "incidental accessory occupancies" and evaluated according to their hazard level. As incidental accessory occupancies, such rooms or areas were inappropriately regulated under the mixed-occupancy provisions relating to accessory occupancies. The guiding concept has been restored with new terminology, "incidental uses," and a separate and distinct code section, Section 509. The term "incidental uses" more accurately reflects the long-held intent on this subject. Table 509, which lists those types of rooms and areas considered as incidental uses, addresses potential hazards based upon the specific use of the space, not the occupancy classification. The introduction of a new code section, outside of the scope of Section 508 addressing mixed occupancies, further emphasizes that incidental uses have no relationship to mixed-occupancy conditions.

New Section 509 begins with general applicability requirements that establish the scope of the incidental use provisions. It is now clearly stated that incidental uses can be located within both single-occupancy and mixed-occupancy buildings, eliminating the past confusion caused by the location of the requirements within the mixed-occupancy portion of the code. It is further stated that incidental uses are ancillary functions included within those occupancy groups that have been established. The scoping provisions also now reinforce the concept that it is the incidental uses that pose a risk to the remainder of the occupancy in which they are located. It is the intent to protect surrounding areas from the hazards that exist due to the incidental uses. Table 509 lists all rooms or areas that are to be regulated as incidental uses.

An important new provision now expressly states that incidental uses are not considered as separate and distinct occupancy classifications, but rather are classified the same as the building occupancies in which they are located. In the past, it was permissible to regulate the listed uses as incidental or, as an alternative, classify them as unique occupancy groups exempt from the incidental use requirements. This option is no longer available, as all rooms and areas identified in Table 509 must be regulated as incidental uses and comply with the requirements of Section 509.

The floor area limitation for incidental uses has been retained to place emphasis on the ancillary function of an incidental use. Each incidental use is limited to a maximum floor area of 10 percent of the floor area of the story in which it is located. Where there are two or more tenants located on the same story, the 10 percent limitation would presumably be based upon the floor area of each individual tenant space rather than that of the entire story. The application of the limit on a tenant-by-tenant basis is consistent with the concept of incidental uses typically being ancillary only to a portion of the building, the specific tenant occupancy.

509

Incidental Uses—Separation and Protection

CHANGE TYPE: Modification

CHANGE SUMMARY: An automatic sprinkler system is now the only fire-extinguishing system specifically permitted as a means of providing any fire protection required for incidental use rooms and areas.

2013 CODE: **509.4 Separation and Protection.** The incidental uses listed in Table 509 shall be separated from the remainder of the building or equipped with an automatic sprinkler system, or both, in accordance with the provisions of that table.

~~508.2.5.1~~ 509.4.1 ~~Fire-resistance-rated~~ Separation. Where Table ~~508.2.5~~ 509 specifies a fire-resistance-rated separation, the incidental ~~accessory occupancies~~ uses shall be separated from the remainder of the building by a fire barrier constructed in accordance with Section 707 or a horizontal assembly constructed in accordance with Section 711, or both. Construction supporting 1-hour fire-resistance-rated fire barriers or horizontal assemblies used for incidental ~~accessory occupancy~~ use separations in buildings of Type IIB, IIIB, and VB construction is not required to be fire-resistance rated unless required by other sections of this code.

~~508.2.5.2~~ 509.4.2 ~~Nonfire-resistance-rated Separation and~~ Protection. Where Table ~~508.2.5~~ 509 permits an automatic ~~fire-extinguishing~~ sprinkler system without a fire barrier, the incidental ~~accessory occupancies~~ uses shall be separated from the remainder of the building by construction capable of resisting the passage of smoke. The walls shall extend from the top of the foundation or floor assembly below to the underside of the ceiling that is a component of a fire-resistance-rated floor assembly or roof assembly above or to the underside of the floor or roof sheathing, deck or slab above. Doors shall be self- or automatic closing

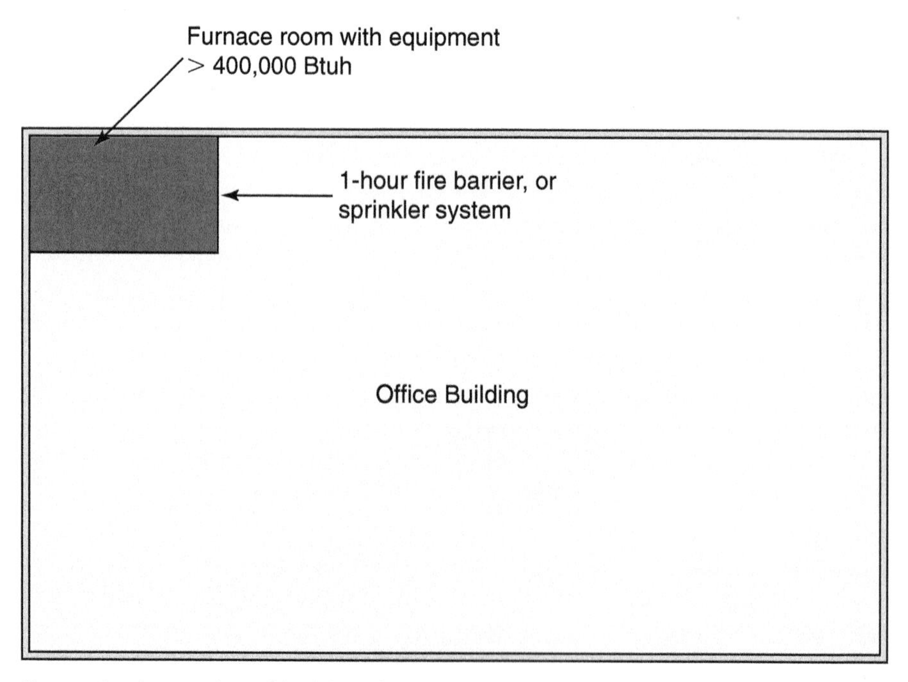

Separation/protection of incidental use.

upon detection of smoke in accordance with Section 716.5.9.3. Doors shall not have air transfer openings and shall not be undercut in excess of the clearance permitted in accordance with NFPA 80. Walls surrounding the incidental use shall not have air transfer openings unless provided with smoke dampers in accordance with Section 710.7.

~~508.2.5.3~~ 509.4.2.1 Protection Limitation. Except as specified in Table ~~508.2.5~~ 509 for certain incidental ~~accessory occupancies~~ uses, where an ~~automatic fire-extinguishing system or an~~ automatic sprinkler system is provided in accordance with Table ~~508.2.5~~ 509, only the space occupied by the incidental ~~accessory occupancy~~ use need be equipped with such a system.

CHANGE SIGNIFICANCE: Where a building contains one or more incidental uses as established in Table 509, such uses must be specifically addressed due to the increased risk their presence poses to the remainder of the building. The code continues to recognize two methods of protection: construction of fire-resistance-rated separation elements and/or installation of a fire protection system. The acceptable protection methods are set forth in Table 509 for each of the incidental uses listed. Where a fire protection system is utilized, the code now mandates that an automatic sprinkler system be provided. Previously, any appropriate fire-extinguishing system was acceptable for protecting most of the incidental use rooms or areas. The change in terminology was made to eliminate any confusion regarding the anticipated results from the fire protection system. It was determined that the term "fire-extinguishing system" could lead the code user to think that a sprinkler system that is designed to control a fire is not adequate. The result of this modification also limits the type of fire-extinguishing permitted for incidental use purposes to an automatic sprinkler system. In order to satisfy the requirements, other types of fire-extinguishing systems are no longer acceptable unless specifically approved by the fire code official as set forth in Section 904.2.

Table 509

Incidental Uses—Rooms or Areas

CHANGE TYPE: Modification

CHANGE SUMMARY: The list of incidental uses now includes waste and linen collection rooms in Group B ambulatory care facilities and such rooms must be separated from the remainder of the building by minimum 1-hour fire-resistance-rated fire barriers and/or horizontal assemblies.

2013 CODE:

TABLE ~~508.2.5~~ 509 Incidental ~~Accessory Occupancies~~ Uses

Room or Area	Separation and/or Protection
Furnace room where any piece of equipment is over 400,000 Btu per hour input	1 hour or provide automatic ~~fire-extinguishing~~ sprinkler system
Rooms with boilers where the largest piece of equipment is over 15 psi and 10 horsepower	1 hour or provide automatic ~~fire-extinguishing~~ sprinkler system
Refrigerant machinery room	1 hour or provide automatic sprinkler system
Hydrogen cutoff rooms, not classified as Group H	1 hour in Group B, F, M, S, and U occupancies; 2 hours in Group A, E, I, and R occupancies.
Incinerator rooms	2 hours and automatic sprinkler system
Paint shops, not classified as Group H, located in occupancies other than Group F	2 hours or 1 hour and provide automatic ~~fire-extinguishing~~ sprinkler system
Laboratories and vocational shops, not classified as Group H, located in a Group E or I-2 occupancy	1 hour or provide automatic ~~fire-extinguishing~~ sprinkler system
[SFM] Rooms or areas with special hazards such as laboratories, vocational shops and other such areas not classified as Group H, located in Group E occupancies where hazardous materials in quantities not exceeding the maximum allowable quantity are used or stored.	*1 hour*
Laundry rooms over 100 square feet	1 hour or provide automatic ~~fire-extinguishing~~ sprinkler system
Group I-3 cells equipped with padded surfaces	1 hour
~~Group I-2~~ Waste and linen collection rooms located in either Group I-2 occupancies or ambulatory care facilities	1 hour
Waste and linen collection rooms over 100 square feet	1 hour or provide automatic ~~fire-extinguishing~~ sprinkler system
Stationary storage battery systems having a liquid electrolyte capacity of more than 50 gallons for flooded lead-acid, nickel cadmium or VRLA, or ~~a lithium-ion capacity of~~ more than 1000 pounds for lithium-ion and lithium metal polymer used for facility standby power, emergency power, or ~~uninterrupted~~ uninterruptable power supplies	1 hour in Group B, F, M, S, and U occupancies; 2 hours in Group A, E, I, and R occupancies.
~~Rooms containing fire pumps in nonhigh-rise buildings~~	~~2 hours; or 1 hour and provide automatic sprinkler system throughout the building~~
~~Rooms containing fire pumps in high-rise buildings~~	~~2 hours~~

CHANGE SIGNIFICANCE: The purpose of Table 509 is twofold: (1) it identifies the rooms or areas that are specifically regulated as "Incidental Uses," and (2) it establishes the type and degree of fire protection that is to be afforded the remainder of the building. The listed rooms and areas have been selected for inclusion because of the increased hazard they present to the other building uses. The intent of the fire separation and fire sprinkler requirements is to provide safeguards because of the increased hazard level presented by the incidental use. Minor changes have been made to the listing of incidental uses, as well as to the type of fire protection systems that are to be installed.

The list of incidental uses now includes all waste and linen collection rooms in Group B ambulatory care facilities. Such rooms have previously only been regulated as incidental uses if they were located in a Group I-2 occupancy or over 100 square feet in floor area. A minimum 1-hour fire-resistance-rated separation, previously required for such rooms in Group I-2 occupancies, is now also applicable to all waste and linen collection rooms that are provided in ambulatory care facilities as regulated by Section 422. Several changes throughout the code, this one included, were made to regulate ambulatory care facilities consistent with the higher level of protection required when some occupants rely on staff for assisted evacuation, similar to nursing homes and hospitals. In another change to the table, rooms containing fire pumps were removed from the listing of incidental uses because they do not meet the criteria for incidental uses. The separation/protection requirements for fire pump rooms comprehensively addressed in Section 913 are intended to protect the fire pump room from risks found in the remainder of the building, the opposite of the intent of the incidental use provisions.

Table 509 also reflects the new requirement that automatic sprinkler systems be utilized for fire protection purposes, where appropriate, rather than automatic fire-extinguishing systems.

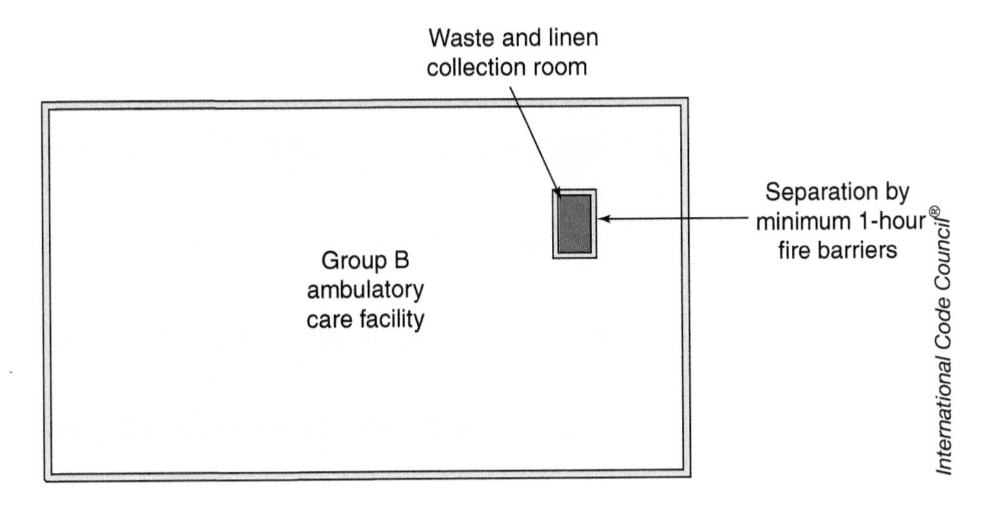

Incidental use in ambulatory care facility.

602.1

Fire-Resistance Rating Requirements for Solar Photovoltaic Systems

CHANGE TYPE: Addition

CHANGE SUMMARY: In most cases, noncombustible supports for solar photovoltaic systems are not required to meet fire-resistance ratings of Tables 601 and 602. Certain limitations apply to systems installed above parking areas.

2013 CODE: 602.1 General. Buildings and structures erected or to be erected, altered or extended in height or area shall be classified in one of the five construction types defined in Sections 602.2 through 602.5. The building elements shall have a fire-resistance rating not less than that specified in Table 601 and exterior walls shall have a fire-resistance rating not less than that specified in Table 602. Where required to have a fire-resistance rating by Table 601, building elements shall comply with the applicable provisions of Section 703.2. The protection of openings, ducts and air transfer openings in building elements shall not be required unless required by other provisions of this code.

> ***Exception:*** *Noncombustible structural members supporting solar photovoltaic panels are not required to meet the fire-resistance rating for the following:*
>
> *1. Photovoltaic panel supported by a structure and having no use underneath. Signs may be provided, as determined by the enforcing agency, prohibiting any use underneath including storage.*
>
> *2. Solar photovoltaic (PV) panels supported by noncombustible framing that have sufficient uniformly distributed and unobstructed openings throughout the top of the array (horizontal plane) to allow heat and gases to escape, as determined by the enforcing agency.*
>
> *3. Solar photovoltaic panels supported by a structure over parking stalls where the panels constitute the roof and all the following conditions are met (see Figure 5-1):*
>
> ***3.1.*** *The area within the perimeter of the solar photovoltaic array has maximum rectangular dimension of 40 feet by 150 feet.*
>
> ***3.2.*** *The distance between solar photovoltaic array structures is a minimum of 10 feet clear.*

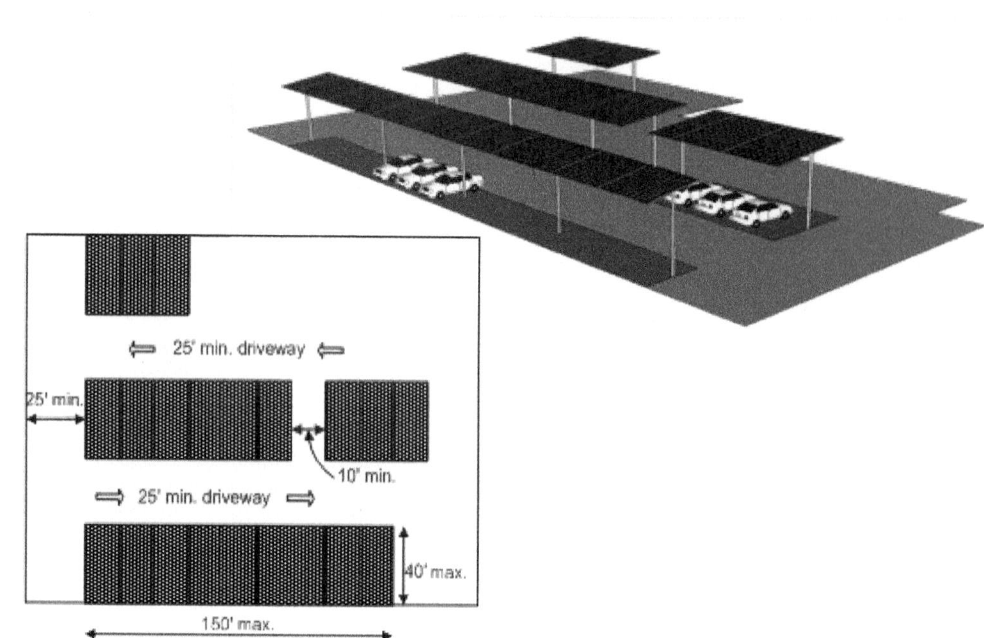

Solar PV parking structure.

3.3. *The driveway aisle separating solar photovoltaic array structures has a minimum width of 25 feet clear.*

3.4. *Solar photovoltaic array structure is used only for parking purposes with no storage.*

3.5. *Completely open on all sides (other than necessary structural supports) with no interior partitions.*

CHANGE SIGNIFICANCE: Table 601 determines the minimum fire-resistance ratings of certain building elements based on a classification of the type of construction. Similarly, Table 602 sets the minimum fire-resistance ratings for exterior walls based on fire separation distance, occupancy group and type of construction. The revision provides clarification that a fire-resistance rating is not required for noncombustible structural members supporting photovoltaic panels. Given the light weight of solar panels and the limited fire hazard, the application of fireproofing or fire-resistant materials on noncombustible supports for those panels was considered unnecessary. Fireproofing of solar PV structures can be very costly, making such installations infeasible.

The code does place a number of limitations on the exemption from fire-resistance ratings based on the use or function of the space below the solar PV panels. If there is no use underneath, no additional requirements apply. Solar PV panel assemblies that have a use underneath require adequate openings to allow heat and gases to escape. Preventing heat accumulation provides an added measure of fire safety. Solar PV panels installed over parking stalls require a minimum spacing of 10 feet between adjacent solar arrays. Likewise, the service drive between separate solar array structures must be at least 25 feet wide to allow fire department access and provide a fire break. The solar photovoltaic array is limited to plan dimensions of 40 feet by 150 feet and must be open on all sides. Storage and interior partitions for these parking structures are not permitted.

PART 3

Fire Protection

Chapters 7 through 9

- **Chapter 7** Fire and Smoke Protection Features
- **Chapter 8** Interior Finishes
- **Chapter 9** Fire-Protection Systems

The fire-protection provisions of the *California Building Code* are found primarily in Chapters 7 through 9. There are two general categories of fire protection: active and passive. The fire and smoke resistance of building elements and systems in compliance with Chapter 7 provides for passive protection. Chapter 9 contains requirements for various active systems often utilized in the creation of a safe building environment, including automatic sprinkler systems, standpipe systems, and fire alarm systems. To further address the rapid spread of fire, the provisions of Chapter 8 are intended to regulate interior-finish materials, such as wall and floor coverings. ■

701.2

Multiple-Use Fire Assemblies

703.4

Establishing Fire Resistance Ratings

703.7

Identification of Fire and Smoke Separation Walls

705.2

Extent of Projections beyond Exterior Walls

705.12

Exterior Graphics on Exterior Walls of High-Rise Buildings

706.2

Double Fire Walls

707.8, 707.9

Intersections of Fire Barriers at Roof Assemblies

712

Vertical Openings

714.4.1.1.2

Floor Penetrations of Horizontal Assemblies

714.4.1.2

Interruption of Horizontal Assemblies

715.4

Exterior Curtain Wall/Floor Intersection

TABLE 716.5

Opening Protection Ratings and Markings

716.5.5.1

Glazing in Exit Enclosure and Exit Passageway Doors

TABLE 716.6

Fire-Protection-Rated Glazing

716.6.4

Wired Glass in Fire Window Assemblies

717.5.4

Fire Damper Exemption for Fire Partitions

903.2.2

Sprinklers in Ambulatory Care Facilities

903.2.4, 903.2.7, 903.2.9

Furniture Storage and Display in Group F-1, M, and S-1 Occupancies

903.2.6, 907.2.6.3, 907.3.2

Fire Protection Systems in Group I-3 Occupancies

903.2.11.1.3

Sprinkler Protection for Basements

903.3.1.1.1

Sprinkler Exemption for Solar Photovoltaic Systems

903.3.5.2

Secondary Water Supply

904.3.2

Actuation of Multiple Fire-Extinguishing Systems

906.1

Portable Fire Extinguishers in Group R-2 Occupancies

907.2.1.2

Emergency Voice/Alarm Communication Captions

907.2.9.3

Smoke Detection in Group R-2 College Buildings

907.2.11.2, 907.2.11.5

Smoke Alarms for Groups R-2, R-2.1, R-3, R-3.1 and R-4 and I-1

907.6

Fire Alarm Systems for High-Rise Buildings

911.1.6

Fire Command Center Ventilation in High-Rise Buildings

913.6

Fire Pump Fuel Supply in High-Rise Buildings

701.2

Multiple-Use Fire Assemblies

CHANGE TYPE: Clarification

CHANGE SUMMARY: Where a single fire assembly serves multiple purposes, such as a wall being utilized as both a fire barrier and a fire partition, it has been clarified that all of the applicable requirements for both types of fire separation walls must be met.

2013 CODE: **701.2 Multiple-Use Fire Assemblies.** Fire assemblies that serve multiple purposes in a building shall comply with all of the requirements that are applicable for each of the individual fire assemblies.

CHANGE SIGNIFICANCE: Fire assemblies are utilized throughout the code for a variety of purposes. Fire walls, fire barriers, fire partitions, smoke barriers, and smoke partitions are selectively mandated in order to provide the appropriate fire separation necessary for the situation under consideration. There are often times where the placement of one type of fire assembly coincides with that of another type. For example, a corridor wall required to be constructed as a fire partition may also serve as the boundary of a fire area, necessitating the use of a fire barrier. It is important to recognize that where such multiple uses exist, the requirements for each of the fire assemblies must be met. This approach is consistent with the accepted concept of applying the most restrictive provisions where multiple requirements are applicable and clarifies the method to deal with such situations.

The most common characteristic that must be evaluated is the minimum required fire-resistance rating of the fire assembly. A single wall assembly serving as both a 3-hour fire wall and a 2-hour fire barrier must be designed and constructed to the higher fire-resistance level, in this case 3 hours. However, the primary intent of separation in regard to fire and/or smoke protection must also be evaluated. In the example of a corridor fire partition also being utilized as fire barrier, the primary purpose of the fire partition can be viewed as smoke containment. On the other hand, the fire barrier is considered more of a fire separation feature. Where both types of wall assemblies occur at the same location, the necessary elements to provide both smoke resistance and fire resistance must be in place.

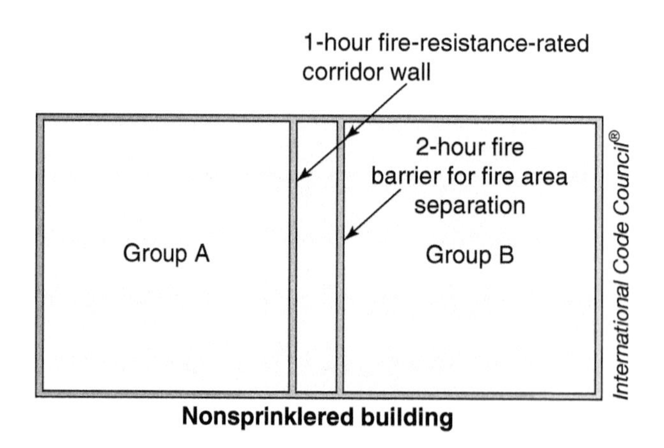

Wall assembly used for multiple separations.

The variation in minimum requirements is typically most evident in the opening protectives that maintain the integrity of the fire assembly. Although the fire door assembly located in a 2-hour fire barrier must have a minimum fire-protection rating of 1½ hours, only a minimum 20-minute fire-protection rating is required for a corridor door installed in a fire partition. However, the corridor door must also meet the requirements for a smoke and draft control assembly tested in accordance with UL 1784 with a maximum air leakage rate. In the single fire assembly under discussion, a door opening would need to be protected with a minimum 1½-hour fire door assembly that also qualifies as a complying smoke and draft control door assembly.

703.4

Establishing Fire-Resistance Ratings

International Code Council®

ASTM E 119 vertical furnace.

CHANGE TYPE: Clarification

CHANGE SUMMARY: Specific language has been added to clarify that a fire suppression system is not permitted to be included as part of a tested building element, component, or assembly in order to establish the fire-resistance rating.

2013 CODE: **703.4 Automatic Sprinklers.** Under the prescriptive fire resistance requirements of the *California Building Code*, the fire-resistance rating of a building element, component, or assembly shall be established without the use of automatic sprinklers or any other fire suppression system being incorporated as part of the assembly tested in accordance with the fire exposure, procedures, and acceptance criteria specified in ASTM E 119 or UL 263. However, this section shall not prohibit or limit the duties and powers of the building official allowed by Sections 104.10 and 104.11.

CHANGE SIGNIFICANCE: As a general rule, the fire-resistance ratings of building elements, components, and assemblies established throughout the CBC are to be determined in accordance with the test procedures as established in ASTM E 119 or UL 263. In addition, alternative methods for determining fire-resistance set forth in Section 703.3 are acceptable where such methods are based on the fire exposure and acceptance criteria specified in ASTM E 119 or UL 263. Specific language has now been added to clarify that a fire suppression system is not permitted to be included as part of the tested element, component, or assembly in order to establish the fire-resistance rating. It has been generally accepted that the various fire resistance ratings mandated throughout the code have been established based on an assumption that the fire assembly would pass the standardized tests without the assistance of water cooling during fire exposure. The new provision clarifies this assumption.

It is important to note that these provisions are not intended to limit the use of Section 104 by building officials for the approval of alternative methods on a case-by-case basis. While the prescriptive provisions of the code are based upon fire-resistance ratings established without the benefit of any automatic fire suppression system, the building official continues to maintain the authority to evaluate and approve alternative materials, designs, and methods of construction that meet the intent and purpose of the code.

703.7

Identification of Fire and Smoke Separation Walls

CHANGE TYPE: Modification

CHANGE SUMMARY: The size and location of identifying markings required on vertical fire assemblies in accessible above-ceiling spaces have been modified to increase the potential for such markings to be seen.

2013 CODE: 703.7 Marking and Identification. Fire walls, fire barriers, fire partitions, smoke barriers, and smoke partitions or any other wall required to have protected openings or penetrations shall be effectively and permanently identified with signs or stenciling. Such identification shall:

1. Be located in accessible concealed floor, floor/ceiling, or attic spaces
2. Be located within 15 feet (4572 mm) of the end of each wall and ~~repeated~~ at intervals not exceeding 30 feet (9144 mm) measured horizontally along the wall or partition
3. Include lettering not less than ~~0.5 inch (12.7 mm)~~ 3 inches (76 mm) in height with a minimum ⅜-inch (9.5-mm) stroke in a contrasting color incorporating the suggested wording: "FIRE AND/OR SMOKE BARRIER—PROTECT ALL OPENINGS" or other wording.

Exception: Walls in Group R-2 occupancies that do not have a removable decorative ceiling allowing access to the concealed space.

703.7 continues

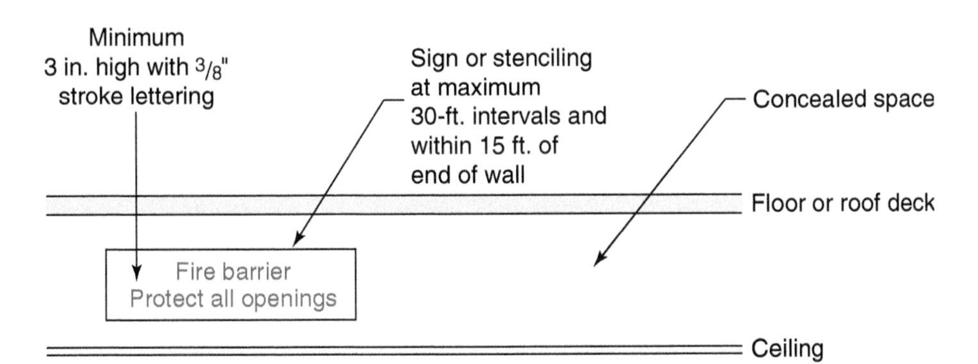

Identification sign for fire barrier.

703.7 continued

CHANGE SIGNIFICANCE: The integrity of fire and/or smoke separation walls is subject to compromise during the life of a building. During maintenance and remodel activities, it is not uncommon for new openings and penetrations to be installed in a fire separation wall without the recognition that the integrity of the construction must be maintained or that some type of fire or smoke protective is required. Provisions mandating the appropriate identification of such walls under certain conditions have been modified to better ensure that tradespeople, maintenance workers, and inspectors will recognize the required level of protection that must be maintained.

It is intended that the identification marks be located in areas not visible to the general public. Specific locations set forth in the provisions indicate that the identification is to be provided above any lay-in panel ceiling or similar concealed space that is deemed to be accessible. In addition to previous requirements for locating the identifying markings at maximum 30-foot intervals, it is now also necessary that such markings be provided no more than 15 feet from the end of each wall requiring such identification. This additional requirement increases the possibility that the identifying markings will be visible during any work on the wall assemblies. The minimum required letter height has also been increased from ½ inch to 3 inches to make the markings much more visible. In addition, a minimum stroke width has been established at ⅜ inch and the lettering must be of a color that contrasts with its background. All of the code modifications are intended to increase the possibility that the identification of the information will be achieved.

The requirements apply to all wall assemblies where openings or penetrations are required to be protected. This would include exterior fire-resistance-rated walls as well as fire walls, fire barriers, fire partitions, smoke barriers, and smoke partitions.

705.2

Extent of Projections beyond Exterior Walls

CHANGE TYPE: Modification

CHANGE SUMMARY: The permitted extent of projections beyond exterior walls is now regulated in a straightforward manner that establishes a minimum clear distance that is required between the leading edge of the projection and the line used to establish the fire separation distance.

2013 CODE: 705.2 Projections. Cornices, eave overhangs, exterior balconies, and similar projections extending beyond the exterior wall shall conform to the requirements of this section and Section 1406. Exterior egress balconies and exterior exit stairways shall also comply with Sections 1019 and 1026, respectively. Projections shall not extend ~~beyond the distance determined by the following three methods, whichever results in the lesser projection:~~ any closer to the line used to determine the fire separation distance than shown in Table 705.2.

1. ~~A point one-third the distance from the exterior face of the wall to the lot line where protected openings or a combination of protected and unprotected openings are required in the exterior walls.~~
2. ~~A point one-half the distance from the exterior face of the wall to the lot line where all openings in the exterior wall are permitted to be unprotected or the building is equipped throughout with an automatic sprinkler system installed under the provisions of Section 705.8.2.~~
3. ~~More than 12 inches (305 mm) into areas where openings are prohibited.~~

Exception: Buildings on the same lot and considered as portions of one building in accordance with Section 705.3 are not required to comply with this section.

TABLE 705.2 Minimum Distance of Projection

Fire Separation Distance (FSD)	Minimum Distance From Line Used To Determine FSD
0 feet to less than 2 feet	Projections not permitted
2 feet to less than 5 feet	24 inches
5 feet or greater	40 inches

705.2 continued

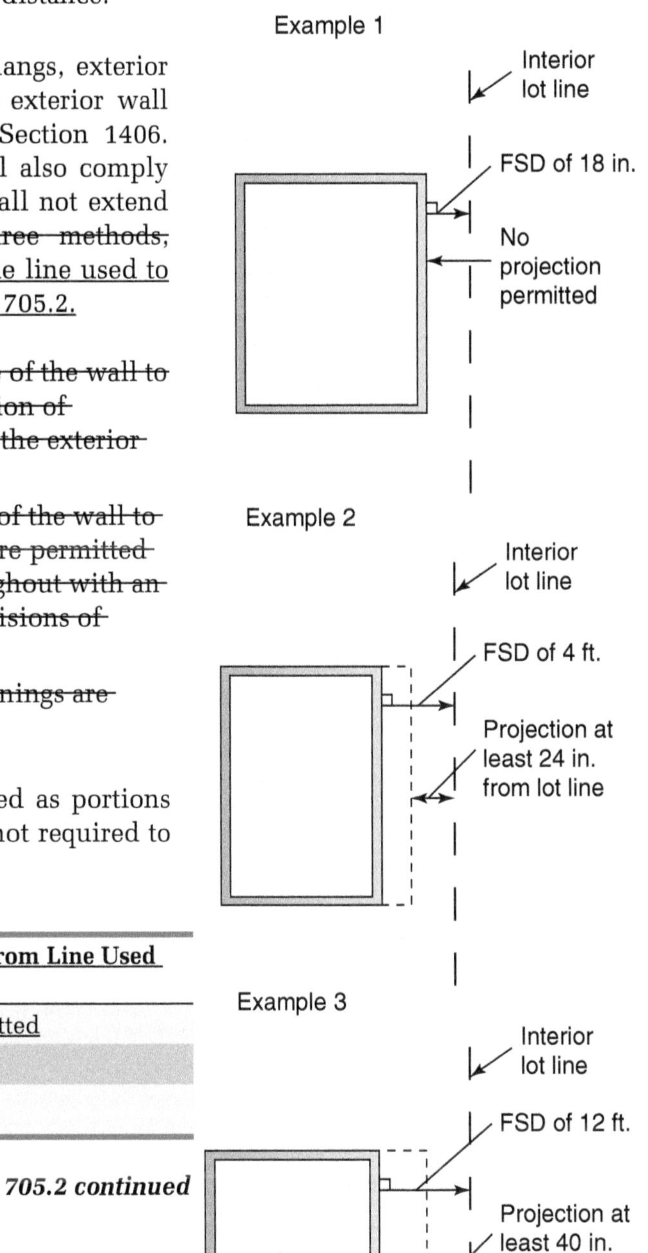

Maximum permitted projections.

705.2 continued

CHANGE SIGNIFICANCE: Where projections like cornices, eave overhangs, and balconies are located such that there is a limited fire separation distance, they create problems due to the trapping of convected heat from a fire in an adjacent building. Therefore, the extent of such projections is addressed. By providing some degree of physical horizontal separation from adjacent buildings and lots, the concerns associated with such trapped heat can be substantially reduced. The permitted extent of projections has been modified and simplified from previous requirements that were viewed as complex, confusing, and inconsistent. The permitted extent of projections is now regulated in a manner that establishes a minimum required clear distance between the leading edge of the projection and the line used to establish the fire separation distance. This methodology is in contrast to the previous approach, which limited the distance a projection could extend beyond the building's exterior wall.

The permitted extent of projections is established by new Table 705.2 and based on the distance between the building's exterior wall and an interior lot line, centerline of a public way, or assumed imaginary line between two buildings on the same lot. Under these new limitations, no projections are permitted beyond the exterior wall where the wall has a fire separation distance of less than 2 feet. Where the exterior wall is located such that the fire separation distance is at least 2 feet, a projection is permitted but its extent is regulated. For example, if a building's exterior wall is located 54 inches from an adjacent interior lot line, at least 24 inches must be maintained between the edge of the projection and the lot line. This results in a maximum permitted projection beyond the exterior wall of 30 inches. If an exterior wall is located 96 inches from an interior lot line, the projection may not extend within 40 inches of the lot line. In this case, a projection of up to 56 inches is permitted.

705.12

Exterior Graphics on Exterior Walls of High-Rise Buildings

CHANGE TYPE: Addition

CHANGE SUMMARY: When exceeding the prescribed dimensions and installed more than 40 feet above grade on the exterior of a high-rise building, materials used for graphics must be noncombustible or have a maximum flame spread of 25. Graphics must be securely attached and not impair ventilation or any safety systems of the building.

2013 CODE: **705.12 Exterior Graphics on Exterior Walls of High-Rise Buildings.** *Where installed on the exterior walls of high-rise buildings, exterior graphics, both permanent and temporary, greater than 100 square feet in area or greater than 10 feet in either dimension shall comply with the following conditions subject to the review and approval of the fire code official and building official:*

1. *The materials used for graphics installed at a height greater than 40 feet above the grade plane shall be noncombustible materials or shall have a flame spread index not greater than 25 when tested in accordance with ASTM E84 or UL 723.*

2. *The method of attachment and mounting of the graphics to the exterior wall shall be such that the graphics are securely attached.*

3. *The graphics shall not interfere with the active or passive ventilation required for the building and the required smoke control systems in the building.*

4. *The graphics shall not impair the functions of any fire or life safety systems in the building.*

705.12 continued

For high-rise buildings, the materials used for large graphics must be noncombustible or have a maximum flame spread of 25.

705.12 continued

CHANGE SIGNIFICANCE: Local fire departments have concerns regarding the application of graphics or wall signs on multi-story buildings when covering large areas of the exterior wall. This applies to temporary mylar-type advertising graphics adhesively-applied to the exterior glazing and permanent signage mounted on the exterior wall. Previously, there was no language in the code pertaining to large graphic applications on the exterior of high-rise buildings. Graphics and signs should not be more combustible than the materials used on the exterior wall. To reduce the possibility of the spread of fire on the exterior of high-rise buildings, the code now requires noncombustible materials or materials having a maximum flame spread index of 25. However, Section 1406.2.2 allows combustible materials to be used up to 40 feet in height above grade, so the proposed amendment for noncombustible or reduced flame spread graphics materials applies only to graphics located above 40 feet in height.

The risk of the graphics falling off the building needs to be minimized. This applies both to the appropriate engineering of mechanical attachment for permanent graphics and the adhesive attachment of temporary graphics directly to the surface of the exterior wall.

Graphics applied to the exterior wall of buildings should in no way interfere with building ventilation or fire and life safety systems in the building. An example of this would be open parking structures that rely on portions of the exterior wall remaining open for natural ventilation and passive smoke evacuation and should therefore not have these openings blocked by graphic elements. Another example would be glazing on the exterior wall that is designed to be broken out for passive smoke evacuation—the break-away functionality of the glass should not be impeded by adhesively-applied graphic banners on the surface of the glass or exterior wall.

706.2

Double Fire Walls

CHANGE TYPE: Addition

CHANGE SUMMARY: In order to satisfy the intended objective of structural stability, the use of a double fire wall complying with NFPA 221 is now permitted as an alternative to a single fire wall.

2013 CODE: 706.2 Structural Stability. Fire walls shall have sufficient structural stability under fire conditions to allow collapse of construction on either side without collapse of the wall for the duration of time indicated by the required fire-resistance rating or shall be constructed as double fire walls in accordance with NFPA 221.

CHANGE SIGNIFICANCE: Fire walls are fire-resistance-rated building elements constructed within a structure that are utilized to create two or more smaller-area buildings. Each portion of the structure so separated may be considered a separate and unique building for all purposes of the code. One of the key criteria to the design and construction of a fire wall is that it performs structurally under fire conditions in a manner that will maintain the integrity of the fire separation. A new allowance permits the use of a double fire wall in lieu of a single fire wall that satisfies the intended objective of structural stability.

Double fire walls are simply two back-to-back walls, each having an established fire-resistive rating. While acceptable for use in a new structure, double fire walls are most advantageous where an addition is being constructed adjacent to an existing building and the intent is to regulate the addition as a separate building under the fire wall provisions. The exterior wall of the existing building, if compliant, can be utilized as one wall of the double wall system, with the new wall of the addition providing the second wall.

Double fire wall assemblies are to comply with the applicable provisions of NFPA 221, *Standard for High Challenge Fire Walls, Fire Walls,*

706.2 continued

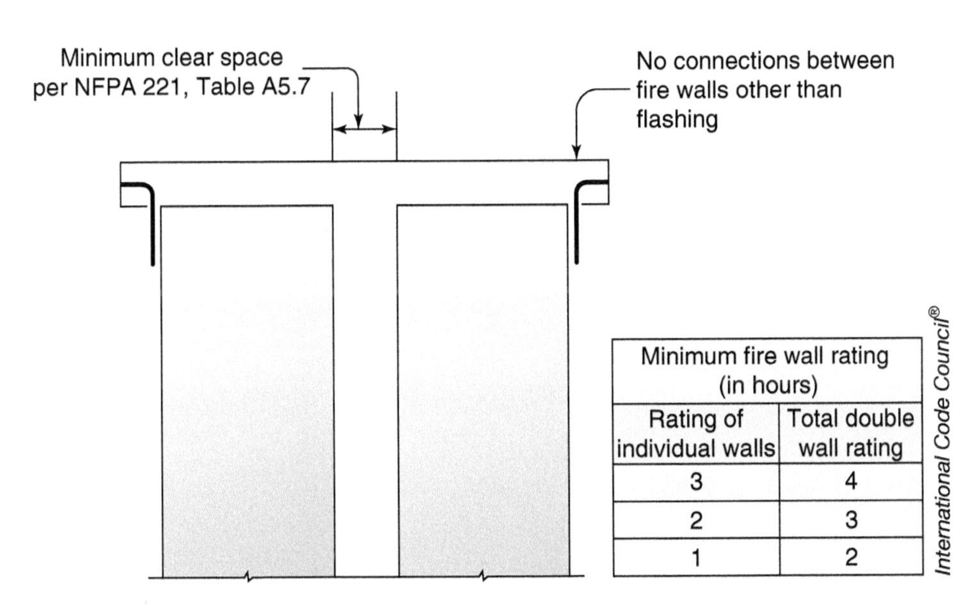

Minimum fire wall rating (in hours)	
Rating of individual walls	Total double wall rating
3	4
2	3
1	2

Double fire wall.

706.2 continued

and Fire Barrier Walls. This standard addresses a number of criteria for double fire walls, including fire-resistance rating, connections, and structural support. In order to meet the minimum fire-resistance rating for a fire wall as set forth in Table 706.4, each individual wall of a double fire wall assembly is permitted to be reduced to 1 hour less than the minimum required rating for a single fire wall. For example, where Table 706.4 requires the use of a minimum 3-hour fire wall, two 2-hour fire-resistance-rated (double) fire walls can be utilized. Similarly, two 3-hour fire walls in a double wall system can be considered as a single 4-hour fire wall, and two 1-hour fire walls used as a double wall qualify as a single 2-hour fire wall.

Because the intended goal of fire wall construction is to allow collapse of a building on either side of the fire wall while maintaining an acceptable level of fire separation, the only connection permitted by NFPA 221 between the two walls that make up the double fire wall is the flashing, if provided. Illustrated in the explanatory material to the standard, the choice of flashing methods must provide for separate flashing sections in order to maintain a complete physical separation between the walls. Each individual wall of the double wall assembly must be supported laterally without any assistance from the adjoining building. In addition, a minimum clear space between the two walls is recommended by NFPA 221 in order to allow for thermal expansion between unprotected structural framework, where applicable, and the wall assemblies that make up the double fire wall.

707.8, 707.9

Intersections of Fire Barriers at Roof Assemblies

CHANGE TYPE: Modification

CHANGE SUMMARY: The void at the intersection between a fire barrier and a nonfire-resistance rated roof assembly now need only be protected with an approved material rather than a fire-resistant joint system.

2013 CODE: **707.8 Joints.** Joints made in or between fire barriers and joints made at the intersection of fire barriers with the underside of ~~the~~ a fire-resistance rated floor or roof sheathing, slab, or deck above, and the exterior vertical wall intersection shall comply with Section 715.

707.9 Voids at Intersections. The voids created at the intersection of a fire barrier and a non-fire-resistance-rated roof assembly shall be filled. An approved material or system shall be used to fill the void, shall be securely installed in or on the intersection for its entire length so as not to dislodge, loosen, or otherwise impair its ability to accommodate expected building movements and to retard the passage of fire and hot gases.

CHANGE SIGNIFICANCE: A fire barrier is one of several specific elements established in the IBC to provide a fire-resistance-rated separation of adjacent spaces to safeguard against the spread of fire and smoke. Limited to fire-resistance-rated wall assemblies, fire barriers must extend from the floor to the bottom of the floor or roof sheathing, deck, or slab directly above. This high degree of required continuity minimizes the potential for fire spread from one area to another over the top of the wall. Historically, where a head-of-wall or similar joint was created at the intersection of the fire barrier and the floor or roof sheathing, deck, or slab above, a fire-resistant joint system complying with ASTM E 1966 or UL 2079 has been required. New language addressing the void at the intersection between a fire barrier and a non-fire-resistance-rated roof assembly now allows for a reduced degree of protection.

707.8, 707.9 continued

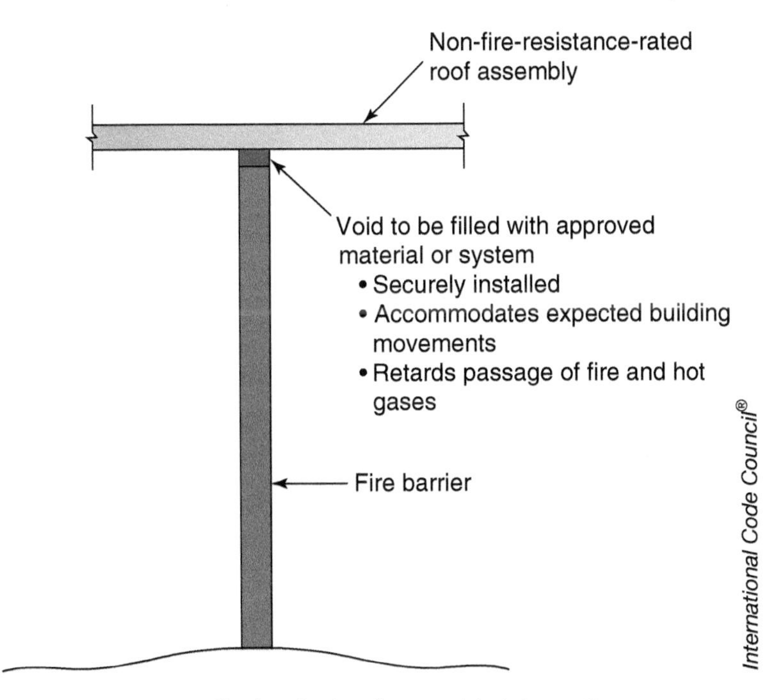

Joint protection at fire barrier/roof assembly intersection.

707.8, 707.9 continued

The two conditions of top-of-wall joints at fire barriers are now addressed differently based upon the type of floor or roof construction involved. Where a fire barrier intersects with a floor or a fire-resistance-rated roof assembly above, the joint must continue to comply with the provisions of Section 715 addressing fire-resistant joint systems. However, a reduced degree of joint protection is now afforded where a fire barrier intersects with a non-fire-resistance-rated roof assembly. The void at the joint need only be an approved material that is securely installed and capable of retarding the passage of fire and hot gases. It is important to note that the allowance for use of an approved material rather than a complying fire-resistant joint system is not applicable where the joint occurs at a non-fire-resistance-rated floor assembly.

712

Vertical Openings

CHANGE TYPE: Clarification

CHANGE SUMMARY: A significant reformatting in Chapter 7 now places the emphasis on the presence of vertical openings rather than on shaft enclosures, recognizing that the use of shaft enclosures is just one of many acceptable protective measures that can be utilized to address the hazards related to vertical openings.

2013 CODE:

SECTION ~~708~~ 712
~~SHAFT ENCLOSURES~~ VERTICAL OPENINGS

~~708.1~~ 712.1 General. The provisions of this section shall apply to the vertical opening applications listed in Sections 712.1.1 through 712.1.18. ~~shafts required to protect openings and penetrations through floor/ceiling and roof/ceiling assemblies. Shaft enclosures shall be constructed as fire barriers in accordance with Section 707 or horizontal assemblies in accordance with Section 712, or both~~.

~~708.2 Shaft Enclosure Required.~~ ~~Openings through a floor ceiling assembly shall be protected by a shaft enclosure complying with this section.~~

> **~~Exceptions:~~** (Exceptions 1 through 16 have been reformatted as Sections 712.1.2 through 712.1.18 with limited editorial changes.)

712.1.1 Shaft Enclosures. Vertical openings contained entirely within a shaft enclosure complying with Section 713 shall be permitted.

712 continues

International Code Council®

Piping extending through opening in floor.

712 continued

SECTION 713
SHAFT ENCLOSURES

713.1 General. The provisions of this section shall apply to shafts required to protect openings and penetrations through floor/ceiling and roof/ceiling assemblies. Exit access stairways and exit access ramps shall be protected in accordance with the applicable provisions of Section 1009. Interior exit stairways and interior exit ramps shall be protected in accordance with the requirements of Section 1022.

713.2 Construction. Shaft enclosures shall be constructed as fire barriers in accordance with Section 707 or horizontal assemblies in accordance with Section 711, or both.

(remainder of section remains relatively unchanged from 2010 CBC Section 708)

CHANGE SIGNIFICANCE: In multi-story buildings, the upward transmission of fire, smoke, and toxic gases through openings in the floor/ceiling assemblies continues to be a hazard of the highest degree. Historically, the provisions of the code intended to address such concerns have primarily been located under the requirements for shaft enclosures. The fundamental premise has been that a shaft enclosure is mandated to protect openings within a floor/ceiling assembly. Other methods of protection were simply identified as exceptions to the shaft enclosure approach. The code has been reformatted in a manner that now places the emphasis on the presence of vertical openings, while identifying the use of shaft enclosures as one of many protective measures that can be utilized to address the concern.

The criteria for shaft enclosures have been maintained as Section 713 for those situations where a shaft enclosure is used as the desired method of opening protection. Limited technical changes were made to the shaft enclosure provisions.

714.4.1.1.2

Floor Penetrations of Horizontal Assemblies

CHANGE TYPE: Modification

CHANGE SUMMARY: An approved through-penetration firestop system used to protect floor penetrations of horizontal assemblies due to the presence of floor, tub, and shower drains is no longer required to have a T rating.

2013 CODE: **~~713.4.1.1.2~~ 714.4.1.1.2 Through-Penetration Firestop System.** Through penetrations shall be protected by an approved through-penetration firestop system installed and tested in accordance with ASTM E 814 or UL 1479, with a minimum positive pressure differential of 0.01 inch of water (2.49 Pa). The system shall have an F rating/T rating of not less than 1 hour but not less than the required rating of the floor penetrated.

Exceptions:

1. Floor penetrations contained and located within the cavity of a wall above the floor or below the floor do not require a T rating.
2. Floor penetrations by floor drains, tub drains, or shower drains contained and located within the concealed space of a horizontal assembly do not require a T rating.

714.4.1.1.2 continued

International Code Council®

Shower drain penetration of horizontal assembly.

714.4.1.1.2 continued

CHANGE SIGNIFICANCE: Through penetrations are permitted in a horizontal assembly where such penetrations are protected by an approved through-penetration firestop system. The firestop system must be tested and installed in accordance with either ASTM E 814, or UL 1479. The firestop system must always have an appropriate F rating to indicate that it is capable of stopping fire, flame, and hot gases from passing through the horizontal assembly at the point of penetration. In addition, as a general rule the system must also have an appropriate T rating demonstrating that the firestop system adequately limits the temperature transfer to the unexposed side of the assembly. A second exception to the requirement for T ratings now allows those floor penetrations of horizontal assemblies due to the presence of floor, tub, and shower drains to be provided with only an F rating.

It is common for most floor penetrations of horizontal assemblies to occur within the cavity of a wall above or below the floor. In such cases, a T rating is not required for the penetrating item due to the allowance granted by Exception 1. However, drain piping from floor drains, bathtubs, and showers typically penetrates at a point where no such wall exists. Thus, those drains cannot be addressed under the previous T rating exception. It was determined that the concealed space in a horizontal assembly is comparable in construction and protection to that of a wall cavity, thus providing a degree of protection equivalent to that of Exception 1.

714.4.1.2

Interruption of Horizontal Assemblies

CHANGE TYPE: Modification

CHANGE SUMMARY: The ceiling membrane of a 1-hour or 2-hour fire-resistance-rated floor/ceiling or roof/ceiling assembly is now permitted to be interrupted by a double wood top plate of a fire-resistance-rated wall.

2013 CODE: **~~713.4.1.2~~ 714.4.1.2 Membrane Penetrations.** Penetrations of membranes that are part of a horizontal assembly shall comply with Section 714.4.1.1.1 or 714.4.1.1.2. Where floor/ceiling assemblies are required to have a fire-resistance rating, recessed fixtures shall be installed such that the required fire resistance will not be reduced.

Exceptions:

1.-5. (no changes to text)

6. Noncombustible items that are cast into concrete building elements and that do not penetrate both top and bottom surfaces of the element.
7. The ceiling membrane of 1-hour and 2-hour fire-resistance-rated horizontal assemblies is permitted to be interrupted with the double wood top plate of a fire-resistance wall assembly, provided that all penetrating items through the double top plates are protected in accordance with Section 714.4.1.1.1 or 714.4.1.1.2. The fire-resistance rating of the wall shall not be less than the rating of the horizontal assembly.

714.4.1.2 continued

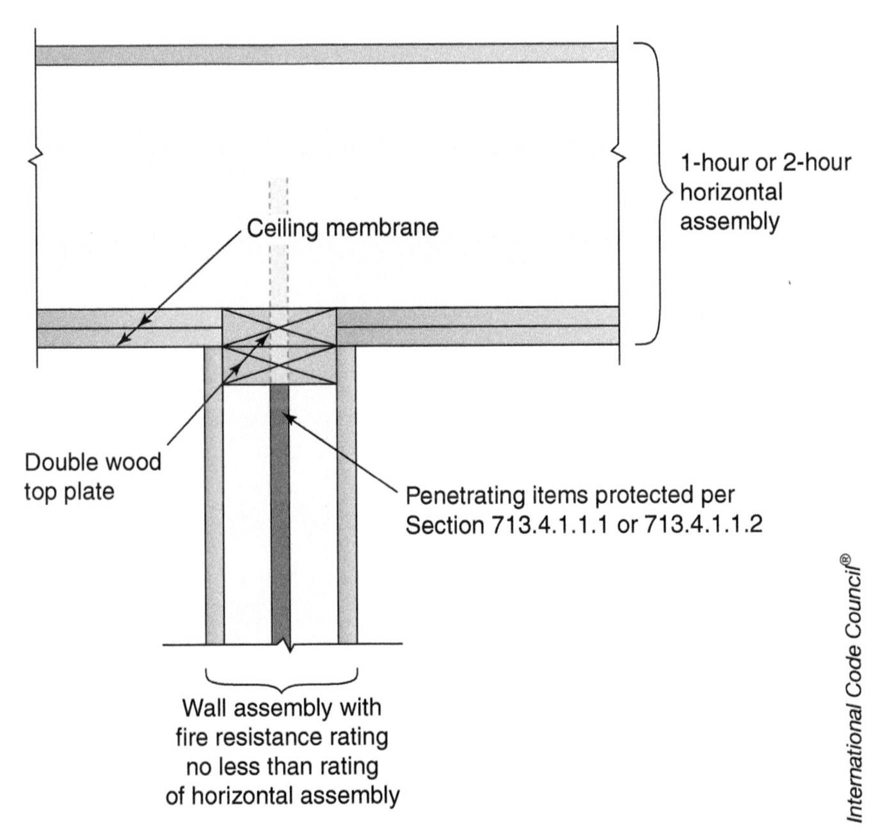

Horizontal assembly continuity at fire-rated wall.

714.4.1.2 continued

CHANGE SIGNIFICANCE: A horizontal assembly, defined as "a fire-resistance-rated floor or roof assembly of materials designed to restrict the spread of fire in which continuity is maintained," is required to be continuous without openings, penetrations, or joints unless specifically permitted. Based on the recognition that some degree of penetrations is necessary, acceptable membrane penetration methods are established in Section 714.4.1.2. In addition to five existing specific allowances that permit various membrane penetrations, a new exception allows the ceiling membrane of a 1-hour or 2-hour fire-resistance-rated floor/ceiling or roof/ceiling assembly to be interrupted by a double wood top plate of a fire-resistance-rated wall. There are two conditions of use: (1) the wall must have fire-resistance rating no less than that of the horizontal assembly, and (2) any penetrations of the double wood top plate must be adequately addressed.

The new exception allows for the practical application of the code where wood-framed walls extend up and attach directly to the underside of wood floor joists/trusses or roof joists/trusses for structural requirements. However, there are limits to its use. Non-fire-rated wall top plates are not allowed to interrupt the gypsum board membrane of the floor/ceiling or roof/ceiling membrane. The allowance is only permitted where the horizontal assembly has a required fire-resistance-rating of 2 hours or less, and the intersecting wall must have a fire-resistance rating equal or greater than that of the horizontal assembly. Piping, conduit, and similar items within the fire-resistance-rated wall must be adequately protected where they penetrate the double wood top plate.

Compliance with the established criteria was deemed to provide for an equivalent degree of fire resistance at the discontinuous portion of the ceiling membrane at the intersection of a horizontal assembly and a fire-resistance-rated wall with a double wood top plate.

Another new exception addresses the partial penetration of noncombustible items into fire-resistance-rated concrete building elements.

715.4

Exterior Curtain Wall/ Floor Intersection

CHANGE TYPE: Modification

CHANGE SUMMARY: The use of ASTM E 119 test criteria is now recognized as an acceptable evaluation method for addressing voids at the intersection of fire-resistance-rated floor assemblies and exterior curtain wall assemblies, but only for those curtain wall assemblies where the vision glass extends down to the finished floor level.

2013 CODE: ~~714.4~~ 715.4 Exterior Curtain Wall/Floor Intersection. Where fire resistance-rated floor or floor/ceiling assemblies are required, voids created at the intersection of the exterior curtain wall assemblies and such floor assemblies shall be sealed with an approved system to prevent the interior spread of fire. Such systems shall be securely installed and tested in accordance with ASTM E 2307 to ~~prevent the passage of flame~~ provide an F rating for ~~the~~ a time period at least equal to the fire-resistance rating of the floor assembly ~~and prevent the passage of heat and hot gases sufficient to ignite cotton waste~~. Height and fire-resistance requirements for curtain wall spandrels shall comply with Section 705.8.5.

> **Exception:** Voids created at the intersection of the exterior curtain wall assemblies and such floor assemblies where the vision glass extends to the finished floor level shall be permitted to be sealed with an approved material to prevent the interior spread of fire. Such material shall be securely installed and capable of preventing the passage of flame and hot gases sufficient to ignite cotton waste where subjected to ASTM E 119 time–temperature fire conditions under a minimum positive pressure differential of 0.01 inch (0.254 mm) of water column (2.5 Pa) for the time period at least equal to the fire-resistance rating of the floor assembly.

715.4 continued

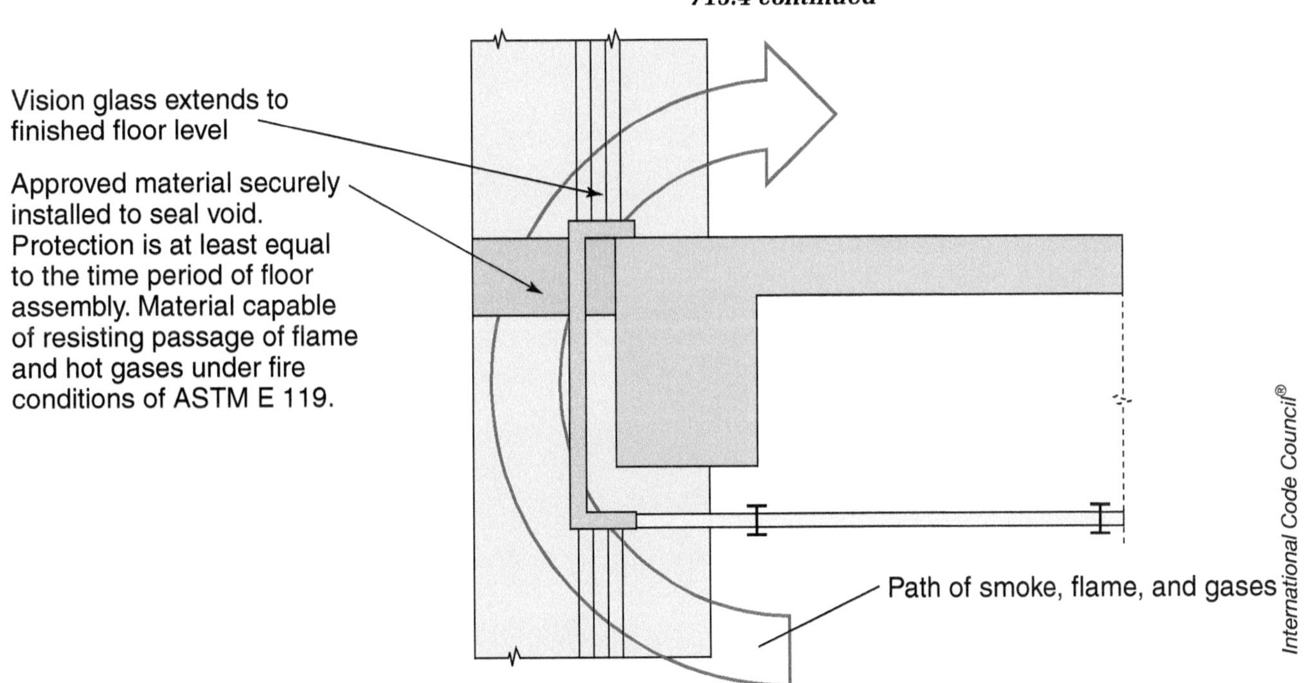

Joint protection at exterior curtain wall/floor intersection.

715.4 continued

CHANGE SIGNIFICANCE: Vertical passages—including those that occur at the intersection of an exterior curtain wall and floor system—allow fire, smoke, and hot gases to quickly travel from story to story if they are not appropriately addressed. Where such openings occur in relationship to a fire-resistance-rated floor or floor assembly, the provisions mandate an approved barrier at the intersection at least equal to the required fire resistance of the floor or floor assembly. The necessary degree of protection has been clarified by specifying that the perimeter fire barrier system provide an F rating equal to that of the fire-resistance rating of the floor assembly. Accordingly, the performance language has been removed because the "F" rating as determined in accordance with ASTM E 2307 evaluates the effectiveness of the material or assembly for passage of flame, heat, and hot gases. The revision also clarifies that the provisions only call for an F rating and a T rating is not required. Previous performance language addressed the prevention of heat passage which potentially brought in the issue of regulating temperature rise.

The use of ASTM E 2307, *Standard Test Method for Determining Fire Resistance of Perimeter Fire Barrier Systems Using Intermediate-scale, Multistory Test Apparatus*, as the test method for perimeter fire barrier systems first occurred in the 2006 edition of the IBC. Prior to that time, the materials and systems were required to comply with the ASTM E 119,*Test Methods for Fire Tests of Building Construction and Materials*, time–temperature fire conditions. Although the 2007 CBC allowed perimeter fire barrier systems to comply with either ASTM E 119 or ASTM E 2307, the 2010 edition of the CBC only recognized those systems complying with ASTM E 2307. The use of ASTM E 119 test criteria has now again been viewed as an acceptable evaluation method, but only for those curtain wall assemblies where the vision glass extends down to the finished floor level. Where the curtain wall consists of full height vision panels, acceptance under the criteria of ASTM E 2307 cannot be attained, although compliance in accordance with the traditional ASTM E 119 criteria is possible. Therefore, the previous IBC allowance utilizing ASTM E 119 has been reinstated for this specific condition. The language in the exception is consistent with the text in previous code editions recognizing the E 119 test method.

Table 716.5

Opening Protection Ratings and Markings

CHANGE TYPE: Clarification

CHANGE SUMMARY: The information previously available in Table 715.4 addressing the minimum required fire-protection ratings of fire door and fire shutter assemblies has been extensively expanded to also include the maximum size and marking requirements for door vision panels and the minimum assembly rating and glazing marking requirements for sidelights and transoms.

2013 CODE:

TABLE ~~715.4~~ 716.5 ~~Fire Door and Fire Shutter Fire Protection Ratings~~
Opening Fire-Protection Assemblies, Ratings, and Markings

Type of Assembly	Required Wall Assembly Rating (Hours)	Minimum Fire Door and Fire Shutter Assembly Rating (Hours)	Door Vision Panel Size	Fire-Rated Glazing Marking Door Vision Panel[e]	Minimum Sidelight/ Transom Assembly Rating (Hours)		Fire-Rated Glazing Marking Sidelite/ Transom Panel	
					Fire protection	Fire resistance	Fire protection	Fire resistance
Fire walls and fire barriers having a required fire-resistance rating greater than 1 hour	4	3	Not Permitted	Not Permitted	Not Permitted	4	Not Permitted	W-240
	3	3[a]	Not Permitted	Not Permitted	Not Permitted	3	Not Permitted	W-180
	2	1½	100 sq. in.[c]	≤100.in.² = D-H--90 >100 in.² = D-H-W-90 ≤100 in.² = D-H-90	Not Permitted	2	Not Permitted	W-120
	1½	1½	100 sq. in.[c]	>100.in.² = D-H-W-90 <100 in.² = D-H-90	Not Permitted	1½	Not Permitted	W-90
Shaft, exit enclosures, and exit passageway walls	2	1½	100 in.²[c, d]	≤100 in.² = D-H -T-or D-H-T-W-90	Not Permitted	2	Not Permitted	W-120

continued

Table 716.5 continued

Type of Assembly	Required Wall Assembly Rating (Hours)	Minimum Fire Door and Fire Shutter Assembly Rating (Hours)	Door Vision Panel Size	Fire-Rated Glazing Marking Door Vision Panel[e]	Minimum Sidelight/ Transom Assembly Rating (Hours)		Fire-Rated Glazing Marking Sidelite/Transom Panel	
					Fire protection	Fire resistance	Fire protection	Fire resistance
Fire barriers having a required fire-resistance rating of 1 hour: Enclosures for shafts, eixt access stairways, exit access ramps, interior exit stairways, interior exit ramps, and exit passageway walls	1	1	100 in.^{2} [c, d]	≤100 in.^{2} = D-H-60 >100 in.^{2} = D-H-T-60 or D-H-T-W-60	Not Permitted	1	Not Permitted	W-60
					Fire protection			
Other fire barriers	1	¾	Maximum size tested	D-H-NT-45	¾		D-H-NT-45	
	1	⅓[b]	Maximum size tested	D-20	¾[b]		D-H-OH-45	
Fire partitions Corridor walls	0.5	⅓[b]	Maximum size tested	D-20	⅓		D-H-OH-20	
Other fire partitions	1	¾	Maximum size tested	D-H-45	¾		D-H-45	
	0.5	⅓	Maximum size tested	D-H-20	⅓		D-H-20	
					Fire protection	Fire resistance	Fire protection	Fire resistance
Exterior walls	3	1½	100 in.^{2} [c]	≤100 in.^{2} = D-H-90 >100 in.^{2} = D-H-W-90	Not Permitted	3	Not Permitted	W-180
	2	1½	100 in.^{2} [c]	≤100 in.^{2} = D-H-90 >100 in.^{2} = D-H-W-90	Not Permitted	2	Not Permitted	W-120
					Fire protection			
	1	¾	Maximum size tested	D-H-45	¾		D-H-45	
					Fire protection			
Smoke barriers	1	⅓[b]	Maximum size tested	D-20	¾		D-H-OH-45	

a. Two doors, each with a fire protection rating of 1-½ hours, installed on opposite sides of the same opening in a fire wall, shall be deemed equivalent in fire protection rating to one 3-hour fire door.

b. For testing requirements, see Section 716.6.3.

c. Fire-resistance-rated glazing tested to ASTM E 119 per Section 716.2 shall be permitted, in the maximum size tested.

d. Except where the building is equipped throughout with an automatic sprinkler and the fire-rated glazing meets the criteria established in Section 716.5.5.

e. Under the column heading "Fire-Rated Glazing Marking Door Vision Panel," W refers to the fire-resistance rating of the glazing, not the frame.

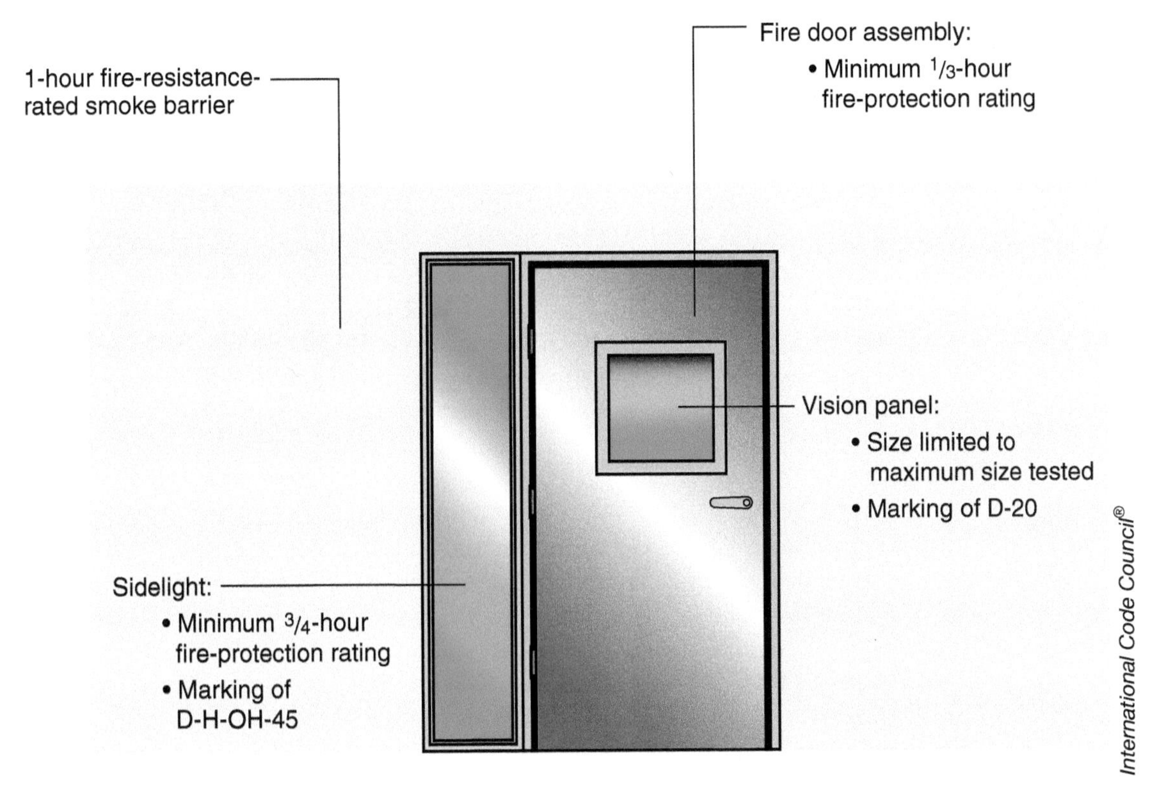

Markings for fire door assembly, vision panel, and sidelight.

CHANGE SIGNIFICANCE: Intended to maintain the integrity of the fire separation elements in which they are located, fire door and fire shutter assemblies used as opening protectives in fire-resistance-rated walls are uniquely regulated. Under certain conditions, door assemblies must provide a high degree of smoke resistance as well. Vision panels, sidelights, and transoms have their own specific requirements. It is critical that all aspects related to the installation of a fire door or fire shutter assembly be evaluated in order to provide a complete fire separation. The information previously available in Table 715.4 addressing the minimum required fire-protection ratings of fire door and fire shutter assemblies has been extensively expanded to also include the maximum size and marking requirements for door vision panels and the minimum assembly rating and glazing marking requirements for sidelights and transoms. The inclusion of this information in the table retains the technical requirements while making them more convenient for the code user. As a result, all text provisions used to define and relate test standards to marking designations have been deleted in favor of the tabular format.

716.5.5.1

Glazing in Exit Enclosure and Exit Passageway Doors

CHANGE TYPE: Modification

CHANGE SUMMARY: The allowance for glazing in fire door assemblies in interior stairways and ramps and exit passageways has been revised in regard to the maximum permitted size of the glazing and the limitations where the building is fully sprinklered.

2013 CODE: ~~715.4.4~~ 716.5.5 Doors in ~~Exit Enclosures~~ Interior Exit Stairways and Ramps and Exit Passageways. Fire door assemblies in ~~exit enclosures~~ interior exit stairways and ramps and exit passageways shall have a maximum transmitted temperature rise of not more than 450°F (250°C) above ambient at the end of 30 minutes of standard fire test exposure.

> **Exception:** The maximum transmitted temperature rise is not required in buildings equipped throughout with an automatic sprinkler system installed in accordance with Section 903.3.1.1 or 903.3.1.2.

~~715.4.4.1~~ 716.5.5.1 Glazing in Doors. Fire-protection-rated glazing in excess of 100 square inches (0.065 m^2) is not permitted. Fire-resistance rated glazing in excess of 100 square inches (0.065 m^2) shall be permitted in fire door assemblies when tested as components of the door assemblies, and not as glass lights, and shall have a maximum transmitted temperature rise of 450°F (250°C) in accordance with Section 716.5.5.

Glazing in interior exit stairway or ramp or exit passageway door.

Exception: ~~The maximum transmitted temperature rise is not required in buildings equipped throughout with an automatic sprinkler system installed in accordance with Section 903.3.1.1 or 903.3.1.2.~~

CHANGE SIGNIFICANCE: Interior exit stairways and ramps and exit passageways are intended to provide a high degree of occupant protection within the means of egress system. As such, fire door assemblies in such exit elements of nonsprinklered buildings must provide for a maximum temperature rise of 450°F above ambient after 30 minutes of standard fire test exposures. The end-point limitation on temperature transmission through the fire door assembly is to protect the person inside the enclosure from excessive heat radiation at the fire door as he or she passes through the fire floor. The allowance for glazing in such fire door assemblies has been revised in regard to two issues: (1) the maximum permitted size of the glazing and (2) the limitations where the building is fully sprinklered.

Fire-protection-rated glazing in a fire door assembly in an interior exit stairway or ramp or exit passageway is no longer permitted to exceed 100 square inches in area. This limitation is now consistent with those for fire-protection-rated glazing installed in 1-hour and 1½-hour fire door assemblies in other types of fire separation elements, such as horizontal exits, control area separations, and occupancy separations. Previously, there was no maximum permitted amount of fire-protection-rated glazing provided the glazing was tested as a component of the door assembly. Where the glazing is fire-resistance-rated, the limit of 100 square inches does not apply if tested as a fire door component.

Table 716.6

Fire-Protection-Rated Glazing

CHANGE TYPE: Clarification

CHANGE SUMMARY: In addition to fire window assembly fire-protection ratings, Table 716.6 now identifies the markings required on the fire-rated glazing for acceptance in specified applications.

2013 CODE: ~~715.5~~ 716.6 Fire-Protection-Rated Glazing. Glazing in fire window assemblies shall be fire-protection rated in accordance with this section and Table 716.6. Glazing in fire door assemblies shall comply with Section 716.5.8. Fire-protection-rated glazing in fire window assemblies shall be tested in accordance with and shall meet the acceptance criteria of NFPA 257 or UL 9. Fire-protection-rated glazing shall also comply with NFPA 80. Openings in nonfire-resistance-rated exterior wall assemblies that require protection in accordance with Section 705.3, 705.8, 705.8.5, or 705.8.6 shall have a fire-protection rating of not less than ¾ hour. Fire protection-rated glazing in 0.5-hour fire-resistance-rated partitions is permitted to have a 0.33-hour fire-protection rating.

~~**Exceptions:**~~

~~2. Fire protection-rated glazing in 0.5-hour fire-resistance-rated partitions is permitted to have an 0.33-hour fire-protection rating.~~

TABLE ~~715.5~~ 716.6 Fire Window Assembly Fire-Protection Ratings

Type of Wall Assembly	Required Wall Assembly Rating (Hours)	Minimum Fire Window Assembly Rating (Hours)	Fire-Rated Glazing Marking
Interior walls			
Fire walls	All	NP[a]	W-xxx[b]
Fire barriers	>1	NP[a]	W-xxx[b]
	1	NP[a]	W-xxx[b]
Incidental-use areas (707.3.6) Mixed-occupancy separations (707.3.8)	1	¾	OH-45 or W-60
Fire partitions	1	¾	OH-45 or W-60
	0.5	⅓	OH-20 or W-30
Smoke barriers	1	¾	OH-45 or W-60
Exterior walls	>1	1½	OH-90 or W-XXX[b]
	1	¾	OH-45 or W-60
	0.5	⅓	OH-20 or W-30
Party wall	All	NP	Not applicable

NP – Not Permitted

a. Not permitted except fire-resistance-rated glazing assemblies tested to ASTM E 119 or UL 263, as specified in Section 716.2.

b. XXX = The fire rating duration period in minutes, which shall be equal to the fire resistance rating required for the wall assembly.

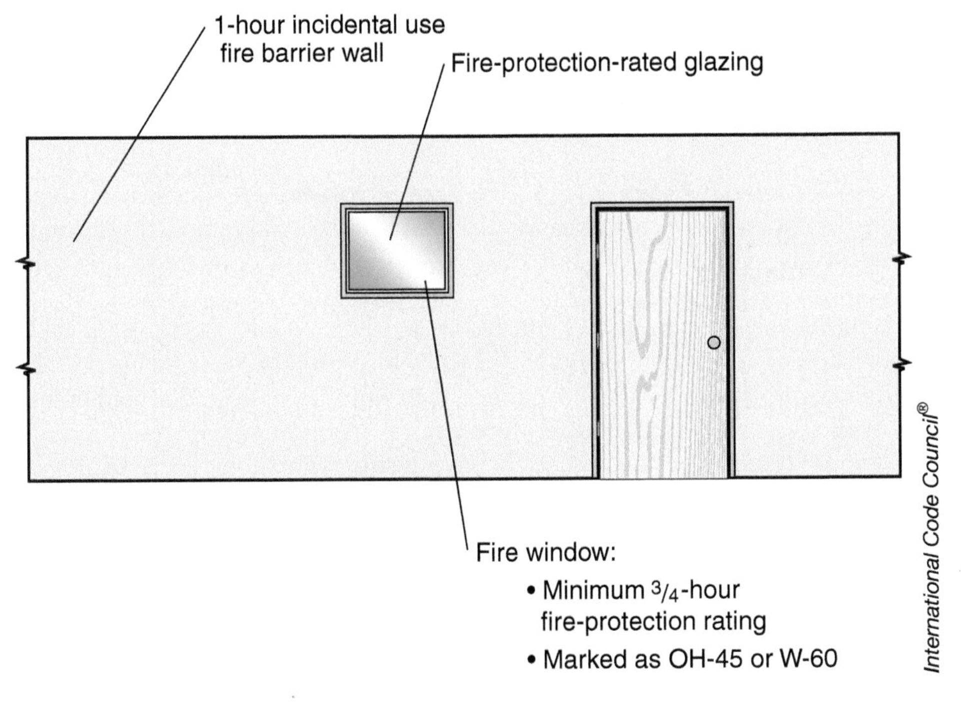

Fire window in incidental-use fire barrier wall.

CHANGE SIGNIFICANCE: In many situations, it is necessary to provide glazed openings in fire-resistance-rated walls. Fire window assemblies satisfy this need as opening protectives in fire partitions, smoke barriers, exterior walls, and specified fire barriers. Table 716.6 has historically identified the minimum fire-protection rating required for fire windows based upon the type of wall assembly and the required wall assembly rating. The table now also identifies the marking required on the fire-rated glazing for acceptance in specified applications. By inserting the marking information into Table 716.6, it is intended to provide building and fire code officials with easy access to all of the information needed when inspecting fire window installations, including required marking designations.

As part of the table's expansion, the allowance for 3/4-hour fire windows in fire barriers utilized as incidental use separations and occupancy separations has been relocated from the text. In addition, fire window requirements for ½-hour fire-resistance-rated exterior walls have been included, however the code currently has no requirement for the use of such walls.

716.6.4

Wired Glass in Fire Window Assemblies

CHANGE TYPE: Deletion

CHANGE SUMMARY: The allowance for the use of wired glass without compliance with the appropriate test standards has been deleted.

2013 CODE: ~~**715.5**~~ **716.6 Fire-Protection-Rated Glazing.** Glazing in fire window assemblies shall be fire-protection rated in accordance with this section and Table 716.6. Glazing in fire door assemblies shall comply with Section 716.5.8. Fire-protection-rated glazing in fire window assemblies shall be tested in accordance with and shall meet the acceptance criteria of NFPA 257 or UL 9. Fire-protection-rated glazing shall also comply with NFPA 80. Openings in non-fire-resistance-rated exterior wall assemblies that require protection in accordance with Section 705.3, 705.8, 705.8.5, or 705.8.6 shall have a fire-protection rating of not less than ¾ hour. Fire protection-rated glazing in 0.5-hour fire-resistance-rated partitions is permitted to have a 0.33-hour fire-protection rating.

~~**Exceptions:**~~

~~1. Wired glass in accordance with Section 715.5.4.~~

~~**715.5.4 Wired glass.** Steel window frame assemblies of 0.125-inch (3.2 mm) minimum solid section or of not less than nominal 0.048-inch-thick (1.2 mm) formed sheet steel members fabricated by pressing, mitering, riveting, interlocking or welding and having provision for glazing with ¼-inch (6.4 mm) wired glass where securely installed in the building construction and glazed with ¼-inch (6.4 mm) labeled wired glass shall be deemed to meet the requirements for a ¾-hour fire window assembly. Wired glass panels shall conform to the size limitations set forth in Table 715.5.4.~~

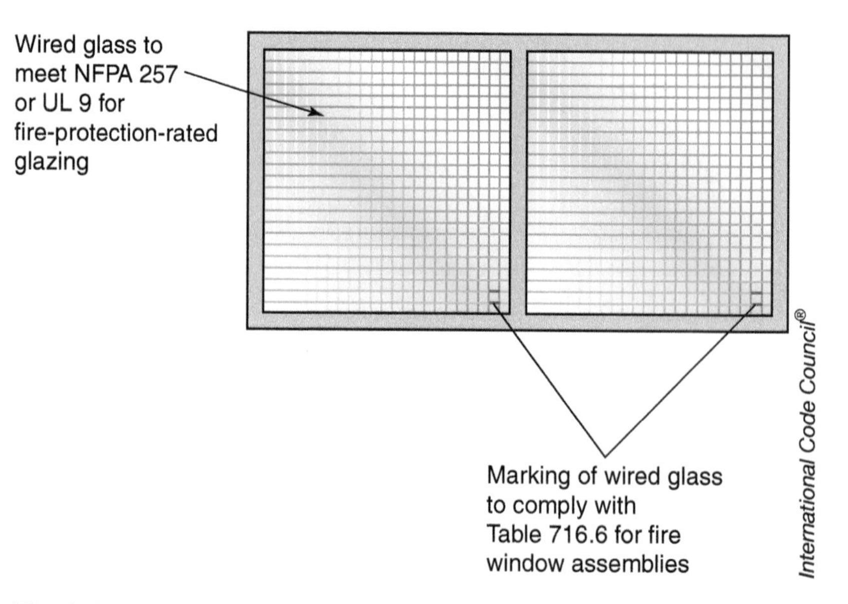

Wired glass used in a fire window assembly.

~~**TABLE 715.5.4 Limiting Sizes Of Wired Glass Panels**~~

~~Opening Fire Protection Rating~~	~~Maximum Area (Square Inches)~~	~~Maximum Height(Inches)~~	~~Maximum Width (Inches)~~
~~3 hours~~	~~0~~	~~0~~	~~0~~
~~1½-hour doors in exterior walls~~	~~0~~	~~0~~	~~0~~
~~1 and 1½ hours~~	~~100~~	~~33~~	~~10~~
~~¾ hours~~	~~1,296~~	~~54~~	~~54~~
~~20 minutes~~	~~Not Limited~~	~~Not Limited~~	~~Not Limited~~
~~Fire window assemblies~~	~~1,296~~	~~54~~	~~54~~

~~**715.5.5 Nonwired glass.**~~ **716.6.4 Glass and Glazing.** Glazing ~~other than wired glass~~ in fire window assemblies shall be fire-protection-rated glazing installed in accordance with and complying with the size limitations set forth in NFPA 80.

CHANGE SIGNIFICANCE: Where glazing occurs in walls that require openings to have a fire-protection rating, such glazing (fire windows) must be tested in accordance with either NFPA 257, *Standard for Fire Test for Window and Glass Block Assemblies*, or UL 9, *Fire Tests of Window Assemblies*. Other than fire-resistance-rated glazing, the only glazing permitted without such a fire-protection rating has historically been wired glass installed within a steel frame in accordance with specific prescriptive provisions established by the code. The allowance for the use of wired glass without compliance with the appropriate test standards has been removed, along with the companion Table 715.5.4, which addressed the maximum size of wired glass panels. Specific reference to the use of wired glass in fire window assemblies has also been deleted from NFPA 80, *Fire Doors and Other Opening Protectives,* which regulates the installation and size limitations of such assemblies. With the removal of Exception 1 to Section 715.5, all glazing in fire-window assemblies must now be fire protection rated, including wired glass.

The use of traditional wired glass has been prohibited for some time in fire doors because it does not meet the CPSC safety glazing requirements of Section 2406.1. Table 715.5.4 has been confusing to many code users because it appears to prescribe permitted size limits for wired glass in doors which are no longer allowed of any significant size. The only accepted application for wired glass is in fire assemblies in nonhazardous locations, and it was determined that a table was not needed to prescribe those size limitations.

717.5.4

Fire Damper Exemption for Fire Partitions

CHANGE TYPE: Modification

CHANGE SUMMARY: The omission of fire dampers in fire partitions is now permitted under the same criteria that have been previously established for fire barriers.

2013 CODE: ~~**716.5.4**~~ **717.5.4 Fire Partitions.** *In other than Group A, E, I and R occupancies, high-rise buildings, and other applications listed in Section 1.11 regulated by the Office of the State Fire Marshal,* ducts and air transfer openings that penetrate fire partitions shall be protected with listed fire dampers installed in accordance with their listing.

> **Exceptions:** In occupancies other than Group H, fire dampers are not required where any of the following apply:
>
> **1.-3.** (no changes to text)
>
> **4.** Such walls are penetrated by ducted HVAC systems, have a required fire-resistance rating of 1 hour or less, and are in buildings equipped throughout with an automatic sprinkler system in accordance with Section 903.3.1.1 or 903.3.1.2. For the purposes of this exception, a ducted HVAC system shall be a duct system for conveying supply, return, or exhaust air as part of the structure's HVAC system. Such a duct system shall be constructed of sheet steel not less than 26 gage thickness and shall be continuous from the air-handling appliance or equipment to the air outlet and inlet terminals.

CHANGE SIGNIFICANCE: Where a vertical fire assembly, such as a fire barrier or fire partition, is penetrated by a duct or air transfer opening,

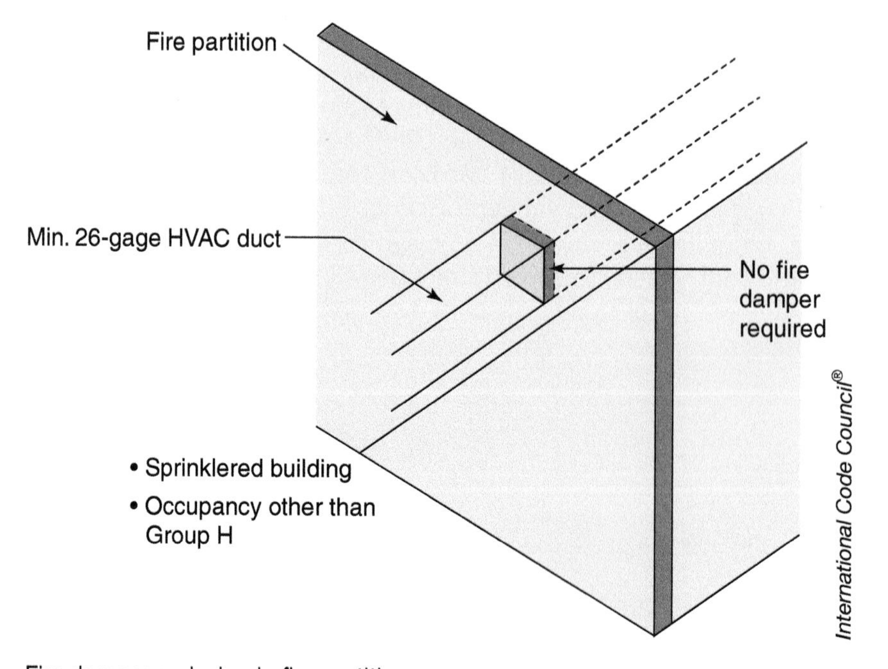

Fire damper omission in fire partition.

the integrity of the assembly must typically be maintained through the installation of a listed fire damper. Exception 3 to Section 717.5.2 has historically allowed the omission of fire dampers at penetrations of fire barriers where the specific conditions of the exception are met; however, such an allowance has not previously been available for fire partitions. The new exception to Section 717.5.4 now permits the omission of fire dampers in fire partitions under the same criteria that have been established for fire barriers. Fire dampers are no longer required in duct and air transfer openings that penetrate fire partitions provided:

- the penetration consists of a duct that is a portion of a ducted HVAC system.
- the fire-resistance rating of the fire partition is 1 hour or less.
- the area is not a Group H occupancy.
- the building is fully protected by an automatic fire-sprinkler system.

The limitations established continue to provide for an acceptable alternative to fire dampers in fully sprinklered buildings.

There are two important considerations regarding the application of this new exception. First, the exception is applicable only to the omission of fire dampers and does not eliminate any smoke damper requirements that may be imposed by the code. Second, the exception has no application to fire-resistance-rated corridors because there is no requirement for fire dampers in such corridors in fully sprinklered buildings.

903.2.2

Sprinklers in Ambulatory Care Facilities

CHANGE TYPE: Modification

CHANGE SUMMARY: Automatic sprinkler requirements for Group B ambulatory care facilities are now regulated on a floor-by-floor basis.

2013 CODE: 903.2.2 ~~Group B~~ Ambulatory ~~Health~~ Care Facilities. An automatic sprinkler system shall be installed throughout ~~all fire areas~~ the entire floor containing an ~~Group B~~ ambulatory ~~health~~ care facility, where either of the following conditions exist at any time:

1. Four or more care recipients are incapable of self-preservation, whether rendered incapable by staff or staff has accepted responsibility for care recipients already incapable.
2. One or more care recipients that are incapable of self-preservation are located at other than the level of exit discharge serving such ~~an~~ facility ~~occupancy~~.

In buildings where care is provided on levels other than the level of exit discharge, an automatic sprinkler system shall be installed throughout the entire floor where such care is provided as well as all floors below, and all floors between the level of ambulatory care and the nearest level of exit discharge, including the level of exit discharge.

CHANGE SIGNIFICANCE: Requirements for ambulatory care facilities were introduced in the 2010 code and previously defined as Ambulatory Health Care Facilities. Ambulatory care facilities, also known as ambulatory surgery centers, are designed so health care practitioners can deliver

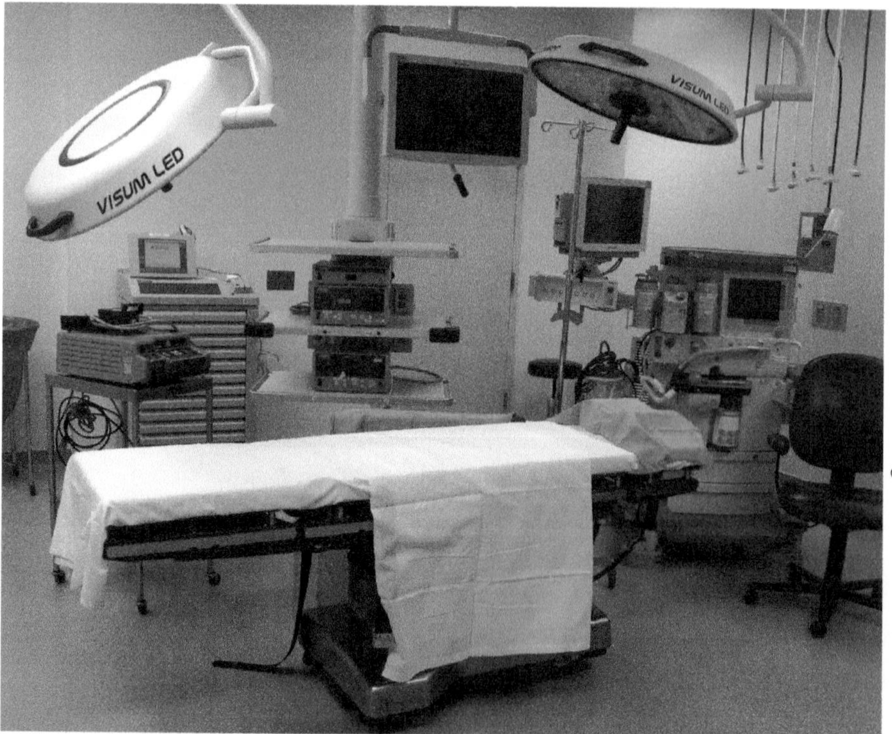

International Code Council®

Operating suite in an ambulatory care facility.

surgical procedures that do not require the patient to have such a treatment within a hospital. Within ambulatory care facilities (ACF), the patient is capable of entering and leaving the building on the same day of the procedure. Conversely, hospitalization of an individual normally requires a 24-hour stay, which is the basis for the institutional (Group I) occupancy classification and code requirements. Many of the procedures performed in an ACF require that the patient be incapacitated by anesthesia or sedation of the body's central nervous system, which means the individual is no longer capable of self-rescue and preservation in the event a fire or other emergency occurs within the building. Patients undergoing treatment in an ACF are capable of being placed under home health care within a few hours of the treatment and do not require an overnight stay in a hospital.

ACFs remain classified as Group B occupancies in the 2013 CBC. The 2010 CBC required automatic sprinkler protection for an ACF based on its location in relation to the level of exit discharge or the number of patients who were incapable of self-preservation. However, the requirement for the sprinkler system was limited only to the fire area containing the ACF. Under the 2013 CBC, automatic sprinkler protection is now required to be extended throughout the entire story where the ACF is located, not just within its fire area. In addition, where the ACF is located on a story other than the level of exit discharge, the automatic sprinkler system is required on the level of exit discharge and all of the stories between it and the ACF.

Because occupants are incapable of self-preservation, it is important that the sprinkler protection be extended over the entire floor because occupant evacuation times will be greater when compared to buildings where occupants are capable of self-preservation and able to initiate self-rescue. That same rationale about the increased evacuation times is also one of the reasons protecting the stories between the ACF and the level of exit discharge is important. This will provide a safe route for evacuating the occupants to the exterior of the building and will ensure they do not leave a sprinklered area to egress through a nonsprinklered area.

903.2.4, 903.2.7, 903.2.9

Furniture Storage and Display in Group F-1, M, and S-1 Occupancies

International Code Council®

Storage area containing upholstered furniture.

CHANGE TYPE: Modification

CHANGE SUMMARY: Automatic sprinkler systems are now required in occupancies where upholstered furniture or mattresses are manufactured, stored, or displayed.

2013 CODE: 903.2.4 Group F-1. An automatic sprinkler system shall be provided throughout all buildings containing a Group F-1 occupancy where one of the following conditions exists:

1. A Group F-1 fire area exceeds 12,000 square feet (1115 m^2).
2. A Group F-1 fire area is located more than three stories above grade plane.
3. The combined area of all Group F-1 fire areas on all floors, including any mezzanines, exceeds 24,000 square feet (2230 m^2).
4. A Group F-1 occupancy used for the manufacture of upholstered furniture or mattresses exceeds 2,500 square feet (232 m^2).

903.2.7 Group M. An automatic sprinkler system shall be provided throughout buildings containing a Group M occupancy where one of the following conditions exists:

1. A Group M fire area exceeds 12,000 square feet (1115 m^2).
2. A Group M fire area is located more than three stories above grade plane.
3. The combined area of all Group M fire areas on all floors, including any mezzanines, exceeds 24,000 square feet (2230 m^2).
4. A Group M occupancy area used for the display and sale of upholstered furniture or mattresses exceeds 5,000 square feet (464 m^2).
5. *The structure exceeds 24,000 square feet (465 m^2), contains more than one fire area containing a Group M occupancy, and is separated into two or more buildings by fire walls of less than 4-hour fire-resistance rating without openings.*

903.2.9 Group S-1. An automatic sprinkler system shall be provided throughout all buildings containing a Group S-1 occupancy where one of the following conditions exists:

1. A Group S-1 fire area exceeds 12,000 square feet (1115 m^2).
2. A Group S-1 fire area is located more than three stories above grade plane.
3. The combined area of all Group S-1 fire areas on all floors, including any mezzanines, exceeds 24,000 square feet (2230 m^2).
4. A Group S-1 fire area used for the storage of commercial trucks or buses where the fire area exceeds 5,000 square feet (464 m^2).
5. A Group S-1 occupancy used for the storage of upholstered furniture or mattresses exceeds 2,500 square feet (232 m^2).

CHANGE SIGNIFICANCE: The 2010 CBC introduced a new requirement that prescribed the installation of an automatic sprinkler system in any Group M occupancy that displayed and sold upholstered furniture, regardless of fire area size. The provision was not tied to the amount or height of furniture storage and it was unclear whether the requirement could be applied to bedding such as mattresses or box springs. Mattresses and box springs are not considered to be "upholstered furniture" under current Consumer Products Safety Commission regulations found in 16 CFR Part 1633, which is a performance standard that measures the ignition resistance of mattresses. Therefore, further refinement was deemed necessary for the requirement to be effective.

New limits have now been established for the presence of upholstered furniture and mattresses in Group F-1, M, and S-1 occupancies. Sections 903.2.4 and 903.2.9 addressing Group F-1 and Group S-1 occupancies, respectively, now establish a threshold of 2500 square feet for the storage or manufacturing of upholstered furniture and mattresses. In Group M occupancies, Section 903.2.7 establishes a threshold of 5000 square feet. These floor area values are arbitrary but are intended to reduce the burden on the regulated businesses while providing reasonable thresholds as to when automatic sprinkler protection is required.

The requirements in Section 903.2.4, 903.2.7, and 903.2.9 are tied to the floor area devoted to the manufacture, display, or storage of upholstered furniture rather than building fire area. Jurisdictions may want to develop some type of policy on these provisions because the exceptions all are tied to the area "used for" manufacturing, display, sale, or storage of the upholstered furniture or mattresses. The code does not clearly state how the storage or display area's size and quantity of the materials are to be measured. For example, can the occupancy have multiple areas within it, provided each area is below the size threshold, or would a single sofa in a large retail store trigger the requirements? Using a Group M occupancy in a nonsprinklered 11,000-square-foot space as an example, is it permissible to divide the display and storage of upholstered furniture or mattresses into areas of 4,900 square feet, each separated by exit access aisles and consider that each area is beneath the 5,000-square-foot threshold? Or, on the other hand, could a single piece of upholstered furniture in the store trigger the requirement because the store itself is over the area limitation? Jurisdictions should consider these scenarios and develop a policy to address how the floor area and quantity of the materials will be measured for the purpose of applying these requirements to determine when automatic sprinkler protection is required.

Another consideration when applying these provisions is the height of storage. Upholstered furniture or mattresses are commonly classified as high-hazard commodities in accordance with the fire code because they commonly are composed of large amounts of expanded Group A plastics.

903.2.6, 907.2.6.3, 907.3.2

Fire Protection Systems in Group I-3 Occupancies

CHANGE TYPE: Modification

CHANGE SUMMARY: The exception for sprinkler systems in cells of Group I-3 occupancies has been removed. Smoke detection is not required in temporary holding cells and, under certain conditions, is not required in inmate cells, day rooms, and sleeping units of I-3 occupancies. Except for single-story buildings, smoke detectors are required in all occupied areas and mechanical/electrical spaces of any story using delayed egress devices.

2013 CODE: ***903.2.6.2 Group I-3.*** *Every building, or portion thereof, where inmates or persons are in custody or restrained shall be protected by an automatic sprinkler system conforming to NFPA 13. The main sprinkler control valve or valves and all other control valves in the system shall be locked in the open position and electrically supervised so that at least an audible and visual alarm will sound at a constantly attended location when valves are closed. The sprinkler branch piping serving cells may be embedded in the concrete construction.*

An automatic smoke detection system is not required within temporary holding cells.

~~***Exception:*** *Sprinklers are not required in cells housing two or fewer inmates and the building shall be considered sprinklered throughout when all the following criteria are met:*~~

~~*1. Automatic fire sprinklers shall be mounted outside the cell a minimum of 6 feet (1829 mm) on center and 12 inches (305 mm) from the wall with quick response sprinkler heads. Where spacing permits, the head shall be centered over the cell door opening.*~~

~~*2. The maximum amount of combustibles, excluding linen and clothing, shall be maintained at three pounds per inmate.*~~

~~*3. For local detention facilities, each individual housing cell shall be provided with a two-way inmate or sound-actuated audio monitoring system for communication directly to the control station serving the cell(s).*~~

~~*4. The provisions of the exception in Section 804.4.2 shall not apply.*~~

907.2.6.3 Group I-3 Occupancies. Group I-3 occupancies shall be equipped with a manual fire alarm system and automatic smoke detection system installed for alerting staff.

Exception: *An automatic smoke detection system is not required within temporary holding cells.*

907.2.6.3.3 Automatic Smoke Detection System. An automatic smoke detection system shall be installed throughout resident housing areas, including sleeping units and contiguous day rooms, group activity spaces and other common spaces normally accessible to ~~residents~~ *inmates*.

Exceptions:

1. Other approved smoke detection ~~providing equivalent protection including, but not limited to, placing detectors in exhaust ducts from cells or behind protective guards listed for the purpose are allowed when necessary to prevent damage or tampering.~~ *arrangements may be used to prevent damage or tampering or for other purposes provided the function of detecting any fire is fulfilled and the location of the detectors is such that the speed of detection will be equivalent to that provided by the spacing and location required in accordance with NFPA 72 as referenced in Chapter 35. This may include the location of detectors in return air ducts from cells, behind grilles or in other locations. Spot type, combination duct and open area smoke detectors may be used when located not more than 14 inches (356 mm) from the return air grill. For initiation and annunciation purposes, these detectors may be combined in groups of four. The fire code official having jurisdiction, however, must approve the proposed equivalent performance of the design.*

~~2. Sleeping units in Use Conditions 2 and 3 as described in Section 308.~~

~~3. Smoke detectors are not required in sleeping units with four or fewer occupants in smoke compartments that are equipped throughout with an automatic sprinkler system installed in accordance with Section 903.3.1.1.~~

2. ~~*Department of Corrections, prison cell or cell complex*~~*For detention housing and/or mental health housing area(s), including correctional medical and mental health uses*, automatic

903.2.6, 907.2.6.3, 907.3.2 continued

903.2.6, 907.2.6.3, 907.3.2 continued

smoke detection system in sleeping units shall not be required when all of the following conditions are met:

2.1. *All rooms, including the inmate cells, are provided with an automatic sprinkler system in accordance with Section 903.3.1.1.*

2.2. *Building is continuously staffed by a correctional officer at all times.*

2.3. *The exception to Section 903.2.6.2 shall not apply.*

3. *Smoke detectors are not required to be installed in inmate cells with two or fewer occupants in detention facilities which do not have a correctional medical and mental health use.*

4. *Smoke detectors are not required to be installed in inmate day rooms of detention facilities where 24-hour direct visual supervision is provided by a correctional officer(s) and a manual fire alarm box is located in the control room.*

907.3.2.1 *In other than Group I, R-2.1 and Group R-4, occupancies for single-story buildings smoke detectors shall be installed at ceilings throughout all occupied areas and mechanical/electrical spaces. For multiple-story buildings smoke detectors shall be installed throughout all occupied areas and mechanical/electrical spaces for the story where delayed egress devices are installed. Additional detectors are required on adjacent stories where occupants of those stories utilize the same means of egress.*

Exception: *Refer to 907.3.2.4 for Group A courthouse occupancies.*

CHANGE SIGNIFICANCE: The I-3 Occupancy Codes Task Group reviewed the history and current correctional operation associated with Section 903.2.6.2 and its exceptions and proposed to repeal the exceptions. The exceptions were a holdover from barred cell front construction. With solid cell fronts commonly used, the exception for omitting sprinklers is no longer permitted.

The change to Section 907.2.6.3 intends to clarify that smoke detection is not required in temporary holding cells in I-3 occupancies as is allowed for sleeping rooms in Section 907.2.6.3.3. Temporary holding cells have far less combustible content and sources of ignition. Occupants of these spaces are there for limited periods of time. These spaces impose less risk than sleeping cells and day rooms which are exempted.

Changes to Exception 2 of Section 907.2.6.3.3 intends to clarify that the exemption from fire and smoke detection in cells in I-3 facilities also applies to correctional medical and mental health facilities.

Exception 3 eliminates smoke detection in inmate cells or cell cases that house two or fewer inmates. These inmate cells located in housing units are being continuously monitored by correction staff. The cells are constructed with noncombustible materials. Inmate cells are required to have automatic fire sprinkler protection and smoke detection in corridors. Inmate cells are also limited in the amount of combustible materials. Correctional staff can manually activate the fire alarm if needed. This exception does not apply to medical facilities.

Exception 4 removes the need for smoke detection in dayrooms located in inmate housing units of detention facilities where 24-hour direct supervision is provided by correctional staff. The high ceilings in these dayrooms prohibit the operational effectiveness of smoke detectors installed on the ceiling. Dayrooms are constructed with noncombustible materials and have automatic fire sprinklers throughout. Dayrooms are under continuous supervision by correctional staff that can manually activate the fire alarm if needed.

903.2.11.1.3

Sprinkler Protection for Basements

CHANGE TYPE: Modification

CHANGE SUMMARY: Basements provided with walls, partitions, or fixtures that can obstruct water from hose streams now require automatic sprinkler protection.

2013 CODE: 903.2.11.1.3 Basements. Where any portion of a basement is located more than 75 feet (22 860 mm) from openings required by Section 903.2.11.1, or where walls, partitions, or other obstructions are installed that restrict the application of water from hose streams, the basement shall be equipped throughout with an approved automatic sprinkler system.

CHANGE SIGNIFICANCE: Interior structural firefighting is a high-risk operation for firefighters. Numerous complications can arise when commencing an interior fire attack, including (but not limited to), problems with the water supply, protective clothing, breathing apparatus, or the structure. One area of buildings that can complicate interior firefighting is basements. IBC Section 202 defines a basement as a *story that is not a story above grade plane.* Basements can be partially or completely underground. Basements present some of the more challenging complications for firefighters because entering the area is analogous to entering a building through the chimney of a fireplace. All of the heat will collect at the highest point, which can be the entry doorway into the basement, so firefighters must push their way through these fire gases before commencing the application of water. Basements almost always contain building load-bearing elements so a fire involving this area can adversely affect structural stability when the area is involved in fire.

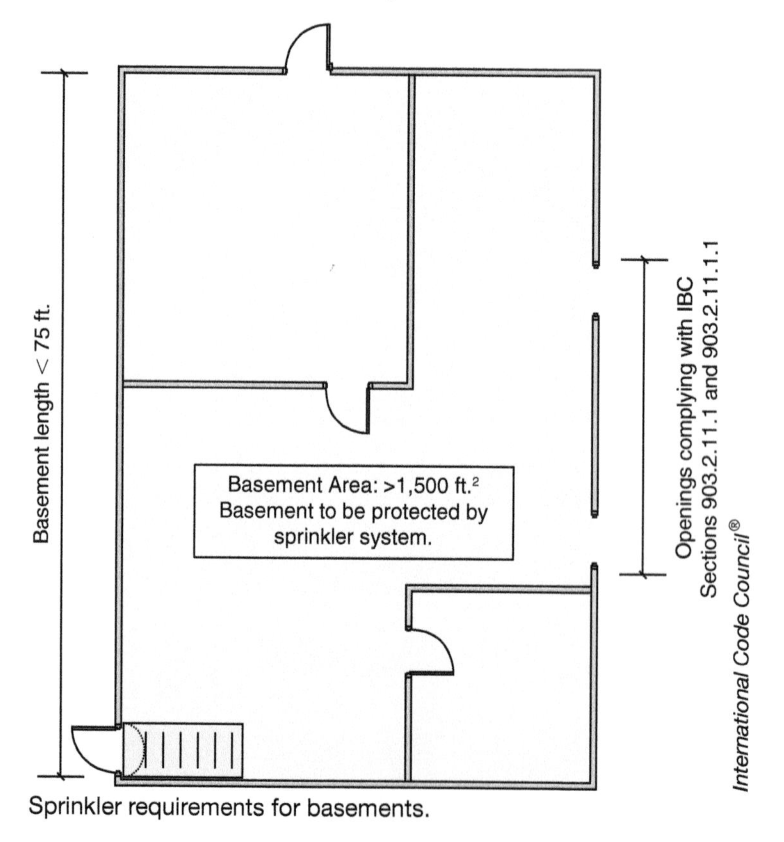

Sprinkler requirements for basements.

One concern during interior firefighting operations is obstruction of fire streams. Obstructions such as walls or partitions may prevent the application of water onto the area of fire involvement. The installation of an automatic sprinkler system in basements over 1500 square feet in floor area is now required when obstructions such as walls, partitions or similar elements are introduced which could obstruct the application of hose streams. It should be noted that whether the wall contains door openings or not has no effect on the application of the provision. While some code requirements such as exit access travel distance (Section 1016) and the location of Class II standpipes (Section 905.5) allow measuring along an available route through the building and through doors, the presence of doorways has no bearing on the code's application. Because a wall of any size has the potential to "restrict the application of water," the building official should be consulted if the design indicates anything other than a wide-open, unfurnished space and sprinklers are not intended to be installed.

903.3.1.1.1

Sprinkler Exemption for Solar Photovoltaic Systems

CHANGE TYPE: Modification

CHANGE SUMMARY: Solar photovoltaic panel structures with no use underneath and PV solar areas that are spaced to allow heat and gases to escape do not require automatic sprinkler protection.

2013 CODE: 903.3.1.1.1 Exempt Locations. *In other than Group I-2, I-2.1 and I-3 occupancies,* automatic sprinklers shall not be required in the following rooms or areas where such rooms or areas are protected with an approved automatic fire detection system in accordance with Section 907.2 that will respond to visible or invisible particles of combustion. Sprinklers shall not be omitted from any room merely because it is damp, of fire-resistance-rated construction or contains electrical equipment.

1. Any room where the application of water, or flame and water, constitutes a serious life or fire hazard.

2. Any room or space where sprinklers are considered undesirable because of the nature of the contents, when approved by the fire code official.

3. ~~Generator and transformer rooms separated from the remainder of the building by walls and floor/ceiling or roof/ceiling assemblies having a fire-resistance rating of not less than 2 hours.~~

4. ~~Rooms or areas that are of noncombustible construction with wholly noncombustible contents.~~

53. Fire service access elevator machine rooms and machinery spaces.

Solar PV structures with adequate spacing do not require fire sprinkler protection.

~~6~~4. Machine rooms and machinery spaces associated with occupant evacuation elevators designed in accordance with Section 3008.

5. *Spaces or areas in telecommunications buildings used exclusively for telecommunications equipment, and associated electrical power distribution equipment, provided those spaces or areas are equipped throughout with an automatic smoke detection system in accordance with Section 907.2 and are separated from the remainder of the building by not less than 1-hour fire barriers constructed in accordance with Section 707 or not less than 2-hour horizontal assemblies constructed in accordance with Section 712, or both.*

6. *Solar photovoltaic panel structures with no use underneath. Signs may be provided, as determined by the enforcing agency prohibiting any use underneath including storage.*

7. *Solar photovoltaic (PV) panels supported by framing that have sufficient uniformly distributed and unobstructed openings throughout the top of the array (horizontal plane) to allow heat and gases to escape, as determined by the enforcing agency.*

CHANGE SIGNIFICANCE: There was previously no specific exemption for solar PV systems from the automatic fire sprinkler requirements. In buildings that are required to be provided with fire sprinklers throughout, the code requires that all parts of the building be provided with fire sprinkler coverage. Some local governments have interpreted that to require fire sprinklers underneath elevated photovoltaic panels on the roof, which can be very costly. The code now specifically provides exemption from sprinklers for photovoltaic systems that have no use underneath. In addition, solar PV panel assemblies that may or may not have a use underneath but have adequate openings to allow heat and gases to escape are also exempt from the sprinkler provisions. Since there is no heat accumulation, the fire sprinklers would not have proper activation and operation. Additionally, configurations meeting the exemptions are considered equipment and are not subject to the requirement for sprinklers.

903.3.5.2

Secondary Water Supply

International Code Council®

Tank providing secondary water supply.

CHANGE TYPE: Modification

CHANGE SUMMARY: Secondary water supplies must now be designed to operate automatically.

2013 CODE: 903.3.5.2 Secondary Water Supply. *An automatic secondary on-site water supply having a usable capacity of not less than the hydraulically calculated sprinkler demand, including the hose stream requirement, shall be provided for high-rise buildings and Group I-2 occupancies having occupied floors located more than 75 feet above the lowest level of fire department vehicle access assigned to Seismic Design Category C, D, E or F as determined by the California Building Code. An additional fire pump shall not be required for the secondary water supply unless needed to provide the minimum design intake pressure at the suction side of the fire pump supplying the automatic sprinkler system. The secondary water supply shall have ~~a usable capacity of not less than the hydraulically calculated sprinkler demand plus 100 GPM for the inside hose stream allowance, for~~ a duration of not less than 30 minutes or as determined by the ~~sprinkler system design~~ occupancy hazard classification in accordance with NFPA 13, whichever is greater. The Class I standpipe system demand shall not be required to be included in the secondary on-site water supply calculations. In no case shall the secondary on-site water supply be less than 15,000 gallons.*

Exception: Existing buildings.

CHANGE SIGNIFICANCE: Any high-rise building constructed in accordance with the code requires a secondary water supply when it is located on property classified as a Seismic Design Category (SDC) C, D, E, or F. SDC is a classification assigned to a building based on its structural occupancy category and the severity of the design earthquake ground motion at the site. Buildings located with SDCs categorized as C, D, E, or F are susceptible to damage as a result of soil liquefaction or the level of ground motion it may be subjected to during an earthquake.

Because an earthquake can break underground water pipes, Section 903.3.5.2 requires high-rise buildings within the indicated SDCs to have a secondary water supply. The secondary water supply must be sized to provide the hydraulic demand of the building's automatic sprinkler system, including hose streams, for a minimum flow duration of 30 minutes. In most high-rise buildings, the hydraulic demand is based on an ordinary hazard group I or II occupancy classification in mechanical rooms or similar spaces and the hose stream.

Section 903.3.5.2 was revised by prescribing automatic operation of the secondary water supply; in other words, switchover to the secondary water source cannot be manually activated. This change is consistent with definitions of "automatic sprinkler system" and "classes of standpipe systems" in that both systems are required to be connected to a reliable water supply. This code change ensures that if an earthquake disables the primary water supply, the secondary source is available for service.

The second revision to this provision clarifies the requirements for a second fire pump. Section 903.3.5.2 does not require a second fire pump in high-rise buildings located in the indicated SDCs unless the water supply cannot provide the minimum suction pressure necessary to supply the hydraulic demand. In such a case, the installation of a second fire pump is now mandated to ensure that a sufficient volume of water at the required pressure is available at the primary fire pump.

904.3.2

Actuation of Multiple Fire-Extinguishing Systems

CHANGE TYPE: Modification

CHANGE SUMMARY: When two or more alternative automatic fire-extinguishing systems are required to protect a hazard, all of the systems must now be designed to simultaneously operate.

2013 CODE: 904.3.2 Actuation. Automatic fire-extinguishing systems shall be automatically actuated and provided with a manual means of actuation in accordance with Section 904.11.1. Where more than one hazard could be simultaneously involved in a fire due to their proximity, all hazards shall be protected by a single system designed to protect all hazards that could become involved.

> **Exception:** Multiple systems shall be permitted to be installed if they are designed to operate simultaneously.

CHANGE SIGNIFICANCE: Section 904.3.2 requires alternative fire-extinguishing systems to be designed for automatic activation. Activation commonly occurs when a heat, fire, or smoke detection system operates. In Type I commercial kitchen hoods, Section 904.11 requires a manual and automatic means of activating the fire-extinguishing system. Designing a fire-extinguishing system to only operate upon manual actuation is prohibited by the IBC and many of the NFPA fire-protection system standards.

The requirements for fire-extinguishing system actuation in Section 904.3.2 have been revised to correlate the requirements in the code with existing provisions in NFPA 17, *Standard for Dry Chemical*

International Code Council®

Activated hood fire-extinguishing system.

Extinguishing Systems, and NFPA 17A, *Standard for Wet Chemical Extinguishing Systems.* The new requirement prescribes that when a hazard is protected by two or more fire-extinguishing systems, all of the systems must be designed to operate simultaneously. The reason for the revision is that a typical alternative automatic fire-extinguishing system has a limited amount of fire-extinguishing agent. The amount of agent that is available is based on the area or volume of the hazard and the fire behavior of the fuel. Because the amount of agent is limited, the simultaneous operation of all the fire-extinguishing systems ensures that enough agent is applied to extinguish the fire and prevent its spread from the area of origin.

It is fairly common for a single hazard to be protected by two or more alternative automatic fire-extinguishing systems. For example, protection of a spray booth used for the application of flammable finishes using dry chemical commonly requires two or three alternative automatic fire-extinguishing systems since many dry chemical and all wet chemical systems are preengineered systems. Utilizing listed nozzles, preengineered systems are designed and constructed based on the manufacturer's installation requirements. Because these systems are assembled using listed nozzles and extinguishing agents, one system may not be able to protect the spraying space and exhaust plenum. As a result, two or more systems may be required as a provision of an extinguishing system's listing to protect certain hazards.

Another example is commercial kitchen cooking operations. Consider a flat grill broiler and a deep fat fryer located beneath the same Type I hood. It is quite common for each of these commercial cooking appliances to be protected by separate automatic fire-extinguishing systems. Based on the revision to Section 904.3.2, both extinguishing systems must simultaneously operate in the event a fire involves either of the example appliances.

906.1

Portable Fire Extinguishers in Group R-2 Occupancies

International Code Council®

Portable fire extinguisher provided within dwelling unit in lieu of common areas.

CHANGE TYPE: Modification

CHANGE SUMMARY: Portable fire extinguishers are no longer required in many public and common areas of Group R-2 occupancies provided a complying extinguisher is provided within each individual dwelling unit.

2013 CODE: 906.1 Where Required. Portable fire extinguishers shall be installed in the following locations.

1. In ~~new and existing~~ Group A, B, E, F, H, I, M, R-1, R-2, R-4, and S occupancies.

Exception: ~~In new and existing Group A, B and E occupancies equipped throughout with quick response sprinklers, portable fire extinguishers shall be required only in locations specified in Items 2 through 6.~~ In Group R-2 occupancies, portable fire extinguishers shall be required only in locations specified in Items 2 through 6 where each dwelling unit is provided with a portable fire extinguisher having a minimum rating of 1-A:10-B:C.

Items 2 through 6 remain unchanged.

CHANGE SIGNIFICANCE: The installation of portable fire extinguishers (PFEs) in low-hazard areas of new and existing Group A, B, and E occupancies where the occupancies are equipped with an automatic sprinkler system utilizing quick-response automatic sprinklers is now required. The removal of the exception reflects a reluctance to place complete reliance on automatic sprinkler systems for the protection of assembly, business, and educational occupancies.

Another issue expressed by code officials was the retrofitting of an automatic sprinkler system into existing buildings. In several cases, these retrofits resulted in the removal of PFEs. The removal of PFEs is widely considered as a reduction in the level of protection in the building. Given that the exception to Section 906.1 only included Groups A, B, and E occupancies, its deletion was viewed as appropriate.

The new exception to item 1 permits smaller PFEs in dwelling units of Group R-2 occupancies. Under the revised exception, the installation of 1-A:10-B:C PFEs within individual dwelling units now allows apartment owners to eliminate their installation in common areas such as corridors, laundry rooms, and swimming pool areas. PFEs in these areas are susceptible to vandalism or theft. Another issue is larger PFEs are more difficult for the infirmed and elderly to safely deploy and operate.

It is more logical to place PFEs inside dwelling units versus common areas because the extinguisher is located in an area that statistically has been shown to be where most fires occur. If the occupant cannot control the fire using the PFE, he or she can escape and allow the automatic sprinkler system to operate and control the fire. The safety of Group R-2 residents should be enhanced because they will not be required to leave a dwelling involved in a fire, find a PFE, and then return to the fire-involved dwelling unit to attempt incipient fire attack.

Including this requirement in the building code alerts designers and building officials that the extinguishers are required. This will allow designers to plan for recessed cabinets that may be used or to design locations where the extinguishers will not project into or obstruct the egress or circulation path.

907.2.1.2

Emergency Voice/ Alarm Communication Captions

CHANGE TYPE: Addition

CHANGE SUMMARY: Mass notification fire alarm signals in large stadiums, arenas, and grandstands now require captioned messages.

2013 CODE: **907.2.1.2 Emergency Voice/Alarm Communication Captions.** Stadiums, arenas, and grandstands required to caption audible public announcements shall be in accordance with Section 907.5.2.2.4.

907.5.2.2.4 Emergency Voice/Alarm Communication Captions. Where stadiums, arenas, and grandstands are required to caption audible public announcements in accordance with Section 1108.2.7.3, the emergency/voice alarm communication system shall also be captioned. Prerecorded or live emergency captions shall be from an approved location constantly attended by personnel trained to respond to an emergency.

International Code Council®

Emergency voice/alarm communication required in large Group A occupancies.

CHANGE SIGNIFICANCE: The court ruled in a 2008 U.S. federal court case that persons with hearing impairments who attend events at stadiums, grandstands, and arenas require a means of equivalent communications in lieu of the public address system. Providing occupant notification in these structures is challenging because of the building area and the number and diversity of occupants. Provisions were added in the code to require captioned messages in these buildings and grandstands when public address (PA) systems are prescribed by the accessibility requirements.

Section 1108.2.7.3 sets forth requirements for audible PA systems in stadiums, arenas, and grandstands. It requires that equivalent text information be provided to the audience and that the delivery time for these messages be the same as those broadcasted from the PA system. These requirements apply to prerecorded and real-time messages. The captioning

907.2.1.2, continued

Control elements for mass notification system *(Courtesy of Cooper Notifications, Long Branch, NJ).*

907.2.1.2, continued

Example of EV/ACS captioning. *(Courtesy of the Alertus Technologies LLC, Beltsville MD)*

of messages is mandated in stadiums, arenas, and grandstands that have more than 15,000 fixed seats.

Because messages being broadcasted can include instructions to building or site occupants explaining the actions they need to take in the event of an emergency, the requirements of NFPA 72, *National Fire Alarm and Signaling Code,* are applicable for alarm captioning systems. Such a system falls within the scope of NFPA 72's Chapter 24, "Emergency Communication Systems." NFPA 72 defines an emergency communications system (ECS) as a system designed for life safety that indicates the existence of an emergency and communicates the appropriate response and action. The ECS is required to be classified as either a one-way or two-way path system. Emergency responder radio coverage systems specified in IFC Section 510 are a part of the NFPA 72 ECS requirements. The messages that will be broadcast are based on an emergency response plan developed during a risk analysis by the project stakeholders and is approved by the fire code official.

Further information can be found in *Significant Changes to the International Fire Code,* 2012 Edition, authored by Scott Stookey.

907.2.9.3

Smoke Detection in Group R-2 College Buildings

CHANGE TYPE: Addition

CHANGE SUMMARY: A smoke detection system, tied into the occupant notification system, is now required in certain public and common spaces of Group R-2 college and university buildings, and the required smoke alarms within individual dwelling and sleeping units must be interconnected with the building's fire alarm and detection system.

2013 CODE: **907.2.9 Group R-2.** Fire alarm systems and smoke alarms shall be installed in Group R-2 occupancies as required in Section 907.2.9.1 ~~and 907.2.9.2~~ through 907.2.9.3.

907.2.9.3 Group R-2 College and University Buildings. An automatic smoke detection system that activates the occupant notification system in accordance with Section 907.5 shall be installed in Group R-2 college and university buildings in the following locations:

1. Common spaces outside of dwelling units and sleeping units.
2. Laundry rooms, mechanical equipment rooms, and storage rooms.
3. All interior corridors serving sleeping units or dwelling units.

Required smoke alarms in dwelling units and sleeping units in Group R-2 college and university buildings shall be interconnected with the fire alarm system in accordance with NFPA 72.

Exception: An automatic smoke detection system is not required in buildings that do not have interior corridors serving sleeping units or dwelling units and where each sleeping unit or dwelling unit either

907.2.9.3 continued

Dormitory at a university.

907.2.9.3 continues

has a means of egress door opening directly to an exterior exit access that leads directly to an exit or a means of egress door opening directly to an exit.

CHANGE SIGNIFICANCE: The fire alarm provisions for college and university buildings now differ somewhat from those required for other Group R-2 buildings. While a Group R-2 occupancy will generally require only a manual fire alarm system, these new requirements will require the connection of smoke detection systems in public areas to smoke alarms that are within the dwelling and sleeping units, creating an automatic alarm and detection system.

These requirements would seem to apply differently to buildings that are owned by a college or university versus those that are privately owned but may be used as housing for college students. Because this is somewhat of a continuation of requirements that were added into Chapter 4 of the 2006 IFC for emergency preparedness and planning, and those requirements were intended to deal with buildings that were owned by a college or university, it seems reasonable to interpret that this new requirement is also limited to the buildings that are owned by the college or university and does not apply to other privately owned facilities.

Two items differ between these college and university buildings and most other Group R-2 occupancies. The differences are:

- A smoke detection system will be required in public and common spaces and will need to activate the building's fire alarm and detection system. In most other Group R-2 occupancies, smoke alarms are only required to be located within the individual dwelling or sleeping units. The only instance where the IBC requires smoke detection in the corridors of a Group R-2 occupancy is when the corridors serve the sleeping units. Section 907.2.9.3 is more restrictive for college and university Group R-2 buildings in comparison to other Group R-2 uses because it requires automatic smoke detection in corridors serving dwelling and sleeping units as well as common areas.
- Smoke alarms that are installed within the dwelling unit and sleeping units must be interconnected with the building's fire alarm system. Typically, the alarms within the units are only used to notify the occupants of that unit and are not connected to the building's fire alarm control unit.

Previously, the installation of single- or multiple-station smoke alarms were mandated on all levels "within" the dwelling unit, in the sleeping rooms, and in the immediate vicinity of the bedrooms. The new provision will expand the requirement and require a smoke detection system in laundry rooms, mechanical equipment rooms, storage rooms, and into common spaces and interior corridors that serve the units. The requirement for smoke detection in "laundry rooms, mechanical equipment rooms, and storage rooms" is intended to apply to those types of communal spaces that are located in public and common areas outside of the individual units and not to any rooms within the units that are used for those purposes. Because smoke alarms within the units provide coverage for these types of uses within the unit, it seems reasonable to limit the ap-

907.2.9.3 continued

plication of item 2 to the communal laundry, mechanical, and storage areas that are outside of the individual units.

Although smoke detectors are specifically required in the indicated areas of Group R-2 college and university buildings, building officials should be cognizant that the installation of smoke detectors in certain areas may ultimately reduce fire safety by serving as a source of nuisance alarm activations. In common areas where cooking is allowed, experience has found that smoke detection is not appropriate because of the potential for burnt food causing an accidental alarm activation. In communal laundry rooms, accumulations of lint and flocking from dryers that are not well maintained may initiate a false alarm signal. In these areas, the use of listed heat detectors should be considered, and is allowed by Section 907.4.3.

The smoke detection system serving the public and common spaces as well as the smoke alarms within the units are to be connected to the alarm system and notify the occupants when a problem occurs within the building. Connecting the smoke detection systems in the public and common spaces outside of the units with the alarm system will help provide automatic notification if a problem should develop in those areas. Another substantial change is the requirement that the smoke alarms within the dwelling and sleeping units be interconnected with the fire alarm system. Previously, the activation of these smoke alarms provided an alarm notification within the unit but did not activate the building's fire alarm system. This requirement for interconnection of the unit smoke alarms and the building's fire alarm system will be a significant difference between these college and university buildings and any other Group R-2 occupancy such as a typical apartment building.

The exception allows for the elimination of the smoke detection system in a specific situation. The use of the wording "automatic smoke detection system" is important in the exception because it helps distinguish between the system that is required in the public and common areas by the first paragraph (along with its three numbered items) and the smoke alarms that are required within the units. Within the units, Sections 907.2.9.2 and 907.2.11 will require smoke alarms at specific locations. The second paragraph of Section 907.2.9.3 will require these smoke alarms to be interconnected with the fire alarm system. The exception does not eliminate the requirement for these smoke alarms within the units or the requirement that they be interconnected with the fire alarm system. The exception is intended to only apply to the "automatic smoke detection system" of the first paragraph and not to the "smoke alarm" requirement of the second paragraph.

907.2.11.2, 907.2.11.5

Smoke Alarms for Groups R-2, R-2.1, R-3, R-3.1, R-4 and I-1

CHANGE TYPE: Addition

CHANGE SUMMARY: The requirements for smoke alarms have been revised to address concerns related to nuisance alarms and to correlate with the provisions of NFPA 72 as recommended by the California State Fire Marshal's Smoke Alarm Task Force.

2013 CODE: ***907.2.11.2.3 Smoke Alarms.*** *Smoke alarms shall be tested and maintained in accordance with the manufacturer's instructions. Smoke alarms that no longer function shall be replaced. Smoke alarms installed in one- and two-family dwellings shall be replaced after 10 years from the date of manufacture marked on the unit, or if the date of manufacture cannot be determined.*

907.2.11.2.4 Conventional Ionization Smoke Alarms. *Conventional ionization smoke alarms that are solely battery powered shall be equipped with a 10-year battery and have a silence feature.*

Conventional ionization smoke alarm for the purposes of this section is a smoke alarm, listed as complying with ANSI/UL 217, in which the only sensing element is an ionization sensor. The output signal from the ionization sensor must exceed a factory set alarm threshold, without the use discriminating algorithms, to determine when an alarm signal is warranted.

907.2.11.5 Specific Location Requirements.

Extract from NFPA 72 Section 29.8.3.4 Specific Location Requirements.*

This extract has been provided by NFPA as amended by the Office of the State Fire Marshal and adopted by reference as follows:

29.8.3.4 Specific Location Requirements. *The installation of smoke alarms and smoke detectors shall comply with the following requirements:*

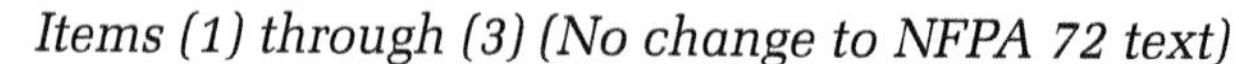
Items (1) through (3) (No change to NFPA 72 text)

Smoke Alarm.

(4) Smoke alarms or smoke detectors shall be installed minimum of 20 feet horizontal distance from a permanently installed cooking appliance.

Exceptions:

1. *Ionization smoke alarms with an alarm-silencing switch or photoelectric smoke alarms shall be permitted to be installed 10 feet (3m) or greater from a permanently installed cooking appliance.*
2. Photoelectric smoke alarms shall be permitted to be installed greater than 6 feet (1.8m) from a permanently installed cooking appliance where the kitchen or cooking area and adjacent spaces have no clear interior partitions and the 10-foot distances would prohibit the placement of a smoke alarm or smoke detector required by other sections of the code.
3. Smoke alarms listed for use in close proximity to a permanently installed cooking appliance.

(5) Installations near bathrooms. Smoke alarms shall be installed not less than a 3-foot (0.91m) horizontal distance from the door or opening of a bathroom that contains a bathtub or shower unless this would prevent placement of a smoke alarm required by other sections of the code.

Items (6) through (12) (No change to NFPA 72 text)

**For additional requirements or clarification see NFPA 72.*

CHANGE SIGNIFICANCE: Section 907.2.11 already requires smoke alarms to be installed in accordance with NFPA 72, which theoretically describes where alarms should and should not be installed. As a convenience to the code user, requirements on where smoke alarms should not be installed in proximity to permanently installed cooking appliances and steam producing bathrooms are now included in this section.

The change to Section 907.2.11.2.3 clarifies the requirements in Section 901.4 for testing and maintaining smoke alarms, and specifies when the devices need to be replaced. The requirements are consistent with NFPA 72 provisions. In particular NFPA 72 requires smoke alarms installed in one- and two-family dwellings to not remain in service longer than 10 years from the date of manufacture, and UL 217 requires the date of manufacture to be marked on the smoke alarms.

It is recognized that it may not always be practical for the code official to enforce the requirements for testing, maintenance and replacement of smoke alarms in residential dwelling units. However realtors and landlords often have checklists that verify that these dwellings comply with codes and other requirements, and they may be in a position to verify compliance with the proposed provisions when the units are sold or leased.

Battery operated smoke alarms previously were not required to have a long life battery which increase the likelihood of the occupant removing the battery or not replacing it twice a year. The activation of a smoke alarm with a reliable battery power will allow timely, accurate notification to the occupants allowing sufficient time for evacuation of the residence.

907.6

Fire Alarm Systems for High-Rise Buildings

CHANGE TYPE: Addition

CHANGE SUMMARY: In high-rise buildings, wiring for fire alarm circuits must be Class A in accordance with NFPA 72 and must be installed in metal conduit or be metallic cable (MC). A matrix format zoning annunciator panel is required and must meet the list of specific conditions.

2013 CODE: **907.6 Installation.** A fire alarm system shall be installed in accordance with this section and NFPA 72.

907.6.1 Wiring. (No change to text)

907.6.1.1 High-Rise Buildings. *Wiring for fire alarm signaling line circuits, initiating circuits, and notification circuits in high-rise buildings shall be in accordance with the following:*

1. Class A in accordance with NFPA 72.

Exception: *Initiating circuits which serve only a single initiating device.*

2. Enclosed in continuous metallic raceways in accordance with the California Electrical Code.

Exception: *Metallic cable (MC) shall be permitted for fire alarm notification circuits where continuous metallic raceways are not required for survivability.*

Class A circuits in metallic raceways are required for fire alarm signal wiring in high-rise buildings.

907.6.3.3 High-Rise Buildings Zoning Annunciator Panel. *In high-rise buildings, a zoning annunciator panel shall be provided in the Fire Command Center. This panel shall not be combined with the Firefighter Smoke Control Panel unless approved. Panel shall be in matrix format or an approved equivalent configuration. All indicators shall be based upon positive confirmation. The panel shall include the following features at a minimum:*

1. *Fire alarm initiating devices with individual annunciation per floor for manual fire alarm boxes, area smoke detectors, elevator lobby smoke detectors, duct smoke detectors, heat detectors, auxiliary alarms, and sprinkler waterflow. (Red LED)*
2. *Sprinkler and standpipe system control valves per floor - supervisory. (Yellow LED)*
3. *Common fire alarm system trouble. (Yellow LED)*
4. *Annunciation Panel Power On. (Green LED)*
5. *Lamp test. (Push Button)*

CHANGE SIGNIFICANCE: In high-rise buildings, the code relies on a high level of performance and reliability by the fire alarm system to maintain life safety. This includes detection of fire incidents, occupant notification, and controlling building systems to minimize the impact of the fire event. High-rise fire alarm circuits must be Class A in accordance with NFPA 72 to enhance the reliability of these critical life safety circuits. Class A circuits will ensure fire alarm performance even if there's a break in the circuit. The code also requires fire alarm circuits to be protected against fire and physical damage by placing the circuits within metallic raceways (i.e., conduit). CBC Section 909.12.1 already requires that all wiring serving smoke control systems including any fire alarm circuits initiating, monitoring, or controlling circuits to be in continuous raceways. The exception allows the use of metallic cable (MC) for fire alarm notification circuits.

Section 907.6.3.3 requires a matrix style fire alarm annunciator in new high-rise buildings. A matrix annunciator facilitates quick evaluation of critical fire alarm conditions by responding emergency personnel. Multiple alarms on multiple floors are shown along with many essential supervisory/ trouble conditions. SFM High-rise Phase I Task Group recommended a graphic annunciator for this purpose.

911.1.6

Fire Command Center Ventilation in High-Rise Buildings

CHANGE TYPE: Addition

CHANGE SUMMARY: Independent ventilation or air conditioning is now required for fire command centers in high-rise buildings.

2013 CODE: ***911.1.6 Ventilation.*** *The fire command center shall be provided with an independent ventilation or air-conditioning system.*

CHANGE SIGNIFICANCE: Common HVAC systems may be shut-down under alarm or other emergency conditions. Equipment in the fire command center is computer based and may malfunction under elevated temperatures. The intent of this code change is to provide an independent HVAC unit within the fire command room. This may include a fan coil within the room even though chilled water is provided from a common building source. Emergency power to the HVAC is not required, but would be desirable. The section is intentionally left performance-based to allow for multiple options based upon building systems. This section is for new high-rise buildings and would only apply to an existing building if the fire command center is relocated or completely renovated.

Independent ventilation is required for fire command centers.

913.6

Fire Pump Fuel Supply in High-Rise Buildings

CHANGE TYPE: Addition

CHANGE SUMMARY: A minimum 8-hour fuel supply is now required for fire pump operation in high-rise buildings.

2013 CODE: ***913.6 Fire Pumps in High-Rise Buildings.*** *Engine-driven fire pumps and electric drive fire pumps supplied by generators shall both be provided with an on-premises fuel supply, sufficient for not less than 8-hour full-demand operation at 100% of the rated pump capacity in addition to all other required supply demands in accordance with Sections 9.6 and 11.4.2 of NFPA 20 and this section. (Also see Section 604.2.14.1.1 of the California Fire Code.)*

CHANGE SIGNIFICANCE: CFC Section 604.14.1 applies to all fuel supplies for generators serving the standby power of high-rise buildings. The standby power serves the systems that focus more on the continued operation of critical equipment in a building such as elevators and fire pumps. It requires the fuel supply to be sufficient to serve the systems for a minimum duration of 6 hours with the exception of fire pumps having a fuel supply capacity of a minimum of 8 hours. There was previously no provision in the CBC to set a threshold for the minimum fuel level for tanks related to fire pump operation before refueling was required. It is possible that the tank fuel level could drop too low due to the system testing. Section 913.6 of the code now requires the fuel supply to be maintained at an 8-hour level at all times for serving fire pumps.

A minimum 8-hour fuel supply is required for fire pump operation in high-rise buildings.

PART 4

Means of Egress

Chapter 10

■ **Chapter 10** Means of Egress

The criteria set forth in Chapter 10 regulating the design of the means of egress are established as the primary method for protection of people in buildings. Both prescriptive and performance language is utilized in the chapter to provide for a basic approach in the determination of a safe exiting system for all occupancies. It addresses all portions of the egress system and includes design requirements as well as provisions regulating individual components. A zonal approach to egress provides a general basis for the chapter's format through regulation of the exit access, exit, and exit discharge portions of the means of egress. ■

1004.1.1

Cumulative Occupant Loads

1004.1.2, TABLE 1004.1.2

Design Occupant Load—Areas without Fixed Seating

1005

Means of Egress Capacity Determination

1008.1.9.7

Delayed Egress Locks for Courtrooms

1008.1.9.9

Electromagnetically Locked Egress Doors

1008.1.9.12

Access-Controlled Elevator Lobby Doors in High-Rise Office Buildings

1009, 1010, 202

Interior Stairways and Ramps

1009.1

Application of Stairway Provisions

1013.1, 1013.8

Guards at Operable Windows

1015.1,1025.4, 1028.1

Means of Egress for Group I-3 Occupancies

1015.2

Exit or Exit Access Doorway Arrangement

1022.5

Enclosure Penetrations of Interior Exit Stairways

1028.1.1.1

Separation of Spaces Under Grandstands and Bleachers

1004.1.1

Cumulative Occupant Loads

Design of egress path capacity is based on the cumulative occupant loads of all rooms, areas or spaces to that point along the path of egress travel.

CHANGE TYPE: Modification

CHANGE SUMMARY: The determination of the cumulative design occupant load for intervening spaces, adjacent levels and adjacent stories has been clarified.

2013 CODE: **1004.1.1 Cumulative Occupant Loads.** Where the path of egress travel includes intervening rooms, areas or spaces, cumulative occupant loads shall be determined in accordance with this section.

1004.1.1.1 Intervening Spaces or *Accessory Areas.* Where occupants egress from one *or more* rooms, areas or spaces through *others*, the design occupant load shall be *the combined occupant load of interconnected accessory or intervening spaces. Design of egress path capacity shall* be based on the cumulative *portion of* occupant loads of all rooms, areas or spaces to that point along the path of egress travel.

1004.1.1.2 Adjacent Levels *for Mezzanines.* *That portion of* occupant load of a mezzanine with *all required* egress through a room, area or space on an adjacent level shall be added to the *occupant load* of that room, area or space.

1004.1.1.3 Adjacent Stories. *Other than for the egress components designed for convergence in accordance with Section 1005.6, the occupant load from separate stories shall not be added.*

CHANGE SIGNIFICANCE: This amendment addresses two areas of concern: Egress on a given level and egress from one story or level through another by way of unenclosed exit access stairways. It reinforces the concept that the occupant load is assigned to each occupied area individually. When there are intervening rooms, each area must be considered both individually and in the aggregate with other interconnected occupied portions of the exit access to determine the number and width of exit access. Portions of the occupant load are accumulated along egress paths to determine the capacity of individual egress elements along those paths. But once occupants from one area make a choice and head out along one of several independent paths of egress travel, their occupant load is not added to some other area to determine how many paths of travel would be required from that different area if a second fire were to occur at the same time in that area.

This amendment also attempts to treat egress design along unenclosed exit access stairways through adjacent stories or through adjacent levels (in the case of mezzanines) in a similar manner recognizing previous limited instances where open exit access stairways from stories were considered as exits and the capacity (width) was required to be maintained but the occupant load was assumed to cascade and was not added to the adjacent story providing exit access.

It also recognizes mezzanines with independent egress can egress similar to a story in a building. Mezzanines with sole egress through a room or area must have the occupant load added to that room or area and when the egress from a mezzanine is split between an independent exit and other exit access through the room below, the portion of occupants with egress through the room below must be added to the occupant load of the room or space below.

1004.1.2, Table 1004.1.2

Design Occupant Load—Areas without Fixed Seating

International Code Council®

Museum exhibit gallery.

CHANGE TYPE: Modification

CHANGE SUMMARY: An occupant load factor for museums and exhibit galleries has been established at 30 square feet per occupant.

2013 CODE: **~~1004.1.1~~ 1004.1.2 Areas without Fixed Seating.** The number of occupants shall be computed at the rate of one occupant per unit of area as prescribed in Table ~~1004.1.1~~ 1004.1.2. For areas without fixed seating, the occupant load shall not be less than that number determined by dividing the floor area under consideration by the occupant load ~~per unit of area~~ factor assigned to the ~~occupancy~~ function of the space as set forth in Table ~~1004.1.1~~ 1004.1.2. Where an intended function ~~use~~ is not listed in Table ~~1004.1.1~~ 1004.1.2, the building official shall establish a function ~~use~~ based on a listed function ~~use~~ that most nearly resembles the intended function ~~use~~.

> **Exception:** Where approved by the building official, the actual number of occupants for whom each occupied space, floor, or building is designed, although less than those determined by calculation, shall be permitted to be used in the determination of the design occupant load.

TABLE ~~1004.1.1~~ 1004.1.2 Maximum Floor Area Allowances per Occupant

Function of Space	Occupant Load Factor[a] ~~Floor Area In Sq. Ft. Per Occupant~~
Assembly	
Gaming floors (keno, slots, etc.)	11 gross
Exhibit gallery and museum	30 net
Mall buildings—covered and open	See Section 402.4.1

For SI: 1 square foot = 0.0929 m^2.
a. Floor area in square feet per occupant.

Note: (no changes to remainder of table)

CHANGE SIGNIFICANCE: A 30-square-foot per person occupant load factor has been added for museums and exhibit galleries in the assembly use entry. The manner in which these spaces function is different than the way most assembly uses are used and the new factor recognizes this difference.

Museums and exhibit areas are typically used in ways that are not typical of other assembly spaces. What must be taken into consideration is the way an exhibit is viewed. Using even an "unconcentrated" occupant load factor of 15 square feet per person is typically not appropriate because the display could not be seen by the vast majority of the people in the room at that density of people. Very few displays are actually viewed from close proximity. In fact, most artworks are best viewed from distances, and most people are not within 10 to 15 feet of the object being viewed. People do make close inspections, but only after viewing the object from a distance and, when approaching a display, most people

1004.1.2, Table 1004.1.2 continues

1004.1.2, Table 1004.1.2 continued

would be courteous and would not step in front of or near the object until other viewers have left the area or completed their distant inspection. Consequently, a museum gallery would not be filled to a high-density design capacity simply because of how the spaces are used.

While museums and galleries do have need for high-occupancy rooms, for gala openings or other special events, most facilities have dedicated spaces for such purposes or would only use a space that was not set up for an exhibit. It is the actual gallery/exhibit spaces that are used at this lower density, and it is only those spaces that this change addresses. When determining the anticipated occupant load of any space listed in the table the intent is to consider how the space will function and be used. To determine the occupant load of these spaces it is appropriate to consider how exhibits are viewed.

It is important to remember that Section 1004.3 continues to require posting of occupant loads within assembly uses. In addition, Section 302.1 addresses the occupant load for spaces where owners want to use the space for more than one use such as parties or lectures. If the intended use is for other than as a gallery or museum, that should be taken into consideration in the design, with an appropriate occupant load for the function being established by the building official.

Several more limited changes can also be found within these provisions. Both Section 1004.1.2 and the second column of Table 1004.1.2 have been modified to use the term "occupant load factor" versus the previous language. The fact that these occupant load factors are based on the floor area per occupant is found by the new footnote a to the table. In addition, an entry for "mall buildings" has been added and will direct the code users to Chapter 4, where the method for establishing an occupant load for a mall building is addressed. Lastly, a somewhat editorial change has been made to Section 1004.1.2 and will relate the title of the first column of the table to the code text by using the word "function" versus looking at the "use or occupancy" of the space.

1005

Means of Egress Capacity Determination

CHANGE TYPE: Modification

CHANGE SUMMARY: Reduced exit width factors have been established for sprinklered buildings provided with an emergency voice/alarm communication system, and the exit width/capacity requirements are now presented in a more logical and organized layout.

2013 CODE: ~~**1004.4 Exiting From Multiple Levels.** Where exits serve more than one floor, only the occupant load of each floor considered individually shall be used in computing the required capacity of the exits at that floor, provided that the exit capacity shall not decrease in the direction of egress travel.~~

~~**1004.5 Egress Convergence.** Where means of egress from floors above and below converge at an intermediate level, the capacity of the means of egress from the point of convergence shall not be less than the sum of the two floors.~~

~~**1005.1 Minimum Required Egress Width.** The means of egress width shall not be less than required by this section. The total width of means of egress in inches (mm) shall not be less than the total occupant load served by the means of egress multiplied by 0.3 inch (7.62 mm) per~~

1005 continues

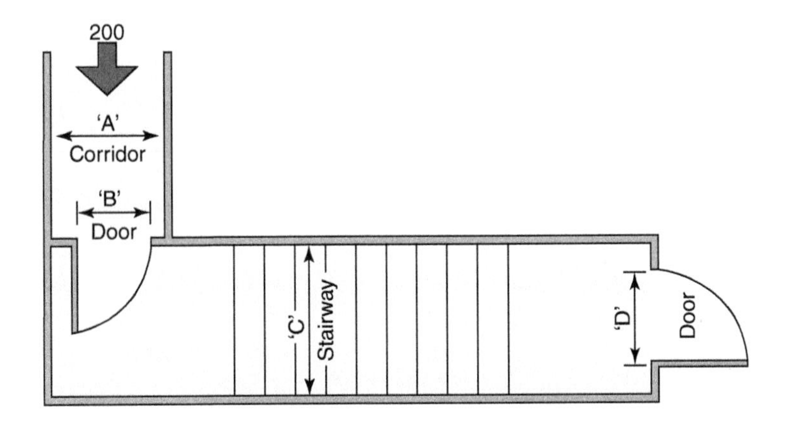

Example : Assuming exit is serving 200 people

Component	Min width based on component (1005.2)	Min width based on occupant load (1005.3)	
		General[1]	Sprinklered building with EV/ACS[2]
Corridor 'A'	44"	40"	30"
Door 'B'	32"	40"	30"
Stairway 'C'	44"	60"	40"
Door 'D'	32"	40"	30"

1. Building without sprinkler system or EV/ACS; (also includes Group H and I-2 occupancies)

2. Other than Group H and I-2 occupancies

International Code Council®

Means of egress sizing.

1005 continued

~~occupant for stairways and by 0.2 inch (5.08 mm) per occupant for other egress components. The width shall not be less than specified elsewhere in this code. Multiple means of egress shall be sized such that the loss of any one means of egress shall not reduce the available capacity to less than 50 percent of the required capacity. The maximum capacity required from any story of a building shall be maintained to the termination of the means of egress.~~

> **Exception:** ~~Means of egress complying with Section 1028.~~

1005.1 General. All portions of the means of egress system shall be sized in accordance with this section.

> **Exception:** Means of egress complying with Section 1028.

1005.2 Minimum Width Based on Component. The minimum width, in inches, of any means of egress components shall not be less than that specified for such component elsewhere in this code.

1005.3 Required Capacity Based on Occupant Load. The required capacity, in inches, of the means of egress for any room, area, space, or story shall not be less than that determined in accordance with the following:

1005.3.1 Stairways. The capacity, in inches, of means of egress stairways shall be calculated by multiplying the occupant load served by such stairway by a means of egress capacity factor of 0.3 inches (7.62 mm) per occupant. Where stairways serve more than one story, only the occupant load of each story considered individually shall be used in calculating the required capacity of the stairways serving that story.

> **Exception:** For other than Group H and I-2 occupancies, the capacity, in inches, of means of egress stairways shall be calculated by multiplying the occupant load served by such stairway by a means of egress capacity factor of 0.2 inches (5.1 mm) per occupant in buildings equipped throughout with an automatic sprinkler system installed in accordance with Section 903.3.1.1 or 903.3.1.2 and an emergency voice/alarm communication system in accordance with Section 907.5.2.2.

1005.3.2 Other Egress Components. The capacity, in inches, of means of egress components other than stairways shall be calculated by multiplying the occupant load served by such component by a means of egress capacity factor of 0.2 inches (5.08 mm) per occupant.

> **Exception:** For other than Group H and I-2 occupancies, the capacity, in inches, of means of egress components other than stairways shall be calculated by multiplying the occupant load served by such component by a means of egress capacity factor of 0.15 inches (3.8 mm) per occupant in buildings equipped throughout with an automatic sprinkler system installed in accordance with Section 903.3.1.1 or 903.3.1.2 and an emergency voice/alarm communication system in accordance with Section 907.5.2.2.

1005.4 Continuity. The capacity of the means of egress required from any story of a building shall not be reduced along the path of egress travel until arrival at the public way.

1005.5. Distribution of Egress Capacity. Where more than one exit, or access to more than one exit, is required, the means of egress shall be configured such that the loss of any one exit, or access to one exit, shall not reduce the available capacity to less than 50 percent of the required capacity.

~~**1004.5**~~ **1005.6 Egress Convergence.** Where the means of egress from stories above and below converge at an intermediate level, the capacity of the means of egress from the point of convergence shall not be less than the sum of the required capacities for the two adjacent stories.

Provisions in 2010 CBC Sections 1005.2 and 1005.3 regulating permissible encroachment of doors also have been reformatted as new Section 1005.7.

CHANGE SIGNIFICANCE: The multiple requirements related to egress width that were previously contained in a single paragraph in Section 1005.1 have been reorganized and clarified, and the related provisions from Section 1004.4 and 1004.5 have been relocated to a more logical location with the other egress width/capacity provisions.

In addition, the reduced egress width factors for sprinklered buildings that had been removed in the previous edition of the code have been reintroduced. The exceptions allow for use of reduced width factors for sprinklered buildings but only where an emergency voice/communications alarm system (EV/ACS) is provided for the building.

The EV/ACS system provides the ability to communicate instructions to the occupants that could facilitate evacuation or relocation during a fire or other emergency. This additional information and direction could lead to more efficient use of the egress system. Studies have shown that most people do not react to an initial alarm; therefore, requiring a voice alarm will increase safety by providing occupants with additional information about the emergency and evacuation.

The following list will help guide code users in finding the new location of the previous requirements and illustrate the editorial nature of this revision:

- Section 1005.1 provides a new charging paragraph and clarifies that it applies to all portions of the egress system.
- Section 1005.2 replaces the second sentence of the previous code's Section 1005.1 and notes that minimum width requirements for means of egress components may be specified in other locations in the code.
- Section 1005.3 provides the egress width factors in subsections that deal with the various types of components. Note the new exceptions in Sections 1005.3.1 and 1005.3.2 for sprinklered buildings that allow for a reduction in the minimum required calculated width.
- The provisions of the former Section 1004.4 have been incorporated as the last sentence of Section 1005.3.1.

1005 continued

1005 continues

- Section 1005.4 replaces the last sentence of the previous code's Section 1005.1, and notes that once a minimum capacity is required along a means of egress, it must be provided along the entire path of egress travel.
- Section 1005.5 is consistent with the fourth sentence of the previous code's Section 1005.1.
- The "egress convergence" provisions from Section 1004.5 can now be found in Section 1005.6. This is basically an issue of egress capacity/ width and is more appropriately located here, instead of within the code section regulating occupant load.
- Revisions have also been made in Sections 3404 and 3412 related to reduced egress width factors.

1008.1.9.7

Delayed Egress Locks for Courtrooms

CHANGE TYPE: Modification

CHANGE SUMMARY: Delayed egress locks are now permitted for Group A courtrooms.

2013 CODE: **1008.1.9.7 Delayed Egress Locks.** *Approved, listed,* delayed egress locks shall be permitted to be installed on doors serving any occupancy except Group A, E, H, and L occupancies.

Group A occupancy courtrooms are permitted to utilize delayed egress locks.

> ***Exception:*** *Group A occupancy courtrooms are permitted to utilize delayed egress locks.*

~~in b~~Buildings that are *with delayed egress locks shall be* equipped throughout with an *automatic sprinkler system* in accordance with Section 903.3.1.1 *and* an approved automatic smoke ~~or heat~~ detection system installed in accordance with Section 907, provided that the doors unlock in accordance with Items 1 through 9 below. A building occupant shall not be required to pass through more than one door equipped with a delayed egress lock before entering an *exit. Delayed egress devices shall conform to all of the following:*

1. through 9. (No significant changes—not shown for clarity)

CHANGE SIGNIFICANCE: Delayed egress doors are necessary to secure secondary exits from courthouses. The alternative would be to allow terrorists or other criminals to open a secondary exit from the inside to allow other armed or otherwise dangerous individuals to enter. Courthouses are heavily staffed and are equipped with sprinklers and smoke detection, and therefore delayed egress poses no threat to life safety.

1008.1.9.9

Electromagnetically Locked Egress Doors

CHANGE TYPE: Modification

CHANGE SUMMARY: Electromagnetically locked egress doors may now be used at locations that require panic hardware provided the operation of the hardware releases the magnetic lock by interrupting the power to the electromagnet.

2013 CODE: 1008.1.9.9 ~~1008.1.9.8~~ Electromagnetically Locked Egress Doors. Doors in the means of egress ~~that are not otherwise required to have panic hardware~~ in buildings with an occupancy in Group A, B, E, M, R-1, or R-2 and doors to tenant spaces in Group A, B, E, M, R-1, or R-2 shall be permitted to be electromagnetically locked if equipped with listed hardware that incorporates a built-in switch and meet the requirements below:

1. The listed hardware that is affixed to the door leaf has an obvious method of operation that is readily operated under all lighting conditions.
2. The listed hardware is capable of being operated with one hand.
3. Operation of the listed hardware directly ~~releases~~ interrupts the power to the electromagnetic lock and unlocks the door immediately.
4. Loss of power to the listed hardware automatically unlocks the door.
5. Where panic or fire exit hardware is required by Section 1008.1.10, operation of the listed panic or fire exit hardware also releases the electromagnetic lock.

International Code Council®

Electromagnet used to lock door.

International Code Council®

Electromagnetic lock shown at top right of door leaf.

CHANGE SIGNIFICANCE: The use of electromagnetic locks on egress doors required to have panic hardware was prohibited under the provisions of the 2010 CBC. The use of such locking devices is now acceptable because there are several "panic" bars that are tested and listed for use in the release of the electromagnetic lock. While these are "listed" for magnetic locking devices, they are generally installed for security or normal locking arrangements and are not specifically intended for panic hardware purposes.

The previous prohibition related to panic hardware has been deleted, while the changes in item 3 and the addition of item 5 ensure a direct connection that will interrupt the power to, and release, the electromagnetic lock. When power is removed from a listed electromagnetic lock, it typically will release in less than ½ second. It is these changes in items 3 and 5 that clarify the release of the lock must be automatic with the operation of the push bar and that these magnetic locks are tested and listed devices.

Directly connecting the hardware to stop the power flow to the magnetic lock ensures that the hardware complies with the single operation required by Section 1008.1.9.5 and that the hardware can open as panic hardware when required by simply pressing against the bar. Panic or fire exit hardware must still be listed in accordance with the standards and requirements found in Section 1008.1.10.

Although the text of Section 1008.1.9.9 appears to clearly allow these magnetic locks on doors with panic hardware when the hardware and magnet are interconnected, the provisions of Sections 1008.1.10 and 1008.1.10.1 have not been completely coordinated with these new provisions. Although Section 1008.1.9.9 permits the magnetic locks, panic and fire exit hardware must still meet the requirements found in Section 1008.1.10. The primary issue is the language of Section 1008.1.10 that indicates the doors "shall not be provided with a latch or lock unless it is panic hardware or fire exit hardware." This generally is interpreted to limit the use of any type of lock or restraint that is not a part of the panic hardware device. It appears that the intended application of Section 1008.1.9.9 establishes it as a specific requirement that would override this general provision if the magnetic locks are arranged to have the hardware "directly interrupt the power" and that the "operation of the listed panic or fire exit hardware also releases the electromagnetic lock." The inconsistency is that panic and fire exit hardware are required to comply with UL 305 (see Section 1008.1.10.1) and that standard views the hardware as a mechanical device. It does not address or evaluate devices with electromagnetic locks included in them. Magnetic locking devices simply are not covered by the currently specified standard. Because of this, it appears that the revisions of Section 1008.1.9.9 will at the least create confusion if not simply conflict with the requirements of Section 1008.1.10 and its subsection.

It is difficult to see how the device can be "listed" as indicated in both Sections 1008.1.9.9 and 1008.10.1 when the applicable standard for the panic hardware does not include the option of the magnetic lock or release for it. It appears that the "listing" for electromagnetically locked devices and the separate listing for panic hardware were intended to be combined—even though they are separate listings and the magnetic locks have not and are not tested as a part of the UL 305 listing for panic and fire exit hardware.

1008.1.9.12

Access-Controlled Elevator Lobby Doors in High-Rise Office Buildings

CHANGE TYPE Clarification

CHANGE SUMMARY: The CBC provisions for access-controlled elevator lobby doors in high-rise office buildings have been reformatted and clarified to make them more user friendly and easier to interpret and enforce.

2013 CODE: ~~1008.1.4.6~~1008.1.9.12 Access-Controlled Elevator Lobby ~~Egress~~ Doors in High-Rise Office Buildings. *For elevator lobbies in high-rise office buildings where the occupants of the floor are not required to travel through the elevator lobby to reach an exit, when approved by the fire chief, the doors separating the elevator lobby from the adjacent occupied tenant space that also serve as the entrance doors to the tenant space shall be ~~the entrance doors within an elevator lobby in a means of egress of high-rise buildings serving offices that are equipped with an automatic sprinkler system in accordance with Section 903.3.1.1 and an approved automatic smoke detection system installed in accordance with Section 907, are~~* permitted to be equipped with an approved entrance and egress access control system *~~which shall be installed in accordance with~~ provided all of the following requirements are met ~~criteria~~:*

In high-rise office buildings, if access is provided to an exit, an elevator lobby door to a tenant space can be access controlled.

1. *The building is provided throughout with an automatic sprinkler system in accordance with Section 903.3.1.1.*

2. *A smoke detector is installed on the ceiling on the tenant side of the elevator lobby doors along the center line of the door opening, not less than 1 foot and not more than 5 feet from the door opening, and is connected to the fire alarm system.*

3. *A remote master switch capable of unlocking the elevator lobby doors shall be provided in the fire command center for use by the fire department.*

~~1~~4. *Locks for the elevator lobby shall be U.L. and California State Fire Marshal listed fail-safe type locking mechanisms. The locking device shall automatically release on activation of any fire alarm device on the floor of alarm (waterflow, smoke detector, manual pull stations, etc.). All locking devices shall unlock, but not unlatch, upon activation.*

~~2~~5. *A two-way voice communication system, utilizing dedicated lines, shall be provided from each locked elevator lobby to the 24-hour staffed location on site, annunciated as to location. Operating instructions shall be posted above each two-way communication device.*

Exception: *When approved by the fire chief, two-way voice communication system to an off-site facility may be permitted where means to remotely unlock the access controlled doors from the off-site facility are provided.*

~~3~~6. *~~Provide~~ An approved momentary mushroom-shaped palm button connected to the doors and installed adjacent to each locked elevator lobby ~~exit~~ door ~~which will~~ shall be provided to release the door locks when operated by an individual in the elevator lobby. The locks shall be reset manually at the door. Mount palm button so that the center line is 48 inches above the finished floor. ~~door.~~*

Provide a sign stating:

"IN CASE OF EMERGENCY, PUSH PALM BUTTON,
DOOR WILL UNLOCK AND
SECURITY ALARM WILL SOUND."

The sign lettering shall be ¾-inch high letters by ⅛-inch width stroke on a contrasting background.

~~4~~7. *Loss of power to that part of the access control system which locks the doors shall automatically unlock the doors.*

CHANGE SIGNIFICANCE: This California State Fire Marshal amendment is a clarification of the intent of the current amendment which is to limit its application to elevator lobbies in office buildings where the required path of egress travel to reach an exit stairway does not pass through the elevator lobby. It also clarifies that the smoke detection system requirement is intended to be a single smoke detector located at each set of the elevator lobby doors on the tenant side ceiling. It also requires a remote master switch for unlocking the elevator lobby doors to be provided in the Fire Command Center similar to the requirement for stairway door locks. This also reformats and edits the section to make it more user friendly and easier to interpret and enforce.

1009, 1010, 202

Interior Stairways and Ramps

CHANGE TYPE: Clarification

CHANGE SUMMARY: Revisions have been made throughout the code to coordinate the provisions for unenclosed interior stairways and ramps that can be used as a portion of the means of egress.

2013 CODE:

202 Definitions.

EXIT. That portion of a means of egress system ~~which is separated from other interior spaces of a building or structure by fire-resistance-rated construction and opening protectives as required to provide a protected path of egress travel~~ between the exit access and the exit discharge or public way. Exit~~s~~ components include exterior exit doors at the level of exit discharge, ~~vertical exit enclosures~~ interior exit stairways, interior exit ramps, exit passageways, exterior exit stairways~~,~~ and exterior exit ramps and horizontal exits.

EXIT ACCESS RAMP. An interior ramp that is not a required interior exit ramp.

EXIT ACCESS STAIRWAY. An interior stairway that is not a required interior exit stairway.

~~**EXIT ENCLOSURE.**~~ ~~An exit component that is separated from other interior spaces of a building or structure by fire-resistance-rated construction and opening protectives, and provides for a protected path of egress travel in a vertical or horizontal direction to the exit discharge or the public way.~~

INTERIOR EXIT RAMP. An exit component that serves to meet one or more means of egress design requirements, such as required number of exits or exit access travel distance, and provides for a protected path of egress travel to the exit discharge or public way.

Interior exit stairway.

International Code Council®

Exit access stairway.

INTERIOR EXIT STAIRWAY. An exit component that serves to meet one or more means of egress design requirements, such as required number of exits or exit access travel distance, and provides for a protected path of egress travel to the exit discharge or public way.

1009.1 General. Stairways serving occupied portions of a building shall comply with the requirements of this section.

1009.2 Interior Exit Stairways. Interior exit stairways shall lead directly to the exterior of the building or shall be extended to the exterior of the building with an exit passageway conforming to the requirements of Section 1023, except as permitted in Section 1027.1.

1009.2.1 Where Required. Interior exit stairways shall be included, as necessary, to meet one or more means of egress design requirements, such as required number of exits or exit access travel distance.

1009.2.2 Enclosure. All interior exit stairways shall be enclosed in accordance with the provisions of Section 1022.

1009.3 Exit Access Stairways. Floor openings between stories created by exit access stairways shall be enclosed.

Exceptions:

1. In other than Group I-2, *I-2.1*, I-3 *and R-2.1* occupancies, exit access stairways that serve, or atmospherically communicate between, only two stories are not required to be enclosed.
2. Exit access stairways serving and contained within a single residential dwelling unit or sleeping unit in Group R-1, R-2, or R-3 occupancies are not required to be enclosed.
3. In buildings with only Group B or M occupancies, exit access stairway openings are not required to be enclosed provided that the building is equipped throughout with an automatic sprinkler system in accordance with Section 903.3.1.1, the area of the floor opening between stories does not exceed twice the horizontal projected area of the exit access stairway, and the opening is protected by a draft curtain and closely spaced sprinklers in accordance with NFPA 13.
4. In other than Group B, *I-2*, *I-2.1*, *I-3* and M occupancies, exit access stairway openings are not required to be enclosed provided that the building is equipped throughout with an automatic sprinkler system in accordance with Section 903.3.1.1, the floor opening does not connect more than four stories, the area of the floor opening between stories does not exceed twice the horizontal projected area of the exit access stairway, and the opening is protected by a draft curtain and closely spaced sprinklers in accordance with NFPA 13.
5. Exit access stairways within an atrium complying with the provisions of Section 404 are not required to be enclosed.

1009, 1010, 202 continues

1009, 1010, 202 continued

6. Exit access stairways and ramps in open parking garages that serve only the parking garage are not required to be enclosed.
7. Stairways serving outdoor facilities where all portions of the means of egress are essentially open to the outside are not required to be enclosed.
8. Exit access stairways serving stages, platforms, and technical production areas in accordance with Sections 410.6.2 and 410.6.3 are not required to be enclosed.
9. Stairways are permitted to be open between the balcony, gallery, or press box and the main assembly floor in occupancies such as theaters, places of religious worship, auditoriums, and sports facilities.
10. In Group I-3 occupancies, exit access stairways constructed in accordance with Section 408.5 are not required to be enclosed.

1010.1 Scope. The provisions of this section shall apply to ramps used as a component of a means of egress.

Exceptions:

1. Other than ramps that are part of the accessible routes providing access in accordance with Sections 1108.2 through 1108.2.4 and 1108.2.6, ramped aisles within assembly rooms or spaces shall conform with the provisions in Section 1028.11.
2. Curb ramps shall comply with ICC A117.1.
3. Vehicle ramps in parking garages for pedestrian exit access shall not be required to comply with Sections ~~1010.3~~ 1010.4 through ~~1010.9~~ 1010.10 when they are not an accessible route serving accessible parking spaces, other required accessible elements, or part of an accessible means of egress.

1010.2 Enclosure. All interior exit ramps shall be enclosed in accordance with the applicable provisions of Section 1022. Exit access ramps shall be enclosed in accordance with the provisions of Section 1009.3 for enclosure of stairways.

CHANGE SIGNIFICANCE: Although generally considered as a clarification of existing requirements, the multiple changes regarding interior stairways and ramps will provide for consistent application of the code requirements. Because so many code sections are affected by this change, including the revision of some of the basic means of egress terminology, it is important that code users are aware of the revisions even if they do not result in major technical changes.

Historically, the code has allowed the limited use of unenclosed exit stairs in a manner that has resulted in inconsistent interpretations. During previous code development cycles, numerous code changes were submitted, with some incorporated into the code, in order to clarify the intent and application of specific provisions. This new revision is considered as a comprehensive change that addresses the entire egress system and how unenclosed stairs affect issues such as exit versus exit access, travel distance measurements, contribution to the minimum number of required exits, etc.

To illustrate the need for a comprehensive revision, consider a two-story building that has one enclosed exit stairway and one open (unenclosed) stairway serving the second floor, which is required to have at least two exits. Because the open stairway did not meet the definition for an "exit," technically only one "exit" is provided from the second story even though the second stairway is permitted to be unenclosed. In the same example, the correct means of measuring exit access travel distance was possibly confusing depending on whether or not the open stairway was considered as an "exit" stairway or an "exit access" stairway from the story.

Code users should be aware of these changes because they will affect means of egress terminology. In addition, modifications result in a number of substantial revisions to Sections 1009, 1010, 1016, 1021, and 1022 as well as sections in Chapters 4, 7, and 8. It should be noted that these revisions are primarily a clarification and are intended to provide consistency throughout the code. The new and revised definitions and those sections that were revised within the code are based on the following concepts:

- All stairs within a building are elements of the means of egress system and must comply with Chapter 10.
- Unenclosed stairways are not considered as an *exit.*
- All exit stairways, to qualify as *exits,* must be enclosed with a fire-resistance-rated enclosure consisting of exit stair shafts and passageways based on the previous exit enclosure provisions.
- All stairways that are permitted to be open, or are not required stairways for egress purposes, are *exit access stairways.*
- *Exit access stairways* must be enclosed with fire-resistance-rated enclosures based on shaft provisions or may be open in accordance with exceptions based on the previous code exceptions.
- Exit access travel distance is measured from an entrance to an *exit.*
- Exit access travel distance includes the travel distance on an *exit access stairway.*
- Entrances to exits on each story are not mandatory and access to exits on other stories is permissible within certain limitations.

1009.1

Application of Stairway Provisions

Example of stairway that should be regulated by the code.

CHANGE TYPE: Clarification

CHANGE SUMMARY: Section 1009.1 has been clarified to apply to any stairway serving occupied portions of a building, including "convenience" stairways that are not a portion of a required means of egress or required means of egress stairways.

2013 CODE: **1009.1 General.** Stairways serving occupied portions of a building shall comply with the requirements of this section.

CHANGE SIGNIFICANCE: With the inclusion of a new scoping provision, it has been clarified that the requirements of Section 1009 apply to any stairway serving an occupied portion of the building. This charging language eliminates the potential for inappropriate interpretations that view stairways not required as a part of the means of egress system as not regulated by Chapter 10 or the provisions of Section 1009.

Whether stairways are serving as a required portion of the egress system or simply installed in additional numbers beyond the code minimum, it is appropriate for the stairways to meet the minimum safeguards that the code intends. Without the broad scope establish by Section 1009.1, it could be debated that items such as the rise and run, width, dimensional uniformity, handrails, etc., could all be considered as unregulated if the stairway was not a required means of egress stairway. This obviously was never the intent because steeper risers or inconsistent rise/run provisions would make the stairway unsafe regardless of whether it was used for convenience or for egress purposes.

element of trim that is below the handrail, the provision now applies the limit to the "side" of the stair or ramp and is not limited to the handrail itself.

In addition, it has been clarified that an intermediate handrail on a stair or in an aisle is to be considered as a permitted projection and not as a reduction in the required egress width. For example the 48-inch aisle stairway required by Section 1028.9.1 that has a 2-inch-wide intermediate handrail would be viewed as providing 48 inches of egress width even though the aisle is arranged to provide 23 inches of clear width between the handrail and seating on both sides with the other 2 inches occupied by the handrail.

CHANGE TYPE: Modification

1013.1, 1013.8

Guards at Operable Windows

CHANGE SUMMARY: The guard requirements for operable windows having a sill height more than 72 inches above the finished grade have been relocated from Chapter 14 to the general guard provisions of Chapter 10 and the minimum window sill height at which a guard is not required has been increased from 24 inches to 36 inches.

2013 CODE: **1013.1 General.** Guards shall comply with the provisions of Sections 1013.2 through 1013.7. Operable windows with sills located more than 72 inches (1.83 m) above finished grade or other surface below shall comply with Section 1013.8.

1013.8 ~~**1405.13.2**~~ **Window Sills.** In Occupancy Groups R-2 and R-3, one- and two-family and multiple-family dwellings, where the opening of the sill portion of an operable window is located more than 72 inches (1829 mm) above the finished grade or other surface below, the lowest part of the clear opening of the window shall be at a height not less than ~~24 inches (610 mm)~~ 36 inches (915 mm) above the finished floor surface of the room in which the window is located. ~~Glazing between the floor and a height of 24 inches (610 mm) shall be fixed or have openings through which a 4-inch (102 mm) diameter sphere cannot pass.~~ Operable sections of windows shall not permit openings that allow passage of a 4-inch (102-mm) diameter sphere where such openings are located within 36 inches (915 mm) of the finished floor.

1013.1 1013.8 continued

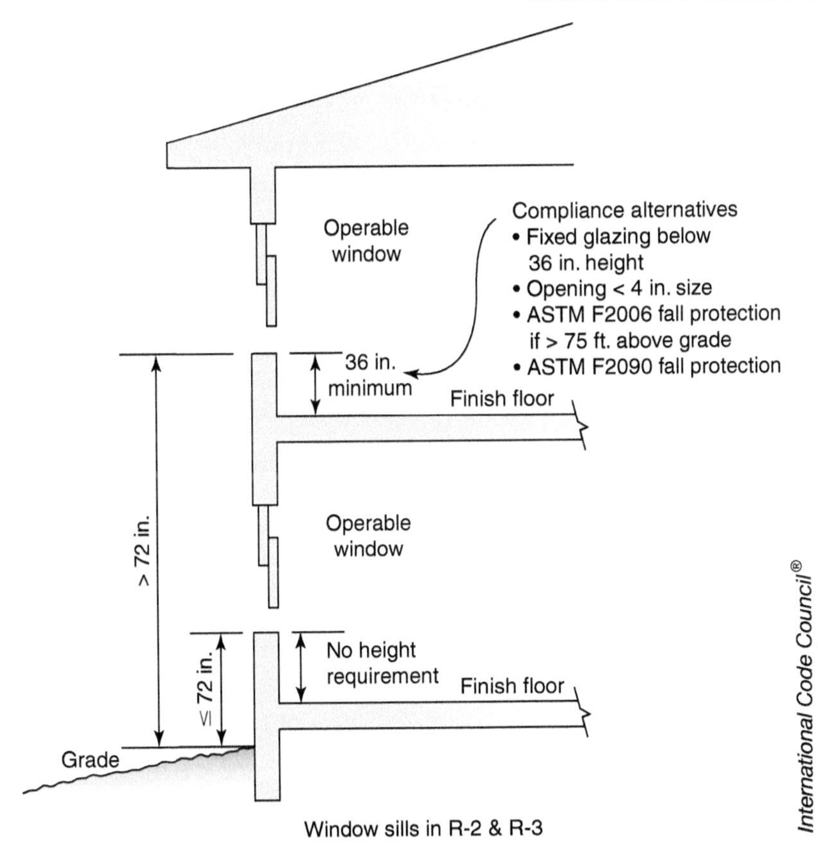

Fall protection at operable windows.

Exceptions:

1. ~~Openings that are~~ Operable windows where the sill portion of the opening is located more than 75 feet (22.86 m) above the finished grade or other surface below and that are provided with window ~~guards~~ fall prevention devices that comply with ASTM F 2006 ~~or F 2090~~.
2. Windows whose openings will not allow a 4-inch (102-mm) diameter sphere to pass through the opening when the window is in its largest opened position.
3. Openings that are provided with window fall prevention devices that comply with ASTM F2090.
4. Windows that are provided with window opening control devices that comply with Section 1013.8.

1013.8.1 Window Opening Control Devices. Window opening control devices shall comply with ASTM F 2090. The window opening control device, after operation to release the control device allowing the window to fully open, shall not reduce the minimum net clear opening area of the window unit to less than the area required by Section 1029.2.

CHANGE SIGNIFICANCE: The fall protection requirements related to low-height window sills have been relocated from Chapter 14 to Section 1013. In addition, the minimum height of the window sill at which a guard is not required has been revised from 24 inches to 36 inches. The 36-inch sill height was chosen to reduce the ability of a child to climb onto the sill and thus enabling them to fall through the opening. While the 24-inch height was above the center of gravity for most children under 4½ years of age, the lower height was easily climbed by most standing children.

The modified Exception 1 makes two changes that better coordinate the code with the scope of the standard addressing window fall prevention devices. Most notable will be the fact that the exception is now limited to only those operable windows that are located more than 75 feet above grade. This revision is coordinated with the scoping provisions found within the ASTM F2006 standard itself. Section 1.2 of the standard states, "This safety specification applies only to window fall prevention devices that are to be used on windows that are not intended for escape (egress) and rescue (ingress)." Further, Section 1.3 states, "This safety specification applies only to devices intended to be applied to windows installed at heights of more than 75 above ground level in multiple-family dwelling buildings. This safety specification is not intended to apply to windows below 75 feet because all windows below 75 feet that are operable could be used as a possible secondary means of escape."

Users will also notice that the ASTM F2090 standard that was previously referenced has been deleted and is now addressed in a new Exception 3. With the revised height limitation in Exception 1 and the fact that emergency escape and rescue openings are not required above 75 feet, the ASTM F2090 standard is no longer applicable. ASTM F 2090 includes window fall prevention devices (the new Exception 3) and window opening control devices (Exception 4 and the new Section 1013.8.1). The standard is specifically written for window openings within 75 feet

1013.1 1013.8 continued

1013.1 1013.8 continued

of grade and specifically allows for windows to be used for emergency escape and rescue. Opening control devices allow for normal operation to result in a 4 inch maximum opening, thus meeting the requirements of the last sentence in the base paragraph, but can be released to allow the window to be fully opened in order to comply with the emergency escape provisions of Section 1029.2. The window control devices and their operation are regulated by the new Section 1013.8.1 to ensure they can serve both the fall protection concerns as well as the escape and rescue opening functions.

The 4-inch opening size limitation specified in Exception 2 is consistent with the guard provisions of Section 1013.4. Although not stated directly within the exception, the requirements of Exception 2 are limited to windows or portions of windows where the opening is located between the floor surface and 36 inches in height above the floor surface. Due to the height limitations within the base paragraph of Section 1013.8, any opening that above the 36-inch height would not be regulated by the 4-inch limitation.

1015.1, 1025.4, 1028.1

Means of Egress for Group I-3 Occupancies

CHANGE TYPE: Modification

CHANGE SUMMARY: Modification to the means of egress provisions specific to Group I-3 occupancies reflects the recommendations of the California State Fire Marshal's Task Force.

2013 CODE: 1015.1 Exits or Exit Access Doorways from Spaces. Two exits or exit access doorways from any space shall be provided where one of the following conditions exists:

The refuge area of a horizontal exit is not required to lead directly to the exterior in I-3 occupancies.

1. The occupant load of the space exceeds one of the values in Table 1015.1.

Exceptions: (No changes to text)

2. and **3.** (No changes to text)

4. *In detention and correctional facilities and holding cells, such as are found in courthouse buildings, ~~a minimum of two means of egress shall be provided~~ when the occupant load is more than 20 (see Section 408.3.11).*

Where a building contains mixed occupancies, each individual occupancy shall comply with the applicable requirements for that occupancy. Where applicable, cumulative occupant loads from adjacent occupancies shall be considered in accordance with the provisions of Section 1004.1.

TABLE 1015.1 Spaces With One Exit Or Exit Access Doorway

Occupancy	Maximum Occupant Load
A, B, E, F, M, U	49
H-1, H-2, H-3	3
H-4, H-5, *I-2.1*, I-3, I-4, R	10
S	29
L	*See Section 443.6.1*

a. For holding cells, see Section 408.3.11.

TABLE 1016.2 Exit Access Travel Distance[a]

OCCUPANCY	WITHOUT SPRINKLER SYSTEM (feet)	WITH SPRINKLER SYSTEM (feet)
A, E, F-1, M, R, S-1	200	250[b]
~~I-1~~*R-2.1*	Not Permitted	250[c]
I-2, *I-2.1*, I-3[d], I-4	150	200[c]

(Portions of table not shown remain unchanged)
a. See the following sections for modifications to exit access travel distance requirements:
Section 408.3.10: For increased limitation in Group I-3.
Section ~~1016.3~~1016.2.2: For increased limitation in Groups F-1 and S-1.
(Other sections not shown for clarity)
b. through d. (No changes to text)

TABLE 1018.1 Corridor Fire-Resistance Rating

(No Changes to table)
a. (No changes to text)
b. For a reduction in the fire-resistance rating for occupancies in Group I-3, see Section*s* *408.1.2 and* 408.8.
c. and d. (No changes to text)

408.3.10 Travel Distance. *The travel distance may be increased to 300 feet for portions of Group I-3 occupancies open only to staff or where inmates are escorted at all times by staff.*

408.3.11 Number of Exits Required. *In temporary holding areas of noncombustible construction, a second means of egress is required when the occupant load is greater than 20.*

1025.4 Capacity of Refuge Area. The refuge area of a horizontal exit shall be a space occupied by the same tenant or a public area and each such refuge area shall be adequate to accommodate the original occupant load of the refuge area plus the occupant load anticipated from the adjoining compartment. The anticipated occupant load from the adjoining compartment shall be based on the capacity of the horizontal exit doors entering the refuge area. The capacity of the refuge area shall be computed based on a net floor area allowance of 3 square feet (0.2787 m^2) for each occupant to be accommodated therein.

Exception: (No change to text)

The refuge area into which a horizontal exit leads shall be provided with exits adequate to meet the occupant requirements of this chapter, but not including the added occupant load imposed by persons entering it through horizontal exits from other areas. *In other than I-3 occupancies,* ~~A~~ *a*t least one refuge area exit shall lead directly to the exterior or to an interior exit stairway or ramp.

1015.1 1025.4, 1028.1 continued

1015.1 1025.4, 1028.1 continued

1028.1 General. ~~*All* occupancies in Group A and assembly occupancies accessory to Group E *including those*~~ A room or space used for assembly purposes which contains seats, tables, displays, equipment or other material shall comply with this section.

Exception: *Group A occupancies within Group I-3 facilities are exempt from egress requirements of Section 1028.*

CHANGE SIGNIFICANCE: Section 1015.1 and the new Footnote a to Table 1015.1 reference the new Section 408.3.11 to clarify when two exits or exit access doorways are required for Group I-3 occupancies. Table 1015.1 limits the occupant load to 10 for Group I-3 occupancies with a single means of egress. However, the footnote directs the user to Section 408.3.11, which does not require a second exit for temporary holding areas until the occupant load exceeds 20. Temporary holding areas occur in courthouses as well as in detention and correctional facilities. To use the higher occupant load threshold, construction must be noncombustible, which is typically the case for these types of occupancies.

The I-3 Occupancy Codes Task Group determined that a 200-foot travel distance was overly conservative for staff areas within an I-3 institution. Staff areas such as storage, control rooms, tunnels and officer areas have a similar or smaller fire load than Group B office areas which are permitted a 300-foot travel distance. Even this distance is based on a slow travel speed to accommodate a wide variety of movement speeds. The staff in an institution should be moving at faster speeds than the average person. The new Footnote a to Table 1016.1 references Section 408.3.10, which permits a 300-foot travel distance for portions of Group I-3 occupancies open only to staff or where inmates are escorted at all times by staff.

Table 1018.1 Footnote b provides a reference to new provisions in Section 408.1.2 for reductions to the fire-resistance rating of corridors serving Group I-3 occupancies.

Often in I-3 occupancies, horizontal exits are required to achieve the exiting requirements and maintain security. In Group I-3 occupancies, an exit is not necessary from each individual fire compartment if there is access to an exit through other fire compartments without passing through the fire compartment of fire origin. This provision is intended to promote the use of horizontal exits in detention and correctional occupancies. Horizontal exits provide an especially effective egress system for an occupancy in which the occupants, due to security concerns, are not commonly released to the outside. The new text in Section 1025.4 clarifies that the refuge area of a horizontal exit is not required to lead directly to the exterior in I-3 occupancies.

The I-3 Occupancy Codes Task Group reviewed the requirements in the previous edition of the code for Group A occupancies found within correctional and detention facilities. The specific means of egress requirements for assembly occupancies in Section 1028 are not compatible with I-3 facilities. Since I-3 facilities are already built to more restrictive requirements than necessary for Group A occupancies, and because quantity and size of exits are spelled out in other areas of Chapter 10, applying Section 1028 to assembly areas of Group I-3 occupancies creates confusion. Assembly areas of Group I-3 occupancies are now excluded from Section 1028.

1015.2

Exit or Exit Access Doorway Arrangement

CHANGE TYPE: Clarification

CHANGE SUMMARY: This clarification addresses the California State Fire Marshal's concerns with the availability and arrangement of exits.

2013 CODE: **1015.2 Exit or Exit Access Doorway Arrangement.** Required exits shall be located in a manner that makes their availability obvious. Exits shall be unobstructed at all times. Exit and exit access doorways shall be arranged in accordance with Sections 1015.2.1 and 1015.2.2. *Exit access doorways, contributing to the total number of exits or exit access doorways required by Sections 1015.1 and 1015.1.1, shall lead to separate exits.*

The third required exit or exit access doorway shall be arranged a reasonable distance apart from the other two.

1015.2.2 Three or More Exits or Exit Access Doorways. Where access to three or more exits is required, at least two exit doors or exit access doorways shall be arranged in accordance with the provisions of Section 1015.2.1. *Additional required exit or exit access doorways shall be arranged a reasonable distance apart so that if one becomes blocked, the others will be available.*

CHANGE SIGNIFICANCE: The previous language appeared to allow two of three required exit access doorways from a space to lead to a single exit and still be counted as two of the required exits or exit access doors from a space. This code amendment clarifies the intent to maintain exit continuity.

1022.5

Enclosure Penetrations of Interior Exit Stairways

CHANGE TYPE: Modification

CHANGE SUMMARY: Penetrations of the outside membrane of a fire barrier utilized to enclose an interior exit stair or ramp are now permitted provided the penetration is properly protected.

2013 CODE: ~~**1022.4**~~ **1022.5 Penetrations.** Penetrations into and openings through ~~an exit enclosure~~ interior exit stairways and ramps are prohibited except for required exit doors, equipment, and ductwork necessary for independent ventilation or pressurization, sprinkler piping, standpipes, electrical raceway for fire department communication systems, and electrical raceway serving the ~~exit enclosure~~ interior exit stairway and ramp and terminating at a steel box not exceeding 16 square inches (0.010 m^2). Such penetrations shall be protected in accordance with Section 714. There shall be no penetrations or communication openings, whether protected or not, between adjacent ~~exit enclosures~~ interior exit stairways and ramps.

> **Exception:** Membrane penetrations shall be permitted on the outside of the interior exit stairway and ramp. Such penetrations shall be protected in accordance with Section 714.3.2.

CHANGE SIGNIFICANCE: Unless specifically permitted, penetrations have historically been prohibited at the fire-resistance-rated enclosure around an interior exit stairway or ramp. The strict limitations were

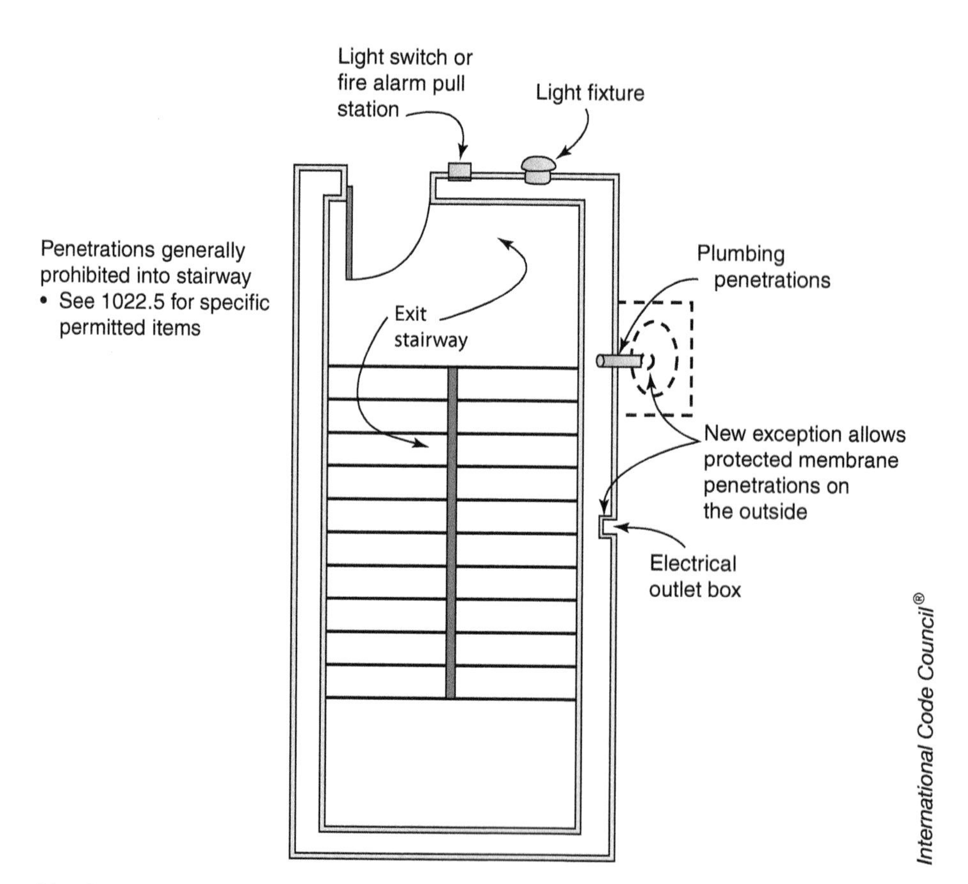

Membrane penetrations of interior exit stairways.

deemed necessary to ensure that the fire-resistive integrity of the exit system was not compromised by penetrations of the protective enclosure. Penetrations of the exterior membrane of the fire-resistance-rated assembly are now permitted provided they are in compliance with the membrane penetration provisions of Section 714.3.2.

Virtually all penetrations have been prohibited in the past, regardless of purpose with very limited exceptions. The prohibition applied to an alarm pull station next to a door into the stair enclosure, fire hose cabinets, fire extinguisher cabinets, alarm notification appliances, electrical wiring for exit signs, electrical outlets, and other items. The new exception will not limit the type of or purpose for the penetration but will simply limit the location to the exterior membrane and require the proper protection.

1028.1.1.1

Separation of Spaces under Grandstands and Bleachers

CHANGE TYPE: Addition

CHANGE SUMMARY: Spaces beneath grandstands and bleachers are now required to be adequately separated to protect the assembly seating area from any potential hazards.

2013 CODE: **1028.1.1.1 Spaces under Grandstands and Bleachers.** When spaces under grandstands or bleachers are used for purposes other than ticket booths less than 100 square feet (9.29 m^2) and toilet rooms, such spaces shall be separated by fire barriers complying with Section 707 and horizontal assemblies complying with Section 711 with not less than 1-hour fire-resistance-rated construction.

CHANGE SIGNIFICANCE: In order to protect the assembly seating area of bleachers and grandstands from an exposure to hazards, a minimum separation of 1-hour fire-resistance-rated construction is now required to protect the seating from the spaces below. This separation requirement applies where the space beneath the seating is used for any purpose other than restrooms of any size or limited size ticket booths, even if the spaces are protected by an automatic sprinkler system in accordance with Section 903.2.1.5. Conceptually this requirement for protection on the underside of the seating is similar to the required protection of enclosed usable space beneath a stairway (see Section 1009.9.3).

The location of the new requirements was chosen for its proximity to the reference to the ICC 300 standard. Placing the provision directly after that reference section will help ensure the protection requirement is not overlooked

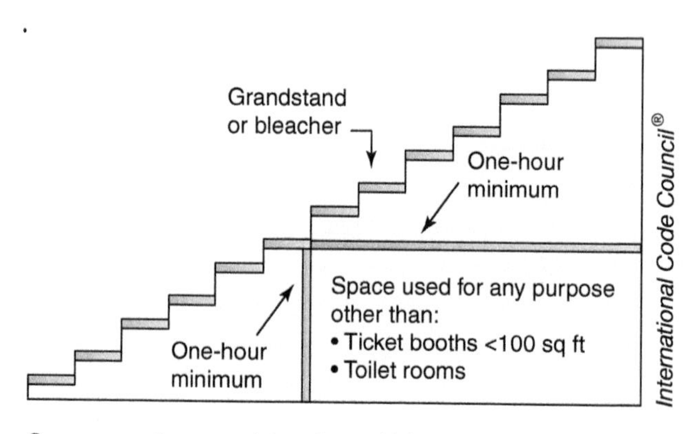

Spaces under grandstands and bleachers.

PART 5

Accessibility

Chapter 11

Chapters 11A and 11B are intended to address the accessibility and usability of buildings and their elements to persons having physical disabilities.

■

Chapter 11A

Housing Accessibility

CHANGE TYPE: Modification

CHANGE SUMMARY: Chapter 11A has been revised in its entirety.

2013 CODE:

CHAPTER 11A

HOUSING ACCESSIBILITY

Chapter 11A has been revised in its entirety.

CHANGE SIGNIFICANCE: Department of Housing and Community Development (HCD) has continued the adoption of Chapter 11A with many amendments throughout. Most of the adopted modifications are intended to incorporate new language from Chapter 11B and the 2010 ADA in an effort to maintain the same technical requirements for common use and public use areas in Chapter 11A and Chapter 11B, respectively. Some editorial corrections and clarifications based on stakeholders' comments are also made. In addition, all definitions, previously located in Section 1107A, are relocated to Chapter 2 for consistency with the new format of 2012 IBC.

All adopted amendments in Chapter 11A and the rationale for their adoption can be found at http://www.hcd.ca.gov/codes/shl/2013codeadoptproj_part2.html.

Apartment building.

Chapter 11B
Accessibility

CHANGE TYPE: Modification

CHANGE SUMMARY: California Division of the State Architect (DSA) has revised Chapter 11B to coordinate the accessibility provisions with the 2010 ADA.

2013 CODE:

CHAPTER 11B

ACCESSIBILITY TO PUBLIC BUILDINGS, PUBLIC ACCOMMODATIONS, COMMERCIAL BUILDINGS AND PUBLICLY FUNDED HOUSING

This chapter has been revised in its entirety.

CHANGE SIGNIFICANCE: The historic update of California accessibility regulations integrated the most accessible provisions of the 2010 Americans with Disabilities Act (ADA) standards and the 2010 CBC into a single comprehensive set of criteria. The new Chapter 11B used the 2004 ADA accessibility guidelines as the base model and the format and organization of the 2010 ADA standards. The revisions and the reasons are found in the Express Terms and Initial Statement of Reasons (ISOR) located at: http://www.dgs.ca.gov/dsa/Programs/progAccess/access2013.aspx.

Public building.

PART 6

Building Envelope, Structural Systems, and Construction Materials

Chapters 12 through 26

- **Chapter 12** Interior Environment
- **Chapter 13** Energy Efficiency No changes addressed
- **Chapter 14** Exterior Walls
- **Chapter 15** Roof Assemblies and Rooftop Structures
- **Chapter 16** Structural Design
- **Chapter 17** Structural Tests and Special Inspections
- **Chapter 18** Soils and Foundations
- **Chapter 19** Concrete
- **Chapter 20** Aluminum No changes addressed
- **Chapter 21** Masonry
- **Chapter 22** Steel
- **Chapter 23** Wood
- **Chapter 24** Glass and Glazing
- **Chapter 25** Gypsum Board and Plaster
- **Chapter 26** Plastic

The interior environment provisions of Chapter 12 include requirements for lighting, ventilation, and sound transmission. Chapter 13 provides a reference to the *California Energy Code* in Title 24, Part 6 for provisions governing energy efficiency. Regulations governing the building envelope are located in Chapters 14 and 15, addressing exterior wall coverings and roof coverings, respectively. Structural systems are regulated through the structural design provisions of Chapter 16, whereas structural testing and special inspections are addressed in Chapter 17. The provisions of Chapter 18 apply to soils and foundation systems. The requirements for materials of construction, both structural and nonstructural, are located in Chapters 19 through 26. Structural materials regulated by the code include concrete, lightweight metals, masonry, steel, and wood. Glass and glazing, gypsum board, plaster, and plastics are included as regulated nonstructural materials. ■

continues

1604.5, 202

Risk Categories

1605.2

Load Combinations Using Strength Design of Load and Resistance Factor Design

1605.3

Load Combinations Using Allowable Stress Design

TABLE 1607.1

Minimum Live Loads

1607.7

Heavy Vehicle Loads

1609, 202

Determination of Wind Loads

1613.3.1, 202

Mapped Acceleration Parameters

1613.5

Ballasted Photovoltaic System

1704.3

Statement of Special Inspections

1705.2

Special Inspection of Steel Construction

TABLE 1705.3

Required Verification and Inspection of Concrete Construction

1705.4

Special Inspection of Masonry Construction

1705.16

Special Inspection of Fire-Resistant Penetration and Joint Systems

1803.5.12

Geotechnical Reports for Foundation Walls and Retaining Walls

CHAPTER 19

Concrete Construction

1905.1.3

Seismic Detailing of Wall Piers

2101.2

Design Methods for Masonry Structures

2206

Composite Structural Steel and Concrete Structures

2210.2

Seismic Requirements for Cold-Formed Steel Structures

2305

General Design Requirements for Lateral-Force-Resisting Systems

2306

Allowable Stress Design

2307

Load and Resistance Factor Design

2406.1, 2406.4

Safety Glazing—Hazardous Locations

2406.2

Safety Glazing—Impact Test

2510.6

Water-Resistive Barriers for Stucco Applications

2603.10, 2603.10.1

Special Approval of Foam Plastics

1203.2

Attic Ventilation

CHANGE TYPE: Modification

CHANGE SUMMARY: The minimum required ventilation area for attics has been clarified.

2013 CODE: **1203.2 Attic Spaces** Enclosed attics and enclosed rafter spaces formed where ceilings are applied directly to the underside of roof framing members shall have cross ventilation for each separate space by ventilation openings protected against the entrance of rain and snow. Blocking and bridging shall be arranged so as not to interfere with the movement of air. ~~A minimum of 1 inch (25 mm)~~ An airspace of not less than 1 inch (25 mm) shall be provided between the insulation and the roof sheathing. The net free ventilating area shall not be less than ~~1/300~~ 1/150th of the area of the space ventilated. ~~with 50 percent of the required ventilating area provided by ventilators located in the upper portion of the space to be ventilated at least 3 feet (914 mm) above eave or cornice vents with the balance of the required ventilation provided by eave or cornice vents~~.

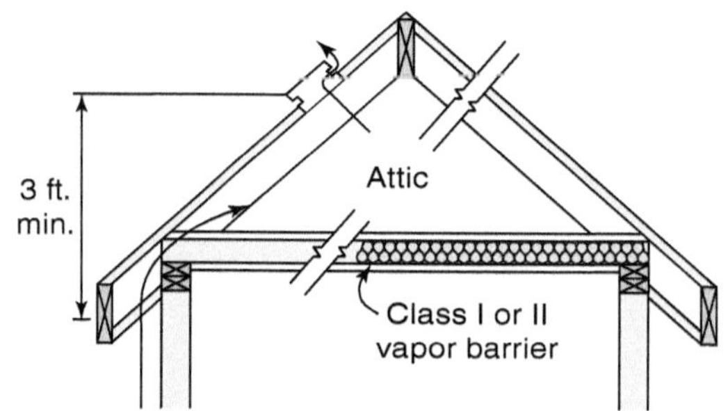

Attic ventilation requirements.

Exceptions:

1. (Not adopted by HCD) The net free cross-ventilation area shall be permitted to be reduced to 1/300 provided that not less than 50 percent and not more than 80 percent of the required ventilating area provided by ventilators located in the upper portion of the space to be ventilated at least 3 feet (914 mm) above eave or cornice vents with the balance of the required ventilation provided by eave or cornice vents.

2. (Not adopted by HCD) The net free cross-ventilation area shall be permitted to be reduced to 1/300 where a Class I or II vapor barrier is installed on the warm-in-winter side of the ceiling.

3. Attic ventilation shall not be required when determined not necessary by the building official due to atmospheric or climatic conditions.

4. (HCD 1 & HCD 2) The net cross-ventilation area shall be permitted to be reduced to 1/300 provided that at least 40 percent and not more than 50 percent of the required ventilating area is provided

by ventilators located in the upper portion of the attic or rafter space. Upper ventilators shall be located no more than 3 feet (914 mm) below the ridge or highest point of the space, measured vertically, with the balance of the required ventilation provided by eave or cornice vents. Where the location of wall or roof framing members conflicts with the installation of upper ventilators, installation more than 3 feet (914 mm) below the ridge or highest point of the space shall be permitted.

5. **(HCD 1 & HCD 2)** The net cross-ventilation area shall be permitted to be reduced to 1/300 in Climate Zones 14 and 16, where a Class I or II vapor retarder is installed on the warm-in-winter side of the ceiling.

CHANGE SIGNIFICANCE: HCD adopted Section 1203.2 from the 2012 *International Building Code* (IBC) into the 2013 *California Building Code* (CBC) with amendment. HCD did not adopt the model code Exceptions 1 and 2, and adopted new Exceptions 4 and 5, which apply to applications under the authority of HCD. The California amendment incorporates provisions for attic ventilation from the 2012 *International Residential Code* (IRC) proposed for adoption into the 2013 *California Residential Code* (CRC), Section R806.2. The amendment will provide clarity to the code user and consistency with the CRC.

There have been numerous changes to the attic ventilation requirements in the IBC and the IRC during the last two code adoption cycles. For purposes of consistency with the IRC, the language in the 2012 IBC was changed and currently is similar to the language in the 2009 IRC. However, the committee developing the 2012 IRC decided that the measures in the 2009 IRC were inadequate to achieve ventilation, in parts, or violated the applicable physics so the language was modified in the 2012 IRC. As a result, the 2012 IRC and the 2012 IBC contain different requirements for the minimum required area for attic ventilation. Currently, there are four proposals for the 2015 IBC related to Section 1203.2. The rationale for the proposed changes is "inadequate ventilation (in the 2012 IBC) and consistency with the IRC."

HCD believes that there is no reason for different requirements to be applicable to the same buildings and applications regulated by HCD. In an effort to avoid confusion and to ease the transition from the current requirements to the future proposed changes, HCD is incorporating the language from the 2012 IRC, which seems to be more accurate and beneficial for use in both codes.

1203.4.2.1

Mechanical Ventilation of Bathrooms

CHANGE TYPE: Modification

CHANGE SUMMARY: The CALGreen requirements for bathroom exhaust fans have been added to the CBC.

2013 CODE: **1203.4.2.1 Bathrooms.** Rooms containing bathtubs, showers, spas and similar bathing fixtures shall be mechanically ventilated in accordance with the *California Mechanical Code.*

The minimum ~~ventilation or~~ exhaust rate shall not be less than that established by Table 4-4 403.7 "Minimum Exhaust Rates." See California Mechanical Code, Chapter 5, for additional provisions related to environmental air ducts.

(HCD 1) In addition to the requirements in this section and in the California Mechanical Code, bathrooms in Group R occupancies shall be mechanically ventilated in accordance with the California Green Building Standards Code (CALGreen), Chapter 4, Division 4.5.

CHANGE SIGNIFICANCE: HCD has included pointers to mandatory CALGreen Code requirements in this code to enhance user convenience and familiarity. These mandatory pointers are excerpts to code sections in CALGreen. Users should consult the actual code text in CALGreen for complete requirements.

The intent of Section 1203.4.2.1 is to reduce the probability of mold and mildew growth. Bathrooms without proper ventilation have a higher history of mold growth than other rooms in a dwelling.

Bathrooms require mechanical ventilation.

1207

Sound Transmission

CHANGE TYPE: Deletion

CHANGE SUMMARY: HCD has elected to not publish the California State Sound Transmission Criteria in the CBC.

2013 CODE: SECTION 1207

~~(HCD 1 & HCD 2)~~ **SOUND TRANSMISSION**

~~***1207.1 Purpose and scope.*** *The purpose of this section is to establish uniform minimum noise insulation performance standards to protect persons within hotels, motels, dormitories, apartment houses and dwellings other than detached single-family dwellings from the effects of excessive noise, including, but not limited to, hearing loss or impairment and interference with speech and sleep. This section shall apply to all buildings for which applications for building permits were made subsequent to August 22, 1974.*~~

1207.1 Scope. This section shall apply to common interior walls, partitions and floor/ceiling assemblies between adjacent dwelling units or between dwelling units and adjacent public areas such as halls, corridors, stairs or service areas.

Insulation to reduce sound transmission.

(The remaining text of the sound transmission provisions is omitted because of length and space limitations, and for clarity.)

CHANGE SIGNIFICANCE: The 2010 CBC implements California Health and Safety Code Sections 17922.6 and 17922.7, which direct the Office of Noise Control in coordination with HCD to adopt regulations that establish noise insulation levels for hotels, motels, apartment houses, and dwellings other than detached single-family dwellings.

Pursuant to the sections cited above, requirements for noise insulation were included in the CBC. HCD has been carrying forward these requirements since 1974. However, most of the measures currently are covered by other regulations, federal, state and local agencies (EPA, Federal Aviation Administration, Federal Highway Administration, California Environmental Quality Act (CEQA), local general plans, local ordinances, etc.) and do not need to be repeated in the CBC. Other measures, including the referenced standards in the amendments, are outdated or superceded by more current standards, and need to be updated. The agency mandated to adopt and amend regulations related to noise insulation is the Office of Noise Control, but this office no longer exists.

There are mandatory provisions in the model code in regards to sound transmission, which overlap most of the provisions in the California amendment. HCD believes that there is no further necessity for the California amendment to be carried forward.

1212

Pollutant Control

CHANGE TYPE: Clarification

CHANGE SUMMARY: A new section on pollutant control has been extracted from the CALGreen requirements and duplicated in the CBC

2013 CODE:

SECTION 1212 (HCD 1)

POLLUTANT CONTROL

1212.1 Finish material pollutant control. *Finish materials, including adhesives, sealants, caulks, paints and coatings, aerosol paints and coatings, carpet systems, carpet cushion, carpet adhesive, resilient flooring systems, and composite wood products shall meet the volatile organic compound (VOC) emission limits in accordance with the California Green Building Standards Code (CALGreen), Chapter 4, Division 4.5.*

CHANGE SIGNIFICANCE: HCD has included pointers to mandatory CALGreen Code requirements in this code to enhance user convenience and familiarity. These mandatory pointers are excerpts to code sections in CALGreen. Users should consult the actual code text in CALGreen for complete requirements.

The required reduction of volatile organic compounds (VOC) in finish materials intends to improve indoor air quality for the occupants of the buildings.

Finish materials including carpet must meet the VOC emission limits.

1507.16

Roof Gardens and Landscaped Roofs

CHANGE TYPE: Addition

CHANGE SUMMARY: The CBC now provides a reference to new CFC provisions on roof gardens and landscaped roofs as a means of controlling the potential hazards these combustible materials on the roof could create.

2013 CODE: **1507.16 Roof Gardens and Landscaped Roofs.** Roof gardens and landscaped roofs shall comply with the requirements of this chapter and Sections 1607.11.2.3 and 1607.11.2.3.1 and the *California Fire Code*.

1507.16.1 Structural Fire-Resistance. The structural frame and roof construction supporting the load imposed upon the roof by the roof gardens or landscaped roofs shall comply with the requirements of Table 601.

Landscaped roof.

International Code Council®

Vegetation on roof must comply with IFC requirements.

International Code Council®

CHANGE SIGNIFICANCE: The addition of rooftop vegetation or landscaping can provide a number of benefits in building construction, such as reducing the heat-gain and cooling demands, helping to control storm water runoff, and simply providing pleasant areas or sites within a community. However, these landscaped roofs also have a potential to place combustible vegetation in an area where it is less accessible to the fire department in the event of an emergency or to increase the potential fire exposure of either the building itself or of buildings nearby. To offset some of these concerns, the CFC has added new provisions (CFC Section 317), and references have been placed in the CBC that will direct users to these new CFC provisions.

The added text in the base paragraph of Section 1507.16 is essentially a reference to the new requirements that were added into CFC Section 317. The fire code provisions have added requirements that limit the size of a single landscaped roof area, require a minimum separation and protection between adjacent areas, and address maintenance issues and separation from other combustible rooftop elements such as penthouses or mechanical equipment. Perhaps the most important CFC provisions are the size limitation on the vegetation and the Class A–rated roof covering requirement for the 6-foot-wide buffer area. These requirements do not exist within the CBC itself.

The clearance/buffer area of at least 6 feet is important because it requires a Class A roof-covering assembly. Table 1505.1 only requires a Class A roof covering in certain areas under the provisions of CBC Chapter 7A or when the fire district requirements of Appendix D are used. In applying the clearance requirement, it is permissible to provide a Class A roof covering for the 6-foot minimum distance and then allow the appropriate roof covering classification for any distance in excess of the minimum dimension.

It is intended that new Section 1507.16 limit the use of Table 601, Footnote a, to situations that do not include a roof garden or landscaped roof based on the premise that the permitted reduction in the roof's fire-resistance rating is only applicable where the structural frame or bearing walls "are supporting a roof only" and that support of the loads imposed by the landscaping and vegetation on a roof is beyond what the original

1507.16 continues

1507.16 continued

limitation intended. The "roof-only" requirement has historically been applied to exclude the footnote's use where the roof system may support portions of other stories as opposed to rooftop mechanical equipment or, in this case, a roof garden or vegetation on top of the roof. Although it may seem unlikely that a fire involving the rooftop vegetation would affect the building's roof structural supports, the fire-resistance rating is not permitted to be reduced based on Footnote a.

For additional information related to this issue, please see the publication *Significant Changes to the International Fire Code, 2012 Edition.*

Construction supporting landscaped roofs must comply with Table 601 fire-resistance.

1507.17, 202

Photovoltaic Systems

CHANGE TYPE: Addition

CHANGE SUMMARY: Photovoltaic elements (modules/shingles or systems) must now meet the general code requirements for roofing materials and rooftop structures.

2013 CODE: **202 Definitions.**

PHOTOVOLTAIC MODULES/SHINGLES. A roof covering composed of flat-plate photovoltaic modules fabricated in sheets that resemble three-tab composite shingles.

1505.8 Building Integrated Photovoltaic Systems. Rooftop-installed *building integrated* photovoltaic systems that *serve as* the roof covering shall be *listed and* labeled *for* fire classification in accordance with Section 1505.1.

1505.9 Photovoltaic Panels and Modules. *Rooftop-mounted photovoltaic systems shall be tested, listed and identified with a fire classification in accordance with UL 1703. The fire classification shall comply with Table 1505.1 based on the type of construction of the building.*

1507.17 Photovoltaic Modules/Shingles. The installation of photovoltaic modules/shingles shall comply with the provisions of this section.

1507.17.1 Material Standards. Photovoltaic modules/shingles shall be listed and labeled in accordance with UL 1703.

1507.17.2 Attachment. Photovoltaic modules/shingles shall be attached in accordance with the manufacturer's installation instructions.

1507.17.3 Wind Resistance. Photovoltaic modules/shingles shall be tested in accordance with procedures and acceptance criteria in ASTM D3161. Photovoltaic modules/shingles shall comply with the classification requirements of Table 1507.2.7.1(2) for the appropriate maximum nominal design wind speed. Photovoltaic modules/shingle packaging shall bear a label to indicate compliance with the procedures in ASTM D3161 and the required classification from Table 1507.2.7.1(2).

1509.7 Photovoltaic Systems. Rooftop-mounted photovoltaic systems shall be designed in accordance with this section.

1509.7.1 Wind Resistance. Rooftop-mounted photovoltaic systems shall be designed for wind loads for component and cladding in accordance with Chapter 16 using an effective wind area based on the dimensions of a single unit frame.

> ***Exception:*** *[BSC, HCD-1, HCD-2, DSA-SS, DSA-SS/CC] The effective wind area shall be in accordance with Chapter 16 and ASCE 7 Section 26.2.*

1509.7.2 Fire Classification. Rooftop-mounted photovoltaic systems shall have the fire classification as required by Section 1505.9.

International Code Council®

Photovoltaic panel on roof.

1507.17, 3111, 202 continues

1507.17, 3111, 202 continued

1509.7.3 Installation. Rooftop-mounted photovoltaic systems shall be installed in accordance with the manufacturer's installation instructions.

1509.7.4 Photovoltaic Panels and Modules. Photovoltaic panels and modules mounted on top of a roof shall be listed and labeled in accordance with UL 1703 and shall be installed in accordance with the manufacturer's installation instructions.

1511.1 Solar Photovoltaic Panels/Modules. *Solar photovoltaic panels/modules installed upon a roof or as an integral part of a roof assembly shall comply with the requirements of this code (see Section 3411) and the California Fire Code.*

1511.1.1 Structural Fire Resistance. *The structural frame and roof construction supporting the load imposed upon the roof by the photovoltaic panels/modules shall comply with the requirements of Table 601 and Section 602.1.*

Photovoltaic modules/shingles being installed. *(Photo courtesy of Atlantis Energy Systems, Inc.)*

CHANGE SIGNIFICANCE: Guidance is now provided related to how photovoltaic systems are to be regulated. Both integrated systems (see definition and Sections 1505.8 and 1507.17) and separate roof-mounted systems (see Sections 1505.8 and 1509.7) are addressed. In general, photovoltaic systems need to comply with the same minimum roof covering classification as the underlying roof assembly that the photovoltaic system is installed on and must meet the same structural requirements as any other roof-mounted equipment.

Section 1505.8 will require that both integrated systems (photovoltaic modules/shingles) and roof-mounted systems comply with the fire classification requirements of Section 1505.1. Depending on the building's type of construction and size, this will typically require that either a Class B or Class C roof covering/assembly be used. Therefore, these systems will be tested and listed so that the designer and building official will only need to verify that the systems have the appropriate classification and are installed in accordance with their listing.

The new definition for photovoltaic modules/shingles along with the requirements of Section 1507.17 provide the guidance needed for the installation of the integrated modules/shingles. These shingles are integrated with the building's roof covering and resemble a typical composite shingle. Because the shingles provide both the roof covering and a source of electrical power, testing using the appropriate UL 1703 standard is required, with the attachment in accordance with the listing and the manufacturer's installation instructions. It is important to realize that even though this type of shingle system may appear similar to an asphalt shingle system, the appropriate design slope and fastening requirements are different for each manufacturer's product. That is the reason why this type of shingle system is included in a separate section of Section 1507 and not included under the asphalt shingle requirements of Section 1507.2.

Section 1509 addresses rooftop-mounted systems (such as a panel array) versus the integrated systems that are covered by Section 1507.17. References are provided to the general code requirements regarding wind resistance, fire classification, and installation, ensuring that the rooftop-mounted systems comply with the same minimum requirements that the underlying roof assembly would need to meet.

See Section 3111 for additional requirements.

1509, 202

Rooftop Structures

CHANGE TYPE: Modification

CHANGE SUMMARY: In addition to several technical changes, the provisions addressing rooftop structures have been reformatted to better organize and clarify the requirements.

2013 CODE:

202 Definitions.

MECHANICAL EQUIPMENT SCREEN. A ~~partially enclosed~~ rooftop structure, not covered by a roof, used to aesthetically conceal ~~heating, ventilating and air conditioning (HVAC)~~ plumbing, electrical, or mechanical equipment from view.

PENTHOUSE. An enclosed, unoccupied rooftop structure ~~above the roof of a building, other than a tank, tower, spire, dome, cupola or bulkhead.~~ used for sheltering mechanical and electrical equipment, tanks, elevators and related machinery, and vertical shaft openings.

ROOF DECK. The flat or sloped surface constructed on top of the exterior walls of a building or other supports for the purpose of enclosing the story below, or sheltering an area, to protect it from the elements, not including its supporting members or vertical supports.

ROOFTOP STRUCTURE. ~~An enclosed~~ A structure erected on ~~or above~~ top of the roof deck or on top of any part of a building.

1509.1 General. The provisions of this section shall govern the construction of rooftop structures.

1509.2 Penthouses. ~~A penthouse or~~ Penthouses in compliance with Sections 1509.2.1 through ~~1509.2.4~~ 1509.2.5 shall be considered as a portion of the story directly below the roof deck on which such penthouses are located. All other penthouses shall be considered as an additional story of the building.

1509, 202 continues

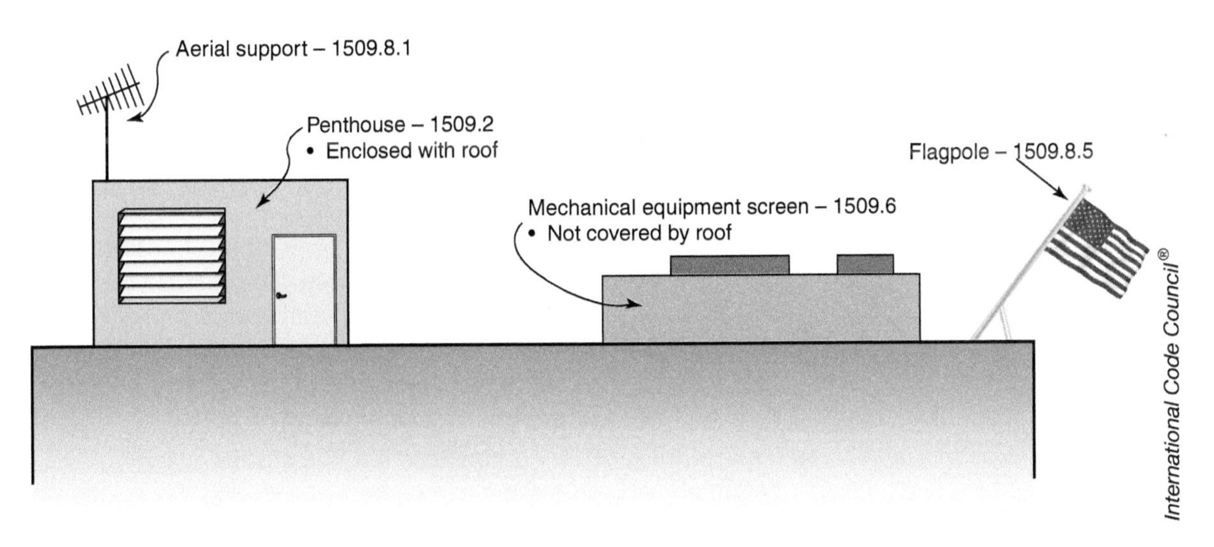

Rooftop structures.

1509, 202 continued

1509.2.1 Height above Roof Deck. ~~A penthouse~~ Penthouses ~~or other projection above the roof in structures~~ constructed on buildings of other than Type I construction ~~shall not exceed 28 feet (8534 mm) above the roof where used as an enclosure for tanks or for elevators that run to the roof and in all other cases~~ shall not exceed ~~extend more than~~ 18 feet (5486 mm) in height above the roof deck as measured to the average height of the roof of the penthouse.

Exceptions:

1. Where used to enclose tanks or elevators that travel to the roof level, penthouses shall be permitted to have a maximum height of 28 feet (8534 mm) above the roof deck.
2. Penthouses located on the roof of buildings of Type I construction shall not be limited in height.

1509.2.2 Area Limitation. The aggregate area of penthouses and other enclosed rooftop structures shall not exceed one-third the area of the supporting roof deck. Such penthouses and other enclosed rooftop structures shall not be required to be included in determining ~~contribute to either~~ the building area or number of stories as regulated by Section 503.1. The area of ~~the penthouse~~ such penthouses shall not be included in determining the fire area ~~defined~~ specified in Section 901.7 ~~902~~.

1509.2.3 Use Limitations. ~~A penthouse~~ Penthouses ~~bulkhead or any other similar projection above the roof~~ shall not be used for purposes other than the shelter of mechanical or electrical equipment, tanks, or ~~shelter of~~ vertical shaft openings in the roof assembly.

1509.2.4 Weather Protection. Provisions such as louvers, louver blades, or flashing shall be made to protect the mechanical and electrical equipment and the building interior from the elements. ~~Penthouses or bulkheads used for purposes other than permitted by this section shall conform to the requirements of this code for an additional story. The restrictions of this section shall not prohibit the placing of wood flagpoles or similar structures on the roof of any building.~~

~~1509.2.4~~ 1509.2.5 Type of Construction. Penthouses shall be constructed with walls, floors, and roof as required for the type of construction of the building on which such penthouses are built.

Exceptions:

1. On buildings of Type I construction, the exterior walls and roofs of penthouses with a fire separation distance ~~of more~~ greater than 5 feet (1524 mm) and less than 20 feet (6096 mm) shall be permitted to have not less than a ~~of at least~~ 1-hour fire-resistance rating ~~rated noncombustible construction~~. The exterior walls and roofs of penthouses with a fire separation distance of 20 feet (6096 mm) or greater shall ~~be of noncombustible construction~~ not be required to have a fire-resistance rating. ~~Interior framing and walls shall be of noncombustible construction.~~
2. On buildings of Type I construction two stories or less in height above grade plane or ~~less in height and~~ of Type II construction, the exterior walls and roofs of penthouses with a fire separation distance ~~of more~~ greater than 5 feet

(1524 mm) and less than 20 feet (6096 mm) shall be permitted to have not less than a ~~of at least~~ 1-hour fire-resistance rating or a lesser fire-resistance rating as required by Table 602 ~~rated noncombustible or~~ and be constructed of fire-retardant-treated wood ~~construction~~. The exterior walls and roofs of penthouses with a fire separation distance of 20 feet (6096 mm) or greater shall be permitted to be constructed of ~~noncombustible or~~ fire-retardant-treated wood ~~construction~~ and shall not be required to have a fire-resistance rating. Interior framing and walls shall be permitted to be constructed of ~~noncombustible or~~ fire-retardant-treated wood.

3. On buildings of Type III, IV, or ~~and~~ V construction, the exterior walls of penthouses with a fire separation distance ~~of more~~ greater than 5 feet (1524 mm) and less than 20 feet (6096 mm) shall be permitted to have not less than a ~~at least~~ 1-hour fire-resistance rating or a lesser fire-resistance rating as required by Table 602 ~~rated construction~~. On buildings of Type III, IV, or VA construction, the exterior walls of penthouses with a fire separation distance of 20 feet (6096 mm) or greater ~~from a common property line~~ shall be permitted to be of Type IV ~~construction~~ or noncombustible construction or fire-retardant-treated wood ~~construction~~ and shall not be required to have a fire-resistance rating. ~~Roofs shall be constructed of materials and fire-resistance rated as required in Table 601 and Section 603, Item 25.3. Interior framing and walls shall be Type IV construction or noncombustible or fire-retardant-treated wood construction.~~

~~4. On buildings of Type I construction, unprotected noncombustible enclosures housing only mechanical equipment and located with a minimum fire separation distance of 20 feet (6096 mm) shall be permitted.~~

~~5. On buildings of Type I construction two stories or less above grade plane in height, or Type II, III, or IV and V construction, unprotected noncombustible or fire-retardant treated wood, enclosures housing only mechanical equipment, and located with a minimum fire separation distance of 20 feet (6096 mm) shall be permitted.~~

~~6. On one-story buildings, combustible unroofed mechanical equipment screens, fences or similar enclosures are permitted where located with a fire separation distance of at least 20 feet (6096 mm) from adjacent property lines and where not exceeding 4 feet (1219 mm) in height above the roof surface.~~

~~7. Dormers shall be of the same type of construction as the roof on which they are placed, or of the exterior walls of the building.~~

1509.3 Tanks. *(See CBC for changes made to Section 1509.3 and its subsections)*

1509.4 Cooling Towers. *(See CBC for changes made to Section 1509.4)*

1509.5 Towers, Spires, Domes, and Cupolas. *(See CBC for changes made to Section 1509.5 and its subsections)*

1509, 202 continues

1509, 202 continued

1509.6 Mechanical Equipment Screens. Mechanical equipment screens shall be constructed of the materials specified for the exterior walls in accordance with the type of construction of the building. Where the fire separation distance is greater than 5 feet (1524 mm), mechanical equipment screens shall not be required to comply with the fire-resistance-rating requirements.

1509.6.1 Height Limitations. Mechanical equipment screens shall not exceed 18 feet (5486 mm) in height above the roof deck, as measured to the highest point on the mechanical equipment screen.

> **Exception:** Where located on buildings of Type IA construction, the height of mechanical equipment screens shall not be limited.

1509.6.2 Types I, II, III, and IV Construction. Regardless of the requirements in Section 1509.6, mechanical equipment screens shall be permitted to be constructed of combustible materials where located on the roof decks of building of Type I, II, III, or IV construction in accordance with any one of the following limitations:

1. The fire separation distance shall not be less than 20 feet (6096 mm) and the height of the mechanical equipment screen above the roof deck shall not exceed 4 feet (1219 mm) as measured to the highest point on the mechanical equipment screen.
2. The fire separation distance shall not be less than 20 feet (6096 mm) and the mechanical equipment screen shall be constructed of fire-retardant-treated wood complying with Section 2303.2 for exterior installation.
3. Where exterior wall-covering panels are used, the panels shall have a flame spread index of 25 or less when tested in the minimum and maximum thicknesses intended for use with each face tested independently in accordance with ASTM E84 or UL 723. The panels shall be tested in the minimum and maximum thicknesses intended for use in accordance with, and shall comply with the acceptance criteria of, NFPA 285 and shall be installed as tested. Where the panels are tested as part of an exterior wall assembly in accordance with NFPA 285, the panels shall be installed on the face of the mechanical equipment screen supporting structure in the same manner as they were installed on the tested exterior wall assembly.

1509.6.3 Type V Construction. The height of mechanical equipment screens located on the roof decks of buildings of Type V construction, as measured from grade plane to the highest point on the mechanical equipment screen, shall be permitted to exceed the maximum building height allowed for the building by other provisions of this code where complying with any one of the following limitations, provided the fire separation distance is greater than 5 feet (1524 mm):

1. Where the fire separation distance is not less than 20 feet (6096 mm), the height above grade plane of the mechanical equipment screen shall not exceed 4 feet (1219 mm) more than the maximum building height allowed.

2. The mechanical equipment screen shall be constructed of noncombustible materials.
3. The mechanical equipment screen shall be constructed of fire-retardant-treated wood complying with Section 2303.2 for exterior installation.
4. Where fire separation distance is not less than 20 feet (6096 mm), the mechanical equipment screen shall be constructed of materials having a flame spread index of 25 or less when tested in the minimum and maximum thicknesses intended for use with each face tested independently in accordance with ASTM E84 or UL 723.

1509.7 Photovoltaic Systems. *(See code for changes made to Section 1509.7 and its subsections. These changes were discussed previously in this book with the page dealing with photovoltaic systems.)*

1509.8 Other Rooftop Structures. Rooftop structures not regulated by Sections 1509.2 through 1509.7 shall comply with Section 1509.8.1 through 1509.8.5 as applicable.

1509.8.1 Aerial Supports. Aerial supports shall be constructed of noncombustible materials.

Exception: Aerial supports not greater than 12 feet (3658 mm) in height as measured from the roof deck to the highest point on the aerial supports shall be permitted to be constructed of combustible materials.

1509.8.2 Bulkheads. Bulkheads used for the shelter of mechanical or electrical equipment or vertical shaft openings in the roof assembly shall comply with Section 1509.2 as penthouses. Bulkheads used for any other purpose shall be considered as an additional story of the building.

1509.8.3 Dormers. Dormers shall be of the same type of construction as required for the roof in which such dormers are located or the exterior walls of the building.

1509.8.4 Fences. Fences and similar structures shall comply with Section 1509.6 as mechanical equipment screens.

1509.8.5 Flagpoles. Flagpoles and similar structures shall not be required to be constructed of noncombustible materials and shall not be limited in height or number.

CHANGE SIGNIFICANCE: The provisions of Section 1509 have been formatted so the requirements in Section 1509.2 are limited to penthouses while the provisions for mechanical equipment screens and other rooftop structures have been relocated in new Sections 1509.6 and 1509.8. Previously, Section 1509.2 also included items such as mechanical equipment screens, flagpoles, fences, and dormers. This formatting change, along with the revisions to some of the definitions, will help focus the application of Section 1509.2 on penthouses, while other rooftop structures that are not covered by a roof will be found either in the provisions

1509, 202 continues

1509, 202 continued

addressing mechanical equipment screens or those dealing with "other roof top structures." Previously, the provisions were somewhat disjointed and inconsistent due to an effort to address all types of rooftop structures within the one code section, even though there clearly are distinctions among the types and hazards of the structures.

While there are several important technical changes, the vast majority of the changes eliminate redundant language, relocate provisions to a more appropriate location, make the terminology more consistent, reformat the text to fit more effectively, and make it easier to distinguish among the various elements.

Section 1509.2 will only address unoccupied rooftop structures that are enclosed (covered by a roof) based on the definition for "penthouse" and the requirements within Section 1509.2. Where a penthouse is not covered by a roof, it will be regulated by either Sections 1509.3 through 1509.8 or it will be considered as an additional story of the building. The restrictions on the use of a penthouse were previously located in the use limitation provisions of Section 1509.2.3.

Section 1509.2.1 now clarifies that the height measurement is made from the roof "deck" and that it is measured to the average height of the penthouse. The code previously did not state how to measure the height if the penthouse had a sloped or gabled roof.

Section 1509.3 dealing with tanks has been editorially revised without any technical revisions.

Section 1509.4 has been revised to clarify that the requirements only apply to cooling towers located on the roof of a building and are not applicable to cooling towers that may be installed on the ground adjacent to a building. It also has been clarified as to how to measure the size of the equipment and where measurements are to be made.

The tower, spire, dome, and cupola construction requirements of Section 1509.5.1 contain technical changes that affect the application of the provisions. In addition, the provisions have been reformatted to distinguish between the requirements for the structures versus those for support of the structures. The 1½ -hour opening protection requirements between the building and any towers have been deleted, and compliance is now required with the general horizontal assembly opening protection requirements of Section 711. The means of protecting—and the type of protection needed for—these openings in the horizontal assembly have also been revised. Typically, either a shaft enclosure or a floor fire-door assembly with a fire-resistive rating is required.

Section 1509.6 is a new section that deals with mechanical equipment screens. The revised definition is important because it serves as a reminder that these screens are "not covered by a roof," whereas it was previously stated they were "partially enclosed" structures. A distinction is now made between roofed penthouses (Section 1509.2) and screens that are not covered by a roof (Section 1509.6). In general, the mechanical equipment screens will need to be constructed of materials consistent with the building's exterior wall type of construction requirements; however, the fire-resistance ratings would not be required. Because the screens are not roofed, they will present less of an exposure hazard than a penthouse. The location and combustibility of the screen itself are the key issues that are addressed.

Sections 1509.6.2 and 1509.6.3 essentially provide exceptions that modify the type of construction or general building height limitations. Item 1 in both of these sections is conceptually based on the previous

Exception 6 from Section 1509.2.4 (now Section 1509.2.5), however the one-story limitation has been deleted because the limited screen height was viewed as not creating a significant hazard. Both of the sections also contain an item to allow the use of fire-retardant-treated wood and will not impose the 4-foot height limit that is found within Item 1 of the provisions.

The last item in Section 1509.6.2 is a new, unique requirement. The limitations are based on a totally new concept where the combustible materials used to construct the mechanical equipment screen are limited to a maximum flame spread index of 25 (which is also required for fire-retardant-treated wood), and the materials are required to be successfully tested in accordance with NFPA 285. This is the same test method that is used to validate the use of foam plastic insulations in exterior walls of Types I, II, III, and IV construction, as well as for the use of metal composite materials (MCM) in accordance with Section 1407.10. Although the material would be tested as the outer face (or skin) of the exterior wall in the NFPA 285 test as part of an exterior wall assembly, the test clearly assesses the surface flame spread resistance of the materials constituting the outer face, as well as, to a certain degree, the inner face where it is exposed to any open cavities in the wall assembly. Because the NFPA 285 test is used to qualify combustible materials for use where noncombustible exterior walls are required, it seems reasonable to allow its use for this application for mechanical equipment screens without the need to have the entire wall assembly constructed as tested for the mechanical equipment screen, instead utilizing the materials tested on the exterior face of the wall system in accordance with NFPA 285.

As mentioned previously, the relationship and wording of the various requirements of Section 1509.6 need to be reviewed carefully. Section 1509.6.2 is essentially intended as an exception to the type of construction materials required by Section 1509.6 and that Section 1509.6.3 was an exception to the height limitations of Section 1509.6.1. Although not clearly stated, the relationship is somewhat apparent when considering how the provisions work together. Although Section 1509.6.3 does indicate that the height of the screens "shall be permitted to exceed the maximum building height allowed for the building by other provisions of this code" when one of the four items is used, the 18-foot height limitation above the roof deck in Section 1509.6.1 should still be applicable. This application would allow the mechanical screens to exceed the height limitations from Table 503, but would still limit the screen heights to 18 feet above the roof deck.

The requirements for photovoltaic systems in Section 1509.7 are also appropriate within Section 1509 because they address elements that are mounted on the roof. See the previous discussion in this publication related to photovoltaic systems for commentary related to the changes in Section 1509.7.

The provisions of Section 1509.8 regulate items that do not fall within the other categories of rooftop structures (penthouses, tanks, cooling towers, spires, or mechanical equipment screens). However, Sections 1509.8.2 and 1509.8.4 reference the penthouse and mechanical equipment screen requirements because bulkheads and fences closely resemble those elements from both an appearance and a hazard standpoint. The flagpole provisions of Section 1509.8.5 were relocated from the previous Section 1509.2.3 (see deleted text in 2012 Section 1509.2.4).

Table 1604.3

Deflection Limits

$$\frac{5wL^3}{384EI} \le \frac{1}{360}$$

Beam deflection

CHANGE TYPE: Modification

CHANGE SUMMARY: Deflection limits for roof and wall members supporting plaster or stucco have been clarified. Footnote f was also modified to account for the new ultimate wind loads in the 2010 edition of ASCE/SEI 7 (ASCE 7-10), *Minimum Design Loads for Buildings and Other Structures.*

2013 CODE:

TABLE 1604.3 Deflection Limits[a, b, c, h, i]

Construction	L	S or W^f	$D + L^{d,g}$
Roof members:[e]			
Supporting plaster or stucco ceiling	$l/360$	$l/360$	$l/240$
Supporting nonplaster ceiling	$l/240$	$l/240$	$l/180$
Not supporting ceiling	$l/180$	$l/180$	$l/120$
Floor members	$l/360$	—	$l/240$
Exterior walls and interior partitions:			
With plaster or stucco finishes	—	$l/360$	—
With other brittle finishes	—	$l/240$	—
With flexible finishes	—	$l/120$	—
Farm buildings	—	—	$l/180$
Greenhouses	—	—	$l/120$

f. The wind load is permitted to be taken as ~~0.7~~ 0.42 times the "component and cladding" loads for the purpose of determining deflection limits herein.
(no changes to other footnotes)

CHANGE SIGNIFICANCE: Table 1604.3 now includes a line item for the deflection limit on roofs and walls with plaster or stucco finishes. The intent is to clarify the terminology and coordinate the language in the deflection limits table with the corresponding IRC table and ASTM C926-98a, *Standard Specification for Application of Portland Cement-Based Plaster.* In preparing the new wind maps for ASCE 7-10, the committee decided to use multiple ultimate event or strength design maps in conjunction with a wind load factor of 1.0 for strength design and 0.6 for allowable stress design. Footnote f of Table 1604.3 was modified to be 0.42 ($0.7 \times 0.6 = 0.42$) because serviceability (deflection) calculations are done at an allowable stress design level.

1604.5, 202

Risk Categories

CHANGE TYPE: Modification

CHANGE SUMMARY: The term "occupancy category" has been changed to "risk category" to better reflect the intended meaning and to coordinate with the terminology used in ASCE 7-10.

2013 CODE: 202 Definitions.

~~**OCCUPANCY CATEGORY** A category used to determine structural requirements based on occupancy.~~

RISK CATEGORY. A categorization of buildings and other structures for determination of flood, wind, snow, ice, and earthquake loads based on the risk associated with unacceptable performance.

1604.5 ~~Occupancy~~ Risk Category. Each building and structure shall be assigned ~~an occupancy~~ a risk category in accordance with Table 1604.5. Where a referenced standard specifies an occupancy category, the risk category shall not be taken as lower than the occupancy category specified therein.

1604.5.1 Multiple Occupancies. Where a building or structure is occupied by two or more occupancies not included in the same ~~occupancy~~ risk category, it shall be assigned the classification of the highest ~~occupancy~~ risk category corresponding to the various occupancies. Where buildings or structures have two or more portions that are structurally separated, each portion shall be separately classified. Where a separated portion of a building or structure provides required access to, required egress from, or shares life safety components with another portion having a higher ~~occupancy~~ risk category, both portions shall be assigned to the higher ~~occupancy~~ risk category.

1604.5, 202 continues

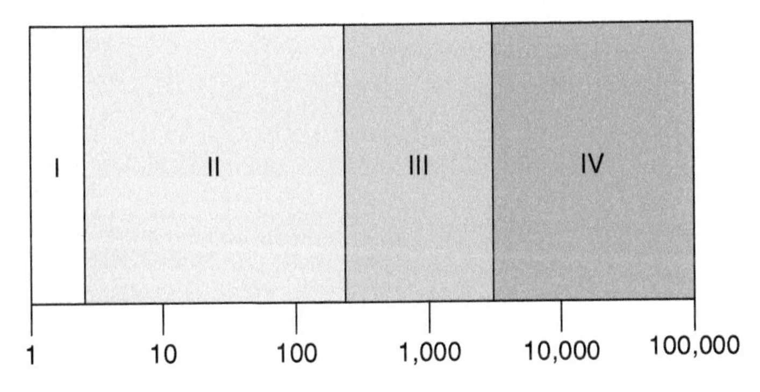

Approximate relationship between number of lives at risk by failure based on risk category. *(ASCE 7-10 Commentary)*

1604.5, 202 continued

TABLE 1604.5 ~~Occupancy~~ Risk Category of Buildings and Other Structures

~~Occupancy~~ Risk Category	Nature of Occupancy
II	Buildings and other structures except those listed in ~~Occupancy~~ Risk Categories I, III, and IV.
III	Buildings and other structures that represent a substantial hazard to human life in the event of failure, including but not limited to: • Buildings and other structures whose primary occupancy is public assembly with an occupant load greater than 300 • Buildings and other structures containing elementary school, secondary school, or day care facilities with an occupant load greater than 250 • Buildings and other structures containing adult education facilities, such as colleges and universities, with an occupant load greater than 500 • Group I-2 occupancies with an occupant load of 50 or more resident ~~patients~~ care recipients but not having surgery or emergency treatment facilities • Group I-3 occupancies • Any other occupancy with an occupant load greater than 5000[a] • Power-generating stations, water treatment for potable water, wastewater treatment facilities, and other public utility facilities not included in ~~Occupancy~~ Risk Category IV • Buildings and other structures not included in ~~Occupancy~~ Risk Category IV containing ~~sufficient~~ quantities of toxic or explosive ~~substances~~ materials that: Exceed maximum allowable quantities per control area as given in Table 307.1(1) or 307.1(2) or per outdoor control area in accordance with the *California Fire Code*; and are sufficient to ~~be dangerous~~ pose a threat to the public if released[b]
IV	Buildings and other structures designated as essential facilities, including but not limited to: • Group I-2 occupancies having surgery or emergency treatment facilities • Fire, rescue, ambulance, and police stations and emergency vehicle garages • Designated earthquake, hurricane, or other emergency shelters • Designated emergency preparedness, communications, and operations centers and other facilities required for emergency response • Power-generating stations and other public utility facilities required as emergency backup facilities for ~~Occupancy~~ Risk Category IV structures • Buildings and other structures containing quantities of highly toxic materials ~~as defined by Section 307 where the quantity of the material~~ that: Exceed~~s~~ ~~the~~ maximum allowable quantities ~~of~~ per control area as given in Table 307.1(2) or per outdoor control area in accordance with the *California Fire Code*; and are sufficient to pose a threat to the public if released[b] • Aviation control towers, air traffic control centers, and emergency aircraft hangars • Buildings and other structures having critical national defense functions • Water storage facilities and pump structures required to maintain water pressure for fire suppression

(Portions of table not shown remain unchanged)

a. (no change to text)

b. Where approved by the building official, the classification of buildings and other structures as Risk Category III or IV based on their quantities of toxic, highly toxic, or explosive materials is permitted to be reduced to Occupancy Category II, provided it can be demonstrated by a hazard assessment in accordance with Section 1.5.3 of ASCE 7 that a release of the toxic, highly toxic, or explosive materials is not sufficient to pose a threat to the public.

Because the term "occupancy category" occurs in so many chapters of the code, the entire code change text is too extensive to be included here. Refer to Code Change S41-09/10 in the *2012 IBC Code Changes Resource Collection* for the complete text and history of the code change.

CHANGE SIGNIFICANCE: The term "occupancy category" is misleading because it implies something about the nature of the building occupants. The term "occupancy" relates primarily to the nonstructural fire and life safety provisions, not the risks associated with structural failure. In fact, some of the structures regulated by the IBC and IEBC are not even occupied but have an occupancy category assigned because their failure could pose a substantial risk to the public. Thus, the term "occupancy category" has been changed to "risk category" to better reflect the intent and provide consistency with the terminology used in ASCE 7-10. Although the terminology changed, the classifications continue to reflect the progression of the consequences of failure from the lowest (Risk Category I) to the highest (Risk Category IV). A detailed discussion of the risk categories is contained in Section C1.5 of the ASCE 7-10 commentary.

1605.2

Load Combinations Using Strength Design of Load and Resistance Factor Design

$$\Sigma\gamma_i Q_i \leq R_n$$

LRFD method limit state

CHANGE TYPE: Modification

CHANGE SUMMARY: The strength design load combinations in the 2013 CBC have been coordinated with Section 2.3 of ASCE 7-10 and expanded to include loads due to fluids, *F*, and other lateral pressures, *H*, as well as ice loads.

2013 CODE: 1605.2~~.1~~ Load Combinations Using Strength Design of Load and Resistance Factor Design. Where strength design or load and resistance factor design is used, buildings and other structures, and portions thereof, shall be designed to resist the most critical effects resulting from the following combinations of factored loads:

$$1.4(D + F) \qquad \textbf{(Equation 16-1)}$$

$$1.2(D + F \cancel{+ T}) + 1.6(L + H) + 0.5(L_r \text{ or } S \text{ or } R) \qquad \textbf{(Equation 16-2)}$$

$$1.2(D + F) + 1.6(L_r \text{ or } S \text{ or } R) + 1.6H + (f_1L \text{ or } \cancel{0.8}\ 0.5W) \qquad \textbf{(Equation 16-3)}$$

$$1.2(D + F) + \cancel{1.6}\ 1.0W + f_1L + 1.6H + 0.5(L_r \text{ or } S \text{ or } R) \qquad \textbf{(Equation 16-4)}$$

$$1.2(D + F) + 1.0E + f_1L + 1.6H + f_2S \qquad \textbf{(Equation 16-5)}$$

$$0.9D + \cancel{1.6}\ 1.0W + 1.6H \qquad \textbf{(Equation 16-6)}$$

$$0.9(D + F) + 1.0E + 1.6H \qquad \textbf{(Equation 16-7)}$$

where:

f_1 = 1 for ~~floors in~~ places of public assembly, ~~for~~ live loads in excess of 100 pounds per square foot (4.79 kN/m^2), and ~~for~~ parking garages,

= and 0.5 for other live loads.

f_2 = 0.7 for roof configurations (such as saw tooth) that do not shed snow off the structure, and

= 0.2 for other roof configurations.

Exceptions:

1. Where other factored load combinations are specifically required by ~~the~~ other provisions of this code, such combinations shall take precedence.
2. Where the effect of *H* resists the primary variable load effect, a load factor of 0.9 shall be included with *H*, where *H* is permanent, and *H* shall be set to zero for all other conditions.

1605.2.1 ~~Flood~~ Other Loads. Where flood loads, F_a, are to be considered in the design, the load combinations of Section 2.3.3 of ASCE 7 shall be used. Where self-straining loads, *T*, are considered in design, their structural effects in combination with other loads shall be determined in accordance with Section 2.3.5 of ASCE 7. Where an ice-sensitive structure is subjected to loads due to atmospheric icing, the load combinations of Section 2.3.4 of ASCE 7 shall be considered.

CHANGE SIGNIFICANCE: The CBC load combinations have been coordinated with the strength design load combinations in Section 2.3 of ASCE 7-10 and loads due to fluids, *F*, and lateral earth pressures, ground water pressures, or the pressure of bulk materials, *H*, have been included. The load factor on the wind load, *W*, has been changed to 1.0 to account for the new ultimate design wind speed and strength level wind forces in ASCE 7-10. Note that *F* and *H* must be considered in ASCE 7-10, but they are indirectly combined with other loads as required by the text in Section 2.3.2. The self-straining load, *T*, was deleted from the load combinations because it is indirectly combined as described under Section 1605.2.2 for other loads. The load and resistance factor design (LRFD) load combinations in Section 1605.2.2 and the allowable stress design (ASD) load combinations in Section 1605.3.1.2 were modified to include ice loads for ice sensitive structures. Where atmospheric ice loads must be considered in the design of ice-sensitive structures, these sections cross reference ASCE 7 Section 2.3.4 for LRFD and Section 2.4.3 for ASD, respectively.

1605.3

Load Combinations Using Allowable Stress Design

$$\Sigma Q_i \leq R_n/\Omega$$

ASD method limit state

CHANGE TYPE: Modification

CHANGE SUMMARY: The allowable stress design load combinations in the 2013 CBC have been coordinated with Section 2.4 of ASCE 7-10 and expanded to include loads due to fluids, F, and other lateral pressures, H, as well as ice loads.

2013 CODE: 1605.3 Load Combinations Using Allowable Stress Design.

1605.3.1 Basic Load Combinations. Where allowable stress design (working stress design), as permitted by this code, is used, structures and portions thereof shall resist the most critical effects resulting from the following combinations of loads:

$D + F$ **(Equation 16-8)**

$D + H + F + L$ ~~$+ T$~~ **(Equation 16-9)**

$D + H + F + (L_r \text{ or } S \text{ or } R)$ **(Equation 16-10)**

$D + H + F + 0.75$~~$(L + T)$~~ $+ 0.75(L_r \text{ or } S \text{ or } R)$ **(Equation 16-11)**

$D + H + F + (0.6W \text{ or } 0.7E)$ **(Equation 16-12)**

$D + H + F + 0.75(0.6W$ ~~$\text{or } 0.7E$~~$)$
$+ 0.75L + 0.75(L_r \text{ or } S \text{ or } R)$ **(Equation 16-13)**

$D + H + F + 0.75(0.7E) + 0.75L + 0.75S$ **(Equation 16-14)**

$0.6D + 0.6W + H$ **(Equation 16-~~14~~ 15)**

$0.6(D + F) + 0.7E + H$ **(Equation 16-~~15~~ 16)**

Exceptions:

1.–2. (no changes to text)

3. Where the effect of H resists the primary variable load effect, a load factor of 0.6 shall be included with H, where H is permanent, and H shall be set to zero for all other conditions.

4. In Equation 16-15, the wind load, W, is permitted to be reduced ~~10 percent for design of the foundation other than anchorage of the structure to the foundation~~ in accordance with Exception 2 of Section 2.4.1 of ASCE 7.

5. In Equation 16-16, $0.6D$ is permitted to be increased to $0.9D$ for the design of special reinforced masonry shear walls complying with Chapter 21.

1605.3.1.2 ~~Flood~~ Other Loads. Where flood loads, F_a, are to be considered in design, the load combinations of Section 2.4.2 of ASCE 7 shall be used. Where self-straining loads, *T*, are considered in design, their structural effects in combination with other loads shall be determined in accordance with Section 2.4.4 of ASCE 7. Where an ice-sensitive structure is subjected to loads due to atmospheric icing, the load combinations of Section 2.3.4 of ASCE 7 shall be considered.

1605.3.2 Alternative Basic Load Combinations. In lieu of the basic load combinations specified in Section 1605.3.1, structures and portions thereof shall be permitted to be designed for the most critical effects resulting from the following combinations. When using these alternative basic load combinations that include wind or seismic loads, allowable stresses are permitted to be increased or load combinations reduced where permitted by the material chapter of this code or the referenced standards. For load combinations that include the counteracting effects of dead and wind loads, only two-thirds of the minimum dead load likely to be in place during a design wind event shall be used. When using allowable stresses which have been increased or load combinations which have been reduced as permitted by the material chapter of this code or the referenced standards, where wind loads are calculated in accordance with Chapters 26 through 31 ~~Chapter 6~~ of ASCE 7, the coefficient ω in the following equations shall be taken as 1.3. For other wind loads, ω shall be taken as 1. When allowable stresses have not been increased or load combinations have not been reduced as permitted by the material chapter of this code or the referenced standards, ω shall be taken as 1. When using these alternative load combinations to evaluate sliding, overturning, and soil bearing at the soil–structure interface, the reduction of foundation overturning from Section 12.13.4 in ASCE 7 shall not be used. When using these alternative basic load combinations for proportioning foundations for loadings, which include seismic loads, the vertical seismic *load effect*, *Ev*, in Equation 12.4-4 of ASCE 7, is permitted to be taken equal to zero.

$$D + L + (L_r \text{ or } S \text{ or } R) \quad \textbf{(Equation 16-17)}$$

$$D + L + (0.6\omega W) \quad \textbf{(Equation 16-18)}$$

$$D + L + 0.6\omega W + S/2 \quad \textbf{(Equation 16-19)}$$

$$D + L + S + 0.6\omega W/2 \quad \textbf{(Equation 16-20)}$$

$$D + L + S + E/1.4 \quad \textbf{(Equation 16-21)}$$

$$0.9D + E/1.4 \quad \textbf{(Equation 16-22)}$$

Exceptions: (no changes to text)

1605.3.2.1 Other Loads. Where *F*, *H*, or *T* are to be considered in design, each applicable load shall be added to the combinations specified in Section 1605.3.2. Where self-straining loads, *T*, are considered in design, their structural effects in combination with other loads shall be determined in accordance with Section 2.4.4 of ASCE 7.

1605.3 continues

1605.3 continued

CHANGE SIGNIFICANCE: The allowable stress design load (ASD) combinations in the CBC have been coordinated with the ASD load combinations in Section 2.4 of ASCE 7-10. The self-straining load, *T*, was deleted from the load combinations because it is indirectly combined as described under Section 1605.3.2.1 for other loads. To improve equivalency with the strength design load combinations and achieve consistency with ASCE 7-10, earthquake load effect, *E*, was removed from Equation 16-13, and the new load combination Equation 16-14 was added. This has the effect of retaining roof live load, L_r, and rain load, *R*, in combination with wind load, *W* (Equation 16-13), but removed these loads in combination with earthquake load, *E*, in Equation 16-14. This was done to achieve consistency between the ASD load combinations and the strength design or LRFD load combinations in Equations 16-4 and 16-5. The load factor on the wind load, *W*, has been changed to 0.6 in both the basic and alternative basic ASD load combinations to account for the new ultimate design wind speed and strength level wind forces in ASCE 7-10 ($W_{ASD} = 0.6W_{ult}$).

Based on deliberations with the Code Resource and Support Committee (CRSC) of the NEHRP, the ω factor in the alternative basic ASD load combinations has been modified to be either 1.3 or 1.0. When allowable stresses have been increased or load combinations have been reduced (as permitted by a material chapter in the code or a referenced standard), the coefficient ω is taken as 1.3. When allowable stresses have not been increased or load combinations have not been reduced, ω is to be taken as 1.0.

Note that although *F* and *H* are not in the ASD load combinations in ASCE 7-10, they are indirectly combined with other loads as described in the text in Section 2.4.1.

The ASD load combinations in Section 1605.3.1.2 and LRFD load combinations in Section 1605.2.2 were also modified to include ice loads for ice-sensitive structures. Where atmospheric ice loads must be considered in the design of ice-sensitive structures, these sections cross reference Section 2.4.3 for ASD and ASCE 7 Section 2.3.4 for LRFD, respectively.

CHANGE TYPE: Modification

Table 1607.1

Minimum Live Loads

CHANGE SUMMARY: The live loads established in Section 1607 and Table 1607.1 have been modified and updated in order to coordinate with the live loads of Chapter 4 and Table 4-1 in ASCE 7-10.

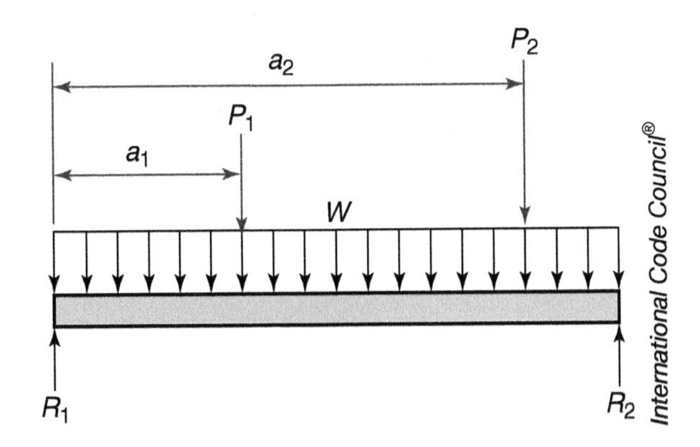

Simple beam load diagram

2013 CODE:

TABLE 1607.1 Minimum Uniformly Distributed Live Loads, L_o, and Minimum Concentrated Live Loads[g]

Occupancy or Use	Uniform (psf)	Concentrated (lb)
3. Armories and drill rooms	150[m]	—
4. Assembly areas ~~and theaters~~		
Fixed seats (fastened to floor)	60[m]	
Follow spot, projections, and control rooms	50	
Lobbies	100[m]	
Movable seats	100[m]	—
Stage~~s and~~ floors	~~125~~ 150[m]	
Platforms (assembly)	~~125~~ 100	
Other assembly areas	100[m]	
5. Balconies ~~(exterior)~~ and decks[h]	Same as occupancy served	
~~6. Bowling alleys~~	~~75~~	—
~~7.~~ 6. Catwalks	40	300
~~9.~~ 8. Corridors~~, except as otherwise indicated~~		
First floor	100	
Other floors	Same as occupancy served except as indicated	—
~~10. Dance halls and ballrooms~~	~~100~~	—
~~11~~ 9. Dining rooms and restaurants	100[m]	—
~~13.~~ 11. Elevator machine room grating (on area of ~~4 in²~~ 2 inches by 2 inches)	—	300
~~14.~~ 12. Finish light floor plate construction (on area of ~~1 in²~~ 1 inch by 1 inch)	—	200
~~16.~~ 14. Garages (passenger vehicles only) Trucks and buses	40[m]	Note a See Section 1607.7

Table 1607.1 continues

Table 1607.1 continued

Occupancy or Use	Uniform (psf)	Concentrated (lb)
~~17. Grandstands (see stadium and arena bleachers)~~	—	—
~~18. Gymnasiums, main floors and balconies~~	~~100~~	—
~~19.~~ 15. Handrails, guards and grab bars	See Section 1607.8	
16. Helipads	See Section 1607.6	
~~22~~ 19. Libraries		
Corridors above first floor	80	1000
Reading rooms	60	1000
Stack rooms	150[b,m]	1000
~~23~~ 20. Manufacturing		
Heavy	250[m]	3000
Light	125[m]	2000
24. Recreational uses:		
Bowling alleys, poolrooms, and similar uses	75[m]	
Dance halls and ballrooms	100[m]	
Gymnasiums	100[m]	
Reviewing stands, grandstands, and bleachers	100[c,m]	
Stadiums and arenas with fixed seats (fastened to floor)	60[c,m]	
~~27.~~ 25. Residential		
One- and two-family dwellings		
Uninhabitable attics without storage[i]	10	
Uninhabitable attics with ~~limited~~ storage[i, j, k]	20	
Habitable attics and sleeping areas[k]	30	—
All other areas	40	
Hotels and multiple-family dwellings		
Private rooms and corridors serving them	40	
Public rooms[m] and corridors serving them	100	
~~28. Reviewing stands, grandstands and bleachers~~		~~Note c~~
~~29.~~ 26. Roofs:		
All roof surfaces subject to maintenance workers		300
Awnings and canopies:		
Fabric construction supported by a ~~lightweight rigid~~ skeleton structure	5 Nonreducible	
All other construction	20	
Ordinary flat, pitched, and curved roofs (that are not occupiable)	20	
Where primary roof members, are exposed to a work floor, at single panel points of lower chord of roof trusses, or any point along primary structural members supporting roofs:		
Over manufacturing, storage warehouses, and repair garages		2000
All other ~~occupancies~~ primary roof members		300
~~Roofs used for other special purposes~~	~~Note l~~	~~Note l~~
~~Roofs used for promenade purposes~~	~~60~~	
~~Roofs used for roof gardens or assembly purposes~~	~~100~~	

Occupancy or Use	Uniform (psf)	Concentrated (lb)
Occupiable roofs:		
Roof gardens	100	
Assembly areas	100[m]	
All other similar areas	Note l	Note l
~~32.~~ 29. Sidewalks, vehicular driveways, and yards, subject to trucking	250[d,m]	8000[e]
~~33. Skating rinks~~	~~100~~	—
~~34. Stadiums and arenas~~		
~~Bleachers~~	~~100[c]~~	—
~~Fixed seats (fastened to floor)~~	~~60[c]~~-	
~~35.~~ 30. Stairs and exits		~~Note f~~
One- and two-family dwellings	40	300[f]
All other	100	300[f]
~~36.~~ 31. Storage warehouses (shall be designed for heavier loads if required for anticipated storage)		
Heavy	250[m]	—
Light	125[m]	
~~37.~~ 32. Stores		
Retail		
First floor	100	1000
Upper floors	75	1000
Wholesale, all floors	125[m]	1000
~~38.~~ 33. Vehicle barriers ~~systems~~	See Section 1607.8.3	
~~40.~~ 35. Yards and terraces, pedestrian	100 [m]	—

(Portions of table not shown are unchanged)

f. The minimum concentrated load on stair treads ~~(~~shall be applied on an area of ~~4 square~~ 2 inches by 2 inches~~)~~ ~~is 300 pounds~~. This load need not be assumed to act concurrently with the uniform load.

g. Where snow loads occur that are in excess of the design conditions, the structure shall be designed to support the loads due to the increased loads caused by drift buildup or a greater snow design determined by the building official (see Section 1608). ~~For special-purpose roofs, see Section 1607.11.2.2.~~

i. Uninhabitable attics without storage are those where the maximum clear height between the joists and rafters is less than 42 inches, or where there are not two or more adjacent trusses with web configurations capable of accommodating an assumed rectangle 42 inches in height by by 24 inches in width, or greater, within the plane of the trusses. ~~For attics without storage,~~ This live load need not be assumed to act concurrently with any other live load requirements.

j. ~~For attics with limited storage and constructed with trusses, this live load need only be applied to those portions of the bottom chord~~ Uninhabitable attics with storage are those where the maximum clear height between the joists and rafters is 42 inches or greater, or where there are two or more adjacent trusses with ~~the same~~ web configurations capable of ~~containing~~ accommodating an assumed rectangle 42 inches ~~high~~ in height by 24 inches ~~wide~~ in width, or greater, ~~located~~ within the plane of the trusses

~~The rectangle shall fit between the top of the bottom chord and the bottom of any other truss member, provided that each of the following criteria is met:~~ The live load need only be applied to those portions of the joists or truss bottom chords where both of the following conditions are met:

i. The attic area is accessible ~~by a pull-dwon stairway or framed opening in accordance with Section 1209.2,~~ from an opening not less than 20 inches in width by 30 inches in length that is located where the clear height in the attic is a minimum of 30 inches; and

ii. The slopes of the joists or truss ~~shall have a~~ bottom chords ~~pitch less than 2:12~~ are no greater than 2 units vertical to 12 units horizontal.

~~iii. Bottom chords of trusses shall be designed for the greater of actual imposed dead load or 10 psf, uniformly distributed over the entire span.~~ The remaining portions of the joists or bottom chords shall be designed for a uniformly distributed concurrent live load of not less than 10 lb/ft^2.

k. Attic spaces served by ~~a fixed stair~~ stairways other than pull-down type shall be designed to support the minimum live load specified for habitable attics and sleeping rooms.

l. ~~Roofs used for other special purposes~~ Areas of occupiable roofs, other than roof gardens and assembly areas, shall be designed for appropriate loads as approved by the building official. Unoccupied landscaped areas of roofs shall be designed in accordance with Section 1607.12.3.

m. Live load reduction is not permitted unless specific exceptions of Section 1607.10 apply.

(Footnotes not shown are unchanged)

Table 1607.1 continues

Table 1607.1 continued

CHANGE SIGNIFICANCE: Many live loads set forth in Chapter 4 of ASCE 7 were updated in the 2010 edition. To coordinate the changes in ASCE 7-10 with the 2013 CBC, corresponding modifications were made to Section 1607 and Table 1607.1. These changes are summarized as follows:

- Footnotes i, j, and k pertaining to residential attic live loads were updated to clarify the intent.
- The live load for stage floors was increased from 125 psf to 150 psf, and the live load for platforms in assembly areas was decreased from 125 psf to 100 psf.
- Various recreational type uses were consolidated under a new item called "recreational uses." These uses include bowling alleys, pool rooms, dance halls and ballrooms, gymnasiums, reviewing stands, grandstands and bleachers, and stadiums and arenas with fixed seats. No technical changes were made to the live loads. The factor, $f_1 = 1$ (See Section 1605.2.1) now applies to floors in places of public assembly areas and recreational uses for live loads in excess of 100 pounds per square foot. Skating rinks are deleted from Table 1607.1 because they are not listed in Table 4-1 of ASCE 7 and Table C4-1 of ASCE-7 specifies uniform live loads of 250 psf for ice skating rinks and 100 psf for roller skating rinks. Footnote m has been added to clarify that a live load reduction is not permitted unless specific exceptions of Section 1607.9 apply. The footnote has been added at each specific use or occupancy in Table 1607.1 where a live load reduction is restricted. With the addition of this footnote, Table 1607.1 clarifies limitations on live load reduction. References are added to Sections 1607.10.1 and 1607.10.2 to correlate with the footnote.
- The 300-pound concentrated load for stair treads has been relocated from footnote f to the table and the clarification is added that the 300-pound concentrated load need not act concurrently with the uniform load.
- New loading requirements for helipads have been added to Section 1607.6. (See a detailed discussion in the commentary to Section 1607.6.)
- The terminology associated with "occupiable roofs" has been clarified and coordinated with ASCE 7-10. Occupiable roof gardens and assembly areas have a live load of 100 psf. Occupiable roofs other than roof gardens and assembly areas must be designed for appropriate loads based on use or as required by the building official. Landscaped areas of roofs that are unoccupied must be designed for a live load of 20 psf plus the weight of the landscaping and saturated soil, which is considered a dead load.

1607.7

Heavy Vehicle Loads

Heavy vehicle. *(Courtesy of Albuquerque Fire Department)*

CHANGE TYPE: Modification

CHANGE SUMMARY: Provisions relating to the design of structures that support heavy vehicle loads in excess of 10,000 pounds gross vehicle weight (GVW) have been updated.

2013 CODE: ~~**1607.6 Truck and Bus Garages.** Minimum live loads for garages having trucks or buses shall be as specified in Table 1607.6, but shall not be less than 50 psf (2.40 kN/m^2), unless other loads are specifically justified and *approved* by the *building official*. Actual loads shall be used where they are greater than the loads specified in the table.~~

~~**1607.6.1 Truck and Bus Garage Live Load Application.** The concentrated load and uniform load shall be uniformly distributed over a 10-foot (3048 mm) width on a line normal to the centerline of the lane placed within a 12-foot-wide (3658 mm) lane. The loads shall be placed within their individual lanes so as to produce the maximum stress in each structural member. Single spans shall be designed for the uniform load in Table 1607.6 and one simultaneous concentrated load positioned to produce the maximum effect. Multiple spans shall be designed for the uniform load in Table 1607.6 on the spans and two simultaneous concentrated loads in two spans positioned to produce the maximum negative moment effect. Multiple span design loads, for other effects, shall be the same as for single spans.~~

~~**Table 1607.6**~~
~~**UNIFORM AND CONCENTRATED LOADS**~~

1607.7 Heavy Vehicle Loads. Floors and other surfaces that are intended to support vehicle loads greater than a 10,000-pound (44.5-kN) gross vehicle weight rating shall comply with Sections 1607.7.1 through 1607.7.5.

1607.7.1 Loads. Where any structure does not restrict access for vehicles that exceed a 10,000-pound gross vehicle weight rating, those portions of the structure subject to such loads shall be designed using the vehicular live loads, including consideration of impact and fatigue, in accordance with the codes and specifications required by the jurisdiction having authority for the design and construction of the roadways and bridges in the same location of the structure.

1607.7.2 Fire Truck and Emergency Vehicles. Where a structure, or portions of a structure, are accessed and loaded by fire department access vehicles and other similar emergency vehicles, the structure shall be designed for the greater of the following loads:

1. The actual operational loads, including outrigger reactions and contact areas of the vehicles as stipulated and approved by the Building Official, or
2. The live loading specified in Section 1607.7.1.

1607.7 continues

1607.7 continued

1607.7.3 Heavy Vehicle Garages. Garages designed to accommodate vehicles that exceed a 10,000-pound gross vehicle weight rating shall be designed using the live loading specified by Section 1607.7.1. For garages the design for impact and fatigue is not required.

Exception: The vehicular live loads and load placement are allowed to be determined using the actual vehicle weights for the vehicles allowed onto the garage floors, provided such loads and placement are based on rational engineering principles and are approved by the building official, but shall not be less than 50 psf (240 kN/m^2). This live load shall not be reduced.

1607.7.4 Forklifts and Movable Equipment. Where a structure is intended to have forklifts or other movable equipment present, the structure shall be designed for the total vehicle or equipment load and the individual wheel loads for the anticipated vehicles as specified by the owner of the facility. These loads shall be posted per Section 1607.7.5.

1607.7.4.1 Impact and Fatigue. Impact loads and fatigue loading shall be considered in the design of the supporting structure. For the purposes of design, the vehicle and wheel loads shall be increased by 30 percent to account for impact.

1607.7.5 Posting. The maximum weight of the vehicles allowed into or on a garage or other structure shall be posted by the owner in accordance with Section 106.1.

CHANGE SIGNIFICANCE: Structures intended to support heavy vehicles loads in excess of 10,000 pounds GVW must now be designed in accordance with the same specifications required by the jurisdiction for the design of roadways and bridges. The new requirements specifically apply to fire truck and emergency vehicles, heavy vehicle parking garages, forklifts, and movable equipment. The owner is required to post the maximum weight of the vehicles allowed in a garage or other structure in accordance with Section 106.1.

1609, 202

Determination of Wind Loads

$$V_{asd} = V_{ult}\sqrt{0.6}$$

Equation 16-33, conversion of wind speed from V_{ult} to V_{ASD}

CHANGE TYPE: Modification

CHANGE SUMMARY: The wind design requirements of Section 1609 have been updated and coordinated with the latest wind load provisions in ASCE/SEI 7 (ASCE 7-10) and the wind load maps in the CBC are now based on ultimate design wind speeds, V_{ult}, which produce a strength level wind load similar to seismic load effects.

2013 CODE: The following are excerpted portions of the subject code text. The entire code change is not shown here for brevity.

202 Definitions.

HURRICANE-PRONE REGIONS. Areas vulnerable to hurricanes defined as:

1. The U. S. Atlantic Ocean and Gulf of Mexico coasts where the ~~basic~~ ultimate design wind speed, V_{ult}, for Risk Category II buildings is greater than 115 ~~90~~ mph (51.4 m/s).
2. Hawaii, Puerto Rico, Guam, Virgin Islands, and American Samoa.

WINDBORNE DEBRIS REGION. Areas within ~~Portions of~~ hurricane-prone regions located: ~~that are~~

1. Within 1 mile (1.61 km) of the coastal mean high water line where the ~~basic~~ ultimate design wind speed, V_{ult}, is 130 ~~110~~ mph (58 m/s) or greater; or
2. In areas ~~portions of hurricane-prone regions~~ where the ~~basic~~ ultimate design wind speed, V_{ult}, is 140 ~~120~~ mph (63.6 m/s) or greater; or Hawaii.

For Risk Category II buildings and structures and Risk Category III buildings and structures, except health care facilities, the windborne debris region shall be based on Figure 1609A. For Risk Category IV buildings and structures and Risk Category III health care facilities, the windborne debris region shall be based on Figure 1609B.

WIND SPEED, V_{ult}. Ultimate design wind speeds.

WIND SPEED, V_{ASD}. Nominal design wind speeds.

1609.1.1 Determination of Wind Loads. Wind loads on every building or structure shall be determined in accordance with Chapters ~~6~~ 26 to 30 of ASCE 7 or provisions of the alternate all-heights method in Section 1609.6. The type of opening protection required, the ~~basic~~ ultimate design wind speed, V_{ult}, and the exposure category for a site is permitted to be determined in accordance with Section 1609 or ASCE 7. Wind shall be assumed to come from any horizontal direction, and wind pressures shall be assumed to act normal to the surface considered.

1609 continues

1609 continued

Exceptions:

1. Subject to the limitations of Section 1609.1.1.1, the provisions of ICC 600 shall be permitted for applicable Group R-2 and R-3 buildings.
2. Subject to the limitations of Section 1609.1.1.1, residential structures using the provisions of the AF&PA WFCM.
3. Subject to the limitations of Section 1609.1.1.1, residential structures using the provisions of AISI S230.
4. Designs using NAAMM FP 1001.
5. Designs using TIA-222 for antenna-supporting structures and antennas, provided the extent of Topographic Category 2, escarpments, in Section 2.6.6.2 of TIA-222 shall extend 16 times the height of the escarpment.
6. Wind tunnel tests in accordance with ~~Section 6.6~~ Chapter 31 of ASCE 7~~, subject to the limitations in Section 1609.1.1.2~~.

The wind speeds in Figure 1609A, 1609B, and 1609C are ultimate design wind speeds, V_{ult}, and shall be converted in accordance with Section 1609.3.1 to nominal design wind speeds, V_{asd}, when the provisions of the standards referenced in Exceptions 1 through 5 are used.

~~**1609.1.1.2 Wind Tunnel Test Limitations.** The lower limit on pressures for main wind-force-resisting systems and components and cladding shall be in accordance with Sections 1609.1.1.2.1 and 1609.1.1.2.2.~~

~~**1609.1.1.2.1 Lower Limits on Main Wind-Force-Resisting System.** Base overturning moments determined from wind tunnel testing shall be limited to not less than 80 percent of the design base overturning moments determined in accordance with Section 6.5 of ASCE 7, unless specific testing is performed that demonstrates it is the aerodynamic coefficient of the building, rather than shielding from other structures, that is responsible for the lower values. The 80-percent limit shall be permitted to be adjusted by the ratio of the frame load at critical wind directions as determined from wind tunnel testing without specific adjacent buildings, but including appropriate upwind roughness, to that determined in Section 6.5 of ASCE 7.~~

~~**1609.1.1.2.2 Lower Limits on Components and Cladding.** The design pressures for components and cladding on walls or roofs shall be selected as the greater of the wind tunnel test results or 80 percent of the pressure obtained for Zone 4 for walls and Zone 1 for roofs as determined in Section 6.5 of ASCE 7, unless specific testing is performed that demonstrates it is the aerodynamic coefficient of the building, rather than shielding from nearby structures, that is responsible for the lower values. Alternatively, limited tests at a few wind directions without specific adjacent buildings, but in the presence of an appropriate upwind roughness, shall be permitted to be used to demonstrate that the lower pressures are due to the shape of the building and not to shielding.~~

1609.1.2 Protection of Openings. In windborne debris regions, glazing in buildings shall be impact resistant or protected with an impact-resistant covering meeting the requirements of an approved impact-resistant standard or ASTM E1996 and ASTM E1886 referenced herein as follows:

1. Glazed openings located within 30 feet (9144 mm) of grade shall meet the requirements of the Large Missile Test of ASTM E1996.
2. Glazed openings located more than 30 feet (9144 mm) above grade shall meet the provisions of the small missile test of ASTM E1996.

Exceptions:

1. Wood structural panels with a minimum thickness of $^7/_{16}$ inch (11.1 mm) and maximum panel span of 8 feet (2438 mm) shall be permitted for opening protection in one- and two-story buildings classified as Group R-3 or R-4 occupancy. Panels shall be precut so that they shall be attached to the framing surrounding the opening containing the product with the glazed opening. Panels shall be predrilled as required for the anchorage method and shall be secured with the attachment hardware provided. Attachments shall be designed to resist the components and cladding loads determined in accordance with the provisions of ASCE 7, with corrosion-resistant attachment hardware provided and anchors permanently installed on the building. Attachment in accordance with Table 1609.1.2 with corrosion-resistant attachment hardware provided and anchors permanently installed on the building is permitted for buildings with a mean roof height of 45 feet (13716 mm) or less where V_{asd} determined in accordance with Section 1609.3.1 ~~wind speeds do~~ does not exceed 140 mph (63 m/s).
2. Glazing in ~~Occupancy~~ Risk Category I buildings as defined in Section 1604.5, including greenhouses that are occupied for growing plants on a production or research basis, without public access shall be permitted to be unprotected.
3. Glazing in ~~Occupancy~~ Risk Category II, III, or IV buildings located over 60 feet (18288 mm) above the ground and over 30 feet (9144 mm) above aggregate surface roofs located within 1500 feet (458 m) of the building shall be permitted to be unprotected.

1609.3 Basic Wind Speed. The ~~basic~~ ultimate design wind speed, V_{ult}, in mph, for the determination of the wind loads shall be determined by ~~Figure 1609~~ Figures 1609A, 1609B, and 1609C. The ultimate design wind speed, V_{ult}, for use in the design of Risk Category II buildings and structures shall be obtained from Figure 1609A. The ultimate design wind speed, V_{ult}, for use in the design of Risk Category III and IV buildings and structures shall be obtained from Figure 1609B. The ultimate design wind speed, V_{ult}, for use in the design of Risk Category I buildings and structures shall be obtained from Figure 1609C. ~~Basic~~ The ultimate design wind speed, V_{ult}, for the special wind regions indicated, near mountainous terrain and near gorges shall be in accordance with local jurisdiction requirements. ~~Basic~~ The ultimate design wind speeds, V_{ult}, determined by the local jurisdiction shall be in accordance with Section 26.5.1 ~~6.5.4~~ of ASCE 7.

1609 continues

1609 continued

In nonhurricane-prone regions, when the ~~basic~~ ultimate design wind speed, V_{ult}, is estimated from regional climatic data, the ~~basic~~ ultimate design wind speed, V_{ult}, shall be ~~not less than the wind speed associated with an annual probability of 0.02 (50-year mean recurrence interval), and the estimate shall be adjusted for equivalence to a 3-second gust wind speed at 33 feet (10 m) above ground in Exposure Category C. The data analysis shall be performed~~ determined in accordance with Section 26.5.3 ~~6.5.4.2~~ of ASCE 7.

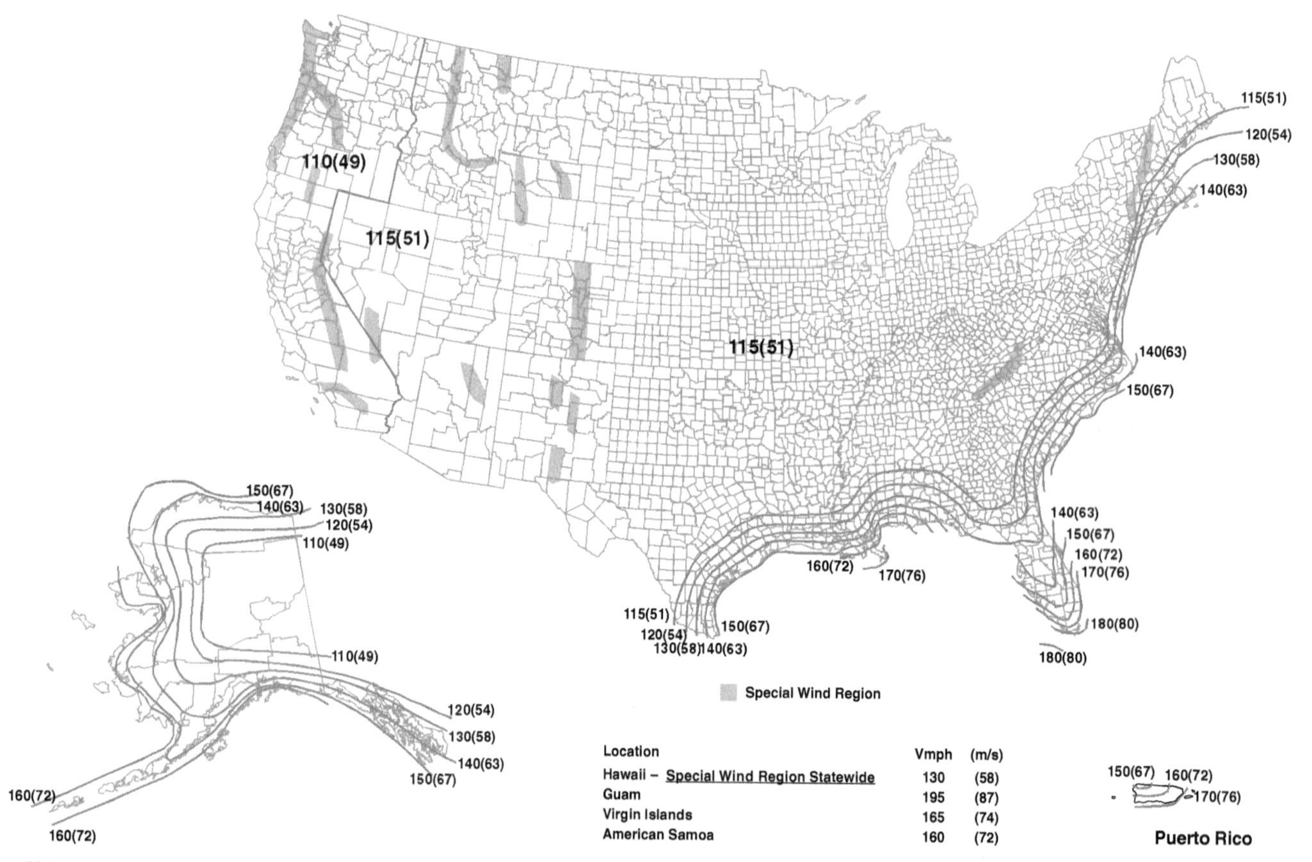

Notes:

1. Values are nominal design 3-second gust wind speeds in miles per hour (m/s) at 33 ft (10m) above ground for Exposure C category.
2. Linear interpolation between contours is permitted.
3. Islands and coastal areas outside the last contour shall use the last wind speed contour of the coastal area.
4. Mountainous terrain, gorges, ocean promontories, and special wind regions shall be examined for unusual wind conditions.
5. Wind speeds correspond to approximately a 7% probability of exceedance in 50 years (Annual Exceedance Probability = 0.00143, MRI = 700 years).

Figure 1609A Ultimate Design Wind Speeds, V_{ult}, For Risk Category II Buildings and Other Structures

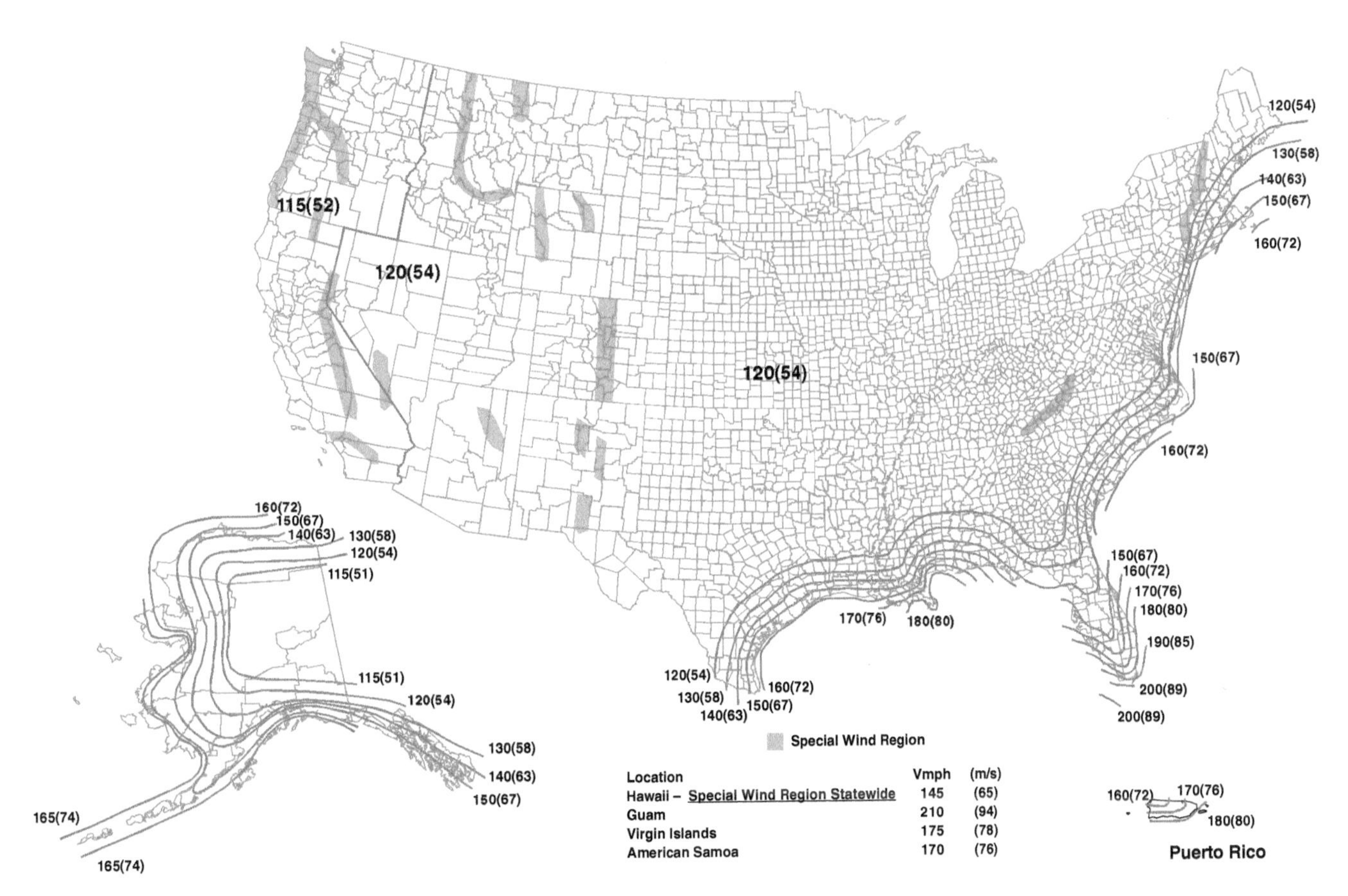

Notes:

1. Values are nominal design 3-second gust wind speeds in miles per hour (m/s) at 33 ft (10m) above ground for Exposure C category.
2. Linear interpolation between contours is permitted.
3. Islands and coastal areas outside the last contour shall use the last wind speed contour of the coastal area.
4. Mountainous terrain, gorges, ocean promontories, and special wind regions shall be examined for unusual wind conditions.
5. Wind speeds correspond to approximately a 3% probability of exceedance in 50 years (Annual Exceedance Probability = 0.000588, MRI = 1700 years).

Figure 1609B Ultimate Design Wind Speeds, V_{ult}, For Risk Categories III And IV Buildings and Other Structures

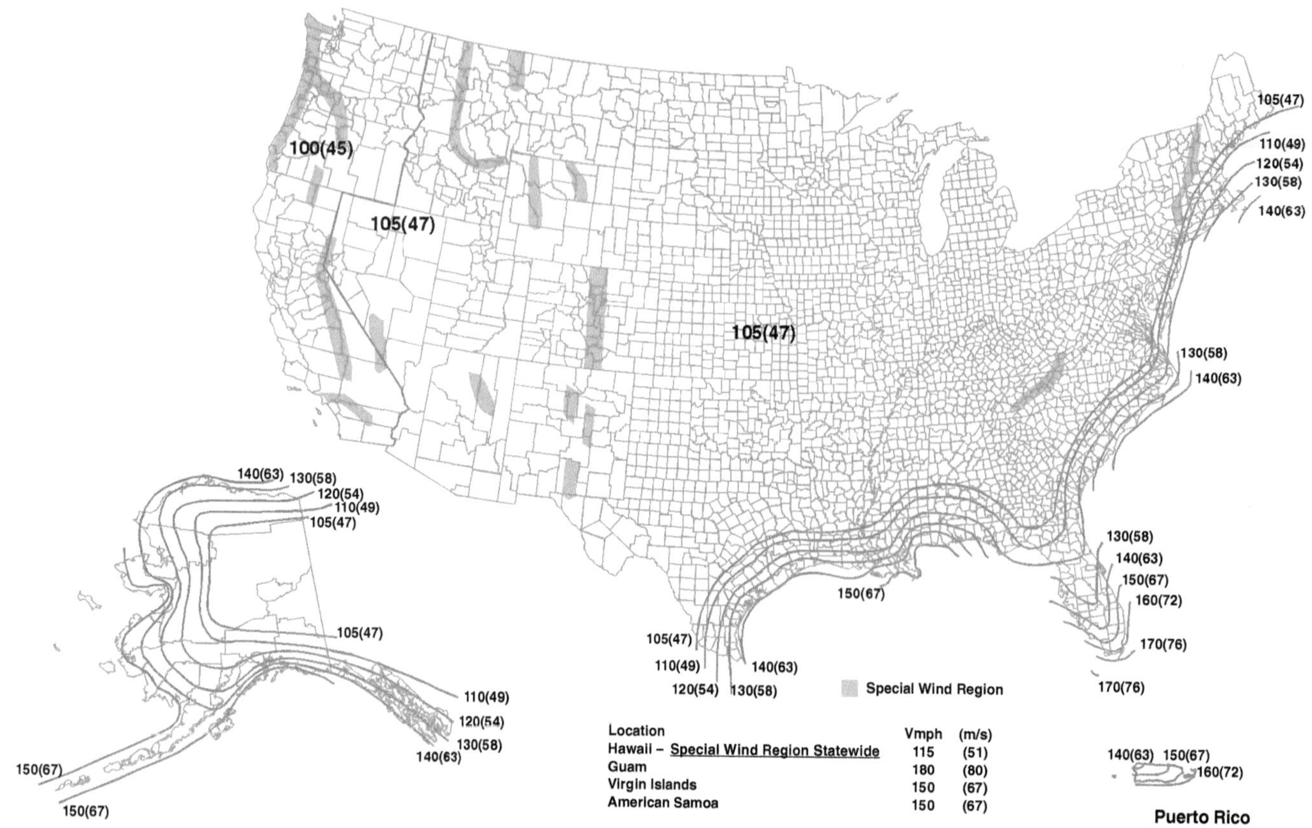

Notes:

1. Values are nominal design 3-second gust wind speeds in miles per hour (m/s) at 33 ft (10m) above ground for Exposure C category.
2. Linear interpolation between contours is permitted.
3. Islands and coastal areas outside the last contour shall use the last wind speed contour of the coastal area.
4. Mountainous terrain, gorges, ocean promontories, and special wind regions shall be examined for unusual wind conditions.
5. Wind speeds correspond to approximately a 15% probability of exceedance in 50 years (Annual Exceedance Probability = 0.00333, MRI = 300 years).

Figure 1609C Ultimate Design Wind Speeds, V_{ult}, For Risk Category I Buildings and Other Structures

1609.3.1 Wind speed conversion. When required, the ~~3-second gust basic~~ ultimate design wind speeds of Figure 1609A, B, and C shall be converted to nominal design wind speeds, V_{asd}, ~~fastest-mile wind speeds, Vfm~~, using Table 1609.3.1 or Equation 16-33.

$$\sout{V_{fm} = \frac{V_{3S} - 10.5}{1.05}} \qquad \text{(Equation 16-33)}$$

~~where:~~

~~V_{3S} = 3-second gust basic wind speed from Figure 1609.~~

$V_{asd} = V_{ult}\sqrt{0.6}$

Where:

V_{asd} = nominal design wind speed applicable to methods specified in Exceptions 1 through 5 of Section 1609.1.1

V_{ult} = ultimate design wind speeds determined from Figures 1609A, 1609B, or 1609C

~~TABLE 1609.3.1 Equivalent Basic Wind Speeds~~[a,b,c]

~~V_{3S}~~	~~85~~	~~90~~	~~100~~	~~105~~	~~110~~	~~120~~	~~125~~	~~130~~	~~140~~	~~145~~	~~150~~	~~160~~	~~170~~
~~V_{fm}~~	~~71~~	~~76~~	~~85~~	~~90~~	~~95~~	~~104~~	~~109~~	~~114~~	~~123~~	~~128~~	~~133~~	~~142~~	~~152~~

~~For SI: 1 mile per hour = 0.44 m/s.~~

~~a. Linear interpolation is permitted.~~

~~b. V3S is the 3-second gust wind speed (mph).~~

~~c. Vfm is the fastest mile wind speed (mph).~~

TABLE 1609.3.1 Wind Speed Conversions[a,b,c]

V_{ul}	100	110	120	130	140	150	160	170	180	190	200
V_{asd}	78	85	93	101	108	116	124	132	139	147	155

a. Linear interpolation is permitted

b. V_{asd} = nominal design wind speed applicable to methods specified in Exceptions 1 through 5 of Section 1609.1.1

c. V_{ult} = ultimate design wind speeds determined from Figures 1609A, 1609B, or 1609C

Because this code change affected substantial portions of Chapters 16 and 17, the entire code change text is too extensive to be included here. Refer to Code Change S84-09/10 in the *2012 IBC Code Changes Resource Collection* for the complete text and history of the code change.

CHANGE SIGNIFICANCE: The most significant aspect of the wind design change is that the wind speed maps were updated to those adopted in ASCE 7-10. Over the past 10 years, new research has indicated that the hurricane wind speeds provided in ASCE 7-05 have been too conservative and should be adjusted downward. As more hurricane data became available, it was also recognized that substantial improvements could be made to the hurricane simulation model used to develop the wind speed maps. The new data resulted in an improved representation of the hurricane wind field, including the modeling of the sea–land transition and the hurricane boundary layer height; new models for hurricane weakening after landfall; and an improved statistical model for the Holland *B* parameter, which controls the wind pressure relationship. Although the new hurricane hazard model yields hurricane wind speeds that are lower than those given in the 2010 CBC and ASCE 7-05, the overall rate of intense storms (as defined by central pressure)

1609 continued

1609 continued

produced by the new model increased compared to those produced by the hurricane simulation model used to develop previous wind speed maps.

In developing the new wind speed maps, it was decided to use multiple ultimate event or strength design based maps in conjunction with a wind load factor of 1.0 for strength design. For allowable stress design (ASD), the load factor has been reduced from 1.0 to 0.6, thus the load combinations in Section 1605 had to be modified accordingly. Several important factors related to more accurate wind load determination were considered that led to the decision to move to strength based ultimate event wind loads:

1. An ultimate event or strength design wind speed map makes the overall approach consistent with the well-established strength-based seismic design procedure in that both wind and seismic load effects are mapped as ultimate events and use a load factor of 1.0 for the strength design load combinations.
2. Utilizing different maps for the different risk categories eliminates previous issues associated with using importance factors that vary according to the risk (occupancy) category of the building. The different importance factors in ASCE 7-05 for hurricane prone versus non-hurricane prone regions for Risk (Occupancy) Category I structures prompted many questions by code users. This is no longer an issue in ASCE 7-10 because Risk Category I, Risk Category II, and Risk Category III and IV have separate wind speed maps, and the importance factor no longer appears in the velocity pressure equation. Note that the importance factor for wind in ASCE 7 Table 1.5-2 is now 1.00 for all risk categories.
3. The use of multiple maps based on risk category eliminates some confusion associated with the recurrence interval associated with the previous wind speed map in ASCE 7-05 because it was not a uniform 50-year return period map. This results in a situation where the level of safety achieved by the overall design was not consistent along the hurricane coast. The wind maps in ASCE/SEI 7-10 have a mean recurrence interval (MRI) of 300 years for Risk Category I, 700 years for Risk Category II, and 1700 years for Risk Categories III and IV.

As a result of the new strength-based wind speed, new terminology was introduced into the 2013 CBC. The former term "basic wind speed" has been changed to "ultimate design wind speed" and is designated V_{ult}. The wind speed that is equivalent to the former basic wind speed is now called the nominal design wind speed, V_{asd}, and the conversion between the two is given by Equation 16-33 as,

$$V_{asd} = V_{ult}\sqrt{0.6}$$

The conversion from V_{asd} to V_{ult} is a result of the wind load being proportional to the square of the velocity pressure and the ASD wind load being 0.6 times the strength level ultimate wind load. Thus,

$$W \cong V^2$$
$$W_{asd} = 0.6W_{ult}$$
$$V_{asd}^2 = 0.6V_{ult}^2$$
$$V_{asd} = \sqrt{0.6}V_{ult}$$

It should also be noted that the term "basic wind speed" in ASCE 7-10 corresponds to the "ultimate design wind speed" in the 2013 CBC.

Because many different code provisions in the code are based upon wind speed, it was necessary to modify the wind speed conversion section so that the many provisions triggered by wind speed were not changed. The terms "ultimate design wind speed" and "nominal design wind speed" were incorporated in numerous locations to help the code user distinguish between them. In cases where wind speed is used to trigger a requirement, the ultimate wind speed, V_{ult}, must be converted to an equivalent wind speed that corresponds to the former basic wind speed. Thus, a new table converts V_{ult} to V_{ASD} so that the mapped wind speed thresholds in various parts of the code can still be used:

V_{ult}	100	110	120	130	140	150	160	170	180	190	200
V_{asd}	78	85	93	101	108	116	124	132	139	147	155

For example, in a case where the previous edition of the code imposed requirements where the basic wind speed exceeds 100 mph, this edition imposes the requirements where V_{asd} exceeds 100 mph. A nominal design speed, V_{asd}, equal to 100 mph corresponds to an ultimate design wind speed, V_{ult}, equal to 129 mph. The following table (which is not in the code) may be more useful to the code user because it gives V_{ult} in terms of V_{asd} in increments of 10 mph:

V_{asd}	85	90	100	110	120	130	140	150
V_{ult}	110	115	126	139	152	164	177	190

For a comparison of ASCE 7-93 fastest mile wind speeds, ASCE 7-05 3-second gust ASD wind speeds, and ASCE 7-10 3-second gust wind speeds, refer to Table C26.5-6 of the ASCE 7-10 commentary. Note that the conversion in ASCE 7-10 is given by $V_{ult} = V_{asd}\sqrt{1.6}$, which produces slightly different values than IBC Equation 16-33.

Beyond the adoption of the new strength design wind speed maps, ASCE/SEI 7-10 also includes a new simplified method for use in the determination of wind loads for buildings up to 160 feet in height. In addition, the wind load calculation provisions that were contained in Chapter 6 of ASCE/SEI 7-05 have been reorganized into six separate chapters (26 through 31) for improved clarity and ease of use. This is similar to the reorganization in ASCE 7-05 where the seismic design provisions were divided into several chapters to facilitate use. This reorganization into multiple chapters required several coordination revisions to the code text.

A few other changes to the wind design provisions in Section 1609 are worth noting:

- To use any of the five standards referenced in the exception in Section 1609.1.1, the ultimate design wind speed must be determined based on the risk category of the building then converted to the nominal design wind speed.
- Wind tunnel test limitations in 2009 IBC Section 2309.1.2 were deleted from the IBC because they are incorporated into Chapter 31 of ASCE 7-10.

1609 continues

- The hurricane-prone region is redefined in terms of the ultimate design wind speed as shown on the Risk Category II wind speed map.
- The windborne debris region is now defined in terms of the ultimate design wind speed and determined from the appropriate risk category wind speed map. For example, for Risk Category II and III buildings and structures, except health care facilities, the windborne debris region is based on Figure 1609A. For Risk Category IV buildings and structures and Risk Category III health care facilities, the windborne debris region is based on Figure 1609B.
- The ultimate design wind speed, V_{ult}, for the special wind regions indicated, near mountainous terrain and near gorges is to be determined in accordance with local jurisdiction requirements and in accordance with Section 26.5.1 of ASCE 7. In nonhurricane-prone regions, when the ultimate design wind speed is estimated from regional climatic data, V_{ult}, is to be determined in accordance with Section 26.5.3 of ASCE 7.

It should be noted that the alternate all-heights wind design procedure is maintained in the 2013 CBC but was updated to conform to the new ultimate wind design procedure in ASCE 7-10.

1613.3.1, 202

Mapped Acceleration Parameters

CHANGE TYPE: Modification

CHANGE SUMMARY: The CBC seismic ground motion maps have been updated to reflect the 2008 maps developed by the United States Geological Survey (USGS) National Seismic Hazard Mapping Project and the technical changes adopted for the 2009 *NEHRP Recommended Seismic Provisions for New Buildings and Other Structures* (FEMA P750).

2013 CODE: 202 Definitions.

RISK-TARGETED MAXIMUM CONSIDERED EARTHQUAKE (MCE_R) GROUND MOTION RESPONSE ACCELERATIONS. The most severe earthquake effects considered by this code, determined for the orientation that results in the largest maximum response to horizontal ground motions and, with adjustment for targeted risk.

~~1613.5.1~~ 1613.3.1 Mapped Acceleration Parameters. The parameters S_S and S_1 shall be determined from the 0.2- and 1-second spectral response accelerations shown on Figures 1613.5(1) through 1613.5(~~14~~6), respectively. Where S_1 is less than or equal to 0.04 and S_S is less than or equal to 0.15, the structure is permitted to be assigned to Seismic Design Category A. The parameters S_S and S_1 shall be, respectively, 1.5 and 0.6 for Guam and 1.0 and 0.4 for American Samoa.

> ***Exception:*** *[OSHPD 2] Seismic Design Category shall be in accordance with exception to Section 613.3.5.*

Because this code change affected substantial portions of Chapters 16, the entire code change text is too extensive to be included here. Refer to Code Change S97-09/10 in the *2012 IBC Code Changes Resource Collection* for the complete text and history of the code change.

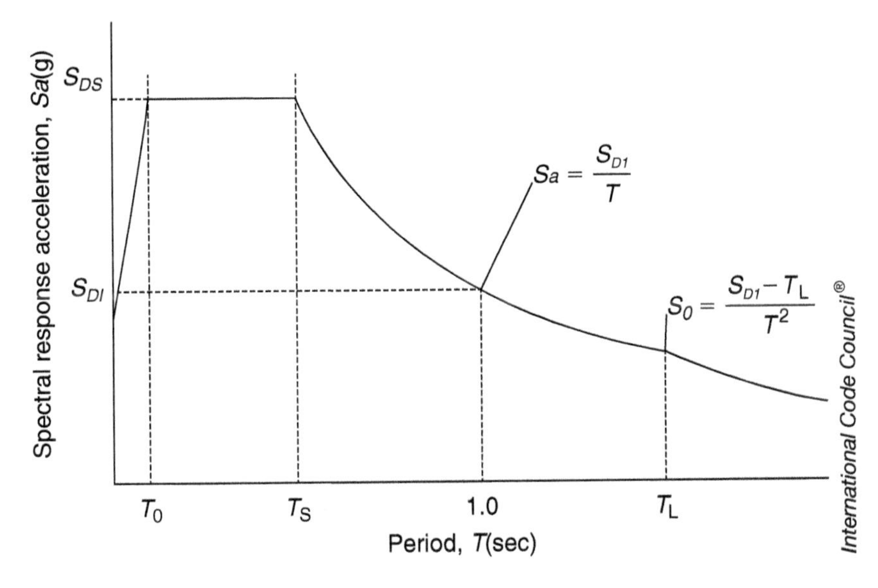

Seismic design response spectrum.

1613.3.1, 202 continues

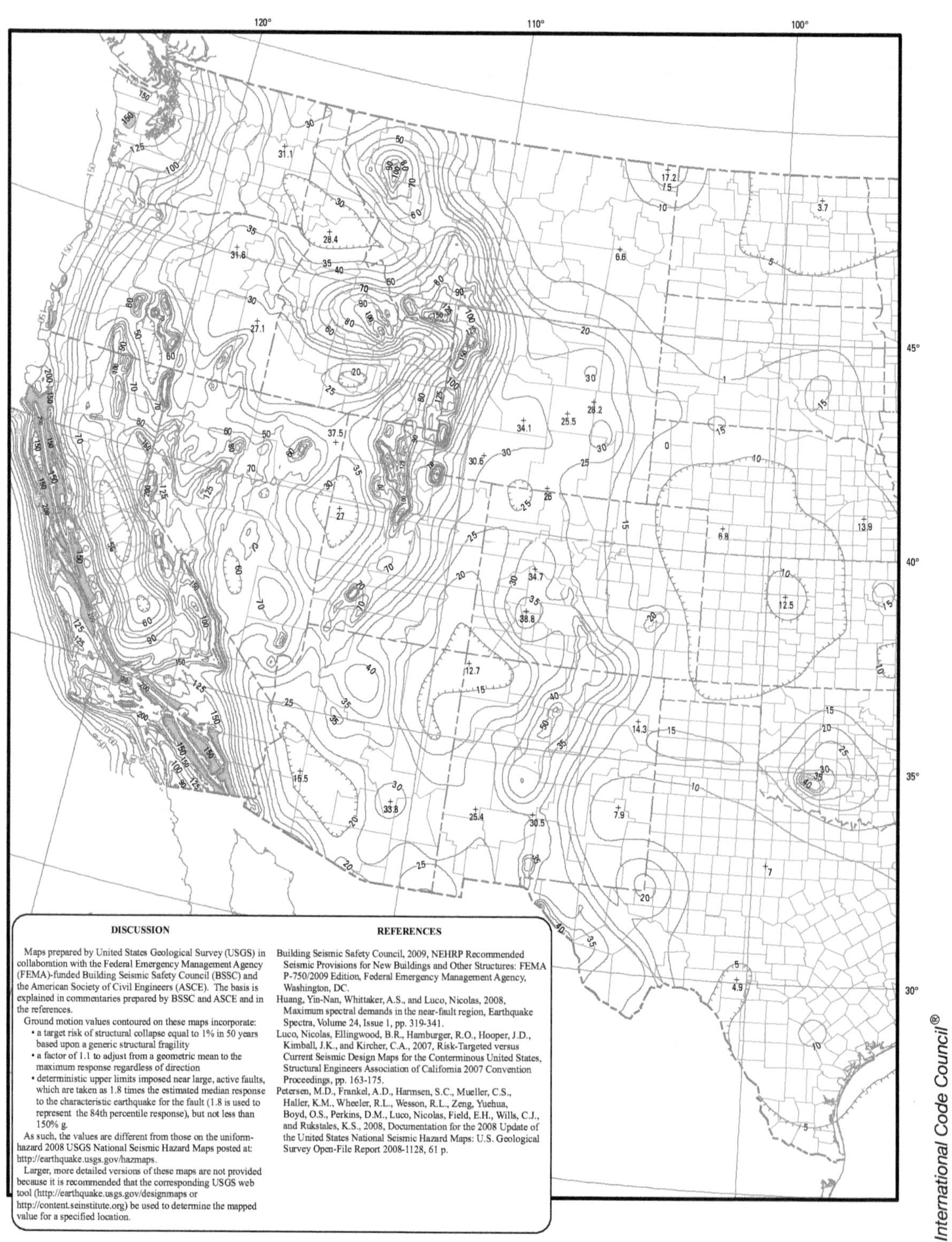

Figure ~~1613.5(1)~~ 1613.3.1(1) Risk-Targeted Maximum Considered Earthquake (MCE$_R$) Ground Motion Response Accelerations for the Conterminous United States of 0.2-Second Spectral Response Acceleration (5% of Critical Damping), Site Class B.

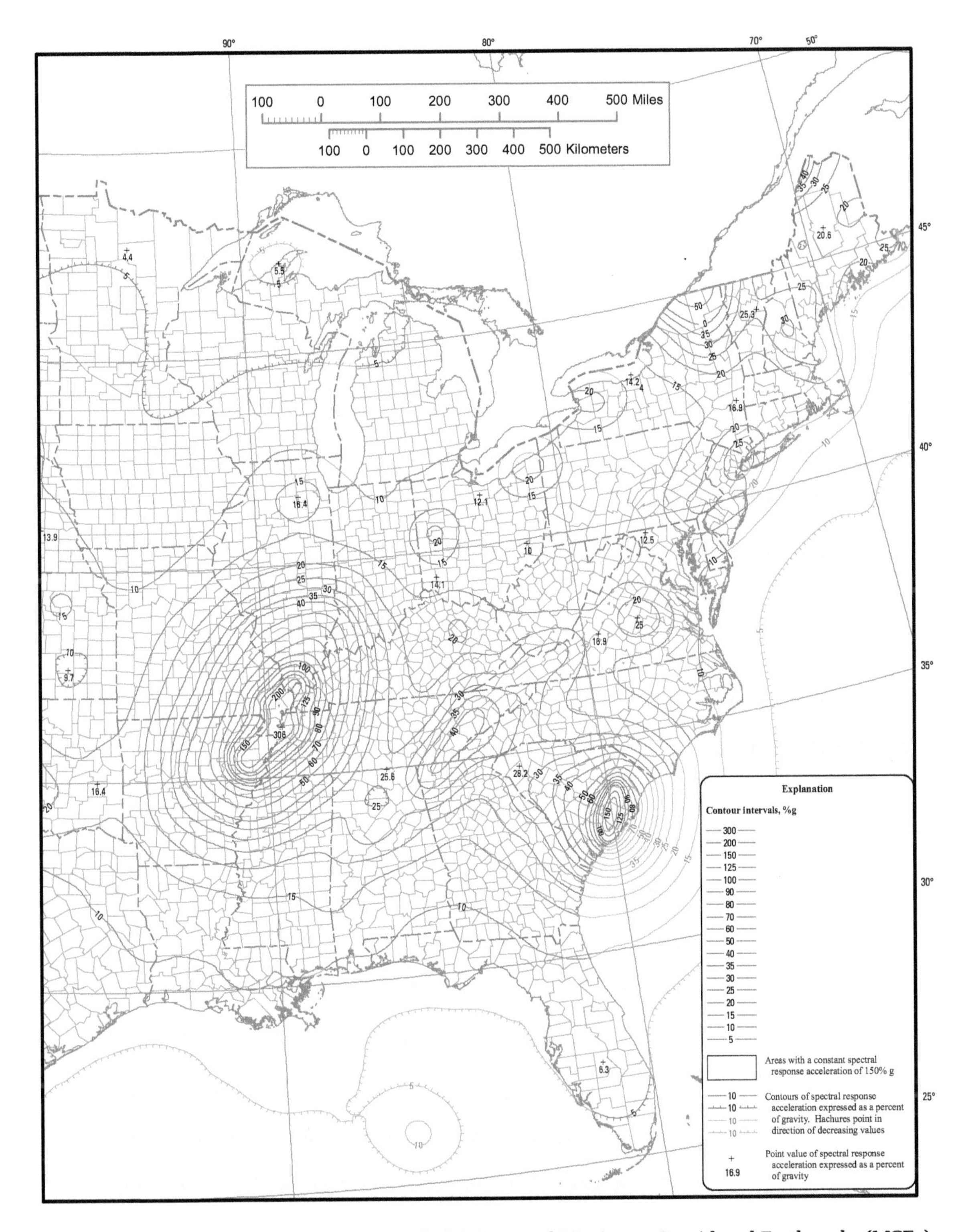

Figure ~~1613.5(1)~~ 1613.3.1(1) - continued Risk-Targeted Maximum Considered Earthquake (MCE$_R$) Ground Motion Response Accelerations for the Conterminous United States of 0.2-Second Spectral Response Acceleration (5% of Critical Damping), Site Class B.

1613.3.1, 202 continued

1613.3.1, 202 continues

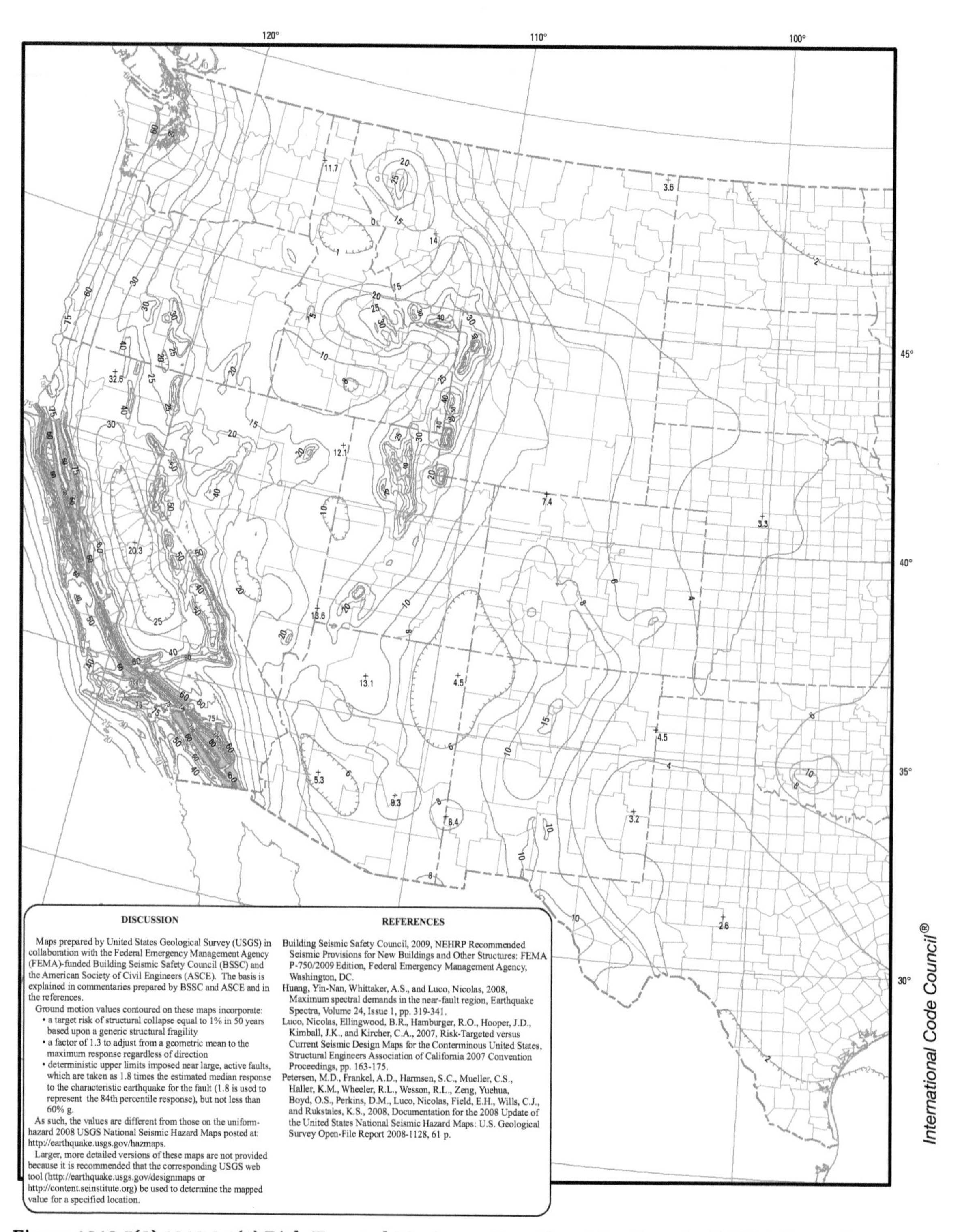

Figure ~~1613.5(2)~~ 1613.3.1(2) Risk-Targeted Maximum Considered Earthquake (MCE_R) Ground Motion Response Accelerations for the Conterminous United States of 1-Second Spectral Response Acceleration (5% of Critical Damping), Site Class B.

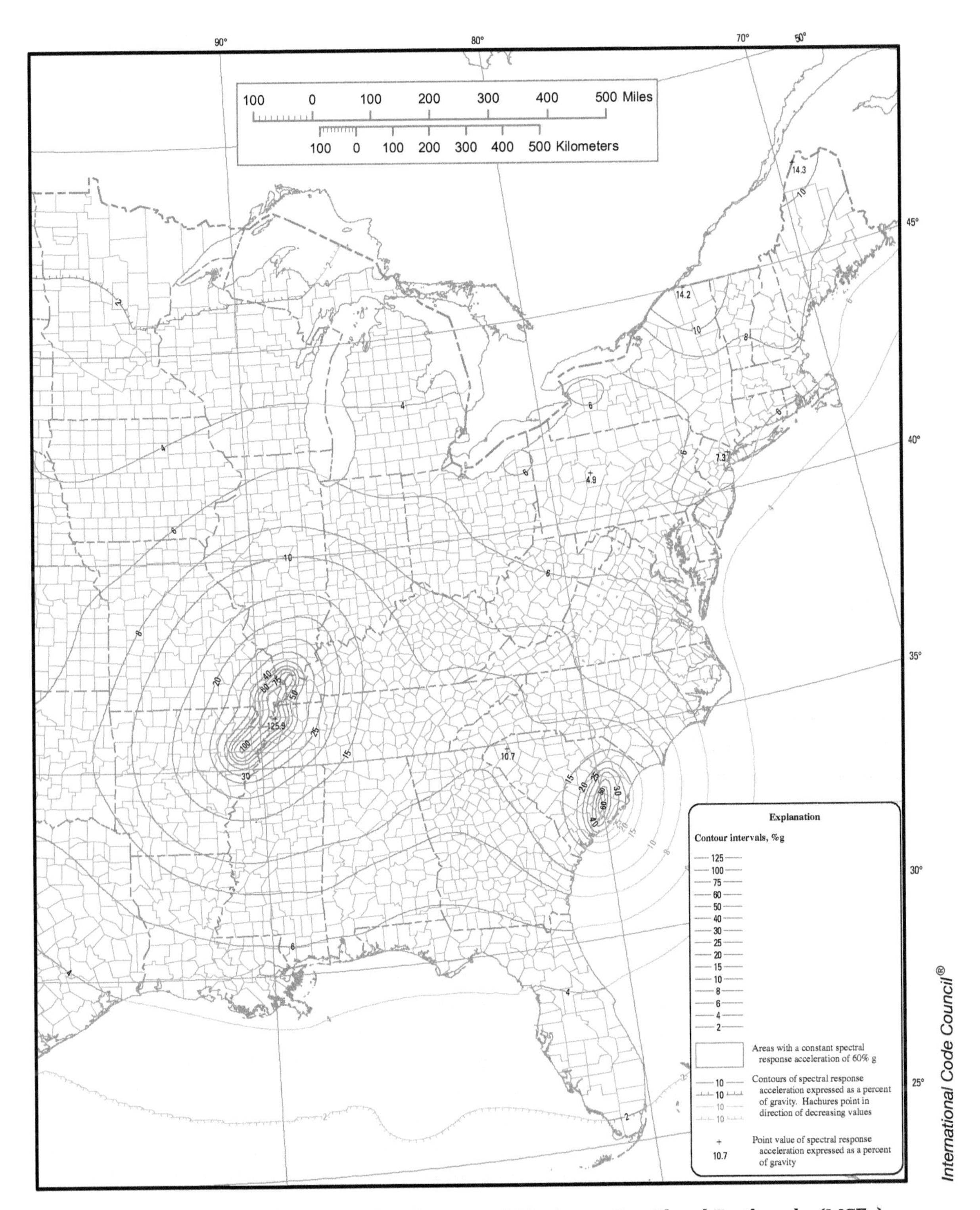

Figure ~~1613.5(2)~~ 1613.3.1(2) - continued Risk-Targeted Maximum Considered Earthquake (MCE$_R$) Ground Motion Response Accelerations for the Conterminous United States of 1-Second Spectral Response Acceleration (5% of Critical Damping), Site Class B.

1613.3.1, 202 continued

CHANGE SIGNIFICANCE: The USGS National Seismic Hazard Mapping Project and the technical changes adopted for the 2009 NEHRP (FEMA P750) are part of the ongoing federal effort to make the most current earthquake hazard information available to users of the IBC. The 2008 USGS seismic hazard maps incorporate new information on earthquake sources and ground motion prediction equations including the new Next-Generation Attenuation (NGA) relations. The ground motion maps in the 2013 CBC also incorporate technical changes adopted for the 2009 *NEHRP Provisions* that include: (1) use of risk-targeted ground motions, (2) the maximum direction ground motions, and (3) near-source 84th percentile ground motions.

The titles of the maps in the code were revised from the former "Maximum Considered Earthquake Ground Motion" to "Risk-Targeted Maximum Considered Earthquake (MCE_R) Ground Motion Response Accelerations" to reflect the changed titles in the 2009 NEHRP and the 2010 edition of *Minimum Design Loads for Buildings and Other Structures*, ASCE/SEI 7 (ASCE 7-10). The number of printed maps in the IBC was reduced from 14 to 6. Although the maps in the IBC are generally illustrative of the earthquake hazard, the contours in some regions cannot be read clearly enough to provide exact design values for specific sites. Precise seismic design values can be obtained from the USGS website (http://earthquake.usgs.gov/) using the longitude and latitude of the building site. Although the seismic design maps are based on corresponding USGS National Seismic Hazard Maps, their values typically differ from the hazard map values. Thus, engineers involved in seismic design of buildings and structures should generally use the maps, data, and tools presented here rather than other hazard map values presented elsewhere on the USGS website. The latitude and longitude of proposed building sites can be obtained from GPS mapping programs or websites such as topozone.com or trails.com.

Detailed descriptions of changes made for the 2009 *NEHRP Recommended Seismic Provisions* developed by the Building Seismic Safety Council and funded by the Federal Emergency Management Agency (FEMA) that served as the basis for the seismic design provisions in the 2013 CBC and ACSE/SEI 7-10 (by reference) are available at www.nibs.org or www.bssconline.org under the explanation of changes made for the 2009 edition of the *Provisions*.

CHANGE TYPE: Modification

CHANGE SUMMARY: Ballasted photovoltaic system design provisions have been added to the CBC.

1613.5

Ballasted Photovoltaic System

2013 CODE: ***1613.5 [BSC, HCD 1 & HCD 2] Modifications to ASCE 7.*** *The text of ASCE 7 shall be modified as indicated in Sections 1613.5.1 through 1613.5.2.*

1613.5.1 [BSC, HCD 1 & HCD 2] Modify ASCE 7 DEFINITIONS *as follows:*

1.2 DEFINITIONS.

BALLASTED PHOTOVOLTAIC SYSTEM: *A roof-mounted system composed of solar photovoltaic panels and supporting members that are unattached or partially attached to the roof and must rely on its weight, aerodynamics and friction to counter the effect of wind and seismic forces.*

Ballasted PV panels are permitted on low-slope roofs.

1613.5.2 [BSC, HCD 1 & HCD 2] Modify ASCE 7 Section 13.4 *as follows:*

Section 13.4 **NONSTRUCTURAL COMPONENT ANCHORAGE.**

Components and their supports shall be attached (or anchored) to the structure in accordance with the requirements of this section and the attachment shall satisfy the requirements for the parent material as set forth elsewhere in this standard. (Remaining text is omitted for clarity and due to space limitations)

> ***Exception:*** *Ballasted photovoltaic systems design is based on Section 13.4.7 and when approved by the enforcing agency.*

***13.4.7** Solar PV panels or modules installed on a roof as a ballasted system need not be rigidly attached to the roof or supporting structure. Ballasted systems shall be designed and installed only on roofs with slopes 1 inch per foot or less. The ballasted system shall be designed to resist sliding and uplift resulting from lateral and vertical forces, using a coefficient of friction determined by acceptable engineering practices. In sites where the Seismic Design Category is C or above, the system shall be designed to accommodate seismic displacement determined by approved analysis or shake table testing, using input motions consistent with ASCE 7 lateral and vertical seismic forces for non-structural components on roofs.*

CHANGE SIGNIFICANCE: Ballasted PV systems are rooftop systems which rely on weight and friction to resist wind and seismic forces without having a positive attachment to the roof. These systems have emerged as an attractive technology especially for large flat rooftops as they reduce costs and limit unnecessary roof penetrations. Currently, ASCE 7 is silent on this technology, does not contain a definition and does not make allowances for the approval of these systems. As a result, the current tendency is to require these systems to be substantially anchored to the roof. While this is appropriate for conventional roof-top equipment, it prohibits ballasted PV systems from being unrestrained which conflicts with the intended design and installation of ballasted systems.

This amendment was developed by the Structural Engineers Association of California – Solar Photovoltaic Systems Committee, and adopted by HCD and the CBSC to provide building officials with additional criteria by which such ballasted PV systems can be permitted.

1613.4 continues

1704.3

Statement of Special Inspections

CHANGE TYPE: Modification

CHANGE SUMMARY: The provisions requiring specific items to have special inspection and what information is required to be included in the statement of special inspections have been clarified and coordinated, with previous conflicts between the two being resolved.

2013 CODE:

~~SECTION 1705~~
~~STATEMENT OF SPECIAL INSPECTIONS~~

~~1705.1 General.~~ 1704.3 Statement of Special Inspections. Where special inspection or testing is required by Section ~~1704, 1707 or 1708~~ 1705, the registered design professional in responsible charge shall prepare a statement of special inspections in accordance with Section ~~1705~~ 1704.3.1 for submittal by the applicant ~~see~~ in accordance with Section ~~1704.1.1~~ 1704.2.3.

> **Exception:** The statement of special inspections is permitted to be prepared by a qualified person approved by the building official for construction not designed by a registered design professional.

~~1705.2~~ 1704.3.1 Content of Statement of Special Inspections. The statement of special inspections shall identify the following:

1. The materials, systems, components, and work required to have special inspection or testing by the building official or by the registered design professional responsible for each portion of the work.
2. The type and extent of each special inspection.
3. The type and extent of each test.

1704.3 continues

STATEMENT OF SPECIAL INSPECTIONS AGREEMENT

To permit applicants of projects requiring special inspection and/or testing per Secti
Building Code (IBC):

Project Address: ______________ Permit No.: __________

BEFORE A PERMIT CAN BE ISSUED, two (2) copies of t
Inspection and the Special Inspection and Testing Schedule
by the owner, or registered design professional in responsi
conference with the parties involved may be required to

APPROVAL OF SPECIAL INSPECTORS: Special i
which they provide special inspection. Special inspectors
performing any duties. Special inspectors shall submit their
prequalification. Special inspectors shall display approved id
performing the function of special inspector.

Special inspection and testing shall meet the minimum requirem
International Building Code. The following conditions are also

International Code Council®

Statement of special inspections agreement.

1704.3 continued

4. Additional requirements for special inspection or testing for seismic or wind resistance as specified in Sections ~~1705.3~~, ~~1705.4~~, 1705.10, ~~1707~~ 1705.11, ~~or~~ and ~~1708~~1705.12.
5. For each type of special inspection, identification as to whether it will be continuous special inspection or periodic special inspection.

~~1705.3.6~~ 1704.3.2 Seismic Requirements in the Statement of Special Inspections. Where Section 1705.11 or 1705.12 specifies special inspection, testing, or qualification for seismic resistance, the statement of special inspections shall identify the designated seismic systems and seismic force-resisting systems that are subject to special inspections.

~~1705.4.1~~ 1704.3.3 Wind Requirements in the Statement of Special Inspections. Where Section 1705.10 specifies special inspection for wind requirements, the statement of special inspections shall identify the main wind-force-resisting systems and wind-resisting components subject to special inspection.

~~**1705.3 Seismic Resistance.** The statement of special inspections shall include seismic requirements for cases covered in Sections 1705.3.1 through 1705.3.5.~~

> **Exceptions:** ~~Seismic requirements are permitted to be excluded from the statement of special inspections for structures designed and constructed in accordance with the following:~~
>
> 1. ~~The structure consists of light-frame construction; the design spectral response acceleration at short periods, S_{DS}, as determined in Section 1613.5.4, does not exceed 0.5 g; and the height of the structure does not exceed 35 feet (10 668 mm) above grade plane; or~~
> 2. ~~The structure is constructed using a reinforced masonry structural system or reinforced concrete structural system; the design spectral response acceleration at short periods, S_{DS}, as determined in Section 1613.5.4, does not exceed 0.5 g, and the height of the structure does not exceed 25 feet (7620 mm) above grade plane; or~~
> 3. ~~Detached one- or two-family dwellings not exceeding two stories above grade plane, provided the structure does not have any of the following plan or vertical irregularities in accordance with Section 12.3.2 of ASCE 7:~~
>
>   ~~3.1 Torsional irregularity.~~
>   ~~3.2 Nonparallel systems.~~
>   ~~3.3 Stiffness irregularity extreme soft story and soft story.~~
>   ~~3.4 Discontinuity in capacity weak story.~~

~~**1705.3.1 Seismic-Force-Resisting Systems.** The seismic force-resisting systems in structures assigned to Seismic Design Category C, D, E or F, in accordance with Section 1613.~~

> **Exceptions:** ~~Requirements for the seismic-force-resisting system are permitted to be excluded from the statement of special inspections for steel systems in structures assigned to Seismic Design Category C that are not specifically detailed for seismic resistance, with a response modification coefficient, R, of 3 or less, excluding cantilever column systems.~~

~~**1705.3.2 Designated Seismic Systems.** Designated seismic systems in structures assigned to Seismic Design Category D, E or F.~~

~~**1705.3.3 Seismic Design Category C.** The following additional systems and components in structures assigned to Seismic Design Category C:~~

1. ~~Heating, ventilating and air-conditioning (HVAC) ductwork containing hazardous materials and anchorage of such ductwork.~~
2. ~~Piping systems and mechanical units containing flammable, combustible or highly toxic materials.~~
3. ~~Anchorage of electrical equipment used for emergency or standby power systems.~~

~~**1705.3.4 Seismic Design Category D.** The following additional systems and components in structures assigned to Seismic Design Category D:~~

1. ~~Systems required for Seismic Design Category C.~~
2. ~~Exterior wall panels and their anchorage.~~
3. ~~Suspended ceiling systems and their anchorage.~~
4. ~~Access floors and their anchorage.~~
5. ~~Steel storage racks and their anchorage, where the importance factor is equal to 1.5 in accordance with Section 15.5.3 of ASCE 7.~~

~~**1705.3.5 Seismic Design Category E or F.** The following additional systems and components in structures assigned to Seismic Design Category E or F:~~

1. ~~Systems required for Seismic Design Categories C and D.~~
2. ~~Electrical equipment.~~

~~**1705.3.6 Seismic requirements in the Statement of Special Inspections.** When Sections 1705.3 through 1705.3.5 specify that seismic requirements be included, the statement of special inspections shall identify the following:~~

1. ~~The designated seismic systems and seismic force- resisting systems that are subject to special inspections in accordance with Sections 1705.3 through 1705.3.5.~~
2. ~~The additional special inspections and testing to be provided as required by Sections 1707 and 1708 and other applicable sections of this code, including the applicable standards referenced by this code.~~

~~**1705.4 Wind Resistance.** The statement of special inspections shall include wind requirements for structures constructed in the following areas:~~

1. ~~In wind Exposure Category B, where the 3-second-gust basic wind speed is 120 miles per hour (mph) (52.8m/s) or greater.~~

1704.3 continues

1704.3 continued

~~2. In wind Exposure Category C or D, where the 3-secondgust basic wind speed is 110 mph (49 m/s) or greater.~~

~~**1705.4.1 Wind Requirements in the Statement of Special Inspections.** When Section 1705.4 specifies that wind requirements be included, the statement of special inspections shall identify the main wind-force-resisting systems and wind-resisting components subject to special inspections as specified in Section 1705.4.2.~~

~~**1705.4.2 Detailed Requirements.** The statement of special inspections shall include at least the following systems and components:~~

1. ~~Roof cladding and roof framing connections.~~
2. ~~Wall connections to roof and floor diaphragms and framing.~~
3. ~~Roof and floor diaphragm systems, including collectors, drag struts and boundary elements.~~
4. ~~Vertical wind-force-resisting systems, including braced frames, moment frames and shear walls.~~
5. ~~Wind-force-resisting system connections to the foundation.~~
6. ~~Fabrication and installation of systems or components required to meet the impact-resistance requirements of Section 1609.1.2.~~

Exception: ~~Fabrication of manufactured systems or components that have a label indicating compliance with the wind-load and impact-resistance requirements of this code.~~

Because this code change deleted and revised substantial portions of Chapter 17, the entire code change text is too extensive to be included here. Refer to Code Changes S129-09/10, S131-09/10, S132-09/10, S133-09/10, and S134-09/10 in the *2012 IBC Code Changes Resource Collection* for the complete text and history of these code changes.

CHANGE SIGNIFICANCE: In the 2010 CBC, Section 1704 covered what specific items required special inspection and Section 1705 covered what is required to be included in the statement of special inspections. In the 2010 CBC, there are a variety of conflicts and inconsistencies between the two sections. The charging sentence of Section 1705 stated that where special inspection or testing was required by Section 1704, 1707, or 1708, the registered design professional in responsible charge must prepare a statement of special inspections in accordance with Section 1705. For example, suspended ceilings in Seismic Design Category D are required to be included in the statement of special inspections, yet Sections 1704, 1707, and 1708 did not specifically require special inspection for suspended ceilings. Additionally, items that required special inspection or testing by Section 1704, 1707, or 1708 were not all covered in the requirements for the statement of special inspections in Section 1705. In other words, not all items that require special inspection under Section 1704, 1707, or 1708 were listed in Section 1705 and not all items required to be in the statement of special inspection in Section 1705 require special inspection in Section 1704, 1707, or 1708. To resolve these issues, many deletions, revisions, and a reorganization of the special inspection and statement of special inspections requirements were undertaken in an effort to clarify the intent and improve proper application and enforcement.

1705.2

Special Inspection of Steel Construction

CHANGE TYPE: Modification

CHANGE SUMMARY: Special inspection requirements for structural steel have been deleted from Chapter 17 because the new standard for structural steel buildings (ANSI/AISC 360-10) includes quality assurance provisions.

2013 CODE: ~~**1704.3**~~ **1705.2 Steel Construction.** The special inspections for steel elements of buildings and structures shall be as required in this section ~~by Section 1704.3 and Table 1704.3~~.

Exceptions:

~~1.~~ Special inspection of the steel fabrication process shall not be required where the fabricator does not perform any welding, thermal cutting, or heating operation of any kind as part of the fabrication process. In such cases, the fabricator shall be required to submit a detailed procedure for material control that demonstrates the fabricator's ability to maintain suitable records and procedures such that, at any time during the fabrication process, the material specification~~,~~ and grade ~~and mill test reports~~ for the main stress-carrying elements are capable of being determined. Mill test reports shall be identifiable to the main stress-carrying elements when required by the approved construction documents.

~~2. The special inspector need not be continuously present during welding of the following items, provided the materials, welding procedures and qualifications of welders are verified prior to the start of the work; periodic inspections are made of the work in progress and a visual inspection of all welds is made prior to completion or prior to shipment of shop welding.~~

~~2.1 Single-pass fillet welds not exceeding 5/16 inch (7.9 mm) in size.~~

~~2.2 Floor and roof deck welding.~~

1705.2 continues

Structural steel building. *(Courtesy of Able Steel Fabricators)*

1705.2 continued

~~2.3 Welded studs when used for structural diaphragm.~~
~~2.4 Welded sheet steel for cold-formed steel members.~~
~~2.5 Welding of stairs and railing systems.~~

1705.2.1 Structural Steel. Special inspection for structural steel shall be in accordance with the quality assurance inspection requirements of AISC 360.

1705.2.2 Steel Construction Other Than Structural Steel. Special inspection for steel construction other than structural steel shall be in accordance with Table 1705.2.2 and this section.

~~1704.3.~~1 1705.2.2.1 Welding. Welding inspection and welding inspector qualification shall be in accordance with this section.

~~**1704.3.1.1 Structural Steel.** Welding inspection and welding inspector qualification for structural steel shall be in accordance with AWS D1.1.~~

~~1704.3.1.2~~ 1705.2.2.1.1 Cold-Formed Steel. Welding inspection and welding inspector qualification for cold-formed steel floor and roof decks shall be in accordance with AWS D1.3.

~~1704.3.1.3~~ 1705.2.2.1.2 Reinforcing Steel. Welding inspection and welding inspector qualification for reinforcing steel shall be in accordance with AWS D1.4 and ACI 318.

~~**1704.3.2 Details.** The special inspector shall perform an inspection of the steel frame to verify compliance with the details shown on the *approved construction documents*, such as bracing, stiffening, member locations and proper application of joint details at each connection.~~

~~**1704.3.3 High-Strength Bolts.** Installation of high-strength bolts shall be inspected in accordance with AISC 360.~~

~~**1704.3.3.1 General.** While the work is in progress, the special inspector shall determine that the requirements for bolts, nuts, washers and paint; bolted parts and installation and tightening in such standards are met. For bolts requiring pretensioning, the special inspector shall observe the preinstallation testing and calibration procedures when such procedures are required by the installation method or by project plans or specifications; determine that all plies of connected materials have been drawn together and properly snugged and monitor the installation of bolts to verify that the selected procedure for installation is properly used to tighten bolts. For joints required to be tightened only to the snug-tight condition, the special inspector need only verify that the connected materials have been drawn together and properly snugged.~~

~~**1704.3.3.2 Periodic Monitoring.** Monitoring of bolt installation for pretensioning is permitted to be performed on a periodic basis when using the turn-of-nut method with matchmarking techniques, the direct tension indicator method or the alternate design fastener (twist-off bolt) method. Joints designated as snug tight need be inspected only on a periodic basis.~~

~~**1704.3.3.3 Continuous Monitoring.** Monitoring of bolt installation for pretensioning using the calibrated wrench method or the turn-of-nut method without matchmarking shall be performed on a continuous basis.~~

TABLE ~~1704.3~~ 1705.2.2 Required Verification and Inspection of Steel Construction Other Than Structural Steel

Verification and Inspection	Continuous	Periodic	Referenced Standard[a]	IBC Reference
~~1. Material verification of high-strength bolts, nuts and washers:~~				
~~a. Identification markings to conform to ASTM standards specified in the approved construction documents.~~	~~—~~	~~X~~	~~AISC 360, Section A3.3 and applicable ASTM material standards~~	~~—~~
~~b. Manufacturer's certificate of compliance required.~~	~~—~~	~~X~~	~~—~~	~~—~~
~~2. Inspection of high-strength bolting:~~				
~~a. Snug-tight joints.~~	~~—~~	~~X~~		
~~b. Pretensioned and slip-critical joints using turn-of-nut with matchmarking, twist-off bolt, or direct tension indicator methods of installation.~~	~~—~~	~~X~~	~~AISC 360, Section M2.5~~	~~1704.3.3~~
~~c. Pretensioned and slip-critical joints using turn-of-nut without matchmarking or calibrated wrench methods of installation.~~	~~X~~	~~—~~		
~~3~~ 1. Material verification of ~~structural steel and~~ cold-formed steel deck:				
~~a. For structural steel, identification markings to conform to AISC 360.~~	~~—~~	~~X~~	~~AISC 360, Section M5.5~~	
~~b.~~ a. ~~For other steel, i~~Identification markings to conform to ASTM standards specified in the approved construction documents.	—	X	Applicable ASTM material standards	
~~c.~~ b. Manufacturers' certified test reports.	—	X		
~~4. Material verification of weld filler materials:~~				
~~a. Identification markings to conform to AWS specification in the approved construction documents.~~	~~—~~	~~X~~	~~AISC 360, Section A3.5 and Applicable AWS A5 documents~~	~~—~~
~~b. Manufacturer's certificate of compliance required.~~	~~—~~	~~X~~	~~—~~	~~—~~
~~5~~ 2. Inspection of welding:				
a. ~~Structural steel and c~~Cold-formed steel deck:				
~~1) Complete and partial joint penetration groove welds.~~	~~X~~	~~—~~	~~AWS D1.1~~	~~1704.3.1~~
~~2) Multipass fillet welds.~~	~~X~~	~~—~~		
~~3) Single-pass fillet welds >5/16"~~	~~X~~	~~—~~		
~~4) Plug and slot welds~~	~~X~~	~~—~~		
~~5) Single-pass fillet welds ≤5/16"~~	~~—~~	~~X~~		
~~6~~ 1) Floor and roof deck welds.	—	X	AWS D1.3	
b. Reinforcing steel:				
1) Verification of weldability of reinforcing steel other than ASTM A 706.	—	X	AWS D1.4 or ACI 318: Section 3.5.2	—

1705.2 continues

1705.2 continued

2) Reinforcing steel-resisting flexural and axial forces in intermediate and special moment frames, and boundary elements of special reinforced concrete shear walls and shear reinforcement.	X	—		
3) Shear reinforcement.	X	—		
4) Other reinforcing steel.	—	X		
~~6. Inspection of steel frame joint details for compliance with approved construction documents:~~				
~~a. Details such as bracing and stiffening.~~	~~—~~	~~X~~	~~—~~	~~1704.3.2~~
~~b. Member locations.~~	~~—~~	~~X~~		
~~c. Application of joint details at each connection.~~	~~—~~	~~X~~		

a. Where applicable, see also Section ~~1707.1~~ 1705.11, Special Inspection for Seismic Resistance.

~~1704.3.4~~ 1705.2.2.2 Cold-Formed Steel Trusses Spanning 60 Feet or Greater. Where a cold-formed steel truss clear span is 60 feet (18288 mm) or greater, the special inspector shall verify that the temporary installation restraint/bracing and the permanent individual truss member restraint/bracing are installed in accordance with the approved truss submittal package.

CHANGE SIGNIFICANCE: Substantial portions of the special inspection requirements for structural steel were deleted from the code because the 2010 edition of ANSI/AISC 360, *Specification for Structural Steel Buildings,* incorporates a new Chapter N, which includes comprehensive quality control and quality assurance requirements for structural steel construction. AISC 360, Chapter N, covers quality control requirements pertaining to the structural steel fabricator and erector, as well as quality assurance requirements pertaining to the owner's inspecting and/or testing agencies. The requirements in ANSI/AISC 360-10 are similar to those that were incorporated into AISC 341-05, Appendix Q. AISC 360-10, Chapter N, provides the foundation for the quality control and quality assurance requirements for general structural steel construction, along with AISC 341-10, Chapter I, thereby extending specific requirements to high-seismic applications. The inspection requirements in AISC 360-10 of the Quality Assurance Inspector are esentially equivalent to those specified for the special inspector in Chapter 17.

Section 1704.3 of the previous edition addressed all forms of steel construction, but the majority of the requirements in the section and Table 1704.3 pertained to structural steel construction and have been deleted. However, some items apply to cold-formed steel construction and rebar welding, which are not covered by AISC 360. Requirements for special inspection of other forms of steel construction are in a separate section and in a reduced table titled, *Required Verification and Inspection of Steel Construction Other Than Structural Steel.* The exception in Section 1705.2 has been retained but modified to clarify the requirement. In practice, the "representative mill test reports" are supplied as described in the AISC Code of Standard Practice, so the added sentence in the exception on mill test reports allows traceability when required by the construction documents and defers to AISC 360 in other cases. For a correlation between the provisions that were deleted from Section 1704.3 that are covered in AISC 360-10, Chapter N, refer to code change S121-09/10 in the *2012 IBC Code Changes Resource Collection.*

Table 1705.3

Required Verification and Inspection of Concrete Construction

CHANGE TYPE: Modification

CHANGE SUMMARY: The type of special inspection required for anchors cast in concrete and post installed anchors in hardened concrete have been clarified.

2013 CODE:

TABLE ~~1704.4~~ 1705.3 Required Verification and Inspection of Concrete Construction

Verification and Inspection	Continuous	Periodic	Referenced Standard[a]	IBC Reference
3. Inspection of ~~bolts to be installed in concrete prior to and during placement of~~ anchors cast in concrete where allowable loads have been increased or where strength design is used.	~~X~~ —	~~—~~ X	ACI 318: 8.1.3, 21.2.8	1908.5, 1909.1
4. Inspection of anchors post-installed in hardened concrete members[b]	—	X	ACI 318: 3.8.6, 8.1.3, 21.2.8	1909.1

(portions of table not shown are unchanged)

a. Where applicable, see also Section ~~1707.1~~ 1705.11, Special Inspection for Seismic Resistance.

b. Specific requirements for special inspection shall be included in the research report for the anchor issued by an approved source in accordance with ACI 355.2 or other qualification procedures. Where specific requirements are not provided, special inspection requirements shall be specified by the registered design professional and shall be approved by the building official prior to the commencement of the work.

Table 1705.3 continues

Screw-bolt anchor. *(Courtesy of Powers Fasteners)*

Table 1705.3 continued

CHANGE SIGNIFICANCE: Anchors cast into concrete are visible for inspection from the time of installation until the concrete is placed, similar to concrete reinforcement, which may have periodic special inspection. Because it is sufficient for special inspectors to be present intermittently during installation of the cast-in-place anchors, the code now allows cast-in-place anchors to have periodic special inspection. The new Footnote b has been added to account for post-installed anchors approved through the alternate methods of construction provisions of Section 104.11, such as anchors installed in accordance with ICC Evaluation Service Reports. It is also intended to distinguish between the requirements for special inspection of anchors designed to comply with the code alone versus those qualified by approved research reports in accordance with ACI 355.2, *Qualification of Post-Installed Mechanical Anchors in Concrete.* Typically, items requiring special inspection that are approved under Section 104.11 are covered by Section 1705.1.1, Special Cases. Where special inspection requirements are not provided in a research report, the special inspection requirements must be specified by the registered design professional, who would indicate whether inspections are continuous or periodic, and be approved by the building official prior to commencement of the work.

1705.4

Special Inspection of Masonry Construction

Masonry special inspector. *(Photo Courtesy of CTC Geotek)*

CHANGE TYPE: Modification

CHANGE SUMMARY: Requirements pertaining to special inspection of masonry construction were deleted from Chapter 17 because the 2011 edition of TMS 402/ACI 530/ASCE 5 and TMS 602/ACI 530.1/ASCE 6, includes requirements for quality assurance of masonry construction.

2013 CODE: ~~1704.5~~ 1705.4 Masonry Construction. Masonry construction shall be inspected and verified in accordance with TMS 402/ACI 530/ASCE 5 and TMS 602/ACI 530.1/ASCE 6 quality assurance program requirements. ~~the requirements of Sections 1704.5.1 through 1704.5.2, depending on the occupancy category of the building or structure~~.

Exceptions: Special inspections shall not be required for:

1. Empirically designed masonry, glass unit masonry, or masonry veneer designed by Section 2109, Section 2110, or Chapter 14, respectively, ~~or by Chapter 5, 7 or 6 of TMS 402/ACI 530/ASCE 5, respectively,~~ where they are part of structures classified as ~~Occupancy~~ Risk Category I, II, or III in accordance with Section 1604.5.
2. Masonry foundation walls constructed in accordance with Table 1807.1.6.3(1), 1807.1.6.3(2), 1807.1.6.3(3), or 1807.1.6.3(4).
3. Masonry fireplaces, masonry heaters, or masonry chimneys installed or constructed in accordance with Section 2111, 2112, or 2113, respectively.

~~1704.5.1~~ 1705.4.1 Empirically Designed Masonry, Glass Unit Masonry, and Masonry Veneer in ~~Occupancy~~ Risk Category IV. The minimum special inspection program for empirically designed masonry, glass unit masonry, or masonry veneer designed by Section 2109, Section 2110, or Chapter 14, respectively, ~~or by Chapter 5, 7 or 6 of TMS 402/ACI ASCE 5, respectively,~~ in structures classified as ~~Occupancy~~ Risk Category IV, in accordance with Section 1604.5, shall comply with TMS 402/ACI 530/ASCE 5 Level B Quality Assurance. ~~Table 1704.5.1~~.

~~**1704.5.2 Engineered Masonry in Occupancy Category I, II or III.** The minimum special inspection program for masonry designed by Section 2107 or 2108 or by chapters other than Chapter 5, 6 or 7 of TMS402/ACI 530/ASCE 5 in structures classified as Occupancy Category I, II or III, in accordance with Section 1604.5, shall comply with Table 1704.5.1.~~

~~**1704.5.3 Engineered Masonry in Occupancy Category IV.** The minimum special inspection program for masonry designed by Section 2107 or 2108 or by chapters other than Chapter 5, 6 or 7 of TMS402/ACI 530/ASCE 5 in structures classified as Occupancy Category IV, in accordance with Section 1604.5, shall comply with Table 1704.5.3.~~

1705.4 continues

1705.4 continued

~~**TABLE 1704.5.1 Level 1 Required Verification and Inspection of Masonry Construction**~~

(deleted table not shown for brevity)

~~**TABLE 1704.5.3 Level 2 Required Verification and Inspection of Masonry Construction**~~

(deleted table not shown for brevity)

~~1704.11~~ <u>1705.4.2</u> Vertical Masonry Foundation Elements. Special inspection shall be performed in accordance with Section ~~1704.5~~ <u>1705.4</u> for vertical masonry foundation elements.

CHANGE SIGNIFICANCE: The basis for the design and construction of masonry structures in Chapter 21 is the 2011 edition of TMS 402/ACI 530/ASCE 5 and TMS 602/ACI 530.1/ASCE 6 by reference. The special inspection provisions for masonry construction in Chapter 17 have been deleted and replaced with references to the standard for quality assurance of masonry construction. Section 1.19 of TMS 402/ACI 530/ASCE 5 and Article 1.6 of TMS 602/ACI 530/ASCE 6 include the requirements for tests, inspections, and verifications of masonry construction. All masonry designed in accordance with Chapter 5, 6, or 7 of TMS 402 is subject to a quality assurance program specified in Section 1.19 of TMS 402. The modifications made to Chapter 17 are as follows:

- For structures in Risk Category IV, reference is now made to Level B Quality Assurance requirements specified in TMS 402 for the list of tests, inspections, and verifications required for masonry designed in accordance with Sections 2109 (empirical design), 2110 (glass unit masonry), and Chapter 14 (veneer).
- Previous Sections 1704.5.2 and 1704.5.3 have been deleted entirely because all masonry designed in accordance with Sections 2107 (allowable stress design) and 2108 (strength design) must comply with Chapter 1 of TMS 402/ACI 530/ASCE 5, which requires masonry construction to be tested, inspected, and verified.
- Previous Tables 1704.5.1 and 1704.5.3 have been deleted entirely because all tests, inspections, and verifications are identified in TMS 402/ACI 530/ASCE 5.

1705.16

Special Inspection of Fire-Resistant Penetration and Joint Systems

CHANGE TYPE: Addition

CHANGE SUMMARY: Where penetration firestop systems and fire-resistant joint systems are used in high-rise buildings and those buildings assigned to Risk Categories III and IV, it is now mandatory that they be inspected by an approved inspection agency as a part of the special inspection process.

2013 CODE: **1705.16 Fire-Resistant Penetrations and Joints.** In high-rise buildings or in buildings assigned to Risk Category III or IV in accordance with Section 1604.5, special inspections for through penetrations, membrane penetration firestops, fire-resistant joint systems, and perimeter fire barrier systems that are tested and listed in accordance with Sections 714.3.1.2, 714.4.1.2, 715.3, and 715.4 shall be in accordance with Section 1705.16.1 or 1705.16.2.

1705.16.1 Penetration Firestops. Inspections of penetration firestop systems that are tested and listed in accordance with Sections 714.3.1.2 and 714.4.1.2 shall be conducted by an approved inspection agency in accordance with ASTM E2174.

1705.16.2 Fire-Resistant Joint Systems. Inspection of fire-resistant joint systems that are tested and listed in accordance with Sections 715.3 and 715.4 shall be conducted by an approved inspection agency in accordance with ASTM E 2393.

Chapter 35.

ASTM E 2174-09, *Standard Practice for On-Site Inspection of Installed Fire Stops*

ASTM E 2393-09, *Standard Practice for On-Site Inspection of Installed Fire Resistive Joint Systems and Perimeter Fire Barrier*

International Code Council®

Penetration protection at fire-resistance-rated floor/ceiling assembly.

CHANGE SIGNIFICANCE: Through-penetration and membrane-penetration firestop systems, as well as fire-resistant joint systems and perimeter fire barrier systems, are critical to maintaining the fire-resistive integrity of fire-resistance-rated construction elements, including fire walls, fire barriers, fire partitions, smoke barriers, and horizontal assemblies. The proper selection and installation of such systems must be in compliance with the code and/or appropriate listing. With thousands of listed firestop systems available—each with variations that multiply possible systems for a building exponentially—the selection of the correct system is not a generic process. Where such systems are used in two types of buildings considered as "high risk," it is now mandatory that they be included as a part of the special inspection process. Such "high-risk" buildings have been identified as:

- Buildings assigned to Risk Category III or IV in accordance with Section 1604.5, and
- High-rise buildings.

Although the proper application of firestop and joint system requirements is very important in all types and sizes of buildings, the requirement for special inspection is limited to specific building types that represent a substantial hazard to human life in the event of a system failure or that are considered to be essential facilities. Inspection to ASTM E2174 for penetration firestop systems and ASTM E2393 for fire-resistant joint systems brings an increased level of review to this important discipline.

1803.5.12

Geotechnical Reports for Foundation Walls and Retaining Walls

Retaining wall. *(Photo Courtesy of Alan D. Wilcox, P.E.)*

CHANGE TYPE: Modification

CHANGE SUMMARY: The requirement that geotechnical reports address earthquake loads on foundation walls and retaining walls in Seismic Design Categories D, E, and F has been modified so that it only applies to those walls supporting more than 6 feet of backfill.

2013 CODE: **1803.5.12 Seismic Design Categories D through F.** For structures assigned to Seismic Design Category D, E, or F, the geotechnical investigation required by Section 1803.5.11 shall also include all of the following as applicable:

1. The determination of dynamic seismic lateral earth pressures on foundation walls and retaining walls supporting more than 6 feet (1830 mm) of backfill height due to design earthquake ground motions.

2.-4. (no significant changes to text)

CHANGE SIGNIFICANCE: Geotechnical reports have previously been required to address earthquake loads on foundation walls and retaining walls for buildings in Seismic Design Categories D, E, and F. In the application of the requirements, there was no exemption based on the height of the wall or the amount of soil supported by the wall. This was deemed to be overly restrictive for foundation walls supporting light-frame construction, small retaining walls, and swimming pools. Evidence from recent earthquakes and recent experimental research results, including work recently completed at the University of California–Berkeley, has demonstrated that retaining wall structures must move in order to develop the failure wedge postulated in the so-called Mononobe and Okabe method. However, the postulated condition can only occur when the wall has already failed due to other causes. The current body of field evidence does not provide any evidence for the existence of this mechanism of failure. It was determined that the requirement in the previous code edition and ASCE 7-05 imposed an unjustifiable burden on the permit applicant to investigate a site for small retaining structures such as foundation walls, retaining walls, and swimming pools that support no more than 6 feet of backfill.

Chapter 19

Concrete Construction

CHANGE TYPE: Modification

CHANGE SUMMARY: The provisions related to concrete construction were deleted from Chapter 19 because they are contained in the 2011 edition of ACI 318, *Building Code Requirements for Structural Concrete and Commentary.*

2013 CODE: ~~**1901.3 Source and Applicability.** The format and subject matter of Sections 1902 through 1907 of this chapter are patterned after, and in general conformity with, the provisions for structural concrete in ACI 318.~~

~~**1901.4**~~ **1901.3 Construction Documents.** The construction documents for structural concrete construction shall include:

1. The specified compressive strength of concrete at the stated ages or stages of construction for which each concrete element is designed.
2. The specified strength or grade of reinforcement.
3. The size and location of structural elements, reinforcement, and anchors.
4. Provision for dimensional changes resulting from creep, shrinkage, and temperature.
5. The magnitude and location of prestressing forces.

International Code Council®

Reinforced concrete foundation.

Chapter 19 continues

6. Anchorage length of reinforcement and location and length of lap splices.
7. Type and location of mechanical and welded splices of reinforcement.
8. Details and location of contraction or isolation joints specified for plain concrete.
9. Minimum concrete compressive strength at time of posttensioning.
10. Stressing sequence for posttensioning tendons.
11. For structures assigned to Seismic Design Category D, E, or F, a statement if slab on grade is designed as a structural diaphragm ~~(see Section 21.12.3.4 of ACI 318)~~.

1903.3 Flat Wall Insulating Concrete Form (ICF) Systems. Insulating concrete form material used for forming flat concrete walls shall conform to ASTM E 2634.

~~**1904.1 Water-Cementitious Materials Ratio.** Where maximum water-cementitious materials ratios are specified in ACI 318, they shall be calculated in accordance with ACI 318, Section 4.1.~~

SECTION 1904
DURABILITY REQUIREMENTS

~~**1904.2**~~ **1904.1 Exposure Categories and Classes.** Concrete shall be assigned to exposure classes in accordance with the durability requirements of ACI 318~~, Section 4.2,~~ based on:

1. Exposure to freezing and thawing in a moist condition or deicer chemicals.
2. Exposure to sulfates in water or soil.
3. Exposure to water where the concrete is intended to have low permeability.
4. Exposure to chlorides from deicing chemicals, salt, saltwater, brackish water, seawater, or spray from these sources, where the concrete has steel reinforcement.

~~**1904.3**~~ **1904.2 Concrete Properties.** Concrete mixtures shall conform to the most restrictive maximum water-cementitious materials ratios, maximum cementitious admixtures, minimum air-entrainment, and minimum specified concrete compressive strength requirements of ACI 318~~, Section 4.3~~, based on the exposure classes assigned in Section ~~1904.2~~ 1904.1.

> ***Exception:*** *For occupancies and appurtenances thereto in Group R occupancies that are in buildings less than four stories above grade plane, normal-weight aggregate concrete is permitted to comply with the requirements of Table ~~1904.3~~ 1904.2 based on the weathering classification (freezing and thawing) determined from Figure ~~1904.3~~ 1904.2 in lieu of the durability requirements of ACI 318 ~~Table 4.3.1~~.*

TABLE ~~1904.3~~ 1904.2 Minimum Specified Compressive Strength (f'_c)

(no changes to table)

a. Concrete in these locations that can be subjected to freezing and thawing during construction shall be of air-entrained concrete in accordance with Section ~~1904.4.1~~ 1904.2.

b. Concrete shall be air entrained in accordance with ~~Section 1904.4.1~~ ACI 318.

c. Structural plain concrete basement walls are exempt from the requirements for exposure conditions of Section ~~1904.3~~ 1904.2 ~~(see Section 1909.6.1)~~.

d. For garage floor slabs where a steel trowel finish is used, the total air content required by ~~Section 1904.4.1~~ ACI 318 is permitted to be reduced to not less than 3 percent, provided the minimum specified compressive strength of the concrete is increased to 4000 psi.

FIGURE ~~1904.3~~ 1904.2
WEATHERING PROBABILITY MAP FOR CONCRETE [a, b, c]
(no changes to map and footnotes)

~~**1904.4 Freezing and Thawing Exposures.** Concrete that will be exposed to freezing and thawing, in the presence of moisture, with or without deicing chemicals being present, shall comply with Sections 1904.4.1 and 1904.4.2.~~

~~**1904.4.1 Air Entrainment.** Concrete exposed to freezing and thawing while moist shall be air entrained in accordance with ACI 318, Section 4.4.1.~~

~~**1904.4.2 Deicing Chemicals.** For concrete exposed to freezing and thawing in the presence of moisture and deicing chemicals, the maximum weight of fly ash, other pozzolans, silica fume or slag that is included in the concrete shall not exceed the percentages of the total weight of cementitious materials permitted by ACI 318, Section 4.4.2.~~

~~**1904.5 Alternative Cementitious Materials for Sulfate Exposure.** Alternative combinations of cementitious materials for use in sulfate-resistant concrete to those listed in ACI 318, Table 4.3.1 shall be permitted in accordance with ACI 318, Section 4.5.1.~~

~~**SECTION 1905**~~
~~**CONCRETE QUALITY, MIXING AND PLACING**~~
(deleted code text not shown for brevity)

~~**SECTION 1906**~~
~~**FORMWORK, EMBEDDED PIPES AND CONSTRUCTION JOINTS**~~
(deleted code text not shown for brevity)

~~**SECTION 1907**~~
~~**DETAILS OF REINFORCEMENT**~~
(deleted code text not shown for brevity)

Because this code change deleted or revised substantial portions of Chapter 19, the entire code change text is too extensive to be included here. Refer to Code Change S160-09/10 in the *2012 IBC Code Changes Resource Collection* for the complete text and history of the code change.

Chapter 19 continued

CHANGE SIGNIFICANCE: Sections 1901 through 1907 of the previous code edition, which contained concrete construction requirements, did not provide any technical content but merely referenced corresponding sections in ACI 318. For example, Section 1906.1, Formwork, reads as follows, "The design, fabrication and erection of forms shall comply with ACI 318, Section 6.1." Therefore, Sections 1905 (Concrete Quality, Mixing, and Placing), 1906 (Formwork, Imbedded Pipes, and Construction Joints), and 1907 (Details of Reinforcement) have been deleted entirely because they do not provide any information other than referencing the corresponding section in the ACI 318 standard. As stated in Section 1901.2, structural concrete is required to be designed and constructed in accordance with ACI 318 as amended in Section 1905.

1905.1.3

Seismic Detailing of Wall Piers

CHANGE TYPE: Addition

CHANGE SUMMARY: ACI 318 Section 21.4 provides seismic requirements for intermediate precast structural walls. Section 1905.1.3 amends ACI 318 Section 21.4 by adding seismic detailing requirements for wall piers in Seismic Design Categories D, E, and F.

Precast concrete wall panel. *(Courtesy of Tilt-Up Concrete Association)*

2013 CODE: 1905.1.3 ACI 318, Section 21.4. Modify ACI 318, Section 21.4, by renumbering Section 21.4.3 to become 21.4.4 and adding new Sections 21.4.3, 21.4.5, ~~and~~ 21.4.6, and 21.4.7 to read as follows:

21.4.3 *Connections that are designed to yield shall be capable of maintaining 80 percent of their design strength at the deformation induced by the design displacement or shall use Type 2 mechanical splices.*

21.4.4 Elements of the connection that are not designed to yield shall develop at least 1.5 S_y.

21.4.5 *Wall piers in Seismic Design Category D, E, or F shall comply with Section 1905.1.4 of the California Building Code.*

~~***21.4.5***~~ ***21.4.6*** *Wall piers not designed as part of a moment frame in buildings assigned to SDC C shall have transverse reinforcement designed to resist the shear forces determined from 21.3.3. Spacing of transverse reinforcement shall not exceed 8 inches (203 mm). Transverse reinforcement shall be extended beyond the pier clear height for at least 12 inches (305 mm).*

Exceptions:

1. *Wall piers that satisfy 21.13.*
2. *Wall piers along a wall line within a story where other shear wall segments provide lateral support to the wall piers and such segments have a total stiffness of at least six times the sum of the stiffnesses of all the wall piers.*

~~***21.4.6***~~ ***21.4.7*** *Wall segments with a horizontal length-to-thickness ratio less than 2.5 shall be designed as columns.*

CHANGE SIGNIFICANCE: ASCE 7 permits intermediate precast structural wall systems in Seismic Design Categories D, E, or F. Section 1908.1.3 previously had no specific seismic detailing requirements for wall piers in Seismic Design Categories D, E, or F. ACI 318 Commentary R 21.1.1 emphasizes that is essential that structures assigned to higher seismic design categories possess a higher degree of toughness and ductility and encourages practitioners to use special structural wall systems in regions of high seismic risk. Commercial buildings constructed using precast panel wall systems often have large window and door openings and narrow wall piers. Wall panels varying in height up to three stories high with openings resembling wall frames have not been recognized under any of the defined seismic-force resisting systems other than by considering them structural wall systems. By requiring wall piers in Seismic Design Category D, E, or F to comply with Section 1905.1.4 for special structural walls, the seismic design and detailing of wall piers will ensure better performance when subjected to the design earthquake. The transverse reinforcing requirements for wall piers in Section 21.9.8.2 will enhance ductile response. The modification clarifies the intent by separating wall piers in structures assigned to Seismic Design Category C from those assigned to Seismic Design Category D, E, or F.

2101.2

Design Methods for Masonry Structures

CHANGE TYPE: Addition

CHANGE SUMMARY: The new TMS 403-10 masonry design standard, now referenced in the code, provides a direct design method for simple, single-story, concrete masonry bearing-wall structures.

2013 CODE: 2101.2 Design Methods. Masonry shall comply with the provisions of one of the following design methods in this chapter as well as the requirements of Sections 2101 through 2104. Masonry designed by the allowable stress design provisions of Section 2101.2.1, the strength design provisions of Section 2101.2.2, ~~or~~ the prestressed masonry provisions of Section 2101.2.3, or the direct design requirements of Section 2101.2.7 shall comply with Section 2105.

2101.2.7 Direct Design. Masonry designed by the direct design method shall comply with the provisions of TMS 403.

Chapter 35. TMS 403—10 Direct Design Handbook for Masonry Structures

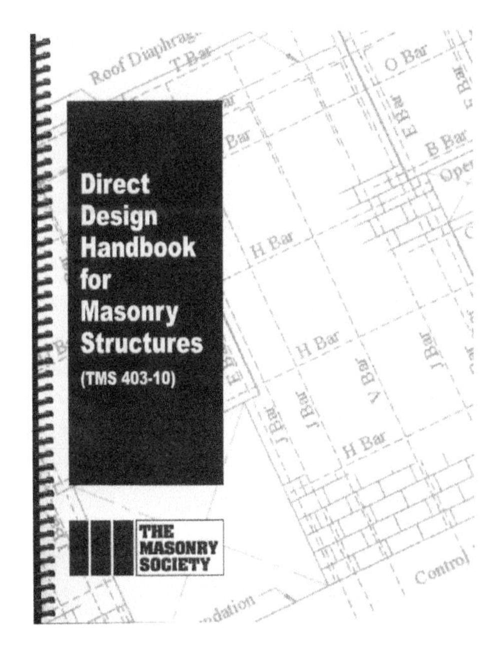

TMS 403-10. *(The Masonry Society)*

CHANGE SIGNIFICANCE: Chapter 21 now includes a simplified design method for single-story, concrete masonry buildings based on the new referenced standard TMS 403, *Direct Design Handbook for Masonry Structures*. The methodology used to develop the standard is based upon the strength design provisions of the 2005 and 2008 editions of TMS 402/ACI 530/ASCE 5 and the factored load combinations for dead, roof live, wind, seismic, snow, and rain loads in accordance with ASCE 7. The new design standard was developed by the masonry industry in response to concerns from the design community that structural loads and design requirements have become too complicated, particularly for relatively small, simple structures. The direct design procedure is a table-based structural design method that permits the user, following a specific series of steps, to design and specify relatively simple, single-story, concrete masonry bearing-wall structures. The method is simple to implement compared to conventional design approaches, but it limits the design to only those configurations addressed by the standard. It introduces slightly more conservatism compared to conventional design procedures as a result of the conditions and assumptions inherent to the design method. Some of the key design limitations in the standard are:

- Snow—ground snow load is limited to 60 psf.
- Wind—3-second gust basic wind speed is limited to 150 mph; wind exposure category is limited to B or C; and site topography is limited to $K_{zt} = 1.0$.
- Seismic—mapped spectral accelerations S_S and S_1 are limited to 3.0g and 1.25g, respectively, and Site Classes are limited to A, B, C, or D.
- Walls—walls are limited to single-story, single-wythe, 8-inch concrete masonry with a maximum height of 30 feet.
- Roof—roof diaphragms are required to be flexible, have rectangular dimensions with an aspect ratio not exceeding 4:1, and a maximum plan dimension of 200 feet.
- Reinforcement—all reinforcing bars are limited to No. 5 and Grade 60.

The *Direct Design Handbook for Masonry Structures* is intended to capture many of the simple load-bearing masonry structures commonly designed today.

2206

Composite Structural Steel and Concrete Structures

CHANGE TYPE: Addition

CHANGE SUMMARY: The requirement that composite structures in Seismic Design Categories D, E, and F provide substantiating evidence demonstrating that they will perform as intended by Part II of AISC 341 has been deleted because these structures are now addressed in the 2010 edition of AISC 341, and a new section for composite structures of structural steel and concrete has been added.

2013 CODE: ~~**2205.3.1 Seismic Design Categories D, E and F.** Composite structures are permitted in *Seismic Design Categories* D, E and F, subject to the limitations in Section 12.2.1 of ASCE 7, where substantiating evidence is provided to demonstrate that the proposed system will perform as intended by AISC 341, Part II. The substantiating evidence shall be subject to *building official* approval. Where composite elements or connections are required to sustain inelastic deformations, the substantiating evidence shall be based on cyclic testing.~~

SECTION 2206
COMPOSITE STRUCTURAL STEEL AND CONCRETE STRUCTURES

2206.1 General. Systems of structural steel acting compositely with reinforced concrete shall be designed in accordance with AISC 360 and ACI 318, excluding ACI 318 Chapter 22. Where required, the seismic design of composite steel and concrete systems shall be in accordance with the additional provisions of Section 2206.2.

2206 continues

Simon headquarters office building. *(Courtesy of Haris Engineering)*

~~2205.3~~ 2206.2 Seismic Requirements for Composite Structural Steel and Concrete Construction. Where a response modification coefficient, *R*, in accordance with ASCE 7, Table 12.2-1, is used for the design of systems of structural steel acting compositely with reinforced concrete, the structures shall be designed and detailed in accordance with the requirements of AISC 341. ~~The design, construction and quality of composite steel and concrete components that resist seismic forces shall conform to the requirements of the AISC 360 and ACI 318. An R factor as set forth in Section 12.2.1 of ASCE 7 for the appropriate composite steel and concrete system is permitted where the structure is designed and detailed in accordance with the provisions of AISC 341, Part II. In Seismic Design Category B or above, the design of such systems shall conform to the requirements of AISC 341, Part II.~~

CHANGE SIGNIFICANCE: The requirement that composite structures in Seismic Design Categories D, E, and F provide substantiating evidence demonstrating that the proposed system will perform as intended by Part II of AISC 341 is no longer necessary because the 2010 edition of AISC 341 contains detailed provisions for testing composite special moment frames, composite partially restrained moment frames, and composite eccentrically braced frames. A new section is added specifically for composite structures of structural steel and concrete, patterned after Section 2305 on structural steel. However, unlike structural steel structures regulated by Section 2305, composite structures must be designed and detailed in accordance with AISC 341 regardless of seismic design category. Therefore, the new section makes no specific reference to Seismic Design Categories D, E, and F.

2210.2

Seismic Requirements for Cold-Formed Steel Structures

CHANGE TYPE: Addition

CHANGE SUMMARY: A reference to the new AISI S110 standard for seismic design of cold-formed steel special moment frames has been added to Chapter 22. The new standard includes design provisions for a new cold-formed steel seismic force resisting system called Cold-Formed Steel—Special Bolted Moment Frames (CFS-SBMF).

2013 CODE: **2210.2 Seismic Requirements for Cold-Formed Steel Structures.** Where a response modification coefficient, *R*, in accordance with ASCE 7, Table 12.2-1, is used for the design of cold-formed steel structures, the structures shall be designed and detailed in accordance with the requirements of AISI S100, ASCE 8, and, for cold-formed steel special bolted moment frames, AISI S110.

Chapter 35. AISI S110-07, *Standard for Seismic Design of Cold-Formed Steel Structural Systems—Special Bolted Moment Frames.*

CHANGE SIGNIFICANCE: The code now references the new AISI S110, *Standard for Seismic Design of Cold-Formed Steel Structural Systems—Special Bolted Moment Frames.* The standard was developed by AISI as a result of research conducted at the University of California at San Diego by Professors Chia-Ming Uang and Atsushi Sato. CFS-SBMF systems experience substantial inelastic deformation during a design seismic event, with most of the inelastic deformation occurring at the bolted connections due to slip and bearing. The CFS-SBMF system was vetted through the Building Seismic Safety Council (BSSC) process for inclusion in the 2009 NEHRP Provisions and subsequently incorporated

2210.2 continues

Cold-formed steel special bolted moment frame. *(Photo Courtesy of FCP Inc. Structures)*

into the ASCE 7-10 standard. Cyclic testing has shown that the system has large ductility capacity and significant hardening. A capacity design procedure is provided in the AISI S110 Commentary so that the designer can explicitly calculate the seismic load effect with overstrength, E_{mh}, at the design story drift. Alternatively, a conservative system overstrength factor of 3.0 is also provided to be compatible with the conventional approach to compute E_{mh} in accordance with ASCE 7. To develop the expected mechanism, requirements based on capacity design principles are provided in the standard for the design of the beams, columns, and their connections. Table 12.2-1 of ASCE 7-10 includes seismic design parameters for CFS-SBMF system of $R = 3.5$, $\Omega_o = 3.0$ and $C_d = 3.5$. It should be noted that ASCE 7 limits structures using CFS-SBMF systems to one story in height and 35 feet. AISI S110 also includes specific requirements for quality assurance and quality control procedures.

2305

General Design Requirements for Lateral-Force-Resisting Systems

International Code Council®

16-gage staples.

CHANGE TYPE: Modification

CHANGE SUMMARY: The provisions in Section 2305 for the lateral design of wood structures have been coordinated with those set forth in the 2008 edition of the AF&PA standard, *Special Design Provisions for Wind and Seismic* (SDPWS-08). Design and deflection values for stapled wood-frame diaphragms and shear walls remain in the code.

2013 CODE: 2305.1 General. Structures using wood frame shear walls ~~and~~ or wood frame diaphragms to resist wind, seismic, ~~and~~ or other lateral loads shall be designed and constructed in accordance with AF&PA SDPWS and the applicable provisions of Sections 2305, 2306, and 2307.

2305.2 Diaphragm Deflection. The deflection of wood frame diaphragms shall be determined in accordance with AF&PA SDPWS. The deflection (Δ) of a blocked wood structural panel diaphragm uniformly fastened throughout with staples is permitted to be calculated in accordance with ~~the following~~ Equation 23-1. If not uniformly fastened, the constant 0.188 (For SI: 1/1627) in the third term shall be modified ~~accordingly~~ by an approved method.

Exception: [DSA-SS, DSA-SS/CC and OSHPD 1, 2 and 4] *Section 2305.2 is not permitted by DSA.*

$$A = \frac{5vL^3}{8EAb} + \frac{vL}{4Gt} + 0.188Le_n + \frac{\sum(\Delta_c X)}{2b} \qquad \textbf{(Equation 23-1)}$$

$$\textit{For SI:}\ A = \frac{0.052vL^3}{EAb} + \frac{vL}{4Gt} + \frac{Le_n}{1627} + \frac{\sum(\Delta_c X)}{2b}$$

where:

A = Area of chord cross section, in square inches (mm^2).
B = Diaphragm width, in feet (mm).
E = Elastic modulus of chords, in pounds per square inch (N/mm^2).
e_n = Staple deformation, in inches (mm) [see Table 2305.2(1)].
Gt = Panel rigidity through the thickness, in pounds per inch (N/mm) of panel width or depth [see Table 2305.2(2)].
L = Diaphragm length, in feet (mm).
V = Maximum shear due to design loads in the direction under consideration, in pounds per linear foot (plf) (N/mm).
Δ = The calculated deflection, in inches (mm).
$\Sigma(\Delta_c X)$ = Sum of individual chord-splice slip values on both sides of the diaphragm, each multiplied by its distance to the nearest support.

2305.3 Shear Wall Deflection. The deflection of wood-frame shear walls shall be determined in accordance with AF&PA SDPWS. The deflection (Δ) of a blocked wood structural panel shear wall uniformly fastened

2305 continues

throughout with staples is permitted to be calculated in accordance with Equation 23-2:

$$\Delta = \frac{8vh^3}{EAb} + \frac{vh}{Gt} + 0.75he_n + d_a\frac{h}{b} \qquad \textbf{(Equation 23-2)}$$

$$For\ SI:\ \Delta = \frac{vh^3}{3EAb} + \frac{vh}{Gt} + \frac{he_n}{407.6} + d_a\frac{h}{b}$$

where:

A = Area of boundary element cross section in square inches (mm^2) (vertical member at shear wall boundary).

b = Wall width, in feet (mm).

d_a = Vertical elongation of overturning anchorage (including fastener slip, device elongation, anchor rod elongation, etc.) at the design shear load (v).

E = Elastic modulus of boundary element (vertical member at shear wall boundary), in pounds per square inch (N/mm^2).

e_n = Staple deformation, in inches (mm) [see Table 2305.2(1)].

Gt = Panel rigidity through the thickness, in pounds per inch (N/mm) of panel width or depth [see Table 2305.2(2)].

h = Wall height, in feet (mm).

v = Maximum shear due to design loads at the top of the wall, in pounds per linear foot (N/mm).

Δ = The calculated deflection, in inches (mm).

CHANGE SIGNIFICANCE: Section 2305 references the 2008 edition of the AF&PA standard, *Special Design Provisions for Wind and Seismic* (*SDPWS*) for lateral design of wood structures. Design values for nailed diaphragms and shear walls have been deleted from the tables in Section 2306 because the values are in the SDPWS standard. However, design values for stapled shear walls and diaphragms still remain in the code. Although the deflection of nailed wood-frame diaphragms and shear walls is determined in accordance with AF&PA SDPWS, the deflection of stapled diaphragms and shear walls is not covered in the standard. Section 2305 provides the formulae and parameters required to calculate the deflection of blocked wood structural panel diaphragms and shear walls fastened with staples.

2306

Allowable Stress Design

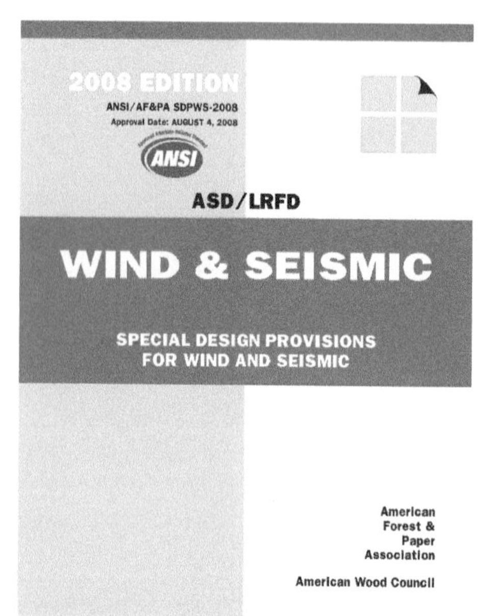

2008 edition of the AF&PA standard.
(American Wood Council, Leesburg, VA)

CHANGE TYPE: Modification

CHANGE SUMMARY: The provisions in Section 2306 addressing the allowable stress design of wood structures have been coordinated with those in the 2008 edition of the AF&PA standard, *Special Design Provisions for Wind and Seismic* (*SDPWS-08*).

2013 CODE: **2306.1 Allowable Stress Design.** The ~~structural analysis~~ design and construction of wood elements in structures using allowable stress design shall be in accordance with the following applicable standards:

(no change to list of allowable stress design standards)

2306.2 Wood-Frame Diaphragms. Wood-frame diaphragms shall be designed and constructed in accordance with AF&PA SDPWS. Where panels are fastened to framing members with staples, requirements and limitations of AF&PA SDPWS shall be met and the allowable shear values set forth in Table 2306.2(1) or 2306.2(2) shall be permitted. The allowable shear values in Tables 2306.2(1) and 2306.2(2) are permitted to be increased 40 percent for wind design.

Exception: [DSA-SS, DSA-SS/CC and OSHPD 1,2 & 4] Wood structural panel diaphragms using staples as fasteners are not permitted by DSA and OSHPD.

~~**2306.2.1 Wood Structural Panel Diaphragms.** Wood structural panel diaphragms shall be designed and constructed in accordance with AF&PA SDPWS. Wood structural panel diaphragms are permitted to resist horizontal forces, using the allowable shear capacities set forth in Table 2306.2.1(1) or 2306.2.1(2). The allowable shear capacities in Tables 2306.2.1(1) and 2306.2.1(2) are permitted to be increased 40 percent for wind design.~~

~~**2306.2.2 Single Diagonally Sheathed Lumber Diaphragms.** Single diagonally sheathed lumber diaphragms shall be designed and constructed in accordance with AF&PA SDPWS.~~

~~**2306.2.3 Double Diagonally Sheathed Lumber Diaphragms.** Double diagonally sheathed lumber diaphragms shall be designed and constructed in accordance with AF&PA SDPWS.~~

~~**2306.2.4**~~ **2306.2.1 Gypsum Board Diaphragm Ceilings.** Gypsum board diaphragm ceilings shall be in accordance with Section 2508.5.

TABLE ~~2306.2.1(1)~~ 2306.2(1) ALLOWABLE SHEAR VALUES (POUNDS PER FOOT) FOR WOOD STRUCTURAL PANEL DIAPHRAGMS UTILIZING STAPLES WITH FRAMING OF DOUGLAS-FIR-LARCH, OR SOUTHERN PINE[a] FOR WIND OR SEISMIC LOADING ~~[h]~~ [f]

TABLE ~~2306.2.1(2)~~ 2306.2(2) ALLOWABLE SHEAR VALUES (POUNDS PER FOOT) FOR WOOD STRUCTURAL PANEL BLOCKED DIAPHRAGMS UTILIZING MULTIPLE ROWS OF ~~FASTENERS~~ STAPLES (HIGH LOAD DIAPHRAGMS) WITH FRAMING OF DOUGLAS FIR, LARCH, OR SOUTHERN PINE[a] FOR WIND OR SEISMIC LOADING[b, g, h]

~~**2306.3 Wood Structural Panel Shear Walls.** Wood structural panel shear walls shall be designed and constructed in accordance with AF&PA SDPWS. Wood structural panel shear walls are permitted to resist horizontal forces, using the allowable capacities set forth in Table 2306.3. Allowable capacities in Table 2306.3 are permitted to be increased 40 percent for wind design.~~

2306.3 Wood-Frame Shear Walls. Wood-frame shear walls shall be designed and constructed in accordance with AF&PA SDPWS. Where panels are fastened to framing members with staples, requirements and limitations of AF&PA SDPWS shall be met and the allowable shear values set forth in Table 2306.3(1), 2306.3(2) or 2306.3(3) shall be permitted. The allowable shear values in Tables 2306.3(1) and 2306.3(2) are permitted to be increased 40 percent for wind design. Panels complying with ANSI/APA PRP-210 shall be permitted to use design values for Plywood Siding in the AF&PA SDPWS.

TABLE ~~2306.3~~ 2306.3(1) ALLOWABLE SHEAR VALUES (POUNDS PER FOOT) FOR WOOD STRUCTURAL PANEL SHEAR WALLS UTILIZING STAPLES WITH FRAMING OF DOUGLAS FIR-LARCH OR SOUTHERN PINE[a] FOR WIND OR SEISMIC LOADING [b, ~~h, i, j, l~~ f, g]

~~**2306.4 Lumber Sheathed Shear Walls.** Single and double diagonally sheathed lumber shear walls shall be designed and constructed in accordance with AF&PA SDPWS. Single and double diagonally sheathed lumber walls shall not be used to resist seismic forces in structures assigned to *Seismic Design Category* E or F.~~

~~**2306.5 Particleboard Shear Walls.** Particleboard shear walls shall be designed and constructed in accordance with AF&PA SDPWS. Particleboard shear walls shall be permitted to resist horizontal forces using the allowable shear capacities set forth in Table 2306.5. Allowable capacities in Table 2306.5 are permitted to be increased 40 percent for wind design. Particleboard shall not be used to resist seismic forces in structures assigned to *Seismic Design Category* D, E or F.~~

~~**2306.6 Fiberboard Shear Walls.** Fiberboard shear walls shall be designed and constructed in accordance with AF&PASDPWS. Fiberboard shear walls are permitted to resist horizontal forces, using the allowable shear capacities set forth in Table 2306.6. Allowable capacities in Table 2306.6 are permitted to be increased 40 percent for wind design. Fiberboard shall not be used to resist seismic forces in structures assigned to *Seismic Design Category* D, E or F.~~

2306 continues

2306 continues

~~**TABLE 2306.5 ALLOWABLE SHEAR FOR PARTICLEBOARD SHEAR WALL SHEATHING**[b]~~

~~PANEL GRADE~~	~~MINIMUM NOMINAL PANEL THICKNESS (inch)~~	~~MINIMUM NAIL PENETRATION IN FRAMING (inches)~~	~~Nail size (common or galvanized box)~~	~~PANELS APPLIED DIRECT TO FRAMING — Allowable shear (pounds per foot) nail spacing at panel edges (inches)~~[a]			
				~~6~~	~~4~~	~~3~~	~~2~~
~~M-S "Exterior Glue" and M-2 "Exterior" Glue"~~	~~3/8~~	~~11/2~~	~~6d~~	~~120~~	~~180~~	~~230~~	~~300~~
	~~3/8~~	~~11/2~~	~~8d~~	~~130~~	~~190~~	~~240~~	~~315~~
	~~1/2~~			~~140~~	~~210~~	~~270~~	~~350~~
	~~1/2~~	~~15/8~~	~~10d~~	~~185~~	~~275~~	~~360~~	~~460~~
	~~5/8~~			~~200~~	~~305~~	~~395~~	~~520~~

TABLE ~~2306.6~~ 2306.3(2) ALLOWABLE SHEAR VALUES (plf) FOR WIND OR SEISMIC LOADING ON SHEAR WALLS OF FIBERBOARD SHEATHING BOARD CONSTRUCTION UTILIZING STAPLES FOR TYPE V CONSTRUCTION ONLY[a,b,c,d,e]

~~**2306.7 Shear Walls Sheathed With Other Materials.** Shear walls sheathed with portland cement plaster, gypsum lath, gypsum sheathing or gypsum board shall be designed and constructed in accordance with AF&PA SDPWS. Shear walls sheathed with these materials p are permitted to resist horizontal forces using the allowable shear capacities set forth in Table 2306.7. Shear walls sheathed with portland cement plaster, gypsum lath, gypsum sheathing or gypsum board shall not be used to resist seismic forces in structures assigned to *Seismic Design Category* E or F.~~

TABLE ~~2306.7~~ 2306.3(3) ALLOWABLE SHEAR VALUES FOR WIND OR SEISMIC FORCES FOR SHEAR WALLS OF LATH AND PLASTER OR GYPSUM BOARD WOOD FRAMED WALL ASSEMBLIES UTILIZING STAPLES

Because this code change affected many tables in Section 2306, the entire code change text is too extensive to be included here. Refer to Code Change S208-09/10 in the *2012 IBC Code Changes Resource Collection* for the complete text and history of the code change.

CHANGE SIGNIFICANCE: Section 2306 references the 2008 edition of the AF&PA standard, *Special Design Provisions for Wind and Seismic (SDPWS)* for lateral design of wood structures. The general term "wood frame" has been added as a clarification of the intent so the code now refers to wood frame diaphragms and shear walls. Design values for nailed diaphragms and shear walls were deleted from the previous tables because the values are in the SDPWS-08 standard. Design values for stapled shear walls and diaphragms remain in the tables in the code. Table footnotes have been revised to account for removal of allowable design values for nailed diaphragms and shear walls. Sections 2306.2 and 2306.3 have been revised to clarify that design and construction as well as limitations in the SDPWS are applicable to stapled diaphragms and shear walls. The sections referring to particleboard, fiberboard, and lumber-sheathed shear walls have been deleted because they are covered under the general term of "wood frame shear walls" and their design provisions are included in the SDPWS standard.

A new national consensus standard, APA PRP-210, has been added to address wood structural panel siding products that were formerly covered under several national standards such as APA PRP-108. Siding products manufactured to the ANSI/APA PRP-210 standard have been developed specifically for wall-covering/weatherproofing applications, carry an exterior exposure durability classification, and have equivalent shear performance on a thickness-by-thickness basis when nailed in accordance with Table 2306.3. The code permits panels complying with ANSI/APA PRP-210 to be designed using the values for plywood siding in the AF&PA SDPWS.

To clarify the intent, the figure that accompanies the diaphragms table has been modified. The figure in previous editions of the code has been difficult to interpret because of improper placement of the annotation lines. The new figure has a legend to better differentiate between blocking and framing members, and the annotation lines are more accurately placed in the figure. The design engineer is concerned with a specific diaphragm sheathing layout pattern with two loading cases, one for each orthogonal direction. Instead of six separate diaphragm configurations, the new figure shows the three diaphragm layout patterns and two load cases for each configuration. Although no technical changes were made to the figure, the new figure better illustrates the intent of the diaphragm design table.

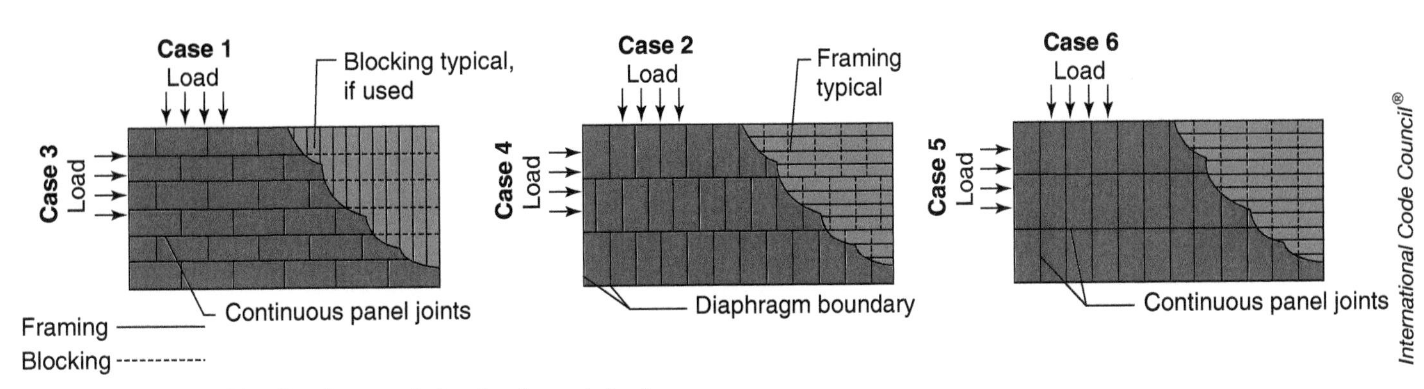

Layout patterns and loading for wood structural panel diaphragms.

2307

Load and Resistance Factor Design

CHANGE TYPE: Modification

CHANGE SUMMARY: The provisions in Section 2307 dealing with the load and resistance factor design of wood structures are now coordinated with the 2008 edition of the AF&PA standard, *Special Design Provisions for Wind and Seismic* (SDPWS-08).

2013 CODE: 2307.1 Load and Resistance Factor Design. The ~~structural analysis~~ design and construction of wood elements and structures using load and resistance factor design shall be in accordance with AF&PA NDS and AF&PA SDPWS.

~~**2307.1.1 Wood Structural Panel Shear Walls.** In structures assigned to Seismic Design Category D, E or F, where shear design values exceed 490 pounds per lineal foot (7154 N/m), all framing members receiving edge nailing from abutting panels shall not be less than a single 3-inch (76 mm) nominal member or two 2-inch (51 mm) nominal members fastened together in accordance with AF&PA NDS to transfer the design shear value between framing members. Wood structural panel joint and sill plate nailing shall be staggered at all panel edges. See Sections 4.3.6.1 and 4.3.6.4.2 of AF&PA SDPWS for sill plate size and anchorage requirements.~~

CHANGE SIGNIFICANCE: The requirements for 3X members at abutting panel joints in Section 2307.1.1 are no longer necessary because similar provisions are contained in Section 4.3.7.1 of SDPWS-08. The SDPWS requires 3X framing at adjoining panel edges and staggered nailing where nail spacing is 2 inches or less on center at adjoining panel edges,

2307 continues

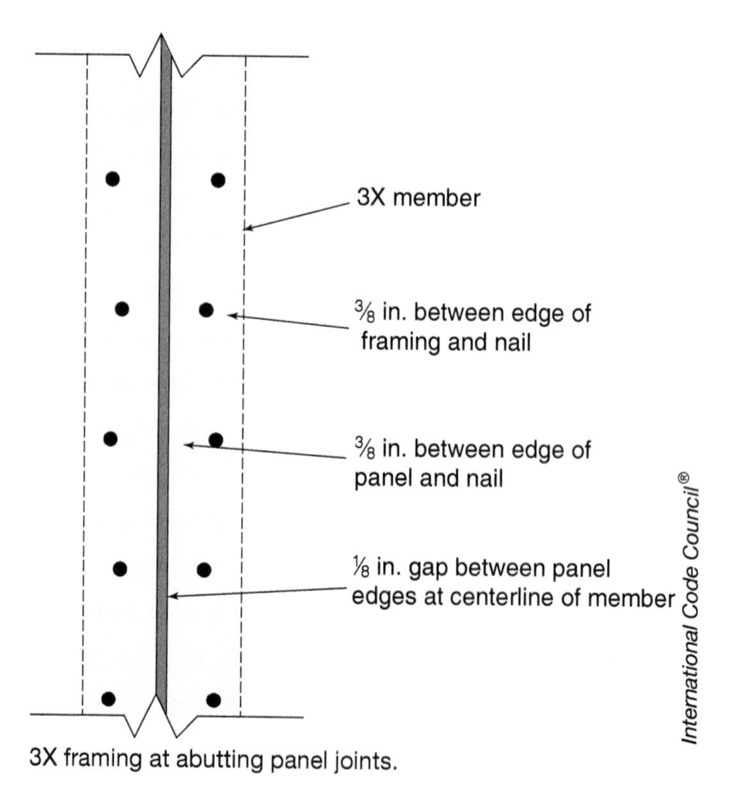

3X framing at abutting panel joints.

or where 10d common nails having penetration into framing members and blocking of more than 1½ inches are nailed at 3 inches or less on center at adjoining panel edges, or where the required nominal unit shear capacity on either side of the shear wall exceeds 700 plf for buildings in Seismic Design Category D, E, or F. An exception permits two 2X framing members provided they are fastened together in accordance with the NDS to transfer the shear between the members. When the fasteners connecting the two framing members are spaced less than 4 inches on center, the fasteners are required to be staggered.

2406.1, 2406.4

Safety Glazing—Hazardous Locations

CHANGE TYPE: Modification

CHANGE SUMMARY: The hazardous locations identified in the safety glazing provisions have been reorganized and clarified in order to provide better consistency between the CBC and CRC.

2013 CODE: 2406.1 Human Impact Loads. Individual glazed areas, including glass mirrors, in hazardous locations as defined in Section 2406.4 shall comply with Sections 2406.1.1 through 2406.1.4.

> **Exception:** Mirrors and other glass panels mounted or hung on a surface that provides a continuous backing support.

2406.4 Hazardous Locations. The ~~following~~ locations specified in Sections 2306.4.1 through 2406.4.7 shall be considered specific hazardous locations requiring safety glazing materials.~~:~~

~~1. Glazing in swinging doors except jalousies (see Section 2406.4.1).~~
~~2. Glazing in fixed and sliding panels of sliding door assemblies and panels in sliding and bifold closet door assemblies.~~
~~3. Glazing in storm doors.~~
~~4. Glazing in unframed swinging doors.~~
~~5. Glazing in doors and enclosures for hot tubs, whirlpools, saunas, steam rooms, bathtubs and showers. Glazing in any portion of a building wall enclosing these compartments where the bottom exposed edge of the glazing is less than 60 inches (1524 mm) above a standing surface.~~

2406.4.1 Glazing in Doors. Glazing in all fixed and operable panels of swinging, sliding, and bifold doors shall be considered a hazardous location.

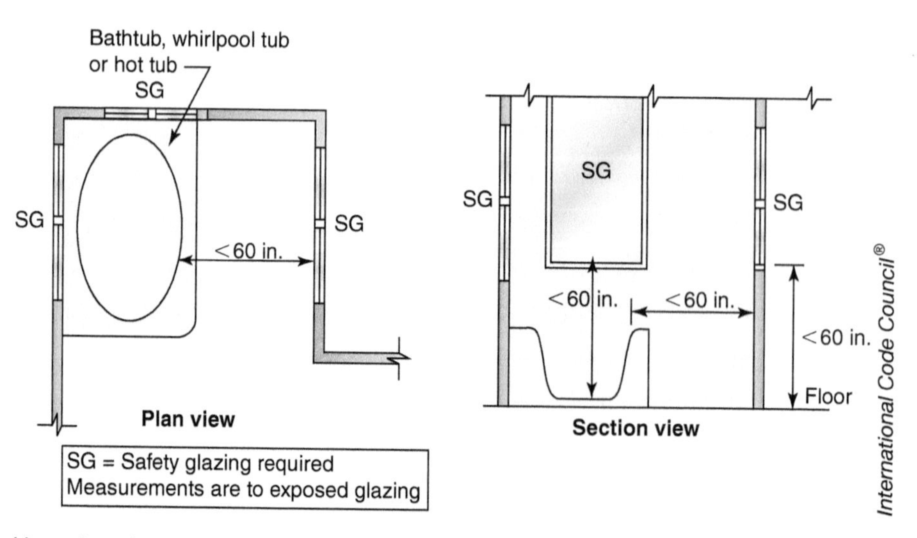

Hazardous locations near wet surfaces.

International Code Council®

Glazing near wet surfaces is considered as being in a hazardous location.

Exceptions:

1. Glazed openings of a size through which a 3-inch (76-mm)-diameter sphere is unable to pass.
2. Decorative glazing.
3. Glazing materials used as curved glazed panels in revolving doors.
4. Commercial refrigerated cabinet glazed doors.

~~6.~~ **2406.4.2 Glazing Adjacent to Doors.** Glazing in an individual fixed or operable panel adjacent to a door where the nearest ~~exposed~~ vertical edge of the glazing is within a 24-inch (610-mm) arc of either vertical edge of the door in a closed position and where the bottom exposed edge of the glazing is less than 60 inches (1524 mm) above the walking surface shall be considered a hazardous location.

Exceptions:

1. Decorative glazing.
2. ~~Panels where~~ Where there is an intervening wall or other permanent barrier between the door and glazing.
3. Where access through the door is to a closet or storage area 3 feet (914 mm) or less in depth. Glazing in this application shall comply with Section ~~2406.4, Item 7~~ 2406.4.3.
4. Glazing in walls ~~perpendicular to the plane of the door in a closed position, other than the wall towards which the door~~

2406.1, 2406.4 continues

2406.1, 2406.4 continued

~~swings when opened,~~ on the latch side of and perpendicular to the plane of the door in a closed position in one- and two-family dwellings or within dwelling units in Group R-2.

~~7.~~ **2406.4.3 Glazing in Windows.** Glazing in an individual fixed or operable panel~~, other than in those locations described in preceding Items 5 and 6, which~~ that meets all of the following conditions shall be considered a hazardous location:

~~7.~~1. ~~Exposed~~ The exposed area of an individual pane is greater than 9 square feet (0.84 m^2).
~~7.~~2. ~~Exposed~~ The bottom edge of the glazing is less than 18 inches (457 mm) above the floor.
~~7.~~3. ~~Exposed~~ The top edge of the glazing is greater than 36 inches (914 mm) above the floor.
~~7.~~4. One or more walking surface(s) are within 36 inches (914 mm), measured horizontally ~~of the plane~~ and in a straight line, of the glazing.

Exceptions: ~~Safety glazing for Item 7 is not required for the following installations:~~

~~1. A protective bar 11/2 inches (38 mm) or more in height, capable of withstanding a horizontal load of 50 pounds plf (730 N/m) without contacting the glass, is installed on the accessible sides of the glazing 34 inches to 38 inches (864 mm to 965 mm) above the floor.~~

1. Decorative glazing.
2. When a horizontal rail is installed on the accessible side(s) of the glazing 34 to 38 inches (864 to 965 mm) above the walking surface. The rail shall be capable of withstanding a horizontal load of 50 pounds per linear foot (730 N/m) without contacting the glass and be a minimum of 1½ inches (38 mm) in cross-sectional height.
~~2~~3. ~~The outboard~~ Outboard panes in insulating glass units or multiple glazing where the bottom exposed edge of the glass is 25 feet (7620 mm) or more above any grade, roof, walking surface, or other horizontal or sloped (within 45 degrees of horizontal) (0.78 rad) surface adjacent to the glass exterior.

~~8.~~ **2406.4.4 Glazing in Guards and Railings.** Glazing in guards and railings, including structural baluster panels and nonstructural in-fill panels, regardless of area or height above a walking surface, shall be considered a hazardous location.

~~9. Glazing in walls and fences enclosing indoor and outdoor swimming pools, hot tubs and spas where all of the following conditions are present:~~

~~9.1. The bottom edge of the glazing on the pool or spa side is less than 60 inches (1524 mm) above a walking surface on the pool or spa side of the glazing; and~~

~~9.2. The glazing is within 60 inches (1524 mm) horizontally of the water's edge of a swimming pool or spa.~~

2406.4.5 Glazing and Wet Surfaces. Glazing in walls, enclosures, or fences containing or facing hot tubs, spas, whirlpools, saunas, steam rooms, bathtubs, showers, and indoor or outdoor swimming pools, where the bottom exposed edge of the glazing is less than 60 inches (1524 mm) measured vertically above any standing or walking surface, shall be considered a hazardous location. This shall apply to single glazing and all panes in multiple glazing.

Exception: Glazing that is more than 60 inches (1524 mm), measured horizontally and in a straight line, from the water's edge of a bathtub, hot tub, spa, whirlpool, or swimming pool.

~~10.~~ **2406.4.6 Glazing Adjacent to Stairs and Ramps.** Glazing ~~adjacent to~~ where the bottom exposed edge of the glazing is less than 60 inches (1524 mm) above the plane of the adjacent walking surface of stairways, landings between flights of stairs, and ramps shall be considered a hazardous location ~~within 36 inches (914 mm) horizontally of a walking surface; when the exposed surface of the glass is less than 60 inches (1524 mm) above the plane of the adjacent walking surface~~.

Exceptions:

1. The side of a stairway, landing, or ramp that has a guard complying with the provisions of Sections 1013 and 1607.8, and the plane of the glass is greater than 18 inches (457 mm) from the railing.
2. Glazing 36 inches (914 mm) or more measured horizontally from the walking surface.

~~11.~~ **2406.4.7 Glazing Adjacent to the Bottom Stair Landing.** ~~Glazing adjacent to stairways within 60 inches (1524 mm) horizontally of the bottom tread of a stairway in any direction when the exposed surface of the glass is less than 60 inches (1524 mm) above the nose of the tread.~~ Glazing adjacent to the landing at the bottom of a stairway where the glazing is less than 36 inches (914 mm) above the landing and within 60 inches (1524 mm) horizontally of the bottom tread shall be considered a hazardous location.

Exception: ~~Safety glazing for Item 10 or 11 is not required for the following installations where:~~

~~1.~~ ~~The side of a stairway, landing or ramp which has~~ Glazing that is protected by a guard ~~or handrail, including balusters or in-fill panels,~~ complying with ~~the provisions of~~ Sections 1013 and 1607.8~~;~~ and ~~2. The~~ the plane of the glass is greater than 18 inches (457 mm) from the ~~railing~~ guard.

~~**2406.4.1 Exceptions.** The following products, materials and uses shall not be considered specific hazardous locations:~~

~~1. Openings in doors through which a 3-inch (76 mm) sphere is unable to pass.~~

~~2. Decorative glass in Section 2406.4, Item 1, 6 or 7.~~

2406.1, 2406.4 continues

2406.1, 2406.4 continued

3. ~~Glazing materials used as curved glazed panels in revolving doors.~~
4. ~~Commercial refrigerated cabinet glazed doors.~~
5. ~~Glass-block panels complying with Section 2101.2.5.~~
6. ~~Louvered windows and jalousies complying with the requirements of Section 2403.5.~~
7. ~~Mirrors and other glass panels mounted or hung on a surface that provides a continuous backing support.~~

CHANGE SIGNIFICANCE: An effective reorganization of the hazardous locations for safety glazing purposes has been accomplished, resulting in the elimination of conflicts, creation of consistency, and ease of use. By taking the 11 hazardous locations and seven exceptions that previously existed in Section 2604.4 and reformatting them into seven individual provisions with the appropriate exceptions located directly within the applicable provision, the understanding of the intent should be much easier. Code users should be aware that although this was predominately a reorganization effort, some technical changes do result from the relocation or combination of provisions. As an example, see the discussion related to Section 2406.4.5.

The point-by-point explanation that follows should assist in understanding the reorganization of the various requirements.

The exception to Section 2406.1 was relocated from Item 7 in Section 2406.4.1 with no change in application because these items were previously exempted.

The "glazing in doors" requirements of new Section 2406.4.1 now include Items 1 through 4 from previous Section 2406.4. In a technical change, jalousie windows were previously exempted from the safety glazing requirement. Because jalousies are no longer listed among the exceptions, they are now required to be safety glazing unless exempted by the limited size or decorative glazing provisions of Exception 1 or 2. The four exceptions that are listed in this section were previously listed as the first four exceptions in Section 2406.4.1.

Section 2406.4.2 dealing with "glazing adjacent to doors" and several of the exceptions were previously found in Item 6 of Section 2406.4. New Exception 1 was previously Exception 2 in Section 2406.4.1. Exception 4 was revised in order to clarify the provisions and to coordinate with similar text in the IRC.

The glazed window requirements of Section 2406.4.3 now combine the provisions of previous Section 2406.4, Item 7, and Exception 2 from Section 2406.4.1. The provisions regarding protecting the window from impact by the use of a horizontal rail have been revised in order to coordinate with the language of the IRC.

Section 2406.4.5 addressing glazing adjacent to wet surfaces is essentially a combination of the previous provisions related to glazing adjacent to hot tubs, bathtubs, and showers (Item 5 in Section 2406.4) as well as pools and spas (Item 9 in Section 2406.4). A single section relating to hazardous glazing adjacent to water will include the criteria that previously applied to walls and fences around a pool as the means to determine if the glazing is in a hazardous location. This revision will affect the application of the requirements to the bathtubs, showers, and other items that were previously included in Item 5 in Section 2406.4. The issue of glazing adjacent to a freestanding bathtub is addressed in the same manner as a hot tub, spa, or whirlpool. To illustrate the most significant impact of the change, consider a bathroom with a shower that is enclosed on three sides by solid walls and on the fourth side by a set of glass doors. Previously, these four sides created the "enclosure" for the shower and the only location regulated for safety glazing purposes was the glass doors. Under the revised provisions, if a person would step out of the enclosed shower and a window in the wall of the bathroom is located within the established 60-inch height and 60-inch horizontal distance, that window is regulated. Previously, because the bathroom window was considered outside of the shower "enclosure," it would have been regulated by the general window requirements (Section 2406.4, Item 7) and not by the shower enclosure provisions of Section 2406.4, Item 5.

The provisions of Sections 2406.4.6 and 2406.4.7 will replace what had previously been Section 2406.4, Items 10 and 11, addressing two different locations related to glazing near stairways. The primary distinction is that Section 2406.4.7 will only regulate the glazing that is adjacent to the bottom landing on a stair. Therefore, when a stairway terminates at a floor level, Section 2406.4.7 would be applicable within 60 inches of the bottom tread, but if the landing were located between two adjacent flights of stairs, then Section 2406.4.6 would be the applicable provision. Code users should note that the provisions dealing with glazing at the bottom of the stair will apply when the bottom edge of the glazing is less than 36 inches above the landing. Previously, any glazing that was less than 60 inches above the nosing of the last tread was regulated. The reduction down to the 36-inch height was made based on an exception within the IRC exempting safety glazing where a solid wall or panel that places the glazing at or above the handrail or guard height is capable of withstanding the guard loading requirements.

2406.2

Safety Glazing—Impact Test

CHANGE TYPE: Modification

CHANGE SUMMARY: The default impact test criteria have been revised to impose the more restrictive test methodology. The higher impact requirements will apply unless the tables in Section 2406.2 allow for a lower impact test to be used.

2013 CODE: 2406.2 Impact Test. Where required by other sections of this code, glazing shall be tested in accordance with CPSC 16 CFR 1201. Glazing shall comply with the test criteria for Category ~~I or~~ II, ~~as~~, unless otherwise indicated in Table 2406.2(1).

> **Exception:** Glazing not in doors or enclosures for hot tubs, whirlpools, saunas, steam rooms, bathtubs, and showers shall be permitted to be tested in accordance with ANSI Z97.1. Glazing shall comply with the test criteria for Class A, ~~or B as~~ unless otherwise indicated in Table 2406.2(2).

CHANGE SIGNIFICANCE: Previously, a reference to Tables 2406.2(1) and 2406.2(2) was simply provided in order to establish the appropriate test criteria for safety glazing based on the size and location of the glazing. However, the tables did not address all of the hazardous locations listed in Section 2406.4. Without any specific test criteria assigned to many of the safety glazing locations, the requirements were confusing and difficult to enforce. As an example, the locations that were previously listed in Items 8, 9, 10, and 11 of Section 2406.4 were not addressed in either of the two glazing classification tables and therefore no appropriate test criteria were identified.

By modifying the base paragraph and exception as indicated, the more severe impact test becomes the default requirement (Class II, or Class A where applicable). Then, by referencing the tables, the lower

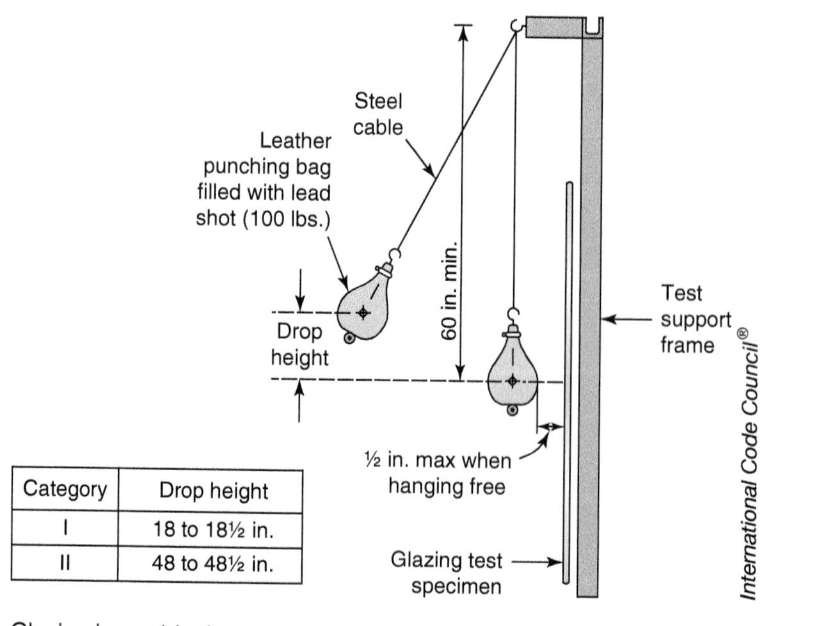

Category	Drop height
I	18 to 18½ in.
II	48 to 48½ in.

Glazing impact test.

impact testing procedures can now be used when the tables indicate those criteria are appropriate, ensuring that the test criteria are addressed for every hazardous location.

The use of the proper test criteria is important to ensure that the safety glazing can truly withstand the anticipated human impact loads it may face.

2510.6

Water-Resistive Barriers for Stucco Applications

CHANGE TYPE: Modification

CHANGE SUMMARY: In order to reduce the likelihood of moisture getting into the building, detailed requirements have been provided for the installation of the two layers of weather-resistive barriers that are required behind stucco-covered exterior walls.

2013 CODE: 2510.6 Water-Resistive Barriers. Water-resistive barriers shall be installed as required in Section 1404.2 and, where applied over wood-based sheathing, shall include a water-resistive vapor-permeable barrier with a performance at least equivalent to two layers of Grade D paper. The individual layers shall be installed independently such that each layer provides a separate continuous plane and any flashing (installed in accordance with Section 1405.4) intended to drain to the water-resistive barrier is directed between the layers.

> **Exception:** Where the water-resistive barrier that is applied over wood-based sheathing has a water resistance equal to or greater than that of 60-minute Grade D paper and is separated from the stucco by an intervening, substantially non-water-absorbing layer or drainage space.

CHANGE SIGNIFICANCE: When installing stucco, a weather-resistive barrier has been required to have a performance level "at least equivalent to two layers" of Grade D paper, however there has been no specific information to indicate how the layers are to be installed. When installing two layers, there are two separate methods of installation, which provide different levels of performance, installing the layers together or installing them separately. These two options are often recognized as a "two-ply system" or a "two-layer system," respectively. Where each layer of the water-resistive barrier is installed individually (the two-layer system), a better level of moisture protection is provided. When installed individually, the interior layer is configured to form a continuous drainage plane and is integrated with the flashing. The independent outboard layer serves to separate and protect the inner layer from the stucco and allows a space

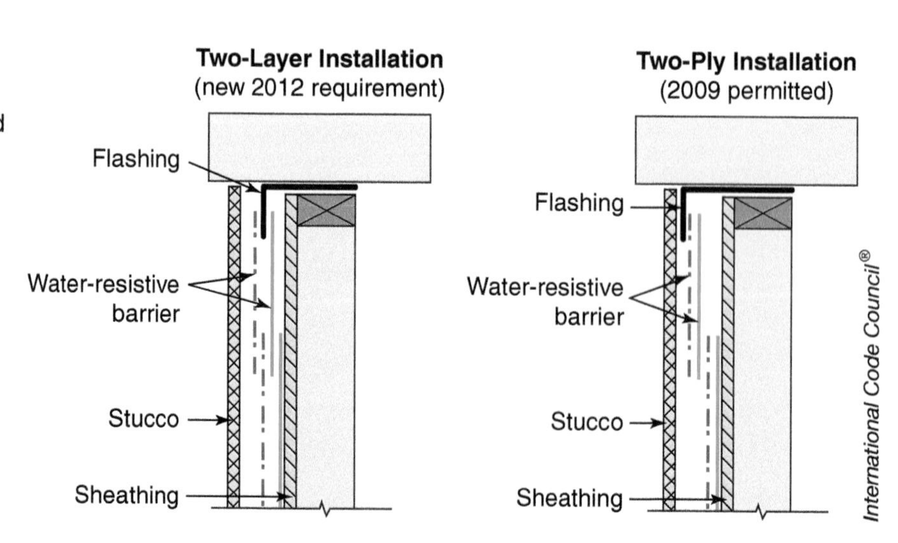

Installation of water-resistive barrier.

between the two layers to improve drainage. If the layers are installed together (the two-ply system), then they function as a single layer, and the only benefit of using two layers is the additional water resistance.

The primary benefit of using two layers of water-resistive barrier (WRB) can only be realized if the method and manner of the installation establishes a continuous drainage plane, separated from the stucco. In a two-layer system, each layer provides a separate and distinct function. The primary function of the inboard layer is to resist water penetration into the building cavity. This interior layer should be integrated with window and door flashings, the weep screed at the bottom of the wall, and any through-wall flashings or expansion joints. The inner layer becomes the drainage plane for any incidental water that gets through the outer layer or at one of the joints or openings or where the outer layer is damaged. The primary function of the outboard layer (layer that comes in contact with the stucco) is to separate the stucco from the water-resistive barrier. This layer has historically been called a sacrificial layer, intervening layer, or bond break layer.

Where each layer is installed independently as the code now requires, it becomes possible to install each layer to meet its intended function. A continuous drainage plane can be established on the inboard layer. However, this is not the case with a two-ply system that functions as a single layer with additional water resistance as the only benefit. If additional water holdout provides no other benefit, then the installation of a superior single-layer WRB would be sufficient.

The new language should ensure that the two required layers are installed "independently" to provide the best level of protection possible based on the two installation options.

2603.10, 2603.10.1

Special Approval of Foam Plastics

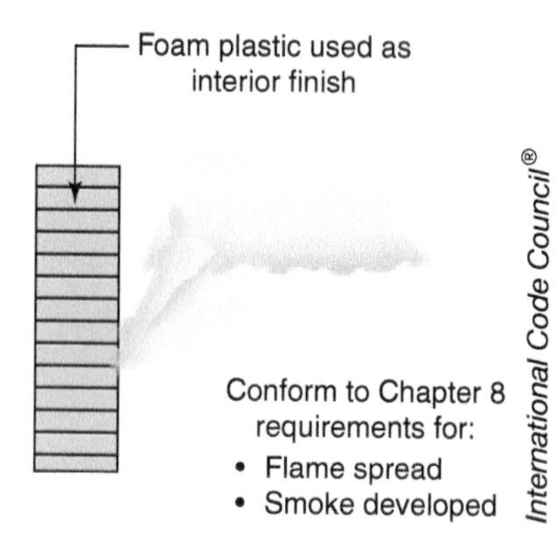

Special approval testing.

CHANGE TYPE: Modification

CHANGE SUMMARY: The specific approval requirements now ensure that the smoke development of all assemblies that contain foam plastic is evaluated, regardless of the test standard used.

2013 CODE: **~~2603.9~~ 2603.10 Special Approval.** Foam plastic shall not be required to comply with the requirements of Sections 2603.4 through ~~2603.7~~ 2603.8, where specifically approved based on large-scale tests such as, but not limited to, NFPA 286 (with the acceptance criteria of Section 803.2), FM 4880, UL 1040, or UL 1715. Such testing shall be related to the actual end-use configuration and be performed on the finished manufactured foam plastic assembly in the maximum thickness intended for use. Foam plastics that are used as interior finish on the basis of special tests shall also conform to the flame-spread and smoke-developed requirements of Chapter 8. Assemblies tested shall include seams, joints, and other typical details used in the installation of the assembly and shall be tested in the manner intended for use.

2603.10.1 Exterior Walls. Testing based on Section 2603.10 shall not be used to eliminate any component of the construction of an exterior wall assembly when that component was included in the construction that has met the requirements of Section 2603.5.5.

CHANGE SIGNIFICANCE: The imposition of the smoke-development requirements when using any of the special approval test standards for assemblies contain foam plastic now ensures that assemblies tested using these special approval options will provide a comparable level of performance and safety as would be required by the general provisions of Chapters 8 and 26. When using the test methods allowed by Section 2603.10, only NFPA 286 by virtue of the reference to Section 803.2 previously imposed any limitation on the smoke development. The other tests—FM 4880, UL 1040, and UL 1715—do not contain any smoke-development criterion and lack any reference to them. Therefore, compliance with the smoke-development requirements of Chapters 7, 8, and 26 was not specified.

In general, all thermal and sound-insulating materials addressed by the code, including noncombustible insulation materials and foam plastics, must meet certain minimum performance levels for the material to be used in the building, including those criteria related to both flame spread (fire growth) and smoke production. When using the special approval tests for foam plastics, testing must relate to the actual end-use configuration based on the finished assembly in the maximum thickness intended for use. But, as mentioned earlier, the previous Section 2603.9 did not clearly state whether it included or excluded smoke development requirements.

Chapter 8 is now referenced and along with the flame-spread and smoke-developed ratings using the ASTM E84 and UL 723 test methods. As a means to illustrate the application of this code change, consider the following example. Under the 2010 CBC, Section 2603.9 was allowed as an alternate to the plenum provisions of Sections 2603.7 and 2604 and would permit foam plastics in a plenum without the installation of a thermal barrier and without any limitation on the smoke-development rating, even if the thermal barrier was eliminated.

It has now been clarified that the "special approval" testing of Section 2603.10.1 cannot be used to eliminate any component of an assembly that was included in the test required by Section 2603.5.5. This ensures that the assemblies used for both of these tests are identical. Section 2603.5.5 requires that exterior walls with foam plastic insulation are tested to the NFPA 285 standard. This standard uses a more severe fire exposure and is run for a longer period of time than most of the tests listed in Section 2603.10. To illustrate this provision, consider the following situation. A single layer of gypsum wallboard is used to cover the interior surface of a wall assembly containing foam plastic insulation when it is tested to the NFPA 285 standard. Because one of the purposes of Section 2603.10 is to allow for the thermal barrier to be removed, it is proposed to test the wall to one of the four listed standards, but in this test, the gypsum would be removed to determine if the thermal barrier could be eliminated. Testing different assemblies to different requirements will not reflect the actual end-use configuration or show that the same assembly can meet both of the code's requirements (Sections 2603.5.5 and 2603.10). This would be an "apples to oranges" comparison and would be of little value in evaluating the acceptability of the wall assembly.

PART 7

Building Services, Special Devices, and Special Conditions

Chapters 27 through 34

- **Chapter 27** Electrical No changes addressed
- **Chapter 28** Mechanical Systems No changes addressed
- **Chapter 29** Plumbing Systems No changes addressed
- **Chapter 30** Elevators and Conveying Systems
- **Chapter 31** Special Construction
- **Chapter 32** Encroachments into the Public Right-of-Way No changes addressed
- **Chapter 33** Safeguards during Construction No changes addressed
- **Chapter 34** Existing Structures No changes addressed

Although building services such as electrical systems (Chapter 27), mechanical systems (Chapter 28), and plumbing systems (Chapter 29) are regulated primarily through separate and distinct codes, a limited number of provisions are set forth in the *California Building Code*. Chapter 30 regulates elevators and similar conveying systems to a limited degree, as most requirements are found in American Society of Mechanical Engineers standards. The special construction provisions of Chapter 31 include those types of elements or structures that are not conveniently addressed in other portions of the code. By special construction, the code is referring to membrane structures, pedestrian walkways, tunnels, awnings, canopies, marquees, and similar building features that are unregulated elsewhere. Chapter 32 governs the encroachment of structures into the public right-of-way, while Chapter 33 addresses safety during construction and the protection of adjacent public and private properties. Provisions regulating the alteration, repair, addition, and change of occupancy of existing structures are established in Chapter 34. ■

3007

Fire Service Access Elevators

3008

Occupant Evacuation Elevators

3111

Solar Photovoltaic Panels/Modules

APPENDIX L

Earthquake-Recording Instruments

APPENDIX M

Tsunami-Generated Flood Hazards

3007

Fire Service Access Elevators

CHANGE TYPE: Modification

CHANGE SUMMARY: Many of the provisions addressing fire service access elevators have now been coordinated with those applicable to occupant evacuation elevators to ensure that the fire service access elevators are able to continue to function and serve their intended purpose during an emergency.

2013 CODE:

SECTION 3007
FIRE SERVICE ACCESS ELEVATOR

3007.1 General. Where required by Section 403.6.1, every floor of the building shall be served by fire service access elevators complying with Sections 3007.1 through 3007.10. Except as modified in this section, fire service access elevators shall be installed in accordance with this chapter and *California Code of Regulations, Title 8, Division 1, Chapter 4, Subchapter 6, Elevator Safety Orders.*

3007.2 Phase I Emergency Recall Operation. Actuation of any building fire alarm initiating device shall initiate Phase I emergency recall operation on all fire service access elevators in accordance with *California Code of Regulations, Title 8, Division 1, Chapter 4, Subchapter 6, Elevator Safety Orders.* All other elevators shall remain in normal service unless Phase I emergency recall operation is manually initiated by a separate, required, three-position, key-operated "Fire Recall" switch or automatically initiated by the associated elevator lobby, hoistway, or elevator machine room smoke detectors. In addition, if the building

3007 continues

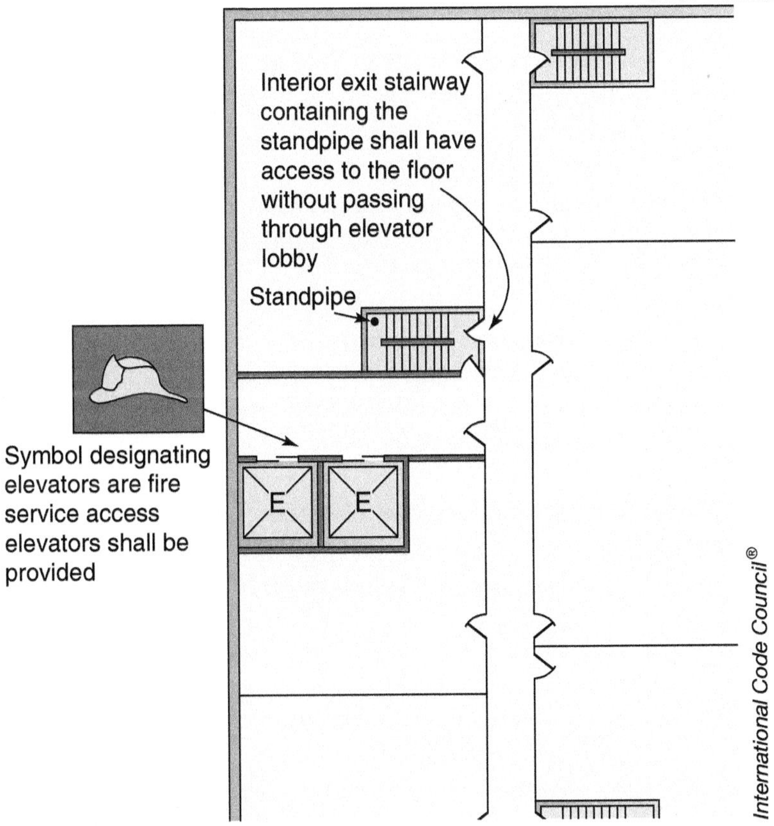

Interior exit stairway containing the standpipe shall have access to the floor without passing through elevator lobby

Standpipe

Symbol designating elevators are fire service access elevators shall be provided

E

E

International Code Council®

Fire service access elevator.

3007 continues

also contains occupant evacuation elevators in accordance with Section 3008, an independent, three-position, key-operated "Fire Recall" switch conforming to the applicable requirements in *California Code of Regulations, Title 8, Division 1, Chapter 4, Subchapter 6, Elevator Safety Orders* shall be provided at the designated level for each fire service access elevator.

3007.3 Automatic Sprinkler System. The building shall be equipped throughout by an automatic sprinkler system in accordance with Section 903.3.1.1, except as otherwise permitted by Section 903.3.1.1.1 and as prohibited by Section 3007.3.1.

3007.3.1 Prohibited Locations. Automatic sprinklers shall not be installed in elevator machine rooms, elevator machine spaces, and elevator hoistways of fire service access elevators.

3007.3.2 Sprinkler System Monitoring. The sprinkler system shall have a sprinkler control valve supervisory switch and waterflow-initiating device provided for each floor that is monitored by the building's fire alarm system.

3007.4 Water Protection. An approved method to prevent water from infiltrating into the hoistway enclosure from the operation of the automatic sprinkler system outside the enclosed fire service access elevator lobby shall be provided.

3007.5 Shunt Trip. Means for elevator shutdown in accordance with Section 3006.5 shall not be installed on elevator systems used for fire service access elevators.

~~3007.2~~ 3007.6 Hoistway Enclosures ~~Protection~~. The fire service access elevator hoistway shall be located in a shaft enclosure complying with Section 713.

3007.6.1 Structural Integrity of Hoistway Enclosures. The fire service access elevator hoistway enclosure shall comply with Sections 403.2.3.1 through 403.2.3.4.

~~3007.3~~ 3007.6.2 Hoistway Lighting. When firefighters' emergency operation is active, the entire height of the hoistway shall be illuminated at not less than 1 foot-candle (11 lux) as measured from the top of the car of each fire service access elevator.

~~3007.4~~ 3007.7 Fire Service Access Elevator Lobby. The fire service access elevator shall open into a fire service access elevator lobby in accordance with Sections 3007.7.1 through 3007.7.5.

> **Exception:** Where a fire service access elevator has two entrances onto a floor, the second entrance shall be permitted to open into an elevator lobby in accordance with Section 708.14.1.

~~3007.4.1~~ 3007.7.1 Access. The fire service access elevator lobby shall have direct access ~~to an exit enclosure~~ *from the enclosed elevator lobby to a smokeproof enclosure complying with Section 909.20.*

Exception: *Access to a smokeproof enclosure shall be permitted to be through a protected path of travel that has a level of fire protection not less than the elevator lobby enclosure. The protected path shall be separated from the enclosed elevator lobby through an opening protected by a smoke and draft control assembly in accordance with Section 716.5.3.*

~~3007.4.2~~ 3007.7.2 Lobby Enclosure. The fire service access elevator lobby shall be enclosed with a smoke barrier having a ~~minimum 1-hour~~ fire-resistance rating of not less than one hour, except that lobby doorways shall comply with Section 3007.7.3.

> **Exception:** Enclosed fire service access elevator lobbies are not required at the levels of exit discharge ~~street floor~~.

~~3007.4.3~~ 3007.7.3 Lobby Doorways. Other than the door to the hoistway, each doorway to a fire service access elevator lobby shall be provided with a ~~doorway that is protected with a~~ ¾-hour fire door assembly complying with Section 716.5. The fire door assembly shall also comply with the smoke and draft control door assembly requirements of Section 716.5.3.1 with the UL 1784 test conducted without the artificial bottom seal.

~~3007.4.4~~ 3007.7.4 Lobby Size. *Regardless of any number of fire service access elevators served by the same elevator lobby, the ~~Each~~* enclosed fire service access elevator lobby shall be a minimum of not less than 150 square feet (14 m^2) in area with a minimum dimension of 8 feet (2440 mm).

3007.7.5 Fire Service Access Elevator Symbol. A pictorial symbol of a standardized design designating which elevators are fire service access elevators shall be installed on each side of the hoistway door frame on the portion of the frame at right angles to the fire service access elevator lobby. The fire service access elevator symbol shall be designed as shown in Figure 3007.7.5 and shall comply with the following:

1. The fire service access elevator symbol shall be not less than 3 inches (76 mm) in height.
2. The vertical centerline of the fire service access elevator symbol shall be centered on the hoistway door frame. Each symbol shall not be less than 78 inches (1981 mm) and not more than 84 (2134 mm) inches above the finished floor at the threshold.

FIGURE 3007.7.5
FIRE SERVICE ACCESS ELEVATOR SYMBOL

~~3007.6~~ 3007.8 Elevator System Monitoring. The fire service access elevator shall be continuously monitored at the fire command center by a standard emergency service interface system meeting the requirements of NFPA 72.

~~3007.7~~ 3007.9 Electrical Power. The following features serving each fire service access elevator shall be supplied by both normal power and Type 60/Class 2/Level 1 standby power:

1. Elevator equipment.

3007 continued

3007 continues

2. Elevator hoistway lighting.
3. Elevator machine room ventilation and cooling equipment.
4. Elevator controller cooling equipment.

~~3007.7.1~~ 3007.9.1 Protection of Wiring or Cables. Wires or cables that are located outside of the elevator hoistway and machine room and that provide normal or standby power, control signals, communication with the car, lighting, heating, air conditioning, ventilation, and fire-detecting systems to fire service access elevators shall be protected by construction having a ~~minimum 1-hour~~ fire-resistance rating of not less than 2 hours, or shall be circuit integrity cable having a ~~minimum 1-hour~~ fire-resistance rating of not less than 2 hours.

> **Exception:** Wiring and cables to control signals are not required to be protected provided that wiring and cables do not serve Phase II emergency in-car operation.

~~3007.5~~ 3007.10 Standpipe Hose Connection. A Class I standpipe hose connection in accordance with Section 905 shall be provided in the ~~exit enclosure~~ interior exit stairway and ramp having direct access from the fire service access elevator lobby.

3007.10.1 Access. The exit enclosure containing the standpipe shall have access to the floor without passing through the fire service access elevator lobby.

CHANGE SIGNIFICANCE: In high-rise buildings that are more than 120 feet in height, fire service access elevators must be provided in accordance with Section 3007. In order to ensure that these elevators function as they are intended and are available for the fire department's use in dealing with emergencies, a number of changes have been made to the requirements.

The emergency recall provisions of Section 3007.2 ensure that the elevator can be recalled quickly to the designated level and is therefore available when the responding firefighters arrive on the scene. Inclusion of these provisions in the code helps coordinate with the requirements of the ASME A17.1 elevator standard and provides a standardized method of recalling the elevators for the use of the fire service.

Sprinkler system provisions were added in order to clarify that a sprinkler system is mandated in those high-rise buildings provided with fire service access elevators, however the sprinkler system is prohibited within the associated elevator machine rooms, elevator machine spaces, or hoistways that serve the fire service elevator. Similar to the requirements for occupant evacuation elevators found in Section 3008.3, the provision differs in that the sprinkler system is not to be installed within the hoistway of the fire service access elevator.

The water protection requirements of Section 3007.4 should be viewed as providing performance language that will permit any number of options to prevent water from an operating sprinkler system from finding its way into the elevator hoistway enclosure, including the installation of drains, a sloped floor, or other solutions. Water does cause problems for elevators during a fire, so providing some means of stopping the water from entering the hoistway is important. It should be noted that the requirements are only applicable to sprinklers that are outside of the lobby and are not applicable for sprinklers that are activated within the lobby. The lobby sprinklers are excluded because the elevators will go into fire department recall if there is smoke or a fire within the lobby.

Due to the restrictions of Section 3007.3 regarding the sprinkler system installation and prohibitions, Section 3007.5 will prohibit the installation of the elevator shutdown system (shunt trip) that would typically be required by Section 3006.5. Because Section 3007.3 prohibits the installation of the sprinkler system in the hoistway and machine rooms, the provisions of Section 3006.5 are not necessary.

Section 3007.6.1 dealing with the structural integrity of the hoistway enclosures was added to ensure the shafts protecting the fire service elevator remain intact and are therefore usable by the responding firefighters. This issue of hardening of the hoistway shafts was one of the recommendations that came out of the NIST World Trade Center Report and has been incorporated elsewhere in the code.

Section 3007.7.5 provides a means to indicate which elevators in a building are designated as the fire service access elevators. The fire hat symbol that is used is already required inside of the elevator car cab by the requirements of the ASME A17.1 elevator standard and therefore will already be easily recognizable by the fire service.

The wiring protection requirements of Section 3007.9.1 address two separate aspects. The base paragraph has been revised so that any wiring outside of the hoistway or machine room is protected to a level of protection equivalent to the shaft enclosure itself. If the wiring is within the hoistway or machine room, it will inherently have this level of protection. Therefore, the provision only needs to address the supply wiring or feeders that are bringing the power into the shaft to ensure they are protected and can continue to power the elevator for the required time it is needed. The required level of protection for the wires or cables has also been increased from 1 hour to 2 hours. The 2-hour rating was selected because it is consistent with the minimum required fire-resistance rating of the hoistway and the fire pump feeder enclosure rating. This degree of protection helps ensure that the elevator is able to continue to function during the time periods that the fire service needs it. The exception recognizes that elevator landing fixtures that provide control signals such as hall call buttons and hall lanterns do not need to be protected to the same fire-resistance rating, because these signals are not necessary to ensure the viability of the fire service elevator during Phase II operation. It also recognizes that the elevator industry does not generally test the elevator landing fixtures to obtain a fire-resistance rating, therefore, protecting the wiring that serves those fixtures is not necessary.

The standpipe access requirements of Section 3007.10.1 will permit the fire department to connect and advance their attack hose onto the fire floor without opening the door between the elevator lobby and the floor. This additional separation helps to limit the possible spread of smoke from the fire floor into the elevator lobby. By minimizing the potential for smoke to spread into the lobby, as it would if the lobby doors had to be opened to run the hose onto the floor, the fire service elevator will be able to continue its operation and serve as a staging area and supply route for the fire department. If smoke did move into the lobby, it would have the potential to affect the operation of the elevator or cause it to go into recall.

3008

Occupant Evacuation Elevators

CHANGE TYPE: Modification

CHANGE SUMMARY: The provisions addressing occupant evacuation elevators are now more closely coordinated with those regulating fire service access elevators.

2013 CODE:

SECTION 3008
OCCUPANT EVACUATION ELEVATORS

3008.1 General. Where elevators are to be used for occupant self-evacuation during fires, all passenger elevators for general public use shall comply with ~~this~~ Sections 3008.1 through 3008.11. Where other elevators are used for occupant self-evacuation, they shall also comply with these sections.

~~3008.4~~ 3008.1.1 Additional Exit Stairway. (no changes to text)

~~3008.2~~ 3008.1.2 Fire Safety and Evacuation Plan. (no changes to text)

3008.2 Phase I Emergency Recall Operation. An independent, three-position, key-operated "Fire Recall" switch complying with *California Code of Regulations, Title 8, Division 1, Chapter 4, Subchapter 6, Elevator Safety Orders* shall be provided at the designated level for each occupant evacuation elevator.

~~3008.3~~ 3008.2.1 Operation. The occupant evacuation elevators shall be used for occupant self-evacuation only in the normal elevator operating mode prior to Phase I emergency recall operation in accordance with *California Code of Regulations, Title 8, Division 1, Chapter 4, Subchapter 6, Elevator Safety Orders* and the building's fire safety and evacuation plan.

3008.2.2 Activation. Occupant evacuation elevator systems shall be activated by any of the following:

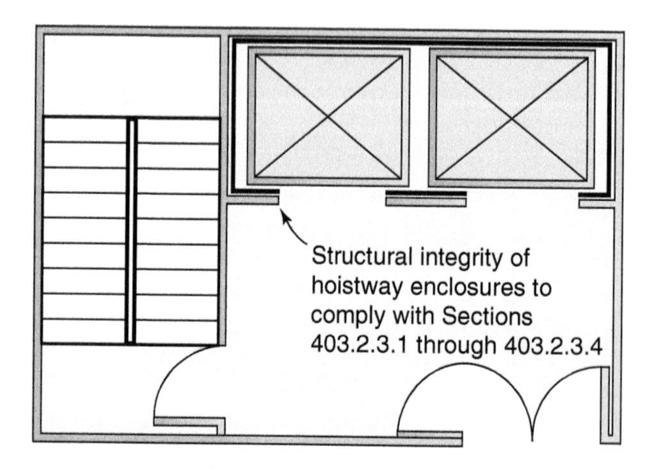

Occupant evacuation elevator system activated by any of the following:
- Operation of sprinkler system per Section 3008.3
- Smoke detectors
- Approved manual means

International Code Council®

Occupant evacuation elevator.

1. The operation of an automatic sprinkler system complying with Section 3008.3.
2. Smoke detectors required by another provision of the code.
3. Approved manual controls.

~~3008.10~~ 3008.4 Water Protection. ~~The occupant evacuation elevator hoistway shall be designed utilizing~~ An approved method to prevent water from infiltrating into the hoistway enclosure from the operation of the automatic sprinkler system ~~from infiltrating into the hoistway enclosure.~~ outside the enclosed occupant evacuation elevator lobby shall be provided.

~~3008.9~~ 3008.6 Hoistway Enclosure Protection. ~~The~~ Occupant evacuation elevator~~s~~ hoistways shall be located in ~~a hoistway~~ shaft enclosure~~(s)~~ complying with Section 713.

3008.6.1 Structural Integrity of Hoistway Enclosures. Occupant evacuation elevator hoistway enclosures shall comply with Sections 403.2.3.1 through 403.2.3.4.

~~3008.11~~ 3008.7 Occupant Evacuation Elevator Lobby. The occupant evacuation elevators shall open into an elevator lobby in accordance with Sections 3008.7.1 through 3008.7.7.

~~3008.11.3~~ 3008.7.3 Lobby Doorways. Other than the door to the hoistway, each doorway to an occupant evacuation elevator lobby shall be provided with a ~~doorway that is protected with a~~ ¾-hour fire door assembly complying with Section 716.5. The fire door assembly shall also comply with the smoke and draft control assembly requirements of Section 716.5.3.1 with the UL 1784 test conducted without the artificial bottom seal.

~~3008.15~~ 3008.9 Electrical Power. The following features serving each occupant evacuation elevator shall be supplied by both normal power and Type 60/Class 2/Level 1 standby power:

1. Elevator equipment.
2. Elevator machine room ventilation and cooling equipment.
3. Elevator controller cooling equipment.

~~3008.15.1~~ 3008.9.1 Protection of Wiring or Cables. Wires or cables that are located outside of the elevator hoistway and machine room and that provide normal or standby power, control signals, communication with the car, lighting, heating, air conditioning, ventilation, and fire-detecting systems to fire service access elevators shall be protected by construction having a ~~minimum 1-hour~~ fire-resistance rating of not less than 2 hours or shall be circuit integrity cable having a ~~minimum 1-hour~~ fire-resistance rating of not less than 2 hours.

> **Exception:** Wiring and cables to control signals are not required to be protected provided that wiring and cables do not serve Phase II emergency in-car operation.

3008 continued

3008 continues

~~3008.7~~ 3008.11 ~~High-Hazard Content~~ Hazardous Material Areas. (no changes to text)

CHANGE SIGNIFICANCE: Where elevators are to be used for occupant self-evacuation during a fire, they are required to be constructed and protected in accordance with Section 3008. The revisions that have been made in this section are intended to ensure the elevators are available during emergencies and can safely be used by the occupants on their own.

Section 3008.2 will allow the occupant evacuation elevators (OEEs) to be quickly recalled by the fire department when they enter the building. The required type of switch is specified (independent, three-position, key-operated), as well as compliance with the ASME A17.1 elevator standard, which contains additional information regarding the installation of the control.

The activation requirements of Section 3008.2.2 are intended to provide the means to initiate automatic activation of the OEE system. This type of system is not required but would be permissible to install and is capable of improving the evacuation process. Automatic operation of the OEE permits the elevator system to evaluate which floors to respond to and evacuate first and allows the OEE to function as an express elevator versus stopping at intermediate floors. These provisions need to be considered in conjunction with the operation provisions of Section 3008.2.1, which permit the OEE to be used for occupant self-evacuation "only in the normal elevator operating mode prior to Phase I emergency recall operation." Once the elevator goes into recall, it would only be used for fire department–assisted evacuations, regardless of whether it had been operating in self-evacuation or in an automatic operation mode.

The water protection requirements of Section 3008.4 should be viewed as providing performance language that will permit any number of options to prevent water from an operating sprinkler system from finding its way into the elevator hoistway enclosure, including the installation of drains, a sloped floor, or other solutions. Water causes problems for elevators during a fire, so providing some means of stopping the water from entering the hoistway is important. It is important to note, however, that the requirements are only applicable to sprinklers that are outside of the lobby and are not required for sprinklers that are activated within the lobby. The lobby sprinklers are excluded because the elevators will go into fire department recall if there is smoke or a fire within the lobby.

Section 3008.6.1 dealing with the structural integrity of the hoistway enclosures was added to ensure the shafts protecting the OEEs remain intact and are therefore usable by the occupants. This issue of hardening of the hoistway shafts was one of the recommendations that came out of the NIST World Trade Center Report and has been incorporated into the CBC in other locations. The reference to the provisions in the high-rise section describe how the hoistway enclosure is to be constructed, and this requirement will apply to any OEE hoistway when it is more than 120 feet above the lowest level of fire department vehicle access.

The lobby doorway requirements of Section 3008.7.3 correlate with the lobby doorway requirements for fire service access elevators in Section 3007.7.3. The integrity and tenability of elevator lobbies used for occupant evacuation are just as critical as those provided for fire service access. The revision to the first sentence clarifies that the requirement for the rated doors applies to all doors into the lobby, except for the hoistway door.

The wiring protection requirements of Section 3008.9.1 address two separate aspects. The base paragraph has been revised so that any wiring outside of the hoistway or machine room is protected to a level of protection equivalent to that of the shaft enclosure itself. If the wiring is within the hoistway or machine room, it will inherently have this level of protection. Therefore, the provision only needs to address the supply wiring or feeders that are bringing the power into the shaft to ensure they are protected and can continue to power the elevator for the required time it is needed. The required level of protection for the wires or cables has also been increased from 1 hour up to 2 hours. The 2-hour rating was selected because it is consistent with the minimum required fire-resistance rating of the hoistway and the fire pump feeder enclosure rating. This should ensure that the elevator is able to continue to function during the time period needed to evacuate the building. The exception recognizes that elevator landing fixtures that provide control signals such as hall call buttons and hall lanterns do not need to be protected to the same fire-resistance rating because these signals are not necessary to ensure the viability of the OEE.

3111

Solar Photovoltaic Panels/Modules

CHANGE TYPE: Clarification

CHANGE SUMMARY: Provisions for solar photovoltaic panels/modules have been added to the CBC.

2013 CODE: **SECTION 3111**
SOLAR PHOTOVOLTAIC PANELS/MODULES

3111.1 Solar Photovoltaic Power Systems. *Solar photovoltaic power systems shall be installed in accordance with Sections 3111.2 through 3111.5 and the California Electrical Code.*

> **Exception:** *Detached, nonhabitable Group U structures including, but not limited to, parking shade structures, carports, solar trellises and similar structures shall not be subject to the requirements of this section.*

3111.2 Marking. *Marking is required on interior and exterior direct-current (DC) conduit, enclosures, raceways, cable assemblies, junction boxes, combiner boxes and disconnects.*

3111.2.1 Materials. *The materials used for marking shall be reflective, weather resistant and suitable for the environment. Marking as required in Sections 3111.2.2 through 3111.2.4 shall have all letters capitalized with a minimum height of $^{3}/_{8}$ inch (9.5 mm) white on red background.*

3111.2.2 Marking Content. *The marking shall contain the words* "WARNING: PHOTOVOLTAIC POWER SOURCE."

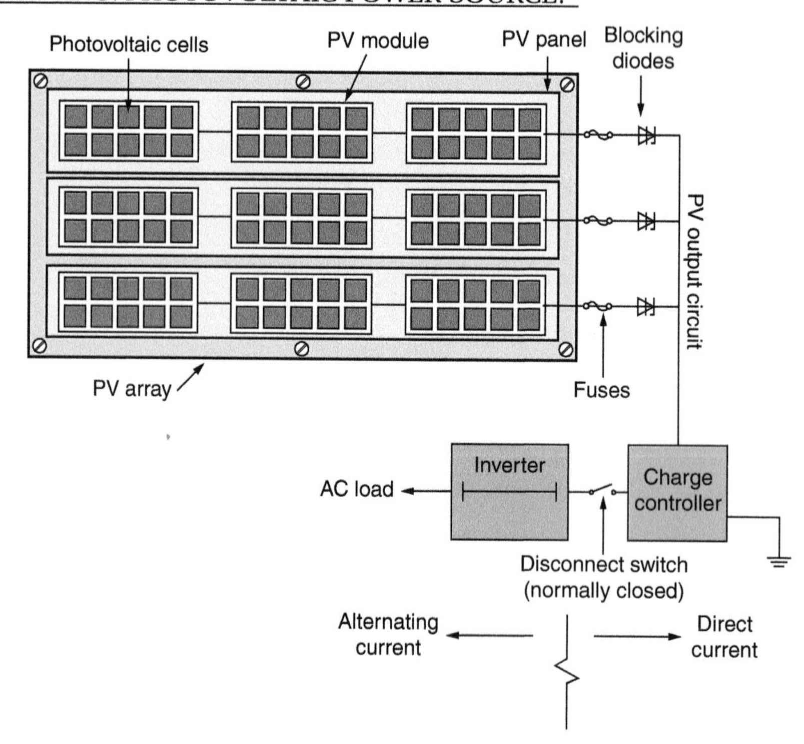

Basic schematic of photovoltaic system.

3111.2.3 Main Service Disconnect. *The marking shall be placed adjacent to the main service disconnect in a location clearly visible from the location where the disconnect is operated.*

3111.2.4 Location of Marking. *Marking shall be placed on interior and exterior DC conduit, raceways, enclosures and cable assemblies every 10 feet (3048 mm), within 1 foot (305 mm) of turns or bends and within 1 foot (305 mm) above and below penetrations of roof/ceiling assemblies, walls or barriers.*

3111.3 Locations of DC Conductors. *Conduit, wiring systems, and raceways for photovoltaic circuits shall be located as close as possible to the ridge or hip or valley and from the hip or valley as directly as possible to an outside wall to reduce trip hazards and maximize ventilation opportunities. Conduit runs between sub arrays and to DC combiner boxes shall be installed in a manner that minimizes the total amount of conduit on the roof by taking the shortest path from the array to the DC combiner box. The DC combiner boxes shall be located such that conduit runs are minimized in the pathways between arrays. DC wiring shall be installed in metallic conduit or raceways when located within enclosed spaces in a building. Conduit shall run along the bottom of load-bearing members.*

3111.4 Access and Pathways. *Roof access, pathways, and spacing requirements shall be provided in accordance with Sections 3111.4.1 through 3111.4.3.3.*

Exceptions:

1. *Residential structures shall be designed so that each photovoltaic array is no greater than 150 feet (45 720 mm) by 150 feet (45 720 mm) in either axis.*

2. *Panels/modules shall be permitted to be located up to the roof ridge where an alternative ventilation method approved by the fire chief has been provided or where the fire chief has determined vertical ventilation techniques will not be employed.*

3111.4.1 Roof Access Points. *Roof access points shall be located in areas that do not require the placement of ground ladders over openings such as windows or doors, and located at strong points of building construction in locations where the access point does not conflict with overhead obstructions such as tree limbs, wires, or signs.*

3111.4.2 Residential Systems for One- and Two-Family Dwellings. *Access to residential systems for one- and two-family dwellings shall be provided in accordance with Sections 3111.4.2.1 through 3111.4.2.4.*

3111.4.2.1 Residential Buildings with Hip Roof Layouts. *Panels/modules installed on residential buildings with hip roof layouts shall be located in a manner that provides a 3-foot-wide (914 mm) clear access pathway from the eave to the ridge on each roof slope where panels/*

3111 continues

3111 continues

modules are located. The access pathway shall be located at a structurally strong location on the building capable of supporting the live load of fire fighters accessing the roof.

Exception: *These requirements shall not apply to roofs with slopes of two units vertical in 12 units horizontal (2:12) or less.*

3111.4.2.2 Residential Buildings with a Single Ridge. *Panels/modules installed on residential buildings with a single ridge shall be located in a manner that provides two, 3-foot-wide (914 mm) access pathways from the eave to the ridge on each roof slope where panels/modules are located.*

Exception: *This requirement shall not apply to roofs with slopes of two units vertical in 12 units horizontal (2:12) or less.*

3111.4.2.3 Residential Buildings with Roof Hips and Valleys. *Panels/modules installed on residential buildings with roof hips and valleys shall be located no closer than 18 inches (457 mm) to a hip or a valley where panels/modules are to be placed on both sides of a hip or valley. Where panels are to be located on only one side of a hip or valley that is of equal length, the panels shall be permitted to be placed directly adjacent to the hip or valley.*

Exception: *These requirements shall not apply to roofs with slopes of two units vertical in 12 units horizontal (2:12) or less.*

3111.4.2.4 Residential Building Smoke Ventilation. *Panels/modules installed on residential buildings shall be located no higher than 3 feet (914 mm) below the ridge in order to allow for fire department smoke ventilation operations.*

3111.4.3 Other than Residential Buildings. *Access to systems for occupancies other than one- and two-family dwellings shall be provided in accordance with Sections 3111.4.3.1 through 3111.4.3.3.*

Exception: *Where it is determined by the fire code official that the roof configuration is similar to that of a one- or two-family dwelling, the residential access and ventilation requirements in Sections 3111.4.2.1 through 3111.4.2.4 shall be permitted to be used.*

3111.4.3.1 Access. *There shall be a minimum 6-foot-wide (1829 mm) clear perimeter around the edges of the roof.*

Exception: *Where either axis of the building is 250 feet (76 200 mm) or less, there shall be a minimum 4-foot-wide (1290 mm) clear perimeter around the edges of the roof.*

3111.4.3.2 Pathways. *The solar installation shall be designed to provide designated pathways. The pathways shall meet the following requirements:*

1. *The pathway shall be over areas capable of supporting the live load of fire fighters accessing the roof.*

2. *The centerline axis pathways shall be provided in both axes of the roof. Centerline axis pathways shall run where the roof structure is capable of supporting the live load of fire fighters accessing the roof.*

3. *Shall be a straight line not less than 4 feet (1290 mm) clear to skylights or ventilation hatches.*

4. *Shall be a straight line not less than 4 feet (1290 mm) clear to roof standpipes.*

5. *Shall provide not less than 4 feet (1290 mm) clear around roof access hatch with at least one not less than 4 feet (1290 mm) clear pathway to parapet or roof edge.*

3111.4.3.3 Smoke Ventilation. *The solar installation shall be designed to meet the following requirements:*

1. *Arrays shall be no greater than 150 feet (45 720 mm) by 150 feet (45 720 mm) in distance in either axis in order to create opportunities for fire department smoke ventilation operations.*

2. *Smoke ventilation options between array sections shall be one of the following:*
   2.1. *A pathway 8 feet (2438 mm) or greater in width.*
   2.2. *A 4-foot (1290 mm) or greater in width pathway and bordering roof skylights or smoke and heat vents.*
   2.3. *A 4-foot (1290 mm) or greater in width pathway and bordering 4-foot by 8-foot (1290 mm by 2438 mm) "venting cutouts" every 20 feet (6096 mm) on alternating sides of the pathway.*

3111.5 Ground-mounted photovoltaic arrays. *Ground-mounted photovoltaic arrays shall comply with Sections 3111.1 through 3111.3 and this section. Setback requirements shall not apply to ground-mounted, free-standing photovoltaic arrays. A clear, brush-free area of 10 feet (3048 mm) shall be required for ground-mounted photovoltaic arrays.*

CHANGE SIGNIFICANCE: The SFM is reproducing the solar PV system provisions of *International Fire Code* Section 605.11 into the *California Building Code* to provide for uniform design and enforcement. Many local enforcing agencies currently provide enforcement of the SFM solar photovoltaic power systems guidelines, which were the basis of the 2012 *International Fire Code* Section 605.11 provisions, or other locally adopted provisions through the building department/official which typically do not enforce the *California Fire Code*. Furthermore, the SFMs intent to have these provisions reproduced into the *California Building Code* is to afford local communities the ability to provide adequate enforcement without the reference to a different code or standard.

Appendix L

Earthquake-Recording Instruments

CHANGE TYPE: Addition

CHANGE SUMMARY: A new appendix requires earthquake-recording instruments to be installed in certain buildings located where the 1-second spectral response acceleration, S_1, is greater than 0.40.

2013 CODE: **1613.8 Earthquake-Recording Instrumentations.** For earthquake-recording instrumentations, see Appendix L.

APPENDIX L
EARTHQUAKE-RECORDING INSTRUMENTATION

SECTION L101
GENERAL

L101.1 General. Every structure located where the 1-second spectral response acceleration, S_1, in accordance with Section 1613.5 is greater than 0.40 that either (1) exceeds six stories in height with an aggregate floor area of 60,000 square feet (5574 m^2) or more or (2) exceeds 10 stories in height regardless of floor area shall be equipped with not less than three approved recording accelerographs. The accelerographs shall be interconnected for common start and common timing.

L101.2 Location. As a minimum, instruments shall be located at the lowest level, midheight, and near the top of the structure. Each instrument shall be located so that access is maintained at all times and is unobstructed by room contents. A sign stating "MAINTAIN CLEAR ACCESS TO THIS INSTRUMENT" in 1-inch (25 mm) block letters shall be posted in a conspicuous location.

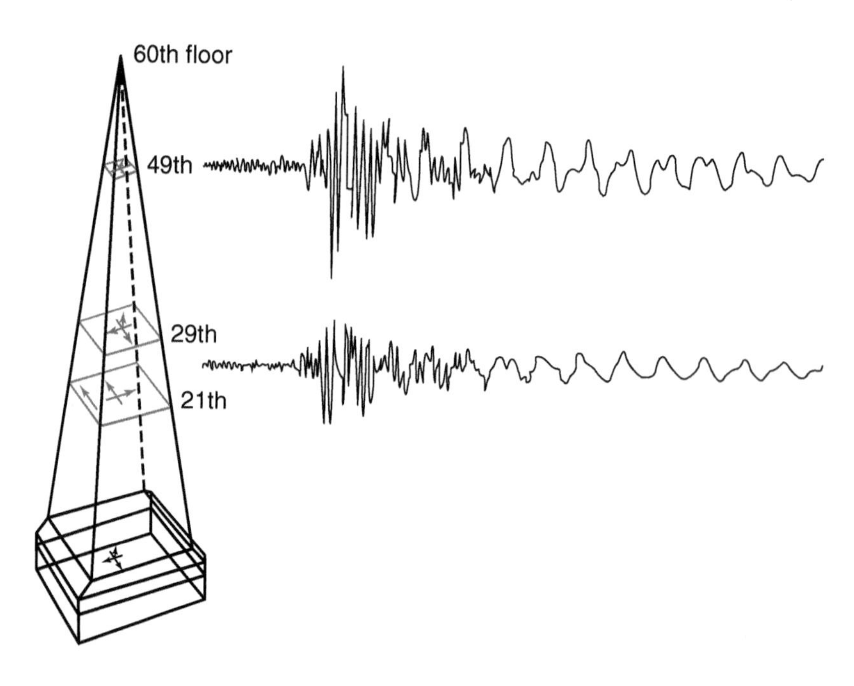

San Francisco transamerica tower. *(Courtesy of U.S. Geological Survey [USGS])*

L101.3 Maintenance. Maintenance and service of the instrumentation shall be provided by the owner of the structure. Data produced by the instrument shall be made available to the building official on request.

Maintenance and service of the instruments shall be performed annually by an approved testing agency. The owner shall file with the building official a written report from an approved testing agency, certifying that each instrument has been serviced and is in proper working condition. This report shall be submitted when the instruments are installed and annually thereafter. Each instrument shall have affixed to it an externally visible tag specifying the date of the last maintenance or service and the printed name and address of the testing agency.

CHANGE SIGNIFICANCE: Earthquake-recording instrumentation measurements provide fundamental information needed to cost effectively improve understanding of the seismic response and performance of buildings subjected to earthquake ground motions. The language of the new provision in the IBC requiring earthquake-recording instrumentation originated with the 1997 *Uniform Building Code* (UBC). When the 2000 IBC was initially developed, this provision was inadvertently left out. The requirement only applies to newly constructed buildings of a specified size and located where the 1-second spectral response acceleration, S_1, is greater than 0.40. Because the provision is in an appendix chapter, it is not mandatory unless specifically adopted by the jurisdiction.

Appendix M

Tsunami-Generated Flood Hazards

CHANGE TYPE: Addition

CHANGE SUMMARY: A new appendix provides requirements for coastal communities that have a potential for being inundated by the effects of tsunami waves.

2013 CODE:

APPENDIX M
TSUNAMI-GENERATED FLOOD HAZARD

SECTION M101
TSUNAMI-GENERATED FLOOD HAZARD

M101.1 General. The purpose of this appendix is to provide tsunami regulatory criteria for those communities that have a tsunami hazard and have elected to develop and adopt a map of their tsunami hazard inundation zone.

M101.2 Definitions. The following words and terms shall, for the purposes of this appendix, have the meanings shown herein.

TSUNAMI HAZARD ZONE MAP. A map adopted by the community that designates the extent of inundation by a design event tsunami. This map shall be based on the tsunami inundation map, which is developed and provided to a community by either the applicable State agency or the

Tsunami hazard zone sign. *(Courtesy of UNESCO)*

National Atmospheric and Oceanic Administration (NOAA) under the National Tsunami Hazard Mitigation Program, but the map shall be permitted to utilize a different probability or hazard level.

TSUNAMI HAZARD ZONE. The area vulnerable to being flooded or inundated by a design event tsunami as identified on a community's Tsunami Hazard Zone Map.

M101.3 Establishment of Tsunami Hazard Zone. Where a community has adopted a Tsunami Hazard Inundation Map, that map shall be used to establish a community's Tsunami Hazard Zone.

M101.4 Construction within the Tsunami Hazard Zone. Buildings and structures designated Occupancy Category III or IV in accordance with Section 1604.5 shall be prohibited within a Tsunami Hazard Zone.

Exceptions:

1. A vertical evacuation tsunami refuge shall be permitted to be located in a Tsunami Hazard Zone provided it is constructed in accordance with FEMA P646.
2. Community critical facilities shall be permitted to be located within the Tsunami Hazard Zone when such a location is necessary to fulfill their function, providing suitable structural and emergency evacuation measures have been incorporated.

SECTION M102
REFERENCED STANDARDS

FEMA P646—08. *Guidelines for Design of Structures for Vertical Evacuation from Tsunamis M101.4*

CHANGE SIGNIFICANCE: The areas designated on State or National Oceanic and Atmospheric Administration (NOAA) Tsunami Hazard Inundation Maps are most likely to suffer significant damage during a design tsunami event. Given the potentially serious life-safety risk presented to structures within these areas, the intent of the new requirement is to limit the presence of high-hazard and high-occupancy structures (Risk Categories III and IV) within the designated Tsunami Hazard Zone. Buildings within the designated hazard zone are only permitted under certain conditions. A vertical evacuation tsunami refuge is permitted when constructed in accordance with FEMA P646 or where critical facilities are located within the hazard zone to fulfill their function and they incorporate adequate structural and emergency evacuation features. Vertical evacuation is a central part of the National Tsunami Hazard Mitigation Program, driven by the fact that there are coastal communities along the West Coast of the United States that are vulnerable to tsunamis that could be generated within minutes of an earthquake on the Cascadia Subduction Zone. Vertical evacuation structures provide a means to create areas of refuge for communities in which evacuation out of the inundation zone is not feasible. The referenced FEMA guide includes information to assist in the planning and design of tsunami vertical evacuation structures. Because the provision is in an appendix chapter, it is not mandatory unless specifically adopted by the jurisdiction.